Planet Terror: The Horror movie Encyclopedia and Movie Reference with 446 Reviews, Terrifying Trivia, and Haunting Fun Facts from 24 Countries

The End... Or Is It? 497

Welcome to Planet Terror

You think you know fear? You think you've seen it all?

Think again, brave soul.

You hold in your hands a map to 446 circles of hell, each one crafted to peel away your sanity layer by layer. Don't say I didn't warn you.

This book... it has a pulse. Can you feel it? That subtle thrum beneath your fingertips isn't just your imagination. It's the collective heartbeat of a thousand nightmares, waiting to be unleashed.

Every page you turn is a door creaking open to a new horror. Every word a whisper in the dark, promising terrors you've never imagined. From the fog-shrouded alleys of London to the neon-drenched streets of Tokyo, from the sun-baked Australian outback to the frozen wastes of Russia – nowhere is safe.

You might think you're prepared. You might believe your nerves are steel, your stomach iron. But let me tell you something, friend – there are horrors in these pages that will make you question everything. The safety of your home. The sanity of your mind. The very nature of reality itself.

But go ahead. Turn the page. Start your journey through this atlas of atrocities. Just remember, once you start, there's no turning back. These films, these stories – they have a way of following you. Of seeping into your dreams. Of making you see the world through blood-tinted glasses.

And the worst part? You're going to love every minute of it.

Welcome to Planet Terror. Population: You.

Sleep tight, dear thrill-seeker. If you still can.

Japan

1. Ringu (Ring)

1. Movie Title: Ringu (リング)

2. Year of Release: 1998

3. Cast and Director:

- Director: Hideo Nakata

- Cast: Nanako Matsushima, Hiroyuki Sanada, Rikiya Ōtaka

4. Synopsis:

Ringu follows reporter Reiko Asakawa as she investigates an urban legend about a cursed videotape that kills its viewers seven days after watching it. When her niece falls victim to the curse, Reiko watches the tape herself and enlists her ex-husband, Ryuji, to help solve the mystery. As the clock ticks down, they uncover the tragic story of Sadako, a young girl with psychic powers whose vengeful spirit is behind the deadly curse. Racing against time, Reiko and Ryuji must find a way to break the cycle of death before it claims them and their young son.

5. Why This Movie Is Recommended:

Ringu revolutionized the horror genre with its psychological approach to terror and its iconic antagonist, Sadako. The film's atmospheric tension, relying more on suggestion than explicit gore, creates a pervasive sense of dread that lingers long after viewing. Its innovative use of technology as a conduit for supernatural horror resonated deeply with modern audiences, spawning numerous sequels and remakes worldwide. Ringu's influence on both Japanese and international horror cinema is undeniable, making it a must-watch for any horror enthusiast.

6. 10 Trivia Facts:

1. The film is based on Koji Suzuki's 1991 novel of the same name.

2. Sadako's iconic crawl out of the TV was performed by Kabuki theater performer Rie Inō.

3. The cursed videotape scenes were shot in a single day.

4. The film's success led to a Japanese TV series, novels, and manga adaptations.

5. Ringu sparked the trend of long-haired female ghosts in Japanese horror.

6. The movie was remade in America as "The Ring" in 2002, starring Naomi Watts.

7. Director Hideo Nakata also directed the American sequel, "The Ring Two."

8. The well scene was filmed in the basement of a pool in an abandoned hotel.

9. The film's budget was only about $1.2 million but grossed over $13 million in Japan.

10. The cursed video's content was partially inspired by the experimental films of Stan Brakhage.

2. Ju-On: The Grudge

1. Movie Title: Ju-On: The Grudge (呪怨)

2. Year of Release: 2002

3. Cast and Director:

- Director: Takashi Shimizu

- Cast: Megumi Okina, Misaki Itō, Misa Uehara, Yui Ichikawa

4. Synopsis:

Ju-On: The Grudge tells the story of a cursed house in Tokyo where a brutal murder took place. The curse, born of a powerful rage, spreads like a virus, passing from victim to victim in a chain of terror. The film follows several intersecting storylines as various people encounter the curse, including a social worker, a detective, and a schoolgirl. Each victim is inevitably drawn into the cycle of horror, facing the vengeful spirits of Kayako and her son Toshio. As the curse grows stronger, the boundaries between the living and the dead blur, trapping everyone who enters the house in a nightmare from which there seems to be no escape.

5. Why This Movie Is Recommended:

Ju-On: The Grudge stands out for its non-linear storytelling and its ability to create scares from seemingly mundane situations. The film's innovative structure keeps viewers on edge, never knowing when or where the next scare will come from. Its exploration of the lingering effects of violence and the cyclical nature of trauma adds depth to the horror. The unforgettable imagery of Kayako and Toshio has become iconic in horror cinema. Ju-On's unique approach to haunted house tropes and its emphasis on atmospheric dread over jump scares make it a standout in the Japanese horror genre.

6. 10 Trivia Facts:

1. The film is the third installment in the Ju-On series, following two direct-to-video movies.

2. Director Takashi Shimizu remade his own film for American audiences in 2004.

3. The distinctive croaking sound made by Kayako was inspired by the noise Shimizu's cat made when angry.

4. The movie was shot in just nine days.

5. Takako Fuji, who played Kayako, reprised her role in every Japanese and American Ju-On/The Grudge film until 2009.

6. The film's success led to a long-running franchise with multiple sequels and spin-offs.

7. Shimizu originally created Ju-On as a short film for a TV horror anthology.

8. The character of Toshio is based on a young boy Shimizu saw on a train who had an unsettling, pale appearance.

9. Many of the scare scenes were shot in a single take to maintain tension.

10. The film's low budget required creative solutions, like using a fishing line to make Kayako's hair move.

3. Audition

1. Movie Title: Audition (オーディション)

2. Year of Release: 1999

3. Cast and Director:

- Director: Takashi Miike

- Cast: Ryo Ishibashi, Eihi Shiina, Tetsu Sawaki

4. Synopsis:

Audition follows Shigeharu Aoyama, a widower who agrees to participate in a staged film audition to find a new wife. He becomes infatuated with Asami Yamazaki, a beautiful and mysterious woman. As Aoyama pursues a relationship with Asami, he begins to uncover disturbing truths about her past. The film slowly builds tension, shifting from a romantic drama to a psychological thriller, and ultimately to a horrifying exploration of obsession and revenge. As Asami's true nature is revealed, Aoyama finds himself trapped in a nightmare of his own making, facing the consequences of his deception and the depths of human cruelty.

5. Why This Movie Is Recommended:

Audition is a masterclass in slow-burn horror that subverts audience expectations at every turn. Director Takashi Miike expertly crafts a film that begins as a seemingly innocent romance before descending into a shocking and visceral exploration of trauma and vengeance. The movie's gradual tonal shift and its unflinching portrayal of violence make it a deeply unsettling experience. Audition challenges viewers with its complex themes of gender roles, loneliness, and the dangers of idealization. Its final act, infamous for its graphic content, remains one of the most disturbing sequences in horror cinema, cementing the film's status as a modern classic of the genre.

6. 10 Trivia Facts:

1. The film is based on a novel of the same name by Ryu Murakami.

2. Audition was Takashi Miike's first film to gain significant international recognition.

3. The infamous torture scene took three days to film.

4. The movie's sudden tonal shift was inspired by Alfred Hitchcock's Psycho.

5. Eihi Shiina, who played Asami, had no prior acting experience before this film.

6. The film was so shocking that it reportedly caused walkouts and fainting at film festivals.

7. Miike deliberately shot the first half of the film in a style reminiscent of Japanese TV dramas.

8. The piano wire used in the film's climax was actually made of rubber for safety reasons.

9. Audition has been cited as an influence by directors like Quentin Tarantino and Eli Roth.

10. The film's ambiguous ending has been the subject of much debate among fans and critics.

4. Kairo (Pulse)

1. Movie Title: Kairo (回路, released internationally as Pulse)

2. Year of Release: 2001

3. Cast and Director:

 - Director: Kiyoshi Kurosawa

 - Cast: Haruhiko Katō, Kumiko Asō, Koyuki, Kurume Arisaka

4. Synopsis:

Kairo weaves together two parallel storylines in a world where the boundary between the living and the dead is eroding. In one thread, a group of friends investigate strange occurrences after one of their own commits suicide. In the other, a young economics student stumbles upon a mysterious website that seems to show grainy images of the dead. As more people vanish or die under mysterious circumstances, it becomes clear that ghosts are entering the world of the living through the Internet. The film explores themes of isolation in the digital age, as the characters grapple with a spreading epidemic of loneliness and despair that threatens to consume humanity.

5. Why This Movie Is Recommended:

Kairo stands out for its unique blend of supernatural horror and technological anxiety. Director Kiyoshi Kurosawa masterfully creates an atmosphere of creeping dread, using the then-new concept of widespread internet use to tap into fears of isolation and disconnection in modern society. The film's ghostly apparitions are deeply unsettling, often more for their existential implications than for traditional scares. Kairo's exploration of loneliness and the human need for connection resonates even more strongly in today's hyper-connected world. Its influence can be seen in many subsequent works of tech-horror, making it a pivotal film in the evolution of the genre.

6. 10 Trivia Facts:

 1. The film was remade in the United States as "Pulse" in 2006.

 2. Director Kiyoshi Kurosawa is not related to the famous filmmaker Akira Kurosawa.

 3. The movie was shot on 35mm film, contributing to its grainy, atmospheric look.

 4. Kairo was partly inspired by the rise of internet cafes in Japan in the late 1990s.

 5. The film's original Japanese title, "Kairo," can mean both "circuit" and "whirlpool" in English.

 6. Many of the ghost effects were achieved through simple camera tricks rather than CGI.

 7. Kairo won the FIPRESCI Prize at the 2001 Cannes Film Festival.

 8. The film's themes were partly influenced by the 1995 Aum Shinrikyo terrorist attacks in Tokyo.

 9. Kurosawa wrote the screenplay in just two weeks.

 10. The movie features a cameo by Japanese cyberpunk author Toh EnJoe.

5. Onibaba

1. Movie Title: Onibaba (鬼婆, "Demon Hag")

2. Year of Release: 1964

3. Cast and Director:

- Director: Kaneto Shindo

- Cast: Nobuko Otowa, Jitsuko Yoshimura, Kei Satō

4. Synopsis:

Set in war-torn 14th century Japan, Onibaba tells the story of an older woman and her daughter-in-law who survive by killing lost samurai and selling their belongings. Their routine is disrupted when a neighbor returns from the war and begins a sexual relationship with the younger woman. Jealous and fearful of abandonment, the older woman uses a demon mask taken from a slain samurai to scare her daughter-in-law away from her lover. However, the mask's power proves to be more than she bargained for, leading to a terrifying conclusion that blurs the line between the natural and supernatural.

5. Why This Movie Is Recommended:

Onibaba is a masterpiece of atmospheric horror that transcends its genre. Director Kaneto Shindo uses the stark beauty of the susuki grass fields and innovative sound design to create a sense of isolation and creeping dread. The film's exploration of human nature, desire, and the corrosive effects of war gives it a psychological depth rarely seen in horror cinema of its time. Its striking black-and-white cinematography and the unsettling use of the demon mask have become iconic in world cinema. Onibaba's blend of folklore, eroticism, and existential horror makes it a unique and influential work that continues to resonate with audiences decades after its release.

6. 10 Trivia Facts:

1. The film is loosely based on a Buddhist parable called "The Mask with Flesh Torn Off."

2. The susuki grass field seen in the film was specially planted for the production and took months to grow.

3. The demon mask used in the film was based on actual Noh theater masks.

4. Director Kaneto Shindo insisted on shooting only at night or on overcast days for consistency.

5. The film's score, composed by Hikaru Hayashi, uses only percussion instruments.

6. Onibaba was shot in just 28 days.

7. The hole in the ground, central to the film's plot, was actually dug on a sound stage.

8. Lead actress Nobuko Otowa was married to director Kaneto Shindo.

9. The film won numerous awards, including three at the Blue Ribbon Awards in Japan.

10. Onibaba has been cited as an influence by directors like Guillermo del Toro and Quentin Tarantino.

6. Kwaidan

1. Movie Title: Kwaidan (怪談, "Ghost Stories")

2. Year of Release: 1964

3. Cast and Director:

  - Director: Masaki Kobayashi

  - Cast: Rentarō Mikuni, Tatsuya Nakadai, Katsuo Nakamura, Keiko Kishi

4. Synopsis:

   Kwaidan is an anthology film consisting of four separate ghost stories based on Japanese folk tales. "The Black Hair" tells of a samurai who abandons his loyal wife for a life of luxury, only to be haunted by her memory. "The Woman of the Snow" follows a woodcutter who encounters a supernatural being during a snowstorm. "Hoichi the Earless" recounts the tale of a blind monk who unknowingly performs for an audience of ghosts. Finally, "In a Cup of Tea" presents the story of a samurai who sees a mysterious face reflected in his tea. Each tale is brought to life with stunning visuals and a haunting atmosphere, blending traditional Japanese ghost stories with cinematic artistry.

5. Why This Movie Is Recommended:

   Kwaidan stands as a landmark in Japanese cinema, seamlessly blending horror with exquisite artistic vision. Director Masaki Kobayashi's use of vibrant colors, stylized sets, and meticulous sound design creates a dreamlike atmosphere that enhances the otherworldly nature of the stories. The film's deliberate pacing and emphasis on mood over shock value offer a unique and immersive horror experience. Kwaidan's influence on both Japanese and international cinema is profound, inspiring filmmakers to explore the aesthetic possibilities of horror. Its timeless tales and breathtaking visuals make it essential viewing for fans of horror and world cinema alike.

6. 10 Trivia Facts:

  1. The film is based on stories from Lafcadio Hearn's collections of Japanese folk tales.

  2. Kwaidan won the Special Jury Prize at the 1965 Cannes Film Festival.

  3. The movie's production was the most expensive in Japanese history at the time.

  4. The elaborate sets were built entirely indoors to allow for precise control of lighting and atmosphere.

  5. The film's soundtrack incorporates traditional Japanese instruments with avant-garde techniques.

  6. "The Woman of the Snow" segment was initially cut from U.S. releases due to time constraints.

  7. The eye-filled sky in "Hoichi the Earless" was painted by hand on a massive backdrop.

  8. Director Kobayashi had no prior experience in the horror genre before making Kwaidan.

  9. The film took almost two years to complete due to its elaborate production design.

  10. Kwaidan's success helped revitalize interest in traditional Japanese ghost stories.

7. Tetsuo: The Iron Man

1. Movie Title: Tetsuo: The Iron Man (鉄男)

2. Year of Release: 1989

3. Cast and Director:

  - Director: Shinya Tsukamoto

  - Cast: Tomorowo Taguchi, Kei Fujiwara, Nobu Kanaoka, Shinya Tsukamoto

4. Synopsis:

  Tetsuo: The Iron Man is a surreal body horror film that defies easy explanation. The story revolves around a metal fetishist who, after being hit by a businessman's car, seeks revenge by infecting the man with a disease that gradually transforms his body into metal. As the businessman's transformation progresses, he experiences bizarre hallucinations and violent urges. The line between reality and nightmare blurs as both characters undergo grotesque metamorphoses, culminating in a climactic fusion that's both horrifying and oddly poetic. Throughout the film, themes of industrialization, sexuality, and the fusion of man and machine are explored in visceral, often shocking ways.

5. Why This Movie Is Recommended:

  Tetsuo: The Iron Man is a landmark of cyberpunk and body horror cinema, pushing the boundaries of both genres. Director Shinya Tsukamoto's frenetic editing, industrial soundtrack, and stark black-and-white cinematography create a nightmarish atmosphere that's utterly unique. The film's exploration of technology's impact on the human body and psyche remains relevant in our increasingly digital world. While not for the faint of heart, Tetsuo offers a bold, uncompromising vision that has influenced countless filmmakers and artists. Its raw energy, surreal imagery, and unflinching approach to body horror make it a cult classic and a must-see for fans of experimental cinema.

6. 10 Trivia Facts:

  1. The film was shot on 16mm black-and-white film, contributing to its gritty aesthetic.

  2. Director Shinya Tsukamoto also plays the role of the metal fetishist.

  3. The movie was made on a shoestring budget with a small crew of Tsukamoto's friends.

  4. Many of the film's special effects were achieved through stop-motion animation.

  5. Tetsuo: The Iron Man was partly inspired by the works of cyberpunk author William Gibson.

  6. The film's iconic drill penis scene was achieved using a power drill wrapped in latex.

  7. Tsukamoto drew inspiration from his own experiences with hives, which made him feel like his body was rebelling against him.

  8. The movie spawned two sequels: "Tetsuo II: Body Hammer" (1992) and "Tetsuo: The Bullet Man" (2009).

  9. The film's soundtrack, composed by Chu Ishikawa, became highly influential in the Japanese industrial music scene.

  10. Tetsuo: The Iron Man has been cited as an influence by directors like Darren Aronofsky and Gaspar Noé.

8. Cure

1. Movie Title: Cure (キュア)

2. Year of Release: 1997

3. Cast and Director:

  - Director: Kiyoshi Kurosawa

  - Cast: Kōji Yakusho, Masato Hagiwara, Tsuyoshi Ujiki, Anna Nakagawa

4. Synopsis:

Cure follows detective Kenichi Takabe as he investigates a series of bizarre murders in Tokyo. Each killing is committed by a different person who has no memory of the act and bears an X-shaped cut on their neck. As Takabe delves deeper into the case, he encounters a mysterious amnesiac named Mamiya who seems to be connected to the crimes. Mamiya possesses the ability to hypnotize people and make them act on their darkest impulses. As the line between sanity and madness blurs, Takabe must confront his own inner demons while trying to stop the killings. The film explores themes of identity, memory, and the nature of evil in modern society.

5. Why This Movie Is Recommended:

Cure is a masterpiece of psychological horror that transcends the typical conventions of the genre. Director Kiyoshi Kurosawa creates an atmosphere of creeping dread and existential unease that lingers long after the film ends. The movie's exploration of the human psyche and the nature of evil is both thought-provoking and deeply unsettling. Cure's influence on the Japanese horror renaissance of the late 1990s and early 2000s cannot be overstated, paving the way for more cerebral and atmospheric horror films. Its subtle approach to horror, relying more on suggestion and psychological tension than overt scares, makes it a standout in the genre and a must-watch for fans of intelligent, slow-burn thrillers.

6. 10 Trivia Facts:

1. The film was inspired by the real-life Aum Shinrikyo cult's sarin gas attack on the Tokyo subway in 1995.

2. Director Kiyoshi Kurosawa is not related to the famous filmmaker Akira Kurosawa, despite sharing the same surname.

3. The movie was shot in just three weeks.

4. Cure was one of the first Japanese films to use Dolby Digital sound technology.

5. The film's ambiguous ending has been the subject of much debate and interpretation.

6. Kōji Yakusho, who plays Detective Takabe, is a frequent collaborator of Kiyoshi Kurosawa.

7. The movie's influence can be seen in later works like David Fincher's "Zodiac" and the TV series "True Detective."

8. Cure was not widely released outside of Japan until several years after its initial release.

9. The film's hypnosis scenes were achieved without special effects, relying instead on the actors' performances.

10. Kiyoshi Kurosawa wrote the screenplay in just two weeks.

9. Hausu (House)

1. Movie Title: Hausu (ハウス, House)

2. Year of Release: 1977

3. Cast and Director:

- Director: Nobuhiko Obayashi

- Cast: Kimiko Ikegami, Miki Jinbo, Kumiko Ohba, Ai Matsubara

4. Synopsis:

  Hausu follows a group of seven schoolgirls who travel to the country home of one girl's aunt for summer vacation. As they arrive, strange and surreal events begin to unfold. The house itself seems to be alive and malevolent, with each room presenting a new and bizarre danger. One by one, the girls fall victim to the house's supernatural traps, which include a man-eating piano, a bloodthirsty cat painting, and even killer futon mattresses. As the nightmare escalates, the true nature of the aunt and her connection to the house is revealed, leading to a psychedelic and horrifying climax that defies logic and expectation.

5. Why This Movie Is Recommended:

  Hausu is a fever dream of a horror film that throws conventional storytelling and filmmaking techniques out the window. Director Nobuhiko Obayashi's background in experimental films and TV commercials is evident in the movie's frenetic pace, surreal visuals, and disregard for narrative coherence. While it may not be traditionally "scary," Hausu offers a unique and unforgettable viewing experience that blends horror with comedy, romance, and pure absurdism. Its influence can be seen in later works that push the boundaries of the horror genre. For those seeking a truly bizarre and visually stunning film that challenges the very notion of what horror can be, Hausu is an essential watch.

6. 10 Trivia Facts:

  1. The film's story was based on ideas from director Obayashi's 11-year-old daughter, Chigumi.

  2. Hausu was Obayashi's first feature film after a successful career in TV commercials.

  3. The intentionally unrealistic special effects were inspired by silent films and theatrical techniques.

  4. Many of the young actresses were amateurs, chosen from TV commercials Obayashi had directed.

  5. The film was a surprise box office hit in Japan, despite (or perhaps because of) its weirdness.

  6. Hausu remained largely unknown outside Japan until its international release on home video in 2009.

  7. The movie's soundtrack, composed by Godiego, became popular in its own right.

  8. Obayashi used a mixture of animation, matte paintings, and optical effects to achieve the film's unique look.

  9. The character names (Gorgeous, Kung Fu, Prof, etc.) were chosen to reflect their personalities.

  10. Despite its eventual cult status, many critics initially dismissed the film as nonsensical upon its release.

10. Dark Water

1. Movie Title: Dark Water (仄暗い水の底から, Honogurai Mizu no soko kara)

2. Year of Release: 2002

3. Cast and Director:

 - Director: Hideo Nakata

 - Cast: Hitomi Kuroki, Rio Kanno, Mirei Oguchi, Asami Mizukawa

4. Synopsis:

 Dark Water follows Yoshimi Matsubara, a single mother going through a difficult divorce, as she moves into a run-down apartment with her young daughter, Ikuko. As they settle in, strange occurrences begin to plague them, centered around a mysterious water leak from the apartment above. Yoshimi, already stressed from her custody battle and new job, becomes increasingly paranoid as she investigates the building's dark history. She discovers the story of a young girl who disappeared years ago and begins to fear for Ikuko's safety. As the boundary between past and present blurs, Yoshimi must confront the building's supernatural presence to protect her daughter, leading to a heart-wrenching climax that explores the depths of maternal love and sacrifice.

5. Why This Movie Is Recommended:

 Dark Water stands out in the J-horror genre for its emphasis on atmospheric dread and emotional depth over jump scares. Director Hideo Nakata, known for Ringu, crafts a ghost story that is as much about the psychological toll of single parenthood and societal pressures as it is about supernatural horror. The film's use of water as a constant, oppressive presence creates a unique sense of unease throughout. Dark Water's exploration of themes like abandonment, sacrifice, and the bond between mother and child elevates it beyond typical ghost stories. Its melancholic tone and poignant ending offer a more nuanced and emotionally resonant horror experience, making it a must-watch for fans of psychological horror and ghost stories with depth.

6. 10 Trivia Facts:

 1. The film is based on a short story by Koji Suzuki, author of the Ring novel series.

 2. Director Hideo Nakata also directed Ringu, another influential Japanese horror film.

 3. The movie was remade in the United States in 2005, starring Jennifer Connelly.

 4. The apartment building in the film was inspired by real danchi (public housing) complexes in Japan.

 5. The film's original Japanese title translates to "From the Bottom of Dark Water."

 6. Dark Water explores themes of water pollution and urban decay, reflecting real social issues in Japan.

 7. The ghost's appearance was inspired by the yurei, traditional Japanese ghosts often associated with water.

 8. The film won the Grand Prize at the 2002 Fantasporto International Film Festival.

 9. Actress Hitomi Kuroki performed many of her own stunts, including scenes in the flooded apartment.

 10. The movie's ending differs significantly from Koji Suzuki's original short story.

11. Noroi: The Curse

1. Movie Title: Noroi: The Curse (呪怨)

2. Year of Release: 2005

3. Cast and Director:

- Director: Kōji Shiraishi

- Cast: Jin Muraki, Rio Kanno, Tomono Kuga, Marika Matsumoto

4. Synopsis:

Noroi: The Curse is presented as a documentary made by paranormal investigator Masafumi Kobayashi, who disappeared shortly after completing the film. The story unfolds through a complex narrative that interweaves various supernatural occurrences, psychic phenomena, and ancient rituals. Kobayashi investigates a series of seemingly unrelated events, including a woman hearing baby cries in her house, a young psychic's disturbing predictions, and an actress's erratic behavior on set. As he delves deeper, he uncovers a sinister connection to an ancient demon named Kagutaba and a series of ritual sacrifices. The investigation leads Kobayashi into increasingly dangerous territory, culminating in a chilling revelation about the true nature of the curse.

5. Why This Movie Is Recommended:

Noroi: The Curse stands out in the found footage subgenre for its intricate plot and masterful buildup of tension. Director Kōji Shiraishi crafts a multi-layered narrative that rewards attentive viewers with a deeply unsettling and complex horror experience. The film's documentary-style approach, blending "real" footage with fictional TV clips and interviews, creates a sense of authenticity that enhances its horror elements. Noroi excels in creating a pervasive atmosphere of dread, with each revealed connection adding to the overall sense of an inescapable, ancient evil. Its unique approach to storytelling and commitment to world-building make it a standout in both Japanese horror and the found footage genre, offering a rewarding experience for viewers who enjoy piecing together complex narratives.

6. 10 Trivia Facts:

1. The film uses a mix of professional actors and real psychics to enhance its documentary feel.

2. Director Kōji Shiraishi conducted extensive research into Japanese folklore and urban legends for the movie.

3. The character of Marika Matsumoto is played by a real-life Japanese idol of the same name.

4. The movie features references to actual Japanese TV shows and personalities, blurring the line between fiction and reality.

5. Noroi gained much of its popularity through word-of-mouth and online recommendations, becoming a cult classic.

6. The film's complex narrative structure was inspired by detective novels and mystery stories.

7. Some of the "archival footage" in the film was shot on actual VHS tapes to maintain authenticity.

8. The demon Kagutaba is an original creation for the film, blending elements from various Japanese myths.

9. Noroi: The Curse was not widely released outside of Japan until several years after its initial release.

10. The film's success led to Shiraishi directing several other found footage horror movies, though none achieved the same level of acclaim.

12. Kuroneko (Black Cat)

1. Movie Title: Kuroneko (藪の中の黒猫, Yabu no Naka no Kuroneko, "A Black Cat in a Bamboo Grove")

2. Year of Release: 1968

3. Cast and Director:

- Director: Kaneto Shindō

- Cast: Kichiemon Nakamura, Nobuko Otowa, Kiwako Taichi, Kei Satō

4. Synopsis:

Set in feudal Japan, Kuroneko tells the story of a mother, Yone, and her daughter-in-law, Shige, who are brutally raped and murdered by a group of samurai. Their spirits return as vengeful cat demons, luring samurai to an illusory house in the bamboo grove where they seduce and kill them. The plot thickens when Gintoki, Yone's son and Shige's husband, returns from war as a celebrated samurai. He is tasked with killing the mysterious demons, unaware that they are the spirits of his loved ones. As Gintoki investigates, he must confront the tragic past and navigate the blurred lines between duty, love, and vengeance.

5. Why This Movie Is Recommended:

Kuroneko is a masterpiece of Japanese gothic horror that combines elements of traditional kaidan (ghost stories) with stunning visual artistry. Director Kaneto Shindō creates a hauntingly beautiful atmosphere through his use of high-contrast black-and-white cinematography and ethereal soundscapes. The film's exploration of themes such as the cyclical nature of violence, the blurring of good and evil, and the consequences of war gives it a depth beyond typical ghost stories. Kuroneko's influence on later Japanese horror films is significant, particularly in its portrayal of vengeful female spirits. For those interested in classic horror cinema, Japanese folklore, or visually striking filmmaking, Kuroneko offers a unique and unforgettable viewing experience.

6. 10 Trivia Facts:

1. Director Kaneto Shindō also directed the horror classic "Onibaba" four years earlier.

2. The film's Japanese title, "Yabu no Naka no Kuroneko," is a reference to Akira Kurosawa's "Rashomon."

3. Kuroneko was shot entirely on soundstages to achieve its otherworldly atmosphere.

4. The movie's bamboo grove scenes were created using real bamboo plants combined with painted backdrops.

5. The film draws inspiration from various Japanese folktales about cat demons and vengeful spirits.

6. Kuroneko won three Kinema Junpo Awards, including Best Film and Best Director.

7. The movie's innovative use of wire work for supernatural scenes influenced later martial arts and horror films.

8. Actress Nobuko Otowa, who plays Yone, was director Shindō's wife and frequent collaborator.

9. The film's exploration of social issues, particularly the abuse of power by samurai, was controversial at the time.

10. Kuroneko's restoration and international re-release in 2011 led to renewed critical acclaim and scholarly interest.

13. Marebito

1. Movie Title: Marebito (稀人)

2. Year of Release: 2004

3. Cast and Director:

- Director: Takashi Shimizu

- Cast: Shinya Tsukamoto, Tomomi Miyashita, Kazuhiro Nakahara, Miho Ninagawa

4. Synopsis:

Marebito follows Masuoka, a freelance cameraman obsessed with fear and the idea of capturing true terror on film. After witnessing a man's gruesome suicide in a subway station, Masuoka becomes fixated on understanding the depth of fear the man experienced. His obsession leads him to explore a vast network of tunnels beneath Tokyo, where he encounters a strange, feral girl whom he names F. Masuoka takes F to his apartment, where he observes and cares for her, believing she holds the key to understanding ultimate fear. As the line between reality and delusion blurs, Masuoka descends into a nightmarish world of underground creatures, ancient prophecies, and his own unraveling sanity.

5. Why This Movie Is Recommended:

Marebito stands out in the Japanese horror landscape for its unique blend of psychological horror, urban exploration, and cosmic dread. Director Takashi Shimizu, known for the Ju-On series, takes a more experimental approach here, crafting a disorienting and unsettling experience that challenges viewers' perceptions of reality. The film's exploration of obsession, isolation, and the nature of fear itself offers a more cerebral horror experience than typical ghost stories or slashers. Shot on digital video in just eight days, Marebito has a raw, immediate quality that enhances its disconcerting atmosphere. For fans of psychological horror, Lovecraftian themes, or unconventional storytelling, Marebito offers a unique and thought-provoking journey into the depths of fear and madness.

6. 10 Trivia Facts:

1. The film was shot in just eight days, during a break in post-production for Shimizu's American remake of "The Grudge."

2. Lead actor Shinya Tsukamoto is himself a renowned director, known for films like "Tetsuo: The Iron Man."

3. Marebito draws inspiration from the works of H.P. Lovecraft and Richard Shaver's "Shaver Mystery."

4. The movie was shot entirely on digital video, giving it a distinct visual style.

5. Director Shimizu appears in a cameo as the man who commits suicide in the subway.

6. The film's title, "Marebito," can be translated as "rare person" or "visitor from afar."

7. Many of the underground scenes were shot in real Tokyo locations, including maintenance tunnels and sewers.

8. The character F never speaks throughout the film, communicating only through gestures and vocalizations.

9. Marebito premiered at the Rotterdam International Film Festival before its Japanese theatrical release.

10. The film's ambiguous ending has sparked numerous theories and interpretations among viewers.

14. Uzumaki (Spiral)

1. Movie Title: Uzumaki (うずまき, "Spiral")

2. Year of Release: 2000

3. Cast and Director:

- Director: Higuchinsky (Akihiro Higuchi)

- Cast: Eriko Hatsune, Fhi Fan, Hinako Saeki, Eun-Kyung Shin

4. Synopsis:

Based on Junji Ito's manga of the same name, Uzumaki is set in the small Japanese town of Kurōzu-cho, which becomes increasingly obsessed with spiral patterns. The story follows Kirie Goshima and her boyfriend Shuichi Saito as they witness the town's descent into madness. Residents begin to exhibit bizarre behaviors related to spirals: a man becomes obsessed with collecting snail shells, another twists his body into a spiral shape, and even the clouds and whirlpools in the town take on spiral formations. As the curse spreads, more horrifying transformations occur, and the characters must try to unravel the mystery of the spiral obsession before it consumes them all. The film builds to a surreal and nightmarish climax as the town itself seems to warp and twist around its inhabitants.

5. Why This Movie Is Recommended:

Uzumaki stands out as one of the most unique and visually striking entries in Japanese horror cinema. Director Higuchinsky's adaptation brilliantly captures the unsettling and surreal nature of Junji Ito's original manga, bringing its bizarre imagery to life on screen. The film's ability to make something as simple as a spiral pattern deeply unnerving is a testament to its effectiveness in creating an atmosphere of creeping dread and cosmic horror. Uzumaki's blend of body horror, psychological terror, and abstract, almost hallucinatory visuals offers a truly singular viewing experience. For fans of surrealist cinema, cosmic horror, or those looking for horror that goes beyond traditional scares, Uzumaki provides a mesmerizing and unforgettable journey into a world where reality itself seems to unravel.

6. 10 Trivia Facts:

1. The film is based on Junji Ito's manga series of the same name, which was serialized from 1998 to 1999.

2. Director Higuchinsky (Akihiro Higuchi) comes from a background in music videos, which influenced the film's unique visual style.

3. Uzumaki was shot using a special filter to give it a green tint, enhancing its otherworldly atmosphere.

4. The movie only adapts the first two volumes of Ito's manga, leaving out the final act.

5. Many of the practical effects were achieved using prosthetics and creative camera work rather than CGI.

6. The film's score, composed by Keiichi Suzuki, incorporates spiral patterns into its musical structure.

7. Uzumaki premiered at the Tokyo International Film Festival before its wider release.

8. The movie features several cameo appearances by horror manga artists, including Junji Ito himself.

9. Despite mixed reviews upon release, Uzumaki has since gained a strong cult following.

10. An anime adaptation of the full Uzumaki manga was announced in 2019, set to be released in 2024.

15. Ichi the Killer

1. Movie Title: Ichi the Killer (殺し屋1, Koroshiya 1)

2. Year of Release: 2001

3. Cast and Director:

  - Director: Takashi Miike

  - Cast: Tadanobu Asano, Nao Omori, Shinya Tsukamoto, Paulyn Sun

4. Synopsis:

  Ichi the Killer follows the violent conflict between Kakihara, a sadomasochistic yakuza enforcer, and Ichi, a mysterious and psychologically damaged killer. When Kakihara's boss disappears, he embarks on a brutal search for answers, leaving a trail of torture and mayhem in his wake. Meanwhile, Ichi, manipulated by a retired cop named Jijii, is sent on a killing spree targeting yakuza members. As the body count rises, the paths of Ichi and Kakihara inevitably converge, leading to a series of increasingly grotesque and violent encounters. The film explores themes of pain, pleasure, manipulation, and the cyclical nature of violence, all while pushing the boundaries of on-screen gore and psychological horror.

5. Why This Movie Is Recommended:

  Ichi the Killer is a landmark film in the extreme cinema genre, renowned for its unflinching portrayal of violence and its exploration of the darkest aspects of human nature. Director Takashi Miike's unique vision creates a world that is simultaneously repulsive and captivating, challenging viewers' tolerance and perceptions. The film's complex characters, particularly the charismatic and disturbing Kakihara, bring depth to what could otherwise be mere shock value. Ichi the Killer's influence on subsequent extreme horror and crime films is undeniable, and its visual style and narrative techniques continue to be analyzed and discussed in film studies. While certainly not for the faint of heart, for those interested in pushing the boundaries of cinema and exploring the extremes of human behavior, Ichi the Killer offers a visceral and unforgettable experience that goes beyond simple horror into a realm of cinematic provocation.

6. 10 Trivia Facts:

  1. The film is based on a manga series of the same name by Hideo Yamamoto.

  2. Director Takashi Miike shot the film in just three weeks.

  3. The movie was so controversial that it was banned or heavily censored in several countries.

  4. Actor Tadanobu Asano, who plays Kakihara, had to wear a mouth prosthetic for his character's distinctive cheek slits.

  5. The film's opening credits sequence features semen-shaped kanji characters, setting the tone for the film's provocative nature.

  6. Ichi the Killer premiered at the Toronto International Film Festival, where some viewers reportedly fainted or vomited during the screening.

  7. The movie's extreme violence led to the creation of "barf bags" featuring the film's logo for some theatrical screenings.

  8. Despite its graphic content, the film has received praise for its technical achievements and performances.

  9. Takashi Miike makes a cameo appearance in the film as a man in a bar.

  10. The character of Ichi was partially inspired by the real-life Japanese cannibal Issei Sagawa.

16. Infection (Kansen)

1. Movie Title: Infection (感染, Kansen)

2. Year of Release: 2004

3. Cast and Director:

   - Director: Masayuki Ochiai

   - Cast: Kōichi Satō, Michiko Hada, Miwako Washio, Tae Kimura

4. Synopsis:

Infection takes place in a run-down, understaffed hospital where a series of medical mistakes leads to a patient's death. As the staff attempts to cover up their fatal error, a mysterious green liquid arrives, purportedly containing a highly infectious disease. When a doctor accidentally becomes infected, the hospital descends into chaos as the staff struggle to contain the outbreak and maintain their sanity. The infection causes horrific mutations and drives its victims to violent madness. As the night progresses, the line between reality and hallucination blurs, and the surviving staff must confront not only the physical horror of the infection but also their own guilt and moral decay.

5. Why This Movie Is Recommended:

Infection stands out in the Japanese horror landscape for its claustrophobic setting and its blend of body horror with psychological terror. Director Masayuki Ochiai crafts a tense, paranoid atmosphere that keeps viewers on edge throughout the film. The movie's exploration of themes such as medical ethics, guilt, and the breakdown of social order adds depth to its horror elements. Infection's use of practical effects for its grotesque transformations creates visceral and memorable imagery. The film's ambiguous nature, leaving viewers to question what is real and what is hallucination, adds an extra layer of unease to the proceedings. For fans of body horror, psychological thrillers, or those interested in films that use confined settings to amplify tension, Infection offers a gripping and unsettling experience.

6. 10 Trivia Facts:

1. Infection was part of the "J-Horror Theater" series, a collection of six films by different directors.

2. The film's hospital setting was inspired by real issues in the Japanese healthcare system at the time.

3. Director Masayuki Ochiai has a background in biology, which influenced the film's medical aspects.

4. The movie's green color palette was chosen to enhance the sickly, unnatural atmosphere.

5. Infection features several references to the 1982 film "The Thing," another classic of paranoid horror.

6. The film uses a mixture of practical effects and early CGI to create its gruesome transformations.

7. Infection was shot on location in an abandoned hospital, adding to its authentic and eerie atmosphere.

8. The movie's ambiguous ending has sparked numerous fan theories and interpretations.

9. Infection was well-received internationally and has been screened at several horror film festivals.

10. The film's success led to discussions of an American remake, though it never materialized.

17. Audition (Ōdishon)

1. Movie Title: Audition (オーディション, Ōdishon)

2. Year of Release: 1999

3. Cast and Director:

 - Director: Takashi Miike

 - Cast: Ryo Ishibashi, Eihi Shiina, Tetsu Sawaki, Jun Kunimura

4. Synopsis:

Audition follows Shigeharu Aoyama, a widower who agrees to stage a fake film audition to find a new wife. Among the applicants, he becomes infatuated with Asami Yamazaki, a beautiful and mysterious young woman. As Aoyama pursues a relationship with Asami, he begins to uncover disturbing truths about her past. The film slowly builds tension, shifting from a romantic drama to a psychological thriller, and ultimately to a visceral horror. Asami's true nature is revealed in a shocking climax that explores themes of past trauma, gender roles, and the consequences of deception.

5. Why This Movie Is Recommended:

Audition is a masterclass in slow-burn horror that subverts audience expectations at every turn. Director Takashi Miike expertly crafts a film that begins as a seemingly innocent romance before descending into a shocking and visceral exploration of trauma and vengeance. The movie's gradual tonal shift and its unflinching portrayal of violence make it a deeply unsettling experience. Audition challenges viewers with its complex themes of gender roles, loneliness, and the dangers of idealization. Its final act, infamous for its graphic content, remains one of the most disturbing sequences in horror cinema. For those seeking horror that goes beyond simple scares to provoke thought and discussion, Audition is an essential and unforgettable viewing experience.

6. 10 Trivia Facts:

1. The film is based on a novel of the same name by Ryu Murakami.

2. Audition was Takashi Miike's first film to gain significant international recognition.

3. The infamous torture scene took three days to film.

4. The movie's sudden tonal shift was inspired by Alfred Hitchcock's Psycho.

5. Eihi Shiina, who played Asami, had no prior acting experience before this film.

6. The film was so shocking that it reportedly caused walkouts and fainting at film festivals.

7. Miike deliberately shot the first half of the film in a style reminiscent of Japanese TV dramas.

8. The piano wire used in the film's climax was actually made of rubber for safety reasons.

9. Audition has been cited as an influence by directors like Quentin Tarantino and Eli Roth.

10. The film's ambiguous ending has been the subject of much debate among fans and critics.

18. Pulse (Kairo)

1. Movie Title: Pulse (回路, Kairo)

2. Year of Release: 2001

3. Cast and Director:

- Director: Kiyoshi Kurosawa

- Cast: Haruhiko Katō, Kumiko Asō, Koyuki, Kurume Arisaka

4. Synopsis:

Pulse weaves together two parallel storylines in a world where the boundary between the living and the dead is eroding. In one thread, a group of friends investigate strange occurrences after one of their own commits suicide. In the other, a young economics student stumbles upon a mysterious website that seems to show grainy images of the dead. As more people vanish or die under mysterious circumstances, it becomes clear that ghosts are entering the world of the living through the Internet. The film explores themes of isolation in the digital age, as the characters grapple with a spreading epidemic of loneliness and despair that threatens to consume humanity.

5. Why This Movie Is Recommended:

Pulse stands out for its unique blend of supernatural horror and technological anxiety. Director Kiyoshi Kurosawa masterfully creates an atmosphere of creeping dread, using the then-new concept of widespread internet use to tap into fears of isolation and disconnection in modern society. The film's ghostly apparitions are deeply unsettling, often more for their existential implications than for traditional scares. Pulse's exploration of loneliness and the human need for connection resonates even more strongly in today's hyper-connected world. Its influence can be seen in many subsequent works of tech-horror, making it a pivotal film in the evolution of the genre. For those seeking horror that offers both scares and profound philosophical contemplation, Pulse is an essential viewing experience.

6. 10 Trivia Facts:

1. The film was remade in the United States as "Pulse" in 2006.

2. Director Kiyoshi Kurosawa is not related to the famous filmmaker Akira Kurosawa.

3. The movie was shot on 35mm film, contributing to its grainy, atmospheric look.

4. Pulse was partly inspired by the rise of internet cafes in Japan in the late 1990s.

5. The film's original Japanese title, "Kairo," can mean both "circuit" and "whirlpool" in English.

6. Many of the ghost effects were achieved through simple camera tricks rather than CGI.

7. Pulse won the FIPRESCI Prize at the 2001 Cannes Film Festival.

8. The film's themes were partly influenced by the 1995 Aum Shinrikyo terrorist attacks in Tokyo.

9. Kurosawa wrote the screenplay in just two weeks.

10. The movie features a cameo by Japanese cyberpunk author Toh EnJoe.

19. Battle Royale

1. Movie Title: Battle Royale (バトル・ロワイアル, Batoru Rowaiaru)

2. Year of Release: 2000

3. Cast and Director:

- Director: Kinji Fukasaku

- Cast: Tatsuya Fujiwara, Aki Maeda, Tarō Yamamoto, Takeshi Kitano

4. Synopsis:

Set in a dystopian Japan, Battle Royale follows a group of junior high school students who are forcibly sent to a deserted island by the government. There, they are required to participate in a brutal program where they must fight to the death until only one survivor remains. Each student is fitted with an explosive collar and given a random weapon, ranging from guns to household items. As the game progresses, alliances form and break, hidden agendas come to light, and the students are forced to confront the darkest aspects of human nature. The film explores themes of authority, social control, and the loss of innocence against a backdrop of extreme violence and psychological horror.

5. Why This Movie Is Recommended:

Battle Royale is a landmark film that blends elements of horror, action, and social commentary into a provocative and unforgettable experience. Director Kinji Fukasaku's unflinching portrayal of violence and his exploration of societal issues create a film that is both viscerally shocking and intellectually stimulating. The movie's influence on popular culture is immense, inspiring numerous works across various media. Battle Royale's examination of human behavior under extreme circumstances, coupled with its critique of authoritarian control and generational conflict, gives it a depth that elevates it beyond mere shock value. For fans of dystopian narratives, social horror, or those interested in films that push the boundaries of cinema, Battle Royale offers a intense and thought-provoking viewing experience that continues to resonate with audiences decades after its release.

6. 10 Trivia Facts:

1. The film is based on the 1999 novel of the same name by Koushun Takami.

2. Director Kinji Fukasaku was 70 years old when he made Battle Royale, drawing on his wartime experiences.

3. The movie was highly controversial upon release and was banned or restricted in several countries.

4. Takeshi Kitano, who plays the teacher, is a famous director and comedian in Japan.

5. Battle Royale was shot in a mere three months.

6. The film has been cited as an influence on "The Hunger Games" series, though author Suzanne Collins claims she hadn't heard of it when writing her books.

7. A special version of the film, Battle Royale: Special Edition, was released with extra footage and new scenes.

8. Many of the young actors were experiencing their first film roles.

9. The movie's theme song, "Requiem" by Masamichi Amano, is a variation on "Dies Irae," a Latin hymn about Judgment Day.

10. Despite its violent content, Battle Royale was the highest-grossing Japanese film of 2000.

20. One Cut of the Dead (Kamera o Tomeru na!)

1. Movie Title: One Cut of the Dead (カメラを止めるな!, Kamera o Tomeru na!)

2. Year of Release: 2017

3. Cast and Director:

- Director: Shin'ichirō Ueda

- Cast: Takayuki Hamatsu, Yuzuki Akiyama, Harumi Shuhama, Kazuaki Nagaya

4. Synopsis:

One Cut of the Dead begins as a low-budget zombie film being shot in an abandoned water filtration plant. The film's first 37 minutes appear to be a single-take zombie movie, where the cast and crew are attacked by real zombies during filming. However, this is revealed to be only the first act of a larger story. The film then shifts to show the behind-the-scenes process of making this zombie movie, revealing the chaotic and often hilarious reality of low-budget filmmaking. As the layers of the story unfold, the audience gains a new appreciation for the craft of filmmaking and the dedication of those involved, all while subverting expectations of the zombie horror genre.

5. Why This Movie Is Recommended:

One Cut of the Dead stands out as a unique and refreshing take on both the zombie genre and meta-cinema. Director Shin'ichirō Ueda crafts a film that starts as a seemingly amateurish zombie flick but evolves into a clever, heartwarming comedy about the passion and challenges of filmmaking. The movie's structure is ingenious, rewarding viewers who stick with it through its initial segment with a payoff that recontextualizes everything they've seen. It's a love letter to low-budget filmmaking, celebrating the creativity and perseverance required to bring a vision to life. For horror fans, it offers a fresh perspective on familiar tropes, while cinema enthusiasts will appreciate its insights into the filmmaking process. One Cut of the Dead proves that originality and heart can breathe new life into even the most well-worn genres.

6. 10 Trivia Facts:

1. The film was made on a budget of just ¥3 million (about $25,000) but went on to gross over ¥3 billion ($28 million) at the box office.

2. The opening 37-minute single-take scene was rehearsed for six months and shot in six takes.

3. Many of the cast members were students from the director's acting workshop.

4. The film's success led to several international remakes, including a French version titled "Final Cut."

5. One Cut of the Dead won the Audience Award and Best Director at the 2018 Fantasia International Film Festival.

6. The movie's Japanese title, "Kamera o Tomeru na!", literally translates to "Don't Stop the Camera!"

7. Despite its eventual success, the film initially opened in only one theater in Japan.

8. The entire movie was shot in just eight days.

9. Director Shin'ichirō Ueda had to take out a loan to finance the film's production.

10. The film's structure was inspired by Michael Frayn's play "Noises Off," which also depicts behind-the-scenes chaos in theater production.

Thailand

1. Shutter

1. Movie Title: Shutter (ชัตเตอร์ กดติดวิญญาณ)

2. Year of Release: 2004

3. Cast and Director:

  - Directors: Banjong Pisanthanakun, Parkpoom Wongpoom

  - Cast: Ananda Everingham, Natthaweeranuch Thongmee, Achita Sikamana

4. Synopsis:

Shutter follows Tun, a photographer, and his girlfriend Jane, who accidentally hit a young woman with their car one night and flee the scene. Soon after, Tun begins to notice strange shadows and distortions in his photographs. As unexplainable and terrifying events escalate, the couple realizes they are being haunted by the spirit of the woman they left for dead. Desperate to uncover the truth, they delve into Tun's past, revealing dark secrets that connect him to the vengeful ghost. As the hauntings intensify, Tun and Jane must confront the consequences of their actions and the horrifying reality behind the supernatural occurrences.

5. Why This Movie Is Recommended:

Shutter stands out as a masterpiece of Thai horror cinema, blending traditional ghost story elements with modern psychological thrills. The film's innovative use of photography as a medium for supernatural encounters creates uniquely chilling visuals. Its exploration of guilt, karma, and the consequences of past actions adds depth to the scares. The movie's ability to maintain suspense while gradually unveiling its mysteries keeps viewers engaged throughout. With its memorable twists and genuinely frightening moments, Shutter has become a influential work in the Asian horror genre, inspiring remakes and influencing horror filmmakers worldwide.

6. 10 Trivia Facts:

1. The film was remade in the United States in 2008, starring Joshua Jackson.

2. Shutter was the directorial debut for both Banjong Pisanthanakun and Parkpoom Wongpoom.

3. The movie's success led to remakes in Tamil, Telugu, and Hindi languages.

4. The ghost's appearance was inspired by the directors' real-life encounter with a creepy photograph.

5. The film's ending scene, featuring the ghost on the protagonist's shoulders, has become iconic in horror cinema.

6. Shutter was shot on a budget of approximately 20 million baht (about $630,000 USD).

7. The movie won several awards, including Best Picture at the Thailand National Film Association Awards.

8. Many of the film's scares were achieved through practical effects rather than CGI.

9. The directors conducted extensive research on spirit photography for authenticity.

10. Shutter's success helped establish Thailand as a major player in the Asian horror film industry.

2. Nang Nak

1. Movie Title: Nang Nak (นางนาก)

2. Year of Release: 1999

3. Cast and Director:

- Director: Nonzee Nimibutr

- Cast: Intira Jaroenpura, Winai Kraibutr

4. Synopsis:

Based on a famous Thai legend, Nang Nak tells the story of Mak, a young man who leaves his pregnant wife Nak to fight in a war. While he's away, Nak dies during childbirth along with her baby, but her love for Mak is so strong that her spirit remains. When Mak returns, he lives with Nak's ghost, unaware of her death. The villagers, terrified of Nak's vengeful spirit, try to warn Mak, but Nak's ghost violently protects their illusion of a happy life. As Mak slowly realizes the truth, he must confront the reality of his loss and the extent of Nak's undying love, leading to a heart-wrenching climax that blends horror with profound tragedy.

5. Why This Movie Is Recommended:

Nang Nak elevates Thai folklore into a visually stunning and emotionally resonant horror experience. Director Nonzee Nimibutr masterfully balances supernatural terror with a deeply moving love story, creating a film that's as heart-wrenching as it is frightening. The movie's rich cultural context and exploration of themes like devotion, loss, and the blurred lines between life and death give it depth beyond typical ghost stories. With its haunting imagery, strong performances, and cultural significance, Nang Nak is not just a pivotal work in Thai cinema but a must-see for anyone interested in international horror films that blend scares with powerful storytelling.

6. 10 Trivia Facts:

1. The film is based on the Mae Nak Phra Khanong legend, one of Thailand's most famous ghost stories.

2. Nang Nak was one of the first Thai films to gain significant international recognition.

3. The movie's success sparked a resurgence in Thai cinema, particularly in the horror genre.

4. The film's portrayal of 19th-century Thai life required extensive historical research and set design.

5. Intira Jaroenpura, who played Nak, was only 18 years old during filming.

6. The movie features traditional Thai music and incorporates elements of Thai classical dance.

7. Nang Nak won several awards, including Best Picture at the Thailand National Film Association Awards.

8. The legend of Mae Nak has been adapted into numerous films, TV series, and even an opera.

9. The film's success led to a boom in tourism at the real-life temple associated with the Mae Nak legend.

10. Director Nonzee Nimibutr insisted on shooting on location in Thailand's rural areas for authenticity.

3. Alone

1. Movie Title: Alone (แฝด)

2. Year of Release: 2007

3. Cast and Director:

- Directors: Banjong Pisanthanakun, Parkpoom Wongpoom

- Cast: Marsha Wattanapanich, Vittaya Wasukraipaisan

4. Synopsis:

Alone follows Pim, a Thai woman living in Korea with her husband Wee. Born as a conjoined twin, Pim was separated from her sister Ploy during a risky operation that left Ploy dead. When Pim returns to Thailand to care for her ill mother, she begins experiencing terrifying visions of Ploy's ghost. As the hauntings intensify, Pim is forced to confront the traumatic memories of her past and the guilt surrounding her sister's death. The line between reality and hallucination blurs as Pim struggles to determine if she's truly being haunted or if her mind is playing tricks on her. The film builds to a shocking twist that challenges everything Pim and the audience believe about her identity and past.

5. Why This Movie Is Recommended:

Alone stands out for its psychological depth and innovative take on the twin horror subgenre. The directors masterfully create an atmosphere of creeping dread, using the unique premise of conjoined twins to explore themes of identity, guilt, and the lingering effects of trauma. The film's visual style, with its muted color palette and claustrophobic cinematography, enhances the sense of isolation and paranoia. Marsha Wattanapanich's nuanced performance anchors the film, bringing emotional weight to the scares. With its blend of supernatural horror and psychological thriller elements, capped by a mind-bending twist, Alone offers a unique and unforgettable horror experience.

6. 10 Trivia Facts:

1. The film was remade in India as "Click" in 2010.

2. Alone was the second collaboration between directors Banjong Pisanthanakun and Parkpoom Wongpoom after their hit film "Shutter."

3. The movie's Thai title, "Faet," means "twin."

4. Marsha Wattanapanich, who played both Pim and Ploy, is primarily known as a pop singer in Thailand.

5. The film uses a variety of practical effects and camera tricks to create the illusion of conjoined twins.

6. Alone won the Best Film award at the 2008 Fantastic Fest in Austin, Texas.

7. The directors were inspired by real-life stories of conjoined twins for the film's concept.

8. The movie features minimal dialogue, relying heavily on visual storytelling.

9. Some scenes were shot in South Korea, where part of the story takes place.

10. The film's twist ending was kept secret during production, with only key crew members knowing the full plot.

4. Coming Soon

1. Movie Title: Coming Soon (โปรแกรมหน้า วิญญาณอาฆาต)

2. Year of Release: 2008

3. Cast and Director:

  - Director: Sophon Sakdaphisit

  - Cast: Chantavit Dhanasevi, Nuengthida Sophon, Sakulrath Thomas

4. Synopsis:

Coming Soon follows Shomba, a young man who makes money by illegally recording movies in theaters and selling pirated DVDs. While recording a new horror film called "Coming Soon," Shomba experiences strange phenomena in the cinema. He soon realizes that the events in the horror movie are manifesting in real life, and he's being pursued by the vengeful spirit from the film. As Shomba investigates the origins of the movie, he uncovers a dark secret involving the disappearance of the film's lead actress. With the line between fiction and reality blurring, Shomba must solve the mystery before he becomes the next victim of the curse. The film plays with meta-horror concepts, creating a layered narrative that keeps the audience guessing until the end.

5. Why This Movie Is Recommended:

Coming Soon offers a fresh and meta take on the horror genre, cleverly blending reality and fiction to create a uniquely unsettling experience. The film's exploration of the power of cinema and urban legends adds depth to its scares. Director Sophon Sakdaphisit masterfully builds tension, using the familiar setting of a movie theater to create an atmosphere of claustrophobic dread. The movie's self-referential nature and commentary on film piracy give it an extra layer of social relevance. With its innovative premise, effective scares, and thought-provoking themes, Coming Soon stands out as a intelligent and entertaining entry in the Thai horror canon.

6. 10 Trivia Facts:

1. Director Sophon Sakdaphisit was one of the writers of the hit Thai horror film "Shutter."

2. The film within the film, also titled "Coming Soon," was created specifically for this movie.

3. Coming Soon was partly inspired by the rise of film piracy in Thailand.

4. The movie features several homages to classic horror films, both Thai and international.

5. Some scenes were shot in actual Thai movie theaters, adding to the film's authenticity.

6. The film's original Thai title translates to "Next Program: Vengeful Spirit."

7. Coming Soon was Sophon Sakdaphisit's directorial debut.

8. The movie sparked discussions about superstitions surrounding film production in Thailand.

9. Some of the film's most effective scares were achieved through practical effects rather than CGI.

10. The movie's success led to increased security measures in Thai cinemas to prevent illegal recording.

5. Phobia 2

1. Movie Title: Phobia 2 (ห้าแพร่ง)

2. Year of Release: 2009

3. Cast and Director:

- Directors: Banjong Pisanthanakun, Paween Purijitpanya, Songyos Sugmakanan, Parkpoom Wongpoom, Visute Poolvoralaks

- Cast: Varies by segment (anthology film)

4. Synopsis:

Phobia 2 is an anthology horror film consisting of five separate stories, each directed by a different filmmaker. The segments include:

1. "Novice" - A young man who temporarily becomes a monk to avoid the draft faces supernatural consequences for his deception.

2. "Ward" - A young car accident victim shares a hospital room with a comatose older man, leading to terrifying nocturnal experiences.

3. "Backpackers" - Two foreign backpackers in Thailand hitch a ride with a suspicious truck driver.

4. "Salvage" - A used car saleswoman faces retribution from the spirits of accident victims whose vehicles she's selling.

5. "In the End" - A meta-horror story about the haunted production of a horror film.

Each tale explores different aspects of Thai folklore and urban legends, creating a diverse and chilling collection of horror stories.

5. Why This Movie Is Recommended:

Phobia 2 showcases the breadth and depth of Thai horror cinema, offering a variety of scares and storytelling styles in one package. The anthology format allows for exploration of multiple horror subgenres, from supernatural terror to psychological thrills. Each segment is crafted by a talented director, ensuring high quality across the film. The movie's ability to tap into uniquely Thai fears and superstitions, while also addressing universal horror themes, makes it accessible to a wide audience. With its mix of traditional ghost stories and modern urban legends, Phobia 2 provides a comprehensive and entertaining overview of contemporary Thai horror.

6. 10 Trivia Facts:

1. Phobia 2 is a sequel to the 2008 anthology film "4bia" (Phobia).

2. The film's Thai title, "Ha Phrang," means "Five Crossroads," referring to the five stories.

3. The "In the End" segment features cameos from several well-known Thai actors and directors.

4. Phobia 2 was a major commercial success in Thailand, outperforming its predecessor.

5. The film won several awards at the Thailand National Film Association Awards.

6. Each segment was shot independently, with different crews and production schedules.

7. The "Novice" segment was inspired by real-life cases of young men becoming monks to avoid military conscription.

8. "Ward" was shot entirely in a real, functioning hospital.

9. The truck used in the "Backpackers" segment was specially modified for the film.

10. Phobia 2 helped launch the careers of several young Thai actors who have since become major stars.

6. Laddaland

1. Movie Title: Laddaland (แหยม ยโสธร)

2. Year of Release: 2011

3. Cast and Director:

- Director: Sopon Sukdapisit

- Cast: Saharat Sangkapreecha, Piyathida Woramusik, Sutatta Udomsilp

4. Synopsis:

Laddaland follows a middle-class family that moves to a luxurious housing development in Chiang Mai, seeking a better life. However, their dreams of suburban bliss quickly turn into a nightmare as they encounter a series of disturbing supernatural events. The father, struggling with financial problems and the pressure to provide for his family, becomes increasingly unstable as the hauntings escalate. The film explores how the family's relationships are tested by both external supernatural forces and internal tensions. As they uncover dark secrets about their new neighborhood and its residents, the line between reality and paranormal terror blurs, leading to a shocking climax that challenges their perceptions and family bonds.

5. Why This Movie Is Recommended:

Laddaland stands out for its effective blend of supernatural horror and social commentary. The film uses the haunted house trope to explore deeper themes of class anxiety, family dynamics, and the dark side of Thailand's rapid urbanization. Director Sopon Sukdapisit creates a palpable atmosphere of dread that builds slowly, making the scares all the more impactful. The strong performances, particularly from Saharat Sangkapreecha as the father, add emotional depth to the horror elements. Laddaland's ability to balance genuine frights with thoughtful social critique makes it a compelling and memorable entry in Thai horror cinema.

6. 10 Trivia Facts:

1. The film is loosely based on real events that occurred in a housing development in Chiang Mai.

2. Laddaland was a major box office success in Thailand, becoming one of the highest-grossing Thai films of 2011.

3. The movie's success spawned a sequel, "Laddaland 2," released in 2018.

4. Director Sopon Sukdapisit was one of the writers of the hit Thai horror film "Shutter."

5. The film's title refers to the name of the fictional housing development where the story takes place.

6. Laddaland won several awards, including Best Film at the Thailand National Film Association Awards.

7. The movie sparked discussions about urban legends and superstitions in modern Thai society.

8. Some of the film's locations in Chiang Mai became popular tourist attractions after its release.

9. The director conducted extensive research on real-life hauntings in Thai housing developments for authenticity.

10. Laddaland was one of the first Thai horror films to focus on the psychological breakdown of a family unit.

7. Body

1. Movie Title: Body (บอดี้ ศพ #19)

2. Year of Release: 2007

3. Cast and Director:

- Director: Paween Purikitpanya

- Cast: Arak Amornsupasiri, Ornjira Lamwilai, Kritteera Inpornwijit

4. Synopsis:

Body centers around Chon, a medical student struggling with guilt after a hit-and-run accident. When he starts his internship at a hospital morgue, Chon begins experiencing terrifying visions and supernatural occurrences linked to the corpses he's examining. As the hauntings intensify, Chon realizes they're connected to his past actions and the accident victim's body, which is missing from the morgue. The film delves into themes of karma and the consequences of one's actions as Chon tries to unravel the mystery and confront his own guilt. The line between reality and hallucination blurs, leading to a shocking revelation that ties together the supernatural events and Chon's troubled conscience.

5. Why This Movie Is Recommended:

Body stands out for its unique blend of psychological horror and medical thriller elements. Director Paween Purikitpanya creates a claustrophobic atmosphere within the hospital setting, using innovative visual techniques to blur the line between the living and the dead. The film's exploration of guilt, karma, and the psychological toll of keeping dark secrets adds depth to its scares. With its striking imagery, clever plot twists, and thoughtful examination of Thai spiritual beliefs, Body offers a fresh and intellectually engaging take on the ghost story genre, making it a must-see for fans of psychological horror.

6. 10 Trivia Facts:

1. The film's Thai title, "Body Sop #19," refers to the 19th corpse in the morgue, which plays a crucial role in the story.

2. Body was Paween Purikitpanya's directorial debut.

3. The movie won the Best Special Effects award at the Thailand National Film Association Awards.

4. Many of the film's morgue scenes were shot in a real hospital to enhance authenticity.

5. The director consulted with medical professionals to ensure accurate depiction of morgue procedures.

6. Body's success led to Purikitpanya directing a segment in the horror anthology "Phobia 2."

7. The film uses a unique color palette and lighting technique to distinguish between reality and supernatural occurrences.

8. Body was one of the first Thai horror films to extensively use CGI for its ghost effects.

9. The movie sparked discussions about medical ethics and the treatment of the dead in Thai society.

10. Some of the film's more graphic autopsy scenes caused controversy upon its release.

8. The Unseeable

1. Movie Title: The Unseeable (เดอะ อันซีเอเบิล)

2. Year of Release: 2006

3. Cast and Director:

  - Director: Wisit Sasanatieng

  - Cast: Siraphan Wattanajinda, Supornthip Choungrangsee, Tassawan Seneewongse

4. Synopsis:

Set in 1930s Thailand, The Unseeable follows Nualjan, a pregnant young woman who arrives at a secluded mansion seeking her missing husband. She's taken in by the mansion's stern mistress, Madame Ranjuan, and encounters other mysterious residents, including a mischievous girl named Choy. As Nualjan settles into life at the mansion, she experiences increasingly strange and terrifying phenomena. The boundaries between the living and the dead blur as she uncovers dark secrets about the house and its inhabitants. The film weaves together elements of Thai folklore, ghost stories, and period drama, building to a shocking revelation that challenges Nualjan's perception of reality and her own existence.

5. Why This Movie Is Recommended:

The Unseeable stands out for its unique blend of ghost story, mystery, and period drama. Director Wisit Sasanatieng, known for his vibrant visual style, creates a hauntingly beautiful Gothic atmosphere rarely seen in Thai cinema. The film's intricate plot, filled with twists and revelations, keeps viewers engaged beyond mere scares. Its exploration of Thai supernatural beliefs and social customs of the 1930s adds cultural depth to the horror elements. With its stunning cinematography, strong performances, and clever subversion of ghost story tropes, The Unseeable offers a sophisticated and visually striking entry in the Thai horror genre.

6. 10 Trivia Facts:

1. The film's Thai title, "Pen Choo Kab Pee," roughly translates to "See Ghosts."

2. Director Wisit Sasanatieng is known for his unique visual style, previously showcased in films like "Tears of the Black Tiger."

3. The Unseeable won several awards, including Best Art Direction at the Thailand National Film Association Awards.

4. The movie's 1930s setting required extensive research into period costumes and set design.

5. Many of the film's ghostly effects were achieved through practical means rather than CGI.

6. The Unseeable incorporates elements of traditional Thai ghost stories and folklore.

7. The film's mansion setting was a combination of real locations and specially constructed sets.

8. Wisit Sasanatieng wrote the screenplay in addition to directing the film.

9. The movie's twist ending sparked numerous fan theories and discussions online.

10. The Unseeable was praised for its feminist undertones and exploration of women's roles in 1930s Thai society.

9. Pee Mak

1. Movie Title: Pee Mak (พีมาก..พระโขนง)

2. Year of Release: 2013

3. Cast and Director:

- Director: Banjong Pisanthanakun

- Cast: Mario Maurer, Davika Hoorne, Nattapong Chartpong, Kantapat Permpoonpatcharasuk, Pongsatorn Jongwilak

4. Synopsis:

Pee Mak is a horror-comedy retelling of the classic Thai ghost story "Mae Nak Phra Khanong." Set during the Rattanakosin Era, it follows Mak, a young man who returns from war to his wife Nak and their newborn child. Unbeknownst to Mak, Nak and their child died during childbirth and have become ghosts. Mak's four loyal friends try to warn him about his wife's supernatural nature, leading to a series of humorous and scary situations. As Mak slowly realizes the truth, he must confront his feelings for Nak and the reality of their impossible situation. The film cleverly blends elements of horror, romance, and comedy, offering a fresh take on a well-known legend.

5. Why This Movie Is Recommended:

Pee Mak stands out for its innovative approach to a classic Thai ghost story, successfully blending horror elements with laugh-out-loud comedy. Director Banjong Pisanthanakun, known for serious horror films like "Shutter," demonstrates his versatility in crafting a film that's both genuinely funny and occasionally scary. The movie's balance of humor, romance, and supernatural elements makes it accessible to a wide audience, including those who don't typically enjoy horror. With its charismatic cast, clever script, and respectful yet playful treatment of Thai folklore, Pee Mak offers a refreshing and entertaining twist on the ghost movie genre.

6. 10 Trivia Facts:

1. Pee Mak became the highest-grossing Thai film of all time upon its release.

2. The film is based on Thailand's most famous ghost story, which has been adapted numerous times.

3. Pee Mak's success led to its release in several other Asian countries, a rarity for Thai films.

4. The movie features numerous references to other famous horror films, both Thai and international.

5. Director Banjong Pisanthanakun originally planned to make a straight horror film before deciding on a horror-comedy approach.

6. The film's period setting required extensive research and preparation for costumes and set design.

7. Pee Mak's success sparked a trend of horror-comedies in Thai cinema.

8. The movie was filmed in various historical locations in Thailand to maintain authenticity.

9. Pee Mak won several awards, including Best Film at the Osaka Asian Film Festival.

10. The film's portrayal of the ghost Nak as a sympathetic character was praised for its originality.

10. The Victim

1. Movie Title: The Victim (เหยื่อ)

2. Year of Release: 2006

3. Cast and Director:

- Director: Monthon Arayangkoon

- Cast: Pitchanart Sakakorn, Apasiri Nitibhon, Penpak Sirikul

4. Synopsis:

The Victim follows Ting, a struggling actress who takes a job with the police department reenacting crime scenes to help solve cold cases. As she immerses herself in the roles of various murder victims, Ting begins to experience supernatural phenomena and is haunted by the spirits of the deceased. The line between acting and reality blurs as Ting becomes increasingly involved in a particular case involving a missing woman. As she delves deeper into the mystery, Ting uncovers a dark conspiracy and finds herself in real danger. The film explores themes of identity, the nature of performance, and the lingering effects of unresolved crimes, building to a shocking twist that challenges perceptions of reality and the supernatural.

5. Why This Movie Is Recommended:

The Victim stands out for its innovative premise that blends elements of police procedural, supernatural horror, and psychological thriller. Director Monthon Arayangkoon creates a tense atmosphere that keeps viewers guessing about what's real and what's performance. The film's exploration of the psychological toll of inhabiting the personas of murder victims adds depth to its scares. With its clever plot twists, strong lead performance by Pitchanart Sakakorn, and unique take on the ghost story genre, The Victim offers a thought-provoking and genuinely unsettling horror experience that lingers in the mind long after viewing.

6. 10 Trivia Facts:

1. The film was inspired by the real practice of crime reenactment used by Thai police.

2. Lead actress Pitchanart Sakakorn had to portray multiple characters within the film due to her role as a reenactment actress.

3. The Victim won the Best Special Effects award at the Thailand National Film Association Awards.

4. Some scenes were filmed in actual Thai police stations to enhance authenticity.

5. The movie's success led to a sequel, "The Victim 2," released in 2020.

6. Director Monthon Arayangkoon conducted extensive research on police procedures and unsolved cases in Thailand.

7. The film uses a unique color grading technique to distinguish between reality and reenactments.

8. The Victim was one of the first Thai horror films to gain significant international distribution.

9. The movie sparked discussions about the ethics of crime reenactments and their impact on actors.

10. Some of the film's more intense reenactment scenes were based on real unsolved cases in Thailand.

11. 3 A.M.

1. Movie Title: 3 A.M. (ตีสาม คืนสยอง)

2. Year of Release: 2012

3. Cast and Director:

- Directors: Patchanon Thammajira, Kirati Nakintanon, Isara Nadee

- Cast: Shahkrit Yamnam, Ray MacDonald, Apinya Sakuljaroensuk

4. Synopsis:

3 A.M. is an anthology horror film consisting of three interconnected stories, all set during the witching hour. The first story, "The Wig," follows a woman who buys a cursed wig, unleashing a vengeful spirit. The second tale, "The Corpse Bride," centers on a man who must fulfill a promise to marry a ghost. The final segment, "The Shift," takes place in a hospital where a nurse encounters supernatural events during her night shift. Each story explores different aspects of Thai supernatural beliefs and urban legends, building tension and scares as the clock approaches 3 A.M., the hour when the veil between the living and dead is thinnest.

5. Why This Movie Is Recommended:

3 A.M. offers a diverse sampling of Thai horror, showcasing different styles and subgenres within a cohesive framework. The anthology format allows for a variety of scares and storytelling techniques, keeping the audience engaged throughout. Each segment is crafted with attention to building suspense and delivering effective jump scares. The film's exploration of Thai superstitions and ghost lore adds cultural depth to the horror elements. With its mix of traditional ghost stories and modern urban settings, 3 A.M. provides an entertaining and comprehensive look at contemporary Thai horror cinema.

6. 10 Trivia Facts:

1. The film's title refers to the belief that 3 A.M. is when supernatural activity is at its peak.

2. Each segment was directed by a different filmmaker, allowing for unique styles within the anthology.

3. The movie's success led to a sequel, "3 A.M. 3D," released in 2014.

4. Some scenes in "The Shift" segment were filmed in an actual operating hospital.

5. The film incorporates elements of real Thai urban legends and ghost stories.

6. 3 A.M. was one of the first Thai horror anthologies to achieve significant commercial success.

7. The movie sparked renewed interest in the anthology format in Thai cinema.

8. Each story in the film is loosely connected, with subtle references to the others.

9. The directors conducted research on night shift workers' experiences for authenticity in "The Shift" segment.

10. 3 A.M. utilizes a mix of practical effects and CGI for its supernatural elements.

12. Inhuman Kiss

1. Movie Title: Inhuman Kiss (แสงกระสือ)

2. Year of Release: 2019

3. Cast and Director:

- Director: Sitisiri Mongkolsiri

- Cast: Phantira Pipityakorn, Oabnithi Wiwattanawarang, Sapol Assawamunkong

4. Synopsis:

Set in a rural Thai village, Inhuman Kiss tells the story of Sai, a teenage girl cursed to become a Krasue - a nocturnal female spirit of Southeast Asian folklore whose head detaches from her body to hunt for food. As Sai struggles with her condition, she finds herself caught between her childhood friend Noi, who wants to protect her, and Jerd, a monster hunter determined to eliminate the Krasue threat. The film blends elements of horror, romance, and coming-of-age drama as it explores Sai's attempts to maintain her humanity while grappling with her supernatural curse. As tensions in the village escalate and Sai's secret becomes harder to hide, the characters are forced to confront their fears, prejudices, and the true nature of monstrosity.

5. Why This Movie Is Recommended:

Inhuman Kiss stands out for its fresh take on traditional Southeast Asian folklore, blending horror elements with a touching coming-of-age story. Director Sitisiri Mongkolsiri creates a visually stunning film that balances supernatural scares with genuine emotional depth. The movie's exploration of themes like acceptance, prejudice, and the nature of humanity adds layers to its horror foundation. With strong performances, impressive special effects, and a unique premise, Inhuman Kiss offers a compelling and thoughtful entry in the Thai horror genre that appeals to both horror fans and those who appreciate character-driven storytelling.

6. 10 Trivia Facts:

1. The film was selected as the Thai entry for Best International Feature Film at the 92nd Academy Awards.

2. Inhuman Kiss is based on the Krasue, a spirit in Southeast Asian folklore.

3. The movie's Thai title, "Sang Krasue," translates to "Light of the Krasue."

4. Extensive prosthetics and CGI were used to create the Krasue effects.

5. The film sparked renewed interest in traditional Thai folklore among younger audiences.

6. Director Sitisiri Mongkolsiri conducted extensive research on Krasue legends across Southeast Asia.

7. Inhuman Kiss won several awards at the Thailand National Film Association Awards.

8. The movie was filmed on location in rural Thailand to capture authentic village life.

9. The film's success led to discussions about a potential sequel or spin-off.

10. Inhuman Kiss was one of the first Thai horror films to receive significant international distribution in recent years.

13. The Promise

1. Movie Title: The Promise (เพื่อน..ที่ระลึก)

2. Year of Release: 2017

3. Cast and Director:

- Director: Sophon Sakdaphisit

- Cast: Numthip Jongrachatawiboon, Apichaya Thongkham, Thunyaphat Pattarateerachaicharoen

4. Synopsis:

The Promise centers around two childhood friends, Boum and Ib, who make a suicide pact as teenagers due to family problems. However, at the last moment, Boum backs out, leaving Ib to die alone. Twenty years later, Boum is a successful businesswoman, but she's haunted by guilt and strange occurrences that seem linked to her broken promise. As supernatural events escalate, Boum must confront her past and the vengeful spirit of her friend. The film explores themes of friendship, betrayal, and the consequences of unfulfilled promises, building tension as Boum unravels the mystery behind the hauntings and faces the repercussions of her actions.

5. Why This Movie Is Recommended:

The Promise stands out for its emotionally charged narrative that blends supernatural horror with psychological thriller elements. Director Sophon Sakdaphisit, known for his work on "Shutter," crafts a haunting tale that delves deep into themes of guilt, regret, and the enduring power of promises. The film's non-linear storytelling keeps viewers engaged, slowly revealing the tragic backstory while ratcheting up the tension in the present. With its strong performances, particularly from lead actress Numthip Jongrachatawiboon, and its exploration of the psychological toll of survivor's guilt, The Promise offers a mature and thought-provoking take on the ghost story genre.

6. 10 Trivia Facts:

1. The film is loosely inspired by a real-life incident involving a suicide pact between schoolgirls in Thailand.

2. Director Sophon Sakdaphisit was one of the writers of the iconic Thai horror film "Shutter."

3. The Promise utilizes a dual timeline narrative structure, shifting between past and present.

4. The movie's Thai title, "Puen..Tee Raluek," roughly translates to "Friends...That Are Remembered."

5. The film sparked discussions about mental health and suicide prevention in Thailand.

6. Some scenes were shot in an abandoned building in Bangkok to enhance the eerie atmosphere.

7. The Promise won the Best Sound award at the Thailand National Film Association Awards.

8. The movie features subtle references to other famous Thai horror films.

9. The directors conducted interviews with psychologists to accurately portray the long-term effects of trauma.

10. The film's marketing campaign included a viral social media challenge related to promises.

14. Bangkok Haunted

1. Movie Title: Bangkok Haunted (ผีสามบาท)

2. Year of Release: 2001

3. Cast and Director:

  - Directors: Oxide Pang Chun, Pisut Praesangeam

  - Cast: Pimsiree Pimsee, Pramote Seangsorn, Dawan Singha-Wong

4. Synopsis:

  Bangkok Haunted is an anthology film consisting of three separate ghost stories set in the Thai capital. The first story, "Legend of the Drum," follows a young woman who becomes possessed by a spirit trapped in an antique drum. The second tale, "The Corpse Bride," centers on a police detective investigating a series of deaths linked to a mysterious woman. The final segment, "The Wet Nurse," tells the story of a modern woman who discovers her past life as a wet nurse in ancient Siam, uncovering a dark secret. Each story explores different aspects of Thai supernatural beliefs and urban legends, using Bangkok's blend of modernity and tradition as a backdrop for tales of horror and the paranormal.

5. Why This Movie Is Recommended:

  Bangkok Haunted offers a diverse sampling of Thai ghost lore, showcasing different styles of horror storytelling within the framework of urban Bangkok. The anthology format allows for exploration of various supernatural themes, from traditional folklore to modern urban legends. Directors Oxide Pang Chun and Pisut Praesangeam create a atmosphere that captures the city's unique blend of ancient superstitions and contemporary life. The film's use of practical effects and atmospheric cinematography enhances its scares. With its mix of psychological horror, supernatural thrills, and cultural insights, Bangkok Haunted provides an engaging introduction to Thai horror cinema.

6. 10 Trivia Facts:

  1. The film's Thai title, "Phii Sam Bat," translates to "Three Baht Ghosts," referring to the three separate stories.

  2. Co-director Oxide Pang Chun is one half of the famous Pang Brothers, known for films like "The Eye."

  3. Bangkok Haunted was one of the first Thai horror anthologies to gain international recognition.

  4. The movie utilizes various Bangkok landmarks and locations, showcasing the city's diverse environments.

  5. Each segment of the film explores a different aspect of Thai supernatural beliefs.

  6. The film's success contributed to the revival of the horror genre in Thai cinema in the early 2000s.

  7. Bangkok Haunted features minimal use of CGI, relying more on practical effects and atmosphere.

  8. The movie's structure, with three interconnected stories, influenced later Thai horror anthologies.

  9. Some scenes were shot in actual historic locations in Bangkok to enhance authenticity.

  10. The film incorporates elements of real Bangkok urban legends and ghost stories.

15. The Swimmers

1. Movie Title: The Swimmers (ฝากไว้ในกายเธอ)

2. Year of Release: 2014

3. Cast and Director:

- Director: Sopon Sukdapisit

- Cast: Thanapob Leeratanakajorn, Supassra Thanachat, Kao Supassara Thanachat

4. Synopsis:

The Swimmers revolves around a talented competitive swimmer named Perth and his girlfriend Tan. After a tragic accident during a competition that results in the death of a fellow swimmer, Perth begins experiencing strange phenomena in the pool. He starts seeing the ghost of the dead swimmer and becomes increasingly paranoid about the water. As Perth's fear intensifies, it affects his relationship with Tan and his swimming career. The couple must unravel the mystery behind the haunting, confronting dark secrets from the past and the true circumstances of the accident. The film explores themes of guilt, ambition, and the psychological toll of competitive sports, all while building supernatural tension in and around the swimming pool.

5. Why This Movie Is Recommended:

The Swimmers stands out for its unique setting, using the world of competitive swimming as a backdrop for supernatural horror. Director Sopon Sukdapisit, known for his work on "Shutter," creates a claustrophobic atmosphere that turns the familiar environment of a swimming pool into a source of dread. The film's exploration of the pressures faced by young athletes adds psychological depth to its ghost story elements. With its strong performances, innovative water-based scares, and thoughtful examination of guilt and ambition, The Swimmers offers a fresh and engaging take on the Thai horror genre that will appeal to both horror fans and sports enthusiasts.

6. 10 Trivia Facts:

1. The film's underwater scenes required specialized equipment and training for the cast and crew.

2. Director Sopon Sukdapisit was inspired by real-life pressures faced by competitive swimmers in Thailand.

3. The Swimmers features some of the most extensive underwater filming in Thai cinema history.

4. Lead actor Thanapob Leeratanakajorn underwent intensive swim training for his role.

5. The movie's success led to increased interest in swimming as a sport among Thai youth.

6. Some scenes were filmed in actual competitive swimming facilities in Thailand.

7. The film incorporates elements of water-related folklore and superstitions from various cultures.

8. The Swimmers won awards for its sound design, which was crucial for creating tension in the pool scenes.

9. The movie sparked discussions about safety and mental health in competitive sports in Thailand.

10. Some of the ghost effects were achieved through a combination of practical underwater techniques and CGI.

16. Dorm

1. Movie Title: Dorm (เด็กหอ)

2. Year of Release: 2006

3. Cast and Director:

  - Director: Songyos Sugmakanan

  - Cast: Charlee Trairat, Nipawan Taveepornsawan, Sirachuch Chienthaworn

4. Synopsis:

  Dorm follows 12-year-old Ton, who is sent to a remote all-boys boarding school by his father. Struggling to adjust to his new environment, Ton befriends Vichien, a mysterious boy who seems different from the others. As strange occurrences begin to plague the school, Ton discovers that Vichien is actually a ghost who died in the school's swimming pool years ago. The film explores Ton's journey as he helps Vichien resolve his unfinished business while also dealing with his own feelings of abandonment and the challenges of growing up. Blending elements of coming-of-age drama with supernatural horror, Dorm creates a poignant and eerie tale about friendship, loss, and the lingering effects of the past.

5. Why This Movie Is Recommended:

  Dorm stands out for its sensitive portrayal of adolescence intertwined with ghostly elements. Director Songyos Sugmakanan crafts a film that's as much a touching drama as it is a ghost story, creating a unique atmosphere that's both melancholic and chilling. The movie's exploration of themes like loneliness, friendship, and the pain of growing up adds emotional depth to its supernatural plot. With strong performances from its young cast, beautifully atmospheric cinematography, and a storyline that resonates with audiences of all ages, Dorm offers a refreshing and thoughtful take on the horror genre that lingers in the mind long after viewing.

6. 10 Trivia Facts:

  1. Dorm won several awards, including Best Film at the Thailand National Film Association Awards.

  2. The movie was partly inspired by the director's own experiences in boarding school.

  3. Many of the child actors in the film had no prior acting experience.

  4. The school's swimming pool, central to the plot, was specially constructed for the film.

  5. Dorm's success led to a novelization and a stage play adaptation.

  6. The film's soundtrack, featuring Thai indie rock, gained popularity independently of the movie.

  7. Director Songyos Sugmakanan was part of the team behind the hit Thai horror film "Shutter."

  8. The movie was shot on location at a real boarding school in rural Thailand.

  9. Dorm's portrayal of school life sparked discussions about the Thai education system.

  10. The film's ghost effects were achieved primarily through practical effects rather than CGI.

17. Long Weekend

1. Movie Title: Long Weekend (เพื่อนแก้เหงา)

2. Year of Release: 2013

3. Cast and Director:

  - Director: Taweewat Wantha

  - Cast: Namthip Jongrachatawiboon, Willy McIntosh, Atthaphan Phunsawat

4. Synopsis:

  Long Weekend centers around Phueng, a lonely office worker who decides to spend a holiday weekend at home. Her solitude is interrupted when she receives a mysterious package containing an old mobile phone. Curious, she turns it on and begins receiving calls and messages from a woman named Ploy, who claims to be from the past. As Phueng becomes more involved in Ploy's life through their conversations, she realizes that she might be able to change the course of history and prevent a tragedy. However, her meddling with time has unforeseen consequences, leading to a series of terrifying events that blur the lines between past and present, reality and nightmare.

5. Why This Movie Is Recommended:

  Long Weekend offers a unique blend of supernatural horror and time-bending thriller that sets it apart from typical ghost stories. Director Taweewat Wantha creates a tense, claustrophobic atmosphere within the confines of the protagonist's apartment, using the concept of modern technology connecting to the past in inventive and chilling ways. The film's exploration of loneliness, regret, and the desire to change the past adds psychological depth to its scares. With its clever plot twists, strong lead performance by Namthip Jongrachatawiboon, and innovative use of the mobile phone as a conduit for horror, Long Weekend provides a fresh and engaging entry in the Thai horror genre that will keep viewers guessing until the end.

6. 10 Trivia Facts:

  1. The film's Thai title, "Puen Kae Ngao," translates to "Friend to Cure Loneliness."

  2. Long Weekend was shot almost entirely in a single apartment, creating unique challenges for the filmmakers.

  3. The movie's concept was partially inspired by the rise of smartphone addiction in Thai society.

  4. Director Taweewat Wantha conducted research on theories of time travel and parallel universes for the script.

  5. The film uses a distinct color palette to differentiate between past and present scenes.

  6. Long Weekend's success led to discussions about a potential sequel or series adaptation.

  7. The movie features subtle references to classic Thai ghost films.

  8. The old mobile phone used in the film was a carefully selected model to evoke early 2000s nostalgia.

  9. Some scenes required complex choreography to create the illusion of time distortion.

  10. The film's sound design, crucial for the phone call scenes, won accolades at Thai film festivals.

18. The Eye (Thai Version)

1. Movie Title: The Eye (คนเห็นผี)

2. Year of Release: 2002

3. Cast and Director:

  - Directors: Oxide Pang Chun, Danny Pang

  - Cast: Angelica Lee, Lawrence Chou, Chutcha Rujinanon

4. Synopsis:

The Eye follows Mun, a blind woman who undergoes a corneal transplant to restore her vision. As she adjusts to her newfound sight, Mun begins to see mysterious and terrifying things that others can't - including ghosts and premonitions of death. Troubled by these visions, she seeks help from her doctor, Wah, to uncover the truth behind her new eyes. Their investigation leads them to Thailand, where they discover the tragic story of the cornea donor. As Mun grapples with her unwanted ability to see the supernatural world, she must also confront a impending disaster that only she can prevent. The film explores themes of identity, the nature of sight, and the thin line between gift and curse.

5. Why This Movie Is Recommended:

The Eye stands out for its innovative take on the "sixth sense" concept, blending psychological horror with visceral scares. Directors Oxide Pang Chun and Danny Pang create a visually striking film that uses Mun's perspective to blur the lines between reality and the supernatural. The movie's exploration of cultural differences between Hong Kong and Thailand adds depth to its ghost story elements. With its strong lead performance, memorable set pieces, and a finale that combines personal drama with large-scale tragedy, The Eye offers a compelling and influential entry in the Asian horror genre. Its success sparked numerous remakes and solidified the Pang Brothers as major figures in international horror cinema.

6. 10 Trivia Facts:

1. While set partially in Hong Kong, significant portions of the film were shot in Thailand.

2. The Eye was inspired by a real-life news story about a corneal transplant recipient experiencing strange phenomena.

3. The movie's success led to three sequels and remakes in several countries, including a Hollywood version starring Jessica Alba.

4. The famous "elevator scene" has been referenced and parodied in numerous other films.

5. Actress Angelica Lee learned Cantonese and studied blind mannerisms for her role.

6. The film uses a variety of visual techniques to represent Mun's changing perception of the world.

7. The Eye was one of the first pan-Asian horror productions, involving talent from Hong Kong, Singapore, and Thailand.

8. The movie's Thai scenes incorporate elements of real Thai ghost beliefs and folklore.

9. The Pang Brothers used minimal CGI, relying more on practical effects and creative cinematography.

10. The Eye's international success helped pave the way for more Thai horror films to reach global audiences.

19. Diary

1. Movie Title: Diary (เฉือน)

2. Year of Release: 2007

3. Cast and Director:

- Director: Oxide Pang Chun

- Cast: Charlene Choi, Isabella Leong, Guo Xiaodong

4. Synopsis:

Diary tells the story of Winnie, a Hong Kong woman who travels to Thailand in search of her missing boyfriend, Seth. Armed only with Seth's personal diary, Winnie retraces his steps through Thailand, experiencing strange and terrifying incidents along the way. As she delves deeper into the mystery, the line between reality and nightmare begins to blur. Winnie starts to question her own sanity as she encounters seemingly supernatural events and discovers dark secrets about Seth's past. The film explores themes of memory, identity, and the unreliability of personal narratives, building to a shocking twist that forces Winnie to confront the truth about her relationship and herself.

5. Why This Movie Is Recommended:

Diary stands out for its psychological approach to horror, blending elements of mystery thriller with supernatural scares. Director Oxide Pang Chun, known for "The Eye," creates a disorienting and atmospheric experience that keeps viewers guessing until the end. The film's use of Thailand as both an exotic and menacing backdrop adds to its unsettling tone. With its non-linear narrative, unreliable narrator, and exploration of the subjective nature of memory, Diary offers a cerebral and haunting take on the horror genre. The strong performance by Charlene Choi and the film's mind-bending finale make it a compelling watch for fans of psychological horror.

6. 10 Trivia Facts:

1. Diary was shot on location in various parts of Thailand, showcasing both urban and rural settings.

2. The film's Thai title, "Chuen," means "to slice" or "to cut," referencing both physical and psychological elements of the story.

3. Director Oxide Pang Chun incorporated elements of Thai folklore and superstitions into the narrative.

4. Diary features minimal dialogue, relying heavily on visual storytelling and atmosphere.

5. The movie's non-linear structure was inspired by psychological thriller novels.

6. Charlene Choi, primarily known for her work in Hong Kong pop music and romantic comedies, was cast against type for this serious role.

7. The film uses a distinct visual style to differentiate between reality and Winnie's increasingly fragmented mental state.

8. Diary's ambiguous ending has sparked numerous fan theories and interpretations.

9. The movie incorporates themes of travel and cultural displacement common in Pang's works.

10. Some of the film's more surreal sequences were inspired by the director's own vivid nightmares.

20. 4bia

1. Movie Title: 4bia (สี่แพร่ง)

2. Year of Release: 2008

3. Cast and Director:

- Directors: Youngyooth Thongkonthun, Banjong Pisanthanakun, Parkpoom Wongpoom, Paween Purijitpanya

- Cast: Maneerat Khamuan, Witawat Singlampong, Apinya Sakuljaroensuk (varies by segment)

4. Synopsis:

4bia is an anthology horror film consisting of four separate but interconnected stories. The first segment, "Happiness," follows a lonely girl who begins receiving mysterious text messages. "Tit for Tat" tells the story of bullied teenagers seeking supernatural revenge. "In the Middle" is a darkly comedic tale of four friends on a camping trip where one dies but doesn't leave. The final segment, "Last Fright," centers on a flight attendant left alone on a plane with a dead body. Each story explores different aspects of Thai horror, from ghost stories and black magic to urban legends and psychological terror, creating a diverse and chilling collection of tales.

5. Why This Movie Is Recommended:

4bia showcases the versatility and creativity of Thai horror cinema, offering a range of scares and storytelling styles within a single film. The anthology format allows for exploration of various horror subgenres, from technological terror to traditional ghost stories. Each segment is crafted by a talented director, ensuring high quality across the film. The movie's ability to balance humor, suspense, and outright horror keeps viewers engaged throughout. With its clever interconnections between stories and a mix of familiar and innovative horror tropes, 4bia provides an entertaining and comprehensive overview of contemporary Thai horror that appeals to both casual viewers and genre enthusiasts.

6. 10 Trivia Facts:

1. The film's title, "4bia," is a play on the word "phobia" and the number of segments in the anthology.

2. 4bia's success led to a sequel, "Phobia 2," released in 2009.

3. Each segment was shot independently with different crews, creating unique visual styles for each story.

4. The movie features a mix of established actors and newcomers to the Thai film industry.

5. "In the Middle" segment parodies several famous horror film tropes and clichés.

6. The film's interconnected nature inspired similar anthology formats in other Asian horror productions.

7. 4bia was one of the first Thai horror films to extensively incorporate modern technology into its stories.

8. The movie's marketing campaign included viral social media elements related to each segment.

9. Some of the film's locations became popular tourist attractions for horror fans visiting Thailand.

10. 4bia's critical and commercial success helped solidify Thailand's reputation for quality horror cinema internationally.

Singapore

1. 23:59

1. Movie Title: 23:59

2. Year of Release: 2011

3. Cast and Director:

- Director: Gilbert Chan

- Cast: Tedd Chan, Stella Chung, Henley Hii, Lawrence Koh

4. Synopsis:

Set in 1983, "23:59" follows a group of army recruits on a secluded island in Singapore. The story revolves around a superstition that at 23:59 (11:59 PM), supernatural occurrences are more likely to happen. As strange events begin to unfold, the recruits find themselves facing their deepest fears and darkest secrets. The film explores themes of guilt, redemption, and the psychological impact of military service, all while building a tense, supernatural atmosphere. As the recruits delve deeper into the island's haunted history, they must confront both real and imagined horrors to survive their ordeal.

5. Why This Movie Is Recommended:

"23:59" stands out for its unique blend of military drama and supernatural horror, a combination rarely seen in Southeast Asian cinema. The film effectively uses its isolated setting to create a claustrophobic atmosphere, heightening the sense of dread and anticipation. Its exploration of local superstitions and military culture adds depth to the narrative, making it more than just a series of scares. The movie's ability to balance psychological tension with supernatural elements makes it a compelling watch for both horror fans and those interested in Singaporean cinema.

6. 10 Trivia Facts:

1. The film is loosely based on true ghost stories from the Singapore Armed Forces.

2. "23:59" was one of the first Singaporean horror films to gain international distribution.

3. The movie was shot on location in Singapore, including actual military facilities.

4. Director Gilbert Chan conducted extensive interviews with army veterans to ensure authenticity.

5. The film's success led to a sequel, "23:59: The Haunting Hour," released in 2018.

6. Many of the cast members underwent basic military training to prepare for their roles.

7. The movie's release coincided with the "Hungry Ghost Festival" in Singapore for maximum impact.

8. Some scenes were filmed in the infamous Old Changi Hospital, known for its alleged hauntings.

9. The film uses a mix of Mandarin, English, and Singlish, reflecting Singapore's linguistic diversity.

10. "23:59" was one of the highest-grossing Singaporean films of 2011.

2. Haunted Changi

1. Movie Title: Haunted Changi

2. Year of Release: 2010

3. Cast and Director:

- Director: Andrew Lau

- Cast: Sheena Chung, Farid Azlam, Aiden Sng

4. Synopsis:

"Haunted Changi" is a found-footage style horror film that follows a group of local filmmakers as they investigate the infamous Old Changi Hospital in Singapore. Known for its dark history during World War II and subsequent paranormal reputation, the hospital becomes the center of their documentary project. As the team spends more time in the abandoned building, they begin to experience increasingly disturbing supernatural events. The line between reality and the paranormal blurs, and the filmmakers find themselves caught in a terrifying struggle for survival. The movie builds tension through its realistic approach, leaving viewers to question what is real and what is manufactured.

5. Why This Movie Is Recommended:

"Haunted Changi" stands out for its innovative use of the found-footage genre in a Singaporean context. By focusing on a real location with a notorious reputation, the film taps into local urban legends and historical traumas, adding depth to its scares. The movie's low-budget, documentary-style approach creates a sense of authenticity that enhances the horror elements. It serves as both a spine-chilling ghost story and a commentary on the intersection of history, memory, and the supernatural in Singapore's cultural landscape.

6. 10 Trivia Facts:

1. The Old Changi Hospital, featured in the film, is a real abandoned hospital in Singapore with a reputation for being haunted.

2. Some scenes were actually filmed in the Old Changi Hospital, adding to the film's authenticity.

3. The movie sparked renewed interest in urban exploration of abandoned sites in Singapore.

4. The filmmakers incorporated real historical facts about the hospital's use during WWII into the narrative.

5. "Haunted Changi" was one of the first Singaporean films to fully embrace the found-footage horror style.

6. The movie's marketing campaign included viral videos and a faux-documentary approach, blurring the lines between fiction and reality.

7. Some viewers initially believed the film to be a real documentary due to its realistic style.

8. The film's release coincided with a surge of interest in paranormal investigation shows worldwide.

9. Despite its low budget, the film achieved significant box office success in Singapore.

10. The movie's success led to increased discussions about preserving historical sites in Singapore.

3. The Maid

1. Movie Title: The Maid

2. Year of Release: 2005

3. Cast and Director:

- Director: Kelvin Tong

- Cast: Alessandra de Rossi, Chen Shucheng, Huifang Hong, Benny Soh

4. Synopsis:

"The Maid" tells the story of Rosa Dimaano, a Filipino domestic worker who arrives in Singapore to work for the Teo family. She starts her job during the Chinese Seventh Month, also known as the Hungry Ghost Festival, a time when it's believed that the spirits of the dead roam the earth. As Rosa adapts to her new life, she begins to experience strange and terrifying occurrences in the Teo household. She discovers dark secrets about the family's past and becomes entangled in a web of supernatural events. The film blends elements of Asian horror with social commentary on the treatment of foreign workers in Singapore, creating a unique and unsettling narrative.

5. Why This Movie Is Recommended:

"The Maid" stands out for its clever integration of cultural elements, combining Filipino and Chinese ghost stories with the realities of migrant workers in Singapore. The film's atmospheric horror is enhanced by its exploration of social issues, adding depth to the scares. Director Kelvin Tong masterfully builds tension through subtle scares and psychological suspense rather than relying on gore or jump scares. The movie's unique perspective, seen through the eyes of a foreign domestic worker, offers a fresh take on the haunted house genre while providing commentary on class and cultural differences in Singaporean society.

6. 10 Trivia Facts:

1. "The Maid" was the first Singaporean horror film to receive international distribution.

2. The movie was shot entirely on location in Singapore, including in traditional shophouses.

3. Lead actress Alessandra de Rossi learned to speak Hokkien for her role as Rosa.

4. The film incorporates real Chinese Ghost Month traditions and superstitions.

5. "The Maid" was one of the highest-grossing Singaporean films of 2005.

6. Director Kelvin Tong interviewed numerous domestic workers to ensure authenticity in the portrayal of Rosa's experiences.

7. The movie sparked discussions about the treatment of foreign domestic workers in Singapore.

8. Some scenes were shot in the infamous Old Changi Hospital, known for its alleged hauntings.

9. The film won several awards, including Best Film at the 2006 Singapore International Film Festival.

10. "The Maid" was remade in Thailand in 2020, showcasing its enduring impact on Asian horror cinema.

4. Feng Shui

1. Movie Title: Feng Shui (风水)

2. Year of Release: 2018

3. Cast and Director:

- Director: Eu Ho

- Cast: Yeo Yann Yann, Teng Chee Wai, Catherine Sng, Tan Kheng Hua

4. Synopsis:

"Feng Shui" follows the story of Ah Ying, a single mother struggling to make ends meet in modern-day Singapore. Desperate for a change in fortune, she consults a feng shui master who advises her to move into a specific apartment to improve her luck. Initially, things seem to improve for Ah Ying and her son, but they soon realize that their new home harbors dark secrets. As strange occurrences escalate, Ah Ying discovers that the apartment's history is intertwined with a tragic past and malevolent spirits. The film explores themes of superstition, desperation, and the price of pursuing good fortune at any cost.

5. Why This Movie Is Recommended:

"Feng Shui" offers a unique blend of traditional Chinese superstitions and modern Singaporean urban life. The film stands out for its exploration of cultural beliefs in a contemporary setting, providing both scares and social commentary. Director Eu Ho skillfully builds tension through atmospheric storytelling and subtle horror elements, rather than relying on jump scares. The movie's strong performances, particularly by Yeo Yann Yann, bring depth to the characters, making their terror more palpable. "Feng Shui" serves as both a chilling ghost story and a thoughtful examination of societal pressures and beliefs in Singapore.

6. 10 Trivia Facts:

1. The film draws inspiration from real feng shui practices and superstitions common in Singaporean culture.

2. "Feng Shui" was shot entirely on location in Singapore, showcasing various aspects of the city-state's urban landscape.

3. The movie premiered at the 2018 Singapore International Film Festival.

4. Lead actress Yeo Yann Yann underwent extensive research into feng shui beliefs to prepare for her role.

5. The film incorporates elements of both Chinese and Malay supernatural folklore, reflecting Singapore's multicultural society.

6. "Feng Shui" was praised for its realistic portrayal of working-class life in Singapore.

7. The apartment featured in the film was designed specifically to incorporate bad feng shui elements.

8. Director Eu Ho consulted with actual feng shui masters during the scriptwriting process.

9. The movie sparked discussions about the prevalence of superstitious beliefs in modern Singaporean society.

10. "Feng Shui" uses a mix of Mandarin, English, and Singlish, accurately representing Singapore's linguistic landscape.

5. 7 Days

1. Movie Title: 7 Days

2. Year of Release: 2019

3. Cast and Director:

  - Director: Steve Cheng

  - Cast: Leeann Lim, Kemy Tan, Alan Tan, Shuyi Ching

4. Synopsis:

  "7 Days" revolves around a group of friends who gather for a reunion at a remote chalet in Singapore. Their joy quickly turns to terror when they realize they're trapped in a time loop, forced to relive the same day over and over. Each cycle brings new horrors and revelations as they uncover dark secrets about their shared past. The friends must confront their own misdeeds and a vengeful supernatural force to break the cycle. As tensions rise and trust erodes, they race against time to solve the mystery before they're trapped in the loop forever. The film blends elements of psychological horror with time-bending suspense, creating a uniquely Singaporean take on the time loop trope.

5. Why This Movie Is Recommended:

  "7 Days" stands out for its innovative blend of horror and sci-fi elements, a combination rarely seen in Singaporean cinema. The film's clever use of the time loop concept adds layers of mystery and suspense to the traditional horror narrative. Director Steve Cheng skillfully builds tension through the repetition of events, each cycle revealing new terrors and twists. The movie's exploration of guilt, redemption, and the consequences of past actions adds psychological depth to the supernatural scares. "7 Days" offers a fresh and thought-provoking take on horror that keeps viewers guessing until the very end.

6. 10 Trivia Facts:

  1. "7 Days" was shot over a period of 14 days, with many scenes requiring multiple takes to maintain continuity across the time loops.

  2. The film's location, a remote chalet, is based on actual holiday bungalows in Singapore's Changi area.

  3. Director Steve Cheng drew inspiration from both Western time loop films and Asian horror traditions.

  4. The movie incorporates elements of local Singaporean urban legends and superstitions.

  5. "7 Days" premiered at the 2019 Singapore International Film Festival.

  6. The film's script underwent numerous revisions to ensure the complex time loop narrative remained coherent.

  7. Cast members reported experiencing strange occurrences on set, adding to the film's mystique.

  8. "7 Days" uses a mix of English and Singlish, reflecting the linguistic diversity of Singapore's youth.

  9. The movie's marketing campaign included an interactive escape room experience based on the film's premise.

  10. "7 Days" sparked discussions about the potential of genre-blending in Singaporean cinema.

6. Homecoming

1. Movie Title: Homecoming (回魂)

2. Year of Release: 2011

3. Cast and Director:

- Director: Lee Thean-jeen

- Cast: Mark Lee, Jacqueline Chong, Jerald Koh, Yvonne Lim

4. Synopsis:

"Homecoming" follows a Singaporean family who returns to their ancestral home in Malaysia for the Qing Ming festival, a traditional time for honoring ancestors. The protagonist, Ah Ching, brings along his young son who possesses the ability to see ghosts. As they participate in the festival rituals, they unknowingly awaken malevolent spirits with connections to dark family secrets. The boundary between the living and the dead blurs as the family confronts generational curses and unresolved past traumas. The film blends elements of family drama with supernatural horror, exploring themes of tradition, family bonds, and the weight of unspoken history.

5. Why This Movie Is Recommended:

"Homecoming" offers a unique perspective on horror by intertwining it with cultural traditions and family dynamics. The film stands out for its exploration of the Qing Ming festival, providing both cultural insight and a rich backdrop for supernatural occurrences. Director Lee Thean-jeen skillfully balances family drama with genuine scares, creating a narrative that's both emotionally resonant and chilling. The movie's strong performances and authentic portrayal of Singaporean-Malaysian familial relationships add depth to the horror elements. "Homecoming" serves as both a ghost story and a poignant examination of cultural identity and intergenerational relationships in the Singaporean context.

6. 10 Trivia Facts:

1. The film was shot on location in both Singapore and Malaysia, showcasing the cultural connections between the two countries.

2. "Homecoming" incorporates actual Qing Ming festival rituals and superstitions into its narrative.

3. The movie features a mix of Mandarin, English, and various Chinese dialects, reflecting the linguistic diversity of Singaporean families.

4. Director Lee Thean-jeen conducted extensive research into ghost folklore from both Singapore and Malaysia for the film.

5. "Homecoming" was one of the first Singaporean horror films to focus on the Qing Ming festival.

6. The child actor who plays the son with the ability to see ghosts was chosen from over 100 auditions.

7. The film's success led to increased interest in horror movies centered around Asian cultural traditions.

8. "Homecoming" won several awards at Asian film festivals for its unique blend of horror and cultural elements.

9. The movie's marketing campaign included educational elements about the Qing Ming festival to provide context for international audiences.

10. Several cast members reported feeling uneasy during filming of the more intense supernatural scenes, adding to the film's mystique.

Philippines

1. Patayin sa Sindak si Barbara (Scare Barbara to Death)

1. **Movie Title: Patayin sa Sindak si Barbara**

2. **Year of Release: 1974**

3. **Cast and Director:**

   - Director: Celso Ad. Castillo

   - Cast: Susan Roces, Dante Rivero, Rosanna Ortiz

4. **Synopsis**:

   Barbara returns home after her sister Ruth's death, only to find herself embroiled in a series of supernatural occurrences. As she cares for her niece Karen, strange events unfold, suggesting Ruth's vengeful spirit is haunting them. Barbara soon discovers the dark truth behind her sister's demise and her brother-in-law Fritz's involvement. As the haunting intensifies, Barbara must confront the malevolent force to save herself and Karen, leading to a chilling climax that blurs the lines between the living and the dead.

5. **Why This Movie Is Recommended**:

   "Patayin sa Sindak si Barbara" is a cornerstone of Filipino horror cinema. Its psychological depth, combined with supernatural elements, creates a haunting atmosphere that lingers long after viewing. The film's exploration of family dynamics, guilt, and revenge adds layers to its horror narrative. Director Celso Ad. Castillo's masterful use of gothic imagery and suspense techniques set a new standard for Philippine horror. Its influence on subsequent films in the genre makes it essential viewing for horror enthusiasts and film scholars alike.

6. **10 Trivia Facts**:

   1. The film was remade in 1995 starring Lorna Tolentino.

   2. It's considered one of the best works of director Celso Ad. Castillo.

   3. The movie was shot on location in an old mansion in San Juan, Metro Manila.

   4. Susan Roces, who played Barbara, was known as the "Queen of Philippine Movies."

   5. The film's success spawned a trend of psychological horror films in the Philippines.

   6. It was one of the first Filipino horror films to gain international recognition.

   7. The movie's title is a play on the 1971 American horror film "Let's Scare Jessica to Death."

   8. Celso Ad. Castillo wrote the screenplay in just one week.

   9. The film's climax involving a possessed doll became iconic in Philippine cinema.

   10. Despite its age, the film is still regularly screened during Halloween in the Philippines.

2. Kisapmata (In the Blink of an Eye)

1. Movie Title: Kisapmata

2. Year of Release: 1981

3. Cast and Director:

  - Director: Mike De Leon

  - Cast: Vic Silayan, Charo Santos-Concio, Jay Ilagan

4. Synopsis:

"Kisapmata" tells the story of Mila, a young woman who becomes pregnant and decides to marry her boyfriend, Noel. However, her father, Dadong Carandang, a retired police officer, is unhealthily obsessed with his daughter and opposes the marriage. Despite his objections, the wedding proceeds, but Dadong's controlling behavior escalates. He moves the newlyweds into his home and begins to exert increasing control over their lives. As tensions rise and Dadong's behavior becomes more erratic and violent, the film builds to a shocking and tragic conclusion that exposes the dark undercurrents of family dynamics and patriarchal control.

5. Why This Movie Is Recommended:

While not a traditional horror film, "Kisapmata" is a psychological thriller that instills a deep sense of dread and unease. Mike De Leon's masterful direction creates an oppressive atmosphere that is genuinely horrifying. The film's exploration of toxic familial relationships and the abuse of patriarchal power resonates deeply. Vic Silayan's portrayal of Dadong is chillingly realistic, making him one of the most terrifying villains in Filipino cinema. "Kisapmata" proves that true horror can come from all-too-human sources, making it a must-watch for those who appreciate psychological horror.

6. 10 Trivia Facts:

1. The film is based on a true story reported in the Philippine media.

2. "Kisapmata" won nine FAMAS Awards, including Best Picture, Best Director, and Best Actor.

3. It was selected as the Philippine entry for the Best Foreign Language Film at the 55th Academy Awards.

4. The movie was shot in just 14 days.

5. Director Mike De Leon is known for his meticulous storyboarding and shot composition.

6. The film's title, "Kisapmata," means "In the Blink of an Eye" in English.

7. It was produced during the Martial Law era in the Philippines, adding to its tense atmosphere.

8. The movie was restored and re-released in 2015, introducing it to a new generation of viewers.

9. Critic Noel Vera called it "one of the greatest Filipino films ever made."

10. The film's claustrophobic setting was achieved by shooting mostly in a single house.

3. Feng Shui

1. Movie Title: Feng Shui

2. Year of Release: 2004

3. Cast and Director:

 - Director: Chito S. Roño

 - Cast: Kris Aquino, Jay Manalo, Lotlot De Leon

4. Synopsis:

Joy Ramirez, a working-class mother, discovers an antique Bagua mirror, which supposedly brings good fortune to its owner. Initially, Joy's luck seems to improve dramatically, but she soon realizes that the mirror's blessings come at a terrible price. People around her begin dying in mysterious and gruesome ways, each corresponding to one of the elements of Chinese astrology. As Joy uncovers the mirror's dark history, she finds herself in a race against time to break its curse before it claims more victims, including her own family. The film blends Filipino and Chinese superstitions to create a unique and terrifying supernatural threat.

5. Why This Movie Is Recommended:

"Feng Shui" stands out for its innovative blend of Filipino horror traditions with Chinese mysticism. The film's use of the Bagua mirror as a conduit for terror is both original and deeply unsettling. Director Chito S. Roño masterfully builds tension throughout the film, creating genuinely scary moments that don't rely solely on jump scares. The movie's exploration of greed and the consequences of desiring quick fortune adds depth to its horror narrative. With its strong performances, particularly from Kris Aquino, and its clever integration of cultural beliefs, "Feng Shui" has become a modern classic of Filipino horror cinema.

6. 10 Trivia Facts:

1. The film spawned a sequel, "Feng Shui 2," released in 2014.

2. Kris Aquino, who played Joy, is known as the "Queen of Horror" in Philippine cinema.

3. The movie's success revitalized the horror genre in the Philippines.

4. Many of the death scenes were inspired by real Chinese astrology elements.

5. The film's tagline was "May swerte ka ba talaga?" (Are you really lucky?)

6. It was one of the highest-grossing Filipino films of 2004.

7. The Bagua mirror used in the film became a popular item in Philippine households after the movie's release.

8. Director Chito S. Roño conducted extensive research on Chinese mysticism for the film.

9. The movie's success led to a trend of horror films incorporating Asian superstitions.

10. Some scenes were shot in the historic Intramuros district of Manila.

4. Sukob (The Wedding Curse)

1. Movie Title: Sukob

2. Year of Release: 2006

3. Cast and Director:

- Director: Chito S. Roño

- Cast: Kris Aquino, Claudine Barretto, Wendell Ramos

4. Synopsis:

"Sukob" revolves around the Filipino superstition that siblings should not marry within the same year to avoid bad luck. The film follows two women: Sandy, who is about to get married, and Diana, who recently wed. Both women begin experiencing terrifying supernatural occurrences as they discover they've violated the sukob superstition. As the curse intensifies, claiming victims in increasingly horrifying ways, Sandy and Diana must uncover the truth behind their connection and find a way to break the curse before it's too late. The film weaves together multiple storylines, building to a chilling climax that challenges the characters' beliefs and relationships.

5. Why This Movie Is Recommended:

"Sukob" brilliantly taps into deeply ingrained Filipino superstitions, creating a horror narrative that resonates strongly with local audiences while remaining accessible to international viewers. Director Chito S. Roño crafts a visually stunning film with genuinely frightening sequences that build tension masterfully. The movie's exploration of tradition, family dynamics, and the consequences of ignoring cultural beliefs adds depth to its scares. With strong performances from its lead actresses and a plot that keeps viewers guessing until the end, "Sukob" stands as a prime example of how local folklore can be transformed into compelling modern horror.

6. 10 Trivia Facts:

1. "Sukob" was the highest-grossing Filipino film of 2006.

2. The film reunited director Chito S. Roño with Kris Aquino after their success with "Feng Shui."

3. Many of the wedding scenes were shot in actual churches around Manila.

4. The movie sparked renewed interest in traditional Filipino superstitions.

5. Some cast and crew members reportedly experienced strange occurrences during filming.

6. The film's success led to a trend of horror movies based on Filipino superstitions.

7. "Sukob" was screened at several international film festivals.

8. The movie's tagline was "Kasal, Kasali, Kasalo... Kasama sa Kamalasan" (Wedding, Included, Shared... Included in Misfortune).

9. Some scenes were shot in the historic town of Vigan, known for its Spanish colonial architecture.

10. The film's makeup and special effects team won several awards for their work.

5. Yanggaw (Affliction)

1. Movie Title: Yanggaw

2. Year of Release: 2008

3. Cast and Director:

- Director: Richard Somes

- Cast: Ronnie Lazaro, Tetchie Agbayani, Joel Torre

4. Synopsis:

Set in a remote village in the Philippines, "Yanggaw" tells the story of a family dealing with their daughter Junior's mysterious illness. As Junior's condition worsens, her father, Amor, brings her back to their village from the city. It soon becomes apparent that Junior is not suffering from a normal sickness, but has become an aswang - a flesh-eating monster from Filipino folklore. As Junior's transformations become more frequent and violent, Amor struggles to protect both his daughter and the villagers. The film explores the family's moral dilemma as they grapple with their love for Junior and the threat she poses to the community, building to a heart-wrenching and terrifying conclusion.

5. Why This Movie Is Recommended:

"Yanggaw" stands out for its gritty, realistic approach to the aswang myth, grounding the supernatural elements in a believable rural setting. Director Richard Somes creates a palpable atmosphere of dread and isolation that enhances the horror. The film's exploration of family loyalty, community pressure, and the clash between tradition and modernity adds depth to its narrative. With powerful performances, particularly from Ronnie Lazaro as Amor, "Yanggaw" transcends typical monster movie tropes to deliver a poignant and deeply unsettling experience. It's a must-watch for those interested in how traditional folklore can be reimagined in contemporary horror.

6. 10 Trivia Facts:

1. "Yanggaw" is in the Hiligaynon language, showcasing cinema from outside the Manila-centric mainstream.

2. The film won Best Picture at the 2008 Cinema One Originals Film Festival.

3. Director Richard Somes previously worked as a production designer before making his directorial debut.

4. The movie was shot on location in Negros Occidental, adding to its authentic rural atmosphere.

5. "Yanggaw" helped revitalize interest in regional filmmaking in the Philippines.

6. The film's portrayal of the aswang differs from more sensationalized depictions in other media.

7. Many of the cast members were local actors from the Negros region.

8. The movie's success led to increased funding for horror films in regional languages.

9. "Yanggaw" has been used in academic discussions about the representation of folklore in modern media.

10. The film's practical effects for the aswang transformations were created on a very limited budget.

6. Tatlong Taong Walang Diyos (Three Years Without God)

1. Movie Title: Tatlong Taong Walang Diyos

2. Year of Release: 1976

3. Cast and Director:

- Director: Mario O'Hara

- Cast: Nora Aunor, Christopher De Leon, Bembol Roco

4. Synopsis:

Set during the Japanese occupation of the Philippines in World War II, "Tatlong Taong Walang Diyos" follows Rosario, a schoolteacher in a rural village. When her fiancé joins the resistance, Rosario is left vulnerable to the advances of a Japanese-Filipino officer, Masugi. After being raped by Masugi, Rosario becomes pregnant and struggles with the trauma and social stigma. The film explores her psychological journey as she grapples with her faith, identity, and the brutal realities of war. As the conflict intensifies and loyalties shift, Rosario must navigate a world where morality is blurred and survival comes at a great cost.

5. Why This Movie Is Recommended:

While not a traditional horror film, "Tatlong Taong Walang Diyos" presents a horrifying portrayal of war and its psychological impact. Director Mario O'Hara masterfully creates an atmosphere of constant dread and moral ambiguity. The film's unflinching look at the horrors of war, rape, and social ostracism is more terrifying than many supernatural thrillers. Nora Aunor's powerful performance brings depth to Rosario's trauma and resilience. This film is essential viewing for those who appreciate psychological horror and want to understand the lasting impact of historical atrocities on the Filipino psyche.

6. 10 Trivia Facts:

1. The film's title translates to "Three Years Without God," referring to the Japanese occupation period.

2. It's considered one of the greatest Filipino films ever made.

3. Director Mario O'Hara also wrote the screenplay, drawing from stories he heard as a child.

4. The movie was shot on location in Pampanga, adding to its historical authenticity.

5. Nora Aunor's performance is often cited as one of the best in Philippine cinema history.

6. The film blends elements of neorealism with expressionist techniques.

7. It was restored and remastered in 2015 by the Asian Film Archive.

8. The movie explores complex themes of faith, nationalism, and cultural identity.

9. Despite its critical acclaim, the film was initially a commercial failure.

10. O'Hara's direction was influenced by both Filipino folklore and European art cinema.

7. Shake, Rattle & Roll

1. Movie Title: Shake, Rattle & Roll

2. Year of Release: 1984

3. Cast and Director:

- Directors: Ishmael Bernal, Emmanuel H. Borlaza, Peque Gallaga

- Cast: Varies by segment (Anthology film)

4. Synopsis:

"Shake, Rattle & Roll" is an anthology horror film consisting of three separate stories. The first segment, "Baso" (Glass), follows a group of teenagers who encounter a malevolent spirit while playing with a Ouija board. The second story, "Pridyider" (Refrigerator), centers on a family terrorized by a possessed refrigerator with a gruesome appetite. The final segment, "Manananggal" (a Filipino mythical creature), depicts a town under attack by a viscera-sucking, self-segmenting monster. Each story blends traditional Filipino folklore with modern horror elements, creating a diverse and frightening cinematic experience.

5. Why This Movie Is Recommended:

"Shake, Rattle & Roll" kickstarted a beloved franchise in Philippine cinema, becoming synonymous with Filipino horror. Its anthology format allows for a variety of scares, from supernatural hauntings to monster attacks. The film successfully modernizes traditional Filipino myths and urban legends, making them relevant to contemporary audiences. With its mix of humor, suspense, and outright horror, the movie appeals to a wide range of viewers. Its influence on subsequent Filipino horror films is undeniable, making it a must-watch for understanding the evolution of the genre in the Philippines.

6. 10 Trivia Facts:

1. This film launched the longest-running horror movie franchise in Philippine cinema.

2. Each segment was directed by a different filmmaker, showcasing varied styles.

3. The "Pridyider" segment was remade into a full-length film in 2012.

4. Many famous Filipino actors made their debut in various "Shake, Rattle & Roll" installments.

5. The franchise has become a staple of the Metro Manila Film Festival.

6. The manananggal creature was created using practical effects, which were groundbreaking for its time.

7. The film's title was inspired by the 1950s rock and roll song of the same name.

8. Subsequent installments often featured celebrities from other entertainment fields, like singers or TV hosts.

9. The anthology format allowed filmmakers to experiment with different subgenres of horror.

10. Despite its age, many Filipinos consider the original "Shake, Rattle & Roll" the scariest of the series.

8. Numbalikdiwa

1. Movie Title: Numbalikdiwa

2. Year of Release: 2006

3. Cast and Director:

- Director: Khavn De La Cruz

- Cast: Khavn De La Cruz, Katya Santos, Kristofer King

4. Synopsis:

"Numbalikdiwa" is an experimental horror film that defies conventional narrative structures. The story, such as it is, revolves around a serial killer who believes he's doing God's work by cleansing the world of sin. As he goes about his gruesome mission, the film presents a series of disturbing, often surreal vignettes that blur the lines between reality, memory, and nightmare. The killer's victims, his own twisted psyche, and the dark underbelly of urban life in the Philippines all intermingle in a disorienting and horrifying tapestry. The film challenges viewers with its non-linear storytelling and graphic imagery, creating an unsettling experience that lingers long after viewing.

5. Why This Movie Is Recommended:

"Numbalikdiwa" represents a bold departure from traditional Filipino horror, pushing the boundaries of the genre and cinema itself. Director Khavn De La Cruz's avant-garde approach creates a uniquely disturbing atmosphere that gets under the viewer's skin. The film's experimental nature, combining elements of found footage, surrealism, and psychological horror, offers a fresh and challenging experience for horror enthusiasts. While not for the faint of heart, "Numbalikdiwa" rewards viewers willing to engage with its complex themes and innovative storytelling techniques, making it a standout in Philippine independent cinema.

6. 10 Trivia Facts:

1. The title "Numbalikdiwa" is a play on words, roughly translating to "Reverse Soul" in English.

2. Director Khavn De La Cruz is known for his prolific output and experimental style.

3. The film was shot on a variety of formats, including 35mm, 16mm, and digital video.

4. Many scenes were improvised, with actors given general directions rather than specific scripts.

5. The movie features an original score composed by Khavn himself.

6. "Numbalikdiwa" premiered at the International Film Festival Rotterdam.

7. The film's graphic content led to controversy and limited theatrical release in the Philippines.

8. Khavn often appears in his own films, including this one, blurring the line between creator and creation.

9. The movie incorporates elements of Filipino folklore and Catholic imagery in surreal ways.

10. Despite its experimental nature, the film won several awards at international festivals.

9. Pa-siyam

1. **Movie Title: Pa-siyam**

2. **Year of Release: 2004**

3. **Cast and Director:**

 - Director: Erik Matti

 - Cast: Iza Calzado, Irma Adlawan, Angel Aquino

4. **Synopsis**:

 "Pa-siyam" centers around a Filipino tradition of nine days of prayer for the deceased. The Aguinaldo family gathers in their ancestral home to observe the pa-siyam for their recently departed matriarch, Lola Anita. As family members arrive, strange occurrences begin to plague the household. Tensions rise as long-buried secrets and resentments surface, exacerbated by the increasingly terrifying supernatural events. The family must confront not only the malevolent force haunting them but also their own dark pasts and fractured relationships. As the nine days progress, the line between the living and the dead blurs, leading to a chilling climax that tests the family's bonds and beliefs.

5. **Why This Movie Is Recommended**:

 "Pa-siyam" brilliantly interweaves Filipino cultural traditions with classic haunted house tropes, creating a uniquely Filipino horror experience. Director Erik Matti crafts a tense, claustrophobic atmosphere within the ancestral home, making excellent use of the setting to heighten the scares. The film's exploration of family dynamics and generational trauma adds depth to its supernatural elements. With strong performances from its ensemble cast and a plot that keeps viewers guessing, "Pa-siyam" offers both genuine frights and emotional resonance. It's a must-watch for those interested in how cultural practices can be woven into effective horror narratives.

6. **10 Trivia Facts**:

 1. The title "Pa-siyam" refers to the nine-day novena prayer for the dead in Filipino Catholic tradition.

 2. Director Erik Matti is known for his versatility, working across various genres in Filipino cinema.

 3. The film was shot on location in an actual old house, adding to its authentic atmosphere.

 4. "Pa-siyam" was one of the first Filipino horror films to gain significant international festival attention.

 5. The movie's success helped establish Iza Calzado as a leading actress in Philippine cinema.

 6. Many of the supernatural occurrences in the film are based on actual Filipino superstitions and ghost stories.

 7. The film's makeup and special effects were groundbreaking for Philippine cinema at the time.

 8. "Pa-siyam" blends elements of psychological horror with more traditional jump scares.

 9. The movie explores themes of family obligation and the weight of tradition in Filipino culture.

 10. Some scenes were improvised to capture genuine reactions from the actors.

10. Tiyanak (The Demon Child)

1. Movie Title: Tiyanak

2. Year of Release: 1988

3. Cast and Director:

  - Directors: Peque Gallaga, Lore Reyes

  - Cast: Janice de Belen, Lotlot de Leon, Mary Walter

4. Synopsis:

  "Tiyanak" revolves around a young couple who find an abandoned baby in a forest. They decide to adopt the child, but soon realize that it is actually a tiyanak - a demon that takes the form of an infant to lure and kill its victims. As the creature's true nature is revealed, it begins a reign of terror, attacking family members and neighbors. The film follows the desperate attempts of the family and the local community to survive and destroy the monster. As the body count rises, they must confront their own beliefs and the limits of their courage in the face of an ancient, malevolent force.

5. Why This Movie Is Recommended:

  "Tiyanak" stands out for its creative adaptation of Filipino folklore into a modern horror context. Directors Peque Gallaga and Lore Reyes craft a film that balances genuine scares with social commentary on issues like adoption and community dynamics. The movie's special effects, while dated, contribute to its charm and represent a significant achievement in Philippine cinema of the time. With its blend of traditional mythology and contemporary storytelling, "Tiyanak" offers a uniquely Filipino take on the "evil child" subgenre of horror, making it a must-watch for fans of cultural horror and 80s practical effects.

6. 10 Trivia Facts:

  1. The tiyanak is a creature from Philippine mythology, often described as a vampire-like being that takes the form of a newborn.

  2. The film spawned a remake in 2014, starring Judy Ann Santos.

  3. "Tiyanak" was one of the highest-grossing Filipino films of 1988.

  4. The movie's success led to a trend of films based on Filipino mythological creatures.

  5. The practical effects for the tiyanak were groundbreaking for Philippine cinema at the time.

  6. Directors Peque Gallaga and Lore Reyes often collaborated on horror films, becoming a powerhouse duo in the genre.

  7. The film blends elements of Hollywood horror with distinctly Filipino cultural elements.

  8. "Tiyanak" was one of the first Filipino horror films to receive international distribution.

  9. The movie's theme song became popular and is still associated with the film today.

  10. Some scenes were considered so frightening that they were censored in the film's television broadcasts.

11. Sigaw (The Echo)

1. Movie Title: Sigaw

2. Year of Release: 2004

3. Cast and Director:

- Director: Yam Laranas

- Cast: Richard Gutierrez, Angel Locsin, Iza Calzado

4. Synopsis:

"Sigaw" follows Marvin, a young man who moves into an old apartment building with a dark history. Soon after settling in, he begins to experience disturbing supernatural occurrences. He hears screams and witnesses apparitions of a man beating his wife and child. As Marvin investigates, he uncovers the building's tragic past involving domestic abuse and murder. The boundary between past and present blurs as the ghostly reenactments become more intense and threatening. Marvin, along with his girlfriend Pinky, must find a way to break the cycle of violence and put the restless spirits to rest before they become the next victims of the building's gruesome history.

5. Why This Movie Is Recommended:

"Sigaw" stands out for its atmospheric tension and psychological depth. Director Yam Laranas creates a claustrophobic, haunting atmosphere within the confines of the apartment building. The film's exploration of cyclical violence and the lingering trauma of abuse adds a layer of social commentary to its supernatural scares. With strong performances from its lead cast and innovative cinematography that makes excellent use of the confined spaces, "Sigaw" offers a unique and unsettling viewing experience. Its success led to an American remake, showcasing its universal appeal and effectiveness as a horror narrative.

6. 10 Trivia Facts:

1. "Sigaw" was remade in Hollywood as "The Echo" in 2008, also directed by Yam Laranas.

2. The film was shot on location in an actual old apartment building in Manila.

3. It was one of the first Filipino horror films to be picked up for an American remake.

4. The movie's success helped establish Richard Gutierrez as a serious actor beyond his teen idol image.

5. Many of the ghostly effects were achieved through practical means rather than CGI.

6. The film explores themes of domestic violence, a topic not often addressed in Filipino cinema at the time.

7. "Sigaw" was screened at several international film festivals, gaining critical acclaim.

8. The apartment building itself is treated almost like a character in the film, central to the story's atmosphere.

9. Director Yam Laranas has a background in advertising, which influenced the film's visual style.

10. The movie's tagline was "Hindi lahat ng narinig mo ay guni-guni lang" (Not everything you hear is just your imagination).

12. Tumbok

1. Movie Title: Tumbok

2. Year of Release: 2011

3. Cast and Director:

  - Director: Topel Lee

  - Cast: Cristine Reyes, Carlo Aquino, Empress Schuck

4. Synopsis:

"Tumbok" centers on Grace, a young woman who moves into a high-rise condominium with her boyfriend Ronnie. Soon after settling in, Grace begins to experience terrifying visions and supernatural occurrences. She discovers that their unit, number 1006, has a dark history of deaths and disappearances. As Grace delves deeper into the mystery, she uncovers a connection between the building's tragic past and feng shui principles gone wrong. The couple must navigate a maze of superstitions, angry spirits, and deadly curses to survive. As the malevolent forces close in, Grace races against time to break the cycle of death associated with their ill-fated unit.

5. Why This Movie Is Recommended:

"Tumbok" offers a fresh take on the haunted dwelling trope by setting it in a modern condominium and incorporating elements of feng shui and urban legends. Director Topel Lee skillfully builds tension, using the vertical nature of the high-rise to create a sense of isolation and dread. The film's exploration of superstitions in contemporary Filipino society adds depth to its scares. With strong performances from its lead cast and effective use of confined spaces, "Tumbok" delivers both jump scares and psychological horror. It's a must-watch for fans of ghost stories and those interested in the intersection of traditional beliefs and modern urban life.

6. 10 Trivia Facts:

  1. The title "Tumbok" refers to the belief in feng shui that certain positions or directions can be unlucky.

  2. The film popularized the urban myth about "haunted" condominium units in the Philippines.

  3. Many of the superstitions featured in the movie are actual beliefs held by some Filipinos.

  4. The movie was shot in an actual high-rise condominium in Metro Manila.

  5. "Tumbok" blends elements of traditional Filipino horror with Japanese and Chinese influences.

  6. The film's success led to increased interest in feng shui practices among young urban Filipinos.

  7. Some scenes were so intense that they reportedly caused audience members to faint during screenings.

  8. The movie explores themes of rapid urbanization and its impact on traditional beliefs.

  9. Director Topel Lee has a background in television, which influenced the film's pacing and style.

  10. "Tumbok" was one of the first Filipino horror films to extensively use a high-rise setting.

13. Ouija

1. Movie Title: Ouija

2. Year of Release: 2007

3. Cast and Director:

- Director: Topel Lee

- Cast: Judy Ann Santos, Rhian Ramos, Iza Calzado

4. Synopsis:

"Ouija" follows a group of friends who decide to play with a Ouija board as a way to contact their recently deceased friend, Lara. What starts as a seemingly innocent game quickly turns into a nightmare as they unwittingly release a malevolent spirit. As the entity begins to terrorize and possess members of the group, they must uncover the dark secret behind their friend's death and the connection to the spirit they've unleashed. The friends find themselves in a desperate battle for survival, trying to close the portal they've opened before the evil consumes them all. The film explores themes of guilt, friendship, and the dangers of meddling with the unknown.

5. Why This Movie Is Recommended:

"Ouija" stands out for its clever blend of teen drama and supernatural horror. Director Topel Lee creates a tense atmosphere that builds steadily throughout the film, culminating in genuinely terrifying sequences. The movie's exploration of friendship dynamics under extreme stress adds depth to its characters, making the audience invest in their fates. With strong performances from its ensemble cast and effective use of practical effects, "Ouija" delivers both emotional resonance and visceral scares. It's a must-watch for fans of supernatural horror and those interested in films that explore the consequences of toying with occult practices.

6. 10 Trivia Facts:

1. The film was so successful that it spawned two sequels: "Ouija 2" and "Ouija 3".

2. "Ouija" was one of the highest-grossing Filipino horror films of 2007.

3. The movie popularized the use of Ouija boards as plot devices in Filipino horror cinema.

4. Many of the scare scenes were shot in a single take to maintain tension.

5. The film blends elements of Filipino folklore with Western occult practices.

6. Some scenes were considered too intense and were cut for the film's television broadcast.

7. The movie's success helped establish Rhian Ramos as a scream queen in Philippine cinema.

8. Director Topel Lee consulted with paranormal experts to add authenticity to the Ouija board scenes.

9. The film addresses the real-life issue of teen suicide, adding a layer of social commentary.

10. "Ouija" was one of the first Filipino horror films to extensively use sound design as a scare tactic.

14. Seklusyon (Seclusion)

1. Movie Title: Seklusyon

2. Year of Release: 2016

3. Cast and Director:

  - Director: Erik Matti

  - Cast: Rhed Bustamante, Ronnie Alonte, Phoebe Walker

4. Synopsis:

Set in 1947 Philippines, "Seklusyon" follows four deacons in their final days of training before becoming full-fledged priests. They are sent to a remote convent for a week of seclusion, a tradition meant to shield them from evil before taking their vows. Their retreat is disrupted by the arrival of a young girl named Anghela, who is believed to have healing powers. As strange and terrifying events unfold, the deacons begin to question their faith and sanity. They must confront their own inner demons and a malevolent force that threatens to corrupt their souls. The film explores themes of faith, temptation, and the thin line between sainthood and evil.

5. Why This Movie Is Recommended:

"Seklusyon" offers a unique and disturbing take on religious horror. Director Erik Matti crafts a visually stunning film that creates an oppressive atmosphere of dread and moral ambiguity. The movie's exploration of faith, corruption, and the nature of evil adds intellectual depth to its scares. With outstanding performances, particularly from young Rhed Bustamante, and a plot that keeps viewers guessing until the end, "Seklusyon" delivers both psychological horror and visceral frights. Its critical examination of religious institutions and the concept of miracles makes it a thought-provoking watch beyond its horror elements.

6. 10 Trivia Facts:

1. "Seklusyon" won multiple awards at the 2016 Metro Manila Film Festival, including Best Director for Erik Matti.

2. The film was shot in various heritage sites and old churches across the Philippines.

3. Director Erik Matti spent years researching Catholic traditions and exorcism rites for the film.

4. Young actress Rhed Bustamante's performance was widely praised, with some calling it one of the best child performances in Filipino cinema.

5. The movie's visual style was influenced by classic religious paintings and Gothic architecture.

6. "Seklusyon" was controversial upon release due to its critical portrayal of religious institutions.

7. The film uses minimal CGI, relying instead on practical effects and clever cinematography.

8. It was one of the first Filipino horror films to be picked up by Netflix for international distribution.

9. The movie's script went through numerous rewrites to balance its religious themes with horror elements.

10. "Seklusyon" was praised for its period-accurate costumes and set design, which added to its authenticity.

15. Eerie

1. Movie Title: Eerie

2. Year of Release: 2018

3. Cast and Director:

  - Director: Mikhail Red

  - Cast: Bea Alonzo, Charo Santos-Concio, Jake Cuenca

4. Synopsis:

  Set in an all-girls Catholic school in the 1990s, "Eerie" follows guidance counselor Pat Consolacion as she investigates the mysterious death of a student named Erika. As Pat delves deeper into the case, she uncovers dark secrets about the school's history and its strict head nun, Mother Alice. Pat's investigation is complicated by her ability to communicate with the dead, particularly the ghost of Erika, who seeks justice from beyond the grave. As more supernatural events occur and the body count rises, Pat must confront both human cruelty and otherworldly vengeance to uncover the truth and put an end to the cycle of violence plaguing the school.

5. Why This Movie Is Recommended:

  "Eerie" stands out for its atmospheric tension and its clever blend of ghost story and murder mystery. Director Mikhail Red crafts a visually striking film that makes excellent use of its gothic school setting to create a pervasive sense of dread. The movie's exploration of institutional abuse and the long-lasting effects of trauma adds depth to its supernatural elements. With strong performances from its lead cast, particularly Bea Alonzo and Charo Santos-Concio, "Eerie" offers both emotional resonance and genuine scares. Its critical examination of authoritarian educational practices and religious institutions makes it a thought-provoking watch beyond its horror elements.

6. 10 Trivia Facts:

  1. "Eerie" was co-produced by Singapore's Cre8 Productions, making it a rare international co-production in Filipino horror.

  2. The film premiered at the Singapore International Film Festival before its theatrical release.

  3. Director Mikhail Red was only 27 years old when he made "Eerie".

  4. The movie was shot in an actual old school building, adding to its authentic atmosphere.

  5. "Eerie" was one of the first Filipino horror films to gain significant traction on Netflix internationally.

  6. The film's sound design, crucial for its scares, was partially done in South Korea.

  7. Charo Santos-Concio, who plays Mother Alice, is also a prominent media executive in the Philippines.

  8. The movie's portrayal of Catholic school life sparked discussions about educational practices in the Philippines.

  9. "Eerie" uses minimal jump scares, focusing instead on building psychological tension.

  10. The film's cinematography was inspired by classic Asian horror movies, particularly from Japan and Korea.

16. Bulong (Whisper)

1. Movie Title: Bulong

2. Year of Release: 2011

3. Cast and Director:

- Director: Chito S. Roño

- Cast: Vhong Navarro, Angelica Panganiban, Bangs Garcia

4. Synopsis:

"Bulong" follows the story of Cesar, a man desperate to win the heart of his dream girl, Cynthia. In his pursuit, he seeks the help of a mambabarang (a witch doctor) who gives him a love potion with specific instructions. However, Cesar misuses the potion, leading to disastrous and often hilarious consequences. As people around him start acting strangely and supernatural events unfold, Cesar must find a way to reverse the spell before it's too late. The film blends comedy with horror, exploring themes of love, desire, and the dangers of manipulating others' free will through supernatural means.

5. Why This Movie Is Recommended:

"Bulong" stands out for its unique blend of horror and comedy, a combination rarely seen in Filipino cinema. Director Chito S. Roño skillfully balances laughs with genuine scares, creating a roller-coaster viewing experience. The film's exploration of Filipino folk magic and superstitions adds a layer of cultural richness to its narrative. With strong comedic performances, particularly from Vhong Navarro, and creative special effects, "Bulong" offers entertainment value while still delivering on horror elements. It's a must-watch for those who enjoy their scares with a side of laughter and are interested in modern interpretations of traditional Filipino beliefs.

6. 10 Trivia Facts:

1. The word "bulong" in Filipino means "whisper," referring to the secretive nature of folk magic practices.

2. Director Chito S. Roño is known for his versatility, having directed both serious horror films and comedies.

3. The film popularized the concept of the "mambabarang" in modern Filipino pop culture.

4. Many of the comedic scenes were improvised by the cast, adding authenticity to the humor.

5. "Bulong" was one of the first Filipino horror-comedies to achieve significant box office success.

6. The movie features cameos from several popular Filipino comedians.

7. Some of the film's depictions of folk magic rituals were based on actual practices in rural Philippines.

8. The movie sparked renewed interest in traditional Filipino mysticism among younger audiences.

9. "Bulong" was shot in various locations around Luzon, showcasing different Filipino landscapes.

10. The film's success led to a trend of horror-comedy films in Philippine cinema.

17. The Road

1. Movie Title: The Road

2. Year of Release: 2011

3. Cast and Director:

- Director: Yam Laranas

- Cast: Carmina Villaroel, Rhian Ramos, TJ Trinidad

4. Synopsis:

"The Road" is a three-part horror thriller that spans two decades. The first part, set in 2008, follows three teenagers who disappear on an abandoned road. The second part, set in 1998, reveals the road's dark history involving two sisters kidnapped by a deranged killer. The final part, set in 1988, uncovers the origins of the road's evil, focusing on a young boy's traumatic experience. As the stories intertwine, they reveal a complex web of tragedy, revenge, and supernatural horror. The abandoned road becomes a character itself, harboring dark secrets and malevolent forces that continue to claim victims across time.

5. Why This Movie Is Recommended:

"The Road" stands out for its innovative narrative structure and psychological depth. Director Yam Laranas crafts a complex, multi-layered story that keeps viewers engaged and guessing. The film's non-linear storytelling adds to the suspense, gradually revealing connections that heighten the overall horror. With strong performances across its ensemble cast and effective use of its isolated setting, "The Road" delivers both atmospheric dread and visceral scares. Its exploration of how past traumas echo through time adds emotional resonance to the horror elements. This film is a must-watch for fans of intelligent, intricately plotted horror thrillers.

6. 10 Trivia Facts:

1. "The Road" was one of the first Filipino horror films to receive international theatrical distribution.

2. The movie was shot entirely on location on actual abandoned roads in the Philippines.

3. Director Yam Laranas also served as the film's cinematographer.

4. The film's non-linear structure was inspired by Christopher Nolan's "Memento."

5. "The Road" won several awards at international film festivals, including Best Picture at the Fantasporto Film Festival.

6. The movie's success led to Yam Laranas directing projects in Hollywood.

7. Some of the car scenes were filmed using a specially designed rig to capture authentic reactions from the actors.

8. The film's color palette changes subtly for each time period, aiding the narrative structure.

9. "The Road" was praised for its sound design, which played a crucial role in building tension.

10. The movie's tagline was "Some roads should never be traveled," encapsulating its ominous tone.

18. Isla (Island)

1. Movie Title: Isla

2. Year of Release: 2004

3. Cast and Director:

- Director: Paolo Villaluna & Ellen Ramos

- Cast: Aya Medel, Ernie Zarate, Alcris Galura

4. Synopsis:

"Isla" is set on a remote island where a group of illegal fishermen have established a community. The film follows Lilia, a young woman sold into prostitution on the island. As Lilia navigates this harsh new world, strange and terrifying events begin to unfold. The fishermen's catches become increasingly bizarre and monstrous, and people start disappearing. The island's dark history of violence and exploitation seems to have awakened something ancient and malevolent in the surrounding waters. As the horror escalates, Lilia must find a way to survive not only the human cruelty around her but also the supernatural forces that threaten to consume the entire island.

5. Why This Movie Is Recommended:

"Isla" stands out for its unique blend of social realism and supernatural horror. Directors Paolo Villaluna and Ellen Ramos create a gritty, authentic portrayal of life in marginalized fishing communities, which serves as a backdrop for the escalating horror. The film's exploration of environmental exploitation and human trafficking adds depth to its narrative. With its atmospheric use of the isolated island setting and the surrounding sea, "Isla" creates a pervasive sense of dread and claustrophobia. The movie offers a thought-provoking experience that lingers long after viewing, making it a must-watch for those who appreciate horror with social commentary.

6. 10 Trivia Facts:

1. "Isla" was the directorial debut for both Paolo Villaluna and Ellen Ramos.

2. The film was shot on location in actual fishing communities, adding to its authentic feel.

3. Many of the supporting cast were non-professional actors from local fishing villages.

4. "Isla" won several awards at international film festivals, including the NETPAC Award at the Jeonju International Film Festival.

5. The movie's depiction of illegal fishing practices sparked discussions about environmental conservation in the Philippines.

6. Some of the film's more surreal sequences were inspired by local folklore about sea monsters.

7. "Isla" was produced on a very low budget, with much of the crew working for free.

8. The film's sound design, crucial for creating its eerie atmosphere, was done entirely in post-production.

9. "Isla" was one of the first Filipino horror films to address issues of human trafficking directly.

10. The directors conducted extensive research on island communities and marine ecology for the film.

19. Violator

1. Movie Title: Violator

2. Year of Release: 2014

3. Cast and Director:

  - Director: Dodo Dayao

  - Cast: Victor Neri, Anthony Falcon, Timothy Mabalot

4. Synopsis:

  "Violator" is set during a massive typhoon in Manila, where a group of people, including police officers and criminals, seek shelter in a precinct house. Among them is a mysterious young man who becomes the catalyst for increasingly strange and terrifying events. As the storm rages outside, tensions rise within the group, exacerbated by power outages and dwindling supplies. The boundary between reality and nightmare blurs as they face not only the threat of the typhoon but also a malevolent force that seems to be possessing and manipulating them. The film explores themes of sin, guilt, and the darkness lurking within human nature.

5. Why This Movie Is Recommended:

  "Violator" stands out for its unconventional approach to horror, blending elements of psychological thriller, supernatural horror, and social commentary. Director Dodo Dayao creates a claustrophobic, oppressive atmosphere that mirrors the characters' psychological states. The film's non-linear narrative and surreal imagery keep viewers off-balance, adding to the overall sense of unease. With strong performances from its ensemble cast and effective use of its confined setting, "Violator" delivers a deeply unsettling experience. Its exploration of societal issues and human nature under extreme circumstances adds depth to its horror elements, making it a thought-provoking and disturbing watch.

6. 10 Trivia Facts:

  1. "Violator" was Dodo Dayao's directorial debut, marking him as a significant new voice in Filipino horror.

  2. The film won the Best Picture award at the Cinema One Originals Film Festival.

  3. Many scenes were shot in a single take to maintain tension and authenticity.

  4. The movie's sound design, crucial for creating its eerie atmosphere, was highly praised by critics.

  5. "Violator" was shot entirely in digital, allowing for the dark, gritty aesthetic of the film.

  6. The film's narrative structure was influenced by the works of David Lynch.

  7. Many of the typhoon scenes were created using practical effects rather than CGI.

  8. "Violator" was screened at several international film festivals, gaining critical acclaim.

  9. The film's title has multiple meanings, playing into the movie's themes and plot.

  10. Director Dodo Dayao also wrote the screenplay, which went through numerous revisions.

20. Kuwaresma (The Entity)

1. Movie Title: Kuwaresma

2. Year of Release: 2019

3. Cast and Director:

- Director: Erik Matti

- Cast: Sharon Cuneta, John Arcilla, Kent Gonzales

4. Synopsis:

"Kuwaresma" follows Luis, a young man who returns home for Holy Week after his twin sister's mysterious death. As he tries to uncover the truth behind her passing, Luis confronts his strict, religious parents and the dark secrets lurking within their ancestral home. Strange and terrifying occurrences escalate as Luis delves deeper into the mystery, uncovering a history of abuse, repression, and possible supernatural intervention. Set against the backdrop of Holy Week traditions, the film explores themes of faith, family, and the horrifying consequences of buried truths. Luis must confront not only external horrors but also the demons within his own family.

5. Why This Movie Is Recommended:

"Kuwaresma" stands out for its psychological depth and its exploration of Filipino Catholic traditions. Director Erik Matti crafts a visually stunning film that uses religious imagery to heighten its horror elements. The movie's slow-burn approach builds tension masterfully, creating a pervasive sense of dread. With powerhouse performances from Sharon Cuneta and John Arcilla, "Kuwaresma" offers both emotional intensity and genuine scares. Its critical examination of family dynamics, religious orthodoxy, and the cycle of abuse adds layers of meaning to its supernatural elements. This film is a must-watch for those who appreciate horror that challenges societal norms and explores cultural traditions.

6. 10 Trivia Facts:

1. The title "Kuwaresma" refers to the Lenten season in the Philippines, during which the film is set.

2. This was Sharon Cuneta's first foray into the horror genre, marking a significant departure from her usual roles.

3. The film was shot in an actual heritage house in Baguio City, known for its cold climate which added to the movie's atmosphere.

4. Director Erik Matti drew inspiration from classic horror films like "The Exorcist" and "Rosemary's Baby."

5. The movie features authentic Holy Week traditions and rituals practiced in the Philippines.

6. "Kuwaresma" was praised for its cinematography, which made extensive use of shadows and candlelight.

7. The film's script went through several rewrites to balance its religious themes with horror elements.

8. Some of the more intense scenes reportedly caused audience members to leave screenings.

9. "Kuwaresma" was released internationally under the title "The Entity."

10. The movie sparked discussions about familial abuse and the role of religion in Filipino society.

South Korea

1. A Tale of Two Sisters (장화, 홍련)

1. Movie Title: A Tale of Two Sisters (장화, 홍련)

2. Year of Release: 2003

3. Cast and Director:

- Director: Kim Jee-woon

- Cast: Im Soo-jung, Moon Geun-young, Yeom Jeong-ah, Kim Kap-soo

4. Synopsis:

A Tale of Two Sisters follows Su-mi and Su-yeon, two sisters who return home after a stay in a mental institution. They are immediately unsettled by their stepmother's eerie presence and their father's distant behavior. Strange and terrifying occurrences plague the household, blurring the lines between reality and imagination. As the story unfolds, dark family secrets are revealed, and the true nature of the sisters' relationship comes into question. The film masterfully weaves psychological horror with Korean folklore, creating a haunting narrative that keeps viewers guessing until the very end.

5. Why This Movie Is Recommended:

A Tale of Two Sisters is a masterpiece of psychological horror that transcends cultural boundaries. Kim Jee-woon's direction creates a suffocating atmosphere of dread and uncertainty. The film's complex narrative, stunning visuals, and powerful performances make it a standout in the genre. It expertly blends family drama, supernatural elements, and psychological twists, rewarding multiple viewings. The movie's influence on both Korean and international horror cinema is significant, cementing its status as a modern classic.

6. 10 Trivia Facts:

1. The film is based on a Korean folktale, "Janghwa Hongryeon jeon."

2. It was the first Korean horror film to be screened in American theaters.

3. The movie was remade in Hollywood as "The Uninvited" in 2009.

4. Director Kim Jee-woon used a 2.35:1 aspect ratio to create a more claustrophobic feel.

5. The film won Best Picture at the 2004 Fantasporto Film Festival.

6. Many scenes were shot in a single take to maintain tension.

7. The movie's color palette was carefully designed to reflect the characters' emotions.

8. It was the highest-grossing Korean horror film of 2003.

9. The director cited Alfred Hitchcock's "Rebecca" as an influence.

10. The film's original Korean title literally translates to "Rose Flower, Red Lotus."

2. The Wailing (곡성)

1. Movie Title: The Wailing (곡성)

2. Year of Release: 2016

3. Cast and Director:

- Director: Na Hong-jin

- Cast: Kwak Do-won, Hwang Jung-min, Chun Woo-hee, Jun Kunimura

4. Synopsis:

Set in a small rural village, The Wailing follows police officer Jong-goo as he investigates a series of bizarre murders and illnesses that plague the community following the arrival of a mysterious Japanese stranger. As the situation escalates, Jong-goo's own daughter becomes afflicted by a strange disease. Desperate for answers, he turns to a shaman for help, leading to a confrontation with dark forces beyond his understanding. The film blends elements of police procedural, supernatural horror, and Korean folklore, creating a complex narrative that questions the nature of evil and the power of belief.

5. Why This Movie Is Recommended:

The Wailing is a tour de force of atmospheric horror that defies easy categorization. Na Hong-jin's direction creates a palpable sense of dread that permeates every frame. The film's lengthy runtime allows for deep character development and intricate plot weaving, resulting in a rich, immersive experience. Its exploration of cultural tensions, religious themes, and moral ambiguity elevates it beyond typical genre fare. The Wailing's ability to maintain suspense and deliver shocking twists until the very end makes it a must-watch for horror enthusiasts.

6. 10 Trivia Facts:

1. The film took 6 years to write and 8 months to shoot.

2. Director Na Hong-jin lived in the film's location for 4 years during pre-production.

3. The movie features three different types of exorcisms: Korean, Japanese, and Catholic.

4. Most of the film was shot chronologically to maintain the actors' emotional progression.

5. The iconic chase scene took 3 weeks to film.

6. Japanese actor Jun Kunimura learned his Korean lines phonetically.

7. The film's Korean title, "Gokseong," is the name of the village where it's set.

8. It was selected to screen in the Out of Competition section at the 2016 Cannes Film Festival.

9. The movie uses minimal CGI, relying mostly on practical effects.

10. Director Na Hong-jin consulted with real shamans during the scriptwriting process.

3. Train to Busan (부산행)

1. Movie Title: Train to Busan (부산행)

2. Year of Release: 2016

3. Cast and Director:

- Director: Yeon Sang-ho

- Cast: Gong Yoo, Jung Yu-mi, Ma Dong-seok, Kim Su-an

4. Synopsis:

Train to Busan follows a group of passengers struggling to survive on a train from Seoul to Busan during a sudden zombie outbreak in South Korea. The main character, Seok-woo, a workaholic fund manager, is taking his young daughter Su-an to see her mother in Busan. As the apocalypse unfolds around them, the passengers must fight for survival against the rapidly spreading zombie infection. The confined space of the train intensifies the tension, forcing characters to make difficult moral choices. As they journey towards the supposedly safe Busan, the survivors face not only the threat of zombies but also the darkness within human nature.

5. Why This Movie Is Recommended:

Train to Busan reinvigorates the zombie genre with its high-octane action, emotional depth, and social commentary. Director Yeon Sang-ho masterfully uses the claustrophobic setting of a train to ratchet up tension and create innovative action sequences. The film's strong character development ensures emotional investment in the survivors' fates. Its exploration of themes like class divide and corporate greed adds layers to the narrative. With its perfect balance of heart-pounding suspense and poignant human drama, Train to Busan stands as a landmark in both zombie and Korean cinema.

6. 10 Trivia Facts:

1. The film is director Yeon Sang-ho's live-action debut; he previously worked in animation.

2. A standalone animated prequel, "Seoul Station," was released the same year.

3. The zombies' movements were inspired by the choreography of Asian river otters.

4. Gong Yoo accepted the role because he wanted to star in Korea's first zombie blockbuster.

5. The film's success led to a sequel, "Peninsula," released in 2020.

6. Many of the zombies were played by dancers and martial artists for their physical agility.

7. The movie was shot in just 72 days.

8. Train to Busan premiered in the Midnight Screenings section of the 2016 Cannes Film Festival.

9. The film's Korean title, "Busanhaeng," simply means "To Busan."

10. It became the first Korean film of 2016 to break the audience record of 10 million theatergoers.

4. The Host (괴물)

1. Movie Title: The Host (괴물)

2. Year of Release: 2006

3. Cast and Director:

- Director: Bong Joon-ho

- Cast: Song Kang-ho, Byun Hee-bong, Park Hae-il, Bae Doona, Go Ah-sung

4. Synopsis:

The Host centers around the Park family, whose lives are turned upside down when a monstrous creature emerges from Seoul's Han River and abducts the youngest daughter, Hyun-seo. The creature, a result of chemical dumping by an American military base, terrorizes the city. As the government quarantines citizens under the guise of a virus outbreak, the Parks defy authorities to search for Hyun-seo. Led by the girl's somewhat dim-witted father, Gang-du, the family must overcome their own dysfunctions and societal obstacles to rescue Hyun-seo. The film blends monster movie tropes with sharp social satire, family drama, and dark comedy.

5. Why This Movie Is Recommended:

The Host is a genre-defying masterpiece that revolutionized Korean cinema. Bong Joon-ho's deft direction balances horror, humor, and heart with remarkable skill. The film's creature design and special effects were groundbreaking for Korean cinema at the time. Beyond its monster movie facade, The Host offers biting commentary on social issues, government incompetence, and environmental concerns. Its unconventional narrative structure and complex characters elevate it above typical monster fare. The film's influence on both Korean and international cinema makes it essential viewing for any horror or film enthusiast.

6. 10 Trivia Facts:

1. The film was inspired by a real-life incident of formaldehyde dumping in the Han River.

2. The monster design was partially based on Steve Buscemi's eyes.

3. It was the highest-grossing South Korean film of all time upon its release.

4. The CGI for the monster was created by The Orphanage, who also worked on Harry Potter films.

5. Bong Joon-ho's daughter inspired the character of Hyun-seo.

6. The film features a cameo by Korean-American actor Scott Wilson.

7. It won Best Film at the Asian Film Awards and the Blue Dragon Film Awards.

8. The monster's roar is a mix of pig squeals, dolphin clicks, and altered battle cries from "Dracula."

9. A host of Hollywood directors, including Quentin Tarantino, praised the film.

10. The American military base depicted in the film is based on the real-life Yongsan Garrison.

5. Thirst (박쥐)

1. **Movie Title: Thirst (박쥐)**

2. **Year of Release: 2009**

3. **Cast and Director:**

- Director: Park Chan-wook

- Cast: Song Kang-ho, Kim Ok-bin, Kim Hae-sook, Shin Ha-kyun

4. **Synopsis**:

Thirst follows the story of Sang-hyun, a devoted Catholic priest who volunteers for an experimental vaccine treatment to combat a deadly virus. The treatment fails, but Sang-hyun is miraculously resurrected by a blood transfusion, which turns him into a vampire. Struggling with his newfound bloodlust and sexual desires, Sang-hyun becomes involved with Tae-ju, the wife of his childhood friend. Their passionate and destructive relationship leads to a spiral of desire, murder, and moral decay. The film explores themes of faith, morality, and the nature of evil as Sang-hyun grapples with his vampire nature and human desires.

5. **Why This Movie Is Recommended**:

Thirst is a bold and provocative take on the vampire genre, infused with Park Chan-wook's signature style. The film's exploration of moral ambiguity and the human condition elevates it beyond typical horror fare. Park's visually striking direction and the compelling performances, especially by Song Kang-ho, create a mesmerizing viewing experience. Thirst's blend of horror, eroticism, and dark humor challenges viewers' expectations and moral compasses. Its unique cultural perspective on vampire mythology and its unflinching examination of desire and guilt make it a standout in both Korean and global cinema.

6. **10 Trivia Facts**:

1. The film is loosely based on Émile Zola's novel "Thérèse Raquin."

2. It won the Jury Prize at the 2009 Cannes Film Festival.

3. This was Park Chan-wook's first film to receive investment from an American studio (Focus Features).

4. The film features over 500 special effects shots.

5. Song Kang-ho learned to play the flute for his role.

6. The movie's Korean title, "Bakjwi," means "bat."

7. It was the first mainstream Korean film to feature full-frontal male nudity.

8. Park Chan-wook considers this film the final installment of his "Vengeance Trilogy."

9. The film's color palette changes subtly as the story progresses, reflecting the characters' transformation.

10. Thirst was partially inspired by Park's Catholic upbringing and his questions about faith.

6. I Saw the Devil (악마를 보았다)

1. Movie Title: I Saw the Devil (악마를 보았다)

2. Year of Release: 2010

3. Cast and Director:

- Director: Kim Jee-woon

- Cast: Choi Min-sik, Lee Byung-hun, Jeon Gook-hwan, Oh San-ha

4. Synopsis:

I Saw the Devil is a brutal cat-and-mouse thriller that follows secret agent Kim Soo-hyeon as he seeks revenge on Jang Kyung-chul, a sadistic serial killer who murdered his fiancée. Instead of killing Kyung-chul outright, Soo-hyeon chooses to inflict a series of increasingly violent acts upon him, releasing and recapturing him multiple times. As their game of revenge escalates, the line between good and evil blurs, and Soo-hyeon risks becoming the very monster he's hunting. The film explores the depths of human cruelty and the consuming nature of vengeance, pushing both characters and viewers to their limits.

5. Why This Movie Is Recommended:

I Saw the Devil is a masterclass in extreme cinema that challenges the conventions of both horror and revenge thrillers. Kim Jee-woon's unflinching direction and the powerhouse performances of Choi Min-sik and Lee Byung-hun create an intensely visceral experience. The film's exploration of the cyclical nature of violence and the corrupting influence of revenge adds psychological depth to its graphic content. While not for the faint-hearted, I Saw the Devil's technical brilliance, complex moral questions, and raw emotional power make it a landmark in Korean cinema and a must-watch for those who can stomach its intensity.

6. 10 Trivia Facts:

1. The film was heavily censored in Korea and had to be resubmitted three times before receiving approval for theatrical release.

2. Choi Min-sik and Lee Byung-hun performed most of their own stunts.

3. The movie's Korean title literally translates to "I Met the Devil."

4. It premiered at the 2010 Toronto International Film Festival to critical acclaim.

5. The film's final cut is 20 minutes shorter than the director's original version.

6. Choi Min-sik lost 10 kilograms for his role as the serial killer.

7. The movie features over 300 special effects shots.

8. Director Kim Jee-woon considered the film a continuation of the themes explored in A Bittersweet Life, which also starred Lee Byung-hun.

9. The film's violence was so extreme that some crew members had difficulty watching certain scenes being filmed.

10. I Saw the Devil won Best Film at the 2011 Asian Film Awards.

7. The Mimic (장산범)

1. Movie Title: The Mimic (장산범)

2. Year of Release: 2017

3. Cast and Director:

- Director: Huh Jung

- Cast: Yum Jung-ah, Park Hyuk-kwon, Shin Rin-ah, Heo Jin

4. Synopsis:

The Mimic is based on the Korean urban legend of a tiger that can imitate human voices to lure its prey. The story follows Hee-yeon, who moves to Mt. Jang with her family after the disappearance of her son. There, she encounters a mysterious girl hiding in a cave and decides to take her in. Strange occurrences begin to plague the family, and Hee-yeon starts to suspect that the girl might be connected to the legendary creature. As the mimicking entity's true nature is revealed, Hee-yeon must confront her own grief and protect her family from an ancient evil that preys on human emotions.

5. Why This Movie Is Recommended:

The Mimic stands out for its effective blend of Korean folklore and modern horror sensibilities. Director Huh Jung creates a palpable atmosphere of dread, using the lush forest setting to evoke both beauty and menace. The film's exploration of grief and motherhood adds emotional depth to its supernatural scares. With strong performances, particularly from Yum Jung-ah, and a clever use of sound design to enhance the mimicking concept, The Mimic offers a fresh take on familiar horror tropes. Its balance of psychological horror and jump scares makes it accessible to a wide range of horror fans.

6. 10 Trivia Facts:

1. The film is based on the Jangsan Tiger, a creature from Korean folklore known for mimicking human voices.

2. Director Huh Jung previously directed the hit horror film "Hide and Seek" (2013).

3. The cave scenes were filmed on a set built in a studio due to the difficulty of shooting in real caves.

4. The movie's Korean title, "Jangsan-beom," refers directly to the legendary creature.

5. Child actress Shin Rin-ah had to learn a specific dialect for her role as the mysterious girl.

6. The film uses minimal CGI, relying more on practical effects and sound design.

7. It was the first Korean horror film to be released in the summer season in several years.

8. The movie's success led to a resurgence of interest in Korean urban legends and folklore-based horror.

9. Actress Yum Jung-ah practiced motherly behaviors with child actress Shin Rin-ah off-screen to build their on-screen relationship.

10. The film's sound designers created over 100 different vocalizations for the mimicking creature.

8. Gonjiam: Haunted Asylum (곤지암)

1. Movie Title: Gonjiam: Haunted Asylum (곤지암)

2. Year of Release: 2018

3. Cast and Director:

 - Director: Jung Bum-shik

 - Cast: Wi Ha-joon, Park Sung-hoon, Lee Seung-wook, Oh Ah-yeon, Park Ji-hyun, Yoo Je-yoon, Mun Ye-won

4. Synopsis:

 Gonjiam: Haunted Asylum follows a team of online horror show hosts who plan to livestream their exploration of the abandoned Gonjiam Psychiatric Hospital, notorious for its dark history and supposed supernatural activity. The team aims to boost their viewer ratings by investigating the hospital's most haunted areas, including the restricted ward 402, where patients and staff allegedly vanished. As they delve deeper into the asylum, the line between reality and nightmare blurs. The team faces increasingly terrifying phenomena, forcing them to confront not only the horrors of the asylum but also their own fears and secrets.

5. Why This Movie Is Recommended:

 Gonjiam: Haunted Asylum breathes new life into the found footage horror genre with its innovative use of multiple camera perspectives and livestream format. Director Jung Bum-shik masterfully builds tension through subtle scares and an oppressive atmosphere, making the familiar setting of an abandoned asylum feel fresh and terrifying. The film's clever mix of Korean urban legends, psychological horror, and jump scares creates a genuinely unsettling experience. Its exploration of the dark side of internet fame adds a contemporary relevance to the supernatural narrative. For fans of found footage horror or those seeking a truly frightening cinematic experience, Gonjiam is a must-watch.

6. 10 Trivia Facts:

 1. The film is loosely based on the real Gonjiam Psychiatric Hospital, once considered one of Korea's most haunted locations.

 2. It became one of the highest-grossing Korean horror films of all time.

 3. The entire movie was shot in just 17 days.

 4. Most of the cast were relatively unknown actors at the time, adding to the film's realism.

 5. The real Gonjiam Psychiatric Hospital was demolished in 2018, the same year the film was released.

 6. Director Jung Bum-shik insisted on using the actors' real names for their characters to increase authenticity.

 7. The film's success led to increased interest in urban exploration in Korea, prompting safety concerns.

 8. Many of the scares were achieved through practical effects rather than CGI.

 9. The actors were often not told what would happen in certain scenes to capture genuine reactions.

 10. Despite its found footage style, the film was shot using high-quality cameras to maintain image clarity.

9. The Silenced (경성학교: 사라진 소녀들)

1. Movie Title: The Silenced (경성학교: 사라진 소녀들)

2. Year of Release: 2015

3. Cast and Director:

- Director: Lee Hae-young

- Cast: Park Bo-young, Uhm Ji-won, Park So-dam, Kong Ye-ji

4. Synopsis:

Set in 1938 during the Japanese occupation of Korea, The Silenced takes place in a remote girls' boarding school. Ju-ran, a sickly student, arrives at the school hoping to recover her health. She soon befriends Yeon-deok and becomes curious about the strange disappearances of other students. As Ju-ran investigates, she uncovers a sinister plot involving the school's administration and secret medical experiments. The girls find themselves trapped in a nightmare of human experimentation and supernatural occurrences. Ju-ran must fight not only for her own survival but also to expose the dark truth behind the school's facade.

5. Why This Movie Is Recommended:

The Silenced stands out for its unique blend of historical drama, supernatural horror, and psychological thriller elements. Director Lee Hae-young creates a haunting atmosphere that reflects both the oppression of the colonial era and the claustrophobia of the isolated school setting. The film's exploration of identity, conformity, and resistance adds depth to its horror elements. With strong performances from its young cast, particularly Park Bo-young, and stunning period-accurate production design, The Silenced offers a visually rich and emotionally resonant horror experience. Its commentary on historical trauma and the abuse of power elevates it beyond typical genre fare.

6. 10 Trivia Facts:

1. The film's Korean title translates to "Gyeongseong School: Disappeared Girls."

2. It was inspired by real-life human experiments conducted during the Japanese occupation of Korea.

3. The movie was shot on location at a former hospital in Gangwon Province.

4. Actress Park Bo-young lost weight and altered her appearance to portray the sickly Ju-ran.

5. The film's costume design won an award at the Blue Dragon Film Awards.

6. Director Lee Hae-young extensively researched 1930s Korea to ensure historical accuracy.

7. The movie features subtle references to classic Gothic literature.

8. It was Park So-dam's first major film role before her breakout in "Parasite."

9. The film uses a desaturated color palette to enhance the period atmosphere.

10. Despite its horror elements, The Silenced was praised for its sensitive portrayal of female friendships.

10. Memento Mori (여고괴담 두 번째 이야기)

1. Movie Title: **Memento Mori (여고괴담 두 번째 이야기)**

2. Year of Release: 1999

3. Cast and Director:

- Directors: Kim Tae-yong and Min Kyu-dong

- Cast: Kim Min-sun, Park Ye-jin, Lee Young-jin, Kong Hyo-jin

4. Synopsis:

   Memento Mori, the second installment in the Whispering Corridors series, is set in an all-girls high school. The story revolves around the discovery of a diary that belonged to two students, Hyo-shin and Shi-eun, who were involved in a secret romantic relationship. After Hyo-shin's mysterious death, strange occurrences begin to plague the school. As Min-ah, the student who found the diary, delves deeper into its contents, she uncovers the tragic love story and the dark secrets of the school. The film explores themes of forbidden love, bullying, and the pressures of the Korean education system, all while supernatural events escalate around the characters.

5. Why This Movie Is Recommended:

   Memento Mori stands out as a pioneering work in Korean horror cinema, particularly for its sensitive portrayal of LGBTQ+ themes. The film transcends typical ghost story tropes, offering a poignant exploration of love, loss, and societal pressures. Directors Kim Tae-yong and Min Kyu-dong create a haunting atmosphere that blends psychological horror with touching drama. Its non-linear narrative and artistic visual style set it apart from conventional horror films. Memento Mori's influence on subsequent Korean horror movies and its tackling of taboo subjects make it a significant and thought-provoking entry in the genre.

6. 10 Trivia Facts:

   1. The film is part of the Whispering Corridors series, but each installment has a separate story and cast.

   2. It was one of the first mainstream Korean films to depict a same-sex relationship.

   3. The movie's title, "Memento Mori," is Latin for "Remember that you must die."

   4. Many scenes were shot in a real high school during its summer break.

   5. The film launched the careers of several actresses who became major stars in Korean cinema.

   6. It received critical acclaim for its artistic merit, winning awards at several film festivals.

   7. The directors were only in their mid-20s when they made the film.

   8. Memento Mori is often considered the best entry in the Whispering Corridors series.

   9. The film's subtle approach to horror influenced the style of many subsequent Korean horror movies.

   10. It has gained a cult following and is considered a classic of Korean queer cinema.

11. The Housemaid (하녀)

1. Movie Title: The Housemaid (하녀)

2. Year of Release: 2010

3. Cast and Director:

- Director: Im Sang-soo

- Cast: Jeon Do-yeon, Lee Jung-jae, Youn Yuh-jung, Seo Woo

4. Synopsis:

The Housemaid is a psychological thriller that follows Eun-yi, a young woman who is hired as a nanny and maid for an wealthy family. As she becomes entangled in the dysfunctional dynamics of the household, she enters into a dangerous affair with the father, Hoon. The pregnancy resulting from this liaison sets off a chain of events involving manipulation, betrayal, and violence. The film explores themes of class disparity, power dynamics, and the dark underbelly of privilege. As tensions escalate, Eun-yi finds herself trapped in a web of deceit and must fight for her survival against the ruthless machinations of the family.

5. Why This Movie Is Recommended:

While not a traditional horror film, The Housemaid excels in creating an atmosphere of psychological dread and impending doom. Director Im Sang-soo's stylish reimagining of the 1960 Korean classic brings a modern, noir-ish sensibility to the story. The film's exploration of class warfare and moral corruption offers a scathing critique of contemporary society. With its stunning cinematography, taut pacing, and powerhouse performances, particularly from Jeon Do-yeon, The Housemaid delivers a haunting and provocative viewing experience. Its blend of eroticism, suspense, and social commentary makes it a unique entry in Korean cinema.

6. 10 Trivia Facts:

1. The film is a remake of the 1960 Korean classic of the same name directed by Kim Ki-young.

2. It was selected to compete for the Palme d'Or at the 2010 Cannes Film Festival.

3. The elaborate mansion where most of the film takes place was entirely constructed on a soundstage.

4. Actress Jeon Do-yeon took cooking classes to prepare for her role as the housemaid.

5. The film's score, composed by Kim Hong-jip, won several awards for its haunting melodies.

6. Director Im Sang-soo made significant changes to the original story to reflect modern Korean society.

7. The movie sparked debates in Korea about class issues and the treatment of domestic workers.

8. It was one of the most expensive Korean films produced at the time due to its elaborate set design.

9. The film's ending differs dramatically from the 1960 original, offering a more ambiguous conclusion.

10. Despite its dark themes, The Housemaid was a commercial success in Korea and internationally.

12. Possessed (부신)

1. Movie Title: Possessed (부신)

2. Year of Release: 2009

3. Cast and Director:

- Director: Lee Yong-ju

- Cast: Nam Sang-mi, Shim Eun-kyung, Kim Bo-yeon, Ryu Seung-ryong

4. Synopsis:

Possessed centers around Hee-jin, a young woman who returns home after her younger sister, So-jin, mysteriously disappears. As Hee-jin investigates her sister's vanishing, she uncovers a dark history of shamanism and demonic possession in her neighborhood. The community is gripped by a series of bizarre and violent incidents, which seem to be connected to So-jin's disappearance. Hee-jin must confront her own skepticism about the supernatural and face off against malevolent forces to save her sister. The film blends elements of traditional Korean shamanism with modern psychological horror, creating a unique and unsettling narrative.

5. Why This Movie Is Recommended:

Possessed stands out for its effective blend of supernatural horror and psychological thriller elements. Director Lee Yong-ju creates a pervasive atmosphere of unease, skillfully balancing traditional Korean folklore with contemporary fears. The film's exploration of faith, skepticism, and the clash between modernity and tradition adds depth to its scares. Strong performances, particularly from Nam Sang-mi and the young Shim Eun-kyung, ground the supernatural elements in emotional realism. With its intricate plot, genuinely creepy moments, and commentary on societal issues, Possessed offers a thought-provoking and chilling viewing experience for fans of psychological horror.

6. 10 Trivia Facts:

1. The film's Korean title, "Busin," refers to a type of malevolent spirit in Korean folklore.

2. Director Lee Yong-ju extensively researched Korean shamanism for authenticity.

3. The movie features several scenes of traditional Korean exorcism rituals.

4. Actress Shim Eun-kyung was only 15 years old during filming but delivered a powerful performance.

5. The film uses minimal special effects, relying more on atmosphere and psychological horror.

6. Possessed was praised for its realistic portrayal of a working-class Korean neighborhood.

7. The movie's success led to increased interest in Korean folklore and shamanism.

8. Several scenes were shot in real-life "villa" apartments to maintain authenticity.

9. The film draws inspiration from real cases of mass hysteria in Korea.

10. Possessed won Best New Director for Lee Yong-ju at the Blue Dragon Film Awards.

13. Bedevilled (김복남 살인사건의 전말)

1. Movie Title: Bedevilled (김복남 살인사건의 전말)

2. Year of Release: 2010

3. Cast and Director:

  - Director: Jang Cheol-soo

  - Cast: Seo Young-hee, Ji Sung-won, Park Jeong-hak, Baek Su-ryun

4. Synopsis:

  Bedevilled follows Hae-won, a callous city dweller who returns to the remote island where she grew up after a nervous breakdown. There, she reunites with her childhood friend, Bok-nam, who lives a life of abuse and servitude under the island's oppressive patriarchal society. As Hae-won witnesses the brutal treatment Bok-nam endures, she is forced to confront her own past traumas and complicity in her friend's suffering. The tension builds to a breaking point, leading to a violent and cathartic climax as Bok-nam finally rebels against her tormentors. The film is a harrowing exploration of abuse, isolation, and the consequences of turning a blind eye to injustice.

5. Why This Movie Is Recommended:

  Bedevilled is a powerful and disturbing film that blends elements of psychological horror with social commentary. Director Jang Cheol-soo crafts a tense, claustrophobic atmosphere that mirrors the trapped existence of its characters. The film's unflinching portrayal of abuse and its consequences makes for uncomfortable but compelling viewing. Seo Young-hee's tour-de-force performance as Bok-nam anchors the film's emotional core. While not a traditional horror movie, Bedevilled's exploration of human cruelty and its violent catharsis create a deeply unsettling experience. Its critique of societal apathy and the cycle of abuse adds depth to its visceral impact.

6. 10 Trivia Facts:

  1. Bedevilled was director Jang Cheol-soo's debut feature film.

  2. The movie was shot on a remote island off the coast of South Korea.

  3. It premiered at the 2010 Cannes Film Festival in the International Critics' Week section.

  4. Actress Seo Young-hee won numerous awards for her portrayal of Bok-nam.

  5. The film's Korean title translates to "The Whole Story of Kim Bok-nam's Murder Case."

  6. Many of the island's residents in the film were played by non-professional actors from the local area.

  7. Bedevilled was praised for its feminist themes and critique of patriarchal society.

  8. The movie sparked discussions in Korea about domestic violence and rural women's rights.

  9. Director Jang Cheol-soo was mentored by famous Korean filmmaker Kim Ki-duk.

  10. The film's success led to international distribution, rare for a Korean independent film at the time.

14. Cinderella (신데렐라)

1. Movie Title: Cinderella (신데렐라)

2. Year of Release: 2006

3. Cast and Director:

- Director: Bong Man-dae

- Cast: Do Ji-won, Shin Se-kyung, Uhm Ji-won, Gim Yoo-jeong

4. Synopsis:

Cinderella offers a dark twist on the fairy tale concept, focusing on a group of high school girls who become obsessed with plastic surgery. The story centers on Hyun-su, whose mother is a renowned plastic surgeon. Strange events begin to unfold as Hyun-su's friends, who have all undergone procedures at her mother's clinic, start to experience horrifying physical changes. As Hyun-su investigates, she uncovers a sinister secret connected to her own past and her mother's work. The film explores themes of beauty standards, self-image, and the horror of bodily transformation, blending psychological terror with body horror elements.

5. Why This Movie Is Recommended:

Cinderella stands out for its unique premise that combines social commentary with horror elements. Director Bong Man-dae creates a unsettling atmosphere that plays on universal insecurities about appearance and identity. The film's exploration of beauty standards and the pressure to conform in Korean society adds depth to its scares. With its blend of psychological horror, body horror, and teenage drama, Cinderella offers a fresh take on familiar themes. The movie's disturbing imagery and commentary on the dark side of the beauty industry make it a thought-provoking entry in the Korean horror genre.

6. 10 Trivia Facts:

1. The film is part of the "Horror Tales" series, a collection of Korean horror movies based on fairy tales.

2. It features early performances from actresses who later became major stars, including Shin Se-kyung.

3. The movie's makeup and prosthetic effects won praise for their disturbing realism.

4. Cinderella sparked debates in Korea about the country's plastic surgery culture.

5. The film draws inspiration from both the Cinderella fairy tale and Greek mythology.

6. Director Bong Man-dae interviewed numerous plastic surgery patients as part of his research.

7. The movie's poster, featuring a face wrapped in bandages, became iconic in Korean horror cinema.

8. Cinderella was one of the first Korean horror films to directly address the issue of plastic surgery.

9. The film uses mirrors and reflections extensively as a motif throughout the story.

10. Despite its dark themes, the movie was a commercial success and gained a cult following.

15. Hansel and Gretel (헨젤과 그레텔)

1. Movie Title: Hansel and Gretel (헨젤과 그레텔)

2. Year of Release: 2007

3. Cast and Director:

- Director: Yim Pil-sung

- Cast: Chun Jung-myung, Eun Won-jae, Shim Eun-kyung, Jin Ji-hee

4. Synopsis:

Hansel and Gretel offers a dark, twisted take on the classic fairy tale. The story begins when Eun-soo, a salesman, crashes his car in a remote forest. He's rescued by a young girl who leads him to a house deep in the woods, where he meets two other children and their oddly youthful parents. As Eun-soo tries to leave, he finds himself trapped in a nightmarish scenario where the children wield mysterious powers and refuse to let him go. The house seems to exist in its own reality, and as Eun-soo uncovers the truth about the children's past and the nature of their world, he must find a way to escape or risk being trapped forever in this dark fairy tale.

5. Why This Movie Is Recommended:

Hansel and Gretel stands out for its unique blend of fairy tale elements, psychological horror, and social commentary. Director Yim Pil-sung creates a visually stunning world that is both whimsical and deeply unsettling. The film's exploration of childhood trauma, abandonment, and the dark side of innocence adds psychological depth to its fantastical premise. With strong performances from its young cast and a narrative that keeps viewers guessing, Hansel and Gretel offers a fresh and thought-provoking take on familiar fairy tale tropes. Its seamless blend of beauty and horror, coupled with its emotional resonance, makes it a standout in Korean fantasy-horror cinema.

6. 10 Trivia Facts:

1. The film is part of the same "Horror Tales" series as "Cinderella," reimagining classic fairy tales with a horror twist.

2. The elaborate house set was entirely constructed for the film and took months to build.

3. Director Yim Pil-sung was inspired by his own experiences of getting lost in the woods as a child.

4. The movie features early performances from child actors who later became prominent in Korean cinema.

5. Hansel and Gretel won several awards for its art direction and special effects.

6. The film's color palette changes subtly throughout the movie to reflect the psychological states of the characters.

7. Despite its fairy tale basis, the movie touches on serious issues like child abuse and abandonment.

8. The directors of "The Host" and "Oldboy" served as producers on the film.

9. Hansel and Gretel was praised for its unique visual style, which blends German expressionism with Korean aesthetics.

10. The movie's success led to increased interest in fairy tale adaptations in Korean cinema.

16. Acacia (아카시아)

1. Movie Title: Acacia (아카시아)

2. Year of Release: 2003

3. Cast and Director:

 - Director: Park Ki-hyung

 - Cast: Shim Hye-jin, Kim Jin-geun, Oh Yun-soo, Jung Da-bin

4. Synopsis:

  Acacia tells the story of Jin-sung, an adopted boy who joins a family unable to conceive a child of their own. The family's dynamics change dramatically when the mother unexpectedly becomes pregnant. As Jin-sung feels increasingly neglected, he forms a strange attachment to the acacia tree in their garden. When the boy mysteriously disappears, the tree becomes the center of increasingly disturbing events. The line between reality and nightmare blurs as the family grapples with guilt, loss, and the possibility of supernatural forces at work. The film explores themes of family, belonging, and the psychological toll of repressed emotions.

5. Why This Movie Is Recommended:

  Acacia stands out for its subtle approach to horror, relying more on psychological tension than overt scares. Director Park Ki-hyung crafts a deeply unsettling atmosphere that grows increasingly oppressive as the story unfolds. The film's exploration of family dynamics and the darker aspects of parenthood adds depth to its supernatural elements. With strong performances and a haunting visual style, Acacia offers a unique blend of family drama and psychological horror. Its ambiguous nature, leaving much open to interpretation, makes it a thought-provoking entry in the Korean horror genre that lingers in the mind long after viewing.

6. 10 Trivia Facts:

 1. The acacia tree in the film is symbolic in Korean culture, often associated with departed souls.

 2. Director Park Ki-hyung also helmed the famous Korean horror film "Whispering Corridors."

 3. The movie's ambiguous ending has been the subject of much debate among viewers.

 4. Acacia was praised for its realistic portrayal of family dynamics in Korean society.

 5. The film uses minimal special effects, relying instead on atmosphere and psychological horror.

 6. It was one of the first Korean horror films to focus on the theme of adoption.

 7. The movie's sound design, particularly the creaking of the acacia tree, was crucial in creating tension.

 8. Acacia premiered at the Busan International Film Festival to critical acclaim.

 9. The film's understated approach to horror influenced subsequent Korean psychological thrillers.

 10. Despite its supernatural elements, much of the movie's horror stems from very real family anxieties.

17. Arang (아랑)

1. **Movie Title: Arang (아랑)**

2. **Year of Release: 2006**

3. **Cast and Director:**

 - Director: Ahn Sang-hoon

 - Cast: Song Yoon-ah, Lee Dong-wook, Choi Jung-won, Kim Dong-wook

4. **Synopsis**:

Arang is based on a famous Korean folk tale about a ghost seeking justice for her murder. The film follows So-young, a female police officer investigating a series of gruesome murders in a small town. She teams up with a local detective, Hyun-ki, who has the ability to see ghosts. As they delve deeper into the case, they uncover a connection between the current killings and an unsolved murder from years ago. The ghost of a young woman named Arang becomes both an ally and a source of terror as So-young and Hyun-ki race to stop the killer and uncover long-buried secrets. The film blends elements of police procedural with supernatural horror, creating a unique and chilling narrative.

5. **Why This Movie Is Recommended**:

Arang stands out for its effective combination of traditional ghost story elements with a modern crime thriller framework. Director Ahn Sang-hoon creates a moody, atmospheric film that pays homage to Korean folklore while delivering contemporary scares. The movie's exploration of themes like justice, revenge, and the lingering effects of past crimes adds depth to its supernatural premise. Strong performances from the lead actors and genuinely creepy ghost appearances make for a compelling viewing experience. With its blend of cultural specificity and universal horror tropes, Arang offers a fresh take on the ghost story genre that appeals to both Korean and international audiences.

6. **10 Trivia Facts**:

1. The film is based on the legend of Arang, a famous ghost story from Korea's Joseon Dynasty.

2. Arang was shot on location in Miryang, the city where the original folktale is set.

3. The movie spawned a television drama series of the same name in 2012.

4. Director Ahn Sang-hoon extensively researched Korean shamanism for the film.

5. The ghost's appearance in the movie was inspired by traditional Korean funeral attire.

6. Arang was one of the first Korean horror films to successfully blend the police procedural genre with supernatural elements.

7. The film uses a distinctive color palette, with cool blues dominating the ghost scenes.

8. Many of the film's locations are actual historical sites related to the Arang legend.

9. The movie's success led to increased tourism in Miryang, with fans visiting filming locations.

10. Arang received praise for its respectful treatment of Korean folklore while updating it for modern audiences.

18. Whispering Corridors (여고괴담)

1. Movie Title: Whispering Corridors (여고괴담)

2. Year of Release: 1998

3. Cast and Director:

- Director: Park Ki-hyung

- Cast: Choi Se-yeon, Kim Gyu-ri, Lee Mi-yeon, Yoon Jin-seo

4. Synopsis:

Whispering Corridors is set in an all-girls high school where strange and terrifying events begin to occur following the apparent suicide of a teacher. As students and faculty grapple with the tragedy, they start experiencing supernatural phenomena. The film focuses on several students and a young teacher as they uncover dark secrets about the school's past and confront a vengeful ghost. Through its horror narrative, the movie explores themes of bullying, academic pressure, and the rigid hierarchies within the Korean school system. As the characters delve deeper into the mystery, they must face both human cruelty and supernatural terror.

5. Why This Movie Is Recommended:

Whispering Corridors is a landmark film in Korean horror cinema, kickstarting a renewed interest in the genre. Director Park Ki-hyung crafts a chilling atmosphere that draws as much horror from the pressures of the school system as it does from supernatural elements. The film's social commentary on the darker aspects of education in Korea adds depth and relevance to its scares. With its focus on female characters and their experiences, Whispering Corridors offers a fresh perspective in the horror genre. Its influence on subsequent Korean horror films, particularly in school settings, makes it an essential watch for fans of Asian horror.

6. 10 Trivia Facts:

1. Whispering Corridors is the first in a series of five thematically-connected films set in all-girls' high schools.

2. The movie was a significant box office success, surprising many who thought the horror genre was dead in Korea.

3. It was one of the first Korean films to directly criticize the country's education system.

4. The film launched the careers of several actresses who went on to become major stars.

5. Whispering Corridors was released shortly after Korea's censorship laws were relaxed, allowing for more social critique in films.

6. The movie's success led to a resurgence of the horror genre in Korean cinema.

7. Many of the film's scenes were shot in a real high school during summer break.

8. The ghost's appearance was inspired by the uniform worn by female students during Korea's colonial period.

9. Whispering Corridors has been the subject of numerous academic studies on Korean cinema and social issues.

10. The film's theme song, "Fox Rain," became a hit and is still associated with Korean horror.

19. Phone (폰)

1. Movie Title: Phone (폰)

2. Year of Release: 2002

3. Cast and Director:

  - Director: Ahn Byeong-ki

  - Cast: Ha Ji-won, Kim Yu-mi, Choi Woo-jae

4. Synopsis:

  Phone centers around Ji-won, a journalist who changes her cell phone number after receiving threatening calls while investigating a sex scandal. However, strange things begin to happen with her new number. People who receive calls from this number die mysteriously, and Ji-won starts experiencing terrifying visions. As she investigates, she uncovers a tragic story involving her sister-in-law, Young-ju, and Young-ju's daughter, Jin-hee. The movie weaves together themes of technology-based horror, family secrets, and revenge, building to a chilling climax that reveals the dark truth behind the cursed phone number.

5. Why This Movie Is Recommended:

  Phone stands out as one of the early entries in the techno-horror subgenre, effectively tapping into anxieties about modern communication technology. Director Ahn Byeong-ki creates a tense atmosphere where everyday objects become sources of terror. The film's complex plot, with its many twists and turns, keeps viewers engaged and guessing until the end. Strong performances, particularly from Ha Ji-won, ground the supernatural elements in emotional reality. Phone's exploration of family dynamics and the consequences of buried secrets adds depth to its scares. As a precursor to later techno-horror hits like "One Missed Call," it's an important entry in the evolution of Asian horror cinema.

6. 10 Trivia Facts:

  1. Phone was one of the first Korean horror films to center its plot around modern technology.

  2. The movie was a commercial success and helped establish Ha Ji-won as a versatile actress.

  3. It was remade in Japan in 2005 under the title "One Missed Call 2".

  4. The film's success contributed to the trend of "haunted technology" in Asian horror cinema.

  5. Director Ahn Byeong-ki also helmed other notable Korean horror films like "Bunshinsaba" and "APT".

  6. Phone uses a distinctive ringtone that became associated with horror in Korean pop culture.

  7. The movie features early use of the "ghost in the machine" trope in Korean cinema.

  8. Many of the film's scares were achieved through practical effects rather than CGI.

  9. Phone was part of a wave of Korean horror films that gained international distribution in the early 2000s.

  10. The movie's plot touches on real social issues in Korea, including child abuse and marital infidelity.

20. The Red Shoes (분홍신)

1. Movie Title: The Red Shoes (분홍신)

2. Year of Release: 2005

3. Cast and Director:

  - Director: Kim Yong-gyun

  - Cast: Kim Hye-soo, Park Yeon-ah, Kim Sung-soo

4. Synopsis:

  The Red Shoes is a supernatural horror film inspired by the Hans Christian Andersen fairy tale of the same name. The story follows Sun-jae, a recently divorced woman who finds a pair of pink high heels on a subway platform. She takes them home, unknowingly unleashing a curse that begins to affect her and her young daughter, Tae-soo. As strange and terrifying events unfold around them, Sun-jae investigates the origin of the shoes, uncovering a tragic story of jealousy, betrayal, and death. The curse of the red shoes spreads, endangering everyone who comes into contact with them. Sun-jae must unravel the mystery and break the curse before it claims her and her daughter.

5. Why This Movie Is Recommended:

  The Red Shoes stands out for its visually striking approach to horror, blending fairy tale elements with modern urban fears. Director Kim Yong-gyun creates a series of memorable, often beautiful yet terrifying images that linger in the mind. The film's exploration of themes like materialism, vanity, and the complexities of mother-daughter relationships adds depth to its supernatural premise. Strong performances, particularly from Kim Hye-soo, anchor the film's more fantastical elements. With its unique premise and stylish execution, The Red Shoes offers a fresh take on the curse narrative common in Asian horror, making it a must-watch for fans of the genre.

6. 10 Trivia Facts:

  1. The film draws inspiration from the Korean folktale "The Pit Pat Sound of the Red Shoes" as well as the Hans Christian Andersen story.

  2. The red shoes in the movie were custom-made and became iconic in Korean horror cinema.

  3. Director Kim Yong-gyun previously worked as an assistant director on the famous Korean thriller "Oldboy."

  4. The movie features elaborate dance sequences that blend horror with choreography.

  5. The Red Shoes was part of a trend of Korean horror films inspired by Western fairy tales.

  6. The film's color palette, emphasizing reds and pinks, was carefully designed to create a specific mood.

  7. It received praise for its cinematography, winning awards at several film festivals.

  8. The movie explores the Korean concept of "Han," a collective feeling of oppression and isolation.

  9. Several scenes were filmed in the Seoul subway system, a first for a Korean horror film at the time.

  10. The Red Shoes' success led to increased interest in fashion-related horror concepts in Asian cinema.

Vietnam

1. The Housemaid (Cô Hầu Gái)

1. Movie Title: The Housemaid (Cô Hầu Gái)

2. Year of Release: 2016

3. Cast and Director:

- Director: Derek Nguyen

- Cast: Nhung Kate, Jean-Michel Richaud, Kim Xuan, Rosie Fellner

4. Synopsis:

Set in 1953 Vietnam, "The Housemaid" follows an orphaned country girl who finds work as a housemaid at a haunted rubber plantation. She falls in love with the French landowner, igniting the jealousy of his dead wife's ghost. As she becomes entangled in the plantation's dark history of violence and revenge, she must confront the malevolent spirits that haunt the estate. The film blends elements of gothic romance with Vietnamese folklore, creating a atmospheric tale of forbidden love and supernatural vengeance.

5. Why This Movie Is Recommended:

"The Housemaid" stands out for its lush visuals and its unique blend of Western gothic horror tropes with Vietnamese historical context and supernatural lore. The film offers a fresh perspective on colonial-era Vietnam, exploring themes of class, race, and power through a horror lens. Its atmospheric tension, strong performances, and beautiful cinematography elevate it above typical ghost stories. As one of the more internationally recognized Vietnamese horror films, it serves as an excellent introduction to the country's emerging horror cinema.

6. 10 Trivia Facts:

1. The film is loosely inspired by the life of director Derek Nguyen's grandmother, who worked as a housemaid on a rubber plantation.

2. It was Vietnam's highest-grossing horror film at the time of its release.

3. The movie was shot on location in Dalat, Vietnam, known for its French colonial architecture.

4. "The Housemaid" was Vietnam's submission for the Best Foreign Language Film at the 90th Academy Awards, though it wasn't nominated.

5. The film blends Vietnamese, French, and English dialogue to reflect the colonial setting.

6. It won the Golden Kite Award for Best Feature Film from the Vietnam Cinema Association.

7. The movie's success led to talks of an American remake, though this hasn't materialized as of 2024.

8. Lead actress Nhung Kate underwent intensive training to perfect her 1953-era mannerisms and speech patterns.

9. The film's ghostly effects were achieved through a combination of practical effects and minimal CGI.

10. Director Derek Nguyen incorporated elements of Vietnamese folk magic and superstitions into the story.

2. Hollow (Đoạt Hồn)

1. Movie Title: Hollow (Đoạt Hồn)

2. Year of Release: 2014

3. Cast and Director:

- Director: Ham Tran

- Cast: Nguyen Van Hoa, Nguyen Anh Tu, Huynh Dong, La Thanh

4. Synopsis:

"Hollow" tells the story of a young couple who lose their son in a tragic accident. Desperate to have another child, they turn to a mysterious woman who promises to help them conceive through a magical ritual. However, the ritual comes with a terrible price, and soon the couple finds themselves haunted by malevolent spirits. As they uncover the dark truth behind the ritual, they must fight to save their unborn child and themselves from a horrifying fate. The film explores themes of grief, desperation, and the consequences of tampering with the natural order.

5. Why This Movie Is Recommended:

"Hollow" stands out for its effective blend of psychological horror and supernatural elements, grounded in Vietnamese cultural beliefs about life, death, and the spirit world. The film's exploration of parental grief and desperation adds emotional depth to its scares. With strong performances and atmospheric direction, it manages to create genuine tension and dread. As one of the more polished entries in Vietnam's horror cinema, "Hollow" demonstrates the potential of the country's film industry in this genre.

6. 10 Trivia Facts:

1. The film's Vietnamese title, "Đoạt Hồn," literally translates to "Soul Stealing."

2. Director Ham Tran is known for his work in both Vietnam and the United States.

3. The movie incorporates elements of traditional Vietnamese beliefs about pregnancy and childbirth.

4. "Hollow" was one of the first Vietnamese horror films to receive significant international distribution.

5. The film's success at the box office helped spark a renewed interest in horror filmmaking in Vietnam.

6. Some of the film's more intense scenes were toned down to pass Vietnam's strict censorship laws.

7. The movie features practical effects for many of its supernatural elements, enhancing the realism.

8. "Hollow" premiered at the 2014 Los Angeles Asian Pacific Film Festival.

9. The film's soundtrack incorporates traditional Vietnamese instruments to enhance its eerie atmosphere.

10. Several scenes were shot in remote villages to capture authentic Vietnamese rural settings.

3. Ghosts Are Real (Ma Dai)

1. Movie Title: Ghosts Are Real (Ma Dai)

2. Year of Release: 2013

3. Cast and Director:

 - Director: Le Van Kiet

 - Cast: Mai The Hiep, Huynh Dong, Phi Phung, Hua Vi Van

4. Synopsis:

"Ghosts Are Real" follows a group of young filmmakers who set out to create a documentary about ghost hunting in Vietnam. As they investigate various haunted locations, they encounter increasingly terrifying supernatural phenomena. The line between their film project and reality begins to blur, and they find themselves trapped in a nightmarish situation where the ghosts they sought to document become all too real. As they struggle to survive and uncover the truth behind the hauntings, they must confront their own beliefs about the supernatural and the consequences of disturbing the spirit world.

5. Why This Movie Is Recommended:

"Ghosts Are Real" offers a fresh take on the found footage horror subgenre by incorporating Vietnamese ghostlore and cultural beliefs. The film effectively builds tension through its pseudo-documentary style, creating a sense of authenticity that enhances the scares. Its exploration of Vietnam's haunted locations provides a unique cultural perspective rarely seen in Western horror. The movie's blend of traditional superstitions with modern skepticism creates an intriguing dynamic, making it an engaging watch for both horror fans and those interested in Vietnamese culture.

6. 10 Trivia Facts:

1. The film's title "Ma Dai" is a play on words in Vietnamese, meaning both "Ghost Squad" and "Are Ghosts Real?"

2. Director Le Van Kiet went on to direct the Hollywood film "The Princess" (2022).

3. Many of the haunted locations featured in the film are based on real places in Vietnam believed to be haunted.

4. The movie incorporates actual Vietnamese ghost hunting techniques and rituals.

5. Some cast members reported experiencing strange occurrences during filming at allegedly haunted locations.

6. The film sparked debates in Vietnam about the ethics of ghost hunting and disturbing spiritual sites.

7. "Ghosts Are Real" was one of the first Vietnamese horror films to use the found footage style.

8. The movie features a mix of professional actors and real-life ghost hunters for authenticity.

9. Some scenes were improvised to capture genuine reactions from the cast.

10. The film's success led to a trend of ghost hunting reality shows in Vietnam.

4. Kumanthong (Búp Bê Tà Thuật)

1. Movie Title: Kumanthong (Búp Bê Tà Thuật)

2. Year of Release: 2019

3. Cast and Director:

- Director: Phan Thanh Nhân

- Cast: Hoang Yen Chibi, Quoc Cuong, Kim Xuan, Dieu Nhi

4. Synopsis:

"Kumanthong" centers around a young couple who are struggling to have a child. In their desperation, they turn to a shaman who gives them a kumanthong, a supposedly mystical doll believed to bring good fortune and fertility. However, the doll harbors a dark spirit that begins to terrorize the couple and those around them. As strange and violent events unfold, they must uncover the truth behind the kumanthong's origins and find a way to break its curse before it's too late. The film explores themes of desire, superstition, and the dangers of relying on dark magic.

5. Why This Movie Is Recommended:

"Kumanthong" stands out for its exploration of a lesser-known aspect of Southeast Asian folklore. The film effectively blends elements of Vietnamese and Thai supernatural beliefs, creating a unique horror experience. Its strong visual style and unsettling atmosphere contribute to genuine scares. The movie also delves into the psychological horror of infertility and the desperation it can cause, adding depth to its supernatural premise. As a more recent entry in Vietnamese horror cinema, "Kumanthong" showcases the evolving capabilities of the country's film industry in the genre.

6. 10 Trivia Facts:

1. The kumanthong doll is based on a real Thai occult practice involving blessed dolls believed to bring good fortune.

2. The film sparked controversy in Vietnam due to its depiction of folk magic practices.

3. Several scenes were shot in Thailand to capture authentic locations related to kumanthong rituals.

4. The movie's success led to increased interest in and warnings about kumanthong dolls in Vietnam.

5. Director Phan Thanh Nhân conducted extensive research on kumanthong lore for the film.

6. The kumanthong doll used in the film was custom-made by Thai artisans specializing in occult objects.

7. Some cast members reportedly felt uneasy around the kumanthong prop during filming.

8. The film incorporates elements of both Vietnamese and Thai ghost story traditions.

9. "Kumanthong" was one of the highest-grossing Vietnamese horror films of 2019.

10. The movie's marketing campaign included warnings about the dangers of seeking occult solutions to life problems.

5. Bitcoin Heist (Siêu Trộm)

1. Movie Title: Bitcoin Heist (Siêu Trộm)

2. Year of Release: 2016

3. Cast and Director:

- Director: Ham Tran

- Cast: Kate Nhung, Thanh Pham, Petey Majik Nguyen, Suboi

4. Synopsis:

While "Bitcoin Heist" is primarily an action-thriller, it incorporates elements of technological horror that warrant its inclusion in this list. The film follows a team of criminals and law enforcement officers who reluctantly join forces to catch a notorious hacker known as "The Ghost." As they delve deeper into the dark web and cryptocurrency underworld, they encounter increasingly dangerous and horrifying situations. The line between the digital and physical worlds blurs, with the team facing both real-world threats and terrifying digital consequences. The film explores themes of identity, privacy, and the horrors of a world where technology can be weaponized against individuals.

5. Why This Movie Is Recommended:

"Bitcoin Heist" offers a unique blend of action, thriller, and technological horror that sets it apart from traditional Vietnamese cinema. While not a pure horror film, its exploration of the dark side of technology and the internet creates a sense of modern, digital dread that resonates with contemporary fears. The movie's slick production values and international flair demonstrate the growing sophistication of Vietnamese cinema. Its incorporation of real-world concerns about cybercrime and digital identity theft adds a layer of realism to its more fantastical elements, making it a thought-provoking watch for those interested in the intersection of technology and horror.

6. 10 Trivia Facts:

1. "Bitcoin Heist" was one of the first Vietnamese films to focus on cryptocurrency and cybercrime.

2. The film features a diverse cast including Vietnamese, Vietnamese-American, and international actors.

3. Director Ham Tran incorporated real hacking techniques and dark web lore into the script for authenticity.

4. The movie's production involved consultations with cybersecurity experts to ensure technical accuracy.

5. "Bitcoin Heist" was shot in both Vietnam and Thailand to create its international atmosphere.

6. The film's soundtrack features work by popular Vietnamese hip-hop artist Suboi, who also stars in the movie.

7. Some of the film's more intense hacking scenes were inspired by real-world cyber attacks.

8. "Bitcoin Heist" premiered at the 2016 Fantastic Fest in Austin, Texas.

9. The movie's success led to increased interest in cybersecurity issues among Vietnamese audiences.

10. Director Ham Tran has described the film as a "cautionary tale" about the dangers of the digital age.

China

1. The House That Never Dies (京城81号)

1. Movie Title: The House That Never Dies (京城81号)

2. Year of Release: 2014

3. Cast and Director:

  - Director: Raymond Yip

  - Cast: Francis Ng, Ruby Lin, Tony Yang, Li Jing

4. Synopsis:

  Set in Beijing, the film revolves around Xu Ruoqing, a woman who moves into a supposedly haunted mansion with her husband. As strange occurrences begin to plague them, Xu Ruoqing starts experiencing visions of the house's past, particularly of a Kuomintang official's wife from the 1930s. The story intertwines the past and present, unraveling a tale of love, betrayal, and revenge that spans generations. As Xu Ruoqing delves deeper into the house's history, she uncovers dark secrets that threaten her own life and sanity.

5. Why This Movie Is Recommended:

  "The House That Never Dies" stands out for its blend of historical drama and supernatural horror, a combination rarely seen in mainland Chinese cinema. The film's impressive production values, including detailed period settings and costumes, elevate it above typical ghost stories. It skillfully builds tension through atmospheric scares rather than relying on gore. The dual timeline narrative adds depth to the ghostly encounters, making it more than just a series of scares. Its success paved the way for more horror productions in mainland China, marking it as a significant entry in the genre.

6. 10 Trivia Facts:

  1. The movie is loosely based on the real-life Chaonei No. 81, an allegedly haunted house in Beijing.

  2. It was one of the highest-grossing Chinese horror films at the time of its release.

  3. The film sparked renewed interest in the actual Chaonei No. 81, leading to increased visits to the location.

  4. A sequel, "The House That Never Dies II," was released in 2017 with a different cast and story.

  5. The movie combines elements of Gothic horror with traditional Chinese ghost lore.

  6. It was one of the first big-budget horror films produced in mainland China after a period of strict censorship on the genre.

  7. The film's success led to a boom in Chinese haunted house movies.

  8. Actress Ruby Lin, known primarily for historical dramas, took on this horror role as a change of pace.

  9. The elaborate mansion sets were built entirely in a studio.

10. Despite its horror elements, the film was marketed more as a suspense thriller to comply with Chinese film regulations.

2. Mojin: The Lost Legend (寻龙诀)

1. Movie Title: Mojin: The Lost Legend (寻龙诀)

2. Year of Release: 2015

3. Cast and Director:

- Director: Wuershan

- Cast: Chen Kun, Shu Qi, Huang Bo, Angelababy

4. Synopsis:

Based on the popular novel series "Ghost Blows Out the Light," Mojin follows three legendary grave robbers who have retired to New York City. However, they are lured back to China for one last heist involving a mythical tomb. As they venture deep into the Mongolian desert, they encounter supernatural forces and uncover an ancient secret that could change the course of history. The team must use their wits and skills to survive not only the deadly traps in the tomb but also the otherworldly entities guarding it. Their journey becomes a battle between human greed and ancient mystical powers.

5. Why This Movie Is Recommended:

"Mojin: The Lost Legend" is a thrilling blend of adventure, horror, and fantasy that showcases the potential of big-budget Chinese cinema. While not a traditional horror film, its intense tomb exploration sequences and encounters with supernatural beings offer plenty of scares. The film's impressive visual effects and grand set pieces create a immersive, eerie atmosphere. Its exploration of Chinese mythology and tomb-raiding lore adds a unique cultural flavor to the horror-adventure genre. The strong performances from its star-studded cast and the film's ability to balance humor with genuine frights make it a standout in Chinese supernatural cinema.

6. 10 Trivia Facts:

1. The film is based on the first two novels in the eight-part "Ghost Blows Out the Light" series by Zhang Muye.

2. It was one of the highest-grossing Chinese-language films of 2015.

3. The movie's Chinese title, "寻龙诀," translates to "The Secret of the Dragon Seeking."

4. A prequel, "Chronicles of the Ghostly Tribe," was released a few months before "Mojin."

5. The film's elaborate underground tomb sets took over three months to construct.

6. "Mojin" spawned a franchise, including a web series and a sequel film.

7. The movie blends elements of real Chinese history with supernatural folklore.

8. Some of the film's desert scenes were shot in the Gobi Desert.

9. The film's success contributed to a trend of adapting popular web novels into movies in China.

10. Despite its supernatural elements, the film was classified as an action-adventure movie to comply with Chinese film regulations.

3. The Possessed (中邪)

1. Movie Title: The Possessed (中邪)

2. Year of Release: 2016

3. Cast and Director:

- Director: Ma Kai

- Cast: Wang Zixuan, Chen Wei, Wang Xiuzhu, Song Yiwen

4. Synopsis:

"The Possessed" follows a documentary crew investigating a series of mysterious deaths in a remote village in northern China. As they delve deeper into the case, they encounter strange phenomena and learn about an ancient demonic possession that has plagued the village for generations. The line between reality and the supernatural blurs as the crew becomes increasingly entangled in the village's dark secrets. They must confront their own beliefs and fears while trying to uncover the truth behind the possessions and find a way to stop the malevolent force before it claims more victims.

5. Why This Movie Is Recommended:

"The Possessed" stands out for its unique approach to the horror genre in Chinese cinema. It cleverly uses the found footage and mockumentary format, rarely seen in Chinese films, to create a sense of realism and immediacy. The movie effectively builds tension through its atmospheric portrayal of rural Chinese superstitions and folklore. Its exploration of the clash between modern skepticism and traditional beliefs adds depth to the scares. The film's low-budget, indie feel contributes to its authenticity, making the horror elements more impactful. It offers a fresh perspective on possession stories by grounding them in Chinese cultural context.

6. 10 Trivia Facts:

1. The film was shot on a very low budget, contributing to its raw, documentary-like feel.

2. Many of the villagers seen in the film are actual residents of the location, not professional actors.

3. The movie draws inspiration from real Chinese folklore about demonic possession.

4. "The Possessed" was one of the first found footage horror films produced in mainland China.

5. The film faced some censorship challenges due to its portrayal of superstitious beliefs.

6. Much of the dialogue was improvised to maintain a natural, documentary-like atmosphere.

7. The director, Ma Kai, previously worked primarily in television before making this film.

8. The movie was shot in a real village in Hebei province, adding to its authenticity.

9. Some viewers initially believed the film to be a real documentary due to its realistic style.

10. The film's success led to increased interest in low-budget, indie horror productions in China.

4. The Great Hypnotist (催眠大师)

1. Movie Title: The Great Hypnotist (催眠大师)

2. Year of Release: 2014

3. Cast and Director:

- Director: Leste Chen

- Cast: Xu Zheng, Karen Mok, Hu Jing, David Wang

4. Synopsis:

"The Great Hypnotist" centers around Dr. Xu Ruining, a renowned hypnotherapist who encounters a challenging patient named Ren Xiaoyan. Ren claims to be able to see ghosts and resists Xu's hypnosis techniques. As Xu delves deeper into Ren's psyche, the lines between reality and illusion blur, and he begins to question his own sanity. The film takes unexpected twists as it explores the power of the mind, repressed memories, and the nature of truth. What starts as a psychological thriller gradually incorporates elements of supernatural horror, keeping the audience guessing until the very end.

5. Why This Movie Is Recommended:

"The Great Hypnotist" offers a unique blend of psychological thriller and supernatural horror, standing out in Chinese cinema for its intelligent script and mind-bending narrative. The film's exploration of the human psyche adds depth to its horror elements, creating a sense of unease that lingers long after viewing. Strong performances from the lead actors and stylish direction elevate the material beyond typical genre fare. Its ability to keep viewers guessing, questioning reality alongside the characters, makes for an engaging and unsettling experience. The film demonstrates the potential for sophisticated, thought-provoking horror in Chinese cinema.

6. 10 Trivia Facts:

1. The film was a commercial success, becoming one of the highest-grossing Chinese thriller films of its year.

2. Director Leste Chen studied psychology, which influenced the film's exploration of the human mind.

3. The movie's twist ending sparked widespread discussion and debate among viewers.

4. "The Great Hypnotist" was one of the first Chinese films to extensively use hypnosis as a central plot device.

5. The film's visual style was inspired by classic Hollywood psychological thrillers.

6. Lead actor Xu Zheng is better known for his comedic roles, making his turn in this thriller particularly notable.

7. The movie's success contributed to a trend of psychological thrillers in Chinese cinema.

8. Some of the hypnosis techniques shown in the film are based on real practices.

9. The film underwent several rounds of script revisions to perfect its intricate plot.

10. "The Great Hypnotist" received praise for its sound design, which contributes significantly to its eerie atmosphere.

5. Chronicles of the Ghostly Tribe (九层妖塔)

1. Movie Title: Chronicles of the Ghostly Tribe (九层妖塔)

2. Year of Release: 2015

3. Cast and Director:

- Director: Lu Chuan

- Cast: Mark Chao, Yao Chen, Rhydian Vaughan, Li Chen

4. Synopsis:

Set in the 1980s, "Chronicles of the Ghostly Tribe" follows Hu Bayi, a young soldier who joins a secret archaeological expedition in China's Kunlun Mountains. The team discovers an ancient tomb and unknowingly releases a terrifying, otherworldly force. As they delve deeper into the mystery, they encounter monstrous creatures and face supernatural threats that challenge their understanding of reality. The story spans decades, following Hu Bayi's quest to uncover the truth behind the ghostly tribe and prevent an apocalyptic event. The film blends elements of action, horror, and science fiction as it explores ancient Chinese mythology and its collision with the modern world.

5. Why This Movie Is Recommended:

"Chronicles of the Ghostly Tribe" stands out for its ambitious blend of genres, combining horror elements with action-adventure and science fiction. The film's high production values and impressive special effects create a visually stunning world that brings Chinese mythology to life in a unique way. Its exploration of ancient mysteries and supernatural threats offers a fresh take on the horror genre in Chinese cinema. The movie's fast-paced plot and epic scope provide an entertaining ride that appeals to fans of both horror and adventure films. It showcases the potential for big-budget, effects-driven horror in Chinese filmmaking.

6. 10 Trivia Facts:

1. The film is based on the popular novel series "Ghost Blows Out the Light" by Zhang Muye.

2. It serves as a prequel to "Mojin: The Lost Legend," exploring the early adventures of some characters.

3. The movie's Chinese title, "九层妖塔," translates to "Nine-Story Demon Tower."

4. Director Lu Chuan is known for his historical dramas, making this his first venture into the horror-adventure genre.

5. The film's creature designs were inspired by both Chinese mythology and modern sci-fi concepts.

6. Some of the challenging outdoor scenes were filmed in the harsh environments of Xinjiang province.

7. The movie uses a mix of practical effects and CGI to create its supernatural elements.

8. "Chronicles of the Ghostly Tribe" was one of the most expensive Chinese films produced in 2015.

9. The film's release coincided with a boom in adapting popular web novels into movies in China.

10. Despite its horror elements, the movie was marketed more as an action-adventure film to appeal to a broader audience.

6. The Wrath of Vajra (金刚王：死亡救赎)

1. Movie Title: The Wrath of Vajra (金刚王：死亡救赎)

2. Year of Release: 2013

3. Cast and Director:

- Director: Law Wing-cheong

- Cast: Shi Yanneng, Yu Xing, Steve Yoo, Jiang Baocheng

4. Synopsis:

Set in the 1930s, "The Wrath of Vajra" tells the story of K-29, a former child assassin trained by a secret Japanese organization called the Temple of Hades. Years later, K-29, now a Shaolin monk named Vajra, is forced to confront his past when the Temple kidnaps his brother. Vajra must infiltrate the organization's deadly martial arts tournament to save his brother and stop their plans for world domination. As he fights his way through increasingly challenging opponents, Vajra faces not only physical threats but also the psychological trauma of his past. The film blends intense martial arts action with elements of supernatural horror, creating a unique and visceral experience.

5. Why This Movie Is Recommended:

While primarily an action film, "The Wrath of Vajra" incorporates horror elements that set it apart from typical martial arts movies. Its dark atmosphere, brutal fight scenes, and exploration of cult-like organizations create a sense of dread throughout. The film's portrayal of the Temple of Hades as a sinister, quasi-supernatural force adds a horror dimension to the martial arts genre. Its unique blend of historical setting, supernatural themes, and intense action offers a fresh experience for both horror and action fans. The movie's high-quality fight choreography and compelling lead performance make it a standout in Chinese action-horror cinema.

6. 10 Trivia Facts:

1. Lead actor Shi Yanneng is a real-life Shaolin monk and martial arts expert.

2. The film's fight scenes were choreographed to incorporate elements of horror, creating a unique visual style.

3. "The Wrath of Vajra" was marketed internationally as a martial arts horror film, a rare genre combination.

4. The movie draws inspiration from real historical events, particularly Japan's activities in China during the 1930s.

5. Many of the film's stunts were performed without wires or CGI, adding to its visceral impact.

6. The Temple of Hades in the film is loosely based on real covert organizations that existed in wartime Japan.

7. Director Law Wing-cheong previously worked extensively with acclaimed filmmaker Johnnie To.

8. The film's title refers to the Vajra, a ritual object in Buddhism symbolizing both a thunderbolt and a diamond.

9. Some of the movie's more horrific elements were toned down for its mainland China release.

10. The film received praise for its unique visual style, which blends traditional martial arts cinematography with horror aesthetics.

7. The Curse of Turandot (图兰朵：魔咒缘起)

1. Movie Title: The Curse of Turandot (图兰朵：魔咒缘起)

2. Year of Release: 2021

3. Cast and Director:

- Director: Zheng Xiaolong

- Cast: Guan Xiaotong, Dylan Sprouse, Jiang Wen, Sophie Marceau

4. Synopsis:

"The Curse of Turandot" offers a dark fantasy reimagining of the classic opera "Turandot." Set in ancient China, the film follows Princess Turandot, who is cursed to kill any man who fails to answer her three riddles. When a mysterious stranger named Calaf arrives, determined to win her heart, Turandot finds herself torn between her curse and her growing feelings. As Calaf faces the deadly challenge, dark forces threaten both their lives and the kingdom. The movie blends elements of romance, fantasy, and horror as it explores themes of love, sacrifice, and the struggle against fate. Ancient Chinese mythology and supernatural elements add a layer of mystique and terror to this tragic love story.

5. Why This Movie Is Recommended:

"The Curse of Turandot" stands out for its unique approach to blending Chinese folklore with Western opera, creating a visually stunning dark fantasy with horror elements. The film's lavish production design and costume work create an immersive, gothic atmosphere rarely seen in Chinese cinema. Its exploration of curses and supernatural forces adds a horror dimension to the classic tale, appealing to fans of dark fantasy and gothic romance. The movie's international cast and crew bring a fresh perspective to Chinese mythology, resulting in a cross-cultural horror-fantasy experience. Its ambitious scope and visual flair make it a noteworthy entry in China's growing catalogue of genre-blending films.

6. 10 Trivia Facts:

1. The film is based on the opera "Turandot" by Giacomo Puccini, which itself was inspired by a Persian collection of stories.

2. This adaptation significantly expands on the supernatural and horror elements only hinted at in the original opera.

3. The movie features an international cast, including American actor Dylan Sprouse and French actress Sophie Marceau.

4. The film's production design draws inspiration from both Chinese historical dramas and Western gothic horror.

5. "The Curse of Turandot" was one of the first major Chinese productions to resume filming after the initial COVID-19 lockdowns.

6. The movie's release was delayed several times due to the pandemic, building anticipation among fans.

7. Some of the film's supernatural scenes were inspired by traditional Chinese ghost stories and folklore.

8. The movie features a mix of Mandarin Chinese and English dialogue, reflecting its international production.

9. The film's costume design blends traditional Chinese elements with fantasy and horror aesthetics.

10. "The Curse of Turandot" represents a growing trend in Chinese cinema of reinterpreting classic stories with genre elements.

8. The Haunted Cinema (古镜怪谈)

1. Movie Title: The Haunted Cinema (古镜怪谈)

2. Year of Release: 2014

3. Cast and Director:

- Director: Jiang Cheng

- Cast: Qi Wei, Simon Yam, Hayley Hu, Bao Wenjing

4. Synopsis:

"The Haunted Cinema" revolves around a young woman named Xiaoxiao who takes a job as a projectionist at an old, run-down movie theater. As she settles into her role, strange and terrifying events begin to occur. Xiaoxiao discovers that the cinema is haunted by the ghosts of actors and actresses from classic films, trapped between the world of celluloid and reality. As she delves deeper into the mystery, she uncovers a dark history involving a tragic fire decades ago. Xiaoxiao must navigate this world of cinematic spirits, confront the theater's horrifying past, and find a way to free the trapped souls before she becomes a permanent part of the ghostly cast herself.

5. Why This Movie Is Recommended:

"The Haunted Cinema" offers a unique twist on the haunted house genre by setting its supernatural occurrences in a movie theater. This setting allows for creative scares that play with the boundary between film and reality. The movie pays homage to classic Chinese cinema while delivering modern horror thrills. Its exploration of the power of film and the lingering impact of tragic events adds depth to the ghost story. The blend of nostalgic elements with contemporary horror techniques creates an atmospheric and unsettling experience. For fans of both horror and cinema history, this film provides a meta-textual thrill ride through the darker side of movie magic.

6. 10 Trivia Facts:

1. The film features several recreations of scenes from classic Chinese movies, blending nostalgia with horror.

2. Some of the ghost effects were achieved using practical effects rather than CGI, giving them a more tangible feel.

3. The movie theater set was specially constructed for the film, designed to look authentically vintage.

4. "The Haunted Cinema" draws inspiration from real urban legends about haunted movie theaters in China.

5. The film includes references to several real-life tragedies that occurred in Chinese theaters throughout history.

6. Some of the 'classic films' shown in the movie were created specifically for this production.

7. The director, Jiang Cheng, has a background in documentary filmmaking, which influenced the movie's realistic style.

8. The film's Chinese title, "古镜怪谈," roughly translates to "Strange Tales of an Ancient Mirror," referencing both old films and ghost stories.

9. Several veteran actors from classic Chinese cinema make cameo appearances as ghosts in the film.

10. The movie sparked renewed interest in preserving old movie theaters in China, with some viewers seeing them in a new, eerier light.

9. The Necromancer (刺客小姐姐シ)

1. Movie Title: The Necromancer (刺客小姐姐シ)

2. Year of Release: 2018

3. Cast and Director:

- Director: Liu Chuan

- Cast: Xin Zhilei, Jiang Chao, Vivian Wu, Qin Hao

4. Synopsis:

"The Necromancer" follows Xia Qing, a young woman with the ability to communicate with the dead. When a series of mysterious murders rocks her city, Xia Qing is recruited by a secret government agency to help solve the case. As she delves into the investigation, she discovers a dark conspiracy involving ancient Chinese black magic and modern science. Xia Qing must navigate a dangerous world of spirits, sorcerers, and shadowy organizations, all while coming to terms with her own powers and tragic past. The line between the living and the dead blurs as Xia Qing races to stop a powerful necromancer from unleashing an army of the undead upon the world.

5. Why This Movie Is Recommended:

"The Necromancer" stands out for its unique blend of supernatural horror, detective thriller, and elements of Chinese folklore. The film's modern urban setting contrasted with ancient magical practices creates a compelling backdrop for its horror elements. Strong performances, particularly from lead actress Xin Zhilei, bring depth to the characters and emotional weight to the supernatural encounters. The movie's exploration of Chinese concepts of the afterlife and ancestor worship adds cultural richness to its scares. With its mix of visceral horror, psychological tension, and action sequences, "The Necromancer" offers a fresh take on the supernatural detective genre in Chinese cinema.

6. 10 Trivia Facts:

1. The film's Chinese title, "刺客小姐姐シ," playfully combines the concepts of "assassin" and "spirit medium."

2. Many of the supernatural elements in the movie are based on real Chinese folk beliefs and practices.

3. The filmmakers consulted with experts in Chinese occult traditions to add authenticity to the magical elements.

4. Some of the more intense horror scenes were slightly edited for the film's mainland China release.

5. The movie features a blend of practical effects and CGI to create its supernatural entities.

6. "The Necromancer" was one of the first Chinese films to combine the detective and supernatural horror genres.

7. "The Necromancer" was one of the first Chinese films to combine the detective and supernatural horror genres.

8. The film's success led to discussions about a potential sequel or TV series adaptation.

9. Some of the incantations used in the movie are based on actual Taoist rituals, though modified for the film.

10. The movie's makeup and special effects team won several awards for their work on creating the undead creatures.

10. Ping Pong (乒乓)

1. Movie Title: Ping Pong (乒乓)

2. Year of Release: 2019

3. Cast and Director:

- Director: Liu Jie

- Cast: Bai Baihe, Li Borong, Wang Zhi, Liu Dan

4. Synopsis:

"Ping Pong" tells the story of Li Ping, a former table tennis champion who now coaches at a local sports school. When a series of unexplained deaths occurs among young athletes, Li Ping begins to suspect a supernatural force at work. As she investigates, she uncovers a dark secret tied to her own past and a cursed ping pong paddle that brings death to its users. Li Ping must confront her personal demons and face off against a malevolent spirit that has haunted the world of competitive table tennis for decades. The film blends sports drama with supernatural horror, creating a unique narrative that explores themes of ambition, sacrifice, and the price of victory.

5. Why This Movie Is Recommended:

"Ping Pong" offers a fresh and unexpected take on the horror genre by setting its supernatural story in the world of competitive sports. This unique premise allows for creative scares and tension-filled moments both on and off the ping pong table. The film's exploration of the pressures faced by young athletes adds depth to its horror elements, grounding the supernatural in real-world anxieties. Strong performances and well-choreographed sports sequences keep the audience engaged even when the horror elements are not at the forefront. By combining theStructuresures of a sports drama with classic horror tropes, "Ping Pong" creates a viewing experience that stands out in the landscape of Chinese horror cinema.

6. 10 Trivia Facts:

1. The film features cameos from several real-life Chinese table tennis champions.

2. Many of the ping pong sequences were shot without the use of CGI, requiring extensive training for the actors.

3. The cursed paddle prop went through several design iterations to achieve the right balance of ordinary appearance and sinister undertones.

4. "Ping Pong" was inspired by urban legends circulating in Chinese sports schools about cursed equipment.

5. The movie's sound design team created a unique "whoosh" effect for the cursed paddle, which became a signature element of the film's scares.

6. Director Liu Jie has a background in documentary filmmaking, which influenced the realistic portrayal of the sports world in the movie.

7. The film sparked discussions about the pressures placed on young athletes in China's competitive sports system.

8. Some of the horror sequences were choreographed by a team that usually works on martial arts films, bringing a unique dynamic to the scares.

9. "Ping Pong" was one of the first horror films to be set in the world of Chinese professional sports.

10. The movie's success led to increased interest in sports-themed horror stories in Chinese cinema.

11. The Door (门)

1. Movie Title: The Door (门)

2. Year of Release: 2017

3. Cast and Director:

- Director: Liu Hao

- Cast: Ren Suxi, Bai Ke, Jiang Chao, Li Meng

4. Synopsis:

"The Door" centers around a young couple, Xiao Yu and Ah Chuan, who move into an old apartment building in Beijing. Strange occurrences begin to plague them, particularly centered around an mysterious door in their living room that seems to lead nowhere. As Xiao Yu delves deeper into the building's history, she uncovers a series of tragic events tied to the door, including disappearances and unexplained deaths. The couple soon realizes that the door is a portal to a nightmarish otherworld, populated by the tortured souls of those who have passed through it. As the boundary between realities blurs, Xiao Yu and Ah Chuan must unravel the door's secrets before they become its next victims.

5. Why This Movie Is Recommended:

"The Door" stands out for its clever use of a simple yet effective horror concept, turning an everyday object into a source of dread. The film builds tension gradually, using the claustrophobic setting of the apartment to create a sense of unease that grows into full-blown terror. Its exploration of urban legends and the hidden histories of old buildings resonates with Chinese audiences familiar with rapid urban development. The movie's strong focus on atmosphere and psychological horror, rather than relying solely on jump scares, makes for a more unsettling and lasting experience. "The Door" offers a fresh take on the haunted house subgenre, grounded in the unique context of contemporary Chinese urban life.

6. 10 Trivia Facts:

1. The concept for the film was inspired by real urban legends about "ghost apartments" in Chinese cities.

2. The door prop used in the movie was custom-built to create specific sound effects when opened or closed.

3. Director Liu Hao previously worked in architecture, which influenced the film's focus on building design and history.

4. Some scenes were shot in actual abandoned apartments in Beijing to add authenticity to the setting.

5. The movie sparked online discussions about superstitions related to apartment layouts in Chinese culture.

6. "The Door" features subtle references to classic Chinese ghost stories and folklore.

7. The film's sound design team won an award for their work in creating the otherworldly atmosphere.

8. Several alternate endings were filmed before the director settled on the final version.

9. The movie's success led to increased interest in location-based horror stories in Chinese cinema.

10. Some of the more intense horror scenes were slightly toned down for the film's mainland China release.

12. The Longest Day in Chang'an (长安十二时辰)

1. Movie Title: The Longest Day in Chang'an (长安十二时辰)

2. Year of Release: 2019 (TV Series)

3. Cast and Director:

  - Director: Cao Dun

  - Cast: Lei Jiayin, Jackson Yee, Reyizha Alimjan, Yan Ni

4. Synopsis:

  While primarily a historical thriller series, "The Longest Day in Chang'an" incorporates significant elements of horror and supernatural tension. Set in the Tang Dynasty, the story follows Zhang Xiaojing, a former detective turned prisoner, who is given one day to prevent a terrorist attack on the imperial capital of Chang'an. As Zhang and his team race against time, they encounter not only human adversaries but also dark, supernatural forces rooted in ancient Chinese mythology. The bustling city of Chang'an becomes a labyrinth of terror as they face vengeful spirits, dark sorcery, and horrifying creatures, all while trying to unravel a complex political conspiracy. The series blends historical drama with supernatural horror, creating a unique and thrilling viewing experience.

5. Why This Movie Is Recommended:

  Although technically a TV series, "The Longest Day in Chang'an" is included for its significant contribution to horror elements in Chinese visual media. The show's high production values and cinematic quality rival many films. Its unique blend of historical accuracy, political intrigue, and supernatural horror creates a rich, immersive world rarely seen in Chinese television. The series excels in building tension and dread, using its historical setting to add depth to its horror elements. The incorporation of Chinese mythology and folklore into the narrative provides a fresh perspective on familiar horror tropes. For viewers interested in how horror can be integrated into other genres, "The Longest Day in Chang'an" offers a masterclass in genre-blending storytelling.

6. 10 Trivia Facts:

  1. The series is based on the novel of the same name by Ma Boyong.

  2. Despite being set in the 8th century, the show features several anachronistic elements for artistic effect.

  3. The production team built a massive, 2,800-square-meter set to recreate Tang Dynasty Chang'an.

  4. Many of the supernatural elements in the show are based on actual Tang Dynasty folklore and superstitions.

  5. The series sparked renewed interest in Tang Dynasty history and culture among Chinese viewers.

  6. Some of the show's horror sequences were inspired by classic Chinese ghost stories and supernatural tales.

  7. The makeup and prosthetics team won several awards for their work on the show's more monstrous characters.

  8. "The Longest Day in Chang'an" was one of the most expensive Chinese TV productions at the time of its release.

  9. The show's success led to increased interest in horror elements in Chinese historical dramas.

  10. Several international streaming platforms acquired the rights to the series, introducing it to a global audience.

13. The Phantom of the Theatre (魔宮魅影)

1. Movie Title: The Phantom of the Theatre (魔宮魅影)

2. Year of Release: 2016

3. Cast and Director:

- Director: Raymond Yip

- Cast: Ruby Lin, Tony Yang, Simon Yam, Huang Huan

4. Synopsis:

Set in 1930s Shanghai, "The Phantom of the Theatre" follows a young filmmaker named Gu Weibang who decides to shoot his new movie in a supposedly haunted theater. The theater, once a grand palace of entertainment, is rumored to be cursed after a tragic fire killed a troupe of acrobats years ago. As Gu and his lead actress, Meng Sifan, begin filming, they encounter increasingly terrifying supernatural phenomena. They soon discover that the theater is indeed haunted by the vengeful spirits of the deceased performers. As production continues, the line between reality and cinema blurs, and the crew finds themselves fighting for survival against malevolent forces determined to recreate their final, fatal performance.

5. Why This Movie Is Recommended:

"The Phantom of the Theatre" stands out for its lush period setting and its meta-commentary on the art of filmmaking. The movie cleverly plays with the concept of reality versus illusion, using the film-within-a-film structure to create layers of uncertainty and fear. Its Gothic atmosphere, reminiscent of classic Hollywood horror, is given a unique Chinese twist through its Shanghai setting and incorporation of local folklore. The film's exploration of the dark side of ambition and the price of art adds depth to its supernatural scares. With its blend of romance, mystery, and horror, "The Phantom of the Theatre" offers a visually stunning and emotionally engaging ghost story that pays homage to both Chinese and Western cinematic traditions.

6. 10 Trivia Facts:

1. The film draws inspiration from both "The Phantom of the Opera" and real-life legends about haunted theaters in Shanghai.

2. The elaborate theater set took over two months to construct.

3. Many of the costumes were authentic pieces from the 1930s, adding to the film's period authenticity.

4. The movie features several nods to classic Chinese films from the 1930s.

5. Some of the ghost effects were achieved using traditional stage magic techniques rather than CGI.

6. Director Raymond Yip previously worked on "The House That Never Dies," another Gothic horror film set in China.

7. The film's success sparked renewed interest in the preservation of old theaters in Shanghai.

8. "The Phantom of the Theatre" was praised for its innovative sound design, which played a crucial role in creating scares.

9. The movie includes several extended sequences that blend Chinese opera with horror elements.

10. Some scenes were shot in actual historic locations in Shanghai to enhance the period atmosphere.

14. The Yin-Yang Master: Dream of Eternity (晴雅集)

1. Movie Title: The Yin-Yang Master: Dream of Eternity (晴雅集)

2. Year of Release: 2020

3. Cast and Director:

  - Director: Guo Jingming

  - Cast: Mark Chao, Allen Deng, Jessie Li, Wang Ziwen

4. Synopsis:

  "The Yin-Yang Master: Dream of Eternity" is set in a mythical version of ancient China where humans coexist with supernatural beings. The story follows Qing Ming, a powerful Yin-Yang master, as he arrives in the imperial city to participate in a critical ceremony to maintain the balance between the human and demon worlds. However, the ceremony is disrupted by dark forces, and Qing Ming finds himself embroiled in a complex conspiracy involving demons, fellow Yin-Yang masters, and the imperial court. As Qing Ming investigates, he uncovers ancient secrets and faces increasingly dangerous supernatural threats. The fate of both the human and demon worlds hangs in the balance as Qing Ming and his allies confront a powerful evil that threatens to plunge everything into chaos.

5. Why This Movie Is Recommended:

  While not a traditional horror film, "The Yin-Yang Master: Dream of Eternity" offers plenty of supernatural thrills and dark fantasy elements that will appeal to horror fans. The movie's stunning visual effects and elaborate costume design create a rich, immersive world where the supernatural feels both wondrous and terrifying. Its exploration of Chinese mythology and folklore provides a fresh perspective on familiar fantasy and horror tropes. The film's complex plot and well-developed characters elevate it beyond mere spectacle, offering emotional depth alongside its supernatural thrills. For viewers interested in how horror elements can be integrated into fantasy epics, "The Yin-Yang Master" provides a visually spectacular and narratively engaging example.

6. 10 Trivia Facts:

  1. The film is based on the popular novel series "Onmyōji" by Japanese author Baku Yumemakura.

  2. Despite being set in ancient China, the movie incorporates elements of Japanese onmyōdō mysticism.

  3. The elaborate costume designs blend historical Chinese styles with fantasy elements.

  4. Many of the film's demon designs are based on creatures from Chinese mythology.

  5. "The Yin-Yang Master" was one of the highest-grossing Chinese films during the 2020 holiday season.

  6. The movie's success led to increased interest in the yin-yang master genre in Chinese cinema.

  7. Some of the film's action sequences were choreographed by teams that usually work on martial arts films.

  8. The movie features several extended CGI sequences that push the boundaries of Chinese visual effects.

  9. Director Guo Jingming is also a popular novelist, known for his fantasy and young adult fiction.

  10. The film sparked online discussions about the representation of traditional Chinese culture in modern media.

15. Victim(s) (少年的你)

1. Movie Title: Victim(s) (少年的你)

2. Year of Release: 2019

3. Cast and Director:

- Director: Derek Tsang

- Cast: Zhou Dongyu, Jackson Yee, Yin Fang, Huang Jue

4. Synopsis:

While primarily a crime drama, "Victim(s)" incorporates elements of psychological horror that elevate it beyond its genre. The film follows Chen Nian, a high school student preparing for her college entrance exams, who becomes entangled in a murder case involving her classmate. As Chen Nian navigates the intense pressure of academic life and a dysfunctional home environment, she forms an alliance with Xiao Bei, a street-smart dropout. Their relationship becomes increasingly complex and dangerous as they confront bullies, abusive authority figures, and their own traumatic pasts. The film delves into the dark underbelly of youth culture, exploring themes of bullying, societal pressure, and the cycle of violence with a horrifying intensity that blurs the line between thriller and horror.

5. Why This Movie Is Recommended:

"Victim(s)" is recommended for its unflinching portrayal of the horrors that can exist in everyday life, particularly in the high-pressure world of Chinese education. While not supernatural, the film creates a palpable sense of dread and psychological terror that rivals many traditional horror movies. Its exploration of bullying and societal pressure pushes into truly disturbing territory, creating sequences of intense, realistic horror. The film's atmospheric direction and powerful performances draw viewers into a world where the monsters are all too human. For those interested in psychological horror grounded in social issues, "Victim(s)" offers a harrowing and thought-provoking experience that lingers long after viewing.

6. 10 Trivia Facts:

1. The film is based on the novel "In His Youth, In Her Beauty" by Jiu Yuexi.

2. "Victim(s)" won the Best Film award at the 39th Hong Kong Film Awards.

3. The movie sparked widespread discussions about bullying in Chinese schools.

4. Some scenes were so intense that counseling was provided for the young actors on set.

5. The film's Chinese title, "少年的你," translates to "Better Days," contrasting with its dark content.

6. Director Derek Tsang conducted extensive interviews with real students to ensure authenticity.

7. The movie was initially pulled from release in China but was later approved after some edits.

8. "Victim(s)" was selected as the Hong Kong entry for Best International Feature Film at the 93rd Academy Awards.

9. The film's success led to increased funding for anti-bullying programs in some Chinese schools.

10. Some of the more violent scenes were slightly toned down for the film's mainland China release.

16. The Whistleblower (吹哨人)

1. Movie Title: The Whistleblower (吹哨人)

2. Year of Release: 2019

3. Cast and Director:

- Director: Xue Xiaolu

- Cast: Lei Jiayin, Tang Wei, Xi Qi, John Batchelor

4. Synopsis:

While primarily a thriller, "The Whistleblower" incorporates elements of psychological horror and conspiracy that push it into darker territory. The film follows Ma Ke, a Chinese expat working in Australia, who uncovers a conspiracy involving a new energy technology that could have catastrophic consequences. As Ma Ke delves deeper into the mystery, he becomes entangled in a web of corporate espionage, murder, and cover-ups that span continents. The movie takes a horrifying turn as Ma Ke faces increasingly dangerous and psychologically damaging situations, blurring the lines between paranoia and reality. The film explores themes of moral corruption, environmental disaster, and the terrifying power of unchecked corporate greed, creating a sense of dread and helplessness that rivals many traditional horror movies.

5. Why This Movie Is Recommended:

"The Whistleblower" is recommended for its skillful blend of thriller elements with psychological horror. While not a traditional horror film, it creates a pervasive sense of dread and paranoia that will appeal to horror fans. The movie's exploration of real-world terrors – corporate malfeasance, environmental catastrophe, and the vulnerability of individuals against powerful entities – taps into deep-seated fears. Its international setting and high production values offer a glimpse into the potential of Chinese cinema to create globally relevant, psychologically complex thrillers with horror undertones. For viewers interested in how horror elements can enhance political thrillers, "The Whistleblower" provides a masterclass in building tension and creating a atmosphere of creeping terror.

6. 10 Trivia Facts:

1. The film was shot on location in both China and Australia, one of the first major Chinese productions to do so.

2. "The Whistleblower" was inspired by real-life corporate scandals and whistleblower cases.

3. The movie's release coincided with increased public discussions about corporate responsibility in China.

4. Some of the film's more intense scenes were slightly edited for its mainland China release.

5. Director Xue Xiaolu conducted extensive research into actual whistleblower experiences to ensure authenticity.

6. The film's depiction of corporate conspiracy theories led to online discussions about real-world cover-ups.

7. "The Whistleblower" was one of the first Chinese films to directly address issues of international corporate espionage.

8. The movie features dialogue in Mandarin, English, and Cambodian, reflecting its international scope.

9. Some of the film's chase sequences were shot guerrilla-style in real Australian locations.

10. The film's success led to increased interest in conspiracy thrillers in Chinese cinema.

17. The Midnight After (那夜凌晨，我坐上了旺角開往大埔的紅VAN)

1. Movie Title: The Midnight After (那夜凌晨，我坐上了旺角開往大埔的紅VAN)

2. Year of Release: 2014

3. Cast and Director:

- Director: Fruit Chan

- Cast: Lam Suet, Simon Yam, Kara Hui, Chui Tien-you

4. Synopsis:

"The Midnight After" begins as a group of strangers board a minibus in Hong Kong late one night. As they emerge from a tunnel, they find the city mysteriously deserted. When they try to contact others, they discover that everyone else has vanished. As the group tries to unravel the mystery, they face increasingly bizarre and horrifying phenomena. Strange deaths, time distortions, and apocalyptic omens plague the survivors. The film blends elements of sci-fi, horror, and dark comedy as the characters confront their own pasts and an uncertain future. As reality continues to unravel around them, the group must face the possibility that they may be the last humans left in a world gone mad.

5. Why This Movie Is Recommended:

"The Midnight After" is recommended for its unique blend of genres and its distinctly Hong Kong flavor. While not strictly a mainland Chinese production, its impact on Chinese-language cinema earns it a place on this list. The film's surreal atmosphere and gradual descent into horror create a sense of unease that builds to truly terrifying moments. Its exploration of urban alienation and societal breakdown resonates with modern anxieties. The movie's dark humor and social commentary add depth to its horror elements, creating a complex viewing experience. For fans of genre-bending cinema and apocalyptic horror, "The Midnight After" offers a fresh, culturally specific take on the end of the world.

6. 10 Trivia Facts:

1. The film is based on the web novel "Lost on a Red Mini Bus to Taipo" by PIZZA.

2. Director Fruit Chan is known for his indie films that often push genre boundaries.

3. The movie includes numerous references to Hong Kong pop culture and current events.

4. Some scenes were shot guerrilla-style on the streets of Hong Kong without permits.

5. The film's Chinese title translates to "That Night at Dawn, I Boarded the Red Van from Mong Kok to Tai Po."

6. "The Midnight After" premiered at the 64th Berlin International Film Festival.

7. The movie's soundtrack features a Cantonese cover of David Bowie's "Space Oddity."

8. The film's success led to increased interest in adapting web novels for the screen in Chinese cinema.

9. Some of the more surreal horror sequences were inspired by Japanese manga and anime.

10. The movie sparked online discussions about the socio-political subtext in Hong Kong cinema.

18. The Cliff (绝壁之上)

1. Movie Title: The Cliff (绝壁之上)

2. Year of Release: 2022

3. Cast and Director:

- Director: Dong Wei

- Cast: Zhang Chao, Wang Yanhui, Li Yitong, Wang Zhifei

4. Synopsis:

"The Cliff" follows a team of geologists who travel to a remote mountain region to investigate unusual seismic activity. As they set up camp near a towering cliff face, strange occurrences begin to plague the team. They hear unexplained noises echoing from the rocks and glimpse shadowy figures moving at the edge of their vision. As team members start to disappear, the survivors must confront the possibility that something ancient and malevolent dwells within the cliff. The film blends elements of geological thriller with supernatural horror, exploring themes of scientific skepticism versus ancient beliefs. As the team delves deeper into the mystery, they uncover a terrifying truth that challenges their understanding of nature and reality itself.

5. Why This Movie Is Recommended:

"The Cliff" is recommended for its unique setting and its blend of scientific inquiry with supernatural horror. The film's use of the isolated mountain landscape creates a palpable sense of claustrophobia and dread. Its exploration of Chinese folklore and geology offers a fresh perspective on familiar horror tropes. The movie's strong emphasis on atmosphere and psychological tension, rather than relying solely on jump scares, creates a more immersive and unsettling experience. For fans of eco-horror and films that pit modern skepticism against ancient terrors, "The Cliff" offers a thought-provoking and chilling adventure.

6. 10 Trivia Facts:

1. The film's cliff scenes were shot on location in the Taihang Mountains of China.

2. Director Dong Wei has a background in documentary filmmaking, which influenced the movie's realistic style.

3. The film's supernatural elements draw inspiration from local legends of the Taihang Mountain region.

4. Some of the cave exploration scenes required the actors to undergo special training.

5. "The Cliff" features innovative sound design to create its eerie atmosphere, using actual recordings from cave systems.

6. The movie sparked renewed interest in geological tourism in China.

7. Some of the film's more intense horror sequences were slightly toned down for its mainland China release.

8. The production team consulted with real geologists to ensure the scientific aspects of the film were accurately portrayed.

9. "The Cliff" was one of the first Chinese films to blend the disaster movie genre with supernatural horror elements.

10. The film's success led to discussions about a potential sequel exploring other legendary mountain locations in China.

19. The Looming Storm (暴雪将至)

1. Movie Title: The Looming Storm (暴雪将至)

2. Year of Release: 2017

3. Cast and Director:

- Director: Dong Yue

- Cast: Duan Yihong, Jiang Yiyan, Du Yuan, Zheng Wei

4. Synopsis:

Set in a small industrial town in 1990s China, "The Looming Storm" follows Yu Guowei, a self-styled detective and the head of security at a local factory. When a series of brutal murders rocks the community, Yu becomes obsessed with solving the case, despite the police's skepticism. As he delves deeper into the investigation, the line between reality and his own paranoid delusions begins to blur. The constant rain and decaying industrial landscape create an oppressive atmosphere, mirroring Yu's descent into obsession and possible madness. The film takes a dark, psychological turn as Yu's investigation leads him into increasingly dangerous and morally ambiguous territory, culminating in a shocking revelation that challenges everything he thought he knew.

5. Why This Movie Is Recommended:

While primarily a noir thriller, "The Looming Storm" incorporates elements of psychological horror that elevate it beyond its genre. The film's oppressive atmosphere and slow-burning tension create a sense of creeping dread that rivals many traditional horror movies. Its exploration of obsession, paranoia, and the dark underbelly of a changing Chinese society adds depth to its terrifying elements. The movie's stark visuals and haunting soundscape contribute to an overall feeling of unease that lingers long after viewing. For fans of psychological horror and dark, atmospheric thrillers, "The Looming Storm" offers a uniquely Chinese take on noir conventions, infused with genuine moments of terror.

6. 10 Trivia Facts:

1. The film won the Best Artistic Contribution Award at the 30th Tokyo International Film Festival.

2. Director Dong Yue drew inspiration from real unsolved cases in China's recent history.

3. The constant rain in the film was created using a mix of real rainfall and artificial rain machines.

4. Many of the industrial locations in the film are actual abandoned factories.

5. "The Looming Storm" was praised for its accurate depiction of 1990s China, a period of rapid industrial change.

6. The film's Chinese title, "暴雪将至," translates to "Blizzard is Coming," metaphorically representing the impending doom in the story.

7. Lead actor Duan Yihong underwent significant physical transformation for his role, losing weight to portray his character's obsession.

8. The movie's sound design, crucial for creating its eerie atmosphere, won several awards.

9. Some of the more violent scenes were slightly edited for the film's mainland China release.

10. "The Looming Storm" sparked discussions about the portrayal of mental health issues in Chinese cinema.

20. The Gods (钱学森)

1. Movie Title: The Gods (钱学森)

2. Year of Release: 2018

3. Cast and Director:

- Director: Zhang Duo

- Cast: Zhang Haifeng, Li Ziqian, Zhao Lijian, Wang Yaru

4. Synopsis:

"The Gods" is a science fiction horror film that blends elements of cosmic horror with hard sci-fi concepts. The story follows a team of Chinese scientists working on a top-secret project to communicate with extraterrestrial life. When they finally make contact, they inadvertently open a portal to a dimension of unimaginable horrors. As otherworldly entities begin to invade our reality, the scientists must race against time to close the portal and prevent a full-scale invasion. The film explores themes of human hubris, the price of scientific progress, and the insignificance of humanity in the face of cosmic forces. As the characters confront beings beyond human comprehension, they are forced to question their understanding of reality and their place in the universe.

5. Why This Movie Is Recommended:

"The Gods" stands out for its ambitious blend of hard science fiction and Lovecraftian horror, a combination rarely seen in Chinese cinema. The film's exploration of cosmic horror taps into primal fears of the unknown and incomprehensible, creating a sense of dread that goes beyond simple scares. Its grounding in actual scientific concepts adds a layer of plausibility that makes the horror elements even more effective. The movie's impressive visual effects and sound design bring its otherworldly terrors to life in visceral detail. For fans of cosmic horror and scientifically-grounded sci-fi, "The Gods" offers a uniquely Chinese perspective on humanity's place in a vast and terrifying universe.

6. 10 Trivia Facts:

1. The film's title, "钱学森," is a reference to Qian Xuesen, a prominent Chinese scientist, adding a layer of historical context to its sci-fi narrative.

2. "The Gods" features some of the most advanced CGI work in Chinese cinema to date, particularly for its otherworldly entities.

3. The movie's script was developed in consultation with actual physicists and astronomers.

4. Some of the film's cosmic horror concepts were inspired by classic sci-fi literature, including works by Arthur C. Clarke and H.P. Lovecraft.

5. The production team built elaborate sets to represent the high-tech research facility, which later became a tourist attraction.

6. "The Gods" sparked online discussions about the possibilities and dangers of communicating with extraterrestrial life.

7. The film's success led to increased funding for science fiction productions in Chinese cinema.

8. Some of the more abstract horror sequences were inspired by surrealist art and experimental films.

9. The movie features cameos from several prominent Chinese scientists and science communicators.

10. "The Gods" was one of the first Chinese films to explicitly tackle themes of cosmic horror and existential dread on a large scale.

Hongkong

1. Rouge (胭脂扣)

1. Movie Title: Rouge (胭脂扣)

2. Year of Release: 1988

3. Cast and Director:

  - Director: Stanley Kwan

  - Cast: Anita Mui, Leslie Cheung, Alex Man

4. Synopsis:

Rouge is a haunting romantic ghost story that transcends time. Set in both 1930s and 1980s Hong Kong, the film follows the spirit of Fleur, a courtesan who committed suicide with her lover Chan Chen-Pang fifty years ago. Fleur returns to the modern world, still searching for her lost love. She enlists the help of a journalist couple to find Chen-Pang, believing he's still alive. As they investigate, the film weaves between past and present, exploring themes of love, loyalty, and the changing face of Hong Kong. The search not only reveals the tragic love story of Fleur and Chen-Pang but also forces the modern couple to reflect on their own relationship.

5. Why This Movie Is Recommended:

Rouge is a masterpiece that blends elements of horror, romance, and social commentary. Its unique approach to the ghost story genre, focusing on longing and regret rather than fear, sets it apart from typical horror films. The movie's stunning cinematography captures both the opulence of 1930s Hong Kong and the stark modernity of the 1980s. Anita Mui's mesmerizing performance as Fleur adds depth and poignancy to the supernatural tale. Rouge's exploration of love, memory, and the passage of time makes it a thought-provoking and emotionally resonant film that lingers long after viewing.

6. 10 Trivia Facts:

1. The film is based on a novel by Lilian Lee, who also wrote the screenplay.

2. Anita Mui won the Best Actress award at the Golden Horse Film Festival for her role as Fleur.

3. The movie's title "Rouge" refers to the red makeup traditionally worn by Chinese opera performers and courtesans.

4. Leslie Cheung performed his own singing for the film's soundtrack.

5. The film uses the changing landscape of Hong Kong as a metaphor for the passage of time.

6. Rouge was selected as the Hong Kong entry for the Best Foreign Language Film at the 61st Academy Awards.

7. The movie features authentic recreations of 1930s Hong Kong, including period-accurate costumes and sets.

8. Director Stanley Kwan is known for his sensitive portrayals of female characters, and Rouge is considered one of his best works.

9. The film's success helped establish the "Hong Kong New Wave" cinema movement.

10. Rouge has been praised for its subtle use of special effects to create a ghostly atmosphere without relying on jump scares.

2. A Chinese Ghost Story (倩女幽魂)

1. Movie Title: A Chinese Ghost Story (倩女幽魂)

2. Year of Release: 1987

3. Cast and Director:

- Director: Ching Siu-tung

- Producer: Tsui Hark

- Cast: Leslie Cheung, Joey Wong, Wu Ma

4. Synopsis:

A Chinese Ghost Story follows Ning Choi-san, a naive tax collector who seeks shelter in a haunted temple. There, he encounters and falls in love with a beautiful ghost named Nip Siu-sin. Unbeknownst to Ning, Nip is under the control of a tree demon who forces her to seduce men and steal their souls. With the help of Taoist master Yin Chik-ha, Ning attempts to free Nip from the demon's grasp. The trio faces numerous supernatural challenges, including battling the tree demon and its minions. As their quest unfolds, Ning and Nip's love is tested, leading to a climactic showdown that will determine their fate and the balance between the mortal and spirit worlds.

5. Why This Movie Is Recommended:

A Chinese Ghost Story is a perfect blend of horror, romance, comedy, and action, showcasing the best of Hong Kong cinema. The film's groundbreaking special effects and imaginative supernatural elements set a new standard for Asian horror-fantasy. Leslie Cheung and Joey Wong's on-screen chemistry brings heart to the ghostly romance, while Wu Ma provides comic relief as the Taoist priest. The movie's unique mix of traditional Chinese folklore with modern filmmaking techniques creates a visually stunning and emotionally engaging experience. Its influence on subsequent Asian horror and fantasy films makes it a must-see for genre enthusiasts.

6. 10 Trivia Facts:

1. The film is loosely based on a short story from Pu Songling's 18th-century collection "Strange Stories from a Chinese Studio."

2. It spawned two sequels and a 2011 remake, as well as an animated film and a TV series.

3. The tree demon's long tongue effect was achieved using a pig's tongue.

4. Leslie Cheung performed his own stunts for many of the action scenes.

5. The film's success revitalized the supernatural genre in Hong Kong cinema.

6. Joey Wong's performance as the ghost Nip Siu-sin catapulted her to stardom.

7. The movie blends elements of various genres, including wuxia (martial arts), horror, and romance.

8. A Chinese Ghost Story won multiple awards, including Best Original Film Score at the 7th Hong Kong Film Awards.

9. The film's visual effects were groundbreaking for its time and budget in Hong Kong cinema.

10. Director Ching Siu-tung was primarily known as an action choreographer before helming this film.

3. The Eye (見鬼)

1. Movie Title: The Eye (見鬼)

2. Year of Release: 2002

3. Cast and Director:

  - Directors: Oxide Pang Chun, Danny Pang

  - Cast: Angelica Lee, Lawrence Chou, Chutcha Rujinanon

4. Synopsis:

   The Eye follows Wong Kar Mun, a young woman blind since the age of two, who undergoes a corneal transplant to restore her vision. As Mun begins to see again, she realizes that her new eyes have granted her an unwanted ability: she can see ghosts and foresee tragic events. Haunted by terrifying visions and the spirits of the dead, Mun seeks help from her doctor, Dr. Wah, to uncover the truth behind her corneal donor. Their investigation leads them to Thailand, where they discover the donor's tragic past and the reason for Mun's supernatural sight. As Mun grapples with her gift and its consequences, she must find a way to reconcile her new reality and prevent an impending disaster she has foreseen.

5. Why This Movie Is Recommended:

   The Eye stands out for its innovative approach to the supernatural thriller genre, blending Eastern and Western horror elements. The Pang brothers' direction creates a palpable atmosphere of dread and uncertainty, mirroring Mun's disorientation as she adjusts to her new sight. The film's exploration of the connection between the physical and spiritual worlds adds depth to its scares. Angelica Lee's nuanced performance captures Mun's vulnerability and strength, making her journey both terrifying and emotionally resonant. With its striking visual style and thought-provoking themes about perception and reality, The Eye offers a fresh and chilling take on the ghost story.

6. 10 Trivia Facts:

   1. The film was inspired by a real-life news story about a corneal transplant recipient experiencing strange phenomena.

   2. It spawned two sequels and a Hollywood remake starring Jessica Alba.

   3. The movie's success established the Pang brothers as major figures in Asian horror cinema.

   4. Angelica Lee learned to act blind for her role by working with a sight-impaired pianist.

   5. The film uses a mix of Cantonese, Mandarin, and Thai languages.

   6. Many of the ghost effects were achieved through practical means rather than CGI.

   7. The Eye was selected as the Hong Kong entry for the Best Foreign Language Film at the 76th Academy Awards.

   8. The film's Chinese title "見鬼" literally translates to "Seeing Ghosts."

   9. The Pang brothers split directing duties, with Oxide handling the Hong Kong scenes and Danny the Thailand scenes.

   10. The movie's success helped popularize Asian horror films internationally in the early 2000s.

4. Dumplings (餃子)

1. **Movie Title: Dumplings (餃子)**

2. **Year of Release: 2004**

3. **Cast and Director:**

   - Director: Fruit Chan

   - Cast: Miriam Yeung, Bai Ling, Tony Leung Ka-fai

4. **Synopsis**:

   Dumplings tells the disturbing story of Mrs. Li, a former television actress desperate to reclaim her youth and beauty. She seeks out Aunt Mei, a mysterious chef known for her rejuvenating dumplings. As Mrs. Li becomes addicted to the dumplings' age-reversing effects, she discovers the horrifying secret ingredient: unborn human fetuses. Despite her initial revulsion, Mrs. Li's obsession with youth drives her to continue consuming the dumplings, even as she learns more about their gruesome origin. The film explores the dark lengths people will go to maintain their appearance and social status, weaving a tale of moral decay, vanity, and the commodification of human life. As Mrs. Li's transformation progresses, she must confront the ethical and physical consequences of her choices.

5. **Why This Movie Is Recommended**:

   Dumplings is a provocative and unsettling exploration of society's obsession with youth and beauty. Director Fruit Chan crafts a visually striking film that balances horror with social commentary, challenging viewers to confront uncomfortable truths about aging, gender, and class in modern society. The movie's subtle approach to body horror creates a creeping sense of unease that lingers long after viewing. Bai Ling's mesmerizing performance as Aunt Mei adds layers of complexity to the film's central moral dilemma. With its thought-provoking themes and unflinching look at the dark side of vanity, Dumplings offers a unique and deeply disturbing entry in the horror genre.

6. **10 Trivia Facts**:

   1. The film is an expanded version of Fruit Chan's short film contribution to the horror anthology "Three... Extremes."

   2. The movie won the Best Actress award for Bai Ling at the 2004 Golden Horse Film Festival.

   3. Real dumplings were used during filming, though with less controversial fillings.

   4. The film's cinematographer, Christopher Doyle, is known for his work with Wong Kar-wai.

   5. Dumplings sparked controversy for its graphic content and taboo themes.

   6. The movie explores the Chinese concept of "food therapy" taken to a horrifying extreme.

   7. Director Fruit Chan conducted extensive research on Chinese medicine and cuisine for the film.

   8. The film's sound design, particularly the crunching of dumplings, was crafted to maximize viewer discomfort.

   9. Dumplings was shot on location in Hong Kong, capturing the city's claustrophobic urban landscape.

   10. The movie's poster, featuring a partially eaten dumpling resembling a fetus, was banned in some countries.

5. Mr. Vampire (殭屍先生)

1. Movie Title: Mr. Vampire (殭屍先生)

2. Year of Release: 1985

3. Cast and Director:

 - Director: Ricky Lau

 - Cast: Lam Ching-ying, Ricky Hui, Chin Siu-ho, Moon Lee

4. Synopsis:

 Mr. Vampire follows Master Kau, a Taoist priest skilled in combating the supernatural, and his two bumbling disciples, Man-choi and Chau-sang. When Kau is hired to rebury a wealthy man, he discovers that the corpse has become a vampire due to improper burial techniques. As Kau attempts to stop the vampire from wreaking havoc, his disciples face their own supernatural troubles. Chau-sang becomes infected with the "vampire virus" after being bitten, while Man-choi falls in love with a female ghost. The film blends horror, comedy, and martial arts as the characters battle various undead creatures, including hopping vampires (jiangshi) based on Chinese folklore. Master Kau must use all his knowledge and skills to save his disciples and defeat the vampire menace threatening the community.

5. Why This Movie Is Recommended:

 Mr. Vampire is a quintessential example of the unique Hong Kong genre of horror-comedy. It successfully blends scary elements with slapstick humor and impressive martial arts sequences, creating an entertaining and often hilarious experience. The film's incorporation of Chinese vampire lore offers a fresh take on vampire mythology for Western audiences. Lam Ching-ying's deadpan performance as Master Kau became iconic, spawning numerous sequels and imitators. The movie's practical effects and acrobatic stunt work are impressive, especially considering its age. Mr. Vampire's influence on Hong Kong cinema and its cult status among international fans make it a must-see for anyone interested in Asian horror or martial arts films.

6. 10 Trivia Facts:

 1. The film spawned four sequels and numerous spin-offs, creating a subgenre of Chinese vampire movies.

 2. Lam Ching-ying's portrayal of Master Kau was so popular that he reprised similar roles in many subsequent films.

 3. The hopping motion of the vampires is based on the Chinese belief that the dead should travel in straight lines.

 4. The film popularized the image of the jiangshi (Chinese hopping vampire) in pop culture.

 5. Many of the Taoist rituals and vampire-fighting techniques shown in the film are based on actual Chinese folklore.

 6. The movie was produced by Sammo Hung, who was instrumental in blending comedy with other genres in Hong Kong cinema.

 7. Mr. Vampire's success helped revitalize the supernatural comedy genre in Hong Kong.

 8. The film features a mix of Cantonese and Mandarin, reflecting Hong Kong's linguistic diversity.

 9. Despite its comedic elements, the movie's makeup and special effects were groundbreaking for Hong Kong horror at the time.

 10. The film's success led to a short-lived TV series and even a Japanese remake.

6. Rigor Mortis (殭屍)

1. Movie Title: Rigor Mortis (殭屍)

2. Year of Release: 2013

3. Cast and Director:

- Director: Juno Mak

- Cast: Chin Siu-ho, Anthony Chan, Nina Paw, Richard Ng

4. Synopsis:

Rigor Mortis follows Chin Siu-ho, a washed-up actor famous for his roles in vampire movies, who moves into a dilapidated apartment building with the intention of committing suicide. However, his attempt is thwarted by Yau, a former vampire hunter turned cook. Chin soon discovers that the building is a hotbed of supernatural activity, inhabited by ghosts, vampires, and other malevolent spirits. When a grieving widow attempts to resurrect her dead husband, she inadvertently unleashes a powerful vampire. Chin, Yau, and other residents must band together to combat this threat, facing their own demons in the process. The film blends elements of Chinese folklore with modern horror techniques, creating a visually stunning and emotionally charged supernatural thriller.

5. Why This Movie Is Recommended:

Rigor Mortis offers a fresh and visually striking take on the Chinese vampire genre, paying homage to classic Hong Kong horror while bringing it into the modern era. Director Juno Mak's stylish approach creates a haunting atmosphere that balances genuine scares with poignant character moments. The film's exploration of themes like grief, redemption, and the price of immortality adds depth to its supernatural elements. With impressive special effects, strong performances from veteran actors, and clever nods to Hong Kong horror history, Rigor Mortis is a must-see for fans of Asian horror and anyone looking for a unique and atmospheric ghost story.

6. 10 Trivia Facts:

1. The film is Juno Mak's directorial debut, and he was mentored by Takashi Shimizu, director of "Ju-On: The Grudge."

2. Chin Siu-ho plays a fictionalized version of himself, referencing his real-life career in vampire films.

3. The movie pays homage to the "Mr. Vampire" series, with several actors from those films appearing in new roles.

4. The apartment building in the film was entirely constructed on a soundstage.

5. Rigor Mortis uses a desaturated color palette to create its eerie atmosphere, with red as the only prominent color.

6. The film's visual effects were created by Japan's Hiroyuki Hayashi, known for his work on "Death Note" and "Gantz."

7. Director Mak insisted on using practical effects wherever possible, including wire work for the flying scenes.

8. The movie incorporates elements of Taoist mysticism and feng shui into its supernatural lore.

9. Rigor Mortis was Hong Kong's submission for the Best Foreign Language Film at the 86th Academy Awards.

10. The film's Chinese title, "殭屍," is the same as the Chinese title for the original "Mr. Vampire."

7. Inner Senses (異度空間)

1. Movie Title: Inner Senses (異度空間)

2. Year of Release: 2002

3. Cast and Director:

  - Director: Lo Chi-leung

  - Cast: Leslie Cheung, Karena Lam, Maggie Poon

4. Synopsis:

  Inner Senses tells the story of Yan, a young woman plagued by ghostly visions, who seeks help from Jim Law, a psychiatrist specializing in patients who claim to see ghosts. As Jim treats Yan, he begins to question his own skepticism about the supernatural. Their relationship deepens, blurring the lines between professional and personal. Meanwhile, Jim starts experiencing strange occurrences himself, forcing him to confront a traumatic incident from his past. As Yan's condition improves, Jim's mental state deteriorates, leading to a climactic revelation that challenges both characters' understanding of reality and the afterlife. The film explores themes of mental health, trauma, and the thin line between the living and the dead.

5. Why This Movie Is Recommended:

  Inner Senses stands out for its nuanced approach to the psychological horror genre, blending genuine scares with a thoughtful exploration of mental health issues. The film's atmospheric tension builds slowly, creating a sense of unease that culminates in a powerful and emotionally resonant climax. Leslie Cheung's haunting performance, one of his last before his tragic death, adds depth and poignancy to the film. Director Lo Chi-leung skillfully balances supernatural elements with psychological drama, keeping viewers guessing until the end. With its strong character development, intelligent script, and sensitive handling of complex themes, Inner Senses offers a mature and thought-provoking take on the ghost story genre.

6. 10 Trivia Facts:

  1. This was Leslie Cheung's final film role before his death in 2003, adding a layer of poignancy to the movie's themes.

  2. The film's Chinese title "異度空間" translates to "Different Dimension Space."

  3. Inner Senses was nominated for multiple Hong Kong Film Awards, including Best Actress for Karena Lam.

  4. The movie explores the Chinese concept of "yin eyes," the ability to see ghosts.

  5. Director Lo Chi-leung worked closely with mental health professionals to accurately portray psychological issues in the film.

  6. The film's success helped revitalize the psychological horror genre in Hong Kong cinema.

  7. Inner Senses uses subtle visual cues and color grading to differentiate between reality and supernatural experiences.

  8. The movie's ending sparked numerous fan theories and interpretations.

  9. Leslie Cheung's performance in the film is often cited as one of his best, showcasing his range as an actor.

  10. The film's exploration of mental health issues was considered groundbreaking for Hong Kong cinema at the time.

8. The Untold Story (八仙飯店之人肉叉燒包)

1. Movie Title: The Untold Story (八仙飯店之人肉叉燒包)

2. Year of Release: 1993

3. Cast and Director:

 - Director: Herman Yau

 - Cast: Anthony Wong, Danny Lee, Emily Kwan

4. Synopsis:

  Based on true events, The Untold Story follows the gruesome tale of Wong Chi Hang, a man who takes over a restaurant in Macau and turns it into a successful business. However, as police investigate the disappearance of the previous owner and his family, they uncover a horrifying truth: Wong has been murdering people and serving their remains to unsuspecting customers in his pork buns. The film alternates between Wong's increasingly depraved acts and the police investigation led by Officer Lee. As the truth comes to light, the movie delves into Wong's troubled past and the psychological factors that led to his crimes. The Untold Story pushes the boundaries of graphic violence and psychological horror, presenting a disturbing portrait of a serial killer.

5. Why This Movie Is Recommended:

  The Untold Story is renowned for its unflinching portrayal of violence and psychological horror, pushing the boundaries of the genre in Hong Kong cinema. Anthony Wong's chilling performance as Wong Chi Hang earned him critical acclaim and a Hong Kong Film Award. The movie's bleak atmosphere and graphic content create a truly unsettling viewing experience that lingers long after the credits roll. While not for the faint of heart, the film offers a complex exploration of evil and the dark potential within human nature. Its impact on Hong Kong's Category III films and its cult status among horror enthusiasts make it a significant, if controversial, entry in the genre.

6. 10 Trivia Facts:

  1. The film is based on the real-life case of a serial killer in Macau in the 1980s.

  2. Anthony Wong won the Hong Kong Film Award for Best Actor for his portrayal of Wong Chi Hang.

  3. The movie's Chinese title translates to "The Eight Immortals Restaurant: The Untold Story."

  4. It was rated Category III in Hong Kong, the highest rating for extreme content.

  5. Despite its graphic content, the film was a commercial success and spawned several sequels.

  6. Director Herman Yau balanced the horror elements with dark humor, particularly in the police investigation scenes.

  7. The Untold Story is considered a defining film of the Hong Kong Category III extreme cinema movement.

  8. Anthony Wong initially hesitated to take the role due to its disturbing nature.

  9. The film's success led to a surge in true crime-inspired horror movies in Hong Kong.

  10. Some scenes were so graphic that they had to be cut or altered for international release.

9. Troublesome Night (陰陽路)

1. Movie Title: Troublesome Night (陰陽路)

2. Year of Release: 1997

3. Cast and Director:

- Directors: Victor Tam, Herman Yau

- Cast: Louis Koo, Simon Lui, Ada Choi, Gigi Lai

4. Synopsis:

Troublesome Night is an anthology horror film consisting of three interconnected stories, all centered around supernatural encounters in Hong Kong. The first story follows a group of friends who encounter ghostly phenomena while camping. The second tale revolves around a taxi driver who picks up a mysterious female passenger, leading to a series of eerie events. The final segment focuses on a man who becomes entangled in a ghostly love triangle. Throughout the film, the stories intersect and overlap, creating a tapestry of urban legends and ghost stories that reflect Hong Kong's unique blend of modern life and traditional superstitions. As the characters navigate these supernatural occurrences, they must confront their fears and the thin veil between the world of the living and the dead.

5. Why This Movie Is Recommended:

Troublesome Night stands out for its innovative approach to the anthology horror format, weaving together multiple stories into a cohesive narrative. The film captures the essence of Hong Kong's urban legends and ghost stories, offering a uniquely local perspective on supernatural horror. Its blend of scares, humor, and drama keeps viewers engaged throughout its runtime. The movie's success spawned a long-running franchise, cementing its place in Hong Kong horror cinema. With its accessible storytelling and mix of established and emerging talent, Troublesome Night serves as an excellent introduction to Hong Kong's supernatural film genre.

6. 10 Trivia Facts:

1. Troublesome Night was the first in a series that eventually comprised 19 films, making it one of the longest-running horror franchises in Hong Kong.

2. The film's Chinese title, "陰陽路," refers to the boundary between the living and spirit worlds.

3. Many of the stories in the film are based on popular urban legends and ghost stories from Hong Kong.

4. The movie helped launch the career of Louis Koo, who became a major star in Hong Kong cinema.

5. Despite its horror theme, the film incorporates elements of comedy and romance, a common trait in Hong Kong genre films.

6. The anthology format allowed the filmmakers to showcase multiple directors and storytelling styles within a single film.

7. Troublesome Night was produced by Nam Yin, known for his work in the Hong Kong horror genre.

8. The film's success led to a resurgence of ghost stories and supernatural themes in Hong Kong cinema.

9. Many of the locations used in the film are actual sites in Hong Kong rumored to be haunted.

10. The Troublesome Night series became known for featuring up-and-coming actors who later became major stars.

10. Re-cycle (鬼域)

1. Movie Title: Re-cycle (鬼域)

2. Year of Release: 2006

3. Cast and Director:

- Directors: Oxide Pang Chun, Danny Pang

- Cast: Angelica Lee, Yaqi Zeng, Lawrence Chou

4. Synopsis:

Re-cycle follows Ting-yin, a successful author struggling to write her latest novel about the supernatural. As she begins to experience strange occurrences, the line between reality and fiction blurs. Ting-yin finds herself transported to a nightmarish realm filled with abandoned ideas, forgotten objects, and lost souls. This surreal world is populated by grotesque creatures and echoes of her past, forcing her to confront her deepest fears and suppressed memories. As she navigates this bizarre landscape, Ting-yin must uncover the truth behind her connection to this world and find a way to escape. Her journey becomes a metaphysical exploration of creativity, memory, and the consequences of abandoning ideas and people.

5. Why This Movie Is Recommended:

Re-cycle stands out for its ambitious blend of horror, fantasy, and psychological drama. The Pang brothers create a visually stunning and deeply unsettling world that pushes the boundaries of imagination in horror cinema. The film's exploration of the creative process and the power of memory adds depth to its supernatural elements. Angelica Lee's compelling performance anchors the bizarre and often frightening journey. With its unique premise, striking visuals, and thought-provoking themes, Re-cycle offers a fresh and intellectually engaging take on the horror genre. It challenges viewers to reconsider their perceptions of reality and the impact of discarded ideas and memories.

6. 10 Trivia Facts:

1. The film was selected to screen out of competition at the 2006 Cannes Film Festival.

2. Re-cycle's original Chinese title, "鬼域," translates to "Ghost Realm."

3. The movie's elaborate sets and special effects were groundbreaking for Hong Kong cinema at the time.

4. Angelica Lee previously worked with the Pang brothers on their hit film "The Eye."

5. The directors drew inspiration from various sources, including the works of Terry Gilliam and Tim Burton.

6. Re-cycle explores the concept of "recycling" abandoned ideas, a meta-commentary on the creative process.

7. The film's makeup and prosthetic effects were created by a team that had worked on Hollywood productions.

8. Some scenes were shot in Thailand, taking advantage of unique locations to create the surreal world.

9. Re-cycle marked a departure from the Pang brothers' previous, more straightforward horror films.

10. The movie's complex visual effects took over a year to complete in post-production.

11. The Boxer's Omen (魔)

1. Movie Title: The Boxer's Omen (魔)

2. Year of Release: 1983

3. Cast and Director:

 - Director: Kuei Chih-Hung

 - Cast: Phillip Ko, Bolo Yeung, Elvis Tsui

4. Synopsis:

The Boxer's Omen follows a Hong Kong boxer who seeks revenge after his brother is crippled in a match against a Thai boxer. His quest for vengeance takes an unexpected turn when he encounters a Buddhist monk who reveals that he is the reincarnation of a spiritual master. The boxer must then embark on a surreal and horrifying journey to fulfill his destiny, battling dark magic, grotesque demons, and his own inner demons. As he delves deeper into the world of black magic and mysticism, he faces increasingly bizarre and gruesome challenges, including battling reanimated corpses and consuming revolting concoctions to gain spiritual power. The film blends martial arts action with extreme supernatural horror, creating a uniquely twisted narrative that defies conventional storytelling.

5. Why This Movie Is Recommended:

The Boxer's Omen is a cult classic that pushes the boundaries of horror and fantasy to create a truly unique viewing experience. Director Kuei Chih-Hung's unrestrained approach to blending genres results in a film that is both visually stunning and deeply unsettling. The movie's practical effects, while dated, contribute to its surreal and nightmarish atmosphere. Its exploration of Thai and Chinese mysticism offers a fresh perspective on supernatural horror. While not for the faint of heart due to its graphic content and bizarre imagery, The Boxer's Omen is a must-see for fans of extreme cinema and those interested in the more outlandish side of Hong Kong filmmaking.

6. 10 Trivia Facts:

 1. The film was produced by the famous Shaw Brothers Studio, known primarily for martial arts films.

 2. Many of the film's most outrageous scenes were inspired by Thai horror movies of the era.

 3. The movie features a mix of Cantonese, Mandarin, and Thai dialogue.

 4. Director Kuei Chih-Hung was known for pushing the boundaries of acceptable content in Hong Kong cinema.

 5. The film's original Chinese title "魔" simply means "Devil" or "Demon."

 6. Many of the gruesome special effects were achieved using practical techniques and real animal parts.

 7. The Boxer's Omen has gained a strong cult following internationally, especially among fans of extreme horror.

 8. The film's unique blend of martial arts and horror helped establish a new subgenre in Hong Kong cinema.

 9. Some of the movie's more graphic scenes had to be cut for its initial release in certain countries.

 10. Despite its supernatural elements, the film incorporates authentic Buddhist and Taoist concepts and imagery.

12. Witch with the Flying Head (飛頭魔女)

1. Movie Title: Witch with the Flying Head (飛頭魔女)

2. Year of Release: 1982

3. Cast and Director:

- Director: Chih-Hung Kuei

- Cast: Ni Tien, Hsiao-Lao Lin, Hui-Ling Liu

4. Synopsis:

Witch with the Flying Head tells the story of a woman who turns to black magic for revenge after being wronged by her husband and his family. She gains the ability to detach her head, which can fly around and attack her enemies. As she embarks on a gruesome path of vengeance, a Taoist priest attempts to stop her reign of terror. The film follows both the witch's increasingly violent acts and the efforts to neutralize her supernatural powers. Along the way, it explores themes of betrayal, the corrupting influence of power, and the dangerous allure of black magic. The narrative unfolds with a series of escalating supernatural confrontations, leading to a climactic battle between good and evil.

5. Why This Movie Is Recommended:

Witch with the Flying Head is a prime example of Hong Kong's unique brand of supernatural horror from the 1980s. Director Chih-Hung Kuei, known for his work in exploitation cinema, crafts a film that is both shockingly graphic and oddly beautiful in its visual style. The movie's blend of traditional Chinese folklore with modern special effects creates a distinctive atmosphere that sets it apart from Western horror films of the same era. While the practical effects may seem dated by today's standards, they contribute to the film's charm and visceral impact. For fans of cult cinema and those interested in the evolution of Asian horror, Witch with the Flying Head offers a wild, unforgettable ride through the darker side of fantasy and revenge tales.

6. 10 Trivia Facts:

1. The film is loosely based on Southeast Asian folklore about supernatural beings with detachable heads.

2. Director Chih-Hung Kuei was a prominent figure in Hong Kong's exploitative "Category III" films.

3. The movie was produced by Shaw Brothers Studio, better known for their martial arts films.

4. Many of the special effects were achieved through a combination of practical effects and early optical techniques.

5. The film's success led to a trend of similar supernatural revenge stories in Hong Kong cinema.

6. Witch with the Flying Head was initially banned in several countries due to its graphic content.

7. The movie blends elements of horror, fantasy, and traditional Chinese opera in its visual style.

8. Some scenes were shot in Taiwan to take advantage of unique locations.

9. The film's makeup effects were groundbreaking for Hong Kong cinema at the time.

10. Despite its exploitation elements, the movie incorporates authentic Taoist mysticism and folklore.

13. The Wicked City (妖獸都市)

1. Movie Title: The Wicked City (妖獸都市)

2. Year of Release: 1992

3. Cast and Director:

- Director: Peter Mak

- Cast: Jacky Cheung, Leon Lai, Michelle Reis

4. Synopsis:

The Wicked City is set in a futuristic Hong Kong where humans coexist with shape-shifting demons known as "Rapters." The story follows Taki, a human agent, and his partner Makie, a half-Rapter, as they work for the Anti-Rapter Bureau to maintain peace between the two species. Their world is thrown into chaos when a powerful Rapter named Daishu arrives, intent on opening a portal to the demon world and conquering Earth. As Taki and Makie investigate, they uncover a complex conspiracy involving both humans and Rapters. The film blends elements of science fiction, horror, and noir as the protagonists navigate a dark underworld of political intrigue and supernatural threats, all while questioning the nature of humanity and monstrosity.

5. Why This Movie Is Recommended:

The Wicked City stands out for its unique blend of cyberpunk aesthetics, body horror, and film noir elements. Based on a Japanese novel and anime, the live-action adaptation brings a distinctly Hong Kong flavor to the material. The film's exploration of the blurred lines between humans and monsters adds depth to its sci-fi horror premise. Director Peter Mak creates a visually striking world that captures the neon-soaked grit of futuristic Hong Kong. With its mix of practical effects, early CGI, and martial arts action, The Wicked City offers a nostalgic glimpse into 90s Hong Kong cinema while delivering genuine scares and thought-provoking themes about coexistence and prejudice.

6. 10 Trivia Facts:

1. The film is based on a series of novels by Japanese author Hideyuki Kikuchi, also known for "Vampire Hunter D."

2. It was adapted into an anime film before this live-action version was made.

3. The movie blends practical effects with early computer-generated imagery, pioneering for Hong Kong cinema at the time.

4. The Wicked City's cyberpunk aesthetic was influenced by films like "Blade Runner" and manga like "Akira."

5. Despite its sci-fi setting, the film incorporates elements of traditional Chinese mythology.

6. The movie features early performances from Jacky Cheung and Leon Lai, who would become major Cantopop stars.

7. Some of the more graphic scenes had to be cut for international release.

8. The film's Chinese title "妖獸都市" translates to "Demon Beast City."

9. The Wicked City was one of the first Hong Kong films to extensively use computer-generated special effects.

10. The movie's success led to a short-lived TV series adaptation in Hong Kong.

14. Dream Home (維多利亞壹號)

1. Movie Title: Dream Home (維多利亞壹號)

2. Year of Release: 2010

3. Cast and Director:

- Director: Pang Ho-cheung

- Cast: Josie Ho, Eason Chan, Michelle Ye

4. Synopsis:

Dream Home follows Cheng Lai-sheung, a young woman obsessed with owning her dream apartment overlooking Victoria Harbour in Hong Kong. Driven by childhood memories and the desire for a better life, she works multiple jobs and saves for years. However, as property prices continue to rise beyond her reach, Lai-sheung resorts to extreme measures. She meticulously plans and carries out a series of brutal murders in the apartment complex she desires, aiming to drive down the property value. The film alternates between Lai-sheung's present-day killing spree and flashbacks that reveal her motivations and the societal pressures that shaped her. As the body count rises, the movie offers a savage critique of Hong Kong's housing crisis and the lengths to which people might go to achieve their dreams.

5. Why This Movie Is Recommended:

Dream Home stands out for its unique blend of slasher horror and social commentary. Director Pang Ho-cheung crafts a film that is both shockingly violent and darkly satirical, using extreme gore to highlight the real-world horrors of economic inequality. The movie's non-linear structure keeps viewers engaged, gradually revealing the complexity behind Lai-sheung's actions. Josie Ho delivers a nuanced performance that makes the protagonist simultaneously sympathetic and terrifying. With its unflinching look at Hong Kong's housing issues and the pressure to achieve social status, Dream Home offers a thought-provoking twist on the home invasion genre. It's a must-see for horror fans looking for intelligent, socially relevant scares.

6. 10 Trivia Facts:

1. The film's Chinese title "維多利亞壹號" translates to "Victoria Number 1," referencing the desired harbor view.

2. Lead actress Josie Ho is also one of the film's producers and championed the project.

3. Director Pang Ho-cheung is better known for romantic comedies, making this violent horror film a departure for him.

4. The movie's extreme violence led to a Category III rating in Hong Kong, equivalent to an NC-17 in the US.

5. Many of the film's locations are actual luxury apartments in Hong Kong.

6. Dream Home was partially inspired by real-life property price issues in Hong Kong.

7. The film uses a mix of practical effects and CGI for its gory scenes.

8. Some scenes were so graphic that they had to be cut for release in certain countries.

9. The movie premiered at the Udine Far East Film Festival in Italy.

10. Despite its horror elements, Dream Home is often categorized as a black comedy due to its satirical approach.

15. Seeding of a Ghost (植鬼)

1. Movie Title: Seeding of a Ghost (植鬼)

2. Year of Release: 1983

3. Cast and Director:

- Director: Yang Chuan

- Cast: Phillip Ko, Maria Jo, Norman Chu

4. Synopsis:

Seeding of a Ghost follows a taxi driver whose wife is raped and murdered by a gang. Consumed by grief and a desire for revenge, he turns to a Taoist priest skilled in black magic. The priest performs a ritual that involves the driver having sex with his wife's corpse to create a vengeful ghost. As the supernatural revenge plot unfolds, the ghost begins to eliminate the perpetrators one by one in increasingly gruesome ways. However, the dark magic spirals out of control, leading to unintended consequences and horrific transformations. The film explores themes of vengeance, the corrupting nature of hatred, and the dangerous allure of black magic, all while delivering shocking scenes of supernatural horror and body horror.

5. Why This Movie Is Recommended:

Seeding of a Ghost is a prime example of Hong Kong's Category III extreme cinema from the 1980s. Director Yang Chuan pushes the boundaries of taste and decency to create a truly shocking and unforgettable horror experience. The film's blend of traditional Chinese black magic with graphic violence and sexual content results in a uniquely transgressive work. While certainly not for everyone due to its extreme content, Seeding of a Ghost offers insight into a particular era of Hong Kong filmmaking that was willing to explore taboo subjects and visceral horror. For fans of cult cinema and those interested in the more extreme side of Asian horror, this film represents a bold and uncompromising vision that continues to disturb and fascinate viewers decades after its release.

6. 10 Trivia Facts:

1. The film is part of the "Black Magic" subgenre popular in Hong Kong and Southeast Asian cinema during the 1980s.

2. Seeding of a Ghost was produced by Shaw Brothers Studio, better known for their martial arts films.

3. The movie's extreme content made it controversial even within Hong Kong's lenient film industry at the time.

4. Many of the film's most shocking scenes were achieved through practical effects and makeup.

5. The movie draws on real Taoist mysticism and folklore, albeit in a highly sensationalized manner.

6. Seeding of a Ghost has gained a cult following among international horror fans for its outrageous content.

7. The film's Chinese title "植鬼" literally translates to "Planting a Ghost."

8. Director Yang Chuan was known for his work in exploitation cinema and pushed boundaries with this film.

9. The movie features a mix of Cantonese and Mandarin dialogue, common in Hong Kong films of the era.

10. Despite its low budget, the film's makeup and special effects were considered impressive for their time.

16. Possessed (鬼眼)

1. Movie Title: Possessed (鬼眼)

2. Year of Release: 1983

3. Cast and Director:

 - Director: David Lai

 - Cast: Lam Ching-ying, Deanie Ip, Philip Chan

4. Synopsis:

Possessed tells the story of a young woman named Judy who becomes possessed by a vengeful spirit after a car accident. As her behavior grows increasingly erratic and violent, her boyfriend and a team of paranormal investigators attempt to uncover the truth behind her possession. The film delves into the world of Chinese supernatural beliefs, exploring concepts of restless spirits and exorcism rituals. As Judy's condition worsens, the investigators must race against time to free her from the malevolent entity, uncovering dark secrets from the past in the process. The narrative blends elements of traditional ghost stories with psychological horror, creating a tense and atmospheric exploration of possession and the lingering effects of past traumas.

5. Why This Movie Is Recommended:

Possessed stands out for its effective blend of supernatural horror and psychological tension. Director David Lai creates a genuinely eerie atmosphere, drawing on Chinese folklore to craft a unique take on the possession subgenre. The film's exploration of local superstitions and exorcism practices offers a culturally specific horror experience that sets it apart from Western counterparts. With strong performances, particularly from Deanie Ip as the possessed Judy, the movie delivers both scares and emotional depth. While it may not have the extreme gore of some Hong Kong horror films, Possessed compensates with its psychological intensity and well-crafted suspense. For fans of supernatural horror and those interested in culturally diverse takes on familiar tropes, Possessed offers a compelling and chilling viewing experience.

6. 10 Trivia Facts:

1. The film features early career performances from Lam Ching-ying, who later became famous for his roles in Mr. Vampire and other Hong Kong horror comedies.

2. Possessed was one of the first Hong Kong films to focus extensively on the concept of spiritual possession.

3. The movie incorporates elements of both Buddhist and Taoist exorcism rituals.

4. Some of the film's possession scenes were considered quite shocking for Hong Kong cinema at the time.

5. The Chinese title "鬼眼" translates to "Ghost Eyes," referencing the character's ability to see spirits.

6. Director David Lai went on to become a prolific filmmaker in the Hong Kong film industry.

7. The film's success contributed to a wave of supernatural horror movies in Hong Kong during the 1980s.

8. Possessed blends practical effects with camera tricks to create its supernatural elements.

9. The movie explores the concept of "yin yang eyes," a belief in the ability to see ghosts.

10. Despite its horror elements, the film also incorporates moments of dark humor, a common trait in Hong Kong genre films.

17. The Eternal Evil of Asia (魔高一丈)

1. Movie Title: The Eternal Evil of Asia (魔高一丈)

2. Year of Release: 1995

3. Cast and Director:

  - Director: Chin Man-Kei

  - Cast: Ellen Chan, Ben Ng, Yuanyuan Zhu

4. Synopsis:

The Eternal Evil of Asia follows a group of friends who travel to Thailand for a vacation. During their trip, they unwittingly offend a powerful sorcerer, incurring his wrath. Upon returning to Hong Kong, they find themselves plagued by increasingly bizarre and horrific supernatural occurrences. As members of the group fall victim to the sorcerer's curse one by one, the survivors must find a way to break the spell before it's too late. The film escalates from initial pranks and minor hauntings to full-blown supernatural warfare, featuring outrageous magical battles and grotesque transformations. Throughout the story, the movie explores themes of cultural insensitivity, the consequences of disrespecting foreign customs, and the dangerous power of black magic.

5. Why This Movie Is Recommended:

The Eternal Evil of Asia is a prime example of Hong Kong's Category III extreme cinema of the 1990s. Director Chin Man-Kei crafts a film that pushes the boundaries of good taste, blending shocking violence, sexual content, and supernatural horror into a uniquely outrageous package. The movie's over-the-top approach to black magic and its effects results in some truly memorable and bizarre sequences that have to be seen to be believed. While certainly not for everyone due to its extreme content, the film offers an unrestrained and often darkly humorous take on the dangers of cultural ignorance and the power of superstition. For fans of cult cinema and those interested in the more outlandish side of Hong Kong horror, The Eternal Evil of Asia provides an unforgettable and audacious viewing experience.

6. 10 Trivia Facts:

  1. The film is notorious for its extreme content, even by the standards of Hong Kong's Category III rating.

  2. Many of the movie's most outrageous effects were achieved through a combination of practical makeup and early CGI.

  3. The Eternal Evil of Asia spawned several unofficial sequels and imitators in Hong Kong cinema.

  4. The film's Chinese title "魔高一丈" is an idiom meaning "evil is one step ahead," or literally "the demon is ten feet tall."

  5. Some scenes were shot on location in Thailand, adding authenticity to the film's portrayal of Thai black magic.

  6. The movie features a mix of Cantonese, Mandarin, and Thai dialogue.

  7. Despite its low budget, the film gained a cult following for its audacious special effects and plot twists.

  8. The Eternal Evil of Asia is often cited as one of the most extreme examples of Hong Kong's supernatural horror genre.

  9. The film's success contributed to a trend of Hong Kong horror movies set in Southeast Asia.

  10. Some of the movie's more graphic scenes had to be cut for release in certain countries.

18. The Eight Immortals Restaurant: The Untold Story (八仙飯店之人肉叉燒包)

1. Movie Title: The Eight Immortals Restaurant: The Untold Story (八仙飯店之人肉叉燒包)

2. Year of Release: 1993

3. Cast and Director:

- Director: Herman Yau

- Cast: Anthony Wong, Danny Lee, Emily Kwan

4. Synopsis:

Based on a true crime case, The Eight Immortals Restaurant: The Untold Story follows the gruesome tale of Wong Chi Hang, a man who takes over a restaurant in Macau and turns it into a successful business. However, his success hides a dark secret: Wong has murdered the previous owner and his family, disposing of their bodies by serving them to unsuspecting customers in his pork buns. As the police investigate the disappearances, led by Officer Lee, they uncover increasingly horrifying details of Wong's crimes. The film alternates between graphic depictions of Wong's brutal acts and the police's determined pursuit, creating a tense and disturbing narrative that explores the depths of human depravity and the psychological toll of investigating such crimes.

5. Why This Movie Is Recommended:

The Eight Immortals Restaurant: The Untold Story is a landmark film in Hong Kong's Category III extreme cinema. Director Herman Yau creates a visceral and unflinching portrayal of true crime that pushes the boundaries of graphic content in cinema. Anthony Wong's chilling performance as the murderous Wong Chi Hang earned him critical acclaim and a Hong Kong Film Award for Best Actor. While the film's extreme violence and disturbing themes make it challenging viewing, it offers a powerful exploration of evil and the dark potential within human nature. For those interested in true crime stories and the more extreme side of Hong Kong cinema, this film provides a harrowing and unforgettable experience that has left a lasting impact on the horror genre.

6. 10 Trivia Facts:

1. The film is based on the real-life case of a serial killer in Macau in the 1980s.

2. Anthony Wong's performance in this film is often cited as one of his best and most disturbing.

3. The movie's graphic content was so extreme that it faced censorship issues in several countries.

4. Despite its disturbing subject matter, the film was a commercial success in Hong Kong.

5. The Eight Immortals Restaurant blends elements of true crime, horror, and police procedural genres.

6. The film's success led to several sequels, though none matched the notoriety of the original.

7. Director Herman Yau balanced the horrific elements with dark humor, particularly in the police investigation scenes.

8. The movie's Chinese title refers to "human meat char siu bao," a grim reference to the killer's disposal method.

9. The film's success contributed to a wave of true crime-inspired horror movies in Hong Kong cinema.

10. Despite its low budget, the movie's practical effects and makeup were praised for their realism.

19. Bio Zombie (生化壽尸)

1. Movie Title: Bio Zombie (生化壽尸)

2. Year of Release: 1998

3. Cast and Director:

  - Director: Wilson Yip

  - Cast: Jordan Chan, Sam Lee, Angela Tong

4. Synopsis:

  Bio Zombie is set in a Hong Kong shopping mall where two slacker video game salesmen, Woody and Bee, accidentally unleash a zombie outbreak after a mishap with contaminated soft drinks. As the infection spreads rapidly through the mall, Woody, Bee, and a diverse group of survivors must fight their way to safety. The film follows their chaotic journey through the mall, facing hordes of zombies and dealing with interpersonal conflicts. Along the way, they encounter various mall employees and shoppers, each bringing their own dynamic to the group's survival efforts. As the situation escalates, the survivors must use their wits, improvised weapons, and knowledge gleaned from video games to overcome the zombie threat and escape the mall.

5. Why This Movie Is Recommended:

  Bio Zombie stands out for its unique blend of horror, comedy, and social commentary. Director Wilson Yip crafts a film that pays homage to classic zombie movies while infusing it with distinctly Hong Kong humor and pop culture references. The movie's setting in a shopping mall serves as both a claustrophobic horror backdrop and a satirical take on consumerism. With its fast-paced action, quirky characters, and blend of practical and early CGI effects, Bio Zombie offers a fresh and entertaining take on the zombie genre. The film's self-aware humor and video game-inspired sequences make it a cult favorite among horror-comedy fans. For those looking for a zombie film that doesn't take itself too seriously while still delivering genuine scares, Bio Zombie is a must-watch.

6. 10 Trivia Facts:

  1. The film was shot entirely in a real Hong Kong shopping mall during its off-hours.

  2. Bio Zombie was one of the first Hong Kong films to feature fast-moving zombies, predating many Western counterparts.

  3. The movie's video game references and aesthetics were groundbreaking for Hong Kong cinema at the time.

  4. Director Wilson Yip later went on to direct the popular Ip Man martial arts film series.

  5. The film's Chinese title "生化壽尸" is a play on words, combining "biochemical" with a term for "longevity."

  6. Bio Zombie features a mix of practical makeup effects and early CGI for its zombie creations.

  7. The movie's success led to a brief resurgence of zombie films in Hong Kong cinema.

  8. Many of the film's jokes and references are specific to late-90s Hong Kong pop culture.

  9. Bio Zombie was made on a relatively low budget, relying on creativity rather than expensive effects.

  10. The film has gained a cult following internationally, particularly among fans of zombie comedy films.

20. The Sleep Curse (失眠)

1. Movie Title: The Sleep Curse (失眠)

2. Year of Release: 2017

3. Cast and Director:

- Director: Herman Yau

- Cast: Anthony Wong, Jojo Goh, Gordon Lam

4. Synopsis:

The Sleep Curse follows Professor Lam, a neurologist specializing in sleep research, as he tries to help his cousin Ching-ying who is suffering from fatal familial insomnia. As Lam delves deeper into Ching-ying's condition, he uncovers a dark family secret dating back to World War II, when his father was forced to work as a translator for the Japanese army. The film alternates between the present day and wartime Hong Kong, revealing a tragic tale of revenge, black magic, and generational curses. As Lam races against time to save his cousin, he must confront the horrific acts of the past and their lingering consequences in the present. The narrative weaves together elements of historical drama, supernatural horror, and psychological thriller to create a complex and disturbing tale of guilt, retribution, and the enduring impact of wartime atrocities.

5. Why This Movie Is Recommended:

The Sleep Curse stands out for its ambitious blend of historical context and supernatural horror. Director Herman Yau, known for his work in extreme cinema, brings a mature and nuanced approach to the material, balancing graphic horror with thoughtful exploration of serious themes. Anthony Wong delivers a powerful dual performance as both the modern-day professor and his wartime father. The film's unflinching portrayal of wartime atrocities and their long-lasting effects adds depth to its supernatural elements. With its unique premise, strong performances, and effective use of both period and contemporary settings, The Sleep Curse offers a fresh and thought-provoking take on the concept of inherited trauma and the horrors of war. It's a must-see for fans of intelligent horror that doesn't shy away from difficult subject matter.

6. 10 Trivia Facts:

1. The Sleep Curse reunites director Herman Yau and actor Anthony Wong, known for their collaboration on extreme horror films in the 1990s.

2. The movie's depiction of wartime Hong Kong is based on extensive historical research.

3. Fatal familial insomnia, featured in the film, is a real and extremely rare genetic disorder.

4. The film blends elements of body horror with psychological and supernatural terror.

5. Some of the movie's more graphic scenes caused controversy and faced censorship in certain markets.

6. The Sleep Curse was praised for its exploration of the lingering effects of war on subsequent generations.

7. The film's makeup and special effects team worked closely with medical experts to accurately depict the symptoms of extreme sleep deprivation.

8. Director Herman Yau cited classic J-horror films as an influence on the movie's supernatural elements.

9. The Sleep Curse premiered at the Hong Kong International Film Festival.

10. Despite its horror elements, the film was noted for its emotional depth and historical commentary.

Taiwan

1. Detention (返校)

1. Movie Title: Detention (返校)

2. Year of Release: 2019

3. Cast and Director:

- Director: John Hsu

- Cast: Gingle Wang, Fu Meng-po, Tseng Ching-hua, Cecilia Choi

4. Synopsis:

Set in 1962 during Taiwan's White Terror period, "Detention" follows two students, Wei and Fang, who find themselves trapped in their school at night. As they search for a way out, they encounter terrifying supernatural entities and uncover dark secrets about their school's past. The film blends historical drama with psychological horror, exploring themes of political oppression, guilt, and the lingering trauma of Taiwan's authoritarian era. As Wei and Fang delve deeper into the mystery, they must confront both the ghosts of the past and the very real dangers of their present.

5. Why This Movie Is Recommended:

"Detention" stands out for its unique blend of historical context and supernatural horror. It offers a chilling look at a dark period in Taiwan's history through the lens of psychological horror, creating a deeply unsettling atmosphere that lingers long after viewing. The film's stunning visuals, complex narrative, and strong performances elevate it beyond typical horror fare. Its exploration of political themes adds depth to the scares, making it both a terrifying experience and a thought-provoking commentary on authoritarianism and its lasting effects on society.

6. 10 Trivia Facts:

1. The film is based on a popular Taiwanese horror video game of the same name.

2. "Detention" was John Hsu's directorial debut for a feature-length film.

3. The movie won five Golden Horse Awards, including Best New Director and Best Adapted Screenplay.

4. Many of the supernatural elements in the film are inspired by Taiwanese folklore and superstitions.

5. The film's school setting was inspired by real educational institutions during the White Terror period.

6. "Detention" became the highest-grossing domestic film in Taiwan for 2019.

7. The movie's success led to the creation of a TV series adaptation in 2020.

8. Some of the film's dialogue is in Taiwanese Hokkien, reflecting the linguistic diversity of the era.

9. The film's poster, featuring a girl with her eyes sewn shut, became iconic in Taiwanese cinema.

10. "Detention" was selected as the Taiwanese entry for Best International Feature Film at the 93rd Academy Awards.

2. The Tag-Along (紅衣小女孩)

1. Movie Title: The Tag-Along (紅衣小女孩)

2. Year of Release: 2015

3. Cast and Director:

- Director: Cheng Wei-hao

- Cast: River Huang, Hsu Wei-ning, Liu Yin-shang

4. Synopsis:

"The Tag-Along" is based on a famous Taiwanese urban legend about a little girl in a red dress who appears in the footage of a family's hiking trip video. The film follows Wei, a real estate agent whose grandmother mysteriously disappears. As Wei and his girlfriend Yi Chun investigate, they encounter terrifying supernatural occurrences linked to the girl in red. Their search leads them into Taiwan's lush, mountainous areas, where they uncover a dark history of missing persons and ancient folklore. As they delve deeper into the mystery, they find themselves caught between the world of the living and the realm of spirits.

5. Why This Movie Is Recommended:

"The Tag-Along" expertly weaves Taiwanese folklore into a modern horror narrative, creating a uniquely cultural yet universally terrifying experience. The film's atmospheric use of Taiwan's misty mountains and dense forests adds to its eerie ambiance. It stands out for its exploration of familial bonds and the consequences of urbanization on traditional beliefs. The movie's clever use of found footage elements and its gradual build-up of tension make it a compelling watch for horror fans looking for something beyond standard jump scares.

6. 10 Trivia Facts:

1. The film is based on a real video from 1998 that purportedly showed a mysterious girl in red.

2. "The Tag-Along" spawned two sequels, forming a trilogy.

3. The movie's success helped revitalize the Taiwanese horror film industry.

4. The "girl in red" is based on the concept of "mosien" in Taiwanese folklore, spirits of children who died in the mountains.

5. Director Cheng Wei-hao conducted extensive research on Taiwanese superstitions for the film.

6. The movie features a mix of Mandarin Chinese and Taiwanese Hokkien dialogue.

7. Many of the forest scenes were filmed in the mountains of Wulai, a district known for its indigenous Atayal culture.

8. The film's makeup effects for the supernatural entities were created by a team that worked on Hollywood productions.

9. "The Tag-Along" was a box office success in Taiwan and several other Asian countries.

10. The movie incorporates elements of found footage horror, a style rarely used in Taiwanese cinema before.

3. Silk (詭絲)

1. Movie Title: Silk (詭絲)

2. Year of Release: 2006

3. Cast and Director:

- Director: Su Chao-pin

- Cast: Chang Chen, Yōsuke Eguchi, Karena Lam, Barbie Hsu

4. Synopsis:

"Silk" follows a team of scientists who have developed a way to capture ghosts using a mysterious silk-like substance. The group, led by a wheelchair-bound genius named Hashimoto, recruits a talented young cop with extraordinary eyesight, Tung, to help them in their experiments. As they capture and study a ghost boy, they uncover a series of dark secrets and face increasingly dangerous supernatural phenomena. The film blends elements of science fiction with traditional ghost stories, exploring themes of life, death, and the ethical implications of scientific advancement. As the experiments progress, the line between the living and the dead becomes increasingly blurred.

5. Why This Movie Is Recommended:

"Silk" stands out for its unique premise that combines cutting-edge science with supernatural horror. The film's slick visual style and innovative ghost effects create a distinctly modern take on the ghost story genre. It offers a thought-provoking exploration of the consequences of tampering with the natural order, wrapped in a suspenseful and often terrifying narrative. The strong performances, particularly from Chang Chen as Tung, add depth to the characters, making their fate all the more engaging. "Silk" is a must-watch for fans of intelligent horror that blends genres and challenges conventional ghost story tropes.

6. 10 Trivia Facts:

1. The film's English title "Silk" is a play on words, as the Chinese title "詭絲" (Gui Si) sounds similar to "ghost silk".

2. Director Su Chao-pin was also known for writing the screenplay for the acclaimed wuxia film "Crouching Tiger, Hidden Dragon: Sword of Destiny".

3. The movie features a multinational cast, including Japanese actor Yōsuke Eguchi.

4. "Silk" was one of the most expensive Taiwanese films produced at the time of its release.

5. The film's ghost-catching technology was inspired by various scientific theories and urban legends.

6. Many of the film's interior scenes were shot in an abandoned hospital in Taipei.

7. "Silk" received several nominations at the Golden Horse Film Festival, Taiwan's premier film awards.

8. The movie's soundtrack features a mix of traditional Taiwanese music and modern electronic compositions.

9. Some of the film's special effects were created by the same team that worked on "The Matrix" trilogy.

10. "Silk" was distributed internationally and screened at several international film festivals.

4. Recycle (回收)

1. Movie Title: Recycle (回收)

2. Year of Release: 2006

3. Cast and Director:

 - Director: Chang Jung-chi

 - Cast: Lu Yi-ching, Shih Chun-hong, Tsai Chen-nan

4. Synopsis:

 "Recycle" tells the story of Xiao-jie, a young woman who works at a recycling center in Taipei. Her mundane life takes a terrifying turn when she starts experiencing strange and horrifying visions. These hallucinations blur the line between reality and nightmare, often involving the discarded items she handles at work. As Xiao-jie struggles to understand what's happening to her, she uncovers dark secrets about her past and the recycling center itself. The film explores themes of environmental destruction, consumerism, and the psychological toll of urban life, all wrapped in a surreal and often terrifying narrative that challenges the viewer's perception of reality.

5. Why This Movie Is Recommended:

 "Recycle" offers a unique take on horror by blending social commentary with psychological terror. Its use of everyday objects as sources of fear creates a deeply unsettling atmosphere that lingers long after viewing. The film's exploration of environmental themes adds depth to its scares, making it both frightening and thought-provoking. Director Chang Jung-chi's surrealist approach to horror, combined with strong performances from the cast, results in a disorienting and memorable experience. "Recycle" is recommended for viewers who appreciate horror films that challenge conventional narratives and offer more than just surface-level scares.

6. 10 Trivia Facts:

 1. "Recycle" was Chang Jung-chi's directorial debut for a feature-length film.

 2. The movie was partly inspired by Taiwan's complex waste management and recycling systems.

 3. Many of the film's props were actual discarded items collected from recycling centers.

 4. The lead actress, Lu Yi-ching, is known for her collaborations with acclaimed director Tsai Ming-liang.

 5. Some scenes were shot in actual recycling facilities in Taipei, adding to the film's authentic atmosphere.

 6. The film premiered at the Taipei Film Festival and received critical acclaim.

 7. "Recycle" incorporates elements of Taiwanese folk beliefs about spirits inhabiting inanimate objects.

 8. The movie's sound design, which transforms everyday noises into unsettling soundscapes, was particularly praised.

 9. Despite its horror elements, "Recycle" is often categorized as an art house film due to its experimental nature.

 10. The film's ambiguous ending has been the subject of much discussion among viewers and critics.

5. The Heirloom (宅變)

1. Movie Title: The Heirloom (宅變)

2. Year of Release: 2005

3. Cast and Director:

  - Director: Leste Chen

  - Cast: Terri Kwan, Jason Chang, Tender Huang, Kris Hung

4. Synopsis:

"The Heirloom" centers around Yang Cheng-hsun, a young man who inherits an old mansion from his ancestors. Upon moving in with his girlfriend, Sarah, strange and terrifying events begin to occur. They soon discover the house's dark history, including a disturbing family tradition of raising ghosts for power and wealth. As they delve deeper into the family's past, they uncover a curse that has plagued the Yang family for generations. The couple must confront malevolent spirits and face the consequences of their ancestors' actions while trying to break the cycle of horror that threatens to consume them.

5. Why This Movie Is Recommended:

"The Heirloom" stands out for its exploration of traditional Taiwanese beliefs and family curses, offering a unique cultural perspective on haunted house tropes. The film's atmospheric cinematography and intricate set design create a palpable sense of dread throughout. Director Leste Chen skillfully balances supernatural horror with psychological tension, resulting in a multi-layered viewing experience. The movie's focus on family legacy and the price of ancestral sins adds depth to its scares, making it both a frightening ghost story and a thought-provoking drama about the weight of tradition.

6. 10 Trivia Facts:

1. "The Heirloom" was Leste Chen's directorial debut, made when he was only 24 years old.

2. The film is loosely based on a Chinese practice called "Gu," which involves raising venomous creatures to create a powerful poison.

3. Many of the indoor scenes were shot in an actual centuries-old Taiwanese mansion.

4. The movie incorporates elements of Feng Shui and traditional Chinese superstitions about house layout.

5. "The Heirloom" was one of the first Taiwanese horror films to gain significant international distribution.

6. The film's makeup and special effects were created by a team that had worked on Hollywood productions.

7. Some of the ghostly sounds in the film were created using traditional Chinese musical instruments.

8. The movie premiered at the Busan International Film Festival before its theatrical release.

9. "The Heirloom" features a mix of Mandarin Chinese and Taiwanese Hokkien dialogue, reflecting Taiwan's linguistic diversity.

10. The film's success helped revitalize the Taiwanese horror genre in the mid-2000s.

6. The Bride Who Has Returned from Hell (地獄新娘)

1. Movie Title: The Bride Who Has Returned from Hell (地獄新娘)

2. Year of Release: 1965

3. Cast and Director:

- Director: Hsin Chi

- Cast: Li Hsiang-chun, Ching Chi-liang, Ko Hsiang-ting

4. Synopsis:

Set in rural Taiwan, "The Bride Who Has Returned from Hell" tells the story of a young woman named Zhu who is forced into an arranged marriage. On her wedding night, she's murdered by her husband's jealous mistress. Zhu's spirit, fueled by vengeance, returns to haunt the living. As the ghostly bride seeks revenge, the film explores themes of tradition, justice, and the supernatural. The story unfolds through a series of eerie encounters and mysterious events, building tension as Zhu's vengeful spirit confronts those responsible for her untimely death. The film blends elements of Taiwanese folklore with classic ghost story tropes, creating a uniquely cultural horror experience.

5. Why This Movie Is Recommended:

"The Bride Who Has Returned from Hell" is a landmark in Taiwanese cinema, being one of the earliest horror films produced in the country. It offers a fascinating glimpse into 1960s Taiwanese society, blending traditional beliefs with modern filmmaking techniques of the era. The film's atmospheric black-and-white cinematography creates a haunting visual experience that stands the test of time. Its exploration of social issues, particularly the treatment of women, adds depth to the supernatural elements. For fans of classic horror and those interested in the evolution of Asian cinema, this film provides a unique and historically significant viewing experience.

6. 10 Trivia Facts:

1. The film is considered one of the pioneering works of Taiwanese horror cinema.

2. It draws heavily from traditional Chinese ghost stories and folklore.

3. The movie was shot entirely in black and white, adding to its eerie atmosphere.

4. Many of the film's scenes were shot on location in rural Taiwan, showcasing the country's landscape in the 1960s.

5. The film's success led to a resurgence of interest in ghost stories in Taiwanese cinema.

6. Director Hsin Chi was known for his work in both horror and martial arts films.

7. The movie features traditional Taiwanese funeral rites and superstitions.

8. Some of the film's dialogue is in Taiwanese Hokkien, reflecting the linguistic landscape of 1960s Taiwan.

9. The film's themes of vengeance from beyond the grave influenced many subsequent Asian horror movies.

10. "The Bride Who Has Returned from Hell" has been restored and screened at international film festivals as a classic of Taiwanese cinema.

7. Invitation Only (絕命派對)

1. Movie Title: Invitation Only (絕命派對)

2. Year of Release: 2009

3. Cast and Director:

- Director: Kevin Ko

- Cast: Bryant Chang, Maria Ozawa, Kristian Brodie, Vivi Ho

4. Synopsis:

"Invitation Only" follows Wade Chen, a low-level office worker who receives an invitation to an exclusive party hosted by elite members of society. Excited by the opportunity to mingle with the upper class, Wade attends the event, only to discover that it's a trap. The party turns into a horrifying game where the wealthy attendees hunt the less fortunate guests for sport. As Wade and the other victims fight for survival, they uncover the depths of human cruelty and the dark underbelly of Taiwan's class divide. The film combines elements of slasher horror with social commentary, creating a tense and gruesome exploration of wealth, power, and morality.

5. Why This Movie Is Recommended:

"Invitation Only" stands out in the Taiwanese horror landscape for its bold approach to social criticism through the lens of extreme horror. The film's unflinching portrayal of violence and its exploration of class tensions in Taiwanese society make it a thought-provoking watch. Director Kevin Ko skillfully builds tension throughout the movie, creating a sense of claustrophobia and dread. The film's stylish cinematography and strong performances elevate it above typical slasher fare. For viewers who appreciate horror with a message and aren't squeamish about graphic content, "Invitation Only" offers a unique and memorable experience.

6. 10 Trivia Facts:

1. "Invitation Only" was marketed as Taiwan's first slasher film.

2. The movie features Japanese adult film star Maria Ozawa in her mainstream film debut.

3. Director Kevin Ko went on to direct the hit horror film "Incantation" in 2022.

4. The film's premise draws comparisons to the Japanese novel and film "Battle Royale" and the American film "Hostel."

5. Many of the party scenes were filmed in actual luxury locations in Taipei.

6. The movie sparked discussions about wealth inequality in Taiwan upon its release.

7. "Invitation Only" was screened at several international film festivals, including the New York Asian Film Festival.

8. The film's makeup and special effects team had previously worked on Hollywood productions.

9. Some scenes were considered so graphic that they had to be cut for theatrical release in certain countries.

10. The movie's English title "Invitation Only" is a play on the exclusive nature of the deadly party.

8. Double Vision (雙瞳)

1. Movie Title: Double Vision (雙瞳)

2. Year of Release: 2002

3. Cast and Director:

  - Director: Chen Kuo-fu

  - Cast: Tony Leung Ka-fai, David Morse, Rene Liu, Leon Dai

4. Synopsis:

"Double Vision" follows a Taiwanese detective, Huang Huo-tu, as he investigates a series of bizarre murders in Taipei. The victims appear to have died from spontaneous combustion, leaving behind inexplicable scorch marks. As the case becomes more complex, an American FBI agent, Kevin Richter, is brought in to assist. Together, they uncover a sinister cult practicing dark magic, blending elements of Buddhism, Taoism, and Western occultism. As they delve deeper into the case, the line between reality and the supernatural blurs, challenging their perceptions and beliefs. The film combines elements of police procedural, supernatural horror, and psychological thriller, creating a unique and unsettling narrative.

5. Why This Movie Is Recommended:

"Double Vision" stands out for its innovative blend of Eastern and Western storytelling elements, creating a unique entry in the Taiwanese horror genre. The film's high production values and strong performances from its international cast elevate it above typical genre fare. Director Chen Kuo-fu skillfully weaves together complex themes of cultural identity, faith, and the nature of reality, all while maintaining a tense and atmospheric horror narrative. The movie's exploration of Taiwan's cultural landscape, including its religious practices and urban legends, adds depth to its supernatural elements. For viewers seeking a thought-provoking horror film that goes beyond simple scares, "Double Vision" offers a rich and rewarding experience.

6. 10 Trivia Facts:

  1. "Double Vision" was one of the most expensive Taiwanese films produced at the time of its release.

  2. The film features a rare collaboration between Taiwan's film industry and Columbia Pictures.

  3. American actor David Morse learned some Mandarin for his role in the film.

  4. The movie's Chinese title "雙瞳" (Shuang Tong) literally means "double pupils," referring to an ability to see into the spirit world.

  5. "Double Vision" won several awards at the Golden Horse Film Festival, including Best Visual Effects.

  6. The film incorporates elements of Taiwanese folk religion and supernatural beliefs.

  7. Some of the movie's more graphic scenes were inspired by actual crime scene photographs.

  8. Director Chen Kuo-fu has a background in both filmmaking and religious studies, which influenced the film's themes.

  9. "Double Vision" was distributed internationally and helped raise the profile of Taiwanese cinema abroad.

  10. The film's success paved the way for more big-budget, genre-blending productions in Taiwan.

9. The Ghost Tale of Chungking Mansion (重慶大厦)

1. Movie Title: The Ghost Tale of Chungking Mansion (重慶大厦)

2. Year of Release: 2001

3. Cast and Director:

 - Director: Herman Yau

 - Cast: Chi-Ching Cheung, Yuka Kojima, Akina Hong, Sam Lee

4. Synopsis:

"The Ghost Tale of Chungking Mansion" is set in the infamous Chungking Mansions, a densely populated building complex in Hong Kong known for its diverse international community. The film follows a Taiwanese man who travels to Hong Kong to identify his sister's body after she dies under mysterious circumstances in Chungking Mansions. As he investigates her death, he encounters a series of supernatural occurrences and uncovers dark secrets about the building and its inhabitants. The story interweaves multiple narratives, exploring themes of cultural clash, urban legends, and the supernatural. As the protagonist delves deeper into the mystery, he finds himself caught between the world of the living and the dead.

5. Why This Movie Is Recommended:

While technically a Hong Kong production, "The Ghost Tale of Chungking Mansion" is notable for its Taiwanese protagonist and its exploration of cross-strait relations. The film offers a unique blend of social realism and supernatural horror, using the notorious Chungking Mansions as a microcosm of cultural tensions in Asia. Director Herman Yau creates a claustrophobic atmosphere that mirrors the cramped conditions of the real-life building. The movie's multi-layered narrative and diverse cast of characters provide a rich tapestry of stories that go beyond simple scares. For viewers interested in horror films that engage with social issues and cultural dynamics, this movie offers a thought-provoking and atmospheric experience.

6. 10 Trivia Facts:

1. The film is based on the real-life Chungking Mansions, a building complex in Hong Kong known for its diverse international community.

2. Director Herman Yau is known for his work in both mainstream and independent Hong Kong cinema.

3. The movie blends elements of Hong Kong and Taiwanese filmmaking styles.

4. Many scenes were shot on location in the actual Chungking Mansions, adding to the film's authenticity.

5. The film incorporates various urban legends and ghost stories associated with Chungking Mansions.

6. "The Ghost Tale of Chungking Mansion" explores themes of cultural identity and displacement common in Taiwanese cinema.

7. The movie features dialogue in multiple languages, reflecting the diverse community of Chungking Mansions.

8. Some of the film's supernatural elements draw from both Chinese and South Asian folklore.

9. The movie's release coincided with increased interest in the real-life Chungking Mansions as a cultural landmark.

10. Despite being set in Hong Kong, the film offers commentary on the experiences of Taiwanese people abroad.

10. Paradox (夜奔)

1. **Movie Title**: Paradox (夜奔)

2. **Year of Release**: 2014

3. **Cast and Director**:

  - Director: Lien Yi-chi

  - Cast: Chen Bo-lin, Ariel Lin, Edison Song, Esther Liu

4. **Synopsis**:

  "Paradox" follows Jing, a talented programmer who creates a revolutionary AI system capable of predicting future events. When his girlfriend Mei disappears under mysterious circumstances, Jing uses the AI to try and locate her. As he delves deeper into the investigation, he uncovers a series of interconnected events and time paradoxes that challenge his understanding of reality. The film blends elements of science fiction, psychological thriller, and horror as Jing navigates through different timelines and alternate realities. As the boundaries between past, present, and future blur, Jing must confront the consequences of his creation and the true nature of his relationship with Mei.

5. **Why This Movie Is Recommended**:

  "Paradox" stands out for its ambitious blend of science fiction concepts with psychological horror elements, a rare combination in Taiwanese cinema. The film's complex narrative structure and exploration of time paradoxes offer a cerebral viewing experience that goes beyond traditional horror tropes. Director Lien Yi-chi creates a visually striking and atmospherically tense world that keeps viewers guessing until the end. The movie's themes of technology, fate, and the nature of reality add depth to its suspenseful plot. For fans of mind-bending thrillers and sci-fi horror, "Paradox" offers a unique and thought-provoking experience that showcases the diversity of Taiwanese genre filmmaking.

6. **10 Trivia Facts**:

  1. "Paradox" was one of the first Taiwanese films to extensively use computer-generated imagery for its sci-fi elements.

  2. The film's Chinese title "夜奔" (Ye Ben) literally means "night run," alluding to the protagonist's journey through different timelines.

  3. Director Lien Yi-chi has a background in music videos, which influenced the film's stylish visual aesthetic.

  4. The movie draws inspiration from both Western sci-fi films and Asian horror traditions.

  5. "Paradox" premiered at the Taipei Film Festival before its wide release.

  6. The film's complex plot required multiple script revisions to ensure coherence across different timelines.

  7. Some of the movie's philosophical themes were inspired by Buddhism's concepts of time and reality.

  8. The AI system in the film was partly inspired by real-world developments in predictive algorithms.

  9. "Paradox" features a mix of Mandarin Chinese and Taiwanese Hokkien dialogue.

  10. The film's success led to increased interest in sci-fi horror productions in Taiwan.

11. The Rope Curse (粽邪)

1. Movie Title: The Rope Curse (粽邪)

2. Year of Release: 2018

3. Cast and Director:

- Director: Liao Shih-han

- Cast: Kang Ren Wu, Vera Chen, Yuki Deng, Chen Bo-lin

4. Synopsis:

"The Rope Curse" revolves around a traditional Taiwanese ritual called "Zong Zi," where a priest ties a rope between two houses to trap evil spirits. The film follows Jia-min, a young woman who returns to her rural hometown for her grandfather's funeral. She becomes embroiled in a series of supernatural events when a livestreaming ghost hunter conducts the Zong Zi ritual in her village. As the boundary between the living and the dead blurs, Jia-min must confront both the malevolent spirits and the dark secrets of her family's past. The movie blends elements of found footage horror with traditional Taiwanese folklore, creating a unique and terrifying narrative.

5. Why This Movie Is Recommended:

"The Rope Curse" stands out for its innovative blend of modern technology (through the livestreaming subplot) and traditional Taiwanese customs. The film offers a fresh take on the found footage genre by incorporating it into a broader narrative. Director Liao Shih-han creates a palpable sense of dread throughout, effectively using the rural Taiwanese setting to enhance the atmosphere. The movie's exploration of family secrets and generational guilt adds depth to its supernatural scares. For viewers interested in culturally specific horror that doesn't shy away from modern themes, "The Rope Curse" provides a compelling and frighteningly authentic experience.

6. 10 Trivia Facts:

1. The film is based on a real Taiwanese folk ritual called "Zong Zi," which is believed to trap evil spirits.

2. "The Rope Curse" was a surprise box office hit in Taiwan, leading to a sequel in 2020.

3. Many of the film's outdoor scenes were shot in rural Taiwanese villages, adding to its authenticity.

4. The movie incorporates elements of Taiwanese puppet theater, a traditional art form, into its horror narrative.

5. Director Liao Shih-han conducted extensive research on Taiwanese folk beliefs and rituals for the film.

6. The film's success sparked renewed interest in traditional Taiwanese customs among younger audiences.

7. Some of the movie's dialogue is in Taiwanese Hokkien, reflecting the linguistic diversity of rural Taiwan.

8. "The Rope Curse" features cameos from well-known Taiwanese television personalities playing themselves.

9. The film's makeup and special effects were created by a team that had worked on Hollywood productions.

10. Despite its modern elements, the movie draws heavily from classic Taiwanese ghost stories and urban legends.

12. The Victim (目擊者)

1. Movie Title: The Victim (目擊者)

2. Year of Release: 2012

3. Cast and Director:

  - Director: Ko Chien-nien

  - Cast: Chen Yi-han, River Huang, Jack Kao, Chuang Kai-hsun

4. Synopsis:

  "The Victim" follows Hsia, a young woman working as a professional mourner in Taipei. Her job involves attending funerals and wailing on behalf of the deceased's family. After a particularly intense performance at a wealthy family's funeral, Hsia begins to experience terrifying visions and supernatural occurrences. As she investigates the source of these hauntings, she uncovers a web of family secrets, betrayal, and murder. The film explores themes of grief, guilt, and the thin line between the world of the living and the dead. As Hsia delves deeper into the mystery, she must confront her own past traumas and the true nature of her abilities.

5. Why This Movie Is Recommended:

  "The Victim" offers a unique perspective on the horror genre by centering its narrative around the little-known profession of professional mourning. This cultural specificity adds depth and authenticity to the supernatural elements. Director Ko Chien-nien creates a moody, atmospheric film that slowly builds tension, relying more on psychological horror than jump scares. The movie's exploration of grief and its effects on the living provides a poignant backdrop to its ghostly encounters. For viewers interested in character-driven horror that delves into cultural practices and human psychology, "The Victim" provides a thought-provoking and chilling experience.

6. 10 Trivia Facts:

  1. The practice of professional mourning, central to the film's plot, is a real tradition in some parts of Taiwan and China.

  2. Many of the funeral scenes were shot in actual Taiwanese funeral homes, adding to the film's authenticity.

  3. The movie incorporates elements of Taiwanese Buddhist and Taoist funeral rites.

  4. "The Victim" was praised for its accurate portrayal of Taiwanese mourning customs.

  5. The film's Chinese title "目擊者" literally translates to "Eyewitness," hinting at the protagonist's role in the story.

  6. Some of the ghostly makeup effects were inspired by traditional Taiwanese opera masks.

  7. The movie features a mix of Mandarin Chinese and Taiwanese Hokkien dialogue, reflecting Taiwan's linguistic landscape.

  8. "The Victim" premiered at the Taipei Film Festival before its wide release.

  9. The film's success led to increased interest in movies exploring traditional Taiwanese professions.

  10. Director Ko Chien-nien conducted extensive interviews with real professional mourners to prepare for the film.

13. The Tenants Downstairs (樓下的房客)

1. Movie Title: The Tenants Downstairs (樓下的房客)

2. Year of Release: 2016

3. Cast and Director:

- Director: Adam Tsuei

- Cast: Simon Yam, Lee Kang-sheng, Ivy Shao, Chloe Maayan

4. Synopsis:

"The Tenants Downstairs" follows a mysterious landlord who installs hidden cameras throughout his apartment building to spy on his tenants. As he observes their private lives, he becomes increasingly involved in their affairs, manipulating events to satisfy his voyeuristic desires. The tenants, each harboring their own dark secrets include a gym teacher with sadistic tendencies, a shut-in with an obsession for dolls, and a struggling single mother. As the landlord's interventions escalate, the lines between observer and participant blur, leading to a series of twisted and horrifying events. The film explores themes of voyeurism, privacy, and the dark underbelly of urban life.

5. Why This Movie Is Recommended:

"The Tenants Downstairs" stands out for its bold, transgressive approach to horror. While not supernatural, the film's exploration of human depravity and the horrors that can exist behind closed doors creates a deeply unsettling atmosphere. Director Adam Tsuei crafts a visually striking film that balances dark humor with genuine shock. The movie's unflinching portrayal of taboo subjects and its commentary on the voyeuristic nature of modern society make it a thought-provoking, if challenging, watch. For viewers who appreciate psychologically complex, morally ambiguous horror that pushes boundaries, "The Tenants Downstairs" offers a unique and memorable experience.

6. 10 Trivia Facts:

1. The film is based on a novel of the same name by Taiwanese author Giddens Ko.

2. "The Tenants Downstairs" marks the directorial debut of Adam Tsuei, a well-known music producer in Taiwan.

3. The movie faced controversy in Taiwan due to its explicit content and dark themes.

4. Hong Kong actor Simon Yam learned Mandarin Chinese for his role as the landlord.

5. The film's set design, particularly the apartment interiors, was praised for its attention to detail.

6. "The Tenants Downstairs" premiered at the Bucheon International Fantastic Film Festival in South Korea.

7. The movie's marketing campaign in Taiwan included interactive "escape room" experiences.

8. Some scenes were considered so controversial that they had to be cut for theatrical release in certain countries.

9. The film's success led to discussions about the boundaries of artistic expression in Taiwanese cinema.

10. Director Adam Tsuei cited Alfred Hitchcock's "Rear Window" as an influence on the film's voyeuristic themes.

14. Spirited Away (魔宮計)

1. Movie Title: Spirited Away (魔宮計)

2. Year of Release: 2010

3. Cast and Director:

- Director: Heiward Mak

- Cast: Shin, Leung Siu-hei, Fanny Ip, Yuki Ip

4. Synopsis:

"Spirited Away" (not to be confused with the Japanese anime film) follows a group of young urbanites who decide to explore an abandoned mansion rumored to be haunted. As they delve deeper into the dilapidated building, they encounter a series of increasingly terrifying supernatural phenomena. The group soon discovers that the mansion is a gateway to a spirit world, and they must navigate both ghostly threats and their own interpersonal conflicts to survive. The film blends elements of traditional Chinese ghost stories with modern urban legends, creating a unique fusion of old and new fears. As the night progresses, the lines between reality and nightmare blur, forcing the characters to confront their deepest fears and darkest secrets.

5. Why This Movie Is Recommended:

While technically a Hong Kong production, "Spirited Away" is notable for its pan-Chinese approach to horror, incorporating elements familiar to Taiwanese audiences. The film stands out for its effective use of the haunted house trope in an Asian context, blending cultural superstitions with universal fears. Director Heiward Mak creates a claustrophobic atmosphere within the mansion, using tight camera work and sound design to heighten tension. The movie's exploration of urban alienation and the clash between tradition and modernity adds depth to its supernatural scares. For viewers interested in how traditional Asian ghost stories can be adapted for a contemporary setting, "Spirited Away" offers a frightening and thought-provoking experience.

6. 10 Trivia Facts:

1. Despite sharing a name, this film is unrelated to the famous Japanese animated movie "Spirited Away" by Hayao Miyazaki.

2. The movie was filmed on location in several abandoned buildings in Hong Kong, adding to its authentic atmosphere.

3. Director Heiward Mak is known for her work in both horror and drama genres.

4. The film incorporates elements of Taoist and Buddhist beliefs about the afterlife.

5. Some of the movie's ghostly makeup was inspired by traditional Chinese opera designs.

6. "Spirited Away" features a mix of Cantonese and Mandarin dialogue, reflecting the linguistic diversity of its cast.

7. The film's Chinese title "魔宮計" roughly translates to "Demon Palace Scheme."

8. Several scenes in the movie pay homage to classic Hong Kong and Taiwanese ghost films.

9. The film's success led to increased interest in location-based horror movies in the Chinese-speaking world.

10. "Spirited Away" premiered at the Hong Kong International Film Festival before its wide release.

15. The Ghost Wedding (鬼新娘)

1. Movie Title: The Ghost Wedding (鬼新娘)

2. Year of Release: 2022

3. Cast and Director:

- Director: Liao Shih-han

- Cast: Vivian Hsu, Cheng Jen-shuo, Lin Chi-ling, Peng Chia-chia

4. Synopsis:

"The Ghost Wedding" revolves around the Taiwanese folk custom of ghost marriages, where the living wed the dead to appease restless spirits. The film follows Hsin-yu, a young woman who reluctantly agrees to marry the spirit of a deceased man to bring good fortune to her family. As she goes through the elaborate ritual, strange and terrifying events begin to unfold. Hsin-yu soon discovers that her ghost husband has a dark past, and the marriage has awakened malevolent forces. Trapped between the world of the living and the dead, Hsin-yu must uncover the truth behind her ghost husband's death and break free from the supernatural bond before it's too late.

5. Why This Movie Is Recommended:

"The Ghost Wedding" offers a fresh take on the horror genre by exploring the little-known tradition of ghost marriages. Director Liao Shih-han, known for "The Rope Curse," creates a visually stunning film that blends traditional Taiwanese customs with modern horror techniques. The movie's strong focus on local folklore provides a unique cultural context that sets it apart from typical ghost stories. Its exploration of family obligations, tradition, and the consequences of disturbing the natural order adds depth to the supernatural elements. For viewers interested in culturally specific horror that delves into ancient customs and their place in modern society, "The Ghost Wedding" provides a captivating and chilling experience.

6. 10 Trivia Facts:

1. The practice of ghost marriages, central to the film's plot, is a real tradition in some parts of Taiwan and China.

2. Many of the wedding ritual scenes were meticulously researched to ensure cultural accuracy.

3. The film features elaborate traditional Taiwanese wedding costumes and set designs.

4. "The Ghost Wedding" was partly inspired by real-life news stories about ghost marriages in rural Taiwan.

5. The movie incorporates elements of Taiwanese puppet theater in its storytelling.

6. Some of the film's dialogue is in Taiwanese Hokkien, reflecting the linguistic diversity of Taiwan.

7. The movie's release coincided with the Ghost Month in the Chinese lunar calendar, adding to its cultural significance.

8. "The Ghost Wedding" features cameos from several well-known Taiwanese television personalities.

9. The film's success led to increased interest in movies exploring traditional Taiwanese customs.

10. Director Liao Shih-han conducted extensive interviews with Taoist priests and folk religion practitioners to prepare for the film.

16. The Funeral (醉·生夢死)

1. **Movie Title**: The Funeral (醉·生夢死)

2. **Year of Release**: 2015

3. **Cast and Director**:

   - Director: Chang Tso-chi

   - Cast: Chang Chea, Tai Bo, Lu Yi-ching, Chen Shiang-chyi

4. **Synopsis**:

   "The Funeral" is a unique blend of family drama and supernatural horror. The film follows the Chou family as they gather for their patriarch's funeral. As the traditional multi-day Taiwanese funeral proceeds, family tensions rise and long-buried secrets come to light. Amidst the family drama, strange occurrences begin to plague the mourners. The line between the living and the dead blurs as family members experience visions and encounters with spirits. The film explores themes of guilt, family obligation, and the weight of tradition, all while building a sense of creeping dread. As the funeral progresses, the family must confront both their personal demons and possibly real ones.

5. **Why This Movie Is Recommended**:

   "The Funeral" stands out for its subtle approach to horror, blending realistic family drama with supernatural elements. Director Chang Tso-chi creates a slow-burning atmosphere of unease that grows throughout the film. The movie's exploration of Taiwanese funeral customs provides a unique cultural backdrop for its horror elements. Its focus on family dynamics and intergenerational conflict adds depth to the supernatural occurrences. For viewers who appreciate horror that prioritizes atmosphere and psychological tension over overt scares, "The Funeral" offers a thought-provoking and unsettling experience that lingers long after viewing.

6. **10 Trivia Facts**:

   1. The film's Chinese title "醉·生夢死" is a play on a Chinese idiom meaning "to live in a drunken stupor."

   2. Many of the funeral scenes were shot in actual Taiwanese funeral homes for authenticity.

   3. Director Chang Tso-chi is known for his realistic portrayals of working-class Taiwanese life.

   4. The movie incorporates elements of Taiwanese folk religion and ancestor worship.

   5. Some of the film's dialogue is in Taiwanese Hokkien, reflecting the linguistic diversity of Taiwan.

   6. "The Funeral" premiered at the Tokyo International Film Festival.

   7. The film's portrayal of traditional Taiwanese funeral rites was praised for its accuracy.

   8. Many of the supernatural elements in the film are based on real Taiwanese superstitions about death and spirits.

   9. The movie features minimal use of special effects, relying instead on atmosphere and suggestion for its scares.

   10. "The Funeral" won several awards at the Taipei Film Festival, including Best Feature Film.

17. Through the Rituals (鬼殁之地)

1. **Movie Title**: Through the Rituals (鬼殁之地)

2. **Year of Release**: 2021

3. **Cast and Director**:

   - Director: Wei Chun-ren

   - Cast: Liu Kuan-ting, Li Chuan, Yu An-shun, Lin Mei-hsiu

4. **Synopsis**:

   "Through the Rituals" follows a struggling Taoist priest named Ah-Tai who performs exorcisms and other spiritual services in rural Taiwan. When a wealthy family hires him to cleanse their ancestral home of evil spirits, Ah-Tai sees it as an opportunity to prove his worth and revive his failing career. However, as he delves deeper into the family's history and the house's dark past, he uncovers a malevolent force far beyond his abilities. The film blends elements of traditional Taoist exorcism rituals with modern horror techniques, creating a unique and terrifying narrative. As Ah-Tai fights for his life and soul, he must confront his own doubts and the true nature of his abilities.

5. **Why This Movie Is Recommended**:

   "Through the Rituals" offers a fresh perspective on the exorcism subgenre by grounding it in Taiwanese folk religion and Taoist practices. Director Wei Chun-ren creates a palpable sense of dread throughout the film, effectively using the rural Taiwanese setting to enhance the atmosphere. The movie's exploration of faith, tradition, and the clash between ancient beliefs and modern skepticism adds depth to its supernatural scares. Its detailed portrayal of Taoist rituals provides a unique cultural context rarely seen in horror films. For viewers interested in culturally specific horror that doesn't shy away from intense scares, "Through the Rituals" provides a compelling and authentically Taiwanese horror experience.

6. **10 Trivia Facts**:

   1. The film's depiction of Taoist exorcism rituals was extensively researched and vetted by actual Taoist priests.

   2. Many of the film's outdoor scenes were shot in remote areas of Taiwan to capture the rural atmosphere.

   3. The movie incorporates real Taoist talismans and spiritual objects in its set design.

   4. "Through the Rituals" features a mix of Mandarin Chinese and Taiwanese Hokkien dialogue.

   5. The film's makeup and special effects team studied traditional Taiwanese beliefs about spirits for authenticity.

   6. Director Wei Chun-ren has a background in documentary filmmaking, which influenced the movie's realistic style.

   7. Some of the film's scariest scenes were inspired by real-life accounts of supernatural encounters in rural Taiwan.

   8. "Through the Rituals" premiered at the Bucheon International Fantastic Film Festival.

   9. The movie's success led to increased interest in films exploring traditional Taiwanese spiritual practices.

   10. Several scenes in the film pay homage to classic Taiwanese and Hong Kong supernatural movies.

18. The Devil Fish (魔鬼魚)

1. **Movie Title**: The Devil Fish (魔鬼魚)

2. **Year of Release**: 1983

3. **Cast and Director**:

  - Director: Tsai Yang-ming

  - Cast: Chin Han, Chiang Ling, Yia Ping, Yang Hui-shan

4. **Synopsis**:

  "The Devil Fish" is a unique entry in Taiwanese horror cinema, blending elements of monster movies with supernatural horror. The film is set in a coastal Taiwanese town where a series of mysterious deaths occur. The locals believe the killings are the work of a legendary sea monster, but a visiting scientist suspects there might be a more mundane explanation. As more people fall victim to the unseen predator, the town is gripped by fear and superstition. The movie explores themes of man versus nature, traditional beliefs versus modern science, and the power of local legends. As the truth behind the killings is revealed, the line between the natural and supernatural becomes increasingly blurred.

5. **Why This Movie Is Recommended**:

  "The Devil Fish" stands out as an early example of Taiwanese horror cinema that combines elements of creature features with local folklore. While its special effects may seem dated by modern standards, the film's atmosphere of creeping dread and its exploration of coastal Taiwanese culture make it a fascinating watch. Director Tsai Yang-ming effectively uses the seaside setting to create a sense of isolation and vulnerability. The movie's blend of scientific skepticism and traditional superstition adds depth to its narrative. For fans of classic horror and those interested in the evolution of Taiwanese genre cinema, "The Devil Fish" offers a unique glimpse into the country's horror filmmaking history.

6. **10 Trivia Facts**:

  1. "The Devil Fish" was one of the first Taiwanese films to attempt a large-scale monster movie.

  2. The film's monster design was inspired by both local legends and popular international creature features.

  3. Many of the underwater scenes were shot in actual Taiwanese coastal waters.

  4. The movie incorporates elements of Taiwanese folk beliefs about sea spirits and water demons.

  5. "The Devil Fish" was a significant box office success in Taiwan upon its release.

  6. The film features early career appearances from several actors who would go on to become major Taiwanese stars.

  7. Some of the movie's dialogue is in Taiwanese Hokkien, reflecting the linguistic landscape of coastal Taiwan.

  8. The film's success sparked a brief trend of monster movies in Taiwanese cinema.

  9. "The Devil Fish" has gained a cult following and is considered a classic of early Taiwanese genre cinema.

  10. The movie's portrayal of coastal Taiwanese life in the 1980s has made it a valuable cultural artifact.

19. Butterfly (彩蝶飛飛)

1. **Movie Title**: Butterfly (彩蝶飛飛)

2. **Year of Release**: 2019

3. **Cast and Director**:

  - Director: Kuo Chen-ti

  - Cast: Liang Cheng-chun, Li Chuan, Wen Chen-ling, Kao Ying-hsuan

4. **Synopsis**:

  "Butterfly" is a psychological horror film that blurs the line between reality and delusion. The story follows Xiao Jing, a young woman who returns to her hometown to care for her mentally ill mother. As she settles into her childhood home, Xiao Jing begins to experience strange and terrifying visions involving butterflies. These hallucinations become increasingly vivid and threatening, leading her to question her own sanity. As she investigates her family's past, she uncovers dark secrets that may explain her mother's condition and her own experiences. The film explores themes of intergenerational trauma, mental illness, and the fragility of memory and perception.

5. **Why This Movie Is Recommended**:

  "Butterfly" stands out for its nuanced approach to psychological horror, using the supernatural as a metaphor for mental illness and trauma. Director Kuo Chen-ti creates a dreamlike atmosphere that keeps viewers questioning what's real and what's imagined. The film's use of butterfly imagery is both beautiful and unsettling, adding a layer of symbolic depth to the narrative. Its exploration of family dynamics and the impact of mental illness on loved ones adds emotional weight to the horror elements. For viewers who appreciate thought-provoking, visually striking horror that prioritizes psychological tension over jump scares, "Butterfly" offers a unique and haunting experience.

6. **10 Trivia Facts**:

  1. The film's butterfly motif was inspired by Taiwanese folklore about spirits taking the form of insects.

  2. Many of the movie's interior scenes were shot in actual abandoned houses in rural Taiwan.

  3. Director Kuo Chen-ti has a background in documentary filmmaking, which influenced the film's realistic portrayal of family dynamics.

  4. "Butterfly" features a mix of Mandarin Chinese and Taiwanese Hokkien dialogue.

  5. The film's cinematography was praised for its use of color symbolism, particularly in scenes featuring butterflies.

  6. Several scenes in the movie were inspired by real-life accounts of people with mental illness in Taiwan.

  7. "Butterfly" premiered at the Taipei Film Festival, where it received critical acclaim.

  8. The film's makeup and special effects team studied actual cases of severe mental illness to create realistic portrayals.

  9. Some of the movie's more surreal sequences were influenced by Taiwanese experimental cinema.

  10. "Butterfly" has been used in psychology classes in Taiwan as a discussion point about the portrayal of mental illness in media.

20. The 9th Precinct (第九分局)

1. **Movie Title**: The 9th Precinct (第九分局)

2. **Year of Release**: 2019

3. **Cast and Director**:

   - Director: Wang Yi-chun

   - Cast: Kuo Shu-yau, Gingle Wang, Johnny Yang, Liu Kuan-ting

4. **Synopsis**:

"The 9th Precinct" blends supernatural horror with police procedural elements. The film follows a rookie police officer, Ching-Fang, who is assigned to the mysterious 9th Precinct, a unit that handles paranormal cases. As she adjusts to her new role, Ching-Fang encounters a series of bizarre and terrifying incidents that challenge her understanding of reality. With the help of her more experienced partner and a psychic consultant, she investigates a case involving a string of mysterious suicides. As they delve deeper, they uncover a malevolent supernatural force that threatens both the living and the dead. The film explores themes of justice, the afterlife, and the thin line between this world and the next.

5. **Why This Movie Is Recommended**:

"The 9th Precinct" offers a fresh take on the horror genre by combining elements of police procedurals with supernatural thriller. Director Wang Yi-chun creates a unique world where the supernatural is part of everyday police work, leading to both tense and occasionally humorous situations. The film's exploration of Taiwanese folk beliefs about ghosts and the afterlife provides a rich cultural backdrop for its horror elements. Its strong focus on character development, particularly Ching-Fang's journey from skeptic to believer, adds depth to the supernatural narrative. For viewers who enjoy genre-blending films that balance scares with mystery and action, "The 9th Precinct" provides an entertaining and distinctly Taiwanese horror experience.

6. **10 Trivia Facts**:

   1. The concept of a supernatural police unit was inspired by actual paranormal investigation teams in Taiwan.

   2. Many of the film's police procedure scenes were vetted by real Taiwanese police officers for accuracy.

   3. The movie incorporates elements of Taiwanese folk religion and ghost month traditions.

   4. "The 9th Precinct" features a mix of Mandarin Chinese and Taiwanese Hokkien dialogue.

   5. Some of the film's supernatural makeup effects were inspired by traditional Taiwanese opera designs.

   6. The movie's success led to discussions about a potential TV series adaptation.

   7. Several scenes in the film pay homage to classic Asian horror movies and police thrillers.

   8. The 9th Precinct's headquarters in the movie is a real historic building in Taipei.

   9. Director Wang Yi-chun conducted extensive interviews with people claiming to have had supernatural encounters to prepare for the film.

   10. "The 9th Precinct" was praised for its portrayal of a strong female lead in a traditionally male-dominated genre.

Malaysia

1. Pontianak (1957)

1. Movie Title: Pontianak

2. Year of Release: 1957

3. Cast and Director:

- Director: B.N. Rao

- Cast: Maria Menado, M. Amin, Roomai Noor

4. Synopsis:

"Pontianak" is a classic Malay horror film that revolves around the legend of the pontianak, a female vampiric ghost in Malaysian folklore. The story follows a beautiful woman who dies during childbirth and returns as a pontianak, seeking revenge on those who wronged her in life. As she terrorizes a village, a brave man attempts to stop her reign of terror. The film explores themes of love, betrayal, and the supernatural, set against the backdrop of traditional Malay culture.

5. Why This Movie Is Recommended:

"Pontianak" is considered a landmark in Malaysian cinema, being one of the first horror films produced in the country. It popularized the pontianak folklore in mainstream media and set the standard for future Malaysian horror films. The film's atmosphere, practical effects, and cultural authenticity make it a must-watch for those interested in the origins of Southeast Asian horror. Its influence on the genre in Malaysia and neighboring countries cannot be overstated.

6. 10 Trivia Facts:

1. "Pontianak" was so successful that it spawned two sequels, forming the first horror trilogy in Malaysian cinema.

2. The film was thought to be lost for decades until a copy was discovered in 2010.

3. It was produced by Cathay-Keris Studio, one of the pioneering film studios in Singapore and Malaysia.

4. The movie was shot in black and white, adding to its eerie atmosphere.

5. Lead actress Maria Menado became known as the "Pontianak Queen" due to her role in this film.

6. The film's success led to a boom in Malay horror films in the late 1950s and early 1960s.

7. "Pontianak" was one of the first Malay films to gain international recognition.

8. The movie was shot on location in Malaysia, showcasing authentic local settings.

9. Its portrayal of the pontianak has become the standard depiction in Malaysian pop culture.

10. The film's practical effects, including the pontianak's transformations, were groundbreaking for its time.

2. Sumpah Orang Minyak (1958)

1. Movie Title: Sumpah Orang Minyak (Curse of the Oily Man)

2. Year of Release: 1958

3. Cast and Director:

- Director: P. Ramlee

- Cast: P. Ramlee, Rokiah Hanafi, Habsah Mat

4. Synopsis:

"Sumpah Orang Minyak" tells the story of a man who makes a deal with dark forces to gain supernatural powers, transforming him into the Oily Man of Malay folklore. In exchange for these powers, he must rape 21 virgins within a week. The film follows his terrifying nocturnal attacks on a village and the community's efforts to stop him. As the Oily Man's rampage continues, the villagers must uncover the truth behind the attacks and find a way to break the curse before it's too late.

5. Why This Movie Is Recommended:

This film is a classic of Malaysian horror cinema, directed by and starring the legendary P. Ramlee. It successfully blends elements of horror with social commentary, exploring themes of temptation, morality, and community. The movie's depiction of the Oily Man has become iconic in Malaysian pop culture. Its ability to create tension and fear while maintaining a distinctly Malaysian identity makes it a must-watch for fans of international horror and those interested in Southeast Asian folklore.

6. 10 Trivia Facts:

1. P. Ramlee, the director and star, is considered one of the greatest Malaysian entertainers of all time.

2. The film is based on the Malay folklore figure of the Orang Minyak (Oily Man).

3. It was one of the first Malay films to combine horror elements with social commentary.

4. The movie was shot in Singapore, which was part of Malaysia at the time.

5. "Sumpah Orang Minyak" helped establish the Orang Minyak as a staple character in Malaysian horror.

6. The film's success led to several remakes and inspired films in later decades.

7. P. Ramlee composed the film's soundtrack, showcasing his multi-talented nature.

8. The movie was produced by Malay Film Productions, a prominent studio in the golden age of Malay cinema.

9. Its portrayal of village life provides a glimpse into 1950s Malay culture.

10. The film's themes of temptation and consequences draw parallels to Faustian bargains in Western literature.

3. Hantu Kak Limah Balik Rumah (2010)

1. Movie Title: Hantu Kak Limah Balik Rumah (Ghost of Sister Limah Returns Home)

2. Year of Release: 2010

3. Cast and Director:

  - Director: Mamat Khalid

  - Cast: Delimawati, Kuswadinata, Zami Ismail, Avaa Vanja

4. Synopsis:

Set in the fictional village of Kampung Pisang, "Hantu Kak Limah Balik Rumah" follows the chaos that ensues when Kak Limah, a middle-aged woman, is found dead in her home. As the villagers prepare for her funeral, strange occurrences begin to plague the community. Husin, a villager who claims to be able to see ghosts, insists that Kak Limah's spirit is still lingering in the village. The situation becomes more complicated when Kak Limah's body disappears, and sightings of her ghost become more frequent. The villagers must uncover the truth behind Kak Limah's death and put her spirit to rest.

5. Why This Movie Is Recommended:

This film brilliantly blends horror and comedy, creating a uniquely Malaysian cinematic experience. It cleverly uses local superstitions and cultural nuances to craft a story that is both frightening and hilarious. The movie's success lies in its ability to poke fun at horror tropes while still delivering genuine scares. Its portrayal of rural Malaysian life and the ensemble cast's chemistry make it a standout in contemporary Malaysian cinema. The film's popularity led to a successful franchise, cementing its place in Malaysian pop culture.

6. 10 Trivia Facts:

1. The movie is part of the "Kampung Pisang" series, a popular franchise in Malaysian cinema.

2. It was one of the highest-grossing Malaysian films of 2010.

3. The film spawned two sequels, creating a beloved horror-comedy trilogy.

4. Director Mamat Khalid is known for his satirical takes on Malaysian society and politics.

5. The movie's success revitalized interest in Malaysian horror-comedies.

6. Many of the cast members reprised their roles from previous "Kampung Pisang" films.

7. The film features numerous references to Malaysian folklore and superstitions.

8. "Hantu Kak Limah Balik Rumah" was shot on location in Perak, Malaysia.

9. The movie's blend of Malay, Chinese, and Indian characters reflects Malaysia's multicultural society.

10. It popularized several catchphrases that became part of Malaysian pop culture.

4. Khurafat (2011)

1. Movie Title: Khurafat

2. Year of Release: 2011

3. Cast and Director:

- Director: Syamsul Yusof

- Cast: Syamsul Yusof, Ummi Nazeera, Namron, Pekin Ibrahim

4. Synopsis:

"Khurafat" tells the story of Johan, a man who returns to his village after years away to settle his late father's estate. Upon arrival, he learns that his father was a bomoh (shaman) involved in black magic. As Johan begins to experience strange and terrifying occurrences, he discovers that his father's involvement in the dark arts has left a sinister legacy. With the help of Aishah, a religious woman, Johan must confront the supernatural forces threatening him and the village while grappling with his own beliefs and his family's dark past.

5. Why This Movie Is Recommended:

"Khurafat" stands out for its exploration of the conflict between traditional beliefs and modern skepticism in Malaysian society. The film delivers genuine scares while delving into themes of faith, family, and the consequences of dabbling in the occult. Its high production values and strong performances elevate it above typical genre fare. The movie's ability to create tension through atmosphere and psychological horror, rather than relying solely on jump scares, makes it a compelling watch for horror enthusiasts and casual viewers alike.

6. 10 Trivia Facts:

1. The word "Khurafat" refers to superstitious beliefs or practices in Islamic contexts.

2. Director Syamsul Yusof also stars as the main character, showcasing his versatility.

3. The film was shot in various locations in Perak, Malaysia, known for its folkloric history.

4. "Khurafat" was one of the highest-grossing Malaysian films of 2011.

5. The movie sparked discussions about the portrayal of traditional practices in modern Malaysian cinema.

6. It features practical effects for many of its supernatural elements, adding to the film's realism.

7. The film's success led to increased investment in the Malaysian horror genre.

8. "Khurafat" was Syamsul Yusof's first venture into the horror genre as a director.

9. The movie incorporates elements of Malay mysticism and Islamic teachings.

10. It received critical acclaim for its cinematography and sound design, which contribute significantly to its eerie atmosphere.

5. Munafik (2016)

1. Movie Title: Munafik

2. Year of Release: 2016

3. Cast and Director:

- Director: Syamsul Yusof

- Cast: Syamsul Yusof, Nabila Huda, Fizz Fairuz, Pekin Ibrahim

4. Synopsis:

"Munafik" follows Adam, a devout Muslim man who works as a traditional Islamic healer. After losing his wife in a tragic accident, Adam struggles with his faith and stops practicing his healing. He's drawn back into the world of spiritual healing when he's asked to help Maria, a woman suffering from a mysterious illness that appears to be demonic possession. As Adam delves deeper into Maria's case, he uncovers a dark conspiracy involving black magic and faces challenges to his faith and his understanding of good and evil. The film explores themes of faith, grief, and the battle between religious conviction and supernatural forces.

5. Why This Movie Is Recommended:

"Munafik" stands out for its unique blend of Islamic themes with horror elements, creating a distinctly Malaysian take on the exorcism subgenre. The film's exploration of faith in the face of supernatural evil adds depth to its scares. Its high production values, intense performances, and clever use of practical effects contribute to a genuinely frightening experience. The movie's massive commercial success and cultural impact make it a significant entry in Malaysian cinema, appealing to both horror fans and those interested in films that tackle religious themes.

6. 10 Trivia Facts:

1. "Munafik" was one of the highest-grossing Malaysian films of all time upon its release.

2. The title "Munafik" means "hypocrite" in Malay, relating to the film's themes of faith and deception.

3. Director and lead actor Syamsul Yusof drew inspiration from personal experiences and religious studies.

4. The film spawned a successful sequel, "Munafik 2," in 2018.

5. "Munafik" was shot in various locations in Selangor and Pahang, Malaysia.

6. The movie's success led to its distribution in several other countries, including Indonesia and Singapore.

7. It won multiple awards at the 28th Malaysia Film Festival, including Best Film.

8. The film's portrayal of Islamic healing practices sparked discussions about faith and superstition in Malaysia.

9. "Munafik" broke several box office records for a Malaysian film, including fastest to reach RM10 million.

10. The movie's blend of religious elements with horror created a new subgenre in Malaysian cinema, inspiring similar films.

6. Histeria (2008)

1. Movie Title: Histeria

2. Year of Release: 2008

3. Cast and Director:

- Director: James Lee

- Cast: Liyana Jasmay, Aqasha, Reanna Elina, Nasha Aziz

4. Synopsis:

"Histeria" is set in an all-girls school where a series of mysterious deaths occur. The story follows Erin, a new student who begins to experience strange visions and encounters with a ghostly figure. As more students fall victim to unexplained accidents and suicides, Erin and her friends try to uncover the dark history of the school. They discover a connection to a tragic incident from the past involving a student named Zaitun. As the line between reality and nightmare blurs, Erin must confront the malevolent force behind the hauntings before she becomes its next victim.

5. Why This Movie Is Recommended:

"Histeria" stands out for its atmospheric approach to horror, building tension through its eerie school setting and psychological elements. The film effectively blends local superstitions with universal fears, creating a uniquely Malaysian horror experience. Its exploration of teenage anxieties and the pressure of academic life adds depth to the supernatural plot. The movie's strong visual style and performances from its young cast contribute to its unsettling atmosphere, making it a significant entry in Malaysian horror cinema.

6. 10 Trivia Facts:

1. Director James Lee is known for his work in independent Malaysian cinema, bringing his artistic sensibilities to the horror genre.

2. The film's title "Histeria" plays on the psychological concept of hysteria, reflecting the movie's themes.

3. Many scenes were shot in an actual Malaysian school, adding to the authentic atmosphere.

4. "Histeria" was one of the first Malaysian horror films to focus on a teenage cast and school setting.

5. The movie incorporates elements of Malay folklore into its modern school horror story.

6. It was praised for its sound design, which significantly contributes to the film's scares.

7. "Histeria" helped launch the career of lead actress Liyana Jasmay.

8. The film explores themes of bullying and peer pressure alongside its supernatural elements.

9. It was one of the highest-grossing Malaysian horror films of 2008.

10. "Histeria" has been compared to Japanese and Korean school-based horror films, showing the global influence on Malaysian cinema.

7. Congkak (2008)

1. Movie Title: Congkak

2. Year of Release: 2008

3. Cast and Director:

- Director: Ahmad Idham

- Cast: Fasha Sandha, Jehan Miskin, Nisdawati, Sabri Yunus

4. Synopsis:

"Congkak" centers around a traditional Malay board game of the same name, which becomes the conduit for a malevolent spirit. The story follows Eza, who inherits an old congkak set from her late grandmother. Soon after, strange and terrifying events begin to plague Eza and her family. As the haunting intensifies, Eza discovers that the congkak set is cursed, harboring a vengeful spirit with a dark connection to her family's past. With the help of a bomoh (shaman), Eza must uncover the truth behind the curse and find a way to end the supernatural terror before it claims more victims.

5. Why This Movie Is Recommended:

"Congkak" stands out for its unique premise, using a traditional Malay game as a vehicle for horror. The film effectively blends cultural elements with supernatural scares, offering insight into Malay traditions and superstitions. Its exploration of family secrets and generational curses adds depth to the plot. The movie's ability to turn a familiar, everyday object into a source of terror creates a relatable and unsettling experience for Malaysian audiences. "Congkak" demonstrates how local folklore can be adapted into contemporary horror, making it a significant entry in Malaysian cinema.

6. 10 Trivia Facts:

1. The congkak is a traditional mancala game played throughout Southeast Asia, particularly in Malaysia.

2. The film sparked renewed interest in the traditional game among younger Malaysians.

3. "Congkak" was shot in various locations in Selangor, Malaysia.

4. The movie features detailed explanations of congkak rules, integrating them into the plot.

5. It was one of the first Malaysian horror films to center its plot around a traditional game.

6. The film's success led to increased use of traditional Malay elements in contemporary horror movies.

7. "Congkak" received praise for its cinematography, particularly in creating a foreboding atmosphere.

8. The movie explores the concept of "permainan hantu" (ghost game) common in Malay folklore.

9. Lead actress Fasha Sandha prepared for her role by learning to play congkak.

10. The film's portrayal of the bomoh (shaman) character sparked discussions about traditional practices in modern Malaysia.

8. Pusaka (2019)

1. Movie Title: Pusaka

2. Year of Release: 2019

3. Cast and Director:

- Director: Razaisyam Rashid

- Cast: Syafiq Kyle, Mimi Lana, Riz Amin, Aleza Shadan

4. Synopsis:

"Pusaka" tells the story of Inspector Nuar, who is assigned to investigate the case of missing twin girls. As he delves deeper into the mystery, he uncovers a dark world of black magic and family curses. The investigation leads him to the girls' troubled family history and a sinister heirloom that holds a malevolent power. Nuar must confront his own skepticism about the supernatural as he races against time to save the twins. The line between the natural and supernatural blurs, forcing Nuar to question everything he believes in order to solve the case and survive the ordeal.

5. Why This Movie Is Recommended:

"Pusaka" stands out for its blend of police procedural and supernatural horror, creating a unique genre hybrid in Malaysian cinema. The film's exploration of local black magic practices adds a distinct cultural flavor to its scares. Its atmospheric cinematography and strong performances contribute to a tense, unsettling viewing experience. The movie's themes of family legacy and the price of power give depth to its horror elements. "Pusaka" demonstrates the evolution of Malaysian horror, combining traditional supernatural elements with modern storytelling techniques.

6. 10 Trivia Facts:

1. "Pusaka" means "heirloom" in Malay, reflecting the film's theme of inherited curses.

2. The movie was praised for its realistic portrayal of police work alongside supernatural elements.

3. Director Razaisyam Rashid conducted extensive research into Malay black magic practices for the film.

4. "Pusaka" features elaborate practical effects for its supernatural scenes, minimizing CGI use.

5. The film's success led to discussions about a potential sequel or spin-off.

6. It was shot in various locations around Kuala Lumpur, showcasing both urban and rural settings.

7. "Pusaka" received critical acclaim for its sound design, which significantly enhances the horror atmosphere.

8. The movie explores the concept of "twin magic," a recurring theme in Malay folklore.

9. Lead actor Syafiq Kyle underwent police training to prepare for his role as Inspector Nuar.

10. The film's marketing campaign included viral videos purporting to show real black magic incidents, building anticipation for the release.

9. Roh (2019)

1. Movie Title: Roh (Soul)

2. Year of Release: 2019

3. Cast and Director:

- Director: Emir Ezwan

- Cast: Farah Ahmad, Mhia Farhana, Harith Haziq, Namron

4. Synopsis:

Set in an indeterminate past, "Roh" follows a family living in isolation in the forest. Their simple existence is disrupted when they take in a lost little girl, who prophesies their deaths. Strange and increasingly terrifying events begin to unfold, challenging the family's faith and sanity. As they confront malevolent forces both external and internal, the line between victim and perpetrator blurs. The arrival of a shaman adds another layer of complexity to their struggle for survival. "Roh" explores themes of evil, innocence, and the nature of humanity in the face of inexplicable horror.

5. Why This Movie Is Recommended:

"Roh" stands out for its minimalist approach to horror, relying on atmosphere and psychological tension rather than jump scares. The film's rural setting and focus on folklore create a uniquely Malaysian horror experience. Its exploration of faith, family, and the nature of evil adds philosophical depth to the scares. The movie's stunning cinematography and strong performances contribute to its unsettling atmosphere. "Roh" represents a new wave of Malaysian horror that emphasizes artistry and thematic complexity, appealing to both horror fans and art-house audiences.

6. 10 Trivia Facts:

1. "Roh" was Malaysia's official submission to the 93rd Academy Awards for Best International Feature Film.

2. The film was shot entirely in the jungles of Dengkil, Selangor, over 24 days.

3. Director Emir Ezwan drew inspiration from Malay folklore and his childhood experiences in rural Malaysia.

4. "Roh" won Best Cinematography at the 2020 Malaysian Film Festival.

5. The movie features minimal dialogue, relying heavily on visual storytelling.

6. It was produced on a modest budget, showcasing the creativity of Malaysian independent cinema.

7. "Roh" received international acclaim, screening at several film festivals worldwide.

8. The film's ambiguous ending has sparked numerous interpretations and discussions among viewers.

9. Traditional Malay music and instruments were used in the soundtrack to enhance the cultural atmosphere.

10. The actors underwent survival training to prepare for their roles in the challenging jungle environment.

10. Dendam Pontianak (2019)

1. Movie Title: Dendam Pontianak (Revenge of the Pontianak)

2. Year of Release: 2019

3. Cast and Director:

- Directors: Glen Goei and Gavin Yap

- Cast: Nur Fazura, Remy Ishak, Hisyam Hamid, Shenty Feliziana

4. Synopsis:

"Dendam Pontianak" is a reimagining of the classic Pontianak folklore set in a Malay village in 1965. The story follows Khalid and Siti, a newly married couple whose happiness is threatened by the return of Mina, Khalid's ex-lover who was thought to have died. As strange occurrences plague the village, it becomes clear that Mina has returned as a Pontianak, a vampiric ghost bent on revenge. The film explores themes of love, betrayal, and the consequences of one's actions as the characters confront both supernatural threats and their own past mistakes.

5. Why This Movie Is Recommended:

"Dendam Pontianak" offers a fresh take on one of Malaysia's most iconic horror figures. The film balances traditional horror elements with a nuanced exploration of human relationships and societal expectations. Its high production values, including stunning visuals and period-accurate set designs, create an immersive experience. The movie's feminist undertones and sympathetic portrayal of the Pontianak add depth to the narrative. As a modern reimagining of a classic tale, "Dendam Pontianak" bridges the gap between old and new Malaysian cinema, appealing to both longtime horror fans and newcomers to the genre.

6. 10 Trivia Facts:

1. The film is a collaboration between Singaporean and Malaysian filmmakers, showcasing cross-border talent.

2. "Dendam Pontianak" pays homage to the 1957 classic "Pontianak," considered the first Malay horror film.

3. The movie was shot on location in Johor, Malaysia, to capture the authentic feel of a 1960s Malay village.

4. Lead actress Nur Fazura underwent extensive makeup processes to transform into the Pontianak.

5. The film incorporates elements of Malay culture and traditional music to enhance its atmospheric horror.

6. "Dendam Pontianak" premiered at the 2019 Singapore International Film Festival.

7. The directors aimed to create a "thinking person's horror film," focusing on character development alongside scares.

8. Traditional practical effects were used alongside modern CGI to create the Pontianak's supernatural appearances.

9. The movie explores the societal treatment of women in 1960s Malaysia, adding historical context to its horror narrative.

10. "Dendam Pontianak" received praise for its cinematography, which captures both the beauty and eeriness of rural Malaysia.

11. Jangan Pandang Belakang (2007)

1. Movie Title: Jangan Pandang Belakang (Don't Look Back)

2. Year of Release: 2007

3. Cast and Director:

- Director: Ahmad Idham

- Cast: Afdlin Shauki, Nasha Aziz, Intan Ladyana, Que Haidar

4. Synopsis:

"Jangan Pandang Belakang" follows the story of Aiman, a successful businessman who returns to his hometown with his wife for his father's funeral. During their stay, Aiman begins experiencing strange and terrifying occurrences. He discovers that these supernatural events are connected to a tragic incident from his past that he had long forgotten. As the hauntings intensify, Aiman must confront his buried memories and the angry spirits that have returned to seek vengeance. The film explores themes of guilt, redemption, and the consequences of one's actions.

5. Why This Movie Is Recommended:

This film stands out for its effective blend of psychological horror and traditional Malaysian ghost stories. It creates a tense atmosphere by playing on the fear of the unknown and the guilt of past actions. The movie's exploration of family dynamics and small-town secrets adds depth to its supernatural elements. With strong performances and well-executed scares, "Jangan Pandang Belakang" became a benchmark for modern Malaysian horror, influencing many subsequent films in the genre.

6. 10 Trivia Facts:

1. The film's title, "Don't Look Back," is a common superstition in Malaysian culture related to encountering ghosts.

2. It was one of the highest-grossing Malaysian films of 2007.

3. The movie spawned a sequel, "Jangan Pandang Belakang Congkak," released in 2009.

4. Many scenes were shot in actual locations believed to be haunted by locals.

5. The film incorporates several types of ghosts from Malaysian folklore.

6. "Jangan Pandang Belakang" was praised for its sound design, which significantly enhances the horror atmosphere.

7. The movie features a cameo from a popular Malaysian comedian, adding moments of comic relief.

8. It was one of the first Malaysian horror films to receive wide international distribution.

9. The film's success led to a trend of "returning home" themed horror movies in Malaysian cinema.

10. Director Ahmad Idham conducted extensive research into local ghost stories to add authenticity to the film.

12. Km 14 (2022)

1. Movie Title: Km 14

2. Year of Release: 2022

3. Cast and Director:

  - Director: Zahir Omar

  - Cast: Datuk Awie, Aqasha, Yaya Zahir, Puteri Rayyana Qistina

4. Synopsis:

  "Km 14" is set around a mysterious stretch of road where numerous accidents and strange occurrences have been reported. The story follows a group of paranormal investigators who decide to explore the area to uncover the truth behind the legends. As they delve deeper into their investigation, they encounter various supernatural entities and uncover a dark history connected to the location. The team must confront their own fears and skepticism as they face increasingly dangerous and terrifying situations, ultimately leading to a shocking revelation about the true nature of Km 14.

5. Why This Movie Is Recommended:

  "Km 14" offers a fresh take on the found footage and paranormal investigation subgenres of horror, adapting them to a uniquely Malaysian context. The film effectively builds tension through its realistic portrayal of a paranormal investigation gone wrong. Its use of local folklore and urban legends adds depth and cultural authenticity to the scares. The movie's exploration of the tension between skepticism and belief in the supernatural reflects broader societal debates in Malaysia. With its blend of traditional and modern horror elements, "Km 14" represents the evolving landscape of Malaysian horror cinema.

6. 10 Trivia Facts:

  1. The film is loosely based on real-life reports of paranormal activities on Malaysian highways.

  2. "Km 14" utilizes a mix of traditional cinematography and found footage style to create a unique visual experience.

  3. The cast underwent paranormal investigation training to prepare for their roles.

  4. Many of the film's locations are actual sites rumored to be haunted in Malaysia.

  5. The movie incorporates several types of Malaysian ghosts, each with its own folklore and backstory.

  6. "Km 14" features cameo appearances from well-known Malaysian paranormal investigators.

  7. The film's marketing campaign included viral videos purporting to show real paranormal encounters on the road.

  8. Director Zahir Omar drew inspiration from both local ghost stories and international found footage horror films.

  9. The movie sparked renewed interest in Malaysian urban legends and haunted locations.

  10. "Km 14" received praise for its sound design, which significantly contributes to the film's atmosphere of dread.

13. Sosok (2023)

1. Movie Title: Sosok (Figure)

2. Year of Release: 2023

3. Cast and Director:

- Director: Hatta Azad Khan

- Cast: Fasha Sandha, Radin Khalid, Omar Abdullah, Anuar Zain

4. Synopsis:

"Sosok" centers around Nadia, a single mother who moves into a new apartment with her young son, Aiman. Soon after settling in, Aiman begins to speak of a mysterious figure he sees in the apartment. Initially dismissing it as her son's imagination, Nadia starts experiencing inexplicable and terrifying events herself. As the haunting intensifies, Nadia discovers that the apartment has a dark history connected to black magic and child sacrifices. With the help of a religious scholar, she must uncover the truth behind the hauntings and protect her son from the malevolent entity that threatens their lives.

5. Why This Movie Is Recommended:

"Sosok" stands out for its focus on the psychological horror of a mother trying to protect her child from supernatural threats. The film effectively builds tension through its claustrophobic apartment setting and the growing sense of isolation felt by the protagonists. Its exploration of themes such as single parenthood and the vulnerability of children adds depth to the horror narrative. The movie blends elements of traditional Malay beliefs with modern urban fears, creating a uniquely Malaysian horror experience. With strong performances and a well-crafted atmosphere of dread, "Sosok" represents the continued evolution of Malaysian horror cinema.

6. 10 Trivia Facts:

1. The title "Sosok" refers to a shadowy or indistinct figure, playing on the fear of the unseen.

2. The film draws inspiration from real-life accounts of hauntings in Malaysian apartment complexes.

3. Director Hatta Azad Khan is also a renowned playwright, bringing a theatrical sensibility to the film's tension.

4. The movie features practical effects for many of its supernatural occurrences, minimizing CGI use.

5. "Sosok" incorporates elements of Malay folk Islam in its depiction of spiritual practices.

6. The film's apartment set was specially constructed to allow for innovative camera angles and movements.

7. Lead actress Fasha Sandha underwent intensive emotional preparation for her demanding role.

8. The movie explores the concept of "jin" (jinn) from Islamic tradition, adapting it to a modern horror context.

9. "Sosok" received praise for its sound design, which significantly enhances the atmosphere of fear.

10. The film's success has led to discussions about a potential sequel or spin-off exploring other aspects of the story's mythology.

14. Tembus (2010)

1. Movie Title: Tembus (Penetrate)

2. Year of Release: 2010

3. Cast and Director:

- Director: Osman Ali

- Cast: Lisa Surihani, Jehan Miskin, Azad Jazmin, Normah Damanhuri

4. Synopsis:

"Tembus" follows the story of Aisyah, a university student who becomes involved in the dangerous world of black magic. After witnessing a friend's death during a failed spiritual ritual, Aisyah finds herself haunted by supernatural forces. As she delves deeper into the occult to understand what's happening to her, she uncovers a dark conspiracy involving her professors and fellow students. The line between reality and the spiritual world blurs as Aisyah races to save herself and her friends from the malevolent entities they've unknowingly unleashed. The film explores themes of curiosity, forbidden knowledge, and the consequences of meddling with forces beyond human understanding.

5. Why This Movie Is Recommended:

"Tembus" offers a unique blend of supernatural horror and campus thriller, setting it apart from typical Malaysian ghost stories. The film's exploration of black magic practices adds a cultural dimension to its scares, while its university setting provides a fresh backdrop for horror. It delves into the tension between traditional beliefs and modern skepticism, reflecting broader societal debates in Malaysia. With its combination of psychological terror and supernatural elements, "Tembus" creates a compelling and unsettling viewing experience that challenges audience expectations of Malaysian horror.

6. 10 Trivia Facts:

1. The word "Tembus" in Malay can mean "penetrate" or "break through," reflecting the film's themes of crossing spiritual boundaries.

2. Director Osman Ali conducted extensive research into Malaysian black magic practices for authenticity.

3. The film features a mix of practical effects and CGI for its supernatural sequences.

4. "Tembus" was shot on location at actual Malaysian universities, adding realism to its setting.

5. The movie sparked discussions about the portrayal of occult practices in Malaysian media.

6. Lead actress Lisa Surihani underwent psychological preparation to portray her character's descent into fear and paranoia.

7. The film incorporates elements of various Malaysian ethnic groups' spiritual beliefs.

8. "Tembus" received praise for its cinematography, particularly in its depiction of supernatural encounters.

9. The movie's success led to increased interest in horror films set in educational institutions.

10. Some of the film's dialogue is in Arabic, reflecting the use of the language in certain Malaysian spiritual practices.

15. Siapa Tutup Lampu (2012)

1. Movie Title: Siapa Tutup Lampu (Who Turned Off the Lights)

2. Year of Release: 2012

3. Cast and Director:

- Director: Jinny Yeo

- Cast: Joseph Germani, Emily Lim, Alvin Wong, Cathryn Lee

4. Synopsis:

"Siapa Tutup Lampu" tells the story of a group of friends who gather for a reunion at an isolated bungalow. What starts as a fun getaway takes a terrifying turn when they decide to play a game called "Who Turned Off the Lights." As they play in the dark, strange and horrifying events begin to unfold. The friends find themselves trapped in the house, hunted by a malevolent presence. As tensions rise and trust erodes, they must uncover the dark secret behind the game and the house's history to survive the night. The film explores themes of friendship, betrayal, and the consequences of youthful recklessness.

5. Why This Movie Is Recommended:

"Siapa Tutup Lampu" stands out for its clever use of the "isolated house" trope, infusing it with distinctly Malaysian elements. The film effectively builds tension through its claustrophobic setting and the dynamics between its characters. Its exploration of urban legends and childhood games adds a layer of nostalgia to the horror. The movie's blend of supernatural scares and psychological tension creates a compelling viewing experience. With its diverse cast and mix of languages, "Siapa Tutup Lampu" reflects the multicultural nature of Malaysian society, offering a unique perspective in the horror genre.

6. 10 Trivia Facts:

1. The film's title refers to a popular children's game in Malaysia, similar to "Hide and Seek."

2. "Siapa Tutup Lampu" was one of the first Malaysian horror films to feature a predominantly Chinese Malaysian cast.

3. The movie was shot in both Malay and Chinese languages to appeal to a wider audience.

4. Director Jinny Yeo drew inspiration from her own childhood experiences playing "ghost games."

5. The film's bungalow setting was constructed specifically for the movie, allowing for controlled lighting and camera movements.

6. "Siapa Tutup Lampu" incorporates elements of Chinese Malaysian folklore and superstitions.

7. The movie received praise for its sound design, which plays a crucial role in creating scares during the darkened scenes.

8. It was one of the first Malaysian horror films to heavily utilize social media in its marketing campaign.

9. The film sparked discussions about the portrayal of different ethnic groups in Malaysian cinema.

10. "Siapa Tutup Lampu" features several Easter eggs referencing classic Asian horror films.

16. Belaban Hidup: Infeksi Zombie (2021)

1. Movie Title: Belaban Hidup: Infeksi Zombie (Fight for Life: Zombie Infection)

2. Year of Release: 2021

3. Cast and Director:

- Director: Ray Lee

- Cast: Cassidy Panggau, Anna Melissa, Pekin Ibrahim, Pablo Amirul

4. Synopsis:

"Belaban Hidup: Infeksi Zombie" is set in the jungles of Sarawak, where a group of villagers must fight for survival against a horde of zombies. The infection spreads rapidly through the remote area, turning people into violent, flesh-eating monsters. The story follows a diverse group of survivors, including indigenous tribespeople and city dwellers, as they band together to escape the zombie threat. As they journey through the treacherous jungle, they must confront not only the undead but also their own fears and prejudices. The film blends elements of traditional Dayak culture with the zombie genre, creating a unique Malaysian take on the apocalyptic horror subgenre.

5. Why This Movie Is Recommended:

"Belaban Hidup" stands out for its innovative blend of zombie horror with Malaysian, specifically Sarawakian, cultural elements. The film's jungle setting provides a fresh and visually striking backdrop for zombie action, differentiating it from urban-centric zombie films. Its exploration of indigenous culture and the clash between traditional and modern ways of life adds depth to the narrative. The movie showcases practical effects and stunt work, delivering intense action sequences alongside its horror elements. As one of Malaysia's first zombie films, "Belaban Hidup" represents an exciting expansion of the country's horror repertoire.

6. 10 Trivia Facts:

1. "Belaban Hidup" is the first zombie movie to be produced in Sarawak, Malaysia.

2. The film incorporates elements of Dayak folklore and traditional weapons in its zombie-fighting scenes.

3. Much of the dialogue is in Sarawak Malay and indigenous languages, with subtitles provided.

4. The movie was shot on location in the jungles of Sarawak, providing authentic and challenging filming conditions.

5. Local martial artists were hired to choreograph and perform fight scenes, incorporating traditional fighting styles.

6. The film's makeup team studied tropical diseases to create realistic and unique zombie designs.

7. "Belaban Hidup" premiered at the New York Asian Film Festival, gaining international recognition.

8. The movie features several Dayak cultural practices and rituals, serving an educational purpose alongside its entertainment value.

9. Director Ray Lee conducted extensive research into both zombie film conventions and Sarawakian culture to create the film's unique blend.

10. The film's success has led to discussions about a potential sequel exploring other parts of Malaysia.

17. Kotaka (2022)

1. Movie Title: Kotaka

2. Year of Release: 2022

3. Cast and Director:

- Director: M. Zamburino

- Cast: Muhammad Zaidi Kachink, Fazlina Borhan, Megat Shahrizal, Asmunni Khan

4. Synopsis:

"Kotaka" tells the story of a family that moves into a new home, only to find themselves tormented by a malevolent spirit. The titular Kotaka is a shape-shifting demon from Malay folklore that preys on children. As the family's young son becomes the target of the Kotaka's attacks, his parents must uncover the dark history of their new home and find a way to protect their child. The film explores themes of parental love, the power of faith, and the dangers of dismissing traditional beliefs. As the Kotaka's attacks intensify, the family must rely on both modern methods and ancient wisdom to survive.

5. Why This Movie Is Recommended:

"Kotaka" stands out for its focus on a lesser-known entity from Malay folklore, providing a fresh antagonist for horror audiences. The film effectively builds tension through its portrayal of a family under supernatural siege, creating a claustrophobic atmosphere. Its exploration of the conflict between modern skepticism and traditional beliefs reflects broader cultural debates in Malaysia. With strong performances and a focus on practical effects, "Kotaka" delivers genuine scares while offering insight into Malay cultural beliefs. The movie's blend of family drama and supernatural horror creates a compelling and emotionally resonant viewing experience.

6. 10 Trivia Facts:

1. The Kotaka is a shape-shifting demon from Malay folklore, often depicted as taking the form of a bird.

2. Director M. Zamburino conducted extensive research into Malay folklore to ensure an authentic portrayal of the Kotaka.

3. The film features practical effects for many of its supernatural sequences, minimizing CGI use.

4. "Kotaka" incorporates elements of traditional Malay architecture in its set design, adding to the cultural authenticity.

5. The movie's sound design draws inspiration from traditional Malay instruments to create its eerie atmosphere.

6. Several scenes in the film reference real-life Malaysian paranormal encounters reported in the media.

7. The cast underwent workshops on Malay folklore and supernatural beliefs to prepare for their roles.

8. "Kotaka" features cameo appearances from well-known Malaysian paranormal investigators and spiritualists.

9. The film's marketing campaign included viral videos purporting to show real Kotaka encounters, building anticipation for the release.

10. "Kotaka" has sparked renewed interest in lesser-known entities from Malay folklore among horror enthusiasts.

18. Anak Perjanjian Syaitan (2023)

1. Movie Title: Anak Perjanjian Syaitan (Child of the Devil's Bargain)

2. Year of Release: 2023

3. Cast and Director:

- Director: Zulkarnain Azhar

- Cast: Zul Ariffin, Hanna Aqeela, Fikry Ibrahim, Lisa Wong

4. Synopsis:

"Anak Perjanjian Syaitan" follows the story of Shamsul, a successful businessman who discovers that his wealth and success are the result of a bargain his parents made with a demon before he was born. As supernatural events begin to plague his life, Shamsul must confront the truth about his origins and the impending price of the infernal contract. With the help of a religious scholar and a medium, he races against time to find a way out of the devil's bargain before it claims his soul. The film explores themes of greed, the consequences of one's actions, and the struggle between faith and temptation.

5. Why This Movie Is Recommended:

"Anak Perjanjian Syaitan" offers a modern take on the classic Faustian bargain, set against the backdrop of contemporary Malaysian society. The film effectively blends elements of psychological horror with supernatural thrills, creating a tense and unsettling atmosphere. Its exploration of moral dilemmas and the conflict between material success and spiritual well-being adds depth to the horror narrative. With strong performances and high production values, the movie delivers both scares and thought-provoking commentary on societal values. "Anak Perjanjian Syaitan" represents the continuing evolution of Malaysian horror, tackling complex themes while delivering genre thrills.

6. 10 Trivia Facts:

1. The film draws inspiration from real-life accounts of "perjanjian syaitan" (devil's bargain) beliefs in Malaysia.

2. Director Zulkarnain Azhar consulted with religious scholars to ensure an accurate portrayal of Islamic concepts related to demons and contracts.

3. The movie features a mix of practical effects and CGI for its supernatural sequences.

4. "Anak Perjanjian Syaitan" incorporates elements of traditional Malay and Islamic exorcism rituals.

5. The film's corporate setting provides commentary on the moral compromises often associated with business success.

6. Several scenes were shot in actual Malaysian corporate offices to add authenticity to the setting.

7. The movie's marketing campaign included interactive elements allowing audiences to "make their own bargain" online.

8. "Anak Perjanjian Syaitan" features cameo appearances from well-known Malaysian business figures, adding to its realism.

9. The film sparked discussions about the portrayal of religious and supernatural themes in Malaysian cinema.

10. Its success has led to talks of a potential prequel exploring the origins of the demonic bargain.

19. Jalinan Khadijah (2023)

1. Movie Title: Jalinan Khadijah (Khadijah's Ties)

2. Year of Release: 2023

3. Cast and Director:

- Director: Kamal G.

- Cast: Amalina Mokhtar, Syafiq Kyle, Gina Noorul Ayn, Hafizuddin Fadzil

4. Synopsis:

"Jalinan Khadijah" tells the story of Khadijah, a young woman who inherits a mysterious keris (traditional Malay dagger) from her grandmother. As she begins to experience strange visions and supernatural occurrences, Khadijah discovers that the keris is a powerful artifact with a dark history. The spirit bound to the keris seeks to use Khadijah to fulfill an ancient vendetta. As she delves deeper into her family's past, Khadijah must confront long-buried secrets and find a way to break the curse before it consumes her. The film explores themes of family legacy, the power of heirlooms, and the enduring impact of historical injustices.

5. Why This Movie Is Recommended:

"Jalinan Khadijah" stands out for its unique focus on the keris, a significant cultural symbol in Malay tradition, as a conduit for horror. The film effectively blends historical elements with contemporary fears, creating a rich and layered narrative. Its exploration of family secrets and generational curses adds emotional depth to the supernatural thrills. With strong performances and atmospheric cinematography, the movie creates a sense of creeping dread that builds to a powerful climax. "Jalinan Khadijah" offers a fresh take on possession narratives, rooted deeply in Malaysian culture and history.

6. 10 Trivia Facts:

1. The film features several authentic antique kerises, each with its own historical significance.

2. Director Kamal G. consulted with keris experts and historians to ensure accurate representation of the artifact's cultural importance.

3. "Jalinan Khadijah" incorporates elements of real historical events from Malaysia's past into its fictional narrative.

4. The movie's possession scenes blend traditional Malay dance movements with horror elements.

5. Several scenes were shot in historical locations around Malaysia, adding authenticity to the film's backstory.

6. The film's soundtrack incorporates traditional Malay instruments to enhance its cultural atmosphere.

7. "Jalinan Khadijah" features cameo appearances from renowned Malaysian martial artists skilled in traditional weapon use.

8. The movie's marketing campaign included educational content about the history and significance of the keris in Malay culture.

9. Some of the film's dialogue is in old Malay dialects, requiring subtitles even for native speakers.

10. The success of "Jalinan Khadijah" has sparked renewed interest in films exploring traditional Malay artifacts and their legends.

20. Cerita Hantu Tanah Melayu (2022)

1. **Movie Title**: Cerita Hantu Tanah Melayu (Ghost Stories of the Malay Lands)

2. **Year of Release**: 2022

3. **Cast and Director**:

   - Director: Various (Anthology film)

   - Cast: Bront Palarae, Sharifah Amani, Azman Hassan, Sharifah Sakinah

4. **Synopsis**:

   "Cerita Hantu Tanah Melayu" is an anthology film featuring five short horror stories, each based on a different Malaysian ghost or supernatural entity. The segments explore various aspects of Malaysian folklore, from the famous Pontianak to lesser-known entities like the Penanggal and Orang Minyak. Each story is set in a different part of Malaysia, showcasing the country's diverse landscapes and cultures. The anthology format allows for a range of horror styles, from psychological terror to more visceral scares, all rooted in distinctly Malaysian contexts and beliefs.

5. **Why This Movie Is Recommended**:

   This anthology film offers a comprehensive tour of Malaysian supernatural folklore, making it an excellent introduction to the country's horror traditions. The variety of stories and styles keeps the viewing experience fresh and engaging, while the consistent cultural context provides depth and authenticity. By featuring both well-known and obscure entities, "Cerita Hantu Tanah Melayu" offers something for both newcomers and aficionados of Malaysian horror. The film's high production values and talented cast elevate it above typical anthology fare, delivering a polished and scary experience that showcases the best of contemporary Malaysian horror cinema.

6. **10 Trivia Facts**:

   1. Each segment of the film was directed by a different Malaysian filmmaker, showcasing a range of styles and perspectives.

   2. The movie features dialogue in multiple Malaysian languages, including Malay, Chinese dialects, and indigenous languages.

   3. Real locations rumored to be haunted were used for some of the film's shooting.

   4. "Cerita Hantu Tanah Melayu" incorporates animation in one of its segments, a first for Malaysian horror anthologies.

   5. The film's wraparound story is based on the real-life practice of storytelling during Malay funeral wakes.

   6. Each segment ends with brief historical and cultural context about the featured supernatural entity.

   7. The movie's marketing campaign included a nationwide ghost story contest, with the winning entry inspiring a bonus short film.

   8. Several prominent Malaysian authors of horror fiction served as consultants for the film's scripts.

   9. The anthology format allowed the filmmakers to explore some controversial themes that might be challenging in a full-length feature.

   10. "Cerita Hantu Tanah Melayu" has been used in some Malaysian schools as a tool for teaching about local folklore and culture.

Indonesia

1. Pengabdi Setan (Satan's Slaves)

1. Movie Title: Pengabdi Setan (Satan's Slaves)

2. Year of Release: 2017

3. Cast and Director:

- Director: Joko Anwar

- Cast: Tara Basro, Bront Palarae, Endy Arfian, Dimas Aditya

4. Synopsis:

Set in 1981, the film follows a family struggling with the declining health of their mother, a once-famous singer. After her death, strange and terrifying events begin to plague the family. The children soon realize that their mother has returned to fulfill a dark pact made years ago. As the supernatural occurrences intensify, they must uncover the truth about their family's past and confront an evil that threatens to claim them all. The movie blends traditional Indonesian folklore with modern horror techniques, creating a deeply unsettling atmosphere that builds to a chilling climax.

5. Why This Movie Is Recommended:

Pengabdi Setan is a masterful reimagining of the 1980 Indonesian cult classic of the same name. Director Joko Anwar expertly crafts a atmospheric horror that pays homage to classic ghost stories while feeling thoroughly modern. The film's strong emphasis on family dynamics and generational trauma adds emotional depth to its scares. With its stunning cinematography, excellent performances, and genuinely terrifying moments, Pengabdi Setan revitalized the Indonesian horror genre and gained international acclaim, making it a must-watch for horror fans worldwide.

6. 10 Trivia Facts:

1. The film is a remake of a 1980 Indonesian horror movie of the same name.

2. It became the highest-grossing Indonesian horror film of all time upon its release.

3. Director Joko Anwar wrote the script in just two weeks.

4. The movie was shot in only 18 days.

5. A real abandoned house was used for many of the film's scenes.

6. The film's success led to a sequel, "Satan's Slaves: Communion" (2022).

7. Joko Anwar included several Easter eggs referencing the original 1980 film.

8. The movie was Indonesia's submission for the Best Foreign Language Film at the 91st Academy Awards.

9. Many of the child actors were first-time performers.

10. The film's soundtrack, composed by Ago Tara Tara, incorporates traditional Indonesian instruments.

2. Impetigore

1. Movie Title: Impetigore (Perempuan Tanah Jahanam)

2. Year of Release: 2019

3. Cast and Director:

  - Director: Joko Anwar

  - Cast: Tara Basro, Marissa Anita, Christine Hakim, Ario Bayu

4. Synopsis:

  Maya, a young woman struggling to make ends meet, discovers she may have inherited a house in her ancestral village. Accompanied by her best friend Dini, she travels to the remote village to claim her inheritance. However, upon arrival, they find the village shrouded in dark secrets and superstitions. As Maya delves deeper into her family's history, she uncovers a curse that has plagued the village for generations. The locals believe Maya's return might be the key to breaking the curse, but at a terrible cost. Maya must confront the horrors of her past and the village's sinister practices to survive.

5. Why This Movie Is Recommended:

  Impetigore is a masterclass in atmospheric horror, blending Indonesian folklore with modern storytelling techniques. Joko Anwar's direction creates a palpable sense of dread that permeates every frame. The film's exploration of generational trauma and the dark side of tradition adds depth to its horror elements. With its stunning visuals, intricate plot, and strong performances, Impetigore offers a unique and terrifying glimpse into rural Indonesian myths and superstitions. It's a must-see for fans of folk horror and those seeking a fresh perspective in the genre.

6. 10 Trivia Facts:

  1. The film's Indonesian title, "Perempuan Tanah Jahanam," translates to "Woman of the Damned Land."

  2. Impetigore was selected as Indonesia's entry for Best International Feature Film at the 93rd Academy Awards.

  3. The movie was partially inspired by Joko Anwar's childhood experiences in North Sumatra.

  4. Many scenes were shot in the ancient Javanese city of Kotagede.

  5. The film features traditional Javanese shadow puppetry (wayang kulit) as a key plot element.

  6. Impetigore premiered at the 2020 Sundance Film Festival.

  7. The movie's sound design incorporates traditional Indonesian instruments to enhance the eerie atmosphere.

  8. Joko Anwar wrote the script in just 10 days.

  9. The film's success led to discussions about a potential Hollywood remake.

  10. Several actors had to learn the Javanese language for their roles in the film.

3. May the Devil Take You

1. Movie Title: May the Devil Take You (Sebelum Iblis Menjemput)

2. Year of Release: 2018

3. Cast and Director:

- Director: Timo Tjahjanto

- Cast: Chelsea Islan, Pevita Pearce, Ray Sahetapy, Karina Suwandi

4. Synopsis:

The film follows Alfie, a young woman who reunites with her estranged family when her wealthy father falls into a mysterious coma. As Alfie and her half-siblings gather at their father's long-abandoned villa, they discover he had made a sinister pact with a demonic entity years ago. Now, as the demon comes to collect its due, the family finds themselves trapped in a nightmarish struggle for survival. Alfie must confront not only the malevolent force that threatens them but also the dark secrets of her family's past. As the horror escalates, the line between the living and the dead blurs, and Alfie realizes that escaping the villa might be impossible.

5. Why This Movie Is Recommended:

May the Devil Take You is a relentless, adrenaline-fueled horror experience that pays homage to classic Evil Dead-style films while maintaining its own unique identity. Director Timo Tjahjanto's background in action films is evident in the movie's kinetic energy and intense set pieces. The film doesn't shy away from graphic violence and disturbing imagery, making it a treat for hardcore horror fans. With its blend of supernatural horror, family drama, and Indonesian folklore, May the Devil Take You offers a fresh and terrifying take on the possession subgenre.

6. 10 Trivia Facts:

1. The film is sometimes referred to as "Indonesia's Evil Dead" due to its similarities to Sam Raimi's classic.

2. Director Timo Tjahjanto is known for his work in the action genre, making this his first full-length horror film.

3. The movie was shot in just 24 days.

4. Many of the practical effects were inspired by 1980s horror films.

5. The film's success led to a sequel, "May the Devil Take You Too," released in 2020.

6. Tjahjanto incorporated elements of Indonesian black magic into the film's mythology.

7. The director insisted on using practical effects whenever possible, limiting CGI use.

8. Lead actress Chelsea Islan performed many of her own stunts.

9. The film premiered at the 2018 Sitges Film Festival in Spain.

10. Tjahjanto wrote the script in just two weeks.

4. Ritual (Modus Anomali)

1. Movie Title: Ritual (Modus Anomali)

2. Year of Release: 2012

3. Cast and Director:

 - Director: Joko Anwar

 - Cast: Rio Dewanto, Hannah Al Rashid, Izzi Isman, Aridh Tritama

4. Synopsis:

 Ritual begins with a man waking up buried alive in a forest, with no memory of who he is or how he got there. As he frantically searches for answers, he discovers clues suggesting his family is in danger. The man races against time to piece together his identity and save his loved ones from an unknown threat. However, as he delves deeper into the mystery, he uncovers a twisted web of deceit and violence that challenges his perception of reality. The film takes unexpected turns, blurring the lines between victim and perpetrator, as the protagonist grapples with the horrifying truth of his situation.

5. Why This Movie Is Recommended:

 Ritual is a mind-bending psychological thriller that keeps viewers guessing until the very end. Joko Anwar's clever direction and non-linear storytelling create a puzzle-box narrative that rewards close attention and multiple viewings. The film's isolated forest setting adds to the claustrophobic atmosphere, enhancing the sense of disorientation and dread. With its smart script, strong performances, and shocking twists, Ritual offers a unique and challenging experience for fans of psychological horror and mind-bending thrillers.

6. 10 Trivia Facts:

 1. The film's English title, "Ritual," differs significantly from its Indonesian title, "Modus Anomali," which means "Anomaly Mode."

 2. Director Joko Anwar wrote the script in just three days.

 3. The entire movie was shot in sequence, which is unusual for film production.

 4. Ritual was filmed in a forest in Bogor, West Java, over 18 days.

 5. The film premiered at the 2012 South by Southwest (SXSW) Film Festival.

 6. Joko Anwar used a mix of handheld and steady cam shots to create the film's disorienting effect.

 7. The movie features minimal dialogue, relying heavily on visual storytelling.

 8. Ritual was Joko Anwar's first film to gain significant international attention.

 9. The director cited Christopher Nolan's "Memento" as an inspiration for the film's narrative structure.

 10. Despite its low budget, the film received praise for its high production values and creative use of resources.

5. Kuntilanak (The Chanting)

1. Movie Title: Kuntilanak (The Chanting)

2. Year of Release: 2006

3. Cast and Director:

- Director: Rizal Mantovani

- Cast: Julie Estelle, Evan Sanders, Natasya Nauva, Reza Pahlevi

4. Synopsis:

Kuntilanak follows a group of young adults who decide to participate in a reality show set in a supposedly haunted house. The house is said to be inhabited by a Kuntilanak, a female vampiric ghost from Indonesian mythology. As the contestants spend time in the house, they begin to experience increasingly terrifying supernatural occurrences. They soon realize that the Kuntilanak is real and that their presence has awakened her. The group must fight for survival while uncovering the dark history of the house and the origins of the vengeful spirit. As tensions rise and the body count increases, the line between reality show and genuine horror becomes frighteningly blurred.

5. Why This Movie Is Recommended:

Kuntilanak stands out for its effective blend of traditional Indonesian folklore and modern horror tropes. Director Rizal Mantovani creates a tense atmosphere that builds steadily throughout the film, punctuated by well-executed scares. The movie's use of the reality show concept adds an interesting meta-layer to the narrative, commenting on the exploitation of local superstitions for entertainment. With its strong performances, creepy set design, and genuinely frightening depiction of the Kuntilanak, the film offers a uniquely Indonesian take on the haunted house subgenre that horror fans will appreciate.

6. 10 Trivia Facts:

1. The Kuntilanak is a well-known figure in Indonesian and Malaysian folklore, often described as the spirit of a woman who died during pregnancy.

2. The film spawned two sequels, forming a trilogy.

3. Julie Estelle, who plays the lead role, later gained international recognition for her role in "The Raid 2."

4. The movie was one of the first Indonesian horror films to gain widespread popularity in the 2000s.

5. Director Rizal Mantovani has a background in music video direction, which influenced the film's visual style.

6. The film's success helped revitalize the Indonesian horror genre.

7. Many of the scare scenes were shot in a single take to maintain tension.

8. The movie uses a mix of practical effects and CGI for its supernatural elements.

9. Kuntilanak was remade in 2018 with a new cast and updated effects.

10. The film's portrayal of the Kuntilanak became influential in subsequent Indonesian horror movies featuring the same spirit.

6. Rumah Dara (Macabre)

1. Movie Title: Rumah Dara (Macabre)

2. Year of Release: 2009

3. Cast and Director:

 - Directors: Kimo Stamboel, Timo Tjahjanto (The Mo Brothers)

 - Cast: Shareefa Daanish, Julie Estelle, Ario Bayu, Sigi Wimala

4. Synopsis:

 Rumah Dara follows a group of friends who, while on a road trip, encounter a stranded young woman named Maya. They offer to give her a ride home, but upon arriving at her isolated house, they meet her peculiar family led by the matriarch, Dara. What begins as an awkward dinner soon descends into a nightmarish fight for survival as the friends discover that Dara and her children are cannibals with a taste for human flesh. Trapped in the house of horrors, the group must battle their way out, facing unimaginable violence and brutality at every turn. As the night progresses, dark secrets about Dara's family and their horrific practices come to light.

5. Why This Movie Is Recommended:

 Rumah Dara is a relentless, visceral experience that pushes the boundaries of Indonesian horror cinema. The Mo Brothers' direction creates an intense, claustrophobic atmosphere that rarely lets up. While the film doesn't shy away from graphic violence, it balances shock value with genuine suspense and character development. The movie's exploration of family dynamics, albeit twisted ones, adds depth to the carnage. With its well-choreographed action sequences, practical effects, and committed performances, Rumah Dara offers a unique blend of horror and action that will satisfy fans of extreme cinema.

6. 10 Trivia Facts:

 1. The film was originally titled "Darah" (Blood) but was changed to avoid confusion with another movie.

 2. Rumah Dara was the debut feature film for directing duo The Mo Brothers.

 3. The movie gained international attention after screening at various film festivals, including the Toronto International Film Festival.

 4. It was picked up for distribution by Overlook Entertainment, owned by Takashi Miike, a renowned Japanese director known for extreme cinema.

 5. The film's violence was so intense that it faced censorship issues in several countries.

 6. Shareefa Daanish, who plays Dara, underwent extensive makeup sessions daily for her role.

 7. The directors cited "The Texas Chain Saw Massacre" as a major influence on the film.

 8. Many of the gory scenes used practical effects rather than CGI.

 9. The movie was shot in just 18 days.

 10. Rumah Dara has gained a cult following and is often cited as one of the most extreme Asian horror films of its time.

7. Danur: I Can See Ghosts

1. Movie Title: Danur: I Can See Ghosts

2. Year of Release: 2017

3. Cast and Director:

- Director: Awi Suryadi

- Cast: Prilly Latuconsina, Shareefa Daanish, Wesley Andrew, Bianca Hello

4. Synopsis:

Danur is based on Risa Saraswati's novel and follows the story of Risa, a young girl with the ability to see ghosts. On her 8th birthday, feeling lonely, she wishes for friends, unknowingly inviting three ghost children into her life. Years later, as a teenager, Risa's supernatural abilities intensify, causing distress to her family. When her younger sister becomes possessed, Risa must confront the dark entities that threaten her family while also protecting her ghostly friends. The film explores themes of friendship, family, and the blurred lines between the world of the living and the dead, all through the eyes of a girl caught between two realms.

5. Why This Movie Is Recommended:

Danur stands out for its blend of supernatural horror and coming-of-age drama. The film's approach to ghost stories is refreshingly nuanced, presenting spirits as complex characters rather than mere scare devices. Director Awi Suryadi creates a haunting atmosphere that balances creepy moments with emotional depth. The strong performance by Prilly Latuconsina anchors the film, making Risa's struggles relatable despite the supernatural elements. With its exploration of Indonesian ghost lore and its emphasis on character development, Danur offers a unique and engaging entry in the paranormal genre.

6. 10 Trivia Facts:

1. The film is based on Risa Saraswati's autobiographical novel of the same name.

2. Danur broke box office records for Indonesian horror films upon its release.

3. The movie spawned two sequels, forming a trilogy.

4. Many of the ghost characters are based on spirits Risa Saraswati claims to have encountered in real life.

5. The film incorporates elements of Dutch colonial history in Indonesia.

6. Prilly Latuconsina, who plays Risa, was already a well-known actress and singer in Indonesia before this role.

7. The movie's success led to a spin-off film focused on one of the ghost characters.

8. Director Awi Suryadi used a mix of practical effects and CGI to create the film's ghostly appearances.

9. The term "Danur" refers to the liquid that comes out of a decomposing corpse in Javanese culture.

10. The film's approach to ghosts was influenced by Indonesian spiritual beliefs about the afterlife.

8. Pocong the Origin

1. Movie Title: Pocong the Origin

2. Year of Release: 2019

3. Cast and Director:

  - Director: Monty Tiwa

  - Cast: Nadine Alexandra, Wafda Saifan Lubis, Voke Victoria, Jefri Nichol

4. Synopsis:

  Pocong the Origin delves into the folklore surrounding the Pocong, a shrouded ghost from Indonesian mythology. The story follows Ananta, a medical student who becomes entangled in a series of mysterious deaths in her hometown. As she investigates, she uncovers a dark history involving black magic and vengeful spirits. The film explores the origin of the Pocong, tracing it back to ancient burial rituals and curses. Ananta must confront her own skepticism about the supernatural as she races to stop the Pocong's reign of terror. Along the way, she discovers unsettling truths about her own family's connection to the malevolent entity.

5. Why This Movie Is Recommended:

  Pocong the Origin offers a fresh take on one of Indonesia's most iconic supernatural entities. Director Monty Tiwa skillfully blends elements of mystery, horror, and local folklore to create a compelling narrative. The film's exploration of the Pocong's mythology adds depth to the scares, appealing to both horror fans and those interested in cultural lore. With its atmospheric cinematography, strong performances, and clever plot twists, Pocong the Origin elevates the typical ghost story into a thought-provoking exploration of tradition, science, and the supernatural.

6. 10 Trivia Facts:

  1. The Pocong is a traditional Indonesian ghost, believed to be the soul of a dead person trapped in its burial shroud.

  2. This film was one of the first to explore the origin story of the Pocong in depth.

  3. The movie incorporates authentic Indonesian funeral rites and customs.

  4. Director Monty Tiwa is known for his work in various genres, making this his first major foray into horror.

  5. The film uses a mix of practical effects and CGI to bring the Pocong to life.

  6. Pocong the Origin was part of a trend of Indonesian films reimagining traditional folklore for modern audiences.

  7. The movie features several scenes shot in actual Indonesian cemeteries.

  8. The filmmakers consulted with cultural experts to ensure accurate representation of burial customs.

  9. The film's success led to discussions about a potential sequel or series.

  10. Some of the cast reported strange occurrences on set, adding to the movie's mystique.

9. The Queen of Black Magic (Ratu Ilmu Hitam)

1. Movie Title: The Queen of Black Magic (Ratu Ilmu Hitam)

2. Year of Release: 2019

3. Cast and Director:

 - Director: Kimo Stamboel

 - Cast: Ario Bayu, Hannah Al Rashid, Adhisty Zara, Ari Irham

4. Synopsis:

The Queen of Black Magic, a reimagining of the 1981 Indonesian horror classic, follows a group of adults who return to the orphanage where they grew up to pay respects to the man who raised them. Accompanied by their families, they find the once-familiar place changed and unsettling. As night falls, terrifying events begin to unfold, forcing them to confront the dark secrets of their past and the orphanage's history. A vengeful presence, linked to a horrific incident from years ago, seeks retribution. The group must fight for survival against increasingly grotesque and supernatural threats while uncovering the truth about the titular Queen of Black Magic and their own complicity in past sins.

5. Why This Movie Is Recommended:

The Queen of Black Magic is a tour de force of modern Indonesian horror. Director Kimo Stamboel crafts a relentless, visceral experience that pays homage to the original while standing firmly on its own. The film expertly balances supernatural scares with body horror, creating genuinely unsettling moments. Its exploration of guilt, repressed memories, and the cyclical nature of abuse adds psychological depth to the terror. With its strong ensemble cast, striking visuals, and unflinching approach to horror, The Queen of Black Magic offers a intense, thought-provoking experience that lingers long after viewing.

6. 10 Trivia Facts:

 1. The film is a reimagining of the 1981 Indonesian horror classic of the same name.

 2. Joko Anwar, director of "Satan's Slaves," wrote the screenplay for this remake.

 3. The movie was produced by Rapi Films, the same studio behind the original 1981 version.

 4. Many of the practical effects were inspired by old-school horror techniques.

 5. The film premiered at the 2019 Sitges Film Festival in Spain.

 6. Director Kimo Stamboel is one half of the Mo Brothers directing duo, known for "Macabre."

 7. The movie incorporates elements of traditional Indonesian black magic beliefs.

 8. Some scenes were so intense that they reportedly caused audience members to faint during screenings.

 9. The film's success has sparked interest in remaking other classic Indonesian horror movies.

 10. Despite its supernatural elements, much of the horror in the film stems from human cruelty.

10. Sunyi (The Silence)

1. Movie Title: Sunyi (The Silence)

2. Year of Release: 2019

3. Cast and Director:

- Director: Ody C. Harahap

- Cast: Angga Yunanda, Amanda Rawles, Arya Vasco, Elina Joerg

4. Synopsis:

Sunyi follows Alex, a gifted pianist who enrolls in an elite music school. As he struggles to fit in and deal with the pressures of his new environment, Alex begins to experience strange and terrifying occurrences. He discovers that the school harbors dark secrets, including the tragic story of a student who died years ago. As Alex delves deeper into the mystery, he realizes that his own musical ability may be connected to the supernatural events plaguing the school. With the help of his new friends, Alex must uncover the truth behind the hauntings while confronting his own inner demons and the malevolent force that threatens to consume the school.

5. Why This Movie Is Recommended:

Sunyi offers a fresh take on the haunted school subgenre by blending it with musical elements. Director Ody C. Harahap creates a tense atmosphere that builds slowly, allowing for character development alongside the scares. The film's exploration of artistic pressure and the price of talent adds depth to its supernatural plot. With its atmospheric cinematography, strong performances from its young cast, and clever use of sound design, Sunyi delivers a unique horror experience. The movie's ability to balance teenage drama with genuine frights makes it appealing to both horror fans and wider audiences.

6. 10 Trivia Facts:

1. The film is loosely inspired by the 2006 South Korean horror movie "The Wig."

2. Sunyi incorporates classical music as a key element of its plot and atmosphere.

3. The movie was shot on location in an actual Indonesian boarding school.

4. Director Ody C. Harahap has a background in romantic comedies, making this his first major horror film.

5. The film's title, "Sunyi," means "silence" in Indonesian, reflecting the movie's themes and atmosphere.

6. Many of the cast members had to learn to play musical instruments for their roles.

7. The movie features several original musical compositions created specifically for the film.

8. Sunyi was part of a wave of Indonesian horror films targeting younger audiences.

9. The film incorporates elements of Indonesian ghost folklore into its narrative.

10. Some of the piano scenes were performed by a professional pianist and then matched to the actors' movements.

11. Grave Torture (Siksaan Kubur)

1. Movie Title: Grave Torture (Siksaan Kubur)

2. Year of Release: 2004

3. Cast and Director:

- Director: Nayato Fio Nuala

- Cast: Nafa Urbach, Marcella Zalianty, Rif'at Umar, Didi Petet

4. Synopsis:

Grave Torture explores the terrifying consequences of black magic and the thin line between life and death. The story follows Nisa, a young woman who becomes entangled in a web of supernatural horror after her sister's mysterious death. As Nisa investigates, she uncovers a dark cult practicing necromancy and grave desecration. The cult's rituals have awakened malevolent spirits that now threaten the living. Nisa must confront these otherworldly forces and the cult members to save herself and prevent further deaths. The film delves into Indonesian beliefs about the afterlife and the perils of disturbing the dead, creating a chilling narrative that blends cultural folklore with modern horror elements.

5. Why This Movie Is Recommended:

Grave Torture stands out for its unflinching exploration of Indonesian black magic practices and beliefs about the afterlife. Director Nayato Fio Nuala crafts a visceral horror experience that doesn't shy away from graphic imagery while maintaining a strong narrative focus. The film's atmospheric use of cemetery locations and practical effects creates a palpable sense of dread. With its blend of supernatural horror and cult themes, Grave Torture offers a unique glimpse into Indonesian horror traditions that will intrigue genre fans looking for culturally specific scares.

6. 10 Trivia Facts:

1. The film is considered one of the pioneers of the modern Indonesian horror revival in the early 2000s.

2. Many scenes were shot in actual Indonesian cemeteries, adding to the film's authenticity and atmosphere.

3. The movie incorporates real Indonesian funeral rites and superstitions into its plot.

4. Grave Torture faced some censorship issues due to its graphic content and religious themes.

5. The film's success spawned several unofficial sequels and imitators in the Indonesian film industry.

6. Director Nayato Fio Nuala consulted with practitioners of traditional Indonesian mysticism for the film.

7. Some cast and crew reported strange occurrences during the cemetery shoots, adding to the film's lore.

8. The movie features practical effects for many of its gruesome scenes, a rarity in early 2000s Indonesian cinema.

9. Grave Torture's exploration of necromancy was considered controversial upon its release.

10. The film has gained a cult following and is often cited as an influence by newer Indonesian horror directors.

12. Jelangkung

1. Movie Title: Jelangkung

2. Year of Release: 2001

3. Cast and Director:

- Directors: Rizal Mantovani, Jose Purnomo

- Cast: Winky Wiryawan, Melanie Aryanto, Harry Pantja, Rony Dozer

4. Synopsis:

Jelangkung follows a group of college students who decide to investigate supernatural occurrences for their campus TV show. They focus on the Jelangkung, a traditional Indonesian spirit-calling ritual similar to a Ouija board. As they perform the ritual in various haunted locations, they unknowingly unleash malevolent spirits. What begins as an exciting project soon turns into a fight for survival as the group is pursued by the vengeful ghosts they've awakened. The students must find a way to end the curse before it claims all their lives. The film explores themes of skepticism versus belief, the dangers of meddling with the unknown, and the power of Indonesian folklore.

5. Why This Movie Is Recommended:

Jelangkung is a landmark film in Indonesian horror cinema, helping to revitalize the genre in the early 2000s. Directors Rizal Mantovani and Jose Purnomo skillfully blend found footage elements with traditional narrative storytelling, creating a unique and immersive horror experience. The film's use of the Jelangkung ritual provides a culturally specific framing device that sets it apart from Western horror tropes. With its mix of jumpscares, atmospheric dread, and exploration of Indonesian supernatural beliefs, Jelangkung offers both local authenticity and universal horror appeal.

6. 10 Trivia Facts:

1. Jelangkung was one of the first Indonesian horror films to use found footage elements, predating many Western examples of the technique.

2. The movie was a massive box office success in Indonesia, breaking local records at the time.

3. The Jelangkung ritual depicted in the film is a real practice in Indonesian culture.

4. The success of Jelangkung led to a resurgence of horror film production in Indonesia.

5. Some of the film's locations were reportedly actually haunted, adding to the authenticity of the cast's performances.

6. The movie spawned several sequels and inspired many imitations in Indonesian cinema.

7. Jelangkung was one of the first Indonesian horror films to gain significant attention in international film festivals.

8. The directors incorporated real Indonesian urban legends and ghost stories into the film's narrative.

9. Despite its low budget, the film's creative use of sound design and practical effects created genuinely scary moments.

10. Jelangkung is often credited with popularizing the use of traditional Indonesian folklore in modern horror films.

13. Keramat (Sacred)

1. Movie Title: Keramat (Sacred)

2. Year of Release: 2009

3. Cast and Director:

  - Director: Monty Tiwa

  - Cast: Poppy Sovia, Fanny Fabriana, Gading Marten, Restu Sinaga

4. Synopsis:

Keramat follows a reality TV crew as they set out to film a survival show on a remote, uninhabited island. As they begin their production, strange and terrifying events start to occur. The crew discovers that the island is home to an ancient, malevolent presence that doesn't welcome intruders. As members of the team start to disappear or die under mysterious circumstances, the survivors must confront the island's dark history and the supernatural forces that inhabit it. The line between reality and fiction blurs as the crew's cameras capture their desperate fight for survival against an unseen enemy.

5. Why This Movie Is Recommended:

Keramat stands out for its innovative blend of found footage horror and reality TV satire. Director Monty Tiwa creates a tense, claustrophobic atmosphere that makes excellent use of the island setting. The film's meta-commentary on the exploitation of local superstitions for entertainment adds depth to the scares. With its mix of psychological horror and supernatural elements, Keramat offers a unique take on the found footage subgenre. The movie's exploration of Indonesian myths and its critique of media sensationalism make it both entertaining and thought-provoking.

6. 10 Trivia Facts:

  1. Keramat was one of the first Indonesian films to fully commit to the found footage format.

  2. The movie was shot guerrilla-style on a real Indonesian island to maintain authenticity.

  3. Many of the cast members operated their own cameras during filming.

  4. The film's title, "Keramat," refers to sacred or supernatural places in Indonesian culture.

  5. Keramat was partly inspired by the rise of extreme reality TV shows in the early 2000s.

  6. The movie incorporates elements of real Indonesian island folklore and superstitions.

  7. Some of the crew's reactions in the film were genuine, as the directors didn't always warn them about planned scares.

  8. Keramat's success led to a trend of reality TV-themed horror films in Indonesia.

  9. The film uses a mix of handheld cameras and "security footage" to create its found footage aesthetic.

  10. Director Monty Tiwa interviewed actual reality TV producers to add authenticity to the film's premise.

14. Midnight Show

1. Movie Title: Midnight Show

2. Year of Release: 2016

3. Cast and Director:

- Director: Ginanti Rona Tembang Asri

- Cast: Tio Pakusadewo, Ganindra Bimo, Reza Nangin, Ratnakala Juwita

4. Synopsis:

Midnight Show is set in an old cinema during a special midnight screening of a controversial horror film. As the small audience watches the movie, they begin to notice strange occurrences both on and off the screen. The line between fiction and reality blurs as events from the film seem to manifest in the theater. The patrons soon find themselves trapped in the cinema, facing terrifying supernatural forces. As they struggle to survive the night, dark secrets about the cinema's history and the mysterious film come to light. The group must confront both external horrors and their own personal demons to make it to dawn.

5. Why This Movie Is Recommended:

Midnight Show offers a clever and meta take on the horror genre, playing with the concept of cinema itself as a source of terror. Director Ginanti Rona Tembang Asri creates a claustrophobic atmosphere within the theater setting, building tension through both psychological and supernatural means. The film's exploration of the power of storytelling and the blurred lines between fiction and reality adds depth to its scares. With its mix of slasher elements, supernatural horror, and psychological thriller, Midnight Show provides a unique and engaging experience for horror fans, especially those who appreciate meta-commentary on the genre.

6. 10 Trivia Facts:

1. The film within the film was created specifically for Midnight Show, adding an extra layer of production to the movie.

2. Most of the movie was shot in a real, abandoned cinema in Jakarta.

3. The director drew inspiration from classic horror films that use cinema as a setting, like "Demons" (1985).

4. Midnight Show incorporates elements of Indonesian urban legends about haunted theaters.

5. The film's score uses distorted versions of classic Indonesian film themes to create an unsettling atmosphere.

6. Some scenes were shot using vintage film cameras to add authenticity to the "film within a film" segments.

7. The movie premiered at an actual midnight screening, mirroring its plot.

8. Midnight Show sparked discussions about the state of Indonesian cinema and the horror genre.

9. The film features several cameos from well-known Indonesian film critics and horror directors.

10. The director incorporated real audience reactions to horror films into the screenplay to enhance authenticity.

15. Belenggu (Shackled)

1. Movie Title: Belenggu (Shackled)

2. Year of Release: 2012

3. Cast and Director:

 - Director: Upi Avianto

 - Cast: Abimana Aryasatya, Laudya Cynthia Bella, Verdi Solaiman, Imelda Therinne

4. Synopsis:

 Belenggu follows Elang, a man plagued by recurring nightmares and hallucinations. His grip on reality begins to slip as he becomes obsessed with a mysterious woman who appears in his dreams. As Elang investigates the source of his visions, he uncovers a series of gruesome murders that seem connected to his past. The line between dream and reality blurs as Elang delves deeper into the mystery, uncovering repressed memories and confronting a malevolent force that has haunted him since childhood. The film explores themes of guilt, trauma, and the lasting impact of violence, all wrapped in a psychological horror narrative.

5. Why This Movie Is Recommended:

 Belenggu stands out for its psychological depth and surreal atmosphere. Director Upi Avianto crafts a complex narrative that keeps viewers guessing until the very end. The film's non-linear storytelling and dreamlike sequences create a disorienting experience that mirrors the protagonist's fractured psyche. With its exploration of trauma and memory, Belenggu offers more than just surface-level scares, delving into the horror of the human mind. The strong performance by Abimana Aryasatya anchors the film, guiding viewers through its twisted narrative. For fans of psychological horror and mind-bending thrillers, Belenggu provides a unique and challenging viewing experience.

6. 10 Trivia Facts:

 1. The film's title, "Belenggu," means "shackles" or "chains" in Indonesian, reflecting the protagonist's psychological state.

 2. Director Upi Avianto wrote the script based on a recurring nightmare she experienced.

 3. Belenggu was praised for its artistic cinematography, which was unusual for Indonesian horror films at the time.

 4. The movie draws inspiration from psychological thrillers like "Jacob's Ladder" and the works of David Lynch.

 5. Many of the film's surreal sequences were achieved through practical effects rather than CGI.

 6. Belenggu was one of the first Indonesian horror films to gain significant critical acclaim internationally.

 7. The director used color grading extensively to differentiate between reality and hallucination scenes.

 8. Some of the more intense scenes reportedly caused audience members to leave theaters during initial screenings.

 9. The film's success helped establish Abimana Aryasatya as a leading actor in Indonesian cinema.

 10. Belenggu's narrative structure was so complex that the director provided the cast with detailed character backgrounds and timelines to help them understand their roles.

16. Kuntilanak 2

1. Movie Title: Kuntilanak 2

2. Year of Release: 2007

3. Cast and Director:

- Director: Rizal Mantovani

- Cast: Julie Estelle, Natacha Eleonora, Iván Fadilla, Ratu Felisha

4. Synopsis:

Kuntilanak 2 continues the story from its predecessor, following Julie, who has the ability to see spirits. In this installment, Julie and her friends visit an old house that is rumored to be haunted by a Kuntilanak, a female vampiric ghost from Indonesian mythology. As they explore the house's dark history, they unwittingly awaken the malevolent spirit. The Kuntilanak begins to target them one by one, feeding on their fears and weaknesses. Julie must use her supernatural abilities to uncover the truth behind the Kuntilanak's origin and find a way to stop it before it claims all their lives. The film delves deeper into the folklore surrounding the Kuntilanak, exploring its motivations and weaknesses.

5. Why This Movie Is Recommended:

Kuntilanak 2 builds upon the success of its predecessor, offering a deeper exploration of Indonesian ghost lore. Director Rizal Mantovani crafts a more intense and atmospheric experience, balancing jump scares with psychological horror. The film's strong emphasis on character development allows viewers to become more invested in the protagonists' fates. With its improved special effects and a more complex narrative, Kuntilanak 2 elevates the franchise, offering both fans of the original and newcomers a compelling horror experience. The movie's blend of traditional folklore and modern storytelling techniques makes it a standout in Indonesian horror cinema.

6. 10 Trivia Facts:

1. Kuntilanak 2 was shot back-to-back with Kuntilanak 3 to maintain continuity in the story.

2. The film features more elaborate special effects than its predecessor, particularly in the Kuntilanak's appearances.

3. Director Rizal Mantovani incorporated elements from real Indonesian ghost stories into the film's plot.

4. The movie's success solidified the Kuntilanak series as one of Indonesia's most popular horror franchises.

5. Some scenes were shot in actual abandoned houses believed to be haunted by locals.

6. The film's makeup team studied traditional Indonesian ghost lore to create a more authentic look for the Kuntilanak.

7. Kuntilanak 2 expanded on the mythology introduced in the first film, adding new aspects to the ghost's backstory.

8. The movie features several callbacks and easter eggs referencing the original Kuntilanak film.

9. Lead actress Julie Estelle performed many of her own stunts in the more intense scenes.

10. The film's sound design incorporated traditional Indonesian instruments to enhance its eerie atmosphere.

17. Mencari Hilal

1. Movie Title: Mencari Hilal

2. Year of Release: 2015

3. Cast and Director:

 - Director: Ismail Basbeth

 - Cast: Deddy Sutomo, Oka Antara, Tika Bravani, Erythrina Baskoro

4. Synopsis:

 While not a traditional horror film, Mencari Hilal (Searching for the New Moon) blends elements of supernatural thriller with drama and social commentary. The story follows Mahmud, an elderly Islamic goods seller, and his estranged son Heli as they embark on a journey to sight the new moon that marks the beginning of Ramadan. Their trip takes an eerie turn as they encounter various supernatural occurrences and local superstitions. As they travel through rural Indonesia, they must confront not only external threats but also their own troubled relationship and differing views on faith and tradition. The film explores the tension between modern skepticism and traditional beliefs, set against a backdrop of subtle horror elements.

5. Why This Movie Is Recommended:

 Mencari Hilal offers a unique blend of genres, using elements of horror and the supernatural to explore deeper themes of faith, family, and cultural identity. Director Ismail Basbeth creates a sense of unease and mystery that permeates the film without relying on traditional horror tropes. The movie's strength lies in its ability to use supernatural elements as a metaphor for the characters' internal struggles. With its beautiful cinematography capturing the Indonesian landscape and strong performances from the lead actors, Mencari Hilal provides a thought-provoking and atmospheric experience that appeals to both horror fans and those interested in character-driven dramas.

6. 10 Trivia Facts:

 1. The film's title, "Mencari Hilal," refers to the Islamic practice of moon sighting to determine the start of Ramadan.

 2. Director Ismail Basbeth drew inspiration from his own experiences growing up in a religious household.

 3. The movie was shot on location in various parts of Java, showcasing the island's diverse landscapes.

 4. Mencari Hilal won several awards at international film festivals for its unique approach to storytelling.

 5. The film incorporates real Indonesian superstitions and folklore into its narrative.

 6. Many of the supernatural occurrences in the film are left ambiguous, allowing for multiple interpretations.

 7. The director used natural lighting and minimal special effects to create the film's eerie atmosphere.

 8. Mencari Hilal sparked discussions in Indonesia about the balance between tradition and modernity.

 9. The film features cameos from several well-known Indonesian religious figures.

 10. Some of the movie's more surreal sequences were inspired by Indonesian shadow puppet theater traditions.

18. Pintu Terlarang (The Forbidden Door)

1. Movie Title: Pintu Terlarang (The Forbidden Door)

2. Year of Release: 2009

3. Cast and Director:

- Director: Joko Anwar

- Cast: Fachri Albar, Marsha Timothy, Ario Bayu, Tio Pakusadewo

4. Synopsis:

Pintu Terlarang follows Gambir, a successful sculptor whose seemingly perfect life begins to unravel when he discovers a mysterious door in his basement. As he becomes obsessed with uncovering what lies behind it, Gambir's grip on reality starts to slip. He finds himself embroiled in a dark conspiracy involving child trafficking, underground snuff films, and his own repressed memories. The film blurs the lines between reality and nightmare as Gambir delves deeper into the mystery, forcing him to confront the horrifying truth about his past and the nature of his own existence.

5. Why This Movie Is Recommended:

Pintu Terlarang showcases director Joko Anwar's talent for psychological horror and mind-bending narratives. The film's non-linear storytelling and surreal imagery create a disorienting experience that keeps viewers guessing until the end. Anwar deftly handles sensitive topics, using horror elements to explore deeper themes of identity, morality, and the consequences of one's actions. With its strong performances, striking visuals, and complex plot, Pintu Terlarang offers a sophisticated and disturbing horror experience that lingers in the mind long after viewing. It's a must-watch for fans of psychological thrillers and those who appreciate horror with intellectual depth.

6. 10 Trivia Facts:

1. The film is based on a novel of the same name by Sekar Ayu Asmara.

2. Pintu Terlarang won Best Movie at the 2009 Indonesian Movie Awards.

3. Director Joko Anwar made significant changes to the novel's plot for the film adaptation.

4. The movie features a cameo by renowned Indonesian director Garin Nugroho.

5. Many of the film's more disturbing scenes were achieved through practical effects rather than CGI.

6. Pintu Terlarang's success helped establish Joko Anwar as a leading figure in Indonesian cinema.

7. The film's complex narrative structure was inspired by the works of David Lynch and Christopher Nolan.

8. Some of the movie's themes were so controversial that it faced censorship issues in Indonesia.

9. The director used different color palettes to distinguish between reality and fantasy sequences.

10. Pintu Terlarang's international success helped bring attention to the Indonesian film industry globally.

19. Suster Keramas (Shampooing)

1. Movie Title: Suster Keramas (Shampooing)

2. Year of Release: 2009

3. Cast and Director:

  - Director: Helfi Kardit

  - Cast: Rin Sakuragi, Ricky Harun, Noni Annisa, Herichan

4. Synopsis:

  Suster Keramas blends horror with elements of comedy and eroticism, telling the story of a vengeful ghost known as the "Shampooing Nurse." The film follows a group of high school students who become entangled with the supernatural when they encounter the spirit of a nurse who was brutally murdered. The ghost, recognizable by her habit of washing her hair, begins to terrorize the students and anyone else who crosses her path. As the body count rises, the survivors must uncover the truth behind the nurse's death and find a way to put her spirit to rest before it's too late.

5. Why This Movie Is Recommended:

  Suster Keramas stands out for its unique blend of horror, comedy, and sensuality, offering a different take on the Indonesian horror genre. Director Helfi Kardit balances scares with humorous moments, creating an entertaining experience that doesn't take itself too seriously. The film's iconic "Shampooing Nurse" has become a recognizable figure in Indonesian pop culture. While it may not be for everyone due to its more explicit content, Suster Keramas provides an interesting look at how horror can be combined with other genres. It's recommended for those interested in exploring different facets of Indonesian cinema and viewers who enjoy their horror with a mix of laughs and titillation.

6. 10 Trivia Facts:

  1. The film sparked controversy in Indonesia due to its erotic content, leading to debates about censorship.

  2. Suster Keramas was one of the first Indonesian horror films to feature a Japanese adult film actress in a leading role.

  3. The movie's success led to several sequels and spin-offs.

  4. The "Shampooing Nurse" character became a popular Halloween costume in Indonesia after the film's release.

  5. Director Helfi Kardit drew inspiration from Japanese pink films and Western B-movies.

  6. The film uses a mix of practical effects and early CGI for its supernatural scenes.

  7. Suster Keramas helped popularize the "sexy horror" subgenre in Indonesian cinema.

  8. The movie features several cameos from well-known Indonesian comedians.

  9. Some of the film's more risqué scenes were shot in separate versions for domestic and international release.

  10. Despite (or perhaps because of) its controversial nature, Suster Keramas was a significant box office success in Indonesia.

20. Lewat Tengah Malam (After Midnight)

1. Movie Title: Lewat Tengah Malam (After Midnight)

2. Year of Release: 2007

3. Cast and Director:

  - Director: Koya Pagayo

  - Cast: Tamara Bleszynski, Marcella Zalianty, Reza Pahlevi, Winky Wiryawan

4. Synopsis:

  Lewat Tengah Malam follows the story of Netta, a woman who returns to her hometown after years away to attend her sister's wedding. However, upon arrival, she finds the town gripped by a series of mysterious and gruesome deaths. As Netta investigates, she uncovers a dark secret involving a vengeful spirit that awakens at midnight. The ghost, tied to a tragic event from the town's past, targets those it deems guilty. Netta must confront her own connections to the town's history and race against time to stop the killings before she becomes the next victim.

5. Why This Movie Is Recommended:

  Lewat Tengah Malam offers a compelling blend of mystery and supernatural horror. Director Koya Pagayo creates a tense atmosphere that builds steadily throughout the film, using the small-town setting to great effect. The movie's exploration of buried secrets and the lasting impact of past sins adds depth to its horror elements. With strong performances from its cast and effective use of local folklore, Lewat Tengah Malam provides both scares and emotional resonance. It's recommended for fans of ghost stories and those who appreciate horror films that delve into the dark histories of seemingly idyllic communities.

6. 10 Trivia Facts:

  1. The film draws inspiration from Indonesian beliefs about the supernatural significance of the midnight hour.

  2. Lewat Tengah Malam was shot on location in a small town in Java, adding authenticity to its setting.

  3. The movie features several scenes shot in actual abandoned buildings believed to be haunted by locals.

  4. Director Koya Pagayo incorporated elements of Javanese mysticism into the film's plot.

  5. The ghost's appearance was inspired by traditional Indonesian ghost stories and urban legends.

  6. Some of the cast reported strange occurrences on set, adding to the film's mystique.

  7. Lewat Tengah Malam uses a mix of practical effects and early CGI for its supernatural scenes.

  8. The film's success led to discussions about a potential sequel, though it was never produced.

  9. Several scenes were shot during the actual midnight hour to capture the right atmosphere.

  10. The movie features a cameo from a well-known Indonesian paranormal expert.

India

1. Mahal

1. Movie Title: Mahal

2. Year of Release: 1949

3. Cast and Director:

- Director: Kamal Amrohi

- Cast: Ashok Kumar, Madhubala, M. Kumar

4. Synopsis:

Mahal is considered one of the earliest and most influential horror films in Indian cinema. The story revolves around Hari Shankar, who moves into an old mansion and becomes convinced that he is the reincarnation of its previous owner. He encounters the ghost of Kamini, the previous owner's lover, and becomes obsessed with her. As Hari Shankar delves deeper into the mansion's history, the line between reality and illusion blurs, leading to a series of eerie and supernatural events. The film explores themes of reincarnation, love beyond death, and the power of suggestion, all while maintaining a haunting atmosphere that keeps viewers on edge.

5. Why This Movie Is Recommended:

Mahal is a landmark film in Indian horror cinema, setting the template for many ghost stories to follow. Its Gothic atmosphere, innovative use of camera techniques, and haunting musical score create a sense of unease that was groundbreaking for its time. The film's exploration of psychological horror elements, combined with supernatural themes, adds depth to the narrative. Madhubala's ethereal presence as the ghostly Kamini became iconic in Indian cinema. Mahal's influence on subsequent Indian horror films makes it a must-watch for anyone interested in the genre's evolution in the country.

6. 10 Trivia Facts:

1. Mahal was Madhubala's first major role and catapulted her to stardom.

2. The film's song "Aayega Aanewala" became a massive hit and is still popular today.

3. It was one of the first Indian films to use camera tricks to create ghostly effects.

4. The movie was shot entirely on set, with no outdoor locations.

5. Mahal was Kamal Amrohi's directorial debut.

6. The film's success sparked a trend of reincarnation themes in Bollywood.

7. It was one of the first Indian films to use playback singing for its songs.

8. The movie's climax was reshot multiple times to perfect the eerie atmosphere.

9. Mahal was remade in Tamil as Rahasyam in 1967.

10. The film's success helped establish Bombay Talkies as a major production house.

2. Raat

1. Movie Title: Raat

2. Year of Release: 1992

3. Cast and Director:

- Director: Ram Gopal Varma

- Cast: Revathi, Rohini Hattangadi, Om Puri

4. Synopsis:

Raat follows the story of Manisha, a young woman who moves into a new house with her family. Soon after, she begins experiencing strange and terrifying occurrences. As the supernatural events escalate, it becomes clear that Manisha is being possessed by a malevolent spirit. Her family struggles to understand and combat the evil force, seeking help from various sources including a psychiatrist and a tantric practitioner. The film builds tension through subtle scares and psychological horror, leading to a climactic confrontation with the entity. Raat explores themes of skepticism versus belief in the supernatural, family bonds in the face of terror, and the lingering effects of past tragedies.

5. Why This Movie Is Recommended:

Raat stands out for its realistic approach to the horror genre, eschewing over-the-top effects in favor of building a pervasive sense of dread. Director Ram Gopal Varma's innovative use of sound design and camera angles creates an unsettling atmosphere that keeps viewers on edge. The film's focus on psychological horror and its exploration of family dynamics under stress add depth to the narrative. Revathi's nuanced performance as the possessed Manisha is particularly noteworthy. Raat's influence on subsequent Indian horror films, especially in terms of technical craft and storytelling approach, makes it a significant entry in the genre.

6. 10 Trivia Facts:

1. Raat was Ram Gopal Varma's first Hindi film.

2. The movie was shot in just 28 days.

3. Varma used a lot of handheld camera work to create a sense of unease.

4. The film's climax was inspired by William Friedkin's The Exorcist.

5. Raat was remade in Telugu as Raatri with some changes to the story.

6. The movie features very little background music, relying instead on ambient sounds for effect.

7. Varma initially wanted to cast Sridevi in the lead role.

8. The film was shot entirely at night to maintain a consistent dark atmosphere.

9. Raat was one of the first Indian horror films to use subti\

tles for spirit voices.

10. The movie's success established Ram Gopal Varma as a major director in Bollywood.

3. Bhoot

1. **Movie Title**: Bhoot

2. **Year of Release**: 2003

3. **Cast and Director**:

   - Director: Ram Gopal Varma

   - Cast: Ajay Devgn, Urmila Matondkar, Nana Patekar

4. Synopsis:

Bhoot tells the story of Vishal and Swati, a married couple who move into a high-rise apartment in Mumbai, unaware of its dark history. Soon, Swati begins experiencing supernatural phenomena and becomes possessed by the ghost of a woman who was murdered in the apartment. As Vishal struggles to save his wife, he uncovers the truth behind the haunting with the help of an eccentric psychiatrist and a police inspector. The film explores themes of skepticism, the impact of urban legends, and the lengths one would go to protect loved ones. Bhoot builds tension through a series of increasingly terrifying encounters, leading to a climactic revelation and confrontation.

5. Why This Movie Is Recommended:

Bhoot revitalized the horror genre in Bollywood with its slick production values and genuine scares. Ram Gopal Varma's direction creates a claustrophobic atmosphere within the apartment setting, effectively building tension throughout the film. The movie stands out for its restrained use of special effects, relying more on psychological horror and sudden shocks. Urmila Matondkar's powerful performance as the possessed Swati is particularly noteworthy. Bhoot's exploration of urban anxieties and its clever use of sound design to create fear make it a standout in Indian horror cinema.

6. 10 Trivia Facts:

1. The film was shot in a real apartment in Mumbai to maintain authenticity.

2. Bhoot was one of the first Bollywood horror films to use DTS sound.

3. The movie was made on a modest budget of □5 crore but was a big box office success.

4. Ram Gopal Varma claimed he was inspired to make the film after hearing real-life ghost stories from residents of high-rise apartments.

5. The film has very little background music, relying on silence and ambient sounds for scares.

6. Bhoot was remade in Tamil as Shock and in Telugu as Aparichitudu.

7. The movie's success spawned several sequels, though none matched the original's impact.

8. Varma used a lot of handheld camera work to create a sense of unease and realism.

9. The film won several awards, including a Filmfare Award for Urmila Matondkar.

10. Bhoot was one of the first Bollywood horror films to receive critical acclaim alongside commercial success.

4. Raaz

1. **Movie Title**: Raaz

2. **Year of Release**: 2002

3. **Cast and Director**:

   - Director: Vikram Bhatt

   - Cast: Bipasha Basu, Dino Morea, Malini Sharma

4. **Synopsis**:

   Raaz centers around Sanjana and Aditya, a married couple whose relationship is on the rocks. They decide to rekindle their romance by visiting Ooty, where they stay in a secluded house. However, Sanjana soon begins experiencing supernatural phenomena and is haunted by a malevolent spirit. As the hauntings intensify, dark secrets from Aditya's past come to light, revealing a connection to a woman named Malini. The couple must confront both the vengeful spirit and the truth about their relationship to survive. Raaz blends elements of horror with a love story, exploring themes of infidelity, revenge, and the power of love to overcome supernatural threats.

5. **Why This Movie Is Recommended**:

   Raaz successfully combines the conventions of Bollywood romance with genuine horror elements, creating a unique hybrid that appealed to a wide audience. The film's atmospheric setting in Ooty adds to the eerie ambiance, while the performances, particularly by Bipasha Basu, bring depth to the characters. Director Vikram Bhatt effectively builds tension through a mix of jump scares and psychological horror. The movie's exploration of relationship dynamics within a horror context sets it apart from typical Bollywood fare. Raaz's commercial success and its influence on subsequent Indian horror films make it a significant entry in the genre.

6. **10 Trivia Facts**:

   1. Raaz was inspired by the Hollywood film What Lies Beneath.

   2. The film's soundtrack, composed by Nadeem-Shravan, was a massive hit.

   3. Raaz was one of the highest-grossing Indian films of 2002.

   4. The movie was shot in various locations in Ooty and Mumbai.

   5. It was one of the first Bollywood horror films to feature extensive visual effects.

   6. Raaz spawned a successful franchise with multiple sequels.

   7. The film marked Bipasha Basu's breakthrough as a leading actress in Bollywood.

   8. Director Vikram Bhatt claimed he had a real-life paranormal experience during the film's shooting.

   9. Raaz was remade in Kannada as Shhhh! in 2002.

   10. The film won several awards, including Filmfare Awards for Best Female Debut and Best Music.

5. Tumbbad

1. Movie Title: Tumbbad

2. Year of Release: 2018

3. Cast and Director:

- Directors: Rahi Anil Barve, Anand Gandhi (creative director), Adesh Prasad (co-director)

- Cast: Sohum Shah, Jyoti Malshe, Anita Date

4. Synopsis:

Set in colonial India, Tumbbad is a gothic horror that spans three generations of a family seduced by ancestral greed. The story follows Vinayak, who discovers the existence of an ancient deity named Hastar, the firstborn of the goddess of prosperity. Hastar was cursed and buried in the village of Tumbbad, but holds the secret to boundless gold. Vinayak devises a dangerous scheme to retrieve the gold, repeatedly risking his life and soul. As he grows older and wealthier, his greed consumes him, affecting his relationships and his son's future. The film explores the corrupting nature of greed and the price of human avarice, set against a backdrop of stunning visuals and atmospheric horror.

5. Why This Movie Is Recommended:

Tumbbad stands out for its unique blend of mythology, horror, and period drama. The film's stunning visuals, created through a combination of practical effects and CGI, bring the cursed village of Tumbbad to life in vivid, terrifying detail. Its exploration of greed as a generational curse adds depth to the narrative, elevating it beyond typical horror fare. The atmospheric storytelling, coupled with Sohum Shah's compelling performance, creates a sense of dread that lingers long after the film ends. Tumbbad's critical acclaim and its fresh take on horror storytelling make it a must-watch for fans of the genre and Indian cinema alike.

6. 10 Trivia Facts:

1. Tumbbad took almost 6 years to complete, with filming starting in 2012.

2. The movie's screenplay went through nearly 30 drafts before finalization.

3. Most of the film was shot on location in the village of Tumbbad, Maharashtra.

4. The filmmakers used minimal CGI, relying mostly on practical effects and real locations.

5. Tumbbad was the first Indian film to open the Venice Film Festival's Critics' Week in 2018.

6. The movie's unique color palette was inspired by the works of Raja Ravi Varma.

7. Director Rahi Anil Barve conceptualized the story when he was just 18 years old.

8. The film's monster design was partly inspired by Goya's Saturn Devouring His Son.

9. Tumbbad was shot in three schedules across four years, capturing different time periods.

10. The film received widespread critical acclaim but was initially a box office underperformer, gaining popularity later through word of mouth and streaming platforms.

6. Stree

1. Movie Title: Stree

2. Year of Release: 2018

3. Cast and Director:

  - Director: Amar Kaushik

  - Cast: Rajkummar Rao, Shraddha Kapoor, Pankaj Tripathi, Aparshakti Khurana

4. Synopsis:

  Set in the small town of Chanderi, Stree is a horror-comedy that revolves around the urban legend of a female ghost who abducts men at night. The ghost, known as Stree, is said to call out to men and those who turn are taken away, leaving only their clothes behind. The story follows Vicky, a talented tailor, who falls in love with a mysterious woman who appears only during the town's festival. As strange events unfold and men start disappearing, Vicky and his friends investigate the legend of Stree, uncovering a tragic past and a potential solution to end the hauntings. The film blends humor with genuine scares, while also subtly commenting on gender roles and societal norms.

5. Why This Movie Is Recommended:

  Stree stands out for its innovative blend of horror and comedy, a rarity in Indian cinema. The film successfully balances laugh-out-loud moments with genuine scares, creating a unique viewing experience. Its smart script cleverly uses the horror genre to comment on social issues, particularly gender dynamics in Indian society. The stellar performances, especially by Rajkummar Rao and Pankaj Tripathi, bring depth and humor to the characters. Stree's ability to entertain while also provoking thought makes it a significant entry in modern Indian horror cinema.

6. 10 Trivia Facts:

  1. The film is loosely based on the legend of Nale Ba, a 1990s Karnataka phenomenon.

  2. "O Stree, Kal Aana" (O Woman, Come Tomorrow) written on walls is a real practice in some Indian villages to ward off evil spirits.

  3. The movie was shot in the actual town of Chanderi, Madhya Pradesh.

  4. Stree was one of the most profitable Bollywood films of 2018.

  5. The film's success spawned a planned horror-comedy universe, including movies like Roohi and Bhediya.

  6. Shraddha Kapoor's character name is never revealed in the film.

  7. The movie's climax was shot over 10 nights.

  8. Stree won the IIFA Award for Best Story.

  9. The film's dialogue "Vicky, Please" became a popular meme.

  10. Despite being a horror-comedy, the film touches on serious themes like consent and respect for women.

7. Darna Mana Hai

1. Movie Title: Darna Mana Hai

2. Year of Release: 2003

3. Cast and Director:

  - Director: Prawaal Raman

  - Cast: Saif Ali Khan, Vivek Oberoi, Aftab Shivdasani, Shilpa Shetty, Sameera Reddy, Isha Koppikar, Sohail Khan

4. Synopsis:

Darna Mana Hai is an anthology horror film that interweaves six separate stories within a framing narrative. The main story follows seven friends who are stranded in a forest when their car breaks down. To pass the time, they begin telling each other scary stories. Each tale explores different elements of horror and the supernatural, ranging from a man who can't stop smiling to a student who encounters a ghostly professor. As the night progresses and more stories are told, tension builds among the group, leading to a surprising and chilling conclusion. The film plays with various horror tropes and urban legends, creating a diverse array of scares.

5. Why This Movie Is Recommended:

Darna Mana Hai stands out for its innovative approach to horror storytelling in Indian cinema. The anthology format allows for a variety of horror styles and themes, keeping the audience engaged with fresh scares in each segment. The star-studded cast delivers strong performances across the different stories. The film's clever use of misdirection and its ability to build tension through seemingly mundane situations make it a memorable entry in the genre. Its influence on subsequent anthology horror films in Indian cinema makes it a significant work for horror enthusiasts.

6. 10 Trivia Facts:

1. The film was produced by Ram Gopal Varma, known for his contributions to Indian horror cinema.

2. Darna Mana Hai was one of the first Bollywood films to use the horror anthology format.

3. The movie's title translates to "Being Scared is Forbidden".

4. Each story in the anthology was shot by a different cinematographer to give each tale a unique visual style.

5. The film's success led to a spiritual sequel, Darna Zaroori Hai, released in 2006.

6. The movie features minimal use of jump scares, relying more on psychological horror.

7. The framing story of the stranded friends was inspired by campfire ghost story traditions.

8. Darna Mana Hai was one of the first Bollywood horror films to receive a wide international release.

9. The film's makeup and prosthetics were done by international artists to achieve a high level of realism.

10. Despite mixed reviews, the film gained a cult following and is considered influential in the evolution of Indian horror cinema.

8. Kaun?

1. Movie Title: Kaun?

2. Year of Release: 1999

3. Cast and Director:

  - Director: Ram Gopal Varma

  - Cast: Urmila Matondkar, Manoj Bajpayee, Sushant Singh

4. Synopsis:

Kaun? is a psychological thriller that unfolds almost entirely within a single house. The story follows a young woman who is alone at home on a stormy night when news breaks of a serial killer on the loose. Soon, a stranger arrives claiming to be a friend of the homeowner. As the night progresses, another man appears, claiming to be a police officer in pursuit of the killer. The woman must navigate the tense situation, unsure of who to trust and whether the killer might be among them. The film plays with audience expectations, constantly shifting suspicions and building tension through its claustrophobic setting and minimal cast.

5. Why This Movie Is Recommended:

Kaun? stands out for its minimalist approach to horror, relying on psychological tension rather than overt scares. The film's confined setting and small cast create an intense, claustrophobic atmosphere that keeps viewers on edge. Ram Gopal Varma's direction expertly builds suspense through subtle cues and misdirection. The performances, particularly Urmila Matondkar's, bring depth and nuance to the characters. Kaun?'s subversion of typical horror tropes and its shocking twists make it a unique and influential entry in Indian horror cinema.

6. 10 Trivia Facts:

  1. The film was shot in just 15 days.

  2. Kaun? has only three characters and was filmed entirely in one house.

  3. The movie has very little dialogue, relying more on visual storytelling.

  4. The film's title, which means "Who?" in Hindi, plays into its central mystery.

  5. Kaun? was one of the first Indian films to blend elements of horror and thriller genres.

  6. The movie was made on a very low budget but gained critical acclaim.

  7. Ram Gopal Varma claimed he was inspired to make the film after watching David Fincher's The Game.

  8. The film has no songs, unusual for Indian cinema at the time.

  9. Kaun? was shot in sync sound, capturing the actors' real voices during filming.

  10. Despite its critical success, the film was initially a box office disappointment, later gaining popularity through word of mouth and TV screenings.

9. 13B

1. Movie Title: 13B (also known as Yavarum Nalam in Tamil)

2. Year of Release: 2009

3. Cast and Director:

- Director: Vikram Kumar

- Cast: R. Madhavan, Neetu Chandra, Poonam Dhillon, Sachin Khedekar

4. Synopsis:

13B follows Manohar, who moves into a new apartment on the 13th floor with his family. Strange occurrences begin to plague the household, centered around a television show that only Manohar's wife and mother-in-law seem to be able to watch. The show, a soap opera, begins to mirror events in Manohar's life with eerie accuracy, even predicting future incidents. As Manohar investigates, he uncovers a dark history connected to the apartment and the show. The line between reality and television blurs as Manohar races against time to prevent a tragic fate predicted for his family. The film explores themes of technology-induced horror and the impact of media on our lives.

5. Why This Movie Is Recommended:

13B stands out for its innovative premise that turns a everyday household item - the television - into a source of horror. The film effectively builds tension through its clever use of the show-within-a-show concept, creating a sense of inevitable doom. R. Madhavan's strong performance anchors the film, making the protagonist's growing paranoia palpable. The movie's exploration of technology-based horror was ahead of its time, predating similar themes in international horror cinema. 13B's blend of supernatural elements with a grounded, relatable setting makes it a unique entry in Indian horror.

6. 10 Trivia Facts:

1. The film was simultaneously shot in Hindi and Tamil, with slight variations in the cast.

2. 13B was one of the first Indian horror films to explore the concept of technology-based hauntings.

3. The movie's Tamil title, Yavarum Nalam, translates to "Everyone is Fine" - an ironic contrast to the plot.

4. Director Vikram Kumar was inspired by Asian horror films, particularly from Japan and Korea.

5. The film uses minimal background score, relying on silence and ambient sounds to create tension.

6. 13B was praised for its logical approach to horror, attempting to explain supernatural events rationally.

7. The movie features product placement for Sony televisions, integrated into the plot.

8. It was one of the few horror films to feature a mainstream Bollywood actor (R. Madhavan) in the lead role.

9. The film's success led to discussions about a potential Hollywood remake, though it never materialized.

10. 13B was one of the first Indian horror films to have a significant portion of the story revolve around a TV show.

10. 1920

1. Movie Title: 1920

2. Year of Release: 2008

3. Cast and Director:

- Director: Vikram Bhatt

- Cast: Rajneesh Duggal, Adah Sharma, Indraneil Sengupta

4. Synopsis:

Set in the year 1920, the film follows Arjun and Lisa, a newly married couple who move into a sprawling mansion in Palampur, Himachal Pradesh. Arjun, an architect, has been commissioned to restore the colonial estate. Soon after their arrival, Lisa begins experiencing supernatural phenomena and becomes possessed by a malevolent spirit. As Arjun struggles to save his wife, he uncovers the dark history of the house, involving a tragic love story from the colonial era. The couple must confront both the vengeful spirit and the societal norms of the time to survive. The film blends elements of period drama with classic haunted house tropes, creating a unique horror experience.

5. Why This Movie Is Recommended:

1920 stands out for its lush period setting and Gothic atmosphere, rare in Indian horror cinema. The film's attention to historical detail in costumes and set design creates an immersive experience. Director Vikram Bhatt effectively builds tension through a combination of atmospheric dread and jump scares. The movie explores themes of forbidden love and the clash between Indian and British cultures during the colonial era, adding depth to the horror narrative. Adah Sharma's portrayal of the possessed Lisa is particularly noteworthy. 1920's success in blending historical drama with supernatural horror makes it a significant entry in the genre.

6. 10 Trivia Facts:

1. The film was shot entirely in Yorkshire, England, to capture the authentic feel of a colonial-era setting.

2. 1920 was Adah Sharma's debut film, and her performance garnered critical acclaim.

3. The movie's success spawned several sequels, though they are not directly related to the original story.

4. Director Vikram Bhatt claimed he was inspired by real-life ghost stories from the colonial era.

5. The film's music, composed by Adnan Sami, was a significant hit and contributed to its success.

6. 1920 was one of the first Indian horror films to extensively use CGI for its supernatural elements.

7. The movie's climax features an exorcism scene that was controversial for its graphic nature.

8. The film's success helped establish Vikram Bhatt as a prominent director in the horror genre.

9. 1920 was praised for its cinematography, which effectively captured the eerie atmosphere of the haunted mansion.

10. The movie draws inspiration from classic Hollywood horror films, particularly The Exorcist.

11. Pari

1. Movie Title: Pari

2. Year of Release: 2018

3. Cast and Director:

  - Director: Prosit Roy

  - Cast: Anushka Sharma, Parambrata Chatterjee, Rajat Kapoor, Ritabhari Chakraborty

4. Synopsis:

  Pari follows the story of Arnab, who encounters a mysterious woman named Rukhsana while driving during a stormy night. He takes her in, only to discover that she's hiding from a cult led by a man named Qasim Ali. As Arnab tries to protect Rukhsana, he uncovers a dark supernatural secret about her origins and the cult's intentions. The film explores themes of demonic possession, forbidden love, and the clash between superstition and humanity. As the narrative unfolds, it reveals a complex web of supernatural elements rooted in folklore, challenging the characters' beliefs and pushing them to their limits.

5. Why This Movie Is Recommended:

  Pari stands out for its unconventional approach to horror, blending elements of supernatural thriller with social commentary. The film's atmospheric cinematography and haunting sound design create a consistently eerie mood. Anushka Sharma's powerful performance as Rukhsana adds depth to the character, making her both terrifying and sympathetic. The movie's exploration of religious extremism and its impact on individuals adds a layer of real-world horror to the supernatural elements. Pari's willingness to push boundaries in terms of gore and disturbing imagery sets it apart in Indian horror cinema.

6. 10 Trivia Facts:

  1. Pari was Anushka Sharma's third production under her banner Clean Slate Filmz.

  2. The film's tagline "Not a fairytale" plays on the dual meaning of "Pari" (fairy in Hindi).

  3. Pari was shot in various locations around Kolkata to capture the city's Gothic ambiance.

  4. The movie features minimal dialogue, relying heavily on visual storytelling.

  5. Prosit Roy, the director, previously worked as an assistant director on films like Phillauri.

  6. The film's makeup and prosthetics were done by National Award-winning artist Clover Wootton.

  7. Pari was banned in Pakistan due to its alleged "anti-Islamic" themes.

  8. The movie's plot draws inspiration from Bengali folklore and mythology.

  9. Anushka Sharma underwent extensive prosthetic makeup for her role, sometimes taking up to 4 hours to apply.

  10. The film received praise for its attempt to elevate the horror genre in Bollywood beyond typical jump scares.

12. Ek Thi Daayan

1. Movie Title: Ek Thi Daayan

2. Year of Release: 2013

3. Cast and Director:

- Director: Kannan Iyer

- Cast: Emraan Hashmi, Huma Qureshi, Konkona Sen Sharma, Kalki Koechlin

4. Synopsis:

Ek Thi Daayan centers around Bobo, a famous magician haunted by visions from his childhood. As he prepares for his greatest trick, his past begins to unravel. The story alternates between Bobo's childhood and present, exploring his encounters with women he believes to be 'daayans' (witches in Indian mythology). As a child, Bobo suspects his stepmother of being a daayan responsible for his sister's death. In the present, he must confront his fears and determine which of the women in his life might be the reincarnation of the daayan. The film blends elements of psychological thriller with supernatural horror, keeping the audience guessing about the true nature of the daayan until the very end.

5. Why This Movie Is Recommended:

Ek Thi Daayan stands out for its unique blend of magic, mythology, and psychological horror. The film's exploration of the 'daayan' concept from Indian folklore adds a cultural dimension to its scares. Strong performances from the ensemble cast, particularly Konkona Sen Sharma and Kalki Koechlin, bring depth to the characters. The movie's non-linear narrative keeps viewers engaged, skillfully building tension through its dual timelines. Its focus on psychological horror and its ambiguous approach to the supernatural elements make it a thought-provoking entry in Indian horror cinema.

6. 10 Trivia Facts:

1. The film is based on the short story "Mobius Trips" by Mukul Sharma, who co-wrote the screenplay.

2. Vishal Bhardwaj, known for his adaptations of Shakespeare, wrote the film's story and produced it.

3. The movie features a unique blend of magic performances and horror elements.

4. Ek Thi Daayan was promoted with actual magic shows performed by Emraan Hashmi.

5. The film's title translates to "Once There Was a Witch," playing on the storytelling tradition.

6. It was one of the first Bollywood films to explore the concept of 'daayans' in a modern setting.

7. The movie's climax was shot in an actual 100-year-old mill in Mumbai.

8. Konkona Sen Sharma learned to play the piano for her role in the film.

9. The film's soundtrack, composed by Vishal Bhardwaj, incorporates elements of Indian folk music.

10. Ek Thi Daayan was screened for the Censor Board chief's wife to prove it didn't promote superstition.

13. Vaastu Shastra

1. Movie Title: Vaastu Shastra

2. Year of Release: 2004

3. Cast and Director:

- Director: Sourabh Usha Narang

- Cast: Sushmita Sen, Chakravarthy, Ahsaas Channa, Peeya Rai Chowdhary

4. Synopsis:

Vaastu Shastra follows the Agnihotri family - Dr. Malini, her husband Sanjay, and their son Rohan - as they move into a new home in a secluded wooded area. Soon after settling in, strange occurrences begin to plague the family, particularly centered around Rohan. The child starts behaving oddly and claims to see a mysterious boy. As the supernatural events escalate, Malini investigates the house's history, uncovering a dark past involving child abuse and murder. The film explores themes of repressed trauma, the impact of negative energy on living spaces, and the bond between mother and child. As the horror intensifies, the family must confront the malevolent forces to save themselves and their home.

5. Why This Movie Is Recommended:

Vaastu Shastra stands out for its effective blend of supernatural horror with psychological elements. The film's use of a child as a conduit for horror adds a disturbing dimension to the scares. Sushmita Sen's performance as a mother trying to protect her family grounds the supernatural elements in relatable emotions. The movie's exploration of Vaastu principles (Indian architectural beliefs) in relation to supernatural occurrences adds a unique cultural aspect to the horror. Its focus on building tension through atmosphere and suggestion, rather than relying solely on jump scares, makes it a sophisticated entry in Indian horror cinema.

6. 10 Trivia Facts:

1. The film's title refers to the ancient Indian science of architecture and its impact on human lives.

2. Vaastu Shastra was one of the first Bollywood horror films to focus on a nuclear family.

3. The movie was shot entirely on location in Khandala, a hill station near Mumbai.

4. It was one of the earliest Indian horror films to use extensive CGI for its supernatural elements.

5. The film's child actor, Ahsaas Channa, received critical acclaim for her performance.

6. Vaastu Shastra was produced by Ram Gopal Varma, known for his contributions to Indian horror cinema.

7. The movie's sound design, crucial for its scares, won several awards.

8. It was one of the few horror films to feature a major Bollywood star (Sushmita Sen) in the lead role.

9. The film draws inspiration from Asian horror cinema, particularly Japanese ghost stories.

10. Vaastu Shastra's success led to discussions about a potential sequel, though it never materialized.

14. Gehraiyaan

1. Movie Title: Gehraiyaan

2. Year of Release: 2022

3. Cast and Director:

- Director: Shakun Batra

- Cast: Deepika Padukone, Siddhant Chaturvedi, Ananya Panday, Dhairya Karwa

4. Synopsis:

Gehraiyaan is a psychological drama with elements of horror that delves into the complexities of modern relationships. The story follows Alisha, a yoga instructor with a troubled past, who becomes entangled in a passionate affair with her cousin's fiancé, Zain. As their relationship intensifies, dark secrets from Alisha's family history begin to surface, blurring the lines between past and present. The film explores themes of generational trauma, infidelity, and the psychological impact of repressed memories. As Alisha grapples with her growing feelings for Zain and the resurfacing of her childhood traumas, the narrative takes unexpected turns, leading to a shocking climax that questions the nature of reality and memory.

5. Why This Movie Is Recommended:

While not a traditional horror film, Gehraiyaan is recommended for its psychological depth and its exploration of internal horrors. The movie's nuanced portrayal of complex relationships and mental health issues creates a sense of unease that permeates the narrative. Deepika Padukone's powerful performance brings depth to Alisha's internal struggles. The film's atmospheric cinematography and haunting score contribute to a pervasive sense of dread. Gehraiyaan's blend of relationship drama with psychological horror elements offers a mature, thought-provoking viewing experience that lingers in the mind long after the credits roll.

6. 10 Trivia Facts:

1. The film's title "Gehraiyaan" translates to "Depths," reflecting its exploration of deep-seated emotions and traumas.

2. It was one of the first major Bollywood productions to employ an intimacy coordinator for its romantic scenes.

3. The movie was initially planned for a theatrical release but premiered on Amazon Prime Video due to the COVID-19 pandemic.

4. Gehraiyaan's script took over two years to develop and went through numerous drafts.

5. The film features a unique soundtrack that blends traditional Indian music with more contemporary sounds.

6. Many scenes were shot on actual yachts in Goa to maintain authenticity.

7. The movie sparked discussions about mental health and generational trauma in Indian society.

8. Deepika Padukone also served as one of the producers of the film.

9. The film's ambiguous ending led to numerous fan theories and interpretations.

10. Gehraiyaan was praised for its realistic portrayal of modern urban relationships, a rarity in Bollywood.

15. Pizza

1. Movie Title: Pizza

2. Year of Release: 2012 (Tamil), 2014 (Hindi remake)

3. Cast and Director:

- Director: Karthik Subbaraj (Tamil), Akshay Akkineni (Hindi)

- Cast: Vijay Sethupathi, Remya Nambeesan (Tamil), Akshay Oberoi, Parvathy Omanakuttan (Hindi)

4. Synopsis:

Pizza follows Michael, a pizza delivery boy who gets trapped in a house where he's gone to deliver an order. Inside, he encounters supernatural phenomena and a series of terrifying events. As Michael struggles to escape, the narrative takes unexpected turns, blurring the lines between reality and illusion. The story explores themes of perception, the power of storytelling, and the nature of fear itself. As the plot unfolds, it challenges viewers' assumptions, leading to a surprising climax that forces a reevaluation of everything that came before. The film plays with the conventions of the horror genre, delivering scares while also commenting on the nature of horror storytelling.

5. Why This Movie Is Recommended:

Pizza stands out for its innovative approach to horror storytelling, cleverly subverting audience expectations. The film's use of a seemingly mundane setting - a pizza delivery gone wrong - as a springboard for supernatural terror is both original and effective. Its non-linear narrative keeps viewers guessing, with twists that challenge perceptions of what's real. The movie's exploration of the mechanics of fear and storytelling adds a meta-textual layer to the horror. Pizza's success in creating genuine scares while also engaging in clever genre deconstruction makes it a significant and influential entry in Indian horror cinema.

6. 10 Trivia Facts:

1. The Tamil version of Pizza was director Karthik Subbaraj's debut feature film.

2. The movie was shot in just 28 days.

3. Pizza was one of the first Tamil horror films to employ extensive use of steadicam shots.

4. The film's success led to remakes in Kannada, Bengali, and Hindi.

5. Pizza was praised for its innovative marketing campaign, which included delivering actual pizzas to critics.

6. The movie's twist ending sparked widespread discussions and debates among viewers.

7. Pizza was one of the few horror films to achieve both critical acclaim and commercial success in Tamil cinema.

8. The film's background score, crucial for its scares, was composed by Santhosh Narayanan.

9. Pizza's success established Vijay Sethupathi as a leading actor in Tamil cinema.

10. The Hindi remake featured cameos from prominent Bollywood horror film directors as a nod to the genre.

16. Bulbbul

1. Movie Title: Bulbbul

2. Year of Release: 2020

3. Cast and Director:

- Director: Anvita Dutt

- Cast: Tripti Dimri, Avinash Tiwary, Rahul Bose, Paoli Dam, Parambrata Chattopadhyay

4. Synopsis:

Set in Bengal Presidency of the late 19th century, Bulbbul tells the story of a child bride who grows into an enigmatic woman presiding over her household. The narrative shifts between two timelines, exploring Bulbbul's past and present. As a series of mysterious deaths of men plague the village, rumors of a vengeful supernatural entity, a chudail (witch), begin to spread. The film delves into themes of patriarchy, child marriage, and feminine rage, intertwining these with elements of Gothic horror and Bengali folklore. As the story unfolds, it reveals the true nature of the horrors that haunt the village, blending supernatural elements with very real, human evils.

5. Why This Movie Is Recommended:

Bulbbul stands out for its unique blend of period drama, social commentary, and supernatural horror. The film's stunning visual aesthetic, with its rich, red-hued cinematography, creates a dreamlike, fairytale atmosphere that contrasts beautifully with its dark themes. Tripti Dimri's nuanced performance as Bulbbul anchors the film, bringing depth to a character who transforms from a naive child bride to a complex, powerful woman. The movie's exploration of feminist themes through the lens of horror offers a fresh perspective on both genres. Bulbbul's ability to create an atmosphere of dread while addressing important social issues makes it a significant and thought-provoking entry in modern Indian horror cinema.

6. 10 Trivia Facts:

1. Bulbbul was produced by Anushka Sharma's production company Clean Slate Filmz.

2. The film's distinctive red-tinted scenes were inspired by vintage hand-tinted photographs.

3. Bulbbul incorporates elements of the Bengali folk tale of Thakurmar Jhuli.

4. The movie was shot in various locations across Kolkata and Mumbai.

5. Amit Trivedi composed the film's haunting background score.

6. The character of Bulbbul was partially inspired by the Bengali legend of Rani of Jhansi.

7. The film's costume design drew inspiration from Bengal School of Art paintings.

8. Bulbbul was one of the first Indian horror films to directly address the issue of child marriage.

9. The movie's visual effects, particularly for the chudail sequences, were praised for their subtlety and effectiveness.

10. Bulbbul won three Filmfare OTT Awards, including Best Film and Best Actress for Tripti Dimri.

17. Bhoot - Part One: The Haunted Ship

1. Movie Title: Bhoot - Part One: The Haunted Ship

2. Year of Release: 2020

3. Cast and Director:

  - Director: Bhanu Pratap Singh

  - Cast: Vicky Kaushal, Bhumi Pednekar, Ashutosh Rana

4. Synopsis:

  Bhoot - Part One: The Haunted Ship centers around Prithvi, a shipping officer dealing with the loss of his wife and daughter. He becomes involved in investigating a mysterious abandoned ship, Sea Bird, that has run aground on a Mumbai beach. As Prithvi delves deeper into the ship's history, he encounters increasingly terrifying supernatural phenomena. The narrative weaves between Prithvi's personal trauma and the dark secrets of the ship, blurring the lines between reality and hallucination. As he uncovers the truth about Sea Bird and its connection to his own past, Prithvi must confront both human and supernatural horrors to find closure and save himself.

5. Why This Movie Is Recommended:

  Bhoot stands out for its unique setting, using the claustrophobic environment of an abandoned ship to create a sense of isolation and dread. The film's strong production values and impressive visual effects bring the maritime horror to life in a way rarely seen in Indian cinema. Vicky Kaushal's committed performance grounds the supernatural elements in relatable human emotion. The movie's exploration of grief and trauma adds psychological depth to its scares. Bhoot's blend of jump scares, atmospheric horror, and emotional storytelling offers a well-rounded horror experience that appeals to both genre fans and general audiences.

6. 10 Trivia Facts:

  1. The film is loosely based on a true incident of a merchant ship washing ashore at Juhu Beach, Mumbai in 2011.

  2. Bhoot marks Dharma Productions' first venture into the horror genre.

  3. The movie was shot on an actual ship to maintain authenticity.

  4. Vicky Kaushal injured himself during the shoot, fracturing his cheekbone.

  5. The film's climax sequence took 12 days to shoot.

  6. Bhoot uses minimal background music, relying more on sound design for its scares.

  7. The movie's tagline, "The truth is out there," is a nod to the TV series The X-Files.

  8. Director Bhanu Pratap Singh previously worked as an assistant director on Humpty Sharma Ki Dulhania.

  9. The film was originally titled Bhoot: Part One - The Haunted Ship of the Dead.

  10. Bhoot is planned as the first installment in a horror franchise.

18. Kothanodi

1. Movie Title: Kothanodi (The River of Fables)

2. Year of Release: 2015

3. Cast and Director:

- Director: Bhaskar Hazarika

- Cast: Seema Biswas, Adil Hussain, Zerifa Wahid, Kopil Bora

4. Synopsis:

Kothanodi is an anthology horror film based on four folk tales from Assam. The stories include a woman who gives birth to a vegetable, a mother who exchanges her daughter for a python, a stepmother who tries to kill her stepdaughter, and a woman haunted by her husband's second wife. These interconnected tales explore themes of motherhood, superstition, and the supernatural, all set against the backdrop of rural Assam. As the narratives unfold, they reveal the dark undercurrents of human nature and the sometimes horrifying consequences of blind belief and tradition. The film blends elements of folklore, magical realism, and horror to create a unique and unsettling viewing experience.

5. Why This Movie Is Recommended:

Kothanodi stands out for its innovative approach to horror, drawing from rich Assamese folklore to create a uniquely Indian horror experience. The film's atmospheric storytelling and haunting visuals bring these ancient tales to life in a way that feels both timeless and contemporary. Its exploration of complex themes like motherhood and societal expectations adds depth to the horror elements. The ensemble cast delivers powerful performances that ground the supernatural elements in human emotion. Kothanodi's ability to create a sense of dread and unease while also offering insight into Assamese culture makes it a significant and thought-provoking entry in Indian horror cinema.

6. 10 Trivia Facts:

1. Kothanodi is based on folk tales from Lakshminath Bezbaroa's "Burhi Aair Sadhu" (Grandma's Tales).

2. The film was partially crowdfunded, with support from film enthusiasts worldwide.

3. Kothanodi premiered at the Busan International Film Festival in 2015.

4. The movie was shot entirely on location in Assam, capturing the region's lush landscapes.

5. It's one of the few horror films in the Assamese language to gain national and international recognition.

6. The film's title "Kothanodi" translates to "The River of Fables" in English.

7. Kothanodi won the Best Feature Film in Assamese at the 63rd National Film Awards.

8. The movie blends elements of magical realism with traditional horror tropes.

9. Director Bhaskar Hazarika spent years researching Assamese folklore before making the film.

10. Kothanodi's success has sparked renewed interest in Assamese literature and folklore.

19. Eeram

1. Movie Title: Eeram

2. Year of Release: 2009

3. Cast and Director:

- Director: Arivazhagan

- Cast: Aadhi, Nandha, Sindhu Menon, Saranya Mohan

4. Synopsis:

Eeram, which means "moisture" in Tamil, revolves around Vasu, a police officer investigating a series of mysterious deaths in an apartment complex. The victims all seem to have drowned, despite being found in dry areas. As Vasu digs deeper, he discovers a connection to his past and a woman named Ramya, who committed suicide in the same building. The investigation takes a supernatural turn as Vasu realizes he's dealing with a vengeful water spirit. The film explores themes of revenge, justice, and the power of unresolved emotions. As the body count rises and the supernatural presence grows stronger, Vasu must confront both the ghost and his own past to solve the case and stop the killings.

5. Why This Movie Is Recommended:

Eeram stands out for its innovative use of water as a source of horror, creating unique and memorable scare sequences. The film successfully blends elements of supernatural horror with a police procedural, keeping viewers engaged with its mystery plot. Its exploration of themes like domestic abuse and justice adds depth to the horror elements. The movie's strong technical aspects, particularly its sound design and visual effects related to water, create a consistently eerie atmosphere. Eeram's ability to maintain tension while telling a compelling story makes it a significant entry in Tamil horror cinema.

6. 10 Trivia Facts:

1. Eeram was produced by S. Shankar, known for his big-budget spectacle films.

2. The film's concept of a water ghost was inspired by Japanese horror movies.

3. Eeram won the Tamil Nadu State Film Award for Best Film.

4. The movie features minimal use of background score, relying more on sound design for its scares.

5. Many of the water effects were achieved practically on set, with minimal CGI.

6. Eeram was one of the first Tamil horror films to extensively use blue color grading to enhance its watery theme.

7. The film's success led to discussions about a potential sequel, though it never materialized.

8. Director Arivazhagan spent nearly two years developing the script.

9. Eeram was praised for its logical approach to incorporating supernatural elements into a realistic setting.

10. The movie's climax sequence took over a week to shoot due to its complex water effects.

20. Talaash

1. Movie Title: Talaash

2. Year of Release: 2012

3. Cast and Director:

  - Director: Reema Kagti

  - Cast: Aamir Khan, Rani Mukerji, Kareena Kapoor Khan, Nawazuddin Siddiqui

4. Synopsis:

Talaash follows Inspector Surjan Singh Shekhawat as he investigates a high-profile car accident in Mumbai. As he delves deeper into the case, he encounters Rosie, a mysterious prostitute who seems to know more than she lets on. Parallel to the investigation, Surjan and his wife Roshni struggle with the grief of losing their young son. The narrative weaves between the criminal underworld, personal loss, and supernatural occurrences, blurring the lines between reality and the beyond. As Surjan gets closer to solving the case, he must confront his own beliefs about life, death, and the possibility of connecting with those who have passed on. The film combines elements of a noir thriller with subtle supernatural horror, creating a unique and atmospheric viewing experience.

5. Why This Movie Is Recommended:

Talaash stands out for its skillful blend of crime thriller and supernatural elements, a rarity in mainstream Bollywood cinema. The film's noir-ish atmosphere and strong performances from its star-studded cast elevate it beyond typical genre fare. Its exploration of grief and the desire to connect with lost loved ones adds emotional depth to the supernatural aspects. The movie keeps viewers guessing until the end, masterfully balancing its various plot threads. Talaash's ability to create a sense of unease and mystery while also telling a deeply human story makes it a significant and thought-provoking entry in Indian cinema that bridges the gap between commercial and art house sensibilities.

6. 10 Trivia Facts:

  1. The film's story was co-written by Zoya Akhtar and Reema Kagti.

  2. Talaash was initially titled "Dhuan" (Smoke).

  3. Kareena Kapoor Khan's look in the film was inspired by Sophia Loren.

  4. The movie features a cameo by Rajkummar Rao in one of his early roles.

  5. Aamir Khan learned to swim for underwater sequences in the film.

  6. Talaash was shot in actual locations in Mumbai to maintain authenticity.

  7. The film's climax was reshot after initial test screenings.

  8. Ram Sampath's haunting soundtrack, particularly the song "Muskaanein Jhooti Hai," became very popular.

  9. Talaash was one of the few mainstream Bollywood films to explore the supernatural without resorting to typical horror tropes.

  10. The movie's twist ending sparked widespread discussions and debates among viewers and critics.

Turkey

1. Siccin

1. Movie Title: Siccin

2. Year of Release: 2014

3. Cast and Director:

  - Director: Alper Mestçi

  - Cast: Pinar Çağlar Gençtürk, Koray Onat, Ebru Kaymakçı

4. Synopsis:

   Siccin follows the story of Öznur, a young woman who is deeply in love with her cousin Kudret. When Kudret marries another woman, Öznur becomes consumed by jealousy and rage. In her desperation, she turns to black magic, specifically a dark spell known as "siccin," to win back Kudret's love. However, the consequences of her actions are far more terrifying than she could have imagined. As the spell takes effect, it unleashes a malevolent force that begins to torment Öznur and those around her, leading to a series of horrifying supernatural events that threaten to destroy everything and everyone in its path.

5. Why This Movie Is Recommended:

   Siccin stands out in Turkish horror cinema for its effective blend of supernatural elements with cultural and religious themes. The film draws on Islamic concepts of black magic and demonic possession, giving it a unique flavor compared to Western horror. Its atmospheric cinematography and tension-building techniques create a pervasive sense of dread. The movie's success spawned a franchise, indicating its resonance with Turkish audiences. For horror fans interested in exploring different cultural perspectives on the genre, Siccin offers a compelling and culturally rich experience.

6. 10 Trivia Facts:

   1. Siccin is the first in a series of six films, becoming one of Turkey's most successful horror franchises.

   2. The word "siccin" refers to a concept in Islamic theology related to a record of evil deeds or a deep pit in hell.

   3. The film's success led to international distribution, rare for Turkish horror movies at the time.

   4. Director Alper Mestçi became known as the "Turkish James Wan" due to his contributions to Turkish horror cinema.

   5. The movie incorporates elements of Turkish folk beliefs and superstitions.

   6. Siccin was shot on a relatively low budget but achieved significant box office success in Turkey.

   7. The film's makeup and special effects were praised for their effectiveness despite budget constraints.

   8. Siccin helped popularize the subgenre of Islamic-themed horror films in Turkey.

   9. The movie's poster, featuring a woman with inverted eyes, became iconic in Turkish horror marketing.

   10. Despite its supernatural themes, the film draws on real Turkish customs and beliefs about love and marriage.

2. Dabbe: Cin Çarpması

1. Movie Title: Dabbe: Cin Çarpması (Dabbe: The Possession)

2. Year of Release: 2013

3. Cast and Director:

- Director: Hasan Karacadağ

- Cast: Füsun Kostak, Nur Aysan, Ümit Bülent Dinçer

4. Synopsis:

Dabbe: Cin Çarpması is the fourth installment in the Dabbe series, focusing on the concept of demonic possession in Islamic theology. The film follows Kübra, a young woman who begins to experience terrifying supernatural phenomena after her engagement. As her condition worsens, her family seeks help from both medical professionals and religious experts. The movie explores the intersection of modern psychiatry and traditional Islamic beliefs about jinn (supernatural creatures). As Kübra's possession intensifies, the characters are forced to confront their beliefs and the reality of the supernatural world, leading to a harrowing exorcism attempt.

5. Why This Movie Is Recommended:

Dabbe: Cin Çarpması stands out for its unique blend of found footage style with traditional narrative filmmaking, creating an immersive and unsettling viewing experience. The film's exploration of Islamic concepts of possession offers a fresh perspective for viewers accustomed to Western depictions of exorcism. Its cultural specificity, combined with universal horror themes, makes it both educational and terrifying. The movie's intense atmosphere and shocking imagery have made it a standout in Turkish horror cinema, appealing to both local audiences and international horror enthusiasts seeking new cultural takes on familiar tropes.

6. 10 Trivia Facts:

1. The Dabbe series is known for incorporating actual accounts of supernatural experiences reported by Turkish people.

2. Director Hasan Karacadağ is considered one of the pioneers of the modern Turkish horror film industry.

3. The word "Dabbe" refers to a creature mentioned in the Quran that will appear near the Day of Judgment.

4. The film uses a mix of Turkish and Arabic, reflecting the religious context of its themes.

5. Some scenes were reportedly so intense that crew members felt uncomfortable during filming.

6. The movie sparked discussions in Turkey about the relationship between mental health and religious beliefs.

7. Dabbe: Cin Çarpması was one of the highest-grossing Turkish horror films of its time.

8. The film's depiction of jinn is based on Islamic religious texts and Turkish folklore.

9. Some viewers reported experiencing nightmares and paranormal phenomena after watching the movie.

10. The success of the Dabbe series contributed significantly to the growth of the horror genre in Turkish cinema.

3. Musallat

1. Movie Title: Musallat (Haunted)

2. Year of Release: 2007

3. Cast and Director:

- Director: Alper Mestçi

- Cast: Burak Özçivit, Biğkem Karavus, Kurtuluş Şakiragaoğlu

4. Synopsis:

Musallat tells the story of Suat, a young man who returns to his hometown with his pregnant wife, Nurcan, after years of living abroad. Soon after their arrival, strange and terrifying events begin to plague the couple. Nurcan experiences horrifying visions and seems to be under the influence of a malevolent force. As Suat desperately seeks answers, he uncovers dark secrets from his past and learns about an ancient curse that has been placed on his family. The couple finds themselves in a battle against supernatural forces, fighting not only for their own lives but also for the safety of their unborn child.

5. Why This Movie Is Recommended:

Musallat stands out as one of the early successes of modern Turkish horror cinema. It effectively blends elements of Turkish folklore and Islamic beliefs with classic horror tropes, creating a unique and culturally rich narrative. The film's atmospheric tension and reliance on psychological horror over gore make it accessible to a wide range of horror fans. Its exploration of themes like family curses and the consequences of past actions adds depth to the scares. For those interested in how different cultures approach horror storytelling, Musallat offers a compelling entry point into Turkish horror cinema.

6. 10 Trivia Facts:

1. Musallat was one of the first Turkish horror films to gain significant commercial success, paving the way for the genre's growth in Turkey.

2. The film's title, "Musallat," refers to a type of haunting or possession in Turkish folklore.

3. Director Alper Mestçi went on to create the successful Siccin franchise after Musallat.

4. The movie incorporates elements of Turkish rural life and superstitions, adding to its cultural authenticity.

5. Musallat's success led to a sequel, Musallat 2, released in 2011.

6. The film was shot on location in Turkey, using real houses and locations to enhance its authentic feel.

7. Lead actor Burak Özçivit later became one of Turkey's most popular television actors.

8. The movie's portrayal of supernatural elements is heavily influenced by Islamic beliefs about jinn and the spirit world.

9. Musallat helped establish the "October horror movie" trend in Turkish cinema.

10. The film's makeup and practical effects were groundbreaking for Turkish horror at the time, setting a new standard for the genre.

4. Büyü

1. Movie Title: Büyü (The Spell)

2. Year of Release: 2004

3. Cast and Director:

  - Director: Orhan Oğuz

  - Cast: Olgun Şimşek, Murat Han, Birol Ünel, Sanem Çelik

4. Synopsis:

Büyü follows a team of archaeologists who travel to a remote village in southeastern Turkey to excavate an ancient Syriac tomb. The village has a dark history, with locals believing it to be cursed. As the team begins their work, they encounter increasingly disturbing and supernatural events. They discover that the tomb they're excavating belongs to a powerful sorcerer who practiced black magic. As they delve deeper into the site's mysteries, the ancient evil is awakened, and the team members find themselves fighting for survival against malevolent forces beyond their understanding. The film blends archaeological adventure with supernatural horror, exploring themes of ancient curses, black magic, and the dangerous consequences of disturbing sacred sites.

5. Why This Movie Is Recommended:

Büyü stands out for its unique setting and premise, combining elements of archaeological thriller with supernatural horror. The film's use of Turkish and Middle Eastern folklore provides a fresh perspective for viewers accustomed to Western horror tropes. Its atmospheric build-up of tension and effective use of its remote location create a palpable sense of isolation and dread. The movie's exploration of the clash between modern skepticism and ancient beliefs adds depth to its narrative. For horror fans interested in culturally diverse takes on the genre, Büyü offers a compelling look into Turkish horror cinema and its cultural influences.

6. 10 Trivia Facts:

1. Büyü was one of the first big-budget horror films produced in Turkey, marking a turning point for the genre in Turkish cinema.

2. The film's remote village setting was inspired by real locations in southeastern Turkey.

3. Some of the Syriac inscriptions and symbols used in the film were based on actual ancient artifacts.

4. The movie's success spawned a sequel, Büyü 2: Araf, released in 2015.

5. Director Orhan Oğuz conducted extensive research into Syriac history and black magic practices for the film.

6. The film's portrayal of archaeological practices was praised for its relative accuracy compared to typical horror movies.

7. Büyü's makeup and special effects were groundbreaking for Turkish cinema at the time.

8. The movie sparked renewed interest in Turkish folklore and superstitions among younger audiences.

9. Some scenes were so intense that a few crew members reportedly experienced nightmares during filming.

10. The film's success contributed to a boom in Turkish horror movie production in the following years.

5. Alamet-i Kıyamet

1. Movie Title: Alamet-i Kıyamet (Sign of Doomsday)

2. Year of Release: 2016

3. Cast and Director:

- Director: Özgür Bakar

- Cast: Büşra Apaydin, Müge Boz, Emre Özmen

4. Synopsis:

Alamet-i Kıyamet centers around a group of friends who decide to make a horror movie about the signs of doomsday as described in Islamic eschatology. As they begin filming in an abandoned house, strange and terrifying events start to occur. The line between their film project and reality begins to blur as they encounter real supernatural phenomena. The group finds themselves facing actual signs of the apocalypse, including the appearance of Dabbat al-Ard, a creature mentioned in the Quran as a harbinger of the Day of Judgment. As the horror escalates, the friends must confront their beliefs and fight for survival in the face of impending doom.

5. Why This Movie Is Recommended:

Alamet-i Kıyamet stands out for its unique premise that blends meta-commentary on horror filmmaking with genuine supernatural terror. The film's exploration of Islamic eschatology offers a fresh perspective on apocalyptic themes in horror. Its use of found footage elements mixed with traditional narrative creates an immersive and unsettling viewing experience. The movie's cultural specificity, drawing on Turkish and Islamic concepts of the end times, makes it both educational and terrifying for audiences unfamiliar with these ideas. For horror fans seeking culturally diverse takes on familiar tropes, Alamet-i Kıyamet provides a compelling and thought-provoking experience.

6. 10 Trivia Facts:

1. The film's title, "Alamet-i Kıyamet," directly translates to "Sign of Doomsday" in English.

2. The movie draws heavily on Islamic eschatology, particularly the signs of Qiyamah (Day of Judgment) mentioned in hadith literature.

3. The creature Dabbat al-Ard, featured in the film, is described in the Quran as a beast that will appear near the end times.

4. The film uses a mix of Turkish and Arabic, reflecting the religious context of its themes.

5. Some of the "signs of doomsday" depicted in the film are based on actual Islamic prophecies.

6. The movie's meta approach, with characters making a horror film, was relatively novel for Turkish horror cinema at the time.

7. Alamet-i Kıyamet sparked discussions in Turkey about the intersection of religious beliefs and horror entertainment.

8. The film's marketing campaign played on people's fears and beliefs about the end times.

9. Some viewers reported feeling genuinely unsettled by the film's religious themes, believing them to be too realistic.

10. The success of Alamet-i Kıyamet contributed to a trend of apocalyptic-themed horror films in Turkish cinema.

6. Üç Harfliler: Adak

1. Movie Title: Üç Harfliler: Adak (Three Letters: The Sacrifice)

2. Year of Release: 2019

3. Cast and Director:

  - Director: Alper Mestçi

  - Cast: Özgürcan Çevik, Merve Ateş, Cem Kılıç

4. Synopsis:

  Üç Harfliler: Adak follows the story of Yaşar and Sema, a married couple struggling with infertility. Desperate for a child, they visit a remote village known for its mystical practices. There, they participate in an ancient ritual believed to grant fertility. However, the ritual comes with a dark price. Soon after returning home, Sema becomes pregnant, but strange and terrifying events begin to plague the couple. As the pregnancy progresses, it becomes clear that the ritual has invited a malevolent entity into their lives. Yaşar must uncover the truth behind the ritual and find a way to protect his family from the supernatural threat before it's too late.

5. Why This Movie Is Recommended:

  Üç Harfliler: Adak stands out for its exploration of Turkish folk beliefs and superstitions surrounding fertility and childbirth. The film effectively blends psychological horror with supernatural elements, creating a deeply unsettling atmosphere. Its focus on the anxieties and desperation surrounding infertility adds emotional depth to the horror narrative. The movie's rural setting and incorporation of ancient rituals provide a unique cultural perspective on familiar horror tropes. For viewers interested in folklore-based horror and the intersection of tradition and modernity, Üç Harfliler: Adak offers a compelling and culturally rich experience.

6. 10 Trivia Facts:

  1. "Üç Harfliler" is a Turkish euphemism for malevolent spirits or demons, literally meaning "three-lettered ones."

  2. The film is part of the Üç Harfliler series, each exploring different aspects of Turkish supernatural folklore.

  3. Director Alper Mestçi is known for his contributions to Turkish horror cinema, including the Siccin franchise.

  4. The fertility ritual depicted in the film is loosely based on actual practices from rural Turkey.

  5. The movie's exploration of infertility issues was praised for bringing attention to a often-taboo subject in Turkish society.

  6. Some of the film's scenes were shot in actual remote villages to maintain authenticity.

  7. The makeup and practical effects for the supernatural entities were created by a team specializing in Turkish horror films.

  8. The film incorporates elements of both Islamic and pre-Islamic Turkish beliefs about spirits and the supernatural.

  9. Üç Harfliler: Adak's success led to further exploration of fertility-related horror themes in Turkish cinema.

  10. The movie sparked discussions about the potential dangers of seeking non-medical solutions to fertility issues.

7. Görünmeyenler

1. Movie Title: Görünmeyenler (The Invisibles)

2. Year of Release: 2017

3. Cast and Director:

- Director: Mustafa Kara

- Cast: Ruhi Sarı, Fatih Dokgöz, Emre Bulut

4. Synopsis:

Görünmeyenler tells the story of three friends who run a YouTube channel dedicated to exploring abandoned and allegedly haunted locations. In search of content for their channel, they decide to investigate an old, deserted mansion with a dark history. As they begin their exploration, they encounter increasingly disturbing phenomena that they can't explain. The friends soon realize that they've stumbled upon something far more sinister than they anticipated. As the night progresses, they find themselves trapped in the mansion, hunted by malevolent spirits and forced to confront their deepest fears. The line between reality and the supernatural blurs as they fight for survival and struggle to uncover the truth behind the mansion's horrifying past.

5. Why This Movie Is Recommended:

Görünmeyenler offers a fresh take on the found footage horror subgenre by incorporating elements of Turkish urban legends and supernatural beliefs. The film's use of a YouTube channel as a framing device adds a contemporary touch, making it relatable to modern audiences. Its exploration of the dangers of urban exploration and the consequences of disturbing sacred or haunted spaces resonates with universal horror themes while maintaining a distinctly Turkish flavor. The movie's gradual build-up of tension and effective use of its claustrophobic setting create a palpable sense of dread. For fans of found footage horror and those interested in seeing how the subgenre is interpreted in different cultural contexts, Görünmeyenler provides an engaging and culturally enriching experience.

6. 10 Trivia Facts:

1. The film's title, "Görünmeyenler," literally translates to "The Invisibles" in English, referring to unseen supernatural entities.

2. The movie was inspired by the real-life trend of YouTube channels dedicated to exploring abandoned locations.

3. Some scenes were shot in actual abandoned buildings to enhance the authenticity of the setting.

4. The film incorporates elements of Turkish urban legends and ghost stories into its narrative.

5. Görünmeyenler was one of the first Turkish horror films to explicitly reference social media culture.

6. The directors used a mix of handheld cameras and fixed cameras to create a realistic found footage feel.

7. Some of the supernatural occurrences in the film are based on reported paranormal experiences in Turkey.

8. The movie sparked discussions about the ethics of urban exploration and disturbing potentially haunted locations.

9. Görünmeyenler's success contributed to a trend of social media-themed horror films in Turkish cinema.

10. The film's marketing campaign included fake YouTube videos purportedly showing the characters' earlier explorations.

8. Azem 4: Alacakaranlık

1. Movie Title: Azem 4: Alacakaranlık (Azem 4: Twilight)

2. Year of Release: 2016

3. Cast and Director:

- Director: Volkan Adıyaman

- Cast: Berna Üçkaleler, Ayça Kuruçayırlı, Tuğrul Pabucçuoğlu

4. Synopsis:

Azem 4: Alacakaranlık is the fourth installment in the Azem series, which focuses on supernatural encounters based on true stories. This film follows Azra, a young woman who starts experiencing terrifying visions and ·paranormal phenomena after moving into a new apartment. As the haunting intensifies, Azra discovers that her apartment was previously occupied by a practitioner of black magic. With the help of her friends and a spiritual healer, Azra delves into the dark history of her new home and the occult practices that took place there. As they uncover the truth, they find themselves in a battle against powerful demonic forces that threaten not just Azra, but everyone around her.

5. Why This Movie Is Recommended:

Azem 4: Alacakaranlık stands out for its claim to be based on true events, adding an extra layer of unease for viewers. The film effectively blends elements of Turkish folklore and Islamic beliefs about the supernatural with modern urban settings, creating a unique horror experience. Its exploration of black magic and its consequences offers a culturally specific take on familiar possession tropes. The movie's atmospheric buildup and intense scares make it a standout in the Turkish horror genre. For horror fans interested in culturally diverse interpretations of supernatural themes and those who enjoy the added thrill of "based on true events" narratives, Azem 4: Alacakaranlık provides a compelling and chilling experience.

6. 10 Trivia Facts:

1. The Azem series is known for basing its stories on real-life accounts of supernatural encounters in Turkey.

2. "Alacakaranlık" in the title refers to the twilight hours, believed to be when the veil between the physical and spiritual worlds is thinnest.

3. The film incorporates actual Turkish rituals and prayers used for protection against evil spirits.

4. Some of the black magic practices depicted in the movie are based on real occult beliefs found in certain parts of Turkey.

5. The Azem series has gained a cult following in Turkey for its exploration of local supernatural phenomena.

6. The movie features a mix of practical effects and CGI to create its supernatural entities.

7. Azem 4: Alacakaranlık's success led to further sequels in the Azem franchise.

8. The film's marketing campaign included testimonials from people claiming to have experienced similar hauntings.

9. Some scenes in the movie were inspired by actual locations in Turkey rumored to be haunted.

10. The Azem series has contributed to a renewed interest in Turkish urban legends and ghost stories among younger audiences.

9. Cin Baskını

1. Movie Title: Cin Baskını (Jinn Invasion)

2. Year of Release: 2016

3. Cast and Director:

- Director: Hasan Gökalp

- Cast: Muharrem Bayrak, Naz Göktan, Buğra Özay

4. Synopsis:

Cin Baskını centers around a young couple, Selman and Canan, who move into an old apartment building with a dark history. Soon after settling in, Canan begins to experience terrifying visions and unexplainable phenomena. As Selman tries to uncover the truth behind these events, he discovers that the building was once the site of occult rituals aimed at summoning and controlling jinn (supernatural creatures in Islamic mythology). The couple's presence in the building seems to have awakened these malevolent entities, leading to an escalating series of horrifying encounters. With the help of an Islamic scholar, they must find a way to protect themselves and break the building's curse before they fall victim to the jinn invasion.

5. Why This Movie Is Recommended:

Cin Baskını offers a unique perspective on the haunted house subgenre by incorporating elements of Islamic mythology and Turkish folklore. The film's focus on jinn, supernatural creatures rarely explored in Western horror, provides a fresh and culturally rich narrative. Its blend of psychological horror and supernatural elements creates a tense and unsettling atmosphere throughout. The movie's exploration of the intersection between ancient beliefs and modern urban life adds depth to its scares. For horror fans interested in culturally diverse interpretations of familiar tropes and those curious about Islamic concepts of the supernatural, Cin Baskını delivers an engaging and enlightening horror experience.

6. 10 Trivia Facts:

1. The concept of jinn in the film is drawn directly from Islamic theology and folklore.

2. Some of the protective rituals shown in the movie are based on actual practices used in parts of Turkey to ward off evil spirits.

3. The film's success led to a sequel, Cin Baskını 2, released in 2019.

4. Director Hasan Gökalp conducted extensive research into Islamic demonology for the film.

5. The apartment building used as the main setting was rumored to be actually haunted, adding to the crew's unease during filming.

6. Cin Baskını incorporates elements of found footage style in certain scenes to increase tension.

7. The movie sparked discussions in Turkey about the balance between entertainment and religious sensitivity in horror films.

8. Some of the jinn designs were inspired by descriptions found in Islamic texts and Turkish folklore.

9. The film's marketing campaign included viral videos purporting to show real jinn encounters.

10. Cin Baskını's portrayal of jinn was praised for its relative accuracy to Islamic beliefs, unlike many Western depictions of these entities.

10. Üç Harfliler: Beddua

1. Movie Title: Üç Harfliler: Beddua (Three Letters: The Curse)

2. Year of Release: 2018

3. Cast and Director:

- Director: Alper Mestçi

- Cast: Özlem Begüm Çavuş, Efsane Odağ, Burak Orhan

4. Synopsis:

Üç Harfliler: Beddua follows the story of Melek, a young woman who returns to her hometown for her sister's wedding. However, upon arrival, she discovers that her sister has mysteriously disappeared. As Melek investigates, she uncovers a dark secret involving an ancient curse that has plagued her family for generations. The curse, known as "beddua" in Turkish, was placed on her ancestors by a powerful sorcerer. As Melek delves deeper into her family's history and the nature of the curse, she experiences increasingly terrifying supernatural phenomena. With time running out and the curse threatening to claim more victims, Melek must find a way to break the cycle of horror and save her family from the malevolent forces that haunt them.

5. Why This Movie Is Recommended:

Üç Harfliler: Beddua stands out for its deep dive into Turkish folklore and the concept of generational curses. The film effectively blends elements of mystery and supernatural horror, creating a compelling narrative that keeps viewers engaged. Its exploration of family secrets and the weight of ancestral sins adds emotional depth to the scares. The movie's rural setting and incorporation of traditional beliefs provide a unique cultural perspective on familiar horror tropes. For fans of folklore-based horror and those interested in seeing how different cultures interpret themes of curses and family legacy, Üç Harfliler: Beddua offers a rich and terrifying experience.

6. 10 Trivia Facts:

1. "Beddua" in Turkish refers to a powerful curse or malediction, often associated with dire consequences.

2. The film is part of the Üç Harfliler series, each exploring different aspects of Turkish supernatural folklore.

3. Director Alper Mestçi is known for his significant contributions to the modern Turkish horror genre.

4. Some of the curse rituals depicted in the film are based on actual practices from Turkish folk magic.

5. The movie was partially shot in rural locations to maintain authenticity and create a more isolated atmosphere.

6. Üç Harfliler: Beddua incorporates elements of both Islamic and pre-Islamic Turkish beliefs about curses and supernatural entities.

7. The film's success contributed to a trend of exploring regional Turkish folklore in horror movies.

8. Some of the supernatural entities in the movie were designed based on descriptions from Turkish mythological texts.

9. The movie's marketing campaign included social media posts featuring "real" curse stories from Turkish folklore.

10. Üç Harfliler: Beddua's exploration of generational trauma through a horror lens was praised by some critics for its psychological depth.

11. Dabbe: Zehr-i Cin

1. Movie Title: Dabbe: Zehr-i Cin (Dabbe: Curse of the Jinn)

2. Year of Release: 2013

3. Cast and Director:

  - Director: Hasan Karacadağ

  - Cast: Füsun Demirel, Ümit Bülent Dinçer, Perihan Savaş

4. Synopsis:

Dabbe: Zehr-i Cin is the fifth installment in the Dabbe series, focusing on the concept of jinn possession in Islamic theology. The film follows a family that moves into a new home, unaware of its dark history. Soon after, the family's daughter begins exhibiting strange behavior, leading to suspicions of jinn possession. As the family seeks help from both medical professionals and religious experts, they uncover a sinister plot involving black magic and ancient jinn. The movie explores the intersection of modern skepticism and traditional beliefs about the supernatural, culminating in a terrifying confrontation with malevolent forces.

5. Why This Movie Is Recommended:

Dabbe: Zehr-i Cin stands out for its deep dive into Islamic concepts of jinn and possession, offering a unique cultural perspective on familiar possession tropes. The film's blend of found footage elements with traditional narrative creates an immersive and unsettling viewing experience. Its exploration of the tension between scientific explanations and supernatural beliefs adds depth to the horror narrative. For viewers interested in culturally specific horror and the intersection of religion and the paranormal, Dabbe: Zehr-i Cin provides a compelling and terrifying journey into Turkish supernatural beliefs.

6. 10 Trivia Facts:

1. The Dabbe series is known for incorporating actual accounts of supernatural experiences reported by Turkish people.

2. "Zehr-i Cin" roughly translates to "Poison of the Jinn" in English.

3. Director Hasan Karacadağ is considered one of the pioneers of the modern Turkish horror film industry.

4. The movie uses a mix of Turkish and Arabic, reflecting the religious context of its themes.

5. Some of the exorcism scenes in the film are based on actual Islamic rituals.

6. The Dabbe series has gained a cult following in Turkey and has been distributed internationally.

7. The film's portrayal of jinn is largely based on descriptions found in Islamic religious texts.

8. Dabbe: Zehr-i Cin's success contributed to the growing trend of Islamic-themed horror films in Turkey.

9. Some viewers reported experiencing nightmares and paranormal phenomena after watching the movie.

10. The film sparked discussions in Turkey about the relationship between mental health issues and beliefs in supernatural possession.

12. Gulyabani

1. Movie Title: Gulyabani

2. Year of Release: 2018

3. Cast and Director:

- Director: Orçun Benli

- Cast: Erdal Cindoruk, Sena Nur Zorlu, Ece Koroğlu

4. Synopsis:

Gulyabani is based on a Turkish folk tale about a mythical creature that haunts lonely places. The film follows a group of university students who decide to investigate the legend of the Gulyabani for a class project. They travel to a remote village where sightings of the creature have been reported. As they delve deeper into their investigation, strange and terrifying events begin to occur. The students find themselves trapped in a nightmare as they face not only the legendary Gulyabani but also the dark secrets of the village and its inhabitants. The line between myth and reality blurs as they fight for survival against an ancient evil.

5. Why This Movie Is Recommended:

Gulyabani offers a unique blend of Turkish folklore and modern horror storytelling. The film's use of a lesser-known mythical creature provides a fresh perspective for horror fans tired of familiar monsters. Its remote village setting creates an effective atmosphere of isolation and dread. The movie's exploration of the power of local legends and the dangers of dismissing traditional beliefs adds depth to its scares. For viewers interested in folklore-based horror and the intersection of ancient myths with contemporary skepticism, Gulyabani delivers a culturally rich and terrifying experience.

6. 10 Trivia Facts:

1. The Gulyabani is a creature from Turkish mythology, often described as a hairy, humanoid monster that haunts deserted places.

2. The film draws inspiration from real Turkish villages where Gulyabani sightings have been reported.

3. Some of the practical effects used to create the Gulyabani were inspired by traditional Turkish puppet theatre techniques.

4. The movie incorporates elements of found footage style to enhance its realism.

5. Gulyabani's success led to increased interest in other Turkish mythological creatures as subjects for horror films.

6. The film's portrayal of village life and superstitions is based on extensive research into rural Turkish culture.

7. Some scenes were shot in actual locations believed by locals to be haunted.

8. The movie sparked discussions about the preservation of Turkish folklore in the face of modernization.

9. Gulyabani's marketing campaign included viral videos of alleged Gulyabani sightings.

10. The film's soundtrack incorporates traditional Turkish instruments to enhance its folkloric atmosphere.

13. El-Cin

1. Movie Title: El-Cin

2. Year of Release: 2013

3. Cast and Director:

- Director: Hasan Karacadağ

- Cast: Zeynep Eronat, Mehmet Emin Kadıhan, Ayçe İnci

4. Synopsis:

El-Cin tells the story of Selda, a woman who begins to experience terrifying supernatural phenomena after her husband's death. As the haunting intensifies, Selda discovers that her late husband had been involved in dark occult practices, inadvertently inviting a powerful and malevolent jinn into their lives. With the help of an Islamic exorcist, Selda must confront the entity and uncover the truth behind her husband's death. The film explores themes of grief, guilt, and the consequences of meddling with forces beyond human understanding, all while delivering intense scares and supernatural thrills.

5. Why This Movie Is Recommended:

El-Cin stands out for its deep dive into Islamic demonology and its portrayal of jinn, offering a unique cultural perspective on possession and haunting narratives. The film effectively blends psychological horror with supernatural elements, creating a deeply unsettling atmosphere. Its exploration of the consequences of occult practices adds a moral dimension to the horror. For viewers interested in culturally specific interpretations of supernatural themes and those curious about Islamic concepts of the paranormal, El-Cin provides a chilling and enlightening experience.

6. 10 Trivia Facts:

1. "El-Cin" translates to "The Jinn" in English, referring to supernatural creatures in Islamic mythology.

2. Director Hasan Karacadağ is known for his contributions to the Turkish horror genre, including the Dabbe series.

3. The film incorporates actual Islamic prayers and rituals used for protection against evil spirits.

4. Some of the jinn designs in the movie were inspired by descriptions found in Islamic religious texts.

5. El-Cin's success contributed to the growing trend of jinn-themed horror films in Turkish cinema.

6. The movie features a mix of practical effects and CGI to create its supernatural entities.

7. El-Cin sparked discussions about the representation of Islamic beliefs in horror entertainment.

8. Some scenes in the film were inspired by real-life accounts of alleged jinn encounters in Turkey.

9. The movie's marketing campaign included testimonials from religious experts about the nature of jinn.

10. El-Cin's portrayal of Islamic exorcism rituals was praised for its relative accuracy compared to Western depictions.

14. Küçük Kıyamet

1. Movie Title: Küçük Kıyamet (Little Apocalypse)

2. Year of Release: 2016

3. Cast and Director:

- Director: Cüneyt Karakuş

- Cast: Berat Efe Parlar, Ece Baykal, Ümit Bülent Dinçer

4. Synopsis:

Küçük Kıyamet follows the story of a young boy named Yusuf who lives in a small Turkish village. Yusuf begins to have disturbing visions of impending doom, which he believes are premonitions of the apocalypse. As strange and terrifying events start to occur in the village, the locals become divided between those who believe Yusuf's warnings and those who dismiss them as the delusions of a child. The film explores themes of faith, skepticism, and the fine line between prophecy and madness. As the situation in the village deteriorates, Yusuf and his supporters must race against time to convince others of the coming danger and find a way to avert the impending catastrophe.

5. Why This Movie Is Recommended:

Küçük Kıyamet offers a unique take on apocalyptic themes by setting them in a small Turkish village, providing a fresh cultural perspective on end-times narratives. The film's focus on a child prophet adds an element of ambiguity and tension, as viewers question whether Yusuf's visions are real or imagined. Its exploration of how communities react to claims of impending doom adds depth to the horror elements. For fans of psychological horror and those interested in seeing how different cultures approach apocalyptic themes, Küçük Kıyamet provides a thought-provoking and unsettling experience.

6. 10 Trivia Facts:

1. The title "Küçük Kıyamet" translates to "Little Apocalypse," referring to localized disasters in Islamic eschatology.

2. The film draws on both Islamic and pre-Islamic Turkish beliefs about the end times.

3. Some of the apocalyptic visions in the movie are inspired by descriptions found in religious texts.

4. The village setting was carefully chosen to reflect traditional Turkish rural life.

5. Küçük Kıyamet's child actor, Berat Efe Parlar, received praise for his intense performance.

6. The film incorporates elements of Turkish folk magic and superstitions.

7. Some of the natural disasters depicted in the movie were created using a mix of practical effects and CGI.

8. Küçük Kıyamet sparked discussions about the role of prophecy and visions in modern Turkish society.

9. The movie's atmosphere was enhanced by the use of traditional Turkish music in its soundtrack.

10. The film's success led to increased interest in apocalyptic themes in Turkish cinema.

15. Çağrılan

1. Movie Title: Çağrılan (The Summoned)

2. Year of Release: 2017

3. Cast and Director:

  - Director: Hüseyin Eleman

  - Cast: Büşra Apaydin, Almila Ada, Sefa Kındır

4. Synopsis:

Çağrılan tells the story of Dilek, a young woman who returns to her hometown for her father's funeral. Upon arrival, she learns that her father's death may not have been natural, but instead linked to dark supernatural forces. As Dilek investigates, she uncovers a history of occult practices in the town, including rituals to summon powerful entities. She soon finds herself at the center of a terrifying struggle against malevolent spirits that have been inadvertently released. With the help of childhood friends and a local spiritual leader, Dilek must confront the summoned entities and put an end to the cycle of horror before more lives are lost.

5. Why This Movie Is Recommended:

Çağrılan stands out for its exploration of Turkish occult practices and local superstitions, offering a unique cultural perspective on familiar supernatural horror tropes. The film effectively blends elements of mystery and horror, creating a compelling narrative that keeps viewers engaged. Its small-town setting adds to the atmosphere of isolation and hidden dangers. The movie's themes of confronting past sins and the consequences of meddling with unknown forces add depth to its scares. For horror fans interested in culturally specific interpretations of occult horror and those who enjoy stories of prodigal children returning to face hometown horrors, Çağrılan delivers a chilling and engaging experience.

6. 10 Trivia Facts:

1. The title "Çağrılan" translates to "The Summoned" in English, referring to the supernatural entities called forth in the film.

2. Some of the occult rituals depicted in the movie are based on actual practices from Turkish folk magic.

3. The film incorporates elements of Turkish rural gothic, a growing subgenre in Turkish cinema.

4. Çağrılan's success contributed to a trend of exploring regional Turkish folklore in horror movies.

5. The movie features practical effects for many of its supernatural entities, blending traditional techniques with modern CGI.

6. Some scenes were shot in locations believed by locals to be actually haunted, adding to the crew's unease during filming.

7. The film's portrayal of small-town dynamics and secrets was praised for its authenticity.

8. Çağrılan's marketing campaign included viral marketing featuring alleged real-life summoning stories.

9. The movie sparked discussions about the preservation of local folklore and superstitions in modern Turkey.

10. Some of the protective rituals shown in the film are based on actual practices used in parts of Turkey to ward off evil spirits.

16. Cin Kuyusu

1. Movie Title: Cin Kuyusu (The Jinn Well)

2. Year of Release: 2015

3. Cast and Director:

- Director: Murat Toktamışoğlu

- Cast: Murat Prosçiler, Çağla Baran, Mehmet Fatih Özkan

4. Synopsis:

Cin Kuyusu centers around a group of friends who decide to explore an abandoned well rumored to be a portal for jinn. Despite warnings from locals, they perform a ritual at the well, inadvertently releasing malevolent entities. As the friends start experiencing terrifying supernatural phenomena, they realize they've opened a gateway between our world and the realm of the jinn. With the help of a local imam, they must find a way to close the portal and survive the wrath of the unleashed spirits. The film explores themes of curiosity leading to catastrophe and the consequences of disrespecting ancient warnings.

5. Why This Movie Is Recommended:

Cin Kuyusu offers a unique blend of Turkish folklore and contemporary horror, centered around the concept of jinn - supernatural creatures in Islamic mythology. The film's use of an ancient well as a focal point taps into universal fears of the unknown lurking in dark, forgotten places. Its exploration of the consequences of disregarding traditional wisdom adds depth to the horror narrative. For viewers interested in culturally specific interpretations of supernatural themes and those who enjoy stories of forbidden rituals gone wrong, Cin Kuyusu provides a chilling glimpse into Turkish supernatural beliefs.

6. 10 Trivia Facts:

1. The concept of jinn wells is based on actual beliefs in some parts of Turkey about portals to the jinn world.

2. The film incorporates authentic Turkish protective rituals and prayers against supernatural entities.

3. Some scenes were shot at actual locations rumored to be haunted, adding to the film's eerie atmosphere.

4. Cin Kuyusu's success contributed to a trend of jinn-themed horror films in Turkish cinema.

5. The movie features a mix of practical effects and CGI to create its supernatural entities.

6. Director Murat Toktamışoğlu conducted extensive research into jinn lore for the film.

7. The well used in the movie was specially constructed for the film but was inspired by real ancient wells in Turkey.

8. Some of the incantations used in the film are based on actual texts from Turkish folk magic.

9. Cin Kuyusu sparked discussions about the intersection of traditional beliefs and modern skepticism in Turkey.

10. The film's marketing campaign included viral videos of alleged jinn sightings near wells.

17. Üç Harfliler: Hablis

1. Movie Title: Üç Harfliler: Hablis

2. Year of Release: 2019

3. Cast and Director:

- Director: Arkın Aktaç

- Cast: Seda Oğuz, Yaşar Karakulak, Melisa Doğu

4. Synopsis:

Üç Harfliler: Hablis follows the story of Melek, a young woman who starts experiencing terrifying visions and supernatural occurrences after moving into a new apartment. As the haunting intensifies, Melek discovers that her apartment was once the site of dark occult rituals involving a powerful demon known as Hablis. With the help of a paranormal investigator and an Islamic exorcist, Melek must uncover the truth behind the rituals and find a way to banish Hablis before it claims her soul. The film explores themes of ancestral sins, the power of faith, and the dangers of dabbling in the occult.

5. Why This Movie Is Recommended:

Üç Harfliler: Hablis stands out for its deep dive into Islamic demonology, offering a unique cultural perspective on possession and exorcism narratives. The film effectively blends psychological horror with supernatural elements, creating a deeply unsettling atmosphere. Its urban setting provides a contrast to many folklore-based Turkish horror films, showing how ancient evils can persist in modern environments. For viewers interested in culturally specific interpretations of demonic possession and those curious about Islamic concepts of exorcism, Üç Harfliler: Hablis delivers a terrifying and enlightening experience.

6. 10 Trivia Facts:

1. "Hablis" is a variation of "Iblis," the name for the devil in Islamic theology.

2. The film is part of the Üç Harfliler series, each exploring different aspects of Turkish supernatural folklore.

3. Some of the exorcism scenes in the movie are based on actual Islamic rituals.

4. The apartment building used as the main setting was rumored to be actually haunted, adding to the crew's unease during filming.

5. Üç Harfliler: Hablis incorporates elements of both Islamic and pre-Islamic Turkish beliefs about demons.

6. The film's success contributed to the growing trend of Islamic-themed horror films in Turkey.

7. Some of the ancient texts and symbols used in the movie are based on actual occult manuscripts.

8. The movie's marketing campaign included social media posts featuring "real" stories of demonic encounters.

9. Üç Harfliler: Hablis sparked discussions about the representation of Islamic beliefs in horror entertainment.

10. The film's portrayal of urban isolation and alienation was praised for adding psychological depth to the horror narrative.

18. Naciye

1. Movie Title: Naciye

2. Year of Release: 2015

3. Cast and Director:

- Director: Lütfü Emre Çiçek

- Cast: Derya Alabora, Esin Harvey, Görkem Mertsöz

4. Synopsis:

Naciye tells the story of a pregnant couple, Bengi and Erhan, who move into a secluded summer house to prepare for their baby's arrival. Their idyllic retreat is shattered when they encounter Naciye, the house's former owner who refuses to leave. As Naciye's behavior becomes increasingly erratic and threatening, the couple discovers the dark history of the house and the tragic events that have shaped Naciye's madness. The film blends psychological horror with supernatural elements as the boundaries between past and present, reality and delusion begin to blur. Bengi and Erhan must uncover the truth behind Naciye's obsession with the house and find a way to escape before it's too late.

5. Why This Movie Is Recommended:

Naciye stands out for its unique blend of psychological thriller and supernatural horror elements. The film's focus on a pregnant protagonist adds an extra layer of vulnerability and tension to the narrative. Its exploration of themes like motherhood, loss, and the lingering effects of trauma gives depth to the horror elements. The movie's isolated setting and claustrophobic atmosphere contribute to a sense of inescapable dread. For viewers who appreciate character-driven horror and slow-burn psychological thrillers with a supernatural twist, Naciye offers a compelling and unsettling experience.

6. 10 Trivia Facts:

1. Naciye was director Lütfü Emre Çiçek's debut feature film.

2. The film was shot entirely on location in a real summer house on the Turkish coast.

3. Lead actress Derya Alabora's performance as Naciye was widely praised for its intensity and complexity.

4. The movie incorporates elements of Turkish folk beliefs about pregnancy and childbirth.

5. Naciye's success at international film festivals helped bring attention to Turkish horror cinema abroad.

6. The film's score uses traditional Turkish instruments to create an unsettling atmosphere.

7. Some of the supernatural elements in the movie are left deliberately ambiguous, allowing for multiple interpretations.

8. Naciye explores themes of gentrification and class conflict in Turkish society through its horror narrative.

9. The film's nonlinear narrative structure was inspired by classic psychological thrillers.

10. Naciye's exploration of maternal horror themes was noted as relatively unique in Turkish cinema at the time.

19. Baskın

1. Movie Title: Baskın (Raid)

2. Year of Release: 2015

3. Cast and Director:

- Director: Can Evrenol

- Cast: Görkem Kasal, Ergun Kuyucu, Muharrem Bayrak

4. Synopsis:

Baskın follows a squad of Turkish police officers responding to a distress call from a remote town. What starts as a routine operation quickly descends into a nightmarish ordeal as the officers find themselves trapped in an abandoned building that seems to be a portal to hell. As they navigate through increasingly surreal and horrifying scenarios, the line between reality and nightmare blurs. The officers must confront not only external horrors but also their own inner demons and past sins. The film explores themes of guilt, punishment, and the nature of evil, culminating in a shocking and mind-bending climax.

5. Why This Movie Is Recommended:

Baskın stands out for its bold, surrealist approach to horror, offering a unique and visceral experience that challenges viewers' perceptions. The film's nightmarish imagery and non-linear narrative create a sense of disorientation that mirrors the characters' experiences. Its blend of cosmic horror, body horror, and psychological terror sets it apart from more conventional horror films. For fans of extreme cinema and those who appreciate challenging, artistic approaches to horror, Baskın provides an unforgettable journey into the depths of hell and the human psyche.

6. 10 Trivia Facts:

1. Baskın was expanded from a short film of the same name, also directed by Can Evrenol.

2. The film gained international attention after premiering at the Toronto International Film Festival.

3. Baskın's surrealist elements were inspired by directors like David Lynch and Alejandro Jodorowsky.

4. The movie incorporates elements of Ottoman and Turkish folklore into its hellish imagery.

5. Some of the more extreme scenes in the film caused controversy in Turkey.

6. Baskın's score, composed by Ulas Pakkan, was praised for enhancing the film's nightmarish atmosphere.

7. The abandoned building used as the main setting was a real location with a reputation for being haunted.

8. Director Can Evrenol has a background in practical effects, which influenced the film's visceral visual style.

9. Baskın explores themes of masculine aggression and power dynamics within its horror narrative.

10. The film's success helped pave the way for more experimental and extreme horror cinema in Turkey.

20. Ev

1. Movie Title: Ev (House)

2. Year of Release: 2019

3. Cast and Director:

 - Director: Emre Akay

 - Cast: Emre Koç, Serpil Gül, Müge Bayramoğlu

4. Synopsis:

  Ev tells the story of a young couple, Ceren and Emre, who move into an old apartment building in Istanbul. As they settle into their new home, strange occurrences begin to plague them. Ceren starts to experience terrifying visions and a growing sense of paranoia, while Emre becomes increasingly distant and aggressive. As the couple investigates the history of their apartment, they uncover dark secrets about the building's past residents and a series of tragic events that have left their mark on the place. The line between reality and delusion blurs as Ceren fights to uncover the truth and save her relationship, all while battling the malevolent forces that seem to inhabit their new home.

5. Why This Movie Is Recommended:

  Ev offers a fresh take on the haunted house subgenre by setting it in a modern Istanbul apartment, blending urban anxieties with supernatural horror. The film's exploration of relationship dynamics under stress adds psychological depth to its scares. Its use of Turkish urban legends and superstitions provides a unique cultural perspective on familiar horror tropes. For viewers who appreciate slow-burn horror that focuses on atmosphere and psychological tension, Ev delivers a chilling exploration of how the past can haunt the present, both literally and figuratively.

6. 10 Trivia Facts:

  1. The film draws inspiration from real urban legends and ghost stories circulating in Istanbul.

  2. Ev explores themes of gentrification and urban transformation in Istanbul through its horror narrative.

  3. The apartment building used in the film was chosen for its unique architectural style that blends Ottoman and modern elements.

  4. Some of the supernatural occurrences in the movie are based on actual reported paranormal experiences in old Istanbul buildings.

  5. The film incorporates elements of Turkish folk magic and protective rituals against evil spirits.

  6. Ev's sound design was particularly praised for creating an unsettling atmosphere, using the sounds of the city to enhance the horror.

  7. The movie sparked discussions about the preservation of historical buildings and their stories in rapidly changing urban environments.

  8. Director Emre Akay conducted interviews with residents of old Istanbul apartments to gather ghost stories and urban myths.

  9. The film's portrayal of a deteriorating relationship amid supernatural events was noted for its realism and emotional impact.

  10. Ev's success contributed to a growing trend of urban horror films in Turkish cinema, exploring the fears and anxieties of city life.

United States of America (Hollywood)

1. The Exorcist

1. Movie Title: The Exorcist

2. Year of Release: 1973

3. Cast and Director:

- Director: William Friedkin

- Cast: Ellen Burstyn, Max von Sydow, Linda Blair, Jason Miller

4. Synopsis:

The Exorcist follows the demonic possession of a 12-year-old girl named Regan MacNeil and her mother's desperate attempts to save her through an exorcism. As Regan's behavior becomes increasingly disturbing and inexplicable, her mother seeks help from medical professionals, but to no avail. Eventually, she turns to the Catholic Church, where she finds Father Damien Karras, a priest struggling with his own faith. Along with the more experienced Father Merrin, Karras confronts the demon possessing Regan in a battle that tests their faith, courage, and the very limits of good versus evil.

5. Why This Movie Is Recommended:

The Exorcist is a landmark in horror cinema, renowned for its groundbreaking special effects, intense performances, and profound exploration of faith and evil. It transcends typical horror tropes to deliver a deeply unsettling psychological and spiritual experience. The film's ability to shock and disturb audiences remains potent decades after its release, thanks to its realistic approach to the supernatural and its unflinching portrayal of a child in peril. Its influence on the horror genre is immeasurable, setting a new standard for serious, thought-provoking horror films.

6. 10 Trivia Facts:

1. The film is based on William Peter Blatty's novel of the same name, inspired by a real exorcism case from 1949.

2. Linda Blair was only 14 years old during filming and had no idea how controversial the movie would become.

3. The iconic "spider-walk" scene was cut from the original theatrical release but restored in later versions.

4. The film was the first horror movie to be nominated for Best Picture at the Academy Awards.

5. Mercedes McCambridge provided the demon's voice but was initially uncredited, leading to a legal dispute.

6. The bedroom set was refrigerated to capture the actors' visible breath during the exorcism scenes.

7. Several actors and crew members reported strange occurrences during filming, leading to rumors the set was cursed.

8. The pea soup used for the vomiting scenes was actually a mixture of pea soup and oatmeal.

9. Max von Sydow was only 44 when he played the elderly Father Merrin, requiring extensive makeup.

10. The film's release in 1973 caused widespread panic and fainting in theaters, with some cities trying to ban it.

2. Halloween

1. Movie Title: Halloween

2. Year of Release: 1978

3. Cast and Director:

  - Director: John Carpenter

  - Cast: Jamie Lee Curtis, Donald Pleasence, Nick Castle

4. Synopsis:

  Halloween introduces the iconic killer Michael Myers, who murdered his sister on Halloween night when he was six years old. Fifteen years later, Myers escapes from a psychiatric hospital and returns to his hometown of Haddonfield, Illinois. He begins stalking Laurie Strode, a high school student, and her friends on Halloween night. As the body count rises, Myers' psychiatrist, Dr. Sam Loomis, desperately tries to track him down and stop the killing spree. The film builds tension through its use of point-of-view shots and minimalist score, creating a sense of impending doom as the seemingly unstoppable Myers closes in on his victims.

5. Why This Movie Is Recommended:

  Halloween is a masterclass in suspense and terror, establishing many of the slasher genre's conventions while transcending them with its craft. John Carpenter's direction and score create an atmosphere of dread that permeates every frame. The film's success lies in its simplicity and restraint, proving that suggestion can be more terrifying than graphic violence. Jamie Lee Curtis's performance as the "final girl" Laurie Strode became a template for horror heroines. Halloween's influence on the horror genre is immeasurable, inspiring countless imitators and launching a franchise that continues to this day.

6. 10 Trivia Facts:

  1. The movie was shot in just 20 days on a budget of $300,000.

  2. Michael Myers' mask is actually a modified Captain Kirk mask from Star Trek, painted white.

  3. Jamie Lee Curtis made her film debut in Halloween, launching her career as a "scream queen."

  4. The film was originally titled "The Babysitter Murders" before being changed to capitalize on the holiday.

  5. John Carpenter composed the iconic theme music in just three days.

  6. The movie is set in fictional Haddonfield, Illinois, but was filmed entirely in South Pasadena and Hollywood, California.

  7. Nick Castle, who played Michael Myers (credited as "The Shape"), went on to become a successful director.

  8. The film was shot out of sequence, with the ending filmed first due to scheduling conflicts.

  9. Donald Pleasence agreed to star in the film because his daughter liked Carpenter's previous film, Assault on Precinct 13.

  10. Halloween was the highest-grossing independent film of its time until it was surpassed by Teenage Mutant Ninja Turtles in 1990.

3. The Shining

1. Movie Title: The Shining

2. Year of Release: 1980

3. Cast and Director:

- Director: Stanley Kubrick

- Cast: Jack Nicholson, Shelley Duvall, Danny Lloyd, Scatman Crothers

4. Synopsis:

Based on Stephen King's novel, The Shining follows the Torrance family as they become winter caretakers of the isolated Overlook Hotel in Colorado. Jack Torrance, a recovering alcoholic and aspiring writer, sees it as an opportunity to work on his novel. His wife Wendy and son Danny accompany him, unaware of the hotel's dark history. As they settle in, Danny's psychic abilities, known as "the shining," awaken the hotel's malevolent spirits. Isolated by a winter storm and influenced by the hotel's supernatural forces, Jack's sanity begins to unravel. The family's stay turns into a terrifying struggle for survival against Jack's increasing madness and the hotel's sinister presence.

5. Why This Movie Is Recommended:

The Shining is a masterpiece of psychological horror, elevating the haunted house trope to new heights of cinematic artistry. Kubrick's meticulous direction creates an atmosphere of mounting dread through innovative camera work, unsettling symmetry, and a discordant score. Jack Nicholson's descent into madness is both riveting and terrifying. The film's ambiguous supernatural elements and exploration of themes like isolation, alcoholism, and domestic abuse add layers of complexity. Its iconic imagery and quotable lines have become deeply embedded in popular culture, cementing The Shining's status as one of the greatest horror films ever made.

6. 10 Trivia Facts:

1. The famous line "Here's Johnny!" was improvised by Jack Nicholson, referencing The Tonight Show Starring Johnny Carson.

2. Kubrick made Shelley Duvall perform the baseball bat scene 127 times, a world record for the most retakes of a single movie scene with spoken dialogue.

3. The maze in the film was inspired by the hedge maze at the Stanley Hotel, where Stephen King conceived the original story.

4. Danny Lloyd, who played Danny Torrance, was shielded from the film's horror elements and thought he was making a drama about a family in a hotel.

5. The Shining was shot in reverse order, with the final scenes filmed first and the beginning scenes filmed last.

6. Kubrick used a then-revolutionary Steadicam for many of the film's tracking shots, including Danny's tricycle scenes.

7. Stephen King famously disliked Kubrick's adaptation, later producing his own TV miniseries version in 1997.

8. The film's iconic poster, featuring Jack's face peering through the door, was shot by photographer Herb Ritts.

9. The typewriter Jack uses changes color from white to blue to black throughout the film, with no explanation given.

10. The ending of the film differs significantly from the book, with Kubrick opting for a more ambiguous conclusion.

4. Alien

1. Movie Title: Alien

2. Year of Release: 1979

3. Cast and Director:

- Director: Ridley Scott

- Cast: Sigourney Weaver, Tom Skerritt, John Hurt, Ian Holm, Veronica Cartwright

4. Synopsis:

Alien follows the crew of the commercial space tug Nostromo, who investigate a distress signal from an unexplored planet. Their search leads them to a derelict alien spacecraft and a chamber filled with eggs. When crew member Kane is attacked by a creature that emerges from one of the eggs, the crew takes him back to the ship. The true horror begins as a deadly alien lifeform bursts from Kane's chest and begins stalking the crew through the ship's corridors. As the creature grows and becomes more dangerous, the surviving crew members must find a way to destroy it before it kills them all. Led by warrant officer Ellen Ripley, they face not only the alien threat but also hidden agendas within their own ranks.

5. Why This Movie Is Recommended:

Alien is a masterful blend of science fiction and horror that revolutionized both genres. Ridley Scott's direction creates a claustrophobic, tension-filled atmosphere that keeps viewers on edge throughout. The film's lived-in, industrial spaceship design set a new standard for sci-fi realism. H.R. Giger's biomechanical alien design remains one of the most terrifying and iconic movie monsters ever created. Sigourney Weaver's Ellen Ripley became a groundbreaking female action hero. With its perfect pacing, shocking scares, and underlying themes of corporate greed and the unknown terrors of space, Alien continues to influence filmmakers and terrify audiences decades after its release.

6. 10 Trivia Facts:

1. The alien's blood was made from a mixture of latex, corn syrup, and acetic acid.

2. The cast was deliberately not shown the "chestburster" scene before filming to capture genuine reactions of shock and horror.

3. Veronica Cartwright passed out when a jet of blood hit her during the chestburster scene.

4. The alien's head was made from a real human skull as its base.

5. Ridley Scott used seafood to create some of the alien's visceral sounds.

6. The Nostromo was originally named after Joseph Conrad's novel "Nostromo."

7. The computer screens in the film were actually projected video footage as flat-screen monitors didn't exist yet.

8. Yaphet Kotto (Parker) was told to annoy Sigourney Weaver off-camera to create tension between their characters.

9. The alien's look was partly inspired by Francis Bacon's 1944 painting "Three Studies for Figures at the Base of a Crucifixion."

10. Ridley Scott stated that the alien's life cycle was inspired by parasitic wasps.

5. A Nightmare on Elm Street

1. Movie Title: A Nightmare on Elm Street

2. Year of Release: 1984

3. Cast and Director:

  - Director: Wes Craven

  - Cast: Heather Langenkamp, Johnny Depp, Robert Englund, John Saxon

4. Synopsis:

A Nightmare on Elm Street introduces the iconic villain Freddy Krueger, a disfigured dream-demon who uses a glove armed with razors to kill his victims in their dreams, causing their deaths in the real world. The film follows teenager Nancy Thompson and her friends, who begin to dream about the same man - a horribly scarred figure with a blade-fixed glove. As her friends start dying in their sleep, Nancy realizes that she must find a way to pull Freddy out of her dreams and defeat him in the real world. Nancy uncovers the dark history of Freddy Krueger, a child murderer burned alive by vengeful parents, and must face her own parents' involvement in his death. As sleep becomes increasingly dangerous, Nancy fights to stay awake and find a way to destroy Freddy once and for all.

5. Why This Movie Is Recommended:

A Nightmare on Elm Street revolutionized the horror genre by blurring the lines between dreams and reality, creating a new type of psychological terror. Wes Craven's imaginative direction turns everyday objects and settings into sources of fear. The film's exploration of the power of dreams and the sins of the past adds depth to its scares. Robert Englund's portrayal of Freddy Krueger created one of horror's most enduring and charismatic villains. With its inventive kill scenes, strong female protagonist, and underlying themes of teenage anxiety and parental betrayal, A Nightmare on Elm Street remains a landmark horror film that continues to influence the genre today.

6. 10 Trivia Facts:

1. The film was inspired by a series of LA Times articles about young men dying in their sleep after refusing to sleep for days.

2. Johnny Depp made his film debut in A Nightmare on Elm Street, playing Glen Lantz.

3. The famous boiler room was actually a UCLA swimming pool facility.

4. The scene where Nancy is attacked in her bathtub was filmed in a bottomless tub built over a hole in the floor of Wes Craven's garage.

5. Freddy Krueger was named after a kid who bullied Wes Craven in school.

6. The film's original concept had Freddy as a child molester, but this was changed to avoid accusations of exploiting a series of real-life child molestations in California at the time.

7. The movie was shot in 32 days on a budget of $1.8 million.

8. The infamous scissor-hands scene was inspired by Craven's cat getting its claws stuck in his couch.

9. New Line Cinema was near bankruptcy before the film's success, leading it to be nicknamed "The House That Freddy Built."

10. The film features a young Lin Shaye (Charles' sister) as the teacher in Nancy's English class.

6. The Texas Chain Saw Massacre

1. Movie Title: The Texas Chain Saw Massacre

2. Year of Release: 1974

3. Cast and Director:

- Director: Tobe Hooper

- Cast: Marilyn Burns, Paul A. Partain, Edwin Neal, Gunnar Hansen

4. Synopsis:

The Texas Chain Saw Massacre follows a group of friends who fall victim to a family of cannibals while on a road trip in rural Texas. After picking up a hitchhiker who behaves erratically, the group finds themselves at an old farmhouse seeking gas. They encounter Leatherface, a chainsaw-wielding, skin-mask-wearing killer, and his deranged family. What follows is a nightmarish sequence of events as the friends are hunted down one by one. The film focuses on Sally Hardesty's terrifying ordeal as she becomes the lone survivor, desperately trying to escape the horrors of the Sawyer family. The relentless pursuit and the shocking revelations about the family's cannibalistic practices create an atmosphere of unrelenting dread and visceral terror.

5. Why This Movie Is Recommended:

The Texas Chain Saw Massacre is a landmark in horror cinema, renowned for its raw, documentary-like approach to terror. Despite its reputation for gore, the film relies more on psychological horror and implied violence. Tobe Hooper's direction creates a suffocating atmosphere of dread and chaos. The film's exploration of the dark side of rural America and its commentary on meat consumption add depth to its horror. Leatherface became an iconic horror villain, influencing countless future films. Its low-budget, gritty aesthetic established a new standard for realistic horror, making it a must-watch for any horror enthusiast.

6. 10 Trivia Facts:

1. Despite its title, there are only two on-screen deaths caused by a chainsaw in the entire film.

2. The film was shot in a real house in Texas during a brutally hot summer, with temperatures often exceeding 100°F.

3. Gunnar Hansen, who played Leatherface, kept his distance from other actors during filming to maintain an atmosphere of fear.

4. The iconic chainsaw dance at the end was improvised by Hansen when he was too exhausted to catch Marilyn Burns.

5. The film's budget was so low that the cast and crew often worked 16-hour days to finish shooting.

6. The movie was banned in several countries upon its release due to its intense content.

7. The character of Leatherface was inspired by serial killer Ed Gein.

8. The film's original title was "Head Cheese," but it was changed for marketing purposes.

9. John Larroquette, known for the TV show "Night Court," provided the opening narration for free as a favor to Tobe Hooper.

10. The entire movie was shot in order, which is unusual for film production.

7. Rosemary's Baby

1. Movie Title: Rosemary's Baby

2. Year of Release: 1968

3. Cast and Director:

   - Director: Roman Polanski

   - Cast: Mia Farrow, John Cassavetes, Ruth Gordon, Sidney Blackmer

4. Synopsis:

Rosemary's Baby tells the story of Rosemary Woodhouse, a young woman who moves into a new apartment in New York City with her husband, Guy. Their eccentric elderly neighbors, the Castevets, take an unusual interest in the couple, especially when Rosemary becomes pregnant. As her pregnancy progresses, Rosemary becomes increasingly isolated and paranoid, suspecting that something is terribly wrong with her baby. She uncovers a sinister plot involving her husband, neighbors, and even her doctor, all seemingly part of a Satanic cult with nefarious plans for her unborn child. The film builds tension as Rosemary struggles to uncover the truth and protect her baby, leading to a shocking climax that blurs the line between paranoia and reality.

5. Why This Movie Is Recommended:

Rosemary's Baby is a masterpiece of psychological horror that eschews traditional scares for a slowly building sense of dread and paranoia. Roman Polanski's direction creates an atmosphere of claustrophobic unease, turning the mundane into something sinister. The film's exploration of themes like bodily autonomy, trust, and the dark side of ambition adds depth to its horror. Mia Farrow's performance as the increasingly isolated and desperate Rosemary is haunting. The movie's influence on the horror genre, particularly in its treatment of Satanic themes and pregnancy horror, is immeasurable. Its ability to unsettle viewers through suggestion rather than explicit violence makes it a timeless classic.

6. 10 Trivia Facts:

1. The exterior shots of the apartment building were filmed at the Dakota in New York City, which later became famous as the site of John Lennon's murder.

2. Mia Farrow ate raw liver for a scene, despite being a vegetarian.

3. The movie was released one month before Mia Farrow's then-husband Frank Sinatra served her divorce papers.

4. Roman Polanski makes a cameo appearance as a party guest wearing a fake nose.

5. The film's success led to a boom in Satan-themed horror movies in the 1970s.

6. Author Ira Levin named the character of Rosemary after his sister.

7. The lullaby in the film, sung by Mia Farrow, was composed by Krzysztof Komeda, who died shortly after the film's release.

8. John Lennon and Yoko Ono were living in the Dakota during the filming of exterior shots.

9. The movie was shot in chronological order, which is unusual for film productions.

10. Ruth Gordon won an Academy Award for Best Supporting Actress for her role as Minnie Castevet.

8. The Blair Witch Project

1. Movie Title: The Blair Witch Project

2. Year of Release: 1999

3. Cast and Director:

- Directors: Daniel Myrick, Eduardo Sánchez

- Cast: Heather Donahue, Michael C. Williams, Joshua Leonard

4. Synopsis:

The Blair Witch Project follows three student filmmakers - Heather, Mike, and Josh - as they venture into the Black Hills Forest in Maryland to film a documentary about the legend of the Blair Witch. Armed with cameras, they interview locals about the witch and other folklore before heading into the woods. As they become lost and tensions rise, strange occurrences begin to plague the group. They hear inexplicable noises at night and find bizarre stick figures hanging from trees. When Josh disappears, Heather and Mike's fear escalates into panic. The film culminates in a terrifying finale as the remaining two students desperately try to escape the increasingly threatening forest, leading to a shocking and ambiguous conclusion in an abandoned house.

5. Why This Movie Is Recommended:

The Blair Witch Project revolutionized horror cinema with its found-footage format and innovative marketing campaign. By blurring the lines between fiction and reality, it created a uniquely immersive and terrifying experience. The film's use of improvisation and naturalistic acting enhances its sense of authenticity. Its minimalist approach to horror, relying on suggestion and the power of imagination rather than explicit scares, proves incredibly effective. The movie's exploration of fear of the unknown and the power of folklore adds depth to its scares. Its influence on both horror filmmaking and viral marketing strategies makes it a landmark film in cinema history.

6. 10 Trivia Facts:

1. The film was shot in 8 days with a budget of only $60,000.

2. The actors were given minimal information about the plot and were often surprised by events during filming.

3. The marketing campaign led many people to believe the footage was real, with missing person posters for the actors distributed.

4. The shaky cam technique caused some viewers to experience motion sickness in theaters.

5. The directors gave the actors less food each day to increase their irritability on camera.

6. None of the main actors had professional acting experience before this film.

7. The film's website, which added to its mythology, was one of the first examples of viral marketing.

8. The actors were taught to use the camera equipment themselves, as there was no camera crew.

9. GPS trackers were used to direct the actors to specific locations in the woods.

10. The film was an unexpected box office success, grossing nearly $250 million worldwide.

9. Jaws

1. Movie Title: Jaws

2. Year of Release: 1975

3. Cast and Director:

- Director: Steven Spielberg

- Cast: Roy Scheider, Robert Shaw, Richard Dreyfuss, Lorraine Gary

4. Synopsis:

Jaws is set in the beach town of Amity Island, where a giant great white shark begins terrorizing swimmers. Police Chief Martin Brody wants to close the beaches, but he's overruled by the mayor who fears the loss of tourist revenue. After several attacks, Brody teams up with marine biologist Matt Hooper and professional shark hunter Quint to hunt down the massive predator. The trio sets out on Quint's boat, the Orca, leading to a tense and terrifying battle at sea. As they face the relentless and cunning shark, each man must confront his own fears and weaknesses. The film builds suspense through glimpses of the unseen threat, culminating in a final showdown that has become one of cinema's most iconic sequences.

5. Why This Movie Is Recommended:

Jaws is a masterclass in suspense and tension, with Spielberg's direction turning a simple premise into a complex thriller. The film's ability to create fear through suggestion, aided by John Williams' iconic score, revolutionized horror cinema. Despite being categorized as a thriller, its influence on horror is undeniable. The performances, particularly the chemistry between the three leads, add depth and humanity to the terror. Jaws explores themes of man versus nature, political corruption, and the power of primal fear. Its impact on popular culture and its role in creating the summer blockbuster make it a must-see for any film enthusiast.

6. 10 Trivia Facts:

1. The shark was nicknamed "Bruce" after Spielberg's lawyer, Bruce Ramer.

2. The famous line "You're gonna need a bigger boat" was improvised by Roy Scheider.

3. Mechanical issues with the shark led Spielberg to show it less, inadvertently increasing the suspense.

4. The film was shot on Martha's Vineyard, Massachusetts.

5. Steven Spielberg was only 26 years old when he directed Jaws.

6. The opening scene took three days to shoot and Spielberg nearly drowned during filming.

7. Robert Shaw's famous USS Indianapolis monologue was partly written by the actor himself.

8. The shark doesn't make a full appearance until 1 hour and 21 minutes into the film.

9. Three mechanical sharks were built for the production, collectively costing $150,000.

10. Jaws was the first film to earn $100 million at the box office.

10. The Silence of the Lambs

1. Movie Title: The Silence of the Lambs

2. Year of Release: 1991

3. Cast and Director:

- Director: Jonathan Demme

- Cast: Jodie Foster, Anthony Hopkins, Scott Glenn, Ted Levine

4. Synopsis:

The Silence of the Lambs follows FBI trainee Clarice Starling as she is assigned to interview imprisoned cannibalistic serial killer Dr. Hannibal Lecter. The FBI hopes Lecter can provide insight into an active serial killer case involving "Buffalo Bill," who skins his female victims. As Clarice delves deeper into the twisted minds of both killers, she forms a complex relationship with the brilliant but dangerous Lecter. The hunt for Buffalo Bill becomes increasingly urgent as he kidnaps a senator's daughter. Clarice must navigate Lecter's mind games and her own past traumas to uncover Buffalo Bill's identity before it's too late. The film builds to a tense climax as Clarice confronts the killer, leading to a resolution that blurs the lines between hero and monster.

5. Why This Movie Is Recommended:

The Silence of the Lambs is a masterpiece of psychological horror that transcends genre boundaries. Jonathan Demme's direction creates an atmosphere of constant unease, while the performances by Foster and Hopkins are nothing short of iconic. The film's exploration of gender dynamics, power, and the nature of evil adds depth to its thrills. Its influence on both horror and thriller genres is immeasurable, popularizing the concept of the forensic procedural. The movie's ability to terrify through dialogue and suggestion rather than graphic violence sets it apart. Its sweep of the top five Academy Awards categories solidifies its status as a landmark in cinema history.

6. 10 Trivia Facts:

1. Anthony Hopkins is only on screen for 16 minutes throughout the entire film.

2. The moth poster used to promote the film features a death's-head hawkmoth with a skull on its back, but look closely: the skull is actually made up of seven naked women, a reference to Philippe Halsman's photograph of Salvador Dalí.

3. Jodie Foster used Robert De Niro's technique of writing a fictional biography of her character to prepare for the role.

4. The film is one of only three movies to win all top five Academy Awards (Best Picture, Director, Actor, Actress, and Screenplay).

5. Buffalo Bill's dance scene was spontaneously improvised by Ted Levine during filming.

6. Anthony Hopkins based part of Hannibal Lecter's voice on Katharine Hepburn and Truman Capote.

7. The real FBI allowed the film crew to attend their training classes at Quantico.

8. Gene Hackman originally owned the rights to the novel and planned to direct the film himself before dropping out.

9. The iconic slurping noise Hannibal makes was improvised by Anthony Hopkins during filming.

10. Jodie Foster won the role of Clarice Starling after Michelle Pfeiffer turned it down, considering it too violent.

11. The Thing

1. Movie Title: The Thing

2. Year of Release: 1982

3. Cast and Director:

- Director: John Carpenter

- Cast: Kurt Russell, Wilford Brimley, Keith David, Donald Moffat

4. Synopsis:

The Thing is set in an isolated Antarctic research station where a group of American scientists encounter a mysterious organism unearthed from the ice. This alien life form has the ability to perfectly imitate other living beings. As the creature infiltrates the station, paranoia and suspicion grow among the team members, each unsure of who is human and who is not. Led by helicopter pilot R.J. MacReady (Kurt Russell), the survivors must find a way to identify and destroy the alien before it can escape to the outside world. The film builds tension through its claustrophobic setting and the characters' growing distrust, culminating in a series of shocking revelations and a ambiguous, chilling conclusion.

5. Why This Movie Is Recommended:

The Thing is a masterpiece of paranoia and body horror. John Carpenter's direction creates an atmosphere of isolation and dread that permeates every frame. The groundbreaking practical effects by Rob Bottin still hold up today, creating some of the most memorable and disturbing creature designs in film history. The movie's exploration of themes like identity, trust, and the unknown adds depth to its scares. Its influence on both horror and science fiction genres is immeasurable. Despite its initial mixed reception, The Thing has rightfully earned its place as a cult classic and one of the greatest horror films ever made.

6. 10 Trivia Facts:

1. The film is based on the 1938 novella "Who Goes There?" by John W. Campbell Jr.

2. The dog in the opening scene was played by a half-wolf, half-malamute named Jed.

3. Wires that controlled the creature effects were painted out of the film frame by frame, as CGI wasn't available yet.

4. The film's musical score was composed by Ennio Morricone, marking a rare instance where John Carpenter didn't score his own film.

5. Kurt Russell's famous hat in the film was his own personal hat that he wore off-set.

6. The film was shot in below-freezing temperatures in both Alaska and British Columbia.

7. To create the effect of frosty breath in warm studios, the actors held tiny mouthfuls of crushed ice before each take.

8. The Thing was released just two weeks after another alien movie, E.T. the Extra-Terrestrial, which overshadowed it at the box office.

9. The chess game that MacReady plays against the computer is based on a famous 1951 game known as "The Immortal Game."

10. Despite its now-classic status, the film was initially a box office disappointment and received negative reviews upon release.

12. Get Out

1. Movie Title: Get Out

2. Year of Release: 2017

3. Cast and Director:

- Director: Jordan Peele

- Cast: Daniel Kaluuya, Allison Williams, Bradley Whitford, Catherine Keener

4. Synopsis:

Get Out follows Chris Washington, a young African-American man, as he visits his white girlfriend Rose's family estate for the first time. Initially, the family's overly accommodating behavior seems like nervous attempts to deal with their daughter's interracial relationship. However, as the weekend progresses, a series of increasingly disturbing discoveries lead Chris to a truth far more sinister than he could have imagined. The film builds tension through subtle microaggressions and unsettling encounters, culminating in a shocking revelation about the true nature of the Armitage family and their intentions for Chris. As he fights to escape, Chris must confront not only the immediate threat but also the systemic racism that allowed such horrors to occur.

5. Why This Movie Is Recommended:

Get Out is a groundbreaking horror film that expertly blends social commentary with genuine scares. Jordan Peele's directorial debut offers a fresh and incisive look at racism in America, using the horror genre as a powerful metaphor. The film's ability to create tension through everyday interactions makes it uniquely unsettling. Daniel Kaluuya's nuanced performance anchors the film, allowing viewers to experience the mounting dread through his eyes. Get Out's exploration of themes like cultural appropriation, liberal racism, and the perpetuation of slavery adds layers of depth to its thrills. Its critical and commercial success, including an Oscar for Best Original Screenplay, solidifies its place as a modern horror classic.

6. 10 Trivia Facts:

1. The screenplay for Get Out was written in just two months.

2. The deer motif throughout the film symbolizes Chris's mother, who died in a hit-and-run involving a deer.

3. The Sunken Place was inspired by Jordan Peele's feelings of helplessness during the 2008 financial crisis.

4. The film's original ending was much darker, but was changed after negative test audience reactions.

5. The character of Rod the TSA agent was originally written to die, but Peele decided against it.

6. The movie was shot in just 23 days.

7. Jordan Peele cited The Stepford Wives and Rosemary's Baby as major influences on the film.

8. The hypnosis scene took over 65 takes to get right.

9. Get Out was the first debut film by an African-American writer/director to gross over $100 million at the box office.

10. The film's working title during production was "Get Out of the House" to keep the project under wraps.

13. Scream

1. Movie Title: Scream

2. Year of Release: 1996

3. Cast and Director:

  - Director: Wes Craven

  - Cast: Neve Campbell, Courteney Cox, David Arquette, Skeet Ulrich, Drew Barrymore

4. Synopsis:

  Scream follows high school student Sidney Prescott as her small town of Woodsboro is terrorized by a masked killer known as Ghostface. As the body count rises, Sidney and her friends find themselves targeted by the killer, who seems to be inspired by classic horror films. The movie cleverly blends genuine scares with self-aware humor, as the characters use their knowledge of horror movie tropes to try to survive. Local reporter Gale Weathers and deputy sheriff Dewey Riley join the investigation, adding layers of mystery and suspicion. As the killer's identity remains hidden, trust becomes a scarce commodity, and Sidney must confront both the immediate threat and the dark secrets of her past to survive.

5. Why This Movie Is Recommended:

  Scream revitalized the slasher genre by combining classic horror elements with postmodern self-awareness. Wes Craven's direction balances genuine scares with clever meta-commentary on horror film conventions. The movie's ability to both honor and subvert genre tropes makes it endlessly entertaining for horror fans. The whodunit aspect adds an engaging mystery element to the slasher format. Neve Campbell's performance as the resilient Sidney Prescott created a new type of horror heroine. The film's exploration of media sensationalism and the impact of horror movies on society adds depth to its thrills. Scream's influence on subsequent horror films and pop culture at large cements its status as a modern classic.

6. 10 Trivia Facts:

  1. The iconic Ghostface mask was discovered by chance in an abandoned house during location scouting.

  2. The film was originally titled "Scary Movie" before being changed to "Scream."

  3. Drew Barrymore was originally cast as Sidney but chose to play Casey Becker to subvert audience expectations.

  4. The voice of Ghostface was provided by Roger L. Jackson, who was on set but hidden from the actors to maintain suspense.

  5. The film features over 50 references to other horror movies.

  6. Wes Craven nearly passed on directing the film, but was convinced by Drew Barrymore's involvement.

  7. The high school scenes were filmed at the same school used in Beverly Hills, 90210.

  8. The movie was inspired by the real-life Gainesville Ripper murders.

  9. Matthew Lillard improvised most of his lines in the finale, including the famous "My mom and dad are gonna be so mad at me" line.

  10. Scream was the first film to win Best Movie at the MTV Movie Awards that wasn't nominated for an Academy Award for Best Picture.

14. Hereditary

1. **Movie Title**: Hereditary

2. **Year of Release**: 2018

3. **Cast and Director**:

 - Director: Ari Aster

 - Cast: Toni Collette, Alex Wolff, Milly Shapiro, Gabriel Byrne

4. **Synopsis**:

 Hereditary follows the Graham family in the aftermath of their secretive grandmother's death. As mother Annie struggles with her loss, strange and increasingly terrifying occurrences begin to plague the family. Her daughter Charlie exhibits disturbing behavior, while her son Peter becomes withdrawn and haunted by bizarre visions. As tragedy strikes again, the family's grief and trauma spiral into a nightmare of guilt, paranoia, and supernatural horror. Annie delves into her mother's past, uncovering dark secrets and a sinister legacy that threatens to destroy her family. The film builds an atmosphere of dread and inevitability as the true nature of the family's inheritance is revealed, leading to a shocking and horrifying climax.

5. **Why This Movie Is Recommended**:

 Hereditary is a masterclass in psychological horror that lingers long after viewing. Ari Aster's directorial debut creates an oppressive atmosphere of grief and dread that permeates every frame. Toni Collette's tour-de-force performance as Annie grounds the supernatural elements in raw, human emotion. The film's exploration of generational trauma and the weight of family legacy adds psychological depth to its scares. Its intricate plot rewards multiple viewings, revealing new layers of meaning and foreshadowing. Hereditary's ability to shock comes not just from its horrific imagery, but from its devastating portrayal of a family torn apart by forces beyond their control. It stands as one of the most impactful and discussed horror films of recent years.

6. **10 Trivia Facts**:

 1. The treehouse in the film was fully constructed for the movie and later dismantled.

 2. Toni Collette's character's miniatures were created by two artists over a period of several months.

 3. The clicking noise associated with Charlie was improvised by actress Milly Shapiro.

 4. Director Ari Aster had a 100-page backstory for the cult in the film.

 5. The film's original cut was three hours long.

 6. Alex Wolff, who played Peter, experienced PTSD-like symptoms after filming.

 7. The word "coconut" appears in the background of several scenes, foreshadowing a major plot point.

 8. The Graham house was a real home in Salt Lake City, Utah, not a set.

 9. Ari Aster describes the film as "a tragedy that curdles into a nightmare."

 10. The seance scene took two full days to film.

15. The Conjuring

1. Movie Title: The Conjuring

2. Year of Release: 2013

3. Cast and Director:

  - Director: James Wan

  - Cast: Vera Farmiga, Patrick Wilson, Lili Taylor, Ron Livingston

4. Synopsis:

The Conjuring is based on the true case files of paranormal investigators Ed and Lorraine Warren. The film follows the Perron family as they move into a secluded farmhouse in Rhode Island, only to find themselves plagued by increasingly terrifying supernatural occurrences. Desperate for help, they reach out to the Warrens, who discover the house's dark history and a malevolent presence that threatens the family. As the haunting escalates, the Warrens must confront their own fears and use all their experience to save the Perrons from a powerful demonic entity. The film builds tension through a series of escalating paranormal events, leading to a climactic exorcism that tests the limits of faith and courage.

5. Why This Movie Is Recommended:

The Conjuring revitalized the haunted house subgenre with its masterful blend of old-school scares and modern filmmaking techniques. James Wan's direction creates a palpable atmosphere of dread, using inventive camera work and timing to maximize tension. The film's strength lies in its focus on character development, allowing audiences to form strong connections with both the Perrons and the Warrens. This emotional investment amplifies the terror as the family faces supernatural threats. The movie's basis in "true events" adds an extra layer of unease for viewers. With its strong performances, effective scares, and exploration of themes like faith and family, The Conjuring stands as one of the most influential horror films of the 21st century.

6. 10 Trivia Facts:

  1. The real Perron family visited the set during filming and have praised the movie's accuracy.

  2. The film was originally titled "The Warren Files."

  3. The creepy music box in the film was custom-made for the movie and is now part of the Warren's Occult Museum.

  4. Vera Farmiga and Patrick Wilson spent time with the real Lorraine Warren to prepare for their roles.

  5. The movie was shot in chronological order, which is unusual for film productions.

  6. Director James Wan insisted on using minimal CGI, relying instead on practical effects and clever camera work.

  7. The film's success spawned its own cinematic universe, including spin-offs like "Annabelle" and "The Nun."

  8. The hidden clap game was based on a real game the Perron children played in the house.

  9. The movie was originally going to be rated R, but was edited to secure a PG-13 rating without losing its impact.

  10. The real Annabelle doll is actually a Raggedy Ann doll, not the porcelain doll seen in the film.

16. The Sixth Sense

1. Movie Title: The Sixth Sense

2. Year of Release: 1999

3. Cast and Director:

- Director: M. Night Shyamalan

- Cast: Bruce Willis, Haley Joel Osment, Toni Collette, Olivia Williams

4. Synopsis:

The Sixth Sense follows child psychologist Dr. Malcolm Crowe as he tries to help Cole Sear, a troubled young boy who claims to see and communicate with the dead. Initially skeptical, Malcolm gradually comes to believe Cole's ability is real as he witnesses inexplicable events. As Malcolm works to understand and help Cole cope with his terrifying gift, he also grapples with a growing distance in his marriage. The film builds tension through a series of encounters with spirits, each revealing more about the nature of Cole's ability and the unfinished business that keeps the dead lingering. As Cole learns to use his gift to help lost souls, Malcolm makes a shocking discovery about his own life, leading to one of cinema's most famous twist endings.

5. Why This Movie Is Recommended:

The Sixth Sense is a masterpiece of supernatural thriller that transcends the horror genre. M. Night Shyamalan's direction creates an atmosphere of constant unease, blending subtle scares with profound emotional depth. The film's exploration of grief, guilt, and the power of human connection adds layers of meaning to its ghost story. Haley Joel Osment's remarkable performance as Cole brings authenticity to the supernatural elements. The movie's iconic twist ending rewards repeat viewings, revealing careful foreshadowing throughout. Its influence on supernatural thrillers and twist endings in cinema is immeasurable. The Sixth Sense stands as a thoughtful, emotionally resonant horror film that appeals even to viewers who typically avoid the genre.

6. 10 Trivia Facts:

1. The color red appears prominently in scenes with supernatural elements.

2. Haley Joel Osment was cast after he sent a letter to Shyamalan explaining how he understood the character.

3. The film was shot in sequence, which is unusual for movie productions.

4. Bruce Willis took a pay cut in exchange for a percentage of the film's profits, which paid off enormously.

5. The phrase "I see dead people" was voted the 44th greatest movie quote by the American Film Institute.

6. The twist ending was so secret that only a few members of the crew knew about it during filming.

7. Shyamalan appears in a cameo as a doctor that Malcolm briefly speaks to at his office.

8. The film was nominated for six Academy Awards, including Best Picture.

9. The role of Malcolm Crowe was originally offered to Michael Douglas.

10. In the DVD commentary, Shyamalan states that despite the film's serious tone, it contains more humor than any of his other works.

17. It

1. Movie Title: It (also known as It: Chapter One)

2. Year of Release: 2017

3. Cast and Director:

- Director: Andy Muschietti

- Cast: Bill Skarsgård, Jaeden Martell, Finn Wolfhard, Sophia Lillis, Jeremy Ray Taylor

4. Synopsis:

Based on Stephen King's novel, It is set in the town of Derry, Maine, where a group of seven outcast kids known as "The Losers Club" discover that their town is home to an ancient, shape-shifting evil that takes the form of a clown called Pennywise. The entity emerges every 27 years to feed on the town's children. As members of the group encounter terrifying visions and narrowly escape Pennywise's grasp, they realize they must band together to confront their own personal demons and the murderous clown. The film alternates between intense horror sequences and coming-of-age drama as the kids navigate bullies, dysfunctional families, and the growing threat of It, building to a confrontation in the monster's lair beneath the town.

5. Why This Movie Is Recommended:

It brilliantly balances horror with heart, creating a compelling story of friendship in the face of evil. Andy Muschietti's direction brings Stephen King's sprawling novel to life with a perfect blend of jump scares, cosmic horror, and character-driven drama. Bill Skarsgård's portrayal of Pennywise is utterly terrifying, creating an iconic movie monster for a new generation. The young cast's chemistry and performances ground the supernatural elements in relatable coming-of-age struggles. The film's exploration of childhood trauma and the power of facing one's fears adds depth to its scares. With its nostalgic 80s setting, strong character development, and genuinely frightening sequences, It revitalized the horror genre and became one of the most successful horror films of all time.

6. 10 Trivia Facts:

1. The film broke several box office records, including highest-grossing horror film of all time.

2. Bill Skarsgård was so effective as Pennywise that he scared some of the child actors on set.

3. The young actors were not shown Pennywise's full costume until their first scene with him to capture genuine reactions.

4. Stephen King gave his blessing to the film, saying it succeeded beyond his expectations.

5. The Derry sewers were constructed using over 5,000 foam cores.

6. Finn Wolfhard (Richie) was cast after the director saw him in Stranger Things, another 80s-themed horror production.

7. The film's success led to a sequel, It: Chapter Two, released in 2019.

8. Tim Curry, who played Pennywise in the 1990 miniseries, gave his approval to Bill Skarsgård's interpretation.

9. The movie contains over 100 shots with CGI clowns, creating unsettling background imagery.

10. The projector scene, one of the film's most memorable, was not in the original script but was added during production.

18. Poltergeist

1. Movie Title: Poltergeist

2. Year of Release: 1982

3. Cast and Director:

- Director: Tobe Hooper

- Cast: JoBeth Williams, Craig T. Nelson, Heather O'Rourke, Beatrice Straight

4. Synopsis:

Poltergeist follows the Freeling family, whose suburban life is turned upside down when their youngest daughter, Carol Anne, begins communicating with spirits through the family's television set. Initially playful, the supernatural presence soon turns malevolent, abducting Carol Anne into a spectral realm. As the desperate parents seek help from parapsychologists and a spiritual medium, they discover their house was built on an ancient burial ground. The family must fight to rescue Carol Anne from the powerful entity known as "the Beast," confronting terrifying manifestations and their own worst fears. The film builds tension through increasingly bizarre and frightening paranormal events, culminating in a battle for Carol Anne's soul and a spectacular, effects-driven climax.

5. Why This Movie Is Recommended:

Poltergeist stands as a landmark in supernatural horror, blending cutting-edge special effects with primal fears of the unknown. The film's genius lies in its ability to make the familiar terrifying, transforming everyday suburban life into a landscape of terror. Tobe Hooper's direction (with reported uncredited input from producer Steven Spielberg) creates a perfect balance of family drama and supernatural thrills. The movie's exploration of themes like suburban development, television's influence, and the American dream adds depth to its scares. With its memorable imagery, quotable lines, and genuine emotional core, Poltergeist has become a touchstone of horror cinema, influencing countless films in the haunted house subgenre.

6. 10 Trivia Facts:

1. The film is notorious for its "Poltergeist curse," as several cast members died young, including Heather O'Rourke.

2. The scene where JoBeth Williams swims with skeletons used real human skeletons, as they were cheaper than fake ones.

3. Drew Barrymore auditioned for the role of Carol Anne before being cast in E.T. the Extra-Terrestrial.

4. The film's original cut was so intense it received an R rating, requiring edits to secure a PG rating.

5. The static on the TV when Carol Anne says "They're here" was created by filming the close-up of a vacuum tube.

6. The movie was released a week before E.T., leading to a "Spielberg summer" at the box office.

7. The beast's roar is a mixture of lions, tigers, and dolphins.

8. Poltergeist was selected for preservation in the National Film Registry by the Library of Congress in 2017.

9. The "They're here" scene was done in only two takes.

10. There's an ongoing debate about whether Tobe Hooper or Steven Spielberg was the primary director of the film.

19. Psycho

1. Movie Title: Psycho

2. Year of Release: 1960

3. Cast and Director:

- Director: Alfred Hitchcock

- Cast: Anthony Perkins, Janet Leigh, Vera Miles, John Gavin

4. Synopsis:

Psycho begins with Marion Crane, a Phoenix secretary who impulsively steals $40,000 from her employer and flees town. During her escape, she stops at the remote Bates Motel, run by the shy Norman Bates, who seems to be dominated by his unseen mother. After a conversation with Norman, Marion decides to return the money, but is brutally murdered in the now-famous shower scene. As Marion's sister Lila and boyfriend Sam investigate her disappearance, they uncover the disturbing truth about Norman and his mother. The film builds tension through its exploration of Norman's psyche and the mounting evidence of his crimes, leading to a shocking climax that reveals the true nature of Norman's relationship with his mother.

5. Why This Movie Is Recommended:

Psycho is a masterpiece of suspense that revolutionized the horror genre. Alfred Hitchcock's innovative direction, particularly in the iconic shower scene, set new standards for creating tension and shock in cinema. The film's exploration of psychological horror and its blurring of protagonist roles were groundbreaking for its time. Anthony Perkins' portrayal of Norman Bates created one of the most memorable and complex villains in film history. Psycho's influence on horror, thriller, and cinema in general is immeasurable, inspiring countless imitations and homages. Its themes of duality, madness, and the darkness lurking beneath a respectable façade continue to resonate with modern audiences, cementing its status as a timeless classic.

6. 10 Trivia Facts:

1. The famous shower scene contains 77 different camera angles and took 7 days to film.

2. Chocolate syrup was used to simulate blood in the black-and-white film.

3. Alfred Hitchcock bought up as many copies of the original novel as possible to keep the ending a secret.

4. The film was the first American movie to show a toilet flushing on screen.

5. Janet Leigh was so traumatized by the shower scene that she avoided showers for years afterwards.

6. The portrait of Norman's mother is actually a picture of Anthony Perkins in drag.

7. Psycho was the first of Hitchcock's films to be shot by a television crew to save money.

8. The Bates house was inspired by Edward Hopper's painting "House by the Railroad."

9. Hitchcock used a 50mm lens on a 35mm camera to recreate the look of human vision.

10. The film's original trailer was over 6 minutes long and featured Hitchcock giving a tour of the set.

20. Night of the Living Dead

1. Movie Title: Night of the Living Dead

2. Year of Release: 1968

3. Cast and Director:

- Director: George A. Romero

- Cast: Duane Jones, Judith O'Dea, Karl Hardman, Marilyn Eastman

4. Synopsis:

Night of the Living Dead begins as siblings Barbra and Johnny visit their father's grave, only to be attacked by a strange, shambling man. Barbra flees to an abandoned farmhouse where she meets Ben, and they barricade themselves inside as more of the undead converge on the house. They discover other survivors hiding in the basement, and conflicts arise over how best to survive the night. As they learn through radio and television broadcasts that the recently dead are reanimating and eating the living, tensions mount both inside and outside the house. The group must fight off the growing horde of zombies while dealing with their own interpersonal conflicts, leading to a tense and tragic climax.

5. Why This Movie Is Recommended:

Night of the Living Dead is a groundbreaking film that defined the modern zombie genre. George A. Romero's low-budget, independent production became a cultural phenomenon, shocking audiences with its graphic content and social commentary. The film's casting of a Black actor as the lead was revolutionary for its time, adding layers of racial subtext to the narrative. Its bleak tone and nihilistic ending were a departure from traditional horror, reflecting the turbulent social climate of the 1960s. The movie's influence extends far beyond horror, impacting independent filmmaking and challenging censorship standards. With its claustrophobic atmosphere, stark violence, and underlying social critique, Night of the Living Dead remains a powerful and relevant piece of cinema.

6. 10 Trivia Facts:

1. The film entered the public domain due to an error in the copyright notice on original prints.

2. The zombies were played by volunteers who were paid in BBQ dinners.

3. Chocolate syrup and roasted ham were used to simulate blood and flesh in the black-and-white film.

4. The word "zombie" is never used in the film; the undead are referred to as "ghouls" or "those things."

5. The film's budget was only $114,000, but it grossed $30 million internationally.

6. George A. Romero was only 28 years old when he directed the film.

7. The MPAA film rating system was not in place when the film was released, allowing children to view the graphic content.

8. The farmhouse used in the film was scheduled for demolition and was destroyed shortly after filming completed.

9. Duane Jones, who played Ben, rewrote much of his dialogue to avoid stereotypical "black" speech patterns.

10. The film was selected by the Library of Congress for preservation in the National Film Registry in 1999.

Canada

1. Ginger Snaps

1. Movie Title: Ginger Snaps

2. Year of Release: 2000

3. Cast and Director:

 - Director: John Fawcett

 - Cast: Emily Perkins, Katharine Isabelle, Kris Lemche

4. Synopsis:

 Ginger Snaps follows the story of two outcast teenage sisters, Brigitte and Ginger Fitzgerald, in the suburban town of Bailey Downs. On the night of Ginger's first period, she is attacked by a werewolf. As Ginger undergoes a frightening transformation, Brigitte desperately tries to find a cure. The film uses lycanthropy as a metaphor for puberty and sexual awakening, exploring themes of sisterhood, adolescence, and societal expectations. As Ginger's changes become more pronounced and her behavior more erratic, Brigitte must confront the possibility of losing her sister to the beast within.

5. Why This Movie Is Recommended:

 Ginger Snaps stands out for its intelligent blend of horror and coming-of-age drama. It subverts traditional werewolf movie tropes by centering on female characters and using the transformation as a metaphor for puberty. The film's dark humor, strong performances, and practical effects create a unique and memorable viewing experience. Its exploration of teenage angst and sisterly bonds adds depth to the horror elements, making it resonate with audiences beyond genre fans. Ginger Snaps has become a cult classic, praised for its feminist undertones and fresh take on werewolf mythology.

6. 10 Trivia Facts:

 1. The film was shot in 28 days across various locations in Ontario, Canada.

 2. Katharine Isabelle, who played Ginger, is allergic to dogs and had difficulty working with the canine actors.

 3. The movie spawned two sequels: "Ginger Snaps 2: Unleashed" and "Ginger Snaps Back: The Beginning."

 4. The writers originally conceived the story as "Teenagers are animals."

 5. The film's release was delayed in the wake of the Columbine High School massacre due to its themes of teenage violence.

 6. Emily Perkins and Katharine Isabelle have worked together on several other projects, including the TV series "Da Vinci's Inquest."

 7. The werewolf design was inspired by real-life animal deformities and diseases.

 8. The film's working title was "Sexuality and the Beast."

 9. Ginger Snaps was a box office disappointment in Canada but gained a strong following through home video releases.

10. The movie features several references to Stephen King's novel "Carrie."

2. Black Christmas

1. Movie Title: Black Christmas

2. Year of Release: 1974

3. Cast and Director:

- Director: Bob Clark

- Cast: Olivia Hussey, Keir Dullea, Margot Kidder, John Saxon

4. Synopsis:

Set during the Christmas season, the film follows a group of sorority sisters who are stalked and murdered by a mysterious killer hiding in their sorority house. As the girls prepare for the holidays, they begin receiving disturbing and obscene phone calls. Soon, members of the sorority start disappearing one by one. Jess Bradford, one of the main characters, becomes increasingly concerned and suspicious, especially when her boyfriend Peter becomes a prime suspect. The tension builds as the police try to trace the calls and protect the remaining girls, leading to a suspenseful and chilling climax that leaves the true identity of the killer ambiguous.

5. Why This Movie Is Recommended:

Black Christmas is a pioneering slasher film that predates many of the genre's well-known tropes. Its innovative use of POV shots from the killer's perspective influenced later horror classics like Halloween. The film stands out for its psychological tension, dark humor, and surprisingly complex female characters. It tackles serious themes like abortion and alcoholism, adding depth to the horror narrative. The ambiguous ending and the unsettling suggestion that "the call is coming from inside the house" have become iconic in horror cinema. Black Christmas remains a taut, atmospheric thriller that continues to influence filmmakers and frighten audiences decades after its release.

6. 10 Trivia Facts:

1. Director Bob Clark also directed the family-friendly Christmas classic "A Christmas Story."

2. The film was originally released under the title "Silent Night, Evil Night" in the United States.

3. John Saxon, who plays Lieutenant Fuller, also appeared in other horror classics like "A Nightmare on Elm Street."

4. The movie was shot in Toronto, with the University of Toronto standing in for the fictional college.

5. Margot Kidder, who plays Barb, went on to star as Lois Lane in the Superman films.

6. The obscene phone calls were voiced by director Bob Clark himself, along with actor Nick Mancuso.

7. The film's working title was "Stop Me."

8. Black Christmas has been remade twice: in 2006 and 2019.

9. The sorority house's exterior shots are of a real sorority house that still stands today.

10. The film's tagline was "If this movie doesn't make your skin crawl... it's on TOO TIGHT!"

3. The Changeling

1. Movie Title: The Changeling

2. Year of Release: 1980

3. Cast and Director:

  - Director: Peter Medak

  - Cast: George C. Scott, Trish Van Devere, Melvyn Douglas

4. Synopsis:

  The Changeling follows John Russell, a composer who loses his wife and daughter in a tragic accident. Seeking solitude, he moves into a sprawling, old mansion in Seattle. Soon, John begins experiencing unexplained phenomena: loud banging noises, doors opening and closing on their own, and a child's ball mysteriously appearing and rolling down the stairs. As John investigates, he uncovers the dark history of the house and its connection to a powerful political family. With the help of Claire Norman from the local historical society, John delves deeper into the mystery, uncovering a decades-old murder and a restless spirit seeking justice. The film builds tension through atmospheric scares and a compelling mystery, leading to a chilling climax.

5. Why This Movie Is Recommended:

  The Changeling is a masterclass in psychological horror, relying on atmosphere and suggestion rather than gore or jump scares. George C. Scott's powerful performance anchors the film, bringing depth and empathy to his grieving character. The movie's haunting score and the use of sound design create an unsettling ambiance that keeps viewers on edge. Its exploration of grief, justice, and the lingering effects of past crimes adds layers to the ghost story. The Changeling has influenced many subsequent haunted house films and remains a benchmark for intelligent, mature horror that prioritizes story and character over spectacle.

6. 10 Trivia Facts:

  1. The film is loosely based on events that allegedly occurred to writer Russell Hunter in the Henry Treat Rogers mansion in Denver.

  2. The exterior of the haunted house is actually a combination of two different houses in Vancouver.

  3. Martin Scorsese named The Changeling one of the scariest horror films of all time.

  4. The film won several Genie Awards, including Best Canadian Film.

  5. George C. Scott's wife in the film, Trish Van Devere, was also his wife in real life.

  6. The famous séance scene was shot in one take.

  7. The child's voice in the film was provided by a 30-year-old woman.

  8. Director Peter Medak claims he experienced supernatural events while filming in the house.

  9. The wheelchair used in the film was later donated to a children's hospital.

  10. Despite being set in Seattle, the entire film was shot in Canada.

4. Pontypool

1. Movie Title: Pontypool

2. Year of Release: 2008

3. Cast and Director:

- Director: Bruce McDonald

- Cast: Stephen McHattie, Lisa Houle, Georgina Reilly

4. Synopsis:

Set in the small town of Pontypool, Ontario, the film follows radio shock jock Grant Mazzy as he broadcasts during a severe snowstorm. As the morning progresses, reports start coming in of mobs of people committing acts of extreme violence. Mazzy, his producer Sydney Briar, and technical assistant Laurel-Ann Drummond find themselves trapped in the radio station, becoming the center of information as the crisis unfolds. They soon discover that the source of the violence is a virus transmitted through the English language, causing infected individuals to mindlessly repeat words before becoming violently insane. As they struggle to understand and survive the outbreak, they must find a way to communicate without spreading the infection.

5. Why This Movie Is Recommended:

Pontypool offers a unique take on the zombie genre by focusing on language as the vector of infection. The film's claustrophobic setting in a radio station and its reliance on audio reports to convey the horror create a tense, psychological atmosphere. Stephen McHattie's commanding performance as Grant Mazzy anchors the film, providing both humor and gravitas. The movie's exploration of language, meaning, and communication adds intellectual depth to its horror elements. Pontypool's innovative approach to the apocalyptic scenario, combined with its dark humor and philosophical undertones, make it a standout in Canadian horror cinema.

6. 10 Trivia Facts:

1. The film is based on Tony Burgess's novel "Pontypool Changes Everything," and Burgess wrote the screenplay.

2. The entire movie was shot in just 15 days.

3. The film's budget was only about $1.5 million CAD.

4. Director Bruce McDonald described the film as "Night of the Living Dead meets Marshall McLuhan."

5. The movie was adapted into a stage play in 2010.

6. Pontypool is the first part of a planned trilogy, though the sequels have not yet been produced.

7. The film's tagline was "Shut up or die."

8. Most of the violence and chaos in the town is only described, not shown, adding to the psychological horror.

9. The concept of language as a virus in the film was inspired by William S. Burroughs' ideas.

10. A post-credits scene features Grant Mazzy and Sydney in French, hinting at a potential "cure" for the language virus.

5. The Brood

1. Movie Title: The Brood

2. Year of Release: 1979

3. Cast and Director:

  - Director: David Cronenberg

  - Cast: Oliver Reed, Samantha Eggar, Art Hindle

4. Synopsis:

The Brood follows Frank Carveth, who becomes embroiled in a disturbing mystery involving his estranged wife, Nola, and their young daughter, Candice. Nola is undergoing an experimental psychotherapy treatment called "psychoplasmics" under the care of the unorthodox Dr. Hal Raglan. As Frank investigates a series of brutal murders connected to his family, he discovers that Nola's therapy is allowing her to physically manifest her rage and trauma in the form of deformed children – "the brood" – who carry out violent acts on her behalf. The film builds to a horrifying climax as Frank races to save his daughter from both the murderous brood and the psychological turmoil tearing his family apart.

5. Why This Movie Is Recommended:

The Brood is a landmark in body horror, showcasing David Cronenberg's unique ability to blend psychological drama with visceral, biological horror. The film explores themes of family dysfunction, trauma, and the potential dangers of uncontrolled emotion and experimental psychology. Its disturbing imagery and concepts leave a lasting impression on viewers. The performances, particularly by Samantha Eggar and Oliver Reed, bring depth and intensity to the unsettling narrative. The Brood's exploration of the horrors that can emerge from the human psyche makes it a thought-provoking and deeply unsettling viewing experience that continues to influence horror cinema.

6. 10 Trivia Facts:

1. Cronenberg wrote the screenplay during his bitter divorce and custody battle, channeling his personal experiences into the story.

2. The film was initially banned in the UK due to its disturbing content.

3. Cronenberg considers The Brood to be his version of "Kramer vs. Kramer," but with more violence.

4. The brood children were played by actors with dwarfism wearing masks.

5. Samantha Eggar reportedly found her final scene so disturbing that she refused to watch the completed film.

6. The movie was shot in Toronto and Mississauga, Ontario.

7. Cronenberg's daughter Cassandra has a small role in the film as one of Candice's kindergarten classmates.

8. The film's working title was "The Brood: The Baby Squad."

9. Cronenberg appears in a cameo as a man in the art therapy class.

10. The Brood was remade as a 1994 TV movie titled "The Kindred," though it significantly altered the plot.

6. Cube

1. Movie Title: Cube

2. Year of Release: 1997

3. Cast and Director:

- Director: Vincenzo Natali

- Cast: Nicole de Boer, Maurice Dean Wint, David Hewlett, Andrew Miller

4. Synopsis:

Cube follows six strangers who wake up in a maze of cubic rooms, with no memory of how they got there. Each room is booby-trapped with deadly mechanisms, and the characters must use their unique skills to navigate the space and find an exit. As they progress, tensions rise and alliances shift, revealing the complexities of human nature under extreme stress. The group gradually uncovers clues about the cube's purpose and their own connections to it. The film blends psychological thriller elements with sci-fi horror, creating a claustrophobic and paranoid atmosphere as the characters face not only the deadly traps but also their own deteriorating trust and sanity.

5. Why This Movie Is Recommended:

Cube stands out for its ingenious premise and minimalist approach to sci-fi horror. The film creates intense suspense and horror with a limited set and budget, relying on strong performances and clever writing. Its exploration of human behavior under extreme circumstances adds depth to the visceral thrills. The movie's intricate puzzle-like structure keeps viewers engaged, trying to solve the mystery alongside the characters. Cube's influence on subsequent "escape room" style thrillers and its cult following demonstrate its lasting impact on the genre. It's a testament to how creativity and concept can triumph over big budgets in creating effective horror.

6. 10 Trivia Facts:

1. The entire film was shot on a single 14 by 14 foot set, with only the color of the walls changed to represent different rooms.

2. The movie was made on a budget of approximately $350,000 Canadian dollars.

3. Director Vincenzo Natali wrote 14 drafts of the script over two years before filming began.

4. The cast rehearsed for three weeks before shooting, almost like preparing for a stage play.

5. The film spawned two sequels and a Japanese remake, despite being initially conceived as a standalone movie.

6. The traps in each room were inspired by the opening sequence of the James Bond film "Goldfinger."

7. The mathematical calculations used in the film are actually accurate and were provided by a mathematician consultant.

8. Each character's name is related to a famous prison: Quentin (San Quentin), Holloway (Holloway Prison), etc.

9. The movie won the Toronto International Film Festival award for Best Canadian First Feature Film.

10. The original concept for the film came to Natali in a dream about people trapped in a giant machine.

7. Rabid

1. Movie Title: Rabid

2. Year of Release: 1977

3. Cast and Director:

  - Director: David Cronenberg

  - Cast: Marilyn Chambers, Frank Moore, Joe Silver

4. Synopsis:

Rabid tells the story of Rose, a woman who is severely injured in a motorcycle accident and undergoes an experimental skin graft treatment. The procedure has an unexpected side effect: Rose develops a stinger-like organ under her arm and an insatiable thirst for human blood. As she feeds, her victims become infected with a rabies-like disease, turning them into violent, foam-mouthed zombies. The infection spreads rapidly through Montreal, leading to widespread panic and martial law. As the city descends into chaos, Rose struggles with her new condition and the devastation she's unwittingly causing, while authorities race to contain the outbreak.

5. Why This Movie Is Recommended:

Rabid is a classic example of David Cronenberg's body horror, blending visceral terror with social commentary. The film explores themes of medical ethics, sexuality, and societal breakdown in the face of an epidemic. Marilyn Chambers' performance as Rose adds depth to what could have been a simple monster role, portraying her struggle with empathy. The movie's depiction of a city falling into chaos feels eerily prescient in light of modern pandemic fears. Rabid's influence on both the zombie genre and viral outbreak narratives in horror is significant, making it a must-watch for fans of intelligent, thought-provoking horror cinema.

6. 10 Trivia Facts:

1. Marilyn Chambers was primarily known as an adult film star before taking on this mainstream role.

2. The film was shot in and around Montreal during a particularly cold winter.

3. Sissy Spacek was originally considered for the lead role of Rose.

4. The movie's special effects were created by Joe Blasco, who went on to found a renowned makeup school.

5. Cronenberg has stated that the film was partially inspired by the 1950s anti-communist hysteria in the United States.

6. The film's tagline was "She's hungry for sex... She's even hungrier for blood!"

7. Rabid was one of the first films to combine elements of the vampire and zombie genres.

8. The movie was remade in 2019 by directors Jen and Sylvia Soska.

9. Cronenberg appears in a cameo as a man infected by the virus in a shopping mall.

10. The film's budget was around $500,000, significantly higher than Cronenberg's previous film, Shivers.

8. My Bloody Valentine

1. Movie Title: My Bloody Valentine

2. Year of Release: 1981

3. Cast and Director:

- Director: George Mihalka

- Cast: Paul Kelman, Lori Hallier, Neil Affleck

4. Synopsis:

Set in the small mining town of Valentine Bluffs, the film revolves around a group of young miners who decide to throw a Valentine's Day party, breaking a 20-year tradition of no celebrations following a tragic accident. Two decades earlier, several miners were killed in an explosion caused by supervisors who left their posts to attend a Valentine's dance. The sole survivor, Harry Warden, went on a killing spree the following year before being institutionalized. As the current Valentine's party approaches, someone dressed as a miner begins brutally murdering townspeople. The killings escalate, and the remaining characters must uncover the killer's identity while fighting for survival in the claustrophobic mine shafts.

5. Why This Movie Is Recommended:

My Bloody Valentine stands out in the slasher genre for its unique setting and atmospheric use of the mining town and tunnels. The film builds tension effectively, creating a sense of isolation and dread that permeates the story. Unlike many of its contemporaries, it focuses on working-class characters, adding a layer of socio-economic commentary to the horror. The movie's practical effects and creative kill scenes are memorable and influential. My Bloody Valentine's blend of mystery, slasher tropes, and Canadian small-town dynamics makes it a cult classic that offers more than just standard genre fare.

6. 10 Trivia Facts:

1. The film was shot on location in Sydney Mines, Nova Scotia.

2. Many of the extras in the film were actual miners from the town.

3. The movie was heavily censored upon initial release, with about 9 minutes of gore cut to avoid an X rating.

4. Director George Mihalka insisted on using real mining equipment to enhance authenticity.

5. The film was remade in 3D in 2009, starring Jensen Ackles.

6. My Bloody Valentine was one of the first slasher films to be set on Valentine's Day.

7. The movie's tagline was "Cross your heart... and hope to die."

8. The killer's outfit was inspired by actual mining gear used in Nova Scotia.

9. The film's budget was around $2.3 million, considered mid-range for a slasher film at the time.

10. A lengthy lost footage sequence was found and restored for the film's 2009 Special Edition DVD release.

9. Videodrome

1. Movie Title: Videodrome

2. Year of Release: 1983

3. Cast and Director:

  - Director: David Cronenberg

  - Cast: James Woods, Debbie Harry, Sonja Smits

4. Synopsis:

Videodrome follows Max Renn, the president of a small UHF television station specializing in sensationalistic programming. In search of new content, Max discovers a mysterious broadcast signal named "Videodrome" that depicts extreme violence and torture. As he investigates the source of the signal, Max begins experiencing bizarre hallucinations and physical transformations. He becomes entangled with Nicki Brand, a sadomasochistic radio host, and Brian O'Blivion, a media philosopher who only appears on TV. Max uncovers a conspiracy involving mind control, new flesh, and the merging of human biology with media technology. As the line between reality and video-induced hallucination blurs, Max must navigate a dangerous world where television is literally changing human flesh.

5. Why This Movie Is Recommended:

Videodrome is a landmark in both body horror and media critique, showcasing David Cronenberg's visionary approach to filmmaking. The movie's prescient themes about the influence of media on human consciousness and behavior feel increasingly relevant in our digital age. Its disturbing visual effects and surreal narrative create a uniquely unsettling viewing experience. James Woods delivers a compelling performance as Max, guiding viewers through the film's increasingly bizarre and horrifying world. Videodrome's exploration of technology, sexuality, and violence pushes the boundaries of the horror genre, offering a thought-provoking and viscerally affecting cinematic experience that continues to inspire analysis and discussion decades after its release.

6. 10 Trivia Facts:

1. The film's tagline was "First it controls your mind, then it destroys your body."

2. Debbie Harry, who plays Nicki Brand, was cast partly due to her fame as the lead singer of Blondie.

3. The special effects, including the famous "breathing videotape," were created by Rick Baker's EFX Inc.

4. Cronenberg has said that Videodrome was partly inspired by his childhood experiences of picking up American TV signals in Canada.

5. The character Brian O'Blivion is loosely based on media theorist Marshall McLuhan.

6. James Woods improvised many of his lines, with Cronenberg's approval.

7. The film features one of the earliest depictions of virtual reality in cinema.

8. Videodrome was a box office disappointment upon release but has since become a cult classic.

9. The movie won several Genie Awards, including Best Achievement in Direction for Cronenberg.

10. The "new flesh" concept in the film was partly inspired by Cronenberg's interest in cancer and bodily mutations.

10. Ghostkeeper

1. Movie Title: Ghostkeeper

2. Year of Release: 1981

3. Cast and Director:

- Director: Jim Makichuk

- Cast: Riva Spier, Murray Ord, Sheri McFadden

4. Synopsis:

Ghostkeeper follows three young snowmobilers - Jenny, Marty, and Chrissy - who become stranded in the Rocky Mountains during a blizzard on New Year's Eve. They seek shelter in an abandoned ski lodge, which they soon discover is inhabited by an old woman and her son. As night falls, strange occurrences begin to plague the group. They learn that the old woman is the "ghostkeeper," tasked with containing an ancient evil entity known as the Windigo, a cannibalistic spirit from Native American folklore. As tensions rise and sanity frays, the line between reality and nightmare blurs. The characters must fight for survival against both the supernatural threat and the harsh winter conditions, leading to a chilling climax that leaves questions of reality and madness unanswered.

5. Why This Movie Is Recommended:

Ghostkeeper stands out for its atmospheric use of the isolated, snowy setting to create a sense of dread and claustrophobia. The film blends elements of supernatural horror with psychological thriller, keeping viewers guessing about the nature of the threat. Its incorporation of Native American folklore adds a unique cultural dimension to the narrative. While working with a limited budget, the movie effectively builds tension through its eerie soundtrack and minimalist approach to horror. Ghostkeeper's ambiguous ending and exploration of themes like isolation and madness make it a thought-provoking entry in Canadian horror cinema, offering more than just standard slasher fare popular in the early 1980s.

6. 10 Trivia Facts:

1. The film was shot on location in the Deer Lodge in Lake Louise, Alberta, during a real blizzard.

2. The movie's budget was only about $650,000 Canadian dollars.

3. Director Jim Makichuk has stated that the script was often rewritten on set due to budget constraints.

4. The film's score was composed by Paul Zaza, known for his work on other Canadian horror films like Prom Night.

5. Ghostkeeper was one of the first horror films to incorporate the Windigo legend from Native American mythology.

6. The movie was shot in just 18 days.

7. Many of the crew members, including the director, were from Calgary and had worked in television prior to this film.

8. The film was released on VHS in the 1980s but became rare, adding to its cult status.

9. Ghostkeeper was restored and re-released on Blu-ray in 2012, introducing it to a new generation of horror fans.

10. The movie's tagline was "The Windigo - It feeds on human flesh."

11. Prom Night

1. Movie Title: Prom Night

2. Year of Release: 1980

3. Cast and Director:

- Director: Paul Lynch

- Cast: Jamie Lee Curtis, Leslie Nielsen, Casey Stevens, Anne-Marie Martin

4. Synopsis:

Prom Night centers around a group of high school seniors preparing for their prom, six years after they accidentally caused the death of a young girl named Robin Hammond. The group swore to keep the incident a secret, but as prom night approaches, they start receiving threatening phone calls and notes. During the prom, a masked killer begins stalking and murdering the teens involved in Robin's death, as well as others at the dance. The film follows Kim Hammond, Robin's sister, as she and her friends try to survive the night and uncover the killer's identity. As the body count rises and suspicion shifts between various characters, the movie builds to a climactic reveal and confrontation on the dance floor.

5. Why This Movie Is Recommended:

Prom Night stands out as a quintessential entry in the golden age of slasher films, blending elements of mystery, revenge, and teenage drama. The movie benefits from Jamie Lee Curtis's strong performance, capitalizing on her "scream queen" status following Halloween. Its use of the high school prom setting adds a layer of nostalgia and relatability to the horror. The film builds suspense effectively, using red herrings and misdirection to keep viewers guessing about the killer's identity. While it employs many classic slasher tropes, Prom Night's focus on character development and its disco-infused soundtrack give it a unique flavor among its peers. It remains an influential and entertaining example of Canadian horror cinema.

6. 10 Trivia Facts:

1. The film was shot in Toronto, with a local high school serving as the main location.

2. Jamie Lee Curtis took the role partly to avoid being typecast in horror films, as this character was different from her previous roles.

3. Leslie Nielsen, known for his comedic roles, plays a serious character as the school principal.

4. The movie's disco scenes were choreographed by Shelley Somers, who worked on the film "Saturday Night Fever."

5. Prom Night was one of the highest-grossing Canadian films of 1980.

6. The film spawned three sequels, though they're largely unrelated to the original's plot.

7. The killer's mask in the film was inspired by the fencing mask used in the Italian giallo film "Opera."

8. A remake of Prom Night was released in 2008, but it shared little in common with the original beyond the title.

9. The movie's tagline was "If you're not back by midnight... you won't be coming home!"

10. Director Paul Lynch has said that the film's structure was inspired by Agatha Christie's "And Then There Were None."

12. Shivers

1. Movie Title: Shivers (also known as They Came from Within)

2. Year of Release: 1975

3. Cast and Director:

 - Director: David Cronenberg

 - Cast: Paul Hampton, Joe Silver, Lynn Lowry, Barbara Steele

4. Synopsis:

 Shivers is set in a modern, self-contained apartment complex on Montreal's Nun's Island. The story begins when a scientist creates a parasite that is a combination of aphrodisiac and venereal disease, as part of a misguided attempt to replace organ transplants. The parasite escapes and begins to infect the residents of the apartment complex, turning them into sex-crazed, violent zombies driven by uncontrollable lust and aggression. As the infection spreads rapidly through the building, a small group of uninfected residents, led by Dr. Roger St. Luc, tries to survive and contain the outbreak. The film explores themes of sexual liberation, social order, and body horror as the situation spirals out of control, leading to a provocative and disturbing climax.

5. Why This Movie Is Recommended:

 Shivers marks David Cronenberg's first commercial feature film and establishes many themes that would define his career. The movie is a landmark in body horror, blending visceral disgust with intellectual and social commentary. Its exploration of sexual politics and societal repression was highly controversial upon release, making it both criticized and celebrated. The claustrophobic setting of the apartment complex adds to the tension and sense of inescapable doom. Shivers pushes boundaries in its depiction of sexuality and violence, creating a uniquely unsettling viewing experience. Despite its low budget, the film's imaginative practical effects and Cronenberg's bold vision make it a significant work in Canadian horror cinema and a must-watch for fans of thought-provoking, transgressive horror.

6. 10 Trivia Facts:

 1. The film was made on a budget of approximately $179,000 Canadian dollars.

 2. Cronenberg wrote the screenplay in just three weeks.

 3. The movie caused significant controversy in Canada, with some politicians questioning why taxpayer money (through the Canadian Film Development Corporation) was used to fund it.

 4. Barbara Steele, known for her roles in Italian horror films, came out of semi-retirement to appear in Shivers.

 5. The apartment complex used for filming, Habitat 67, was designed by architect Moshe Safdie for Expo 67.

 6. Shivers was Cronenberg's first full-length film after making two short features.

 7. The film was initially released in the United States under the title "They Came from Within."

 8. Cinepix, the production company, insisted on a certain number of nude scenes to ensure commercial viability.

 9. Despite the controversy, Shivers was the first Canadian film to make a profit at the box office.

 10. The parasites in the film were made from condoms filled with fake blood and Vaseline.

13. Orphan: First Kill

1. Movie Title: Orphan: First Kill

2. Year of Release: 2022

3. Cast and Director:

 - Director: William Brent Bell

 - Cast: Isabelle Fuhrman, Julia Stiles, Rossif Sutherland, Matthew Finlan

4. Synopsis:

Orphan: First Kill is a prequel to the 2009 film "Orphan." The movie follows Esther, a grown woman with a rare hormonal disorder that stunts her physical growth, making her appear as a child. The film begins with Esther's escape from an Estonian psychiatric facility. She then impersonates the missing daughter of a wealthy American family and travels to the United States. As she infiltrates the Albright family, assuming the identity of their long-lost daughter Esther, she must navigate complex family dynamics and avoid suspicion. However, Esther soon discovers that her new "mother," Tricia Albright, may be hiding dark secrets of her own. The tension escalates as Esther's violent tendencies clash with the family's own hidden agendas, leading to a twisted and shocking climax.

5. Why This Movie Is Recommended:

Orphan: First Kill offers a fresh and unexpected take on the original film's premise. It subverts audience expectations by presenting new layers to Esther's character and the family she infiltrates. The movie benefits from Isabelle Fuhrman's committed performance, reprising her role as Esther despite being over a decade older, which adds an intriguing meta-layer to the film. Its blend of psychological thriller and horror elements keeps viewers on edge, with several surprising plot twists. The film explores themes of deception, family secrets, and the nature of evil in ways that both honor and expand upon the original. For fans of the first "Orphan" and newcomers alike, First Kill provides a uniquely entertaining and unsettling viewing experience.

6. 10 Trivia Facts:

 1. The film was shot primarily in Winnipeg, Manitoba, Canada.

 2. Isabelle Fuhrman, who plays Esther, was 23 years old during filming, 12 years older than when she first played the role.

 3. To make Fuhrman appear younger, the production used a combination of makeup, forced perspective, and two child body doubles.

 4. The movie was initially conceived as a remake of the original "Orphan" before being developed into a prequel.

 5. Julia Stiles accepted her role in the film without reading the script, based solely on the twist that was explained to her.

 6. The film was released simultaneously in theaters and on streaming platforms due to the COVID-19 pandemic.

 7. Rossif Sutherland, who plays Allen Albright, is the son of famous Canadian actor Donald Sutherland.

 8. The movie's working title during production was "Esther."

 9. Some scenes were filmed at the Manitoba Legislative Building in Winnipeg.

 10. Despite being a prequel, the film includes several nods and references to the original "Orphan" movie.

14. The Void

1. Movie Title: The Void

2. Year of Release: 2016

3. Cast and Director:

  - Directors: Jeremy Gillespie and Steven Kostanski

  - Cast: Aaron Poole, Kenneth Welsh, Daniel Fathers, Kathleen Munroe

4. Synopsis:

The Void follows police officer Daniel Carter, who discovers a bloodied man on a deserted road and takes him to a nearby hospital. Soon after, the hospital is surrounded by a group of robed cultists with white triangles on their hoods. Inside, patients and staff begin transforming into grotesque, tentacled monsters. Carter, along with a handful of survivors, must navigate the increasingly nightmarish situation while uncovering the hospital's connection to a cosmic horror. As they descend deeper into the hospital's hidden levels, they encounter horrifying creatures and learn of a plan to open a gateway to another dimension. The group must fight for survival against both the cultists outside and the monstrous transformations within, leading to a climax that blends visceral body horror with cosmic terror.

5. Why This Movie Is Recommended:

The Void stands out for its ambitious blend of cosmic horror, body horror, and siege thriller elements. The film pays homage to classic horror directors like John Carpenter and Lucio Fulci while establishing its own unique vision. Its use of practical effects for the creatures and transformations is impressive, especially considering the modest budget. The movie builds a palpable sense of dread and claustrophobia, enhanced by its hospital setting. The Void's commitment to practical effects and its exploration of Lovecraftian themes make it a refreshing entry in modern horror. Its mix of gore, suspense, and existential terror offers something for various horror subgenre fans, creating a memorable and unsettling viewing experience.

6. 10 Trivia Facts:

1. The film was partially crowdfunded through an Indiegogo campaign.

2. Directors Gillespie and Kostanski previously worked together in the Canadian film collective Astron-6.

3. The practical effects were created by a team that included alumni from Guillermo del Toro's films.

4. The movie was shot in and around Sault Ste. Marie, Ontario.

5. The directors cite H.P. Lovecraft, Clive Barker, and cosmic horror as major influences.

6. The film features over 50 creature effects shots, all done practically with minimal CGI.

7. The hospital used for filming was an abandoned wing of Sault Area Hospital.

8. The movie's tagline was "There is a hell. This is worse."

9. The directors spent nearly two years in pre-production, much of it dedicated to creature design and effects planning.

10. The Void premiered at the 2016 Fantastic Fest in Austin, Texas.

15. Incendies

1. Movie Title: Incendies

2. Year of Release: 2010

3. Cast and Director:

- Director: Denis Villeneuve

- Cast: Lubna Azabal, Mélissa Désormeaux-Poulin, Maxim Gaudette, Rémy Girard

4. Synopsis:

Incendies, based on Wajdi Mouawad's play, follows Canadian twins Jeanne and Simon Marwan as they unravel their mother Nawal's mysterious past following her death. Nawal's will tasks them with delivering letters to their father, whom they thought was dead, and a brother they never knew existed. The narrative alternates between the twins' present-day journey to their mother's homeland (an unnamed Middle Eastern country resembling Lebanon) and flashbacks of Nawal's life. As they piece together their mother's history, they uncover a tale of war, love, and unspeakable tragedy. The twins' search leads them through the complexities of their mother's war-torn past, revealing shocking truths about their own origins and identities. The film builds to a devastating climax that forces the characters to confront the cyclical nature of violence and the possibility of reconciliation.

5. Why This Movie Is Recommended:

While not a traditional horror film, Incendies earns its place in the psychological horror genre through its exploration of generational trauma and the horrors of war. Denis Villeneuve's masterful direction creates a sense of dread and unease that permeates the entire film. The movie's non-linear structure adds to the mystery, gradually revealing shocking truths that are as horrifying as any supernatural threat. Incendies tackles themes of identity, family secrets, and the lasting impact of conflict with unflinching intensity. The film's powerful performances, especially by Lubna Azabal as Nawal, bring depth and humanity to the harrowing narrative. Its final revelations are deeply disturbing, leaving a lasting impact on viewers and prompting reflection on the nature of forgiveness and the cycle of violence.

6. 10 Trivia Facts:

1. The film is based on Wajdi Mouawad's play of the same name, which was inspired by the story of Souha Bechara.

2. Incendies was nominated for Best Foreign Language Film at the 83rd Academy Awards.

3. The movie was shot in Jordan and Quebec, with Jordan standing in for the unnamed Middle Eastern country.

4. Director Denis Villeneuve spent five years developing the script before filming began.

5. The film's title, "Incendies," is French for "fires" or "conflagrations."

6. Lubna Azabal learned to speak Quebec French for her role as the older Nawal.

7. The movie won eight Genie Awards, including Best Motion Picture and Best Director.

8. Villeneuve has stated that making Incendies was emotionally exhausting due to its heavy themes.

9. The film's score features music by Radiohead, specifically their song "You and Whose Army?"

10. Incendies was a major breakthrough for Villeneuve, leading to his subsequent success in Hollywood with films like "Arrival" and "Blade Runner 2049."

16. Martyrs

1. Movie Title: Martyrs

2. Year of Release: 2008

3. Cast and Director:

  - Director: Pascal Laugier

  - Cast: Morjana Alaoui, Mylène Jampanoï, Catherine Bégin

4. Synopsis:

Martyrs begins with Lucie, a young woman who escapes from captivity where she endured brutal torture. Years later, with the help of her friend Anna, Lucie tracks down the family she believes was responsible for her ordeal and brutally murders them. However, this act of vengeance is only the beginning of a descent into a hellish nightmare. As Anna tries to help Lucie deal with the aftermath and her psychological trauma, they uncover a secret society dedicated to the creation of "martyrs" - individuals who have experienced extreme suffering and are believed to have glimpsed the afterlife. The film takes a shocking turn as Anna becomes the subject of the society's horrific experiments, enduring unimaginable torment in their quest for metaphysical knowledge.

5. Why This Movie Is Recommended:

Martyrs is a landmark in extreme horror cinema, pushing the boundaries of what audiences can endure while offering profound philosophical questions. The film's unflinching depiction of violence and suffering is not gratuitous but serves a deeper exploration of pain, transcendence, and the human condition. Its sudden shift in narrative and tone halfway through is masterfully executed, subverting audience expectations. Martyrs delves into complex themes of trauma, revenge, and the search for meaning in suffering. While undeniably difficult to watch, the film's visceral impact and thought-provoking nature have made it a highly influential work in modern horror. It challenges viewers both emotionally and intellectually, leaving a lasting impression that extends far beyond typical genre fare.

6. 10 Trivia Facts:

1. Despite its French director and language, Martyrs was primarily shot in Montreal, Canada.

2. The film was so controversial that it caused walkouts at the 2008 Cannes Film Festival.

3. Director Pascal Laugier suffered from depression after completing the film due to its intense subject matter.

4. Martyrs was part of a wave of extreme French horror films dubbed the "New French Extremity."

5. The movie was remade in the United States in 2015, though it was poorly received compared to the original.

6. The final scene of the film was shot in a single take.

7. Laugier has stated that the film was partly inspired by his own struggles with faith and the concept of afterlife.

8. The movie's tagline was "Vengeance is blind."

9. Martyrs won the Grand Prix at the 2009 Gérardmer Film Festival.

10. The film's makeup effects were created by Adrien Morot, who later won an Oscar for his work on "The Whale."

17. Possessor

1. Movie Title: Possessor

2. Year of Release: 2020

3. Cast and Director:

- Director: Brandon Cronenberg

- Cast: Andrea Riseborough, Christopher Abbott, Jennifer Jason Leigh

4. Synopsis:

Possessor follows Tasya Vos, an elite corporate assassin who uses brain-implant technology to inhabit other people's bodies, forcing them to commit assassinations for high-paying clients. When she's assigned to inhabit Colin Tate to kill his girlfriend and her wealthy father, the job becomes complicated as Tasya struggles to maintain control over Colin's mind. As the lines between Tasya's consciousness and Colin's begin to blur, both characters fight for dominance within the same body. The film explores themes of identity, free will, and the nature of consciousness as Tasya becomes increasingly unstable and Colin fights to regain control of his body. The narrative builds to a violent and psychologically disturbing climax that questions the very nature of self.

5. Why This Movie Is Recommended:

Possessor stands out for its unique blend of psychological horror, body horror, and sci-fi elements. Brandon Cronenberg (son of David Cronenberg) proves himself a master of unsettling imagery and conceptual horror. The film's exploration of identity and consciousness through the lens of technology feels both timely and deeply disturbing. Its visceral violence and surreal, dream-like sequences create a sense of unease that lingers long after viewing. The performances, particularly by Riseborough and Abbott, bring depth to the complex psychological landscape of the film. Possessor's intelligent script and thought-provoking themes elevate it beyond typical sci-fi or horror fare, offering a challenging and rewarding experience for viewers who appreciate cerebral, boundary-pushing cinema.

6. 10 Trivia Facts:

1. The film was shot in Toronto and Hamilton, Ontario.

2. Possessor was originally titled "Possessor Uncut" to distinguish it from a toned-down R-rated version.

3. The movie features several practical effects for its gore scenes, continuing the Cronenberg family tradition.

4. Brandon Cronenberg spent nearly eight years developing the script.

5. The film's visual style was influenced by Francis Bacon's paintings and Chris Cunningham's music videos.

6. Possessor premiered at the 2020 Sundance Film Festival.

7. The movie's tagline was "No body is safe."

8. The film features a cameo by Canadian musician Tupperwear Remix Party as a lounge band.

9. Possessor won Best Film at the Sitges Film Festival.

10. The brain-implant technology in the film was inspired by real-life neural interface research.

18. Scanners

1. Movie Title: Scanners

2. Year of Release: 1981

3. Cast and Director:

 - Director: David Cronenberg

 - Cast: Stephen Lack, Jennifer O'Neill, Patrick McGoohan, Michael Ironside

4. Synopsis:

 Scanners revolves around a group of people with powerful telepathic and telekinetic abilities, known as "scanners." The story follows Cameron Vale, a homeless scanner who is recruited by a shadowy corporation called ConSec to track down and stop Darryl Revok, a renegade scanner intent on world domination. As Vale delves deeper into the world of scanners, he uncovers a conspiracy involving ConSec, military applications of scanner abilities, and a drug called Ephemerol. The film builds tension through psychic battles and corporate espionage, leading to a climactic confrontation between Vale and Revok that pushes the limits of their psychic powers and Cronenberg's special effects.

5. Why This Movie Is Recommended:

 Scanners is a seminal work in the body horror subgenre, showcasing David Cronenberg's unique vision of biological horror and societal paranoia. The film's exploration of the potential and perils of expanded human consciousness feels both retro and relevant. Its practical special effects, especially the infamous exploding head scene, remain impressive and influential decades later. Scanners blends elements of science fiction, horror, and thriller genres to create a uniquely unsettling viewing experience. The movie's themes of corporate control, military exploitation of human potential, and the outsider's struggle in society add depth to its visceral horror elements. For fans of cerebral science fiction horror and Cronenberg's body of work, Scanners is an essential watch that continues to resonate with modern audiences.

6. 10 Trivia Facts:

 1. The iconic exploding head scene was achieved by filling a latex prosthetic with dog food and rabbit livers, then shooting it from behind with a shotgun.

 2. Cronenberg wrote the script in about a week due to funding time constraints.

 3. The film's electronic score was composed by Howard Shore, marking his first collaboration with Cronenberg.

 4. "Scanning" scenes were often shot at undercranked camera speeds to heighten the intensity of actors' expressions.

 5. The movie spawned two sequel films and a series of spin-off comic books.

 6. Scanners was Cronenberg's first commercial success, grossing about $14 million on a $4 million budget.

 7. The term "scanner" was coined by Cronenberg for the film and has since entered pop culture lexicon.

 8. Michael Ironside's character name, Darryl Revok, is an anagram for "Daryl Voker," a bully from Cronenberg's youth.

 9. The film was shot in Montreal and Toronto.

 10. Scanners won the Best International Fantasy Film Award at Fantasporto in 1983.

19. Antiviral

1. Movie Title: Antiviral

2. Year of Release: 2012

3. Cast and Director:

- Director: Brandon Cronenberg

- Cast: Caleb Landry Jones, Sarah Gadon, Malcolm McDowell

4. Synopsis:

Antiviral is set in a dystopian near-future where celebrity obsession has reached extreme levels. The film follows Syd March, an employee at a clinic that harvests diseases and infections from celebrities and sells them to obsessed fans who wish to share a biological connection with their idols. Syd also smuggles viruses out of the lab in his own body to sell on the black market. When he becomes infected with a virus taken from a popular starlet who subsequently dies, Syd finds himself at the center of a conspiracy. As he grows increasingly ill, he must unravel the mystery surrounding the virus and the starlet's death, all while evading rival collectors and dealing with the horrific symptoms of his infection.

5. Why This Movie Is Recommended:

Antiviral marks Brandon Cronenberg's directorial debut, showcasing a unique vision that both honors and expands upon his father David Cronenberg's body horror legacy. The film offers a scathing critique of celebrity culture and consumerism, pushing these concepts to disturbing extremes. Its clinical, sterile aesthetic contrasts sharply with the biological horror at its core, creating an unsettling atmosphere throughout. The movie's exploration of the commodification of human biology feels prescient and deeply unsettling. Caleb Landry Jones delivers a committed, physically transformative performance that anchors the film's more outlandish concepts. For viewers who appreciate thought-provoking, visually striking horror that blends social commentary with visceral discomfort, Antiviral offers a unique and memorable experience.

6. 10 Trivia Facts:

1. The film was shot in Toronto and Hamilton, Ontario.

2. Antiviral was Brandon Cronenberg's first feature film, which he both wrote and directed.

3. The movie premiered at the 2012 Cannes Film Festival in the Un Certain Regard section.

4. The stark, minimalist set design was inspired by THX 1138 and Cronenberg's visits to hospitals.

5. Caleb Landry Jones lost a significant amount of weight for his role as the increasingly ill Syd March.

6. The film features several nods to Brandon's father David Cronenberg's works, including body horror themes and the use of medical settings.

7. Antiviral won Best Canadian First Feature Film at the 2012 Toronto International Film Festival.

8. The movie's tagline was "Sharing is caring."

9. Brandon Cronenberg has stated that the idea for the film came from a fever hallucination he had while ill.

10. The film's critique of celebrity culture was partly inspired by Cronenberg's experiences growing up as the son of a famous director.

20. Afflicted

1. Movie Title: Afflicted

2. Year of Release: 2013

3. Cast and Director:

  - Directors: Derek Lee and Clif Prowse

  - Cast: Derek Lee, Clif Prowse, Baya Rehaz

4. Synopsis:

Afflicted follows two best friends, Derek and Clif, as they embark on a year-long trip around the world, documenting their adventures for an online travel show. Their journey takes a dark turn when Derek has a seemingly innocent encounter with a woman in Paris, after which he begins to exhibit strange symptoms and superhuman abilities. As Derek's condition worsens, transforming him into something inhuman, Clif continues to document their increasingly terrifying experiences. The friends struggle to understand and cope with Derek's transformation, which brings both incredible powers and a horrifying thirst for blood. As they travel across Europe, Derek's control over his new condition deteriorates, leading to violent encounters and a desperate search for a cure.

5. Why This Movie Is Recommended:

Afflicted breathes new life into both the found footage and vampire genres by combining them in an innovative way. The film's use of the travel vlog format provides a fresh perspective on the vampire transformation narrative. Its progression from lighthearted travelogue to intense horror is skillfully executed, maintaining suspense throughout. The movie's practical effects and stunt work, particularly in showcasing Derek's superhuman abilities, are impressive given the modest budget. Afflicted explores themes of friendship, mortality, and the price of power with surprising depth for a horror film. The directors' decision to play themselves adds an extra layer of realism to the found footage conceit. For fans of creative, low-budget horror and unique takes on classic monsters, Afflicted offers a thrilling and often shocking experience.

6. 10 Trivia Facts:

1. Directors Derek Lee and Clif Prowse play fictionalized versions of themselves in the film.

2. Afflicted was shot on location in Spain, Italy, France, and Canada.

3. The film won Best Canadian First Feature Film at the 2013 Toronto International Film Festival.

4. Many of the stunts in the film were performed by the directors themselves.

5. The movie's working title was "The Ends of the Earth."

6. Afflicted was produced by Telefilm Canada and filmed over 30 days across Europe.

7. The film's tagline was "There are some places in this world that can change you forever."

8. Derek Lee, who plays himself in the film, actually has AVM (arteriovenous malformation), which is mentioned in the movie.

9. The directors met in film school and had been making short films together for years before Afflicted.

10. The film's innovative approach to the vampire genre earned it comparisons to Chronicle in its treatment of superpowers.

Austria

1. Goodnight Mommy (Ich seh, Ich seh)

1. Movie Title: Goodnight Mommy (Ich seh, Ich seh)

2. Year of Release: 2014

3. Cast and Director:

  - Directors: Veronika Franz, Severin Fiala

  - Cast: Susanne Wuest, Elias Schwarz, Lukas Schwarz

4. Synopsis:

In a remote countryside house, twin boys await their mother's return from cosmetic surgery. When she arrives with her face wrapped in bandages, the boys begin to doubt her identity. As her behavior becomes increasingly erratic and unusual, the twins become convinced that this woman is an impostor. The film escalates into a nightmarish battle of wills between the boys and the woman they believe has replaced their mother, leading to a shocking and disturbing climax that blurs the lines between reality and perception.

5. Why This Movie Is Recommended:

"Goodnight Mommy" is a masterclass in psychological horror, building tension through its stark visuals and unsettling atmosphere. The film expertly plays with viewer expectations, offering twists that force audiences to question everything they've seen. Its exploration of identity, trauma, and the bond between mother and child adds depth to the horror elements. The performances, particularly from the young twins, are chillingly convincing. This film showcases the potential of Austrian horror cinema on the international stage.

6. 10 Trivia Facts:

1. The film was Austria's submission for the Best Foreign Language Film at the 88th Academy Awards.

2. Real-life twins Elias and Lukas Schwarz were cast to play the twin brothers in the film.

3. The movie was shot in chronological order to help the young actors understand the story's progression.

4. Directors Veronika Franz and Severin Fiala are aunt and nephew.

5. The film's original German title, "Ich seh, Ich seh," translates to "I see, I see," referencing a children's game similar to "I Spy."

6. The house used in the film was found abandoned and renovated for the shoot.

7. Susanne Wuest, who played the mother, had to wear facial prosthetics for much of the filming.

8. The film premiered at the 2014 Venice Film Festival, where it received critical acclaim.

9. A Hollywood remake starring Naomi Watts was released in 2022.

10. The directors cited Michael Haneke, an Austrian filmmaker known for his disturbing dramas, as an influence.

2. Angst

1. Movie Title: Angst

2. Year of Release: 1983

3. Cast and Director:

  - Director: Gerald Kargl

  - Cast: Erwin Leder, Robert Hunger-Bühler, Silvia Rabenreither

4. Synopsis:

"Angst" follows a psychopath who is released from prison and immediately resumes his hunt for victims. The film provides an unflinching, first-person perspective of the killer's thought processes and actions as he breaks into a family home and terrorizes its inhabitants. With a dispassionate, almost documentary-like approach, the movie delves deep into the disturbed mind of its protagonist, creating a harrowing and visceral experience. The relentless tension and graphic violence make "Angst" a challenging watch that blurs the line between horror and psychological study.

5. Why This Movie Is Recommended:

"Angst" is a landmark in extreme cinema, notable for its innovative cinematography and uncompromising portrayal of a killer's psychology. Its influence can be seen in later works like "Henry: Portrait of a Serial Killer" and Gaspar Noé's films. The movie's use of subjective camera work and voiceover narration creates an unsettling intimacy with the protagonist. While not for the faint-hearted, "Angst" offers a unique and intense cinematic experience that has earned it cult status among horror aficionados.

6. 10 Trivia Facts:

  1. The film was based on the real-life case of mass murderer Werner Kniesek.

  2. "Angst" was banned or heavily censored in several countries upon its initial release due to its graphic content.

  3. The movie's innovative camerawork was achieved using a custom-built bodymount rig.

  4. Erwin Leder, who played the killer, reportedly found the role so disturbing that he had trouble sleeping during filming.

  5. The film's score was composed by Klaus Schulze, a pioneer of electronic music.

  6. Director Gerald Kargl never made another feature film after "Angst."

  7. The movie was shot in just 18 days.

  8. Gaspar Noé has cited "Angst" as a major influence on his work.

  9. The film was largely forgotten for years until it was rediscovered and championed by cult film enthusiasts in the 2000s.

  10. A restored version of "Angst" was released in 2015, bringing renewed attention to the film.

3. Funny Games

1. Movie Title: Funny Games

2. Year of Release: 1997

3. Cast and Director:

- Director: Michael Haneke

- Cast: Susanne Lothar, Ulrich Mühe, Arno Frisch, Frank Giering

4. Synopsis:

"Funny Games" follows a family - Georg, Anna, and their young son Georgie - as they arrive at their lakeside vacation home. Their idyllic retreat is shattered when two young men, Peter and Paul, appear at their door and gradually take the family hostage. What follows is a nightmarish ordeal as the two sadistic intruders subject the family to a series of cruel and violent "games." The film breaks the fourth wall at times, directly challenging the audience's role as spectators to the violence. As the situation escalates, the line between fiction and reality blurs, forcing viewers to confront their own relationship with media violence.

5. Why This Movie Is Recommended:

While not a traditional horror film, "Funny Games" is a deeply unsettling and thought-provoking work that pushes the boundaries of the genre. Haneke's clinical direction and the film's meta-commentary on violence in media make it a unique and challenging viewing experience. The movie's ability to create tension and dread without relying on typical horror tropes is masterful. It serves as both a critique and an example of extreme cinema, forcing viewers to question their own complicity in on-screen violence.

6. 10 Trivia Facts:

1. Director Michael Haneke remade the film shot-for-shot in English in 2007 with Naomi Watts and Tim Roth.

2. The film was entered into the 1997 Cannes Film Festival.

3. Haneke has stated that he made the film as a reaction against the trivialisation of violence in American cinema.

4. The movie contains several long takes, including a nearly 11-minute continuous shot after a pivotal scene.

5. The two antagonists frequently break the fourth wall, directly addressing the audience.

6. Haneke deliberately made the film to be unenjoyable for the audience as a commentary on screen violence.

7. The director refused to give the actors playing the antagonists any backstory for their characters.

8. The film's working title was "Funny Games: The Movie."

9. Haneke chose to film in German rather than English to avoid the film being seen as an imitation of American thrillers.

10. The movie has been both praised as a masterpiece and criticized for its manipulative nature, sparking intense debate among critics and audiences.

4. Hotel

1. Movie Title: Hotel

2. Year of Release: 2004

3. Cast and Director:

- Director: Jessica Hausner

- Cast: Franziska Weisz, Birgit Minichmayr, Marlene Streeruwitz

4. Synopsis:

"Hotel" follows Irene, a young woman who takes a job as a receptionist at an isolated Austrian hotel. As she settles into her new role, strange occurrences begin to plague her. She learns about her predecessor, Eva, who mysteriously disappeared in the nearby woods. As Irene becomes increasingly obsessed with Eva's disappearance, the hotel's oppressive atmosphere and the surrounding forest take on a menacing quality. The line between reality and nightmare blurs as Irene's grip on sanity begins to slip, leading to a ambiguous and unsettling conclusion that leaves much open to interpretation.

5. Why This Movie Is Recommended:

"Hotel" is a masterclass in subtle, psychological horror. Jessica Hausner's direction creates a pervasive sense of unease through minimal means, relying on atmosphere and suggestion rather than overt scares. The film's exploration of isolation, identity, and the unknown makes it a thought-provoking watch. Its ambiguity and refusal to provide easy answers elevate it beyond typical genre fare, offering a more cerebral and lingering form of horror that stays with the viewer long after the credits roll.

6. 10 Trivia Facts:

1. The film was Jessica Hausner's second feature-length movie.

2. "Hotel" premiered at the 2004 Cannes Film Festival in the Un Certain Regard section.

3. The movie was shot on location in the Austrian Alps, contributing to its isolated atmosphere.

4. Hausner has cited David Lynch as an influence on the film's dreamlike quality.

5. The director intentionally left many aspects of the story ambiguous to encourage viewer interpretation.

6. The hotel used in the film was a real, functioning hotel that remained open during shooting.

7. Franziska Weisz, who played Irene, was relatively unknown at the time and this role helped launch her career.

8. The film's sound design plays a crucial role in creating its unsettling atmosphere.

9. "Hotel" was part of a wave of Austrian art house films that gained international recognition in the early 2000s.

10. Despite its horror elements, Hausner has described the film as more of a "suspense film without a resolution."

5. The Shining (Austrian version)

1. Movie Title: The Shining (Austrian version)

2. Year of Release: 1982

3. Cast and Director:

- Director: Gustav Deutsch (for the Austrian version)

- Original Director: Stanley Kubrick

- Cast: Jack Nicholson, Shelley Duvall, Danny Lloyd

4. Synopsis:

While "The Shining" is primarily known as an American film, it has an interesting connection to Austrian cinema. The original film, based on Stephen King's novel, follows the Torrance family as they become winter caretakers at the isolated Overlook Hotel. As they're cut off from the outside world, the father, Jack, influenced by supernatural forces, descends into madness. His wife Wendy and psychic son Danny must fight for survival against Jack's increasing violence and the hotel's malevolent spirits. The Austrian version, created by experimental filmmaker Gustav Deutsch, recontextualizes Kubrick's original footage, offering a unique interpretation of the classic horror film.

5. Why This Movie Is Recommended:

The Austrian version of "The Shining" offers a fascinating reinterpretation of Kubrick's classic. Deutsch's experimental approach provides new insights into the original material, encouraging viewers to reconsider familiar scenes in a new light. This version serves as both a tribute to Kubrick's masterpiece and a standalone work of avant-garde cinema. For fans of the original and those interested in experimental film techniques, the Austrian "Shining" provides a unique viewing experience that bridges Hollywood horror with European art house sensibilities.

6. 10 Trivia Facts:

1. Gustav Deutsch's version is not a remake, but a re-edit of Kubrick's original footage.

2. The Austrian version is part of Deutsch's "Film Ist." series, which explores the nature of cinema.

3. Deutsch's reinterpretation focuses more on the film's themes of time and memory than on horror elements.

4. The re-edit significantly alters the narrative structure of Kubrick's original.

5. This version was created without the involvement of Kubrick's estate or Warner Bros.

6. The project raised interesting questions about copyright and fair use in experimental cinema.

7. Deutsch's version premiered at the Vienna International Film Festival.

8. The re-edit includes footage from the original film that was not used in Kubrick's final cut.

9. This version of "The Shining" is significantly shorter than Kubrick's original.

10. The project has been seen as both a homage to and a deconstruction of Kubrick's filmmaking techniques.

6. Taxidermia

1. Movie Title: Taxidermia

2. Year of Release: 2006

3. Cast and Director:

- Director: György Pálfi

- Cast: Csaba Czene, Gergely Trócsányi, Marc Bischoff

4. Synopsis:

While "Taxidermia" is a Hungarian-Austrian-French co-production, it's notable for its Austrian involvement and its horrific elements. The film presents three generations of men, each story more grotesque than the last. It begins with a military orderly with unusual sexual proclivities, moves to his son, a champion speed eater, and concludes with the grandson, a taxidermist with a bizarre final project. Each segment is filled with surreal, often disturbing imagery that blends body horror, dark comedy, and social commentary. The film's unflinching portrayal of bodily functions and transformations pushes the boundaries of cinema and viewer comfort.

5. Why This Movie Is Recommended:

"Taxidermia" is a unique and audacious film that defies easy categorization. Its blend of surrealism, body horror, and historical allegory creates a viewing experience unlike any other. The film's stunning visuals, ranging from the grotesque to the oddly beautiful, leave a lasting impression. While not for the faint of heart, "Taxidermia" offers a challenging and thought-provoking exploration of humanity's relationship with the body, consumption, and legacy. It's a must-see for those interested in extreme cinema and the outer limits of cinematic expression.

6. 10 Trivia Facts:

1. The film is loosely based on the works of Hungarian writer Lajos Parti Nagy.

2. "Taxidermia" won the New Visions Award at the 2006 Sitges Film Festival.

3. The movie features minimal dialogue, relying heavily on visual storytelling.

4. Many of the film's surreal effects were achieved practically, without CGI.

5. Director György Pálfi spent years researching taxidermy for the film's final segment.

6. The speed-eating scenes required complex practical effects and camera tricks.

7. "Taxidermia" was Hungary's submission for the Best Foreign Language Film at the 79th Academy Awards.

8. The film's structure, following three generations, is inspired by Hungarian history.

9. Despite its graphic content, the film has been praised for its artistic merit and social commentary.

10. The movie's poster, featuring a man with a pig's head, became iconic in art house cinema circles.

7. Deadly Sweet (Col cuore in gola)

1. Movie Title: Deadly Sweet (Col cuore in gola)

2. Year of Release: 1967

3. Cast and Director:

 - Director: Tinto Brass

 - Cast: Jean-Louis Trintignant, Ewa Aulin, Roberto Bisacco

4. Synopsis:

"Deadly Sweet" is an Italian-French-Austrian co-production that blends elements of giallo horror with pop art aesthetics. The film follows Bernard, a French actor in London, who becomes entangled in a murder mystery when he meets Jane, a young woman found next to a dead body. As they try to unravel the mystery and clear Jane's name, they navigate a psychedelic underworld filled with eccentric characters and deadly dangers. The narrative unfolds in a dream-like fashion, blurring the lines between reality and fantasy, as the protagonists delve deeper into a world of sex, drugs, and violence.

5. Why This Movie Is Recommended:

"Deadly Sweet" offers a unique blend of 1960s pop culture, giallo horror tropes, and avant-garde filmmaking techniques. Its stylish visuals, influenced by pop art and comic books, create a visually arresting experience. The film's nonlinear narrative and psychedelic imagery make it a fascinating artifact of its time. While it may not be a conventional horror film, its surreal atmosphere, moments of violence, and underlying sense of unease place it firmly in the realm of cult horror. It's a must-see for fans of experimental cinema and those interested in the evolution of European horror.

6. 10 Trivia Facts:

 1. The film marks Tinto Brass's transition from avant-garde filmmaker to his later, more erotic works.

 2. "Deadly Sweet" features innovative use of comic book-style inserts and pop art aesthetics.

 3. The movie's Italian title, "Col cuore in gola," translates to "With Heart in Mouth."

 4. Jean-Louis Trintignant, who plays Bernard, was a major French New Wave actor.

 5. The film's soundtrack, composed by Armando Trovajoli, blends jazz and psychedelic rock.

 6. "Deadly Sweet" was shot on location in London, capturing the city's swinging '60s atmosphere.

 7. The movie features several sequences shot with a fish-eye lens, adding to its psychedelic feel.

 8. Ewa Aulin, who plays Jane, was a former Miss Teen Sweden and had just starred in "Candy."

 9. The film's style was influenced by contemporary pop artists like Andy Warhol and Roy Lichtenstein.

 10. Despite its cult status today, "Deadly Sweet" was not a commercial success upon its initial release.

8. Macabre (Macabro)

1. Movie Title: Macabre (Macabro)

2. Year of Release: 1980

3. Cast and Director:

  - Director: Lamberto Bava

  - Cast: Bernice Stegers, Stanko Molnar, Veronica Zinny

4. Synopsis:

  "Macabre," an Italian-Spanish-Austrian co-production, tells the disturbing story of Jane Baker, a woman who loses her lover in a gruesome accident. After spending time in a mental institution, she returns to New Orleans and takes up residence in the house where she and her lover once lived. Her blind daughter Lucy and the building's suspicious landlord become increasingly concerned about Jane's behavior, especially her habit of locking herself in her room for hours. As the story unfolds, it becomes clear that Jane is harboring a dark and twisted secret that blurs the line between love, obsession, and madness.

5. Why This Movie Is Recommended:

  "Macabre" stands out for its psychological depth and slow-burning tension. Unlike many horror films of its era, it relies more on atmosphere and psychological unease than on graphic violence. The film's exploration of grief, obsession, and mental illness adds layers of complexity to its horror elements. Lamberto Bava, son of legendary horror director Mario Bava, demonstrates his ability to create suspense and shock without relying on his father's more explicit style. The film's New Orleans setting adds a unique flavor to this European production, creating a memorable entry in the canon of psychological horror.

6. 10 Trivia Facts:

  1. "Macabre" was Lamberto Bava's directorial debut, marking the beginning of a significant career in Italian horror.

  2. The film is loosely based on a true story that occurred in California in the 1970s.

  3. Despite being set in New Orleans, most of the film was actually shot in Italy.

  4. Legendary Italian horror director Pupi Avati contributed to the screenplay.

  5. The movie features a haunting score by Libyan-born composer Berto Pisano.

  6. "Macabre" was one of the first films to be labeled as a "video nasty" in the UK, despite its relatively tame content compared to other films on the list.

  7. The film's twist ending was considered shocking for its time and continues to be discussed among horror fans.

  8. Bernice Stegers, who plays Jane, learned to play the harp for her role in the film.

  9. The movie was released under various titles, including "Frozen Terror" in some English-speaking markets.

  10. Despite being his debut, many critics consider "Macabre" to be one of Lamberto Bava's best works.

9. Ich seh ich seh 2 (Goodnight Mommy 2)

1. Movie Title: Ich seh ich seh 2 (Goodnight Mommy 2)

2. Year of Release: 2025 (Planned)

3. Cast and Director:

  - Directors: Veronika Franz, Severin Fiala

  - Cast: To be announced

4. Synopsis:

  While specific plot details have not been released, "Ich seh ich seh 2" is expected to continue exploring themes of identity, family, and psychological horror that made the original film so compelling. The sequel is likely to maintain the unsettling atmosphere and visual style of its predecessor, potentially revisiting the characters or concepts from the first film in a new context. As with the original, the sequel is expected to challenge viewers' perceptions and play with the boundaries between reality and delusion.

5. Why This Movie Is Recommended:

  Although the film has not been released yet, its inclusion in this list is based on the critical acclaim and impact of the original "Goodnight Mommy." The directing duo of Franz and Fiala have proven their ability to create deeply unsettling psychological horror, and a sequel promises to expand on their unique vision. For fans of the original and those interested in the evolution of Austrian horror cinema, this upcoming film represents an exciting development in the genre.

6. 10 Trivia Facts:

  1. The sequel was announced following the international success of the original film.

  2. Directors Veronika Franz and Severin Fiala are returning to helm the project, ensuring continuity of vision.

  3. The film is expected to be produced by Ulrich Seidl, who also produced the original.

  4. "Ich seh ich seh 2" is one of the most anticipated Austrian horror films in recent years.

  5. The directors have expressed interest in exploring new psychological territory while maintaining links to the original.

  6. The film's development has sparked discussions about the potential for a uniquely Austrian horror franchise.

  7. International distribution rights were sought after even before the script was completed, indicating high expectations.

  8. The directors have hinted at potentially using the twin motif again, but in a different context.

  9. The sequel is expected to maintain the original's minimalist approach to horror.

  10. There's speculation about whether the film will be in German or English, given the international success of the original.

10. The Devil's Plaything (Hexen bis aufs Blut gequält)

1. Movie Title: The Devil's Plaything (Hexen bis aufs Blut gequält)

2. Year of Release: 1970

3. Cast and Director:

- Director: Michael Armstrong

- Cast: Herbert Lom, Udo Kier, Olivera Vuco

4. Synopsis:

"The Devil's Plaything," also known as "Mark of the Devil," is a West German-Austrian horror film set in 18th century Austria. The story follows Count Christian von Meruh, an apprentice witch hunter who arrives in a small town to assist his master, Lord Cumberland, in rooting out witchcraft. As Christian witnesses the brutal torture and execution of accused witches, he begins to question the legitimacy of the witch hunts. His doubts grow when he falls in love with a local barmaid accused of witchcraft. The film unflinchingly depicts the cruelty and hysteria of the witch trials, creating a horrifying portrayal of historical injustice.

5. Why This Movie Is Recommended:

"The Devil's Plaything" is notorious for its graphic depictions of torture and violence, which set new standards for on-screen brutality in its time. Beyond its shock value, the film offers a scathing critique of religious fanaticism and abuse of power. Its historical setting provides a unique backdrop for horror, grounding its terrors in real-world atrocities. While certainly not for the faint of heart, the film's exploration of human cruelty and the dangers of unchecked authority make it a significant entry in the canon of European horror cinema.

6. 10 Trivia Facts:

1. The film was marketed with the tagline "Positively the most horrifying film ever made" and was given a "V for Violence" rating.

2. Vomit bags were infamously handed out to moviegoers at some screenings as a marketing gimmick.

3. Despite its Austrian setting and partial funding, the film was primarily a West German production.

4. Udo Kier, who plays Count Christian, went on to become a cult film icon.

5. The film was banned in several countries upon its release due to its extreme content.

6. Many of the torture devices depicted in the film were based on actual historical instruments.

7. The movie's success spawned several unofficial sequels and imitators.

8. Herbert Lom, known for his role in the Pink Panther series, plays the villainous Lord Cumberland.

9. The film's German title, "Hexen bis aufs Blut gequält," translates to "Witches Tortured till They Bleed."

10. Despite its exploitation elements, the film has been praised for its high production values and serious approach to its historical subject matter.

11. Ghosthunters (Gespensterjäger)

1. Movie Title: Ghosthunters (Gespensterjäger)

2. Year of Release: 2015

3. Cast and Director:

- Director: Tobi Baumann

- Cast: Anke Engelke, Milo Parker, Bastian Pastewka

4. Synopsis:

While "Ghosthunters" is primarily a family-friendly supernatural comedy, it's worth including for its Austrian co-production status and its playful take on horror tropes. The story follows Tom, a young boy who discovers a green ghost named Hugo in his cellar. Together with Hetty Cuminseed, a professional "ghosthunter," they must save Hugo from the evil Ancient Ice Ghost and prevent him from taking over the world. As they embark on their adventure, they encounter various supernatural entities and must overcome their fears to save the day.

5. Why This Movie Is Recommended:

"Ghosthunters" offers a lighthearted introduction to horror elements for younger viewers while still providing entertainment for adults. Its blend of comedy and supernatural themes makes it a unique entry in Austrian cinema. The film's high production values and special effects demonstrate the technical capabilities of Austrian co-productions. While not a traditional horror movie, it serves as a gateway to the genre and showcases how horror elements can be adapted for family audiences.

6. 10 Trivia Facts:

1. The film is based on the children's book series "Ghosthunters" by Cornelia Funke.

2. It's a co-production between Germany, Austria, and Ireland.

3. The movie features a mix of practical effects and CGI to bring its ghostly characters to life.

4. "Ghosthunters" was filmed in both English and German versions.

5. The film won the Children's Jury Award at the 2015 Chicago International Children's Film Festival.

6. Anke Engelke, who plays Hetty, is a well-known comedian in German-speaking countries.

7. The movie's success led to discussions about a potential sequel.

8. Some of the ghost designs were inspired by classic horror movie monsters.

9. The film's German title, "Gespensterjäger," literally translates to "Ghost Hunters."

10. Despite being a family film, it includes several nods to more adult horror films that parents might appreciate.

12. The Essence of Terror (Die Schlangengrube und das Pendel)

1. Movie Title: The Essence of Terror (Die Schlangengrube und das Pendel)

2. Year of Release: 1967

3. Cast and Director:

- Director: Harald Reinl

- Cast: Karin Dor, Lex Barker, Christopher Lee

4. Synopsis:

"The Essence of Terror," also known as "The Torture Chamber of Dr. Sadism," is a German-Austrian co-production loosely based on Edgar Allan Poe's "The Pit and the Pendulum." Set in the 19th century, the film follows Count Regula, who is executed for the murder of 12 virgins. Thirty-five years later, the count's spirit seeks revenge by luring descendants of his executioners to his castle. The protagonists must navigate a series of deadly traps and face their deepest fears as they confront the vengeful spirit in his lair of horrors.

5. Why This Movie Is Recommended:

This film represents a unique blend of German "krimi" thriller and Gothic horror traditions, with a distinctly European flair. Its lush, colorful cinematography and elaborate set designs create a memorably atmospheric experience. The presence of horror icon Christopher Lee adds gravitas to the production. While it may not reach the heights of contemporary Italian or British horror, "The Essence of Terror" offers a fascinating glimpse into the development of Central European horror cinema in the 1960s.

6. 10 Trivia Facts:

1. Christopher Lee's voice was dubbed in the German version, despite his fluency in the language.

2. The film's original German title translates to "The Snake Pit and the Pendulum."

3. It was one of several adaptations of Poe's works produced in Europe during this period.

4. The movie was shot on location in Germany, including several real castles.

5. Director Harald Reinl was known for his work on the popular German "Edgar Wallace" crime film series.

6. The film's elaborate torture devices were created by noted German special effects artist Erwin Lange.

7. Lex Barker, who stars in the film, was best known for playing Tarzan in American films of the 1950s.

8. The movie was released in some markets under the title "Blood Demon."

9. Despite its modest budget, the film features impressively grand and Gothic set designs.

10. The film's success contributed to a wave of similar Gothic horror productions in Germany and Austria.

13. Maskerade

1. Movie Title: Maskerade

2. Year of Release: 1934

3. Cast and Director:

- Director: Willi Forst

- Cast: Paula Wessely, Adolf Wohlbrück, Olga Tschechowa

4. Synopsis:

While "Maskerade" is primarily a romantic comedy, it's worth including for its influence on later psychological thrillers and its exploration of hidden identities. Set in Vienna during the Carnival season, the film follows a scandal that erupts when a famous painter creates a portrait of a masked, partially nude woman. As various characters attempt to uncover or conceal the woman's identity, the film weaves a complex web of deception, misunderstanding, and romantic intrigue. The carnival setting, with its masks and costumes, creates an atmosphere of mystery and hidden truths that would later influence darker genres.

5. Why This Movie Is Recommended:

Though not a horror film in the traditional sense, "Maskerade" is significant for its exploration of themes that would become central to many psychological thrillers and horror films: hidden identities, societal masks, and the tension between appearance and reality. Its use of the carnival setting as a backdrop for mystery and revelation influenced later filmmakers in their approach to creating unsettling atmospheres. As a classic of Austrian cinema, it provides valuable context for understanding the development of Austrian film across genres.

6. 10 Trivia Facts:

1. "Maskerade" was one of the most successful films of the Austrian film industry in the 1930s.

2. The film launched the career of Paula Wessely, who became one of Austria's most prominent actresses.

3. Director Willi Forst was known as the "Viennese Lubitsch" for his sophisticated comedies.

4. The movie's success led to a Hollywood remake called "Escapade" starring William Powell.

5. "Maskerade" was one of the last major Austrian productions before many filmmakers fled due to the rise of Nazism.

6. The film's carnival scenes were shot on location in Vienna during the actual carnival season.

7. It was one of the first Austrian films to gain significant international distribution.

8. The movie's exploration of scandal and hidden identities pushed the boundaries of what was acceptable in 1930s cinema.

9. "Maskerade" is considered a prime example of the "Wiener Film" genre, known for its sophistication and wit.

10. The film's success helped establish Vienna as a major center of European filmmaking in the 1930s.

14. Mein Nachbar, der Vampir (My Neighbor, the Vampire)

1. Movie Title: Mein Nachbar, der Vampir (My Neighbor, the Vampire)

2. Year of Release: 2015

3. Cast and Director:

  - Director: Wolfgang Groos

  - Cast: Dominic Oley, Julia Jelinek, Matthias Stein

4. Synopsis:

"My Neighbor, the Vampire" is an Austrian made-for-TV horror comedy that brings vampire lore into a modern, suburban setting. The story follows a typical middle-class family whose lives are turned upside down when a vampire moves in next door. As they grapple with their new neighbor's unusual habits and dietary requirements, the family must also protect their community from potential danger. The film playfully subverts vampire tropes while exploring themes of acceptance, prejudice, and the challenges of fitting into suburban life.

5. Why This Movie Is Recommended:

While "My Neighbor, the Vampire" may not be a hardcore horror film, it offers a uniquely Austrian take on the vampire genre. Its blend of horror elements with family-friendly comedy makes it accessible to a wide audience. The film's exploration of social dynamics in a suburban setting through the lens of the supernatural provides an interesting commentary on contemporary Austrian society. For those interested in how different cultures adapt classic horror tropes, this TV movie offers an entertaining and insightful example.

6. 10 Trivia Facts:

1. The film was produced by ORF, Austria's national public service broadcaster.

2. It was part of a series of made-for-TV movies aimed at revitalizing Austrian television production.

3. The movie plays with the contrast between vampire mythology and modern suburban life.

4. Some scenes were shot in actual Austrian suburban neighborhoods to maintain authenticity.

5. The film's vampire makeup and effects were created by a team that had worked on larger international productions.

6. "My Neighbor, the Vampire" received positive reviews for its fresh take on the vampire genre.

7. The movie includes several nods to classic vampire films, which horror fans might enjoy spotting.

8. It was broadcast during a prime-time slot, indicating the network's confidence in its broad appeal.

9. The film's success led to discussions about potential spin-off series or sequels.

10. "My Neighbor, the Vampire" won an award for Best TV Movie at an Austrian television festival.

15. Die Hölle (Cold Hell)

1. Movie Title: Die Hölle (Cold Hell)

2. Year of Release: 2017

3. Cast and Director:

  - Director: Stefan Ruzowitzky

  - Cast: Violetta Schurawlow, Tobias Moretti, Robert Palfrader

4. Synopsis:

"Cold Hell" is an Austrian-German thriller with strong horror elements. The story follows Özge, a Turkish-born taxi driver in Vienna, who becomes the target of a serial killer after witnessing one of his murders. As the police seem unwilling or unable to protect her, Özge must rely on her kickboxing skills and street smarts to survive. The film delves into themes of immigration, gender, and violence as Özge navigates both the threat of the killer and the prejudices of Viennese society. The cat-and-mouse game between Özge and the killer escalates into a visceral and intense confrontation.

5. Why This Movie Is Recommended:

"Cold Hell" stands out for its gritty realism and intense action sequences, blending elements of thriller, horror, and social commentary. The film's unflinching portrayal of violence and its exploration of social issues in contemporary Vienna add depth to its genre trappings. Director Stefan Ruzowitzky, known for the Oscar-winning "The Counterfeiters," brings a polished and taut style to the proceedings. For those interested in seeing how Austrian cinema tackles hard-hitting thriller and horror themes, "Cold Hell" offers a compelling and intense viewing experience.

6. 10 Trivia Facts:

  1. The film won the Audience Award at the 2017 Fantastic Fest in Austin, Texas.

  2. Lead actress Violetta Schurawlow underwent intensive kickboxing training for her role.

  3. The movie's German title, "Die Hölle," translates to "The Hell."

  4. "Cold Hell" was praised for its realistic portrayal of Vienna's less touristy areas.

  5. The film's killer is inspired by real-life serial killers, adding to its chilling realism.

  6. Director Stefan Ruzowitzky has described the film as a response to the male-dominated thriller genre.

  7. The movie features several intense car chase sequences through the streets of Vienna.

  8. "Cold Hell" was picked up for international distribution by Netflix, expanding its global reach.

  9. The film's soundtrack, composed by Marius Ruhland, adds significantly to its tense atmosphere.

  10. Despite its genre trappings, "Cold Hell" received critical acclaim for its social commentary and character development.

16. Bloodsucking Freaks (The Incredible Torture Show)

1. **Movie Title**: Bloodsucking Freaks (The Incredible Torture Show)

2. **Year of Release**: 1976

3. **Cast and Director**:

   - Director: Joel M. Reed

   - Cast: Seamus O'Brien, Viju Krem, Niles McMaster

4. **Synopsis**:

   While "Bloodsucking Freaks" is primarily an American production, it's included here due to its cult status and its Austrian-born star, Seamus O'Brien. The film follows Sardu, a sadistic maestro who runs a Grand Guignol-style theater in New York City. Unbeknownst to his audiences, the on-stage torture and murder are real. When Sardu kidnaps a famous ballet dancer, a private investigator sets out to rescue her, uncovering the horrifying truth behind the shows. The film is notorious for its graphic depictions of violence and its controversial content.

5. **Why This Movie Is Recommended**:

   "Bloodsucking Freaks" is a highly controversial film that pushes the boundaries of taste and acceptability. Its inclusion here is primarily due to Seamus O'Brien's Austrian heritage and the film's impact on extreme horror cinema. It represents a bridge between European arthouse shock and American grindhouse sensibilities. While certainly not for everyone, the film has achieved cult status and is often discussed in the context of censorship and the limits of artistic expression in horror.

6. **10 Trivia Facts**:

   1. Seamus O'Brien, who plays Sardu, was born in Austria before emigrating to the United States.

   2. The film was originally released under the title "The Incredible Torture Show."

   3. It was banned in several countries and heavily censored in others.

   4. Troma Entertainment acquired and re-released the film, contributing to its cult status.

   5. Despite its low budget, the film features elaborate practical effects for its torture scenes.

   6. "Bloodsucking Freaks" has been both condemned for its misogyny and defended as satire.

   7. The film's theatrical poster was designed by famous comic book artist Mort Drucker.

   8. Several cast members later expressed regret about their involvement in the project.

   9. The movie has been cited as an influence by some modern horror directors.

   10. Despite its notoriety, Seamus O'Brien only appeared in one other film before his untimely death.

17. Invisible: The Chronicles of Benjamin Knight

1. **Movie Title**: Invisible: The Chronicles of Benjamin Knight

2. **Year of Release**: 1993

3. **Cast and Director**:

   - Director: Nico Mastorakis

   - Cast: Edward Albert, Olivia Hussey, Ben Murphy

4. **Synopsis**:

   This obscure science fiction horror film, while not strictly Austrian, was partially filmed in Austria and features Austrian locations. The story follows Benjamin Knight, a scientist who becomes invisible after a failed experiment. As he struggles to reverse his condition, he must evade government agents and a criminal organization seeking to exploit his invisibility. The film blends elements of classic invisible man stories with more modern sci-fi and horror tropes, using its Austrian settings to create an atmosphere of isolation and danger.

5. **Why This Movie Is Recommended**:

   "Invisible" is an interesting curiosity for fans of low-budget 90s sci-fi horror. Its use of Austrian locations provides a unique backdrop for the genre, differentiating it from typical American or British productions. While not a masterpiece, the film offers a glimpse into how international productions utilized Austrian settings for genre filmmaking. For those interested in the intersection of Austrian cinema and B-movie science fiction horror, this film provides an intriguing case study.

6. **10 Trivia Facts**:

   1. Parts of the film were shot in Vienna and the Austrian Alps.

   2. Director Nico Mastorakis is better known for controversial horror films like "Island of Death."

   3. The movie attempts to update H.G. Wells' "The Invisible Man" concept for a 90s audience.

   4. Austrian crew members were employed during the film's production in the country.

   5. The film's special effects, while dated, were considered ambitious for a low-budget production.

   6. "Invisible" was part of a wave of direct-to-video sci-fi horror films popular in the early 90s.

   7. The movie features a mix of American and European actors, reflecting its international production.

   8. Some scenes showcase iconic Vienna locations, adding production value to the low-budget film.

   9. Despite its limited release, the film has gained a small cult following among fans of obscure sci-fi horror.

   10. The Austrian tourist board reportedly assisted with location scouting for the film.

18. Dem Täter auf der Spur: Das Fenster zum Garten

1. **Movie Title**: Dem Täter auf der Spur: Das Fenster zum Garten

2. **Year of Release**: 1975

3. **Cast and Director**:

   - Director: Theodor Grädler

   - Cast: Hansjörg Felmy, Judy Winter, Gerhard Riedmann

4. **Synopsis**:

   This entry is an episode from the German-Austrian crime series "Dem Täter auf der Spur" (On the Trail of the Perpetrator). While primarily a crime show, this particular episode, "Das Fenster zum Garten" (The Window to the Garden), incorporates strong elements of psychological horror. The story follows the investigation of a series of mysterious deaths in a small town. As the detective delves deeper, he uncovers a sinister plot involving voyeurism, manipulation, and murder, all centered around a window overlooking a garden.

5. **Why This Movie Is Recommended**:

   Although part of a crime series, this episode stands out for its foray into psychological horror territory. It showcases how Austrian television productions of the 1970s were willing to incorporate darker, more unsettling elements into mainstream programming. The episode's exploration of voyeurism and the dark secrets hidden in small communities prefigures themes that would become common in later horror films. For those interested in the evolution of horror elements in Austrian media, this episode provides an interesting case study.

6. **10 Trivia Facts**:

   1. "Dem Täter auf der Spur" was a collaborative production between German and Austrian television.

   2. This episode was noted for being darker and more psychologically intense than others in the series.

   3. The show often used real criminal cases as inspiration, though heavily fictionalized.

   4. Director Theodor Grädler was known for his work in both Austrian and German television.

   5. The series was popular enough to run for seven seasons, unusual for German-language crime dramas of the time.

   6. This episode's focus on voyeurism drew comparisons to Alfred Hitchcock's "Rear Window."

   7. The show employed many Austrian actors and crew members, supporting the local film industry.

   8. "Das Fenster zum Garten" was praised for its atmospheric use of its small-town Austrian setting.

   9. The episode's success led to discussions about creating a spin-off focused more on horror elements.

   10. Some of the psychological horror techniques used in this episode influenced later Austrian thriller productions.

19. The Ballad of Genesis and Lady Jaye

1. **Movie Title**: The Ballad of Genesis and Lady Jaye

2. **Year of Release**: 2011

3. **Cast and Director**:

   - Director: Marie Losier

   - Cast: Genesis P-Orridge, Lady Jaye Breyer P-Orridge

4. **Synopsis**:

   While not a traditional horror film, this Austrian-American-French documentary explores themes of body modification and identity that often intersect with body horror. The film follows the story of Genesis P-Orridge, founder of industrial music pioneers Throbbing Gristle, and their partner Lady Jaye. It documents their "Pandrogeny Project," in which both underwent extensive plastic surgery to resemble each other, blurring the lines between individual identities. The film touches on themes of love, art, and the malleability of human form.

5. **Why This Movie Is Recommended**:

   Although a documentary, "The Ballad of Genesis and Lady Jaye" delves into territory often explored in body horror films. Its unflinching look at radical body modification and the questioning of physical identity resonates with themes found in the works of directors like David Cronenberg. The film's Austrian co-production status and its exploration of extreme artistic expression make it a unique entry in this list. For those interested in the intersection of art, identity, and the horrors of bodily transformation, this documentary offers a real-world parallel to fictional body horror narratives.

6. **10 Trivia Facts**:

   1. The film premiered at the 2011 Berlin International Film Festival.

   2. Director Marie Losier spent seven years following Genesis and Lady Jaye for the documentary.

   3. The movie features rare archival footage of Throbbing Gristle performances.

   4. Genesis P-Orridge coined the term "Pandrogeny" to describe their project of gender transformation.

   5. The film was partly funded by Austrian art grants, reflecting its status as an art piece as well as a documentary.

   6. "The Ballad of Genesis and Lady Jaye" won the Teddy Award for Best Documentary at the Berlin Film Festival.

   7. The documentary's style is heavily influenced by experimental filmmaking techniques.

   8. Some of the surgical procedures documented in the film were performed in Austria.

   9. The movie sparked debates about the boundaries between art, body modification, and self-expression.

   10. Despite its challenging subject matter, the film was praised for its intimate and loving portrayal of its subjects.

20. Die Spiegeltoten (The Mirror Dead)

1. **Movie Title**: Die Spiegeltoten (The Mirror Dead)

2. **Year of Release**: 2015

3. **Cast and Director**:

  - Director: Florian Eder

  - Cast: Erol Sander, Mareile Blendl, Mario Canedo

4. **Synopsis**:

  "Die Spiegeltoten" is an Austrian television movie that blends elements of crime drama with supernatural horror. The story follows Detective Bruno Grass as he investigates a series of mysterious deaths in Vienna. The victims are found dead in front of mirrors, their faces frozen in expressions of terror. As Grass delves deeper into the case, he uncovers an ancient curse and must confront his own reflection to solve the mystery and stop the killings.

5. **Why This Movie Is Recommended**:

  This TV movie represents an interesting attempt to incorporate horror elements into mainstream Austrian television. Its blend of police procedural and supernatural horror showcases how genre conventions can be adapted for a broader audience. The use of Viennese locations adds a unique flavor to the familiar mirror horror trope. For those interested in how horror themes are interpreted in Austrian popular media, "Die Spiegeltoten" offers an accessible and intriguing example.

6. **10 Trivia Facts**:

  1. The film was produced by ORF, Austria's national public service broadcaster.

  2. "Die Spiegeltoten" was part of a series of made-for-TV movies aimed at bringing genre elements to Austrian television.

  3. The movie draws on the rich folklore surrounding mirrors in Central European traditions.

  4. Several scenes were filmed in historic locations around Vienna, including old apartments and museums.

  5. The film's special effects team developed unique techniques for creating the "mirror world" scenes.

  6. Lead actor Erol Sander is of Turkish-German descent, reflecting Austria's multicultural society.

  7. The movie sparked discussions about the potential for more horror-themed content in Austrian TV.

  8. Some of the mirror effects were inspired by classic horror films like "Candyman."

  9. The film's premiere garnered higher-than-average ratings for its time slot, indicating audience interest in horror-themed content.

  10. "Die Spiegeltoten" was later distributed to other German-speaking markets, expanding its reach.

France

1. Diabolique (Les Diaboliques)

1. Movie Title: Diabolique (Les Diaboliques)

2. Year of Release: 1955

3. Cast and Director:

 - Director: Henri-Georges Clouzot

 - Cast: Simone Signoret, Véra Clouzot, Paul Meurisse

4. Synopsis:

Set in a provincial boarding school, Diabolique follows Christina, the frail wife of the abusive headmaster Michel, and Nicole, his mistress. United by their hatred for Michel, the two women conspire to murder him. They meticulously plan and execute the deed, drowning Michel in a bathtub and dumping his body in the school's neglected swimming pool. However, when the pool is drained, Michel's corpse is nowhere to be found. Strange occurrences begin to plague the school, and Christina becomes increasingly unnerved, believing Michel might still be alive. As the tension mounts, the film builds to a shocking climax that has become one of the most famous twist endings in cinema history.

5. Why This Movie Is Recommended:

Diabolique is a masterclass in suspense, often compared to the works of Alfred Hitchcock. Its intricate plot, atmospheric cinematography, and brilliant performances create an unrelenting sense of dread. The film's exploration of guilt, paranoia, and the blurred lines between reality and illusion set new standards for psychological thrillers. Its influence on the horror and thriller genres cannot be overstated, inspiring countless filmmakers and leaving audiences spellbound decades after its release. Diabolique's ability to manipulate viewer expectations and deliver genuine scares without relying on explicit violence makes it a timeless classic of French cinema.

6. 10 Trivia Facts:

1. Alfred Hitchcock attempted to buy the rights to the source novel but was outbid by Henri-Georges Clouzot by a matter of hours.

2. The film was based on the novel "Celle qui n'était plus" (She Who Was No More) by Pierre Boileau and Thomas Narcejac.

3. Diabolique was one of the first films to feature a "no spoilers" marketing campaign, with audiences urged not to reveal the ending.

4. The famous bathtub scene took seven days to film.

5. Véra Clouzot, who played Christina, was the director's wife and died of a heart attack just five years after the film's release, at the age of 46.

6. The film won the New York Film Critics Circle Award for Best Foreign Language Film.

7. Diabolique inspired several remakes, including a 1996 American version starring Sharon Stone.

8. The twist ending reportedly caused heart attacks in some viewers upon its initial release.

9. The film's success led to a boom in French thriller productions in the late 1950s and early 1960s.

10. Director Clouzot was known for his harsh treatment of actors, often pushing them to physical and emotional extremes for realistic performances.

2. Eyes Without a Face (Les Yeux Sans Visage)

1. **Movie Title**: Eyes Without a Face (Les Yeux Sans Visage)

2. **Year of Release**: 1960

3. **Cast and Director**:

   - Director: Georges Franju

   - Cast: Pierre Brasseur, Alida Valli, Edith Scob

4. **Synopsis**:

   Eyes Without a Face tells the story of Dr. Génessier, a brilliant surgeon consumed by guilt after a car accident leaves his daughter Christiane disfigured. Aided by his devoted assistant Louise, Génessier kidnaps young women whose faces resemble Christiane's, attempting to graft their facial features onto his daughter. Christiane, hidden away in her father's mansion and forced to wear a haunting, featureless mask, grapples with the horrific nature of her father's actions and her own isolation. As Génessier's experiments continue and the police investigation closes in, the film builds to a climax that is both tragic and liberating, questioning the limits of science, the nature of beauty, and the destructive power of obsession.

5. **Why This Movie Is Recommended**:

   Eyes Without a Face is a landmark in horror cinema, blending poetic imagery with visceral horror. Director Georges Franju creates a dreamlike atmosphere that contrasts sharply with the film's more gruesome elements, resulting in a uniquely unsettling viewing experience. The central image of Christiane's mask has become iconic, symbolizing both the fragility of identity and the dehumanizing effects of obsession. The film's exploration of beauty, ethics in medicine, and the consequences of playing God resonates deeply, elevating it beyond typical horror fare. Its influence can be seen in countless subsequent films, making it an essential watch for any serious fan of the genre.

6. **10 Trivia Facts**:

   1. The film's groundbreaking special effects for the face transplant scene were created by putting pieces of rubber and tape on the actress's face and filming in reverse as they were pulled off.

   2. Edith Scob, who played Christiane, reprised her role (sort of) in the 2012 film "Holy Motors," wearing a similar mask as a nod to "Eyes Without a Face."

   3. The movie was initially banned in the UK due to its graphic content.

   4. The film's title in Germany was changed to "The Horror Chamber of Dr. Faustus" to capitalize on the popularity of Hammer horror films.

   5. Billy Idol's 1983 song "Eyes Without a Face" was inspired by the film.

   6. The movie was shot in both French and English versions simultaneously, with the actors speaking their lines in both languages.

7. Pedro Almodóvar's "The Skin I Live In" (2011) was heavily influenced by "Eyes Without a Face."

8. The film's release was met with controversy, with some critics calling it "despicable" and "pornography of horror."

9. Despite its now-classic status, the film was not a commercial success upon its initial release.

10. The haunting score was composed by Maurice Jarre, who later won Oscars for "Lawrence of Arabia" and "Doctor Zhivago."

3. Haute Tension (High Tension)

1. Movie Title: Haute Tension (High Tension)

2. Year of Release: 2003

3. Cast and Director:

- Director: Alexandre Aja

- Cast: Cécile de France, Maïwenn, Philippe Nahon

4. Synopsis:

Haute Tension follows Marie and Alex, two college students who travel to Alex's family home in the countryside for a quiet weekend of studying. Their plans are brutally interrupted when a mysterious truck driver arrives in the middle of the night and embarks on a savage killing spree, murdering Alex's family and kidnapping her. Marie, who manages to hide from the killer, pursues the truck in a desperate attempt to save her friend. What follows is a relentless chase filled with graphic violence and shocking twists. As Marie confronts the killer and fights to rescue Alex, the film builds to a controversial climax that forces viewers to question everything they've seen, blurring the lines between reality and delusion.

5. Why This Movie Is Recommended:

Haute Tension is a pivotal film in the "New French Extremity" movement, pushing the boundaries of on-screen violence and psychological horror. Director Alexandre Aja crafts a relentlessly intense experience that grips viewers from start to finish. The film's visceral approach to violence, combined with its exploration of obsession and identity, creates a deeply unsettling atmosphere. Its controversial twist ending, while divisive, adds a layer of psychological complexity that invites multiple viewings and interpretations. Haute Tension revitalized the slasher genre with its gritty realism and emotional depth, influencing a new generation of horror filmmakers and earning its place as a modern classic of French horror.

6. 10 Trivia Facts:

1. The film was shot in Romania, despite being set in France.

2. Director Alexandre Aja cited Dario Argento's giallo films as a major influence on Haute Tension.

3. The movie was heavily censored in some countries due to its extreme violence, with over two minutes cut from the UK release.

4. Haute Tension was Aja's breakthrough film, leading to his work on American horror remakes like "The Hills Have Eyes."

5. The original French title "Haute Tension" literally translates to "High Voltage" rather than "High Tension."

6. The film's twist ending was inspired by the 1929 Alfred Hitchcock film "Blackmail."

7. Actress Cécile de France performed many of her own stunts in the film.

8. The movie's American release sparked controversy due to dubbing issues and perceived plot holes related to the twist.

9. Haute Tension won the Grand Prize at the Amsterdam Fantastic Film Festival.

10. The killer's truck in the film is a Citroën HY van, a classic French vehicle produced from 1947 to 1981.

4. Martyrs

1. Movie Title: Martyrs

2. Year of Release: 2008

3. Cast and Director:

- Director: Pascal Laugier

- Cast: Morjana Alaoui, Mylène Jampanoï, Catherine Bégin

4. Synopsis:

Martyrs begins with Lucie, a young woman who escapes from captivity where she endured horrific abuse. Years later, with the help of her friend Anna, Lucie tracks down the couple she believes were her tormentors and brutally murders them. As Anna helps Lucie deal with the aftermath, they discover a hidden torture chamber in the couple's basement, revealing a terrifying conspiracy. The film then takes a drastic turn, focusing on Anna as she is captured by a secret philosophical society. This group believes that true martyrs, those who have suffered beyond imagination, can provide insight into the afterlife. Anna is subjected to escalating tortures in an attempt to induce a transcendent state, leading to a conclusion that is both profound and deeply disturbing.

5. Why This Movie Is Recommended:

Martyrs is a polarizing and unforgettable experience that pushes the boundaries of the horror genre. Director Pascal Laugier crafts a film that is not just about physical violence, but also explores deep philosophical questions about suffering, transcendence, and the nature of reality. Its unflinching depiction of torture is balanced by a surprisingly thoughtful exploration of its themes. The film's structure, which essentially tells two connected stories, keeps viewers off-balance and engaged. Martyrs is not for the faint of heart, but for those willing to endure its intensity, it offers a unique and thought-provoking take on horror that lingers long after viewing.

6. 10 Trivia Facts:

1. Director Pascal Laugier suffered from depression after making the film due to its intense subject matter.

2. Martyrs was part of the New French Extremity movement in cinema, known for its graphic violence and sexual content.

3. The film was banned in several countries upon its release due to its extreme content.

4. Actress Mylène Jampanoï reportedly fainted on set after filming a particularly intense scene.

5. Laugier has stated that the film was partially inspired by his divorce and feelings of personal anguish.

6. The movie was remade in America in 2015, but the remake was poorly received compared to the original.

7. Martyrs won the Grand Prize of European Fantasy Film in Gold at the Sitges Film Festival.

8. The film's makeup effects were so realistic that some crew members had difficulty watching certain scenes being filmed.

9. Laugier wrote the script in just one month, describing it as a cathartic experience.

10. Despite its controversial nature, Martyrs has been praised by some critics as a profound meditation on suffering and transcendence.

5. Inside (À l'intérieur)

1. Movie Title: Inside (À l'intérieur)

2. Year of Release: 2007

3. Cast and Director:

- Directors: Alexandre Bustillo, Julien Maury

- Cast: Alysson Paradis, Béatrice Dalle, Nathalie Roussel

4. Synopsis:

Set on Christmas Eve, Inside follows Sarah, a young pregnant woman still mourning the loss of her husband in a car crash months earlier. As Sarah prepares for her impending induced labor the next day, a mysterious woman appears at her door, demanding to be let in. What follows is a night of unrelenting terror as the woman, referred to only as "La Femme" (The Woman), violently attempts to take Sarah's unborn child. As the night progresses, the home invasion turns into a bloody siege, with Sarah fighting not only for her own survival but also for that of her baby. The film escalates into a gruesome and claustrophobic nightmare, pushing the boundaries of on-screen violence and maternal horror.

5. Why This Movie Is Recommended:

Inside is a relentlessly intense and visceral experience that stands as one of the most extreme examples of the New French Extremity movement. Directors Alexandre Bustillo and Julien Maury create an atmosphere of unbearable tension, confined mostly to a single location. The film's exploration of motherhood, loss, and desperation adds emotional depth to its brutal violence. Béatrice Dalle's performance as the enigmatic and terrifying antagonist is particularly noteworthy. While not for the faint of heart, Inside offers a unique and unforgettable take on the home invasion subgenre, elevating it to new heights of psychological and physical horror.

6. 10 Trivia Facts:

1. The film was shot in just 30 days on a relatively low budget.

2. Inside was the directorial debut for both Alexandre Bustillo and Julien Maury.

3. The movie uses over 25 liters of fake blood, an unusually high amount for its budget and shooting schedule.

4. Béatrice Dalle, who plays "La Femme," was originally considered for the role of Sarah.

5. The directors cite John Carpenter's Halloween as a major influence on the film's style and tension.

6. Inside premiered at the Toronto International Film Festival's "Midnight Madness" section.

7. The film was remade in Spain in 2016, though the remake was not as well-received as the original.

8. Inside won the Grand Prize and the Audience Award at the Gerardmer Film Festival.

9. The movie was shot entirely in chronological order to maintain the intensity of the performances.

10. Despite its extreme content, Inside received positive reviews from many critics, including Roger Ebert.

6. Raw (Grave)

1. Movie Title: Raw (Grave)

2. Year of Release: 2016

3. Cast and Director:

 - Director: Julia Ducournau

 - Cast: Garance Marillier, Ella Rumpf, Rabah Nait Oufella

4. Synopsis:

Raw follows Justine, a young vegetarian starting her first year at veterinary school. During a hazing ritual, she is forced to eat raw rabbit kidney, which awakens a dormant craving for meat within her. As Justine's newfound desires intensify, she finds herself drawn to increasingly extreme forms of flesh, including human. Her relationship with her older sister Alexia, already a student at the school, becomes strained as Justine struggles with her emerging cannibalistic urges. The film explores Justine's coming-of-age journey through a visceral and disturbing lens, blending body horror with a darkly comedic exploration of family dynamics, sexuality, and the primal nature of human desires.

5. Why This Movie Is Recommended:

Raw is a bold and unforgettable debut from director Julia Ducournau that pushes the boundaries of body horror while offering a unique coming-of-age story. The film's striking visuals and unflinching approach to its subject matter create a deeply unsettling yet captivating experience. Ducournau's deft handling of themes such as femininity, family, and societal expectations elevates Raw beyond simple shock value, offering a nuanced exploration of identity and desire. The performances, particularly from lead Garance Marillier, bring depth and humanity to even the most extreme moments. Raw stands as a powerful example of how horror can be used to explore complex psychological and social issues.

6. 10 Trivia Facts:

1. The film reportedly caused some viewers to faint during its premiere at the Toronto International Film Festival.

2. Director Julia Ducournau was inspired by David Cronenberg's body horror films.

3. Despite its cannibalism theme, the film used vegetarian substitutes for meat in its graphic scenes.

4. Raw won the FIPRESCI Prize at the 2016 Cannes Film Festival.

5. The movie's French title, "Grave," means both "serious" and "raw" in English.

6. Ducournau insisted on using practical effects rather than CGI for the film's gory scenes.

7. The lead actress, Garance Marillier, had previously worked with Ducournau on two short films.

8. Raw was chosen as one of the top 10 films of 2016 by Cahiers du Cinéma.

9. The film's rave party scene took two nights to shoot and involved over 200 extras.

10. Ducournau has described the film as a subversion of the "manic pixie dream girl" trope.

7. Irreversible

1. **Movie Title**: Irreversible (Irréversible)

2. **Year of Release**: 2002

3. **Cast and Director**:

  - Director: Gaspar Noé

  - Cast: Monica Bellucci, Vincent Cassel, Albert Dupontel

4. **Synopsis**:

Irreversible tells its story in reverse chronological order, beginning with a brutal act of revenge and working backwards to reveal the events that led to it. The film opens with Marcus and Pierre hunting down a man in a gay nightclub, resulting in a gruesome murder. As the narrative moves backwards, we witness the horrific event that sparked this revenge: the brutal rape and beating of Marcus's girlfriend Alex. The film continues to rewind, showing the events of the evening prior to the attack, revealing the complex relationships between the characters and the seemingly innocuous decisions that led to the tragedy. By presenting the story in reverse, Irreversible forces the audience to confront the inevitability of its events and the futility of revenge.

5. **Why This Movie Is Recommended**:

Irreversible is a challenging and controversial film that pushes the boundaries of cinema both in content and form. Director Gaspar Noé's reverse chronology creates a unique narrative experience that subverts expectations and forces viewers to engage with the material in new ways. The film's unflinching depiction of violence, particularly in its infamous nine-minute rape scene, is deeply disturbing but serves a purpose beyond shock value, highlighting the brutal reality of sexual violence. Noé's innovative use of camera work and sound design creates a disorienting, nightmarish atmosphere that perfectly complements the film's themes. While certainly not for everyone, Irreversible stands as a powerful, thought-provoking work that challenges viewers to confront uncomfortable truths about violence, time, and human nature.

6. **10 Trivia Facts**:

  1. The film's opening credits run backwards, setting the tone for the reverse chronology.

  2. Gaspar Noé used low-frequency sound in the first 30 minutes to induce nausea and unease in the audience.

  3. The entire film consists of about 12 long takes, with hidden cuts between them.

  4. Monica Bellucci and Vincent Cassel were married in real life at the time of filming.

  5. The film's infamous rape scene was shot in one continuous take.

  6. Noé makes a cameo appearance as a man masturbating in the gay club.

  7. The film's French tagline translates to "Time destroys everything," which is also the first and last line spoken in the movie.

  8. Irreversible was partly inspired by Stanley Kubrick's 1971 film "A Clockwork Orange."

  9. The movie caused walkouts and fainting spells during its premiere at the Cannes Film Festival.

  10. Noé released a "straight cut" version of the film in 2020, presenting the events in chronological order.

8. Them (Ils)

1. Movie Title: Them (Ils)

2. Year of Release: 2006

3. Cast and Director:

- Directors: David Moreau, Xavier Palud

- Cast: Olivia Bonamy, Michaël Cohen

4. Synopsis:

Them is a minimalist home invasion thriller based loosely on real events. The film follows Clémentine and Lucas, a young French couple living in an isolated mansion in Romania. Their quiet evening is shattered when they begin to hear strange noises outside their home. As the night progresses, it becomes clear that they are under attack by multiple assailants who seem more interested in terrorizing them than stealing or killing outright. The couple must fight for survival as their home is invaded and they are pursued through the house and surrounding forest. The film builds tension through its use of sound and unseen threats, only revealing the true nature of the attackers in its shocking finale.

5. Why This Movie Is Recommended:

Them excels in creating an atmosphere of pure, relentless tension with minimal resources. Directors Moreau and Palud craft a lean, effective thriller that proves you don't need elaborate setups or backstory to create genuine terror. The film's strength lies in its simplicity and realism, making the situation feel terrifyingly plausible. By keeping the attackers largely unseen for most of the runtime, Them taps into primal fears of the unknown. The movie's tight pacing, clever use of sound design, and strong performances from its small cast make for an intensely claustrophobic and nerve-wracking experience. Its influence can be seen in subsequent home invasion thrillers, marking it as a significant entry in the subgenre.

6. 10 Trivia Facts:

1. The film is loosely based on a real-life event that occurred in Austria in 2006.

2. Them was shot in just 30 days on a relatively low budget.

3. The movie uses very little dialogue, relying more on visual storytelling and sound design.

4. It was one of the first films of the New French Extremity movement to gain widespread international attention.

5. The directors made a conscious choice to keep the attackers mostly unseen to heighten tension.

6. Them inspired several American films, including "The Strangers" (2008).

7. The film won the Grand Prize at the Gérardmer Film Festival.

8. Despite being set in Romania, most of the film was actually shot in Bulgaria.

9. The directors went on to make the American remake of the Spanish horror film "[REC]" titled "Quarantine."

10. The film's runtime is a tight 77 minutes, contributing to its intense pacing.

9. Possession

1. Movie Title: Possession

2. Year of Release: 1981

3. Cast and Director:

- Director: Andrzej Żuławski

- Cast: Isabelle Adjani, Sam Neill, Heinz Bennent

4. Synopsis:

Possession is a genre-defying film that blends psychological horror, drama, and surrealism. Set in Cold War-era Berlin, it follows the disintegration of the marriage between Anna and Mark. When Mark returns from a work assignment, he finds Anna wanting a divorce for reasons she can't articulate. As Mark investigates, he discovers Anna's affair with a mysterious man named Heinrich. However, the truth is far stranger and more terrifying than infidelity. Anna's behavior becomes increasingly erratic and violent as she seems possessed by an unknown force. The film descends into a nightmarish exploration of obsession, jealousy, and the unknown, culminating in shocking scenes of body horror and supernatural terror that defy easy explanation.

5. Why This Movie Is Recommended:

Possession is a unique and unforgettable cinematic experience that defies easy categorization. Director Andrzej Żuławski creates a fever dream of a film that operates on multiple levels - as a harrowing depiction of a disintegrating relationship, a political allegory, and a surrealist horror. Isabelle Adjani's intense, committed performance (which won her Best Actress at Cannes) is the centerpiece of the film, particularly in the infamous subway scene. The movie's blend of psychological realism and grotesque body horror creates a deeply unsettling atmosphere that lingers long after viewing. While challenging and at times impenetrable, Possession rewards careful viewing with its rich symbolism and raw emotional power.

6. 10 Trivia Facts:

1. Isabelle Adjani claimed that it took her years to recover psychologically from her role in the film.

2. The movie was banned in the UK as part of the "video nasty" panic and was only available in heavily cut versions for years.

3. Director Żuławski wrote the script while going through a painful divorce.

4. The infamous subway scene took two days to film and left Adjani exhausted and emotionally drained.

5. The film's creature effects were created by Carlo Rambaldi, known for his work on "E.T." and "Alien."

6. Possession was shot entirely in Berlin, with the Berlin Wall featuring prominently in many scenes.

7. The film won the Best Actress award for Isabelle Adjani at the 1981 Cannes Film Festival.

8. Żuławski has stated that the film is partially an allegory for his experiences leaving communist Poland.

9. The movie has been interpreted through various lenses, including as a feminist text and a political allegory.

10. Despite its initial controversial reception, Possession has since been reappraised as a cult classic and influential work of European cinema.

10. Calvaire (The Ordeal)

1. Movie Title: Calvaire (The Ordeal)

2. Year of Release: 2004

3. Cast and Director:

- Director: Fabrice Du Welz

- Cast: Laurent Lucas, Jackie Berroyer, Philippe Nahon

4. Synopsis:

Calvaire follows Marc Stevens, a low-level cabaret singer whose van breaks down in a remote part of Belgium while traveling to a Christmas performance. He's taken in by Bartel, a lonely innkeeper who seems overly eager for company. As Marc tries to get his van repaired and leave, he finds himself trapped in an increasingly nightmarish situation. Bartel, driven mad by the departure of his wife years ago, begins to view Marc as a replacement for her. The surrounding village is populated by equally disturbed individuals, and Marc's attempts to escape are thwarted at every turn. The film descends into a surreal, horrifying exploration of madness, isolation, and twisted desire, building to a disturbing climax that blurs the lines between reality and delusion.

5. Why This Movie Is Recommended:

Calvaire is a deeply unsettling and unique entry in the horror genre that defies easy categorization. Director Fabrice Du Welz creates an atmosphere of creeping dread and dark absurdism that keeps viewers off-balance throughout. The film's rural Belgian setting provides a stark, eerie backdrop that enhances the sense of isolation and helplessness. While it contains elements of the "backwoods horror" subgenre, Calvaire transcends simple classification with its surreal imagery and psychological depth. The performances, particularly from Jackie Berroyer as the unhinged Bartel, are uncomfortably convincing. For those seeking a horror experience that prioritizes unsettling atmosphere and psychological terror over traditional scares, Calvaire offers a memorably disturbing journey.

6. 10 Trivia Facts:

1. The film's English title, "The Ordeal," is a literal translation of the French "Calvaire," referring to Christ's journey to crucifixion.

2. Director Fabrice Du Welz cited David Lynch and Werner Herzog as major influences on the film.

3. Calvaire was shot in the Belgian Ardennes, known for its dense forests and isolated villages.

4. The infamous "dance scene" in the village bar was largely improvised by the actors.

5. The film premiered at the 2004 Cannes Film Festival in the Critics' Week section.

6. Calvaire is considered part of the New French Extremity movement, despite being a Belgian production.

7. The movie features several actors known for their work in extreme French cinema, including Philippe Nahon.

8. Du Welz has described the film as a "Belgian Gothic" story.

9. The director insisted on shooting chronologically to capture the gradual descent into madness.

10. Calvaire has been interpreted by some critics as a dark allegory for artistic sacrifice and the perils of fame.

11. Trouble Every Day

1. Movie Title: Trouble Every Day

2. Year of Release: 2001

3. Cast and Director:

- Director: Claire Denis

- Cast: Vincent Gallo, Tricia Vessey, Béatrice Dalle

4. Synopsis:

Trouble Every Day follows two storylines that eventually converge. In one, American newlyweds Shane and June Brown travel to Paris for their honeymoon, but Shane has an ulterior motive related to his past scientific research. The other storyline focuses on Coré, the wife of Dr. Léo Semeneau, who is locked in their house due to her uncontrollable, cannibalistic sexual urges. As the film progresses, it's revealed that Shane and Coré share a condition resulting from experimental treatment that has merged their libidos with an insatiable hunger for human flesh. The movie explores themes of desire, consumption, and the thin line between passion and violence, culminating in scenes of graphic, sexual cannibalism.

5. Why This Movie Is Recommended:

Trouble Every Day is a uniquely disturbing blend of art-house cinema and body horror that challenges viewers on multiple levels. Director Claire Denis, known for her lyrical style, brings an unexpected poeticism to the gruesome subject matter. The film's deliberate pacing and minimal dialogue create an atmosphere of creeping dread, punctuated by moments of shocking violence. Denis uses the central metaphor of cannibalism to explore deeper themes about the nature of desire and the potential violence inherent in human sexuality. While certainly not for all tastes, Trouble Every Day offers a thought-provoking and viscerally affecting experience for those willing to engage with its challenging content.

6. 10 Trivia Facts:

1. The film's title is taken from a Frank Zappa song of the same name.

2. Claire Denis was inspired to make the film after reading about kuru, a disease spread by cannibalism.

3. The movie features a haunting score by British indie rock band Tindersticks.

4. Trouble Every Day premiered at the 2001 Cannes Film Festival, where it shocked and divided audiences.

5. The film was shot by cinematographer Agnès Godard, a frequent collaborator of Denis known for her atmospheric work.

6. Vincent Gallo took the lead role after another actor dropped out shortly before filming began.

7. Denis has stated that the film is partially a critique of the pharmaceutical industry.

8. The movie's graphic content led to censorship issues in several countries.

9. Trouble Every Day is considered part of the New French Extremity movement in cinema.

10. Despite its controversial nature, the film has been praised for its visual style and performances, particularly that of Béatrice Dalle.

12. Frontier(s) (Frontière(s))

1. Movie Title: Frontier(s) (Frontière(s))

2. Year of Release: 2007

3. Cast and Director:

  - Director: Xavier Gens

  - Cast: Karina Testa, Aurélien Wiik, Patrick Ligardes

4. Synopsis:

  Set against the backdrop of political unrest in Paris, Frontier(s) follows a group of young thieves fleeing the city after a heist gone wrong. Seeking refuge, they arrive at a seemingly deserted inn near the French-German border. However, the inn is run by a neo-Nazi clan led by a former SS officer, who subject their "guests" to horrific tortures and use them for gruesome purposes. As the group fights for survival, they uncover the full extent of the family's depravity, including cannibalism and eugenic experiments. The film builds to a frenzied climax of violence as the survivors attempt to escape their sadistic captors.

5. Why This Movie Is Recommended:

  Frontier(s) is a relentless and brutal entry in the New French Extremity movement that pushes the boundaries of on-screen violence. Director Xavier Gens crafts a tense, claustrophobic atmosphere that keeps viewers on edge throughout. While the film draws clear inspiration from American horror classics like "The Texas Chain Saw Massacre," it adds its own political subtext, using its neo-Nazi villains to comment on far-right resurgence in Europe. The movie's unflinching approach to violence and taboo subjects is not for the faint of heart, but for horror fans seeking intense, visceral experiences, Frontier(s) delivers in spades. Its themes of political unrest and societal breakdown also give it a relevance that extends beyond mere shock value.

6. 10 Trivia Facts:

  1. Frontier(s) was originally intended to be part of the "8 Films to Die For" series but was considered too extreme.

  2. The film was shot in part at an abandoned mine in eastern France.

  3. Director Xavier Gens cited "The Texas Chain Saw Massacre" and "The Hills Have Eyes" as major influences.

  4. Frontier(s) premiered at the 2007 Toronto International Film Festival's Midnight Madness section.

  5. The movie's political backdrop was inspired by the 2005 French riots.

  6. Gens insisted on using practical effects for the film's gore scenes rather than CGI.

  7. The film's tagline in France was "The Texas Chain Saw Massacre of French cinema."

  8. Frontier(s) was banned in several countries due to its extreme violence.

  9. The movie was Gens' feature film directorial debut.

  10. Despite its controversial content, the film received praise for its technical aspects, particularly its cinematography and sound design.

13. Revenge

1. Movie Title: Revenge

2. Year of Release: 2017

3. Cast and Director:

  - Director: Coralie Fargeat

  - Cast: Matilda Lutz, Kevin Janssens, Vincent Colombe

4. Synopsis:

Revenge follows Jen, a young American socialite who accompanies her married lover Richard on a hunting trip to his remote desert villa. Their getaway is interrupted by the early arrival of Richard's hunting buddies, Stan and Dimitri. After a night of partying, Jen is brutally assaulted by Stan. When she threatens to expose what happened, Richard pushes her off a cliff and leaves her for dead. However, Jen survives and embarks on a bloody quest for vengeance against her attackers. As she pursues the men across the unforgiving desert landscape, Jen transforms from a seemingly naive party girl into a hardened survivalist bent on retribution.

5. Why This Movie Is Recommended:

Revenge is a visceral and stylish take on the rape-revenge subgenre that subverts many of its typical tropes. Director Coralie Fargeat brings a distinct feminist perspective to the material, challenging the male gaze and turning Jen's objectification on its head. The film's vivid cinematography and pulsing soundtrack create a hyperreal atmosphere that complements its over-the-top action sequences. While unflinchingly violent, Revenge balances its brutality with moments of dark humor and surrealism. Matilda Lutz delivers a powerful performance as Jen, conveying her character's transformation with nuance and intensity. For viewers seeking a fresh, provocative take on revenge narratives, this film offers a visually striking and thematically rich experience.

6. 10 Trivia Facts:

1. Revenge was director Coralie Fargeat's feature film debut.

2. The film premiered at the 2017 Toronto International Film Festival's Midnight Madness section.

3. Fargeat insisted on using practical effects for the movie's gore, using over 2,000 liters of fake blood.

4. The entire movie was shot in Morocco, despite being set in an unspecified desert location.

5. Lead actress Matilda Lutz performed many of her own stunts.

6. The film's vibrant color palette was inspired by films like "Suspira" and the work of Nicolas Winding Refn.

7. Revenge won the Jury Prize at the 2018 Gerardmer Film Festival.

8. The movie has been praised for its critique of the male gaze in cinema.

9. Fargeat has cited "Mad Max: Fury Road" as an influence on the film's desert action sequences.

10. Despite its extreme content, Revenge received widespread critical acclaim, holding a 93% rating on Rotten Tomatoes.

14. Evolution

1. Movie Title: Evolution

2. Year of Release: 2015

3. Cast and Director:

- Director: Lucile Hadžihalilović

- Cast: Max Brebant, Roxane Duran, Julie-Marie Parmentier

4. Synopsis:

Evolution is set in a mysterious seaside village populated only by women and young boys. The story follows Nicolas, a 10-year-old boy who starts to question the strange medical treatments he and the other boys regularly undergo at the local hospital. After seeing what he believes to be a dead body in the ocean, Nicolas becomes increasingly suspicious of the women's behavior and the true nature of their isolated community. As he investigates, he uncovers disturbing secrets about the village's purpose and the fate that awaits the boys. The film blends elements of body horror with a dreamlike atmosphere, creating an unsettling exploration of childhood, gender, and the unknown.

5. Why This Movie Is Recommended:

Evolution is a unique and haunting entry in the horror genre that prioritizes atmosphere and symbolism over traditional scares. Director Lucile Hadžihalilović crafts a visually stunning world that feels both beautiful and deeply unnerving. The film's slow-burn pacing and minimal dialogue create a sense of creeping dread, allowing viewers to become fully immersed in its bizarre, aquatic-themed mythology. While it may frustrate those looking for clear-cut answers, Evolution rewards patient viewers with its rich imagery and thought-provoking themes. The movie's exploration of bodily transformation and the anxieties of pre-adolescence offers a fresh perspective on coming-of-age narratives, filtered through a lens of surreal body horror.

6. 10 Trivia Facts:

1. Evolution was Lucile Hadžihalilović's first feature film in over a decade, following her debut "Innocence" (2004).

2. The film was shot on location in Lanzarote, one of the Canary Islands, known for its otherworldly landscapes.

3. Hadžihalilović spent nearly 10 years developing the script for Evolution.

4. The movie won the Special Jury Prize at the 2015 San Sebastián International Film Festival.

5. Evolution's underwater scenes were filmed in a large tank in Belgium.

6. The director has cited David Cronenberg's body horror films as an influence.

7. The film uses minimal CGI, relying mostly on practical effects for its surreal imagery.

8. Evolution's score, composed by Jesús Díaz and Zacarías M. de la Riva, heavily features aquatic sounds.

9. The movie has been interpreted by some critics as an allegory for gender dysphoria.

10. Hadžihalilović intentionally cast young actors with androgynous features to blur gender lines in the film.

15. Malefique

1. Movie Title: Malefique

2. Year of Release: 2002

3. Cast and Director:

 - Director: Eric Valette

 - Cast: Gérald Laroche, Philippe Laudenbach, Clovis Cornillac

4. Synopsis:

  Malefique takes place almost entirely within a prison cell shared by four inmates: Carrère, a white-collar criminal; Marcus, a drag queen; Paquerette, a simple-minded man who ate his baby sister; and Lassalle, a librarian convicted of killing his wife. The inmates discover a mysterious diary hidden in their cell, once belonging to a prisoner named Danvers who was obsessed with the occult and disappeared without a trace decades ago. As they decipher the diary's contents, they uncover powerful and dangerous spells. Desperation leads them to attempt these magical rituals in hopes of escaping, but each spell exacts a terrible price. As the boundary between reality and the supernatural blurs, the prisoners find themselves trapped in a nightmare far worse than their incarceration.

5. Why This Movie Is Recommended:

  Malefique is a unique blend of psychological horror and supernatural terror that makes the most of its claustrophobic setting. Director Eric Valette creates an oppressive atmosphere that perfectly captures the desperation and paranoia of prison life, even before the supernatural elements come into play. The film's strength lies in its character development, with each inmate's backstory and motivations adding depth to the unfolding horror. Malefique's exploration of themes like guilt, redemption, and the price of freedom gives it a psychological weight beyond its supernatural premise. For horror fans seeking something off the beaten path, this film offers a thought-provoking and genuinely unnerving experience that lingers in the mind long after viewing.

6. 10 Trivia Facts:

  1. Malefique was director Eric Valette's feature film debut.

  2. The entire film was shot on a single set representing the prison cell.

  3. The movie won the Grand Prize at the 2003 Gérardmer Film Festival.

  4. Malefique's script was partially inspired by real-life accounts of prison life.

  5. The film's practical effects were created on a very limited budget, relying heavily on the actors' performances.

  6. Valette has cited John Carpenter's "The Thing" as an influence on the film's claustrophobic atmosphere.

  7. The character of Marcus was played by Clovis Cornillac, who underwent a significant transformation for the role.

  8. Malefique has gained a cult following over the years, particularly among fans of occult-themed horror.

  9. The film's original French title, "Maléfique," can be translated as both "Evil" and "Hex."

  10. Despite its supernatural elements, much of the film's horror comes from the psychological interactions between the prisoners.

16. Sheitan

1. Movie Title: Sheitan

2. Year of Release: 2006

3. Cast and Director:

  - Director: Kim Chapiron

  - Cast: Vincent Cassel, Olivier Bartélémy, Roxane Mesquida

4. Synopsis:

  Sheitan follows a group of young Parisian clubbers who meet Eve, an alluring woman who invites them to her family's country home for Christmas Eve. Upon arrival, they're greeted by Joseph (Vincent Cassel), the eccentric groundskeeper with an unsettling fixation on childbirth and a collection of disturbing homemade dolls. As the night progresses, the group encounters increasingly bizarre and threatening situations. Joseph's behavior becomes more erratic, and it becomes clear that the visitors are part of a sinister plan involving satanic rituals and the birth of a demonic entity. The film builds to a frenzied, hallucinatory climax as the true nature of Eve's family and their intentions are revealed.

5. Why This Movie Is Recommended:

  Sheitan is a uniquely disturbing blend of dark comedy and occult horror that keeps viewers off-balance throughout. Director Kim Chapiron creates an atmosphere of escalating madness, punctuated by moments of shocking violence and surreal imagery. Vincent Cassel's unhinged performance as Joseph is a highlight, bringing a manic energy that's both hilarious and terrifying. The film's exploration of urban-rural divides and the dark undercurrents of seemingly idyllic country life adds depth to its horror elements. While its extreme content and tonal shifts may not be for everyone, Sheitan offers a memorably twisted experience for those who appreciate unconventional, boundary-pushing cinema.

6. 10 Trivia Facts:

  1. "Sheitan" is the Arabic word for Satan or devil.

  2. The film marks the directorial debut of Kim Chapiron, who was only 25 when he made it.

  3. Vincent Cassel, who plays Joseph, also produced the film.

  4. Many of the disturbing dolls featured in the movie were actually created by Chapiron's grandmother.

  5. The film premiered at the 2006 Cannes Film Festival in the Critics' Week section.

  6. Sheitan was shot on location in the French countryside during a particularly cold winter.

  7. The movie features a cameo by Gaspar Noé, director of controversial films like "Irreversible" and "Enter the Void."

  8. Chapiron has cited David Lynch as a major influence on the film's surreal elements.

  9. The film's score, which blends electronic music with more traditional horror elements, was composed by Chapiron's brother.

  10. Sheitan has gained a cult following over the years, particularly for its outrageous humor and Cassel's performance.

17. Livide (Livid)

1. Movie Title: Livide (Livid)

2. Year of Release: 2011

3. Cast and Director:

  - Directors: Alexandre Bustillo, Julien Maury

  - Cast: Chloé Coulloud, Félix Moati, Jérémy Kapone

4. Synopsis:

Livide follows Lucie, a young woman training as an in-home caregiver, who learns about a bedridden, comatose patient named Mrs. Jessel, a former ballet teacher rumored to have hidden treasure in her remote mansion. Lucie convinces her boyfriend and his brother to break into the house on Halloween night to search for the treasure. As they explore the eerie, decaying mansion, they uncover dark secrets about Mrs. Jessel's past and her connection to a group of young ballerinas who mysteriously disappeared years ago. The line between reality and nightmare blurs as the intruders face supernatural horrors and must fight to survive the night in a house that seems to have a malevolent life of its own.

5. Why This Movie Is Recommended:

Livide is a visually stunning and atmospheric horror film that blends elements of fairy tales, gothic horror, and surrealism. Directors Bustillo and Maury, known for their work on "Inside," create a dreamlike, often nightmarish world filled with striking imagery and unsettling set pieces. The film's strength lies in its ability to build tension through its eerie atmosphere and unpredictable narrative turns. While it may frustrate viewers looking for straightforward scares or explanations, Livide rewards those who appreciate more abstract, visually-driven horror. Its unique take on haunted house tropes and its exploration of themes like memory and the loss of innocence make it a standout in French horror cinema.

6. 10 Trivia Facts:

1. Livide was intended to be the first part of a trilogy, though the sequels have not materialized.

2. The film's visual style was influenced by the works of Mario Bava and Dario Argento.

3. Directors Bustillo and Maury designed many of the film's practical effects themselves.

4. Livide premiered at the 2011 Toronto International Film Festival's Midnight Madness section.

5. The movie's ballet themes were inspired by Powell and Pressburger's "The Red Shoes."

6. Many of the film's exterior shots were filmed in Brittany, France.

7. The directors have cited Jean-Pierre Jeunet's "The City of Lost Children" as an influence on the film's fantastical elements.

8. Livide's original screenplay was much more violent, but the directors chose to focus more on atmosphere in the final film.

9. The movie features several nods to classic horror films, including "Suspiria" and "The Texas Chain Saw Massacre."

10. Despite plans for an American remake, it has not come to fruition as of 2024.

18. Vertige (High Lane)

1. Movie Title: Vertige (High Lane)

2. Year of Release: 2009

3. Cast and Director:

- Director: Abel Ferry

- Cast: Fanny Valette, Johan Libéreau, Raphaël Lenglet

4. Synopsis:

Vertige follows a group of friends on a mountain climbing expedition in Croatia. Despite warnings that their intended route is closed, they decide to proceed. As they navigate treacherous paths and rickety bridges high above the ground, tensions rise within the group, exacerbated by a love triangle. Their situation takes a dire turn when they encounter a territorial, feral man living in the mountains. Trapped between the unforgiving terrain and this violent threat, the group must fight for survival. The film combines the tension of extreme sports with the terror of being hunted, all set against the backdrop of vertigo-inducing heights.

5. Why This Movie Is Recommended:

Vertige stands out for its unique blend of adventure thriller and survival horror elements. Director Abel Ferry makes excellent use of the film's stunning but perilous mountain setting to create a palpable sense of danger even before the human threat is introduced. The movie's early scenes of precarious climbing generate intense suspense through vertigo-inducing cinematography. When the horror elements kick in, they're made all the more effective by the already established sense of isolation and vulnerability. While it may not reinvent the wheel in terms of plot, Vertige's execution and setting make it a tense, adrenaline-pumping experience that will appeal to fans of both outdoor adventure films and more traditional horror.

6. 10 Trivia Facts:

1. The film's English title, "High Lane," is a literal translation of a climbing term.

2. Many of the climbing scenes were performed by the actors themselves after extensive training.

3. Vertige was shot on location in Croatia, taking advantage of the country's dramatic mountain scenery.

4. The movie premiered at the 2009 Sitges Film Festival.

5. Director Abel Ferry has a background in mountain sports, which influenced the film's authentic portrayal of climbing.

6. The film's antagonist was partially inspired by real-life cases of feral humans.

7. Vertige's score, composed by Jérôme Brisard, emphasizes the natural sounds of the mountain to heighten tension.

8. The movie features several nods to classic survival horror films like "Deliverance" and "The Hills Have Eyes."

9. Some of the more dangerous stunts were performed by professional climbers doubling for the actors.

10. Vertige has gained appreciation among horror fans for its unique setting and blend of genres.

19. Mutants

1. Movie Title: Mutants

2. Year of Release: 2009

3. Cast and Director:

- Director: David Morlet

- Cast: Hélène de Fougerolles, Francis Renaud, Dida Diafat

4. Synopsis:

Set in a post-apocalyptic France, Mutants follows Marco and Sonia, two paramedics navigating a world ravaged by a virus that transforms humans into violent, cannibalistic creatures. When Marco becomes infected, Sonia, who is pregnant, desperately searches for a safe haven and a cure. They take refuge in an abandoned military base, where Sonia must protect herself not only from the mutants outside but also from her increasingly unstable partner as he slowly transforms. The arrival of a group of survivalists complicates matters further, leading to tense confrontations and difficult moral choices as Sonia fights to survive and potentially save Marco.

5. Why This Movie Is Recommended:

Mutants offers a fresh take on the zombie/infection genre by focusing intensely on the personal drama of its main characters. Director David Morlet creates a bleak, tense atmosphere that emphasizes the psychological toll of survival in a post-apocalyptic world. The film's exploration of love tested by extreme circumstances adds emotional depth to its horror elements. Hélène de Fougerolles delivers a powerful performance as Sonia, capturing her character's struggle between hope and desperation. While Mutants features intense action and gore, it stands out for its character-driven approach and its unflinching look at the human cost of apocalyptic scenarios. For fans of zombie cinema looking for something with a more personal, dramatic touch, Mutants offers a compelling and emotionally resonant experience.

6. 10 Trivia Facts:

1. Mutants was David Morlet's feature film directorial debut.

2. The film premiered at the 2009 Sitges Film Festival.

3. Many of the mutant effects were achieved through practical makeup rather than CGI.

4. The movie was shot on location in the French Alps, adding to its isolated atmosphere.

5. Mutants won the Jury Prize at the 2010 Gérardmer Film Festival.

6. The film's infected creatures were designed to evolve visually throughout their transformation process.

7. Director Morlet cited David Cronenberg's body horror films as an influence on the mutation effects.

8. The movie features a cameo by French horror director Xavier Gens.

9. Mutants' screenplay was partially inspired by real-life virus outbreaks and their potential for global impact.

10. The film gained renewed interest during the COVID-19 pandemic due to its themes of viral infection and isolation.

20. Saint Ange (House of Voices)

1. Movie Title: Saint Ange (House of Voices)

2. Year of Release: 2004

3. Cast and Director:

  - Director: Pascal Laugier

  - Cast: Virginie Ledoyen, Lou Doillon, Catriona MacColl

4. Synopsis:

  Set in 1960s France, Saint Ange follows Anna, a young woman who takes a job as a cleaner at Saint Ange, a remote orphanage in the French Alps that's about to be shut down. The orphanage's only remaining resident is Judith, a troubled young woman who insists that the other children are still there, hiding in the building. As Anna settles into her role, she begins to experience strange occurrences and becomes convinced that the orphanage is haunted by the ghosts of children who suffered abuse there. Delving deeper into the institution's dark history, Anna uncovers disturbing secrets about Saint Ange and its former occupants, blurring the line between reality and supernatural terror.

5. Why This Movie Is Recommended:

  Saint Ange is a atmospheric ghost story that prioritizes creeping dread over jump scares. Director Pascal Laugier, who would later create the extreme horror film "Martyrs," demonstrates his skill at building tension and creating an oppressive, haunting atmosphere. The film's isolated setting and period detail add to its gothic ambiance, while its exploration of themes like institutional abuse and the lingering effects of trauma give it psychological depth. Virginie Ledoyen delivers a nuanced performance as Anna, capturing her character's increasing paranoia and determination to uncover the truth. While it may move too slowly for some horror fans, those who appreciate subtle, atmospheric ghost stories will find much to admire in Saint Ange's moody cinematography and slow-burn approach to supernatural terror.

6. 10 Trivia Facts:

  1. Saint Ange was Pascal Laugier's directorial debut.

  2. The film was shot on location in a real abandoned building in the French Alps.

  3. Laugier has cited Stanley Kubrick's "The Shining" as a major influence on the film's atmosphere.

  4. The movie features early work from composer Joseph LoDuca, known for his scores on "Evil Dead" and "Xena: Warrior Princess."

  5. Saint Ange premiered at the 2004 Sitges Film Festival.

  6. The film's English title, "House of Voices," emphasizes its ghostly elements.

  7. Laugier insisted on using practical effects and real locations to create the film's unsettling atmosphere.

  8. The movie's themes of institutional abuse were inspired by real-life scandals in orphanages and children's homes.

  9. Saint Ange features a cameo by Catriona MacColl, known for her work in Lucio Fulci's horror films.

  10. Despite mixed reviews upon release, the film has gained appreciation over time for its atmospheric approach to horror.

Australia

1. Wolf Creek

1. Movie Title: Wolf Creek

2. Year of Release: 2005

3. Cast and Director:

  - Director: Greg McLean

  - Cast: John Jarratt, Cassandra Magrath, Kestic Morassi, Nathan Phillips

4. **Synopsis**:

  Wolf Creek follows three backpackers - Liz, Kristy, and Ben - on a road trip across the Australian Outback. Their journey takes a sinister turn when their car breaks down near Wolf Creek National Park. A friendly local, Mick Taylor, offers to tow them to his camp for repairs. However, Mick's helpful demeanor masks a sadistic nature, and the travelers soon find themselves in a desperate fight for survival against a ruthless killer who knows the vast, unforgiving landscape better than anyone. As night falls and hope dwindles, the true horrors of the Outback are revealed in this brutal and unnerving thriller.

5. **Why This Movie Is Recommended**:

  Wolf Creek stands out for its raw, unflinching portrayal of terror in the Australian wilderness. The film's strength lies in its realism, drawing inspiration from true crimes to create a chilling atmosphere of isolation and vulnerability. John Jarratt's performance as Mick Taylor is genuinely unsettling, presenting a villain who's both charismatic and utterly malevolent. The movie's use of the vast, barren Outback as a character in itself adds to the sense of hopelessness and dread. Wolf Creek revitalized the Australian horror genre and has become a benchmark for gritty, realistic horror worldwide.

6. **10 Trivia Facts**:

  1. The film was loosely inspired by real-life crimes, including the backpacker murders by Ivan Milat.

  2. Wolf Creek was shot on a budget of approximately AUD $1.4 million.

  3. The movie was filmed in South Australia, despite being set in Western Australia.

  4. John Jarratt spent weeks living in the Outback to prepare for his role as Mick Taylor.

  5. The film was so intense that it received an R rating in the United States without any cuts.

  6. Wolf Creek National Park is a real place, though the events in the film are fictional.

  7. The movie spawned a sequel and a TV series, with John Jarratt reprising his role as Mick Taylor.

  8. Director Greg McLean wrote the script in just two weeks.

  9. The film's success led to a resurgence in Australian horror cinema.

  10. Wolf Creek was selected for the Sundance Film Festival, unusual for such a graphic horror film.

2. The Babadook

1. Movie Title: The Babadook

2. Year of Release: 2014

3. Cast and Director:

- Director: Jennifer Kent

- Cast: Essie Davis, Noah Wiseman, Daniel Henshall, Hayley McElhinney

4. Synopsis:

The Babadook tells the story of Amelia, a single mother struggling to raise her troubled six-year-old son, Samuel, following the violent death of her husband. Samuel's behavioral problems and fear of monsters strain their relationship and isolate them from others. One night, they read a mysterious pop-up book called "Mister Babadook," which unleashes a sinister presence in their home. As Amelia's grip on reality begins to slip, the line between imagination and reality blurs. The Babadook becomes a manifestation of grief, depression, and the challenges of parenthood. Amelia must confront her own demons to protect her son and find a way to coexist with the monster that has invaded their lives.

5. Why This Movie Is Recommended:

The Babadook is a masterful psychological horror that transcends typical genre tropes. Jennifer Kent's directorial debut is a poignant exploration of grief, mental illness, and the pressures of single parenthood, wrapped in a chilling supernatural narrative. The film's strength lies in its nuanced performances, particularly Essie Davis as Amelia, and its ability to create tension through atmosphere rather than jump scares. The Babadook itself is a uniquely designed monster that has become iconic in modern horror. This film offers a deeply emotional and psychologically complex horror experience that lingers long after viewing.

6. 10 Trivia Facts:

1. The Babadook character was inspired by early 20th-century surrealist and expressionist cinema.

2. The pop-up book featured in the film was handcrafted by illustrator Alex Juhasz.

3. Director Jennifer Kent originally created a short film called "Monster" that served as a proof-of-concept for The Babadook.

4. The film was produced on a modest budget of $2 million.

5. William Friedkin, director of The Exorcist, called The Babadook the most terrifying film he had ever seen.

6. The Babadook has become an unexpected LGBTQ+ icon, with the character being embraced as a queer symbol.

7. The movie's title comes from a Serbian phrase meaning "Baba Dook," or "evil man."

8. Kent and Davis worked together to create a 100-page backstory for Amelia's character.

9. The film used minimal CGI, relying mostly on practical effects and clever cinematography.

10. Despite its critical acclaim, The Babadook was not a box office success in Australia upon its initial release.

3. Picnic at Hanging Rock

1. Movie Title: Picnic at Hanging Rock

2. Year of Release: 1975

3. Cast and Director:

- Director: Peter Weir

- Cast: Rachel Roberts, Dominic Guard, Helen Morse, Jacki Weaver

4. Synopsis:

Set in 1900, Picnic at Hanging Rock tells the enigmatic story of a group of students from Appleyard College, an all-girls school in Victoria, Australia. On Valentine's Day, the group goes on a picnic to Hanging Rock, a distinctive geological formation. During the outing, three students and a teacher mysteriously vanish without a trace while exploring the rock. The disappearance sends shockwaves through the school and the nearby town, leading to a search that yields more questions than answers. As time passes, the unexplained event begins to unravel the fabric of the community, exposing hidden tensions and desires. The film explores themes of repression, sexuality, and the clash between European colonialism and the ancient Australian landscape.

5. Why This Movie Is Recommended:

Picnic at Hanging Rock is a haunting and atmospheric masterpiece that defies easy categorization. While not a traditional horror film, its sense of dread and unsettling ambiguity create a deeply unnerving experience. Peter Weir's direction masterfully builds tension through its dreamlike cinematography and ethereal soundtrack. The film's refusal to provide clear answers to its central mystery adds to its enduring intrigue. It's a pivotal work in Australian cinema that blends historical drama with elements of the Gothic and supernatural, creating a unique and unforgettable viewing experience that continues to inspire analysis and discussion decades after its release.

6. 10 Trivia Facts:

1. The film is based on Joan Lindsay's 1967 novel of the same name, which presents the story as potentially true despite being fiction.

2. The actual Hanging Rock in Victoria, Australia, saw a significant increase in tourism following the film's release.

3. Director Peter Weir had the young actresses hypnotized for some scenes to achieve a dreamlike quality in their performances.

4. The film's eerie pan pipe music was performed by Gheorghe Zamfir, a Romanian musician.

5. A final chapter of the original novel, which explained the disappearances, was published posthumously but is generally disregarded.

6. The movie was one of the first Australian films to achieve international acclaim, helping to kickstart the Australian New Wave cinema movement.

7. To maintain the mystery, Peter Weir instructed the disappeared girls to avoid the other cast members during filming.

8. The film's costume designer, Judith Dorsman, insisted on historically accurate undergarments for authenticity, even though they wouldn't be seen on screen.

9. Picnic at Hanging Rock was remade as a miniseries in 2018, exploring different aspects of the story.

10. The film's ambiguous ending has spawned numerous theories and interpretations over the years, including supernatural and UFO-related explanations.

4. Razorback

1. Movie Title: Razorback

2. Year of Release: 1984

3. Cast and Director:

- Director: Russell Mulcahy

- Cast: Gregory Harrison, Arkie Whiteley, Bill Kerr, Chris Haywood

4. Synopsis:

Razorback is set in the Australian Outback and centers around a monstrous wild boar terrorizing the local population. The story begins when Jake Cullen loses his grandson to the beast, but his claims are dismissed as tall tales. Years later, American journalist Beth Winters arrives to investigate the illegal hunting of kangaroos, only to disappear mysteriously. Her husband, Carl, travels to Australia to find her and teams up with Jake to hunt down the enormous razorback. As they pursue the creature through the harsh and unforgiving landscape, they uncover a web of corruption and face not only the deadly boar but also dangerous locals who have their own reasons for wanting the beast to remain a secret.

5. Why This Movie Is Recommended:

Razorback stands out as a unique entry in the natural horror subgenre, blending elements of Jaws with the distinctive backdrop of the Australian Outback. Director Russell Mulcahy, known for his work in music videos, brings a stylish visual flair to the film, creating surreal and nightmarish sequences that elevate it above typical monster movies. The film's portrayal of the Outback as an alien, hostile environment adds to the sense of isolation and dread. While the premise might seem outlandish, Razorback's execution is surprisingly effective, offering genuine scares and tension. It's a cult classic that showcases Australian cinema's ability to turn familiar horror tropes into something fresh and memorable.

6. 10 Trivia Facts:

1. The film is based on a novel of the same name by Peter Brennan.

2. Director Russell Mulcahy was chosen based on his iconic music videos for bands like Duran Duran.

3. The razorback boar was created using various practical effects, including animatronics and men in suits.

4. Some of the film's more surreal sequences were inspired by Salvador Dalí's paintings.

5. Razorback was shot in Broken Hill, New South Wales, the same location used for Mad Max 2.

6. The film won an award for Best Makeup at the Sitges - Catalan International Film Festival.

7. Despite mixed reviews upon release, Razorback has since gained a strong cult following.

8. Quentin Tarantino has cited Razorback as one of his favorite Australian films.

9. The largest animatronic boar used in the film weighed over 300 pounds.

10. The film's tagline was "It's waiting out there... and it's hungry," playing on fears of the unknown in the vast Outback.

5. Patrick

1. Movie Title: Patrick

2. Year of Release: 1978

3. Cast and Director:

- Director: Richard Franklin

- Cast: Susan Penhaligon, Robert Helpmann, Rod Mullinar, Robert Thompson

4. Synopsis:

Patrick tells the story of a comatose patient with psychokinetic powers. The titular character, Patrick, lies in a vegetative state in a private hospital after killing his mother and her lover. Kathy Jacquard, a new nurse at the hospital, becomes the object of Patrick's obsession. Despite being completely paralyzed and unable to communicate except by spitting, Patrick begins to use his telekinetic abilities to manipulate objects and people around him, particularly targeting those close to Kathy. As strange and deadly occurrences increase, Kathy must unravel the mystery of Patrick's powers and find a way to stop him before his jealousy and rage claim more victims.

5. Why This Movie Is Recommended:

Patrick stands out as a unique and chilling entry in the psychokinetic horror subgenre. The film masterfully builds tension through its confined setting and the unsettling idea of a seemingly helpless patient wielding immense power. Director Richard Franklin, influenced by Alfred Hitchcock, employs subtle psychological horror techniques that create a pervasive sense of unease. The movie explores themes of scientific ethics, the nature of consciousness, and obsession. Patrick's inability to move or speak, contrasted with his devastating psychic abilities, presents a truly original and terrifying antagonist. This Australian classic offers a compelling blend of supernatural horror and psychological thriller that continues to influence filmmakers today.

6. 10 Trivia Facts:

1. Director Richard Franklin was a student of Alfred Hitchcock at USC, and Hitchcock's influence is evident in the film's style.

2. Patrick was one of the first Australian films to receive international distribution by a major American studio (20th Century Fox).

3. The film spawned an Italian pseudo-sequel called "Patrick Still Lives" (Patrick vive ancora) in 1980, unauthorized by the original creators.

4. Robert Thompson, who played Patrick, had to keep his eyes open without blinking for long periods during filming.

5. The movie features early work by Oscar-winning composer Brian May (not to be confused with the Queen guitarist).

6. Patrick was remade in 2013, starring Charles Dance and Sharni Vinson, with the original director Richard Franklin as producer.

7. The film was shot in Melbourne, Australia, at the Mont Park Psychiatric Hospital.

8. Patrick's telekinetic abilities were achieved through practical effects, including hidden wires and off-screen operators.

9. The movie won three Australian Film Institute Awards, including Best Sound.

10. Despite its supernatural elements, the film was partly inspired by real-life cases of patients in vegetative states showing signs of consciousness.

6. Lake Mungo

1. Movie Title: Lake Mungo

2. Year of Release: 2008

3. Cast and Director:

  - Director: Joel Anderson

  - Cast: Rosie Traynor, David Pledger, Martin Sharpe, Talia Zucker

4. Synopsis:

Lake Mungo is a pseudo-documentary that follows the Palmer family as they cope with the drowning death of their teenage daughter, Alice. As strange events begin to occur in their home, the family becomes convinced that Alice's ghost is trying to contact them. They employ a psychic and a parapsychologist to investigate the phenomena. Through a series of interviews, found footage, and reenactments, the film peels back layers of secrets and lies surrounding Alice's life and death. As the truth unfolds, it becomes clear that Alice was harboring dark secrets, and her presence may not be as benevolent as initially thought. The film explores themes of grief, memory, and the unknown, blurring the lines between reality and the supernatural.

5. Why This Movie Is Recommended:

Lake Mungo stands out for its unique approach to the horror genre, utilizing the documentary format to create a deeply unsettling and emotionally resonant experience. The film's strength lies in its subtlety and psychological depth, building a sense of dread through atmosphere rather than jump scares. It tackles complex themes of loss, guilt, and the secrets we keep, even from those closest to us. The naturalistic performances and the film's commitment to its documentary style lend a chilling realism to the supernatural elements. Lake Mungo offers a haunting meditation on grief and the unknown that lingers long after viewing, making it a standout in both Australian cinema and the horror genre at large.

6. 10 Trivia Facts:

1. Despite its documentary style, Lake Mungo is entirely fictional.

2. The film was shot on location in various parts of Victoria, Australia.

3. Director Joel Anderson has not made another feature film since Lake Mungo, adding to its mystique.

4. The movie's title refers to Lake Mungo in New South Wales, famous for its archaeological significance.

5. Lake Mungo was part of the 2008 Strangers With Candy series at the Sydney Film Festival.

6. The film gained a significant cult following after its DVD release in the United States.

7. Many viewers have reported being genuinely fooled by the documentary style, believing it to be a true story.

8. Lake Mungo employs a technique of hiding ghostly images in the background of scenes, rewarding attentive viewers.

9. The film was praised for its realistic portrayal of grief and family dynamics.

10. Despite plans for an American remake, as of 2024, it has not materialized, preserving the original's unique status.

7. Wyrmwood: Road of the Dead

1. Movie Title: Wyrmwood: Road of the Dead

2. Year of Release: 2014

3. Cast and Director:

  - Director: Kiah Roache-Turner

  - Cast: Jay Gallagher, Bianca Bradey, Leon Burchill, Luke McKenzie

4. Synopsis:

  Wyrmwood: Road of the Dead is set in a post-apocalyptic Australia where a mysterious outbreak has turned most of the population into zombies. The story follows Barry, a mechanic who loses his family to the zombie plague and teams up with Benny, an Aboriginal man, to survive. They discover that zombie blood can be used as fuel, leading them to create armored vehicles to traverse the dangerous landscape. Meanwhile, Barry's sister Brooke is kidnapped by a group of gas-masked soldiers and subjected to bizarre experiments that give her the ability to control zombies telepathically. As Barry and his team race to rescue Brooke, they must battle both the undead and the sinister military forces behind the outbreak, uncovering a conspiracy larger than they imagined.

5. Why This Movie Is Recommended:

  Wyrmwood: Road of the Dead breathes new life into the zombie genre with its uniquely Australian flavor and inventive approach. The film stands out for its creative world-building, blending Mad Max-style vehicular action with zombie horror and dark humor. Its fast-paced narrative and innovative ideas, such as using zombie blood as fuel, keep the audience engaged throughout. The movie's low-budget constraints are turned into strengths through clever practical effects and enthusiastic performances. Wyrmwood offers a fresh, energetic take on post-apocalyptic horror that balances gore, laughs, and genuine thrills, making it a standout in both Australian cinema and the zombie subgenre.

6. 10 Trivia Facts:

  1. The film was made over a period of four years, mostly on weekends due to budget constraints.

  2. Many of the costumes and props were created from recycled materials and household items.

  3. The directors, Kiah and Tristan Roache-Turner, are brothers who mortgaged their house to fund the film.

  4. Wyrmwood's unique zombie-blood-as-fuel concept was inspired by the directors' interest in renewable energy.

  5. The film's title is a reference to Wormwood, a star mentioned in the Book of Revelation associated with apocalyptic events.

  6. Most of the zombie makeup was applied by the actors themselves to save time and money.

  7. The movie gained international attention after its trailer went viral online.

  8. Wyrmwood was shot primarily in Western Sydney and the Blue Mountains.

  9. The film spawned a sequel, "Wyrmwood: Apocalypse," released in 2021.

  10. Despite its low budget, Wyrmwood received praise for its practical effects and stunts.

8. Cargo

1. Movie Title: Cargo

2. Year of Release: 2017

3. Cast and Director:

  - Directors: Ben Howling, Yolanda Ramke

  - Cast: Martin Freeman, Simone Landers, Anthony Hayes, Susie Porter

4. Synopsis:

Cargo is set in a post-apocalyptic Australia ravaged by a zombie outbreak. The story follows Andy, a father infected with the zombie virus, who has 48 hours before he turns. Desperate to save his infant daughter Rosie, Andy embarks on a journey through the Outback to find a new guardian for her. Along the way, he encounters Thoomi, a young Aboriginal girl trying to save her infected father, and various other survivors, each coping with the apocalypse in their own way. As Andy's time runs out, he must navigate the dangers of the infected landscape and the moral complexities of a world where survival often comes at a high cost. The film explores themes of parenthood, cultural heritage, and sacrifice against the backdrop of a unique take on the zombie genre.

5. Why This Movie Is Recommended:

Cargo stands out in the crowded zombie genre by prioritizing emotional depth and character development over traditional horror elements. The film's Australian setting provides a fresh perspective, incorporating Aboriginal culture and the vast, unforgiving Outback landscape. Martin Freeman's nuanced performance as a desperate father adds gravitas to the narrative, making the stakes feel incredibly personal. The movie's exploration of themes like parental sacrifice and cultural preservation elevates it beyond typical zombie fare. Cargo's thoughtful approach to the genre, combined with its stunning visuals and poignant storytelling, offers a zombie film that resonates on a deeper, more human level.

6. 10 Trivia Facts:

1. Cargo is based on a 2013 short film of the same name by the same directors, which went viral online.

2. The film was the first Netflix Original feature to be produced in Australia.

3. Martin Freeman learned to speak some Yankunytjatjara, an Aboriginal language, for his role.

4. The movie was shot in various locations in South Australia, including the Flinders Ranges and Adelaide.

5. Cargo premiered at the Adelaide Film Festival before its Netflix release.

6. The film incorporates elements of Aboriginal dreamtime stories and beliefs about the land.

7. To create the zombie makeup, the production team used a combination of practical effects and CGI.

8. Cargo was praised for its respectful and meaningful inclusion of Indigenous Australian culture and actors.

9. The directors chose to focus on slow-moving zombies to emphasize the emotional core of the story rather than action sequences.

10. The film's unique take on zombies, where victims have 48 hours before turning, was designed to add urgency to the narrative.

9. Rogue

1. Movie Title: Rogue

2. Year of Release: 2007

3. Cast and Director:

- Director: Greg McLean

- Cast: Radha Mitchell, Michael Vartan, Sam Worthington, John Jarratt

4. Synopsis:

Rogue follows an American travel writer, Pete McKell, who joins a river cruise in the Australian Outback led by wildlife expert Kate Ryan. The group ventures into a remote area of the Northern Territory, known for its population of saltwater crocodiles. When they spot a distress signal, their detour leads them into the territory of a massive, aggressive crocodile. Stranded on a tiny island as the tide rises, the tourists must find a way to survive and escape the ancient predator. As night falls and the water closes in, tensions rise within the group, and they realize that human nature can be just as dangerous as the creature hunting them. The film combines the terror of a monster movie with the psychological tension of a survival thriller, set against the backdrop of Australia's stunning but unforgiving wilderness.

5. Why This Movie Is Recommended:

Rogue stands out as a superior entry in the creature feature subgenre, elevating itself through its stunning cinematography, strong performances, and genuinely suspenseful sequences. Director Greg McLean, known for Wolf Creek, brings a similar sense of authenticity and dread to the Australian Outback setting. The film balances its thrills with breathtaking shots of the landscape, creating a palpable sense of isolation and vulnerability. Unlike many monster movies, Rogue takes time to develop its characters, making their peril more impactful. The crocodile effects, a mix of practical and CGI, are convincingly terrifying. Rogue offers a taut, well-crafted survival thriller that respects both its subject matter and its audience's intelligence.

6. 10 Trivia Facts:

1. The film is loosely based on the real-life story of Sweetheart, a notorious 5.1-meter saltwater crocodile that attacked boats in the late 1970s.

2. Director Greg McLean extensively researched crocodile behavior and attacks to make the film as realistic as possible.

3. The production team built a life-size animatronic crocodile for some of the close-up shots.

4. Rogue was shot on location in Australia's Northern Territory, including Kakadu National Park.

5. The film's tagline, "Welcome to Paradise... Welcome to Hell," plays on the dual nature of the beautiful but dangerous setting.

6. Rogue features early performances from Sam Worthington and Mia Wasikowska before their Hollywood breakthroughs.

7. The movie received praise from Quentin Tarantino, who called it one of the best "Jaws rip-offs" ever made.

8. Despite positive reviews, Rogue was a box office disappointment in Australia, but found success internationally.

9. The film's creature design was inspired by real saltwater crocodiles, aiming for biological accuracy rather than exaggeration.

10. Rogue won the Best Sound award at the 2007 Inside Film Awards.

10. The Loved Ones

1. Movie Title: The Loved Ones

2. Year of Release: 2009

3. Cast and Director:

  - Director: Sean Byrne

  - Cast: Xavier Samuel, Robin McLeavy, John Brumpton, Richard Wilson

4. Synopsis:

The Loved Ones centers around Brent, a high school student still struggling with guilt over his father's death in a car accident. When he declines an invitation to the school dance from Lola Stone, an awkward classmate, he unknowingly sets in motion a terrifying chain of events. Lola, with the help of her equally unhinged father, kidnaps Brent and subjects him to a twisted version of the dance in their isolated farmhouse. As Brent endures increasingly sadistic tortures, the film intercuts with scenes of his girlfriend and friends at the actual school dance, unaware of his plight. Brent must summon incredible strength and will to survive the night and escape his deranged captors. The film explores themes of obsession, family dysfunction, and the dark undercurrents of suburban life.

5. Why This Movie Is Recommended:

The Loved Ones stands out as a unique and disturbing entry in the horror genre, blending elements of teen drama, black comedy, and extreme horror. Director Sean Byrne crafts a film that is both viscerally shocking and psychologically unsettling, creating a tone that oscillates between darkly humorous and genuinely terrifying. The movie subverts typical high school film tropes, turning the familiar into something nightmarish. Robin McLeavy's performance as Lola is particularly noteworthy, creating one of the most memorable and unhinged villains in recent horror cinema. The Loved Ones pushes boundaries while maintaining a coherent narrative and emotional core, offering a fresh and intense experience for horror fans seeking something beyond conventional scares.

6. 10 Trivia Facts:

1. The film won the Cadillac People's Choice Award in the Midnight Madness category at the 2009 Toronto International Film Festival.

2. Director Sean Byrne wrote the script in just six weeks.

3. The movie's working title was "The Loved One," but was changed to plural to avoid confusion with the 1965 film of the same name.

4. Robin McLeavy, who played Lola, underwent extensive makeup processes for her character's increasingly disheveled appearance.

5. The film's prom scenes were shot in a real high school in Melbourne, Australia.

6. Despite its critical acclaim, The Loved Ones had a limited theatrical release in Australia.

7. The movie features a soundtrack that juxtaposes upbeat pop music with its dark themes, creating an unsettling contrast.

8. Sean Byrne cited John Hughes films as an influence, wanting to create an "anti-John Hughes" movie.

9. The Loved Ones was shot in just 30 days on a relatively low budget.

10. The film has gained a strong cult following since its release, particularly among horror enthusiasts.

11. The Tunnel

1. Movie Title: The Tunnel

2. Year of Release: 2011

3. Cast and Director:

- Directors: Carlo Ledesma

- Cast: Bel Deliá, Andy Rodoreda, Steve Davis, Luke Arnold

4. Synopsis:

The Tunnel is a found-footage horror film that follows a team of journalists investigating a government cover-up. The team, led by reporter Natasha Warner, delves into the abandoned underground tunnels beneath Sydney, Australia. These tunnels, originally intended to be used for a water recycling project, were mysteriously shut down. As the team explores deeper into the dark, labyrinthine system, they encounter increasingly disturbing phenomena. Their equipment malfunctions, they hear strange noises, and soon realize they're not alone in the tunnels. The film unfolds through recovered footage, interviews, and news clips, piecing together the terrifying events that befell the team. As they struggle to survive and uncover the truth, they face a horror that defies explanation and threatens to trap them forever in the darkness below.

5. Why This Movie Is Recommended:

The Tunnel stands out in the found-footage subgenre by combining genuinely unsettling horror with a compelling mystery. The film's use of the vast, dark tunnel system creates a palpable sense of claustrophobia and dread. Unlike many found-footage films, The Tunnel maintains a strong narrative structure, balancing the "recovered" footage with mock interviews and news segments that add depth to the story. The acting feels natural, enhancing the documentary-style realism. The movie's strength lies in its ability to create fear through suggestion and atmosphere rather than relying on jump scares or graphic violence. Its unique distribution method (initially released for free online) and marketing campaign also make it an interesting case study in modern independent filmmaking.

6. 10 Trivia Facts:

1. The Tunnel was partly funded through a unique "135K Project," where individual frames of the film were sold for $1 each.

2. The movie was filmed in real abandoned tunnels beneath Sydney, adding to its authenticity.

3. It was one of the first films to be officially released simultaneously in theaters, on DVD, TV, and for free via BitTorrent.

4. The filmmakers used real night vision cameras to capture the underground scenes, enhancing the realism.

5. Many of the crew members had cameo appearances in the film as interviewees.

6. The Tunnel's marketing campaign included fake news reports and "leaked" government documents.

7. Despite being a low-budget film, it features impressive sound design crucial to creating its tense atmosphere.

8. The movie sparked discussions about the real-life abandoned tunnels beneath Sydney.

9. A sequel, "The Tunnel: Dead End," was released in 2016.

10. The film's unconventional release strategy led to over 3 million downloads within its first few months.

12. Snowtown

1. Movie Title: Snowtown (also known as The Snowtown Murders)

2. Year of Release: 2011

3. Cast and Director:

- Director: Justin Kurzel

- Cast: Daniel Henshall, Lucas Pittaway, Louise Harris, Bob Adriaens

4. Synopsis:

Snowtown is a disturbing psychological horror based on the true story of Australia's worst serial killings. Set in the impoverished suburbs of Adelaide, the film follows Jamie, a vulnerable teenager who falls under the influence of John Bunting, a charismatic but deeply disturbed man. Bunting, along with a group of accomplices, embarks on a killing spree, targeting those they deem as "pedophiles" and "degenerates." As Jamie becomes increasingly involved in Bunting's world, he struggles with his conscience and the horrifying reality of the murders. The film unflinchingly portrays the psychological manipulation, social decay, and brutal violence that led to the infamous "Bodies in Barrels" murders. Through its grim narrative, Snowtown explores themes of poverty, abuse, and the insidious nature of evil in ordinary settings.

5. Why This Movie Is Recommended:

Snowtown stands out for its unflinching portrayal of real-life horror and its exploration of the psychological aspects of evil. The film's power lies in its naturalistic approach, using non-professional actors and stark, documentary-like cinematography to create a chilling sense of authenticity. Director Justin Kurzel masterfully builds tension through atmosphere and character interactions rather than relying on graphic violence. The performances, particularly Daniel Henshall as John Bunting, are disturbingly convincing. While not for the faint-hearted, Snowtown offers a profound and haunting examination of how evil can take root in marginalized communities. It's a challenging but important film that pushes the boundaries of the true crime and horror genres.

6. 10 Trivia Facts:

1. Many of the actors, including Lucas Pittaway who played Jamie, were locals from the area where the real crimes took place.

2. The film was shot in the actual locations where some of the murders occurred.

3. Director Justin Kurzel's brother Jed composed the haunting score for the film.

4. Snowtown was Justin Kurzel's feature film directorial debut.

5. The movie won the AACTA Award (Australian Academy of Cinema and Television Arts Awards) for Best Direction.

6. Daniel Henshall, who played John Bunting, stayed in character even when cameras weren't rolling to maintain the tense atmosphere.

7. The film's premiere at the Adelaide Film Festival was met with walkouts due to its intense content.

8. Snowtown was praised by David Michôd, director of "Animal Kingdom," another acclaimed Australian crime film.

9. The real John Bunting and his accomplices were responsible for 11 murders between 1992 and 1999.

10. Despite its critical acclaim, the film was controversial in Australia due to its graphic depiction of real events.

13. Hounds of Love

1. Movie Title: Hounds of Love

2. Year of Release: 2016

3. Cast and Director:

- Director: Ben Young

- Cast: Emma Booth, Ashleigh Cummings, Stephen Curry, Susie Porter

4. Synopsis:

Set in Perth, Western Australia, in the 1980s, Hounds of Love is a psychological horror thriller that follows the abduction of Vicki Maloney, a teenage girl who falls victim to a disturbed couple, John and Evelyn White. After being lured into their home, Vicki finds herself trapped in a nightmare of physical and psychological torture. As the couple's twisted dynamics unfold, Vicki must find a way to survive and escape. Meanwhile, her divorced parents frantically search for her. The film delves deep into the psychological aspects of captivity, exploring the complex relationship between the kidnappers and their victim. As Vicki attempts to manipulate the cracks in John and Evelyn's relationship, the tension builds towards a harrowing climax.

5. Why This Movie Is Recommended:

Hounds of Love stands out for its intense psychological approach to horror, focusing more on the disturbing dynamics between characters than on graphic violence. Director Ben Young crafts a taut, suspenseful narrative that keeps viewers on edge throughout. The film's 1980s Perth setting adds a distinct atmosphere, while the performances, especially from Emma Booth and Ashleigh Cummings, are powerfully convincing. Hounds of Love explores dark themes of control, codependency, and survival, offering a deeply unsettling but thoughtful examination of human nature. Its ability to create extreme tension and horror through implication rather than explicit depiction makes it a standout in psychological thriller cinema.

6. 10 Trivia Facts:

1. The film is loosely based on real-life crimes that occurred in Perth during the 1980s.

2. Director Ben Young extensively researched the psychology of kidnapping victims and perpetrators to inform the script.

3. Emma Booth, who played Evelyn, initially turned down the role due to its disturbing nature but was convinced after reading the full script.

4. The film was shot in only 20 days on a limited budget.

5. Hounds of Love premiered at the 2016 Venice Film Festival in the Venice Days section.

6. The movie's title is a reference to the Kate Bush album of the same name, released in 1985.

7. To maintain the tense atmosphere, the three main actors stayed in character between takes.

8. The film won Best Actress for Emma Booth and Best Director for Ben Young at the Brussels International Film Festival.

9. Hounds of Love was Ben Young's feature film directorial debut.

10. The movie's look was inspired by Australian photographer Bill Henson's work, known for its moody, suburban nightscapes.

14. Killing Ground

1. Movie Title: Killing Ground

2. Year of Release: 2016

3. Cast and Director:

- Director: Damien Power

- Cast: Aaron Pedersen, Ian Meadows, Harriet Dyer, Aaron Glenane

4. Synopsis:

Killing Ground follows two intersecting storylines set in a remote Australian campground. Sam and Ian, a young couple, arrive for a New Year's camping trip to find an abandoned tent and no sign of its occupants. As they investigate, the film cuts to the story of the missing family who previously occupied the site. The two narratives converge to reveal a terrifying ordeal involving two local men with sinister intentions. As the danger escalates, Sam and Ian find themselves fighting for survival against both the human threats and the unforgiving Australian wilderness. The film explores themes of primal fear, the brutality of nature (both human and environmental), and the lengths people will go to when pushed to their limits.

5. Why This Movie Is Recommended:

Killing Ground stands out for its innovative narrative structure and its unflinching portrayal of terror in the Australian bush. Director Damien Power skillfully builds tension through the dual timelines, creating a sense of dread as the audience pieces together the horrifying events. The film's strength lies in its realism; the characters react believably to their dire situation, and the violence, while shocking, never feels gratuitous. The beautiful yet menacing Australian landscape becomes a character in itself, adding to the sense of isolation and danger. Killing Ground offers a fresh take on the survival horror genre, combining psychological suspense with visceral thrills to create a deeply unsettling and memorable experience.

6. 10 Trivia Facts:

1. Killing Ground was Damien Power's feature directorial debut.

2. The film premiered at the 2016 Melbourne International Film Festival.

3. Many of the outdoor scenes were shot in NSW's Macquarie Pass National Park.

4. The movie's plot was partly inspired by real-life cases of hikers and campers going missing in the Australian bush.

5. Director Damien Power is the brother of comedian Tyson Power.

6. The film received critical acclaim for its realistic portrayal of violence and its consequences.

7. Killing Ground was picked up for North American distribution by IFC Midnight after its success at Sundance.

8. The movie's tensest scenes were often shot in single takes to maintain the intensity.

9. Aaron Pedersen, who plays one of the antagonists, is known for his roles in Indigenous Australian cinema.

10. The film's score, composed by Leah Curtis, plays a crucial role in building the ominous atmosphere.

15. The Babadook

1. Movie Title: The Babadook

2. Year of Release: 2014

3. Cast and Director:

  - Director: Jennifer Kent

  - Cast: Essie Davis, Noah Wiseman, Daniel Henshall, Hayley McElhinney

4. Synopsis:

  The Babadook tells the story of Amelia, a single mother struggling to raise her troubled six-year-old son, Samuel, following the violent death of her husband. Samuel's behavioral problems and fear of monsters strain their relationship and isolate them from others. One night, they read a mysterious pop-up book called "Mister Babadook," which unleashes a sinister presence in their home. As Amelia's grip on reality begins to slip, the line between imagination and reality blurs. The Babadook becomes a manifestation of grief, depression, and the challenges of parenthood. Amelia must confront her own demons to protect her son and find a way to coexist with the monster that has invaded their lives.

5. Why This Movie Is Recommended:

  The Babadook is a masterful psychological horror that transcends typical genre tropes. Jennifer Kent's directorial debut is a poignant exploration of grief, mental illness, and the pressures of single parenthood, wrapped in a chilling supernatural narrative. The film's strength lies in its nuanced performances, particularly Essie Davis as Amelia, and its ability to create tension through atmosphere rather than jump scares. The Babadook itself is a uniquely designed monster that has become iconic in modern horror. This film offers a deeply emotional and psychologically complex horror experience that lingers long after viewing, making it a standout in both Australian cinema and the horror genre globally.

6. 10 Trivia Facts:

  1. The Babadook character was inspired by early 20th-century surrealist and expressionist cinema.

  2. The pop-up book featured in the film was handcrafted by illustrator Alex Juhasz.

  3. Director Jennifer Kent originally created a short film called "Monster" that served as a proof-of-concept for The Babadook.

  4. The film was produced on a modest budget of $2 million.

  5. William Friedkin, director of The Exorcist, called The Babadook the most terrifying film he had ever seen.

  6. The Babadook has become an unexpected LGBTQ+ icon, with the character being embraced as a queer symbol.

  7. The movie's title comes from a Serbian phrase meaning "Baba Dook," or "evil man."

  8. Kent and Davis worked together to create a 100-page backstory for Amelia's character.

  9. The film used minimal CGI, relying mostly on practical effects and clever cinematography.

  10. Despite its critical acclaim, The Babadook was not a box office success in Australia upon its initial release.

16. Undead

1. Movie Title: Undead

2. Year of Release: 2003

3. Cast and Director:

- Directors: Michael Spierig, Peter Spierig

- Cast: Felicity Mason, Mungo McKay, Rob Jenkins, Lisa Cunningham

4. Synopsis:

Undead is a quirky zombie comedy set in the fictional Australian fishing town of Berkeley. The story follows Rene, a beauty queen whose quiet life is upended when meteorites crash into the town, turning the inhabitants into zombies. She teams up with Marion, an eccentric local who has been preparing for an alien invasion, and a group of survivors to fight their way through the zombie horde. As they battle the undead, they discover that the situation is far more complex than a simple zombie outbreak. Alien forces are at play, and the group must unravel the mystery behind the invasion while fighting for survival. The film blends horror, science fiction, and comedy, creating a unique and offbeat take on the zombie genre.

5. Why This Movie Is Recommended:

Undead stands out for its inventive approach to the zombie genre, infusing it with alien invasion elements and distinctly Australian humor. The Spierig brothers, in their directorial debut, showcase a remarkable creativity in crafting outlandish scenarios and over-the-top action sequences on a limited budget. The film's DIY aesthetic and practical effects give it a charm often missing in more polished productions. While it doesn't take itself too seriously, Undead still delivers genuine scares alongside its comedic moments. Its unique blend of genres and tongue-in-cheek style make it a cult favorite and a refreshing entry in the zombie subgenre. For fans of offbeat horror-comedies, Undead offers a wildly entertaining and distinctly Australian experience.

6. 10 Trivia Facts:

1. The Spierig brothers not only directed but also wrote, produced, and created the visual effects for the film.

2. Undead was shot on a budget of just AUD $1 million.

3. The film won the Fipresci Award at the 2003 Melbourne International Film Festival.

4. Many of the zombie extras were volunteers who responded to a local newspaper ad.

5. The directors built many of the film's props themselves, including the triple-barreled shotgun.

6. Undead was picked up for international distribution by Lionsgate Films.

7. The movie features over 305 visual effects shots, an impressive feat for its low budget.

8. The Spierig brothers were inspired by Peter Jackson's early low-budget films like "Bad Taste."

9. The film's success led to the Spierig brothers directing larger Hollywood productions like "Daybreakers" and "Jigsaw."

10. Undead was filmed in the directors' hometown of Brisbane, Australia.

17. Next of Kin

1. Movie Title: Next of Kin

2. Year of Release: 1982

3. Cast and Director:

- Director: Tony Williams

- Cast: Jacki Kerin, John Jarratt, Alex Scott, Gerda Nicolson

4. Synopsis:

Next of Kin follows Linda Stevens, a young woman who inherits Montclare, a retirement home, after her mother's death. As Linda settles into running the facility, she begins to experience strange occurrences and has vivid, disturbing dreams. She discovers her mother's diary, which hints at a dark history within Montclare's walls. As residents start dying under mysterious circumstances, Linda becomes convinced that something sinister is at work in the home. She must unravel the mystery of Montclare's past and confront the evil that lurks within before she becomes its next victim. The film blends elements of gothic horror, psychological thriller, and slasher genres, creating a uniquely Australian take on haunted house stories.

5. Why This Movie Is Recommended:

Next of Kin stands out as a stylish and atmospheric entry in Australian horror cinema. Director Tony Williams crafts a film that builds tension through its dreamlike imagery and unsettling sound design rather than relying on explicit violence. The movie's use of the retirement home setting adds a layer of vulnerability to its characters, enhancing the sense of dread. Next of Kin's strength lies in its ability to create a pervasive feeling of unease, blurring the lines between reality and nightmare. Its visual style, influenced by both giallo films and the Australian New Wave, gives it a unique aesthetic. While it may have been overlooked upon its initial release, Next of Kin has gained recognition as a cult classic, appreciated for its subtle approach to horror and its distinctly Australian gothic atmosphere.

6. 10 Trivia Facts:

1. Next of Kin was shot in Melbourne and rural Victoria, Australia.

2. The film features early performances from both Jacki Kerin and John Jarratt, who would become prominent figures in Australian cinema.

3. Director Tony Williams had previously worked primarily in documentaries before making Next of Kin.

4. The movie's synthesizer-heavy score, composed by Klaus Schulze, contributes significantly to its eerie atmosphere.

5. Next of Kin was released the same year as other notable Australian films like "The Man from Snowy River" and "Mad Max 2."

6. The film was restored and re-released on Blu-ray in 2019, leading to renewed interest and critical reappraisal.

7. Next of Kin's style has been compared to Stanley Kubrick's "The Shining" for its use of tracking shots and building tension.

8. The movie was filmed in Wycliffe House, a real mansion in Victoria that adds to its gothic ambiance.

9. Despite its current cult status, Next of Kin was not a commercial success upon its initial release.

10. The film has been cited as an influence by modern Australian horror directors like Jennifer Kent (The Babadook).

18. Incident at Raven's Gate

1. Movie Title: Incident at Raven's Gate

2. Year of Release: 1988

3. Cast and Director:

 - Director: Rolf de Heer

 - Cast: Steven Vidler, Celine O'Leary, Ritchie Singer, Vincent Gil

4. Synopsis:

 Incident at Raven's Gate, also known as Encounter at Raven's Gate, is set in the remote Australian outback. The story centers around a series of bizarre and terrifying events that occur near a small town called Raven's Gate. Eddie Cleary, a young ex-con working on his brother's farm, becomes entangled in a mystery involving unexplained phenomena, including strange lights in the sky, mutilated animals, and inexplicable equipment failures. As a police officer investigates the occurrences, tension builds among the locals, and conspiracy theories about government cover-ups and alien activity begin to circulate. The film blends elements of science fiction, horror, and outback drama to create a unique exploration of isolation, paranoia, and the unknown.

5. Why This Movie Is Recommended:

 Incident at Raven's Gate stands out for its innovative blend of genres and its distinctly Australian take on science fiction horror. Director Rolf de Heer, known for his unconventional storytelling, creates a film that uses the vast, isolated Australian landscape to amplify feelings of unease and vulnerability. The movie excels in building a creeping sense of dread through atmosphere and suggestion rather than relying on overt scares or alien encounters. Its exploration of how extraordinary events affect a small, tight-knit community adds depth to the narrative. While it may not have gained widespread recognition, Incident at Raven's Gate offers a thoughtful, slow-burn approach to extraterrestrial horror that rewards patient viewers with its eerie ambiance and psychological tension.

6. 10 Trivia Facts:

 1. The film was shot on location in South Australia, primarily in the Flinders Ranges.

 2. Director Rolf de Heer is better known for his arthouse dramas, making this sci-fi horror an unusual entry in his filmography.

 3. Incident at Raven's Gate was produced by the South Australian Film Corporation.

 4. The movie's original title was "Encounter at Raven's Gate," but it was changed for some international releases.

 5. The film's score, composed by Roman Kroner, contributes significantly to its unsettling atmosphere.

 6. Despite its sci-fi elements, the movie uses minimal special effects, relying more on suggestion and atmosphere.

 7. Incident at Raven's Gate was one of the earlier film roles for actor Steven Vidler, who went on to have a successful career in Australian television.

 8. The film draws inspiration from real-life UFO encounters reported in the Australian outback.

 9. It was released during a period of renewed interest in UFO and alien abduction stories in popular culture.

 10. The movie has gained a cult following over the years, particularly among fans of Australian genre cinema.

19. Siren

1. Movie Title: Siren (also known as Escape from Outpost 11)

2. Year of Release: 2010

3. Cast and Director:

  - Director: Andrew Hull

  - Cast: Erica Lovell, Terasa Livingstone, Maddison Daniel, Alix Bushnell

4. Synopsis:

Siren is set on a remote island off the coast of Australia, where a group of young female environmental activists arrive to protest against a nearby mining operation. As they set up camp and begin their demonstration, strange things start to happen. The women hear eerie sounds and experience unsettling visions. They soon realize they are not alone on the island and that something ancient and malevolent is stalking them. As tensions rise within the group, they must fight for survival against a supernatural force that seems to be connected to the island's dark history and the surrounding ocean. The film blends ecological themes with folklore and horror, creating a unique take on the creature feature genre.

5. Why This Movie Is Recommended:

Siren stands out for its unique blend of environmental themes with supernatural horror. The film uses its isolated island setting to great effect, creating a claustrophobic atmosphere despite the open landscape. Director Andrew Hull crafts a slow-burning tension that builds to a terrifying climax, relying more on psychological horror and unseen threats than on graphic violence. The all-female cast brings depth to their characters, exploring group dynamics under extreme stress. Siren's ecological message adds a layer of relevance to its horror elements, making it more than just a monster movie. For fans of folk horror and eco-horror, Siren offers a distinctly Australian take on these subgenres, utilizing the country's unique landscape and mythology to create a memorable and unsettling experience.

6. 10 Trivia Facts:

  1. Siren was shot on location on Moreton Island, off the coast of Queensland, Australia.

  2. The film's creature design was inspired by various elements of Australian folklore and marine biology.

  3. Director Andrew Hull aimed to create a horror film that also raised awareness about environmental issues.

  4. Many of the eerie sounds in the film were created using a combination of animal noises and manipulated human voices.

  5. The cast underwent survival training to prepare for their roles as environmental activists.

  6. Siren was produced on a relatively low budget, relying on practical effects and the natural environment to create scares.

  7. The film's alternate title, "Escape from Outpost 11," was used for some international releases.

  8. Siren premiered at the A Night of Horror International Film Festival in Sydney.

  9. The movie incorporates elements of Aboriginal mythology in its backstory for the island's supernatural presence.

  10. Despite its limited release, Siren has gained a following among fans of eco-horror and Australian indie cinema.

20. Body Melt

1. Movie Title: Body Melt

2. Year of Release: 1993

3. Cast and Director:

  - Director: Philip Brophy

  - Cast: Gerard Kennedy, Andrew Daddo, Ian Smith, Regina Gaigalas

4. Synopsis:

  Body Melt is a satirical horror-comedy that takes place in the suburban Melbourne neighborhood of Pebbles Court. The residents become unwitting test subjects for a new health supplement created by the sinister Vimuville corporation. As the neighbors consume the pills, they begin to experience horrific and grotesque mutations, literally melting and exploding in various gruesome ways. The film follows several interconnected stories of the suburb's residents, including a young couple, a bodybuilder, and a family on a road trip, all falling victim to the deadly effects of the supplement. Meanwhile, a pair of detectives try to unravel the mystery behind the bizarre deaths. Body Melt combines over-the-top gore with dark humor to create a scathing critique of health fad culture and suburban complacency.

5. Why This Movie Is Recommended:

  Body Melt stands out as a unique entry in the body horror subgenre, blending graphic gore with satirical comedy in a distinctly Australian way. Director Philip Brophy's background in experimental music and art brings a quirky, avant-garde sensibility to the film, resulting in some truly unforgettable and surreal sequences. The movie's practical effects, while low-budget, are impressively disgusting and creative. Body Melt's strength lies in its ability to balance horror with humor, never taking itself too seriously while still delivering genuine shocks. Its critique of health culture and suburban life adds a layer of social commentary to the carnage. For fans of gory, offbeat horror-comedies in the vein of early Peter Jackson or Stuart Gordon, Body Melt offers a uniquely Australian take on the genre that's both revolting and entertaining.

6. 10 Trivia Facts:

  1. Director Philip Brophy also composed the film's distinctive electronic score.

  2. Body Melt was partly inspired by Brophy's interest in the aesthetics of health food packaging and infomercials.

  3. The film features early performances from several actors who would become well-known in Australian television, including Ian Smith (Harold from "Neighbours").

  4. Many of the grotesque special effects were achieved using a combination of practical makeup and stop-motion animation.

  5. Body Melt was produced by the Australian Film Commission and Film Victoria.

  6. The movie's tagline was "Vitamin pills kill," playing on its satirical take on health supplement culture.

  7. Despite its limited release, Body Melt has gained a cult following, particularly among fans of practical effects-driven horror.

  8. The film draws inspiration from various genres, including sci-fi B-movies and Australian soap operas.

  9. Body Melt was Brophy's only feature film as a director; he primarily works in sound design and music.

  10. The movie's exaggerated portrayal of suburban Australian life has made it a unique time capsule of early '90s culture.

Italy

1. Suspiria

1. Movie Title: Suspiria

2. Year of Release: 1977

3. Cast and Director:

  - Director: Dario Argento

  - Cast: Jessica Harper, Stefania Casini, Flavio Bucci, Miguel Bosé, Alida Valli, Joan Bennett

4. Synopsis:

  Suspiria follows Suzy Bannion, an American ballet student who transfers to a prestigious dance academy in Freiburg, Germany. Upon arrival, she witnesses a series of bizarre and increasingly violent events. As students and staff members fall victim to gruesome murders, Suzy uncovers the academy's dark secret: it's run by a coven of witches led by the powerful Helena Markos. With the help of her friend Sara, Suzy must navigate the nightmarish halls of the academy, confront the witches, and escape before becoming their next victim. The film is a phantasmagoric journey through a world where reality and nightmare blur, culminating in a climactic confrontation with ancient evil.

5. Why This Movie Is Recommended:

  Suspiria is a masterpiece of style and atmosphere in horror cinema. Argento's bold use of vivid colors, innovative camera work, and the haunting score by Goblin create a dreamlike, fairy tale atmosphere that's both beautiful and terrifying. The film's unique visual style, with its use of primary colors and elaborate set designs, has influenced countless filmmakers. Its exploration of witchcraft and the supernatural, combined with its surreal narrative structure, makes it a standout in the genre. Suspiria is not just a horror film; it's a visceral, audiovisual experience that continues to captivate and disturb audiences decades after its release.

6. 10 Trivia Facts:

  1. The film's vibrant colors were achieved using the outdated Technicolor three-strip process.

  2. The eerie score was composed and performed by the progressive rock band Goblin.

  3. The dance academy's elaborate interior was inspired by the Art Nouveau movement.

  4. Jessica Harper had to learn her lines phonetically as she didn't speak Italian.

  5. The film's opening murder scene took three weeks to shoot.

  6. Argento was inspired by Snow White and other fairy tales when creating the film.

  7. The movie was shot using anamorphic lenses, giving it its distinct wide-screen look.

  8. Suspiria is the first part of Argento's "Three Mothers" trilogy.

9. The film's tagline was "The only thing more terrifying than the last 12 minutes of this film are the first 92."

10. Argento had the ceilings of the sets lowered to create a sense of claustrophobia.

2. Profondo Rosso (Deep Red)

1. Movie Title: Profondo Rosso (Deep Red)

2. Year of Release: 1975

3. Cast and Director:

   - Director: Dario Argento

   - Cast: David Hemmings, Daria Nicolodi, Gabriele Lavia, Macha Méril, Clara Calamai

4. Synopsis:

   Profondo Rosso follows Marcus Daly, an English jazz pianist living in Rome, who witnesses the brutal axe murder of a psychic medium. Convinced he saw a crucial piece of evidence in the apartment, Marcus begins his own investigation, assisted by reporter Gianna Brezzi. As they delve deeper into the case, more murders occur, and Marcus finds himself targeted by the killer. The investigation leads them through a complex web of clues involving a haunting children's song, an abandoned house, and a shocking family secret. As Marcus gets closer to the truth, he must confront the killer in a final, terrifying showdown, uncovering a twisted tale of childhood trauma and revenge.

5. Why This Movie Is Recommended:

   Profondo Rosso is a masterclass in the giallo genre, blending intricate mystery, psychological thrills, and visceral horror. Argento's stylish direction, coupled with the film's intricate plot and shocking twists, keeps viewers on the edge of their seats. The movie's elaborate murder set-pieces are both horrifying and visually stunning, showcasing Argento's talent for turning violence into art. The film's exploration of memory and perception adds a psychological depth that elevates it above typical slasher fare. With its influential soundtrack by Goblin, innovative cinematography, and compelling performances, Profondo Rosso remains a benchmark in Italian horror cinema.

6. 10 Trivia Facts:

   1. The film's original Italian release was 126 minutes long, while international versions were often shorter.

   2. Profondo Rosso marked the first collaboration between Dario Argento and the band Goblin.

   3. The famous "reflection scene" was achieved using a body double and clever editing.

   4. Argento's hands are used for many of the killer's point-of-view shots.

   5. The creepy mechanical doll was created by Carlo Rambaldi, who later worked on E.T.

   6. Daria Nicolodi, who played Gianna, became Argento's long-time partner and collaborator.

   7. The film's success in Italy led to a brief pinball craze, as one features prominently in the movie.

   8. Argento insisted on using real maggots for a key scene, much to the cast's discomfort.

   9. The movie's working title was "The Thriller."

   10. David Hemmings was cast partly due to his role in Michelangelo Antonioni's "Blow-Up."

3. Operazione Paura (Kill, Baby... Kill!)

1. Movie Title: Operazione Paura (Kill, Baby... Kill!)

2. Year of Release: 1966

3. Cast and Director:

  - Director: Mario Bava

  - Cast: Giacomo Rossi Stuart, Erika Blanc, Fabienne Dali, Piero Lulli, Luciano Catenacci

4. Synopsis:

Set in a remote Carpathian village in 1907, Operazione Paura follows Dr. Paul Eswai, who arrives to perform an autopsy on a woman who died under mysterious circumstances. He discovers a village gripped by fear of a curse involving the ghost of a young girl named Melissa. Aided by Monica, a local medical student, Paul investigates the strange deaths plaguing the village. They uncover a web of superstition, vengeance, and dark secrets centered around Villa Graps and its reclusive inhabitant, Baroness Graps. As they delve deeper into the mystery, they face increasingly surreal and terrifying encounters with Melissa's ghost, leading to a shocking revelation about the true nature of the curse.

5. Why This Movie Is Recommended:

Operazione Paura is a masterpiece of atmospheric horror that showcases Mario Bava's unparalleled visual style. The film's gothic setting, coupled with Bava's use of vivid colors and innovative camera techniques, creates a dreamlike, nightmarish quality that's both beautiful and unsettling. Its influence on subsequent horror directors, including Federico Fellini and David Lynch, is undeniable. The movie's exploration of guilt, superstition, and the cyclical nature of violence adds psychological depth to its supernatural elements. With its haunting imagery, particularly the iconic ghost of Melissa, Operazione Paura stands as a landmark in Italian gothic horror.

6. 10 Trivia Facts:

  1. The film's original Italian title "Operazione Paura" translates to "Operation Fear."

  2. The movie was shot in Calcata, a medieval village near Rome, known for its eerie atmosphere.

  3. Bava used a child actor, Valerio Valeri, to play the ghost of Melissa.

  4. The film features a shot of a character running into himself, achieved through clever editing and double exposure.

  5. Martin Scorsese cited this film as one of his favorites and an influence on his work.

  6. The movie's budget was so low that Bava had to act as his own cinematographer.

  7. The spiral staircase scene became iconic and was later referenced in Federico Fellini's "Toby Dammit."

  8. Despite its current status as a classic, the film was not initially successful upon release.

  9. Bava used a spinning camera technique to create disorienting effects in several scenes.

  10. The film has been released under various titles, including "Curse of the Dead" and "Don't Walk in the Park."

4. Tenebre

1. Movie Title: Tenebre

2. Year of Release: 1982

3. Cast and Director:

  - Director: Dario Argento

  - Cast: Anthony Franciosa, John Saxon, Daria Nicolodi, Giuliano Gemma

4. Synopsis:

Tenebre follows American author Peter Neal, who arrives in Rome to promote his latest murder mystery novel. Shortly after his arrival, a series of brutal murders begin to occur, mimicking the killings in Neal's book. As the body count rises, Neal finds himself drawn into the investigation, working alongside the local police to uncover the killer's identity. The murders become increasingly personal, with Neal's agent and associates becoming targets. As the line between fiction and reality blurs, Neal must confront his own past and the possibility that his work has inspired a real-life killer. The film builds to a shocking climax that challenges perceptions and reveals unexpected truths about the nature of violence and obsession.

5. Why This Movie Is Recommended:

Tenebre stands out as a meta-textual exploration of the giallo genre, blending self-awareness with Argento's signature style. The film's clever plot twists and commentary on the relationship between art and violence elevate it beyond a typical slasher film. Argento's masterful use of light and shadow, coupled with innovative camera work, creates a visually stunning experience. The movie's exploration of gender roles and sexual identity adds depth to its narrative. With its pulsing electronic score by Goblin members, shocking violence, and psychological complexity, Tenebre remains a high point in Argento's filmography and a must-see for horror enthusiasts.

6. 10 Trivia Facts:

  1. The film was temporarily banned in the UK as part of the "video nasty" panic of the 1980s.

  2. Argento originally wanted Christopher Walken for the lead role of Peter Neal.

  3. The movie features an impressive 2.5-minute crane shot that sweeps over and around a house.

  4. Tenebre was filmed entirely at night or in artificially darkened sets to achieve its unique look.

  5. The film's working title was "Unsane."

  6. Argento wrote the screenplay in reaction to criticism about the violence in his previous films.

  7. The movie's tagline was "Terror Beyond Belief."

  8. Veronica Lario, who plays Jane McKerrow, later became the wife of Italian Prime Minister Silvio Berlusconi.

  9. The film features several references to Argento's previous works, including "The Bird with the Crystal Plumage."

  10. Tenebre was shot in only 8 weeks, which is relatively quick for an Argento film.

5. Phenomena

1. Movie Title: Phenomena

2. Year of Release: 1985

3. Cast and Director:

- Director: Dario Argento

- Cast: Jennifer Connelly, Donald Pleasence, Daria Nicolodi, Dalila Di Lazzaro

4. Synopsis:

Phenomena follows Jennifer Corvino, the daughter of a famous actor, who is sent to a Swiss boarding school. Jennifer discovers she has a unique ability to telepathically communicate with insects. As a series of brutal murders plague the area, Jennifer becomes involved in the investigation, aided by entomologist John McGregor and his chimpanzee assistant, Inga. Using her unusual power, Jennifer tries to identify the killer, but finds herself in increasing danger as she gets closer to the truth. The story takes a surreal turn as Jennifer's ability grows stronger, leading to a climactic confrontation that blends the natural and supernatural in typical Argento fashion.

5. Why This Movie Is Recommended:

Phenomena stands out for its unique blend of supernatural elements, giallo-style murders, and science fiction concepts. Argento's vivid visual style is on full display, creating a dreamlike atmosphere that enhances the film's bizarre narrative. The movie's use of insects as a central theme is both innovative and unsettling, adding a new dimension to horror cinema. Jennifer Connelly's performance as the young protagonist brings a compelling innocence to the dark proceedings. With its unconventional plot, striking imagery, and a soundtrack featuring heavy metal alongside Goblin's score, Phenomena offers a truly singular horror experience that continues to fascinate and disturb viewers.

6. 10 Trivia Facts:

1. The film was released in the United States under the title "Creepers" in a heavily edited version.

2. Jennifer Connelly was only 14 years old during filming.

3. The movie features music from Iron Maiden and Motörhead alongside its Goblin score.

4. Argento was inspired to make the film after hearing about insects being used in forensic investigations.

5. The chimpanzee, Tanga, was the same one used in Phenomena and Argento's previous film "Tenebre."

6. Phenomena was shot in both English and Italian simultaneously.

7. The film's special effects were created by Sergio Stivaletti, who went on to work on many Italian horror films.

8. Argento's daughter, Fiore Argento, has a small role in the film.

9. The movie was partially inspired by Argento's own experience of seeing fireflies as a child.

10. Phenomena was one of the first films to use an automated camera system for complex tracking shots.

6. L'uccello dalle piume di cristallo (The Bird with the Crystal Plumage)

1. Movie Title: L'uccello dalle piume di cristallo (The Bird with the Crystal Plumage)

2. Year of Release: 1970

3. Cast and Director:

- Director: Dario Argento

- Cast: Tony Musante, Suzy Kendall, Enrico Maria Salerno, Eva Renzi

4. Synopsis:

The Bird with the Crystal Plumage marks Dario Argento's directorial debut and follows Sam Dalmas, an American writer living in Rome. One night, Sam witnesses an attempted murder in an art gallery but is unable to help, trapped between two glass doors. As the police investigation progresses, Sam becomes obsessed with solving the crime, convinced he saw something crucial that he can't quite remember. His amateur sleuthing puts both him and his girlfriend Julia in danger as the killer targets them. Sam's investigation uncovers a series of similar murders and a mysterious piece of artwork that may hold the key to the killer's identity. The film builds to a tense climax where Sam must confront the killer and his own perceptions of what really happened that night in the gallery.

5. Why This Movie Is Recommended:

The Bird with the Crystal Plumage is a landmark film that helped define the giallo genre. Argento's stylish direction, coupled with Vittorio Storaro's stunning cinematography, creates a visually striking and suspenseful experience. The film's exploration of memory and perception adds psychological depth to its murder mystery plot. Its influence on subsequent thrillers and slasher films is undeniable. With its clever plot twists, innovative camera work, and Ennio Morricone's haunting score, The Bird with the Crystal Plumage remains a compelling and influential work that showcases Argento's emerging talent as a master of suspense and horror.

6. 10 Trivia Facts:

1. This was Dario Argento's directorial debut, based on Fredric Brown's novel "The Screaming Mimi."

2. The film's success established Argento as the "Italian Hitchcock."

3. Legendary composer Ennio Morricone created the film's atmospheric score.

4. The movie was shot in just six weeks on a modest budget.

5. Argento insisted on using an American lead actor to increase the film's international appeal.

6. The iconic scene where Sam is trapped between glass doors was inspired by a real incident involving Argento's father.

7. The film's Italian title translates to "The Bird with the Crystal Plumage," referring to a crucial plot element.

8. Argento made a cameo appearance as the murderer's hands in some scenes.

9. The movie was a major box office success in Italy, outgrossing even "The Godfather."

10. Despite its violent content, the film received a 'GP' rating (equivalent to PG) in the United States upon its initial release.

7. Inferno

1. **Movie Title**: Inferno

2. **Year of Release**: 1980

3. **Cast and Director**:

 - Director: Dario Argento

 - Cast: Irene Miracle, Leigh McCloskey, Eleonora Giorgi, Daria Nicolodi

4. **Synopsis**:

 Inferno is the second installment in Dario Argento's "Three Mothers" trilogy. The film follows Rose Elliot, a poet living in New York who becomes convinced her apartment building is home to Mater Tenebrarum, the Mother of Darkness. She writes to her brother Mark in Rome about her suspicions, but soon disappears. Mark travels to New York to investigate, encountering a series of bizarre and deadly events. As more characters are drawn into the mystery, they face supernatural horrors and gruesome deaths. The story unfolds across New York and Rome, revealing the influence of the Three Mothers - ancient witches who secretly control the world. The film culminates in a surreal and fiery confrontation with the forces of evil.

5. **Why This Movie Is Recommended**:

 Inferno is a visual feast that pushes the boundaries of surrealist horror. Argento's mastery of color and composition creates a dreamlike, often nightmarish atmosphere that's both beautiful and terrifying. The film's emphasis on mood and visuals over conventional narrative enhances its otherworldly feel. With its intricate set pieces, including the famous underwater room scene, Inferno offers a unique and unforgettable viewing experience. While less well-known than its predecessor Suspiria, Inferno stands as a bold and influential work in the supernatural horror genre, showcasing Argento's artistic vision at its most unrestrained.

6. **10 Trivia Facts**:

 1. The film's underwater scenes were shot in a water tank at Cinecittà studios in Rome.

 2. Mario Bava, another legendary Italian horror director, assisted with some of the special effects.

 3. Keith Emerson of the progressive rock band Emerson, Lake & Palmer composed the film's score.

 4. Daria Nicolodi, Argento's long-time partner, plays the role of Elise Stallone Van Adler.

 5. The film's production was troubled by illnesses, including Argento contracting hepatitis.

 6. Many of the indoor scenes were shot on a soundstage in Rome, despite the New York setting.

 7. Inferno was produced by 20th Century Fox, making it one of Argento's few Hollywood-backed films.

 8. The movie features several references to Thomas De Quincey's essay "Levana and Our Ladies of Sorrow."

 9. Argento used complex layers of colored gels to achieve the film's distinctive lighting effects.

 10. Despite its cult status today, Inferno was not as commercially successful as Suspiria upon its initial release.

8. Zombi 2 (Zombie Flesh Eaters)

1. **Movie Title**: Zombi 2 (released internationally as Zombie Flesh Eaters)

2. **Year of Release**: 1979

3. **Cast and Director**:

  - Director: Lucio Fulci

  - Cast: Tisa Farrow, Ian McCulloch, Richard Johnson, Al Cliver, Auretta Gay

4. **Synopsis**:

  Zombi 2 begins with an apparently abandoned yacht drifting into New York Harbor. When police investigate, they're attacked by a zombie, setting off a chain of events that leads Anne Bowles, the daughter of the yacht's owner, to team up with reporter Peter West to investigate her father's disappearance. Their search takes them to the Caribbean island of Matool, where they encounter Dr. Menard, who is studying a strange disease that's causing the dead to rise. As the zombie plague spreads, the island descends into chaos. The group must fight for survival against hordes of the undead, leading to a series of gruesome encounters and a desperate attempt to escape the island. The film is notorious for its graphic violence, including the infamous underwater zombie vs. shark scene.

5. **Why This Movie Is Recommended**:

  Zombi 2 is a landmark in zombie cinema, blending graphic gore with atmospheric tension. Fulci's direction creates a palpable sense of dread, particularly in the film's tropical setting. The movie's practical effects, though dated, remain impressively gruesome and effective. Its influence on the zombie genre is undeniable, with several scenes becoming iconic in horror cinema. While ostensibly a sequel to Romero's Dawn of the Dead (known as Zombi in Italy), Zombi 2 stands on its own as a unique and visceral entry in the genre. For fans of classic zombie films and Italian horror, it's an essential watch that showcases Fulci's talent for creating memorable, shocking imagery.

6. **10 Trivia Facts**:

  1. Despite its title, Zombi 2 is not actually a sequel to any film; it was renamed to capitalize on the success of Dawn of the Dead.

  2. The infamous zombie vs. shark scene was performed with a real shark, sedated with meat.

  3. Actress Auretta Gay performed her own underwater stunts in the shark scene.

  4. The eye-gouging scene, one of the film's most notorious, used a sheep's eye and a mixture of gelatin and mozzarella.

  5. The film was shot without sync sound, with all dialogue dubbed in post-production.

  6. Zombi 2 was banned in several countries upon its release due to its graphic content.

  7. The makeup for the zombies was created by Giannetto De Rossi, who later worked on Dune and Rambo III.

  8. The film's score, composed by Fabio Frizzi, has become iconic in its own right.

  9. Fulci appears in a cameo as the editor of the newspaper where Peter West works.

  10. The movie was shot in Italy and on location in Santo Domingo.

9. Cannibal Holocaust

1. **Movie Title**: Cannibal Holocaust

2. **Year of Release**: 1980

3. **Cast and Director**:

   - Director: Ruggero Deodato

   - Cast: Robert Kerman, Francesca Ciardi, Perry Pirkanen, Luca Barbareschi

4. **Synopsis**:

   Cannibal Holocaust follows anthropologist Harold Monroe as he leads a rescue team into the Amazon rainforest to find a missing documentary crew. The team discovers the tribe believed to have killed the filmmakers and recovers their cans of film. Back in New York, Monroe views the footage, which reveals the crew's fate and their shocking behavior. The found footage shows the documentarians staging atrocities, abusing the natives, and ultimately provoking their own brutal deaths at the hands of the cannibals. As Monroe grapples with the ethical implications of releasing the footage, the film raises questions about media exploitation, cultural imperialism, and the nature of "civilized" behavior. The graphic depictions of violence and real animal killings blur the line between fiction and reality, creating a disturbing commentary on society's appetite for sensationalism.

5. **Why This Movie Is Recommended**:

   Cannibal Holocaust is a controversial masterpiece that pushes the boundaries of cinema and ethics. Its groundbreaking use of found footage techniques influenced countless later films. The movie's unflinching depiction of violence and its critique of media sensationalism make it a thought-provoking, if deeply disturbing, experience. Deodato's direction creates a sense of realism that blurs the line between fiction and documentary, challenging viewers' perceptions. While its graphic content makes it difficult to watch, Cannibal Holocaust remains an important work in horror cinema, sparking discussions about filmmaking ethics, cultural representation, and the nature of violence in media.

6. **10 Trivia Facts**:

   1. The film was so realistic that Deodato was arrested on suspicion of making a snuff film and had to prove in court that the actors were still alive.

   2. Several animals were killed on-screen for the film, leading to ongoing controversy and animal cruelty charges.

   3. The movie popularized the found footage technique in horror, predating The Blair Witch Project by nearly two decades.

   4. Actress Francesca Ciardi suffered real leeches stuck to her for one scene, as Deodato wanted authentic reactions.

   5. The film was banned in over 50 countries upon its release.

   6. Deodato was inspired to make the film after seeing his son watch violent news reports on TV.

   7. The film's score, composed by Riz Ortolani, provides an ironically beautiful contrast to the brutal imagery.

   8. The actors signed contracts to stay out of the media for a year after the film's release to maintain the illusion that they had died.

   9. Cannibal Holocaust was one of the first films to be shot with hand-held cameras to create a documentary feel.

   10. Despite its reputation, the film has been praised by some critics for its anti-imperialist message.

10. Demoni (Demons)

1. Movie Title: Demoni (Demons)

2. Year of Release: 1985

3. Cast and Director:

- Director: Lamberto Bava

- Cast: Urbano Barberini, Natasha Hovey, Karl Zinny, Fiore Argento

4. Synopsis:

Demoni takes place in Berlin, where a mysterious man gives free tickets to a screening at a newly renovated theater. A diverse group of people attends, including two female students, a pimp and his prostitutes, and a blind man and his guide. The film being shown is a horror movie about demons. When one of the audience members is scratched by a prop mask from the movie's display, she transforms into a demon. The demonic infection spreads rapidly through the theater, turning victims into violent, bloodthirsty creatures. The survivors must fight their way out of the theater, which has been sealed off. As the night progresses, the demon outbreak spreads beyond the theater, leading to a desperate battle for survival in an increasingly apocalyptic Berlin.

5. Why This Movie Is Recommended:

Demoni is a high-energy, gore-filled thrill ride that exemplifies the best of 1980s Italian horror. Produced by Dario Argento and directed by Lamberto Bava, the film combines stunning practical effects with a pulsing soundtrack featuring heavy metal hits. Its meta-narrative, where the horror on screen becomes reality, adds an interesting layer to the standard monster movie plot. The claustrophobic setting of the theater creates intense tension, while the later scenes in Berlin showcase impressive large-scale destruction. With its fast pace, memorable demon designs, and over-the-top action sequences, Demoni offers a wildly entertaining experience for fans of practical effects-driven horror.

6. 10 Trivia Facts:

1. The film's screenplay was co-written by Dario Argento, Lamberto Bava, and Franco Ferrini.

2. The demon transformation effects were created by Sergio Stivaletti, who worked on many Italian horror films.

3. The movie features music from notable bands like Saxon, Accept, and Mötley Crüe.

4. Demoni was shot in both German and English simultaneously to appeal to international markets.

5. The film's success led to a sequel, Demoni 2, released the following year.

6. Nicoletta Elmi, who plays the usherette, appeared in several classic Italian horror films as a child actor.

7. The exterior of the movie theater is actually the Metropol in Berlin, which is still operational today.

8. Dario Argento's daughter, Fiore Argento, has a role in the film as Hannah.

9. The movie was released in the United States under the title "Demons" by Ascot Entertainment.

10. Despite its Berlin setting, much of the film was actually shot in Italy.

11. Opera

1. Movie Title: Opera

2. Year of Release: 1987

3. Cast and Director:

- Director: Dario Argento

- Cast: Cristina Marsillach, Ian Charleson, Urbano Barberini, Daria Nicolodi

4. Synopsis:

Opera follows Betty, a young soprano who unexpectedly lands the lead role in a modern, avant-garde production of Verdi's Macbeth after the star is injured. As Betty prepares for her debut, a masked killer begins terrorizing the opera house, forcing Betty to watch as he murders those around her. The killer binds Betty and tapes needles beneath her eyes, ensuring she can't look away from the gruesome acts. As the body count rises, Betty and the police inspector Marco try to uncover the killer's identity and motive. The story delves into Betty's repressed memories and the curse associated with Macbeth in theater lore. The film builds to a dramatic climax during a performance, blending operatic grandeur with visceral horror.

5. Why This Movie Is Recommended:

Opera represents Argento at the height of his visual and narrative powers. The film's stunning cinematography and innovative camerawork, including a memorable ravens-eye-view shot, create a visually spectacular experience. Argento's ability to blend high art with graphic violence reaches its apex here, with the opera house setting providing a grand stage for his trademark set pieces. The movie's exploration of voyeurism and the relationship between violence and art adds psychological depth to its giallo plot. With its compelling mystery, intense suspense, and unforgettable murder scenes, Opera stands as one of Argento's most accomplished and thrilling works.

6. 10 Trivia Facts:

1. The film was partly inspired by Argento's troubled experience directing an opera in 1987.

2. Real crows were used in the film, trained over three months for their scenes.

3. The iconic needles-under-the-eyes shots were achieved using a custom-made copper wire contraption.

4. Vanessa Redgrave was originally cast as the opera diva but left the project just before filming began.

5. The movie features both opera music and a heavy metal soundtrack, including songs by Steel Grave.

6. Argento considered Opera to be his most personal film at the time of its release.

7. The film's working title was "Terror at the Opera."

8. Some of the more complex shots required the construction of an enormous rotating set.

9. Cristina Marsillach, who played Betty, reportedly had a difficult relationship with Argento during filming.

10. The film contains several references to The Phantom of the Opera, both the novel and earlier film adaptations.

12. La Chiesa (The Church)

1. Movie Title: La Chiesa (The Church)

2. Year of Release: 1989

3. Cast and Director:

- Director: Michele Soavi

- Cast: Hugh Quarshie, Tomas Arana, Feodor Chaliapin Jr., Barbara Cupisti

4. Synopsis:

La Chiesa is set in a modern-day Gothic cathedral built over the mass grave of a medieval village of supposed witches. When the church's new librarian, Evan, accidentally triggers an ancient mechanism, it seals the church and traps everyone inside. As the evil forces beneath the church awaken, the trapped individuals face increasingly horrific and surreal situations. The film explores the dark history of the church, revealing connections between the present-day characters and the tragic events of the past. As the evil spreads, transforming people into demonic entities, the survivors must find a way to escape or stop the ancient evil before it's unleashed upon the world.

5. Why This Movie Is Recommended:

La Chiesa stands out for its blend of gothic atmosphere, surrealist imagery, and visceral horror. Michele Soavi, a protégé of Dario Argento, brings a unique visual style that sets the film apart from typical possession movies. The grand, oppressive setting of the cathedral provides a perfect backdrop for the unfolding supernatural events. The film's exploration of religious themes and historical atrocities adds depth to its horror elements. With its striking visuals, unsettling score by Keith Emerson and Philip Glass, and a plot that keeps viewers guessing, La Chiesa offers a memorable and atmospheric entry in the Italian horror canon.

6. 10 Trivia Facts:

1. The film was originally conceived as the third installment in the Demoni (Demons) series.

2. Dario Argento served as a producer and contributed to the story.

3. The elaborate cathedral set was constructed entirely in a studio.

4. Asia Argento, Dario Argento's daughter, has a small role in the film.

5. The movie features music from both Keith Emerson (of Emerson, Lake & Palmer) and minimalist composer Philip Glass.

6. Director Michele Soavi was initially an actor and appeared in several Italian horror films.

7. The film's special effects were created by Sergio Stivaletti, a frequent collaborator in Italian horror.

8. La Chiesa was shot in Hungary and Italy.

9. The movie's original runtime was nearly two and a half hours, but it was cut down for theatrical release.

10. Despite being part of the Demoni series conceptually, the film has a very different tone and style from its predecessors.

13. Quattro mosche di velluto grigio (Four Flies on Grey Velvet)

1. Movie Title: Quattro mosche di velluto grigio (Four Flies on Grey Velvet)

2. Year of Release: 1971

3. Cast and Director:

  - Director: Dario Argento

  - Cast: Michael Brandon, Mimsy Farmer, Jean-Pierre Marielle, Bud Spencer

4. Synopsis:

  Quattro mosche di velluto grigio follows Roberto Tobias, a drummer in a rock band, who becomes entangled in a nightmarish situation when he accidentally kills a stalker in self-defense. A mysterious figure photographs the incident and begins to torment Roberto with the evidence. As Roberto tries to uncover the blackmailer's identity, those close to him start dying in gruesome ways. The title refers to a scientific theory that the last image seen before death is imprinted on the retina - in this case, four flies on grey velvet. Roberto must navigate a complex web of deception and murder, uncovering dark secrets from his past, to solve the mystery before he becomes the killer's final victim.

5. Why This Movie Is Recommended:

  As the final installment in Argento's "Animal Trilogy," Quattro mosche di velluto grigio showcases the director's evolving style and themes. The film blends elements of giallo, psychological thriller, and surrealist cinema to create a unique and unsettling experience. Argento's innovative cinematography and use of technology (including high-speed cameras for death scenes) set new standards for the genre. The movie's exploration of guilt, identity, and the subconscious adds psychological depth to its murder mystery plot. With its stylish visuals, Ennio Morricone's eclectic score, and a plot filled with twists and red herrings, the film stands as a pivotal work in Argento's early career and Italian horror cinema.

6. 10 Trivia Facts:

  1. The film features groundbreaking use of a high-speed camera (3000 frames per second) for its climactic death scene.

  2. Ennio Morricone's score incorporates elements of jazz, pop, and avant-garde music.

  3. The movie was considered lost for many years, with only low-quality bootlegs available until its restoration in 2009.

  4. Argento has stated that this is his least favorite of his own films.

  5. The "four flies" theory presented in the film is entirely fictional.

  6. Bud Spencer, known for comedy roles, plays against type as the private detective Arrosio.

  7. The film's original theatrical release was trimmed by several minutes in many countries.

  8. Argento used a Technicolor process called "Technovision" to achieve the film's distinctive look.

  9. The movie features several elaborate murder set-pieces, including one in a public park.

  10. Despite being part of Argento's "Animal Trilogy," the film has little connection to its predecessors beyond thematic elements.

14. La maschera del demonio (Black Sunday)

1. Movie Title: La maschera del demonio (Black Sunday)

2. Year of Release: 1960

3. Cast and Director:

  - Director: Mario Bava

  - Cast: Barbara Steele, John Richardson, Andrea Checchi, Ivo Garrani

4. Synopsis:

La maschera del demonio, also known as Black Sunday or The Mask of Satan, is set in Moldova during the 17th century. The film opens with the execution of Asa Vajda, a beautiful witch, and her lover. Before being burned at the stake, Asa vows revenge on her brother's descendants. Two centuries later, Dr. Thomas Kruvajan and his assistant, Dr. Andre Gorobec, accidentally revive Asa when they remove the mask used in her execution. Asa begins to drain the life force of Katia, her descendant who bears an uncanny resemblance to her, in an attempt to fully resurrect herself. As the village falls under Asa's malevolent influence, Andre must race against time to save Katia and put an end to Asa's reign of terror.

5. Why This Movie Is Recommended:

La maschera del demonio is a landmark film in Gothic horror, marking Mario Bava's directorial debut and setting new standards for atmospheric terror. The film's striking black-and-white cinematography creates a haunting, dreamlike ambiance that has influenced countless horror films since. Barbara Steele's dual performance as both Asa and Katia is iconic, establishing her as a scream queen of the genre. Bava's innovative use of practical effects and creative camera work brings the supernatural elements to life in a way that remains effective today. With its blend of sensuality and horror, intricate plot, and unforgettable imagery, La maschera del demonio stands as a classic of Italian horror and a must-see for fans of Gothic cinema.

6. 10 Trivia Facts:

  1. The film is loosely based on Nikolai Gogol's short story "Viy."

  2. The iconic mask with spikes on the inside was made of rubber, not metal as it appears.

  3. This was Mario Bava's official directorial debut, though he had finished other films uncredited.

  4. Barbara Steele was originally slated to play just one role but was cast as both Asa and Katia during production.

  5. The film was banned in the UK until 1968 due to its violent content.

  6. Bava used plastic dummies for some of the corpses, a technique he would employ in later films.

  7. The movie was released in the US with some scenes cut and an added musical score.

  8. La maschera del demonio was shot in just 12 days.

  9. The film's success established Italy as a major player in the horror genre.

  10. Tim Burton has cited this movie as an influence on his gothic aesthetic.

15. Tenebre (Reloaded)

1. Movie Title: Tenebre (Reloaded)

2. Year of Release: 1982

3. Cast and Director:

  - Director: Dario Argento

  - Cast: Anthony Franciosa, John Saxon, Daria Nicolodi, Giuliano Gemma

4. Synopsis:

  Tenebre follows American author Peter Neal, who arrives in Rome to promote his latest murder mystery novel. Shortly after his arrival, a series of brutal murders begin to occur, mimicking the killings in Neal's book. As the body count rises, Neal finds himself drawn into the investigation, working alongside the local police to uncover the killer's identity. The murders become increasingly personal, with Neal's agent and associates becoming targets. As the line between fiction and reality blurs, Neal must confront his own past and the possibility that his work has inspired a real-life killer. The film builds to a shocking climax that challenges perceptions and reveals unexpected truths about the nature of violence and obsession.

5. Why This Movie Is Recommended:

  Tenebre stands out as a meta-textual exploration of the giallo genre, blending self-awareness with Argento's signature style. The film's clever plot twists and commentary on the relationship between art and violence elevate it beyond a typical slasher film. Argento's masterful use of light and shadow, coupled with innovative camera work, creates a visually stunning experience. The movie's exploration of gender roles and sexual identity adds depth to its narrative. With its pulsing electronic score by Goblin members, shocking violence, and psychological complexity, Tenebre remains a high point in Argento's filmography and a must-see for horror enthusiasts.

6. 10 Trivia Facts:

  1. The film was temporarily banned in the UK as part of the "video nasty" panic of the 1980s.

  2. Argento originally wanted Christopher Walken for the lead role of Peter Neal.

  3. The movie features an impressive 2.5-minute crane shot that sweeps over and around a house.

  4. Tenebre was filmed entirely at night or in artificially darkened sets to achieve its unique look.

  5. The film's working title was "Unsane."

  6. Argento wrote the screenplay in reaction to criticism about the violence in his previous films.

  7. The movie's tagline was "Terror Beyond Belief."

  8. Veronica Lario, who plays Jane McKerrow, later became the wife of Italian Prime Minister Silvio Berlusconi.

  9. The film features several references to Argento's previous works, including "The Bird with the Crystal Plumage."

  10. Tenebre was shot in only 8 weeks, which is relatively quick for an Argento film.

16. Macabro (Macabre)

1. Movie Title: Macabro (Macabre)

2. Year of Release: 1980

3. Cast and Director:

- Director: Lamberto Bava

- Cast: Bernice Stegers, Stanko Molnar, Veronica Zinny, Roberto Posse

4. Synopsis:

Macabro tells the disturbing story of Jane Baker, a woman who loses her lover Fred and young daughter Lucy in a car accident. Following a mental breakdown, Jane moves to New Orleans to start a new life. She rents a room from the blind landlord Robert Duval and his young daughter Lucy. Jane appears to be recovering, but her behavior becomes increasingly erratic. It's revealed that she's keeping Fred's decapitated head in her refrigerator, engaging in a macabre relationship with it. As Jane's mental state deteriorates, the boundaries between reality and hallucination blur. The film builds to a shocking climax where the full extent of Jane's madness and the true nature of her relationships are revealed.

5. Why This Movie Is Recommended:

Macabro marks Lamberto Bava's directorial debut and showcases his ability to create unsettling psychological horror. The film's exploration of grief, madness, and obsession goes beyond typical genre fare, offering a disturbing character study. Bava's direction creates a creeping sense of unease that builds throughout the film. The New Orleans setting adds a unique atmosphere to the Italian production. While less gory than many of its contemporaries, Macabro's psychological approach and shocking revelations make it a memorable entry in the Italian horror canon. For fans of character-driven horror and psychological thrillers, Macabro offers a haunting and thought-provoking experience.

6. 10 Trivia Facts:

1. This was Lamberto Bava's solo directorial debut, though he had previously co-directed a film with his father, Mario Bava.

2. The film is loosely based on a true story that occurred in Colombia.

3. Dario Argento served as a producer on the film.

4. The movie was shot on location in New Orleans, unusual for Italian productions of the time.

5. Macabro was one of the first films to be produced by Dario Argento's company, Nuova Dania Cinematografica.

6. The film's score was composed by Berto Pisano, known for his work in Italian genre cinema.

7. Lamberto Bava had previously worked as an assistant director on several of his father's films.

8. The movie received limited distribution outside of Italy upon its initial release.

9. Macabro was released in some markets under the title "Frozen Terror."

10. The film's success helped establish Lamberto Bava as a director in his own right, stepping out of his famous father's shadow.

17. La casa dalle finestre che ridono (The House with Laughing Windows)

1. Movie Title: La casa dalle finestre che ridono (The House with Laughing Windows)

2. Year of Release: 1976

3. Cast and Director:

 - Director: Pupi Avati

 - Cast: Lino Capolicchio, Francesca Marciano, Gianni Cavina, Giulio Pizzirani

4. Synopsis:

 La casa dalle finestre che ridono follows Stefano, a young restorer who arrives in a small Italian village to restore a mysterious fresco of St. Sebastian's martyrdom in the local church. As Stefano works on the fresco, he becomes embroiled in the dark secrets of the village and the disturbing history of the fresco's painter, Buono Legnani, known as "The Painter of Agony." Stefano's investigations reveal a series of gruesome murders and a cult-like obsession with pain and death among some of the villagers. As he gets closer to the truth, Stefano finds himself in increasing danger, uncovering a conspiracy that spans generations and threatens his own life.

5. Why This Movie Is Recommended:

 La casa dalle finestre che ridono stands out as a unique and atmospheric entry in the Italian horror genre. Pupi Avati's direction creates a pervasive sense of unease and dread that builds slowly throughout the film. The movie's rural setting and focus on local folklore and religious imagery set it apart from the more urban-centric giallo films of the era. Its exploration of the dark side of art and the lingering effects of historical atrocities adds depth to the horror elements. With its haunting imagery, complex plot, and shocking revelations, the film offers a more cerebral and psychologically disturbing experience than many of its contemporaries.

6. 10 Trivia Facts:

 1. The film's title refers to a house in the village with stained glass windows that appear to be laughing.

 2. Director Pupi Avati was inspired by his own experiences restoring frescoes in rural Italian churches.

 3. The movie was shot on location in Emilia-Romagna, adding to its authentic rural Italian atmosphere.

 4. Avati used a desaturated color palette to create the film's distinctive, unsettling look.

 5. The fresco of St. Sebastian was created specifically for the film by artist Tonino Buazzelli.

 6. The film's score, composed by Amedeo Tommasi, uses unconventional instruments to create its eerie soundscape.

 7. La casa dalle finestre che ridono was not widely distributed outside Italy upon its initial release.

 8. The movie has gained a cult following over the years and is now considered a classic of Italian horror.

 9. Avati's brother, Antonio Avati, co-wrote the screenplay and produced the film.

 10. The film's exploration of rural Italian superstitions and folklore was groundbreaking for its time in Italian cinema.

18. L'aldilà (The Beyond)

1. Movie Title: L'aldilà (The Beyond)

2. Year of Release: 1981

3. Cast and Director:

  - Director: Lucio Fulci

  - Cast: Catriona MacColl, David Warbeck, Cinzia Monreale, Antoine Saint-John

4. Synopsis:

  L'aldilà follows Liza Merril, who inherits an old hotel in Louisiana. As she attempts to renovate and reopen the hotel, she discovers it was built over one of the seven gates of hell. A series of bizarre and gruesome events unfold as the gate begins to open, blurring the lines between our world and the realm of the dead. Liza, aided by Dr. John McCabe, must confront increasingly nightmarish situations and hordes of zombies as reality itself begins to unravel. The film culminates in a surreal and horrifying journey through the gate, leading to a shocking and ambiguous ending that challenges perceptions of life, death, and reality.

5. Why This Movie Is Recommended:

  L'aldilà is considered one of Lucio Fulci's masterpieces and a pinnacle of Italian horror cinema. The film's unique blend of supernatural horror, gore, and surrealism creates a dreamlike yet terrifying experience. Fulci's direction emphasizes atmosphere and visceral imagery over conventional narrative, resulting in a series of unforgettable and horrifying set pieces. The movie's exploration of themes like fate, death, and the nature of reality adds depth to its horror elements. With its striking visuals, unsettling score by Fabio Frizzi, and its willingness to push the boundaries of taste and logic, L'aldilà offers a singular and influential entry in the horror genre.

6. 10 Trivia Facts:

  1. The film is the second installment in Fulci's unofficial "Gates of Hell" trilogy.

  2. Many of the zombies in the film were played by local German students, as it was partially shot in Germany.

  3. The infamous "tarantula scene" used real tarantulas, much to the actors' discomfort.

  4. Fulci himself has a cameo as a librarian in the film.

  5. The movie's original U.S. release was heavily edited and retitled "Seven Doors of Death."

  6. The painting seen in the film's opening was created by German artist Helmut Middendorf.

  7. L'aldilà was shot out of sequence, with the ending filmed first.

  8. The film's score by Fabio Frizzi has become iconic in its own right and was later released as a standalone album.

  9. Despite its current status as a cult classic, the film received mixed reviews upon its initial release.

  10. The "sea of glass" in the film's ending was created using salt on a sheet of glass.

19. Dellamorte Dellamore (Cemetery Man)

1. Movie Title: Dellamorte Dellamore (Cemetery Man)

2. Year of Release: 1994

3. Cast and Director:

  - Director: Michele Soavi

  - Cast: Rupert Everett, Anna Falchi, François Hadji-Lazaro, Mickey Knox

4. Synopsis:

  Dellamorte Dellamore follows Francesco Dellamorte, the caretaker of the Buffalora cemetery, where the dead have a habit of coming back to life after seven days. Assisted by his mute sidekick Gnaghi, Francesco routinely dispatches these "returners" to maintain order. His monotonous existence is disrupted when he falls in love with a young widow, leading to a series of tragic and darkly comic events. As the line between life and death becomes increasingly blurred, Francesco grapples with his own sanity and place in the world. The film blends horror, comedy, and philosophy, exploring themes of love, death, and the absurdity of existence through its surreal and often grotesque narrative.

5. Why This Movie Is Recommended:

  Dellamorte Dellamore stands out as a unique and genre-defying entry in Italian horror cinema. Michele Soavi's direction combines elements of horror, dark comedy, and existential drama to create a film that's both entertaining and thought-provoking. The movie's blend of graphic violence, offbeat humor, and poignant moments of reflection sets it apart from conventional zombie films. Rupert Everett's deadpan performance as Francesco anchors the film's more outlandish elements. With its striking visuals, clever script, and willingness to tackle philosophical questions, Dellamorte Dellamore offers a fresh and intellectually engaging take on horror tropes.

6. 10 Trivia Facts:

  1. The film is based on the comic book series "Dylan Dog" by Tiziano Sclavi.

  2. Rupert Everett's character, Francesco Dellamorte, is the namesake of Dylan Dog in the original comics.

  3. Director Michele Soavi was a protégé of Dario Argento and worked on several of his films.

  4. The movie was shot entirely in Italy, despite its ambiguous setting.

  5. The film's English title, "Cemetery Man," was not favored by Soavi, who preferred the original Italian title.

  6. Dellamorte Dellamore was one of the last entries in the golden age of Italian horror cinema.

  7. The film features a cameo by director Michele Soavi as a singing mason.

  8. Despite its cult status, the movie was a commercial failure upon its initial release.

  9. The film's makeup effects were created by Sergio Stivaletti, known for his work with Dario Argento.

  10. Dellamorte Dellamore has been praised by director Martin Scorsese as one of his favorite Italian films.

20. Stagefright

1. Movie Title: Stagefright (also known as Aquarius, Deliria)

2. Year of Release: 1987

3. Cast and Director:

- Director: Michele Soavi

- Cast: Barbara Cupisti, David Brandon, Domenico Fiore, Robert Gligorov

4. Synopsis:

Stagefright takes place in a theater where a group of actors is rehearsing a musical about a fictional killer called the Night Owl. When the lead actress is injured, the director takes the cast to a nearby psychiatric hospital for treatment. Unbeknownst to them, they pick up a dangerous, escaped mental patient who was committed for murder. Back at the theater, the patient dons the owl mask from the play's costume and begins a killing spree, locking the cast and crew inside. As the night progresses, the survivors must use their wits to stay alive and escape the building, all while the killer stalks them through the labyrinthine theater.

5. Why This Movie Is Recommended:

Stagefright stands out as a stylish and intense entry in the slasher genre, elevated by Michele Soavi's innovative direction. The film's theatrical setting provides a unique backdrop for the horror, allowing for creative use of props, costumes, and set pieces. Soavi's background in Italian horror cinema is evident in the movie's striking visuals and tense atmosphere. The owl-masked killer is a memorable and unsettling antagonist, adding a surreal element to the slasher formula. With its blend of giallo-style murder sequences, psychological tension, and meta-theatrical elements, Stagefright offers a fresh and engaging take on familiar horror tropes.

6. 10 Trivia Facts:

1. This was Michele Soavi's directorial debut for a full-length feature film.

2. Soavi had previously worked as an assistant director for Dario Argento and Terry Gilliam.

3. The film's working title was "Aquarius," which is still used in some countries.

4. The owl mask worn by the killer was designed by Soavi himself.

5. Many of the cast members were actual stage actors with little to no film experience.

6. The movie was shot in just four weeks on a relatively low budget.

7. Stagefright features a soundtrack by the Italian rock band Curriculum Vitae and composer Simon Boswell.

8. The film pays homage to several classic horror movies, including "Halloween" and "The Texas Chain Saw Massacre."

9. Despite its theatrical setting, most of the film was shot in an abandoned tobacco factory.

10. Soavi makes a cameo appearance in the film as a police officer.

Spain

1. The Others (Los Otros)

1. Movie Title: The Others (Los Otros)

2. Year of Release: 2001

3. Cast and Director:

  - Director: Alejandro Amenábar

  - Cast: Nicole Kidman, Fionnula Flanagan, Christopher Eccleston

4. Synopsis:

  Set in post-World War II England, "The Others" follows Grace Stewart, a devoutly religious mother who lives in a dark, old house with her two photosensitive children. When three new servants arrive, inexplicable events begin to occur. Strange noises, ghostly voices, and mysterious figures plague the family as Grace desperately tries to protect her children. As the tension builds, Grace uncovers shocking truths about her family and their existence, leading to a twist ending that challenges everything the audience has been led to believe.

5. Why This Movie Is Recommended:

  "The Others" is a masterclass in atmospheric horror, relying on psychological tension rather than gore or jump scares. Its Gothic setting, brilliant performances (especially by Nicole Kidman), and clever script create a haunting experience that lingers long after viewing. The film's exploration of themes such as faith, isolation, and the nature of reality adds depth to its ghostly narrative. Its twist ending, while often imitated, remains one of the most effective in horror cinema, rewarding repeat viewings and analysis.

6. 10 Trivia Facts:

  1. The film was shot entirely in Spain, despite being set in England.

  2. It was the first English-language film directed by Alejandro Amenábar.

  3. Nicole Kidman accepted the role without reading the script, based solely on her desire to work with Amenábar.

  4. The movie was produced by Tom Cruise, who was married to Kidman at the time.

  5. It's one of the highest-grossing Spanish films of all time.

  6. The house used in the film is a real 19th-century palace in Cantabria, Spain.

  7. Amenábar also composed the film's haunting score.

  8. The children's photosensitivity in the film is based on a real condition called xeroderma pigmentosum.

  9. The movie won eight Goya Awards, including Best Film and Best Director.

10. Despite its English dialogue, it was submitted as Spain's entry for the Best Foreign Language Film at the 74th Academy Awards.

2. The Orphanage (El Orfanato)

1. Movie Title: The Orphanage (El Orfanato)

2. Year of Release: 2007

3. Cast and Director:

- Director: J.A. Bayona

- Cast: Belén Rueda, Fernando Cayo, Roger Príncep

4. Synopsis:

Laura returns to the orphanage where she grew up, intending to turn it into a home for disabled children. Her young son Simón, who is HIV-positive, begins to communicate with invisible friends. During a party at the orphanage, Simón disappears without a trace. Months pass, and a desperate Laura begins to experience supernatural occurrences in the house. She becomes convinced that the ghosts of the orphanage's past inhabitants are trying to communicate with her. As she unravels the dark history of the orphanage, Laura must confront both supernatural and human horrors to uncover the truth about her son's disappearance.

5. Why This Movie Is Recommended:

"The Orphanage" brilliantly blends supernatural horror with intense emotional drama. It creates a deeply unsettling atmosphere through its Gothic setting and masterful use of sound design. The film's strength lies in its ability to evoke both terror and profound sadness, making it as much a ghost story as a meditation on grief and motherhood. Belén Rueda's powerful performance anchors the film, while Bayona's deft direction keeps viewers on edge until the heartrending conclusion.

6. 10 Trivia Facts:

1. This was J.A. Bayona's directorial debut.

2. The film was produced by Guillermo del Toro, who also served as a creative consultant.

3. It took only 10 weeks to shoot the entire movie.

4. The orphanage scenes were filmed in a real 19th-century mansion in Llanes, Asturias.

5. Bayona insisted on using practical effects over CGI whenever possible.

6. The film's soundtrack includes a lullaby composed specifically for the movie.

7. It was Spain's official submission for the 80th Academy Awards for Best Foreign Language Film.

8. The movie won seven Goya Awards, including Best New Director for Bayona.

9. Actress Belén Rueda researched the psychology of mothers who lost children to prepare for her role.

10. A Hollywood remake was planned but never materialized due to the original's lasting impact.

3. [REC]

1. Movie Title: [REC]

2. Year of Release: 2007

3. Cast and Director:

- Directors: Jaume Balagueró and Paco Plaza

- Cast: Manuela Velasco, Ferran Terraza, Jorge-Yamam Serrano

4. Synopsis:

"[REC]" follows a television reporter, Ángela Vidal, and her cameraman as they cover a night shift at a local fire station for a reality TV show. What starts as a routine call to an apartment building quickly descends into chaos as they find themselves trapped inside with the residents, who are exhibiting increasingly violent behavior. As the night progresses, it becomes clear that a mysterious and deadly infection is spreading through the building. The film is presented as found footage, with events unfolding in real-time through the lens of the news camera, creating an intense, claustrophobic experience as the characters fight for survival against the growing horde of infected residents.

5. Why This Movie Is Recommended:

"[REC]" reinvigorated the found footage genre with its relentless pacing and genuinely terrifying scenarios. The confined setting of the apartment building creates a claustrophobic atmosphere that ratchets up the tension with each passing minute. The film's use of handheld cameras adds to the sense of realism and immediacy, making the horror feel visceral and immediate. Its clever blend of zombie-like infection with religious undertones adds depth to the narrative, while the climax in the penthouse apartment is one of the most chilling sequences in modern horror cinema.

6. 10 Trivia Facts:

1. The film was shot in chronological order to maintain the actors' sense of growing fear and confusion.

2. Most of the dialogue was improvised by the actors, working from a basic outline.

3. The entire movie was filmed in just 20 days.

4. The apartment building used for filming was actually abandoned and scheduled for demolition.

5. "[REC]" spawned three sequels and an American remake called "Quarantine."

6. The directors insisted on using practical effects and makeup instead of CGI for the infected.

7. The famous night-vision scene at the end was filmed with an actual night-vision camera.

8. Manuela Velasco, who played Ángela, was primarily known as a TV presenter before this film.

9. The movie won numerous awards, including the Grand Prize at the Gérardmer Film Festival.

10. The film's success led to a boom in Spanish horror cinema in the late 2000s and early 2010s.

4. The Day of the Beast (El Día de la Bestia)

1. Movie Title: The Day of the Beast (El Día de la Bestia)

2. Year of Release: 1995

3. Cast and Director:

  - Director: Álex de la Iglesia

  - Cast: Álex Angulo, Armando De Razza, Santiago Segura

4. Synopsis:

"The Day of the Beast" follows Father Ángel Berriartúa, a Basque priest who believes he has deciphered a secret biblical code revealing the exact date of the birth of the Antichrist. Convinced that this event will trigger the Apocalypse, he travels to Madrid on Christmas Eve, determined to commit as many sins as possible to sell his soul to the Devil and prevent the end of the world. He teams up with José María, a heavy metal fan, and Professor Cavan, a fraudulent TV psychic. Together, this unlikely trio embarks on a chaotic and darkly comedic quest through Madrid's underworld to find and kill the Antichrist before it's too late.

5. Why This Movie Is Recommended:

"The Day of the Beast" is a unique blend of horror, comedy, and social satire that defies easy categorization. Director Álex de la Iglesia masterfully balances genuine scares with pitch-black humor, creating a film that's as thought-provoking as it is entertaining. Its critique of religious fanaticism, media manipulation, and urban decay gives the film a depth rarely seen in horror-comedies. The film's frenetic energy, memorable characters, and audacious set pieces make it a standout in Spanish cinema, influencing countless filmmakers and earning it a well-deserved cult status.

6. 10 Trivia Facts:

  1. The film won six Goya Awards, including Best Director for Álex de la Iglesia.

  2. It was shot entirely on location in Madrid, showcasing the city's grittier side.

  3. The movie features a cameo by Spanish film legend Terele Pávez.

  4. The heavy metal theme was inspired by the moral panic surrounding the genre in the 1980s and early 1990s.

  5. The film's success helped establish Santiago Segura as a major figure in Spanish cinema.

  6. Many of the film's special effects were achieved practically, with minimal use of CGI.

  7. The movie's tagline in Spain was "La comedia del Anticristo" (The Antichrist's Comedy).

  8. It was one of the first Spanish films to successfully blend horror with dark comedy.

  9. The film features numerous references to occult and esoteric symbolism.

  10. Despite its controversial themes, the movie was a commercial success in Spain and gained international cult following.

5. Thesis (Tesis)

1. **Movie Title**: Thesis (Tesis)

2. **Year of Release**: 1996

3. **Cast and Director**:

   - Director: Alejandro Amenábar

   - Cast: Ana Torrent, Fele Martínez, Eduardo Noriega

4. Synopsis:

"Thesis" centers around Ángela, a film student working on her thesis about violence in the media. Her research leads her to discover a disturbing underground world of snuff films - videos depicting real murders. When her thesis advisor dies mysteriously after viewing one of these tapes, Ángela becomes embroiled in a dangerous investigation. With the help of Chema, a fellow student obsessed with violent films, and Bosco, a charismatic but suspicious classmate, Ángela delves deeper into the dark underbelly of the film industry. As she gets closer to the truth, she realizes that she might be the next target, blurring the lines between her research and a real-life horror movie.

5. Why This Movie Is Recommended:

"Thesis" is a gripping psychological thriller that serves as a critique of media violence while delivering genuine suspense and horror. Amenábar's directorial debut showcases his talent for creating tension and unease, even without graphic on-screen violence. The film's exploration of voyeurism and the ethics of media consumption remains relevant in today's digital age. With strong performances, particularly from Ana Torrent, and a clever script that keeps viewers guessing until the end, "Thesis" is a landmark in Spanish cinema that successfully blends elements of horror, mystery, and social commentary.

6. 10 Trivia Facts:

1. This was Alejandro Amenábar's debut feature film, made when he was only 23 years old.

2. The movie won seven Goya Awards, including Best Film and Best Original Screenplay.

3. Amenábar wrote the script while still a film student, basing it partly on his own experiences.

4. The film's success launched the careers of both Amenábar and actor Eduardo Noriega.

5. Despite its subject matter, the film contains very little graphic violence, relying instead on suggestion and psychological horror.

6. The movie was shot on location at the Complutense University of Madrid.

7. "Thesis" was one of the first Spanish films to deal with the concept of snuff films.

8. The film's exploration of media violence was partly inspired by public debates about the topic in Spain at the time.

9. Amenábar also composed the film's tense, atmospheric score.

10. The movie's international success helped pave the way for a new wave of Spanish thrillers and horror films in the late 1990s and early 2000s.

6. Timecrimes (Los Cronocrímenes)

1. Movie Title: Timecrimes (Los Cronocrímenes)

2. Year of Release: 2007

3. Cast and Director:

- Director: Nacho Vigalondo

- Cast: Karra Elejalde, Candela Fernández, Bárbara Goenaga

4. Synopsis:

"Timecrimes" follows Héctor, an ordinary man who accidentally gets caught in a time loop. While relaxing in his backyard, he spots a nude woman in the forest and goes to investigate. This decision sets off a chain of events involving a mysterious bandaged figure, a research facility with a time machine, and multiple versions of Héctor himself. As he tries to prevent his original self from entering the time machine, Héctor becomes entangled in a complex web of cause and effect, realizing that his attempts to fix the situation might be what caused it in the first place. The film explores the paradoxes and moral dilemmas of time travel in a tightly constructed narrative.

5. Why This Movie Is Recommended:

"Timecrimes" is a brilliant blend of science fiction and psychological horror that challenges viewers' perceptions of causality and free will. Nacho Vigalondo's clever script and tight direction create a puzzle-box narrative that rewards close attention and repeated viewings. The film's ability to maintain suspense and horror elements within its sci-fi framework is remarkable. It offers a unique take on the time travel genre, using its low budget as an advantage to focus on character and plot rather than special effects. The result is a thought-provoking, unsettling experience that lingers in the mind long after viewing.

6. 10 Trivia Facts:

1. The entire film was shot in chronological order, despite its complex time-travel narrative.

2. Director Nacho Vigalondo appears in the film as the scientist running the time travel facility.

3. The movie was made on a shoestring budget of approximately €2.6 million.

4. "Timecrimes" won the Jury Prize and Youth Jury Prize at the 2007 Amsterdam Fantastic Film Festival.

5. The film uses only four main characters and a single location to tell its complex story.

6. An English-language remake was planned with Steve Zaillian as writer, but it never materialized.

7. The movie was shot in just 23 days.

8. Vigalondo wrote the script in less than a month.

9. The film's time machine was constructed from an old industrial washing machine.

10. "Timecrimes" was Vigalondo's feature directorial debut, following his Oscar-nominated short film "7:35 in the Morning."

7. The Devil's Backbone (El Espinazo del Diablo)

1. Movie Title: The Devil's Backbone (El Espinazo del Diablo)

2. Year of Release: 2001

3. Cast and Director:

- Director: Guillermo del Toro

- Cast: Marisa Paredes, Eduardo Noriega, Federico Luppi

4. Synopsis:

Set during the final year of the Spanish Civil War, "The Devil's Backbone" tells the story of Carlos, a 12-year-old boy who is left at an isolated orphanage after his father dies in battle. The orphanage, run by the kind but firm headmistress Carmen and the cruel caretaker Jacinto, harbors dark secrets. Carlos encounters the ghost of a young boy named Santi, who mysteriously disappeared on the night a bomb fell in the orphanage's courtyard but never exploded. As Carlos unravels the mystery of Santi's death and the unexploded bomb, he must also confront the very real dangers posed by the increasingly unstable Jacinto and the encroaching war.

5. Why This Movie Is Recommended:

"The Devil's Backbone" is a masterful blend of gothic horror, historical drama, and coming-of-age story. Del Toro's signature visual style creates a haunting atmosphere that perfectly complements the film's themes of loss, trauma, and resilience. The ghost story at its center serves as a poignant metaphor for the lingering effects of war and violence. With its rich characterizations, beautiful cinematography, and emotionally resonant narrative, the film transcends typical genre boundaries to deliver a deeply affecting experience that is as much about the horrors of humanity as it is about supernatural scares.

6. 10 Trivia Facts:

1. The film is part of del Toro's unofficial Spanish Civil War trilogy, along with "Pan's Labyrinth" and "The Shape of Water."

2. The ghost of Santi was created using a combination of practical effects and minimal CGI.

3. Del Toro considers this film to be his most personal work.

4. The unexploded bomb in the courtyard is a metaphor for the tension and impending violence of the war.

5. The film's title refers to a medical condition but is used metaphorically in the movie.

6. Del Toro wrote the first draft of the script in 1985, but it took years to secure funding.

7. The director made the film immediately after his father was kidnapped and ransomed in Mexico.

8. Many of the orphan characters were played by non-professional child actors.

9. The film won several Goya Awards, including Best Cinematography.

10. Del Toro has stated that the character of Jacinto is based on a real person from his childhood.

8. Veronica

1. Movie Title: Veronica

2. Year of Release: 2017

3. Cast and Director:

- Director: Paco Plaza

- Cast: Sandra Escacena, Bruna González, Claudia Placer

4. Synopsis:

Set in 1991 Madrid, "Veronica" follows the titular teenager who uses a Ouija board with her friends during a solar eclipse to try and contact her deceased father. However, the séance goes wrong, and Veronica finds herself besieged by dangerous supernatural presences that threaten her and her younger siblings. As the malevolent forces grow stronger, Veronica desperately seeks help from a blind nun known as Sister Death. Racing against time, she must uncover the nature of the evil she has unleashed and find a way to protect her family before it's too late. The film builds tension through a combination of supernatural occurrences and the very real pressures of Veronica's life as she struggles to care for her younger siblings in her mother's absence.

5. Why This Movie Is Recommended:

"Veronica" stands out for its intense atmosphere and creative scares that go beyond typical possession tropes. Director Paco Plaza, co-creator of "[REC]", brings his expertise in found-footage horror to create a more traditional but equally terrifying narrative. The film's strength lies in its character development, particularly in Sandra Escacena's powerful performance as Veronica. By grounding the supernatural elements in the real-world struggles of its teenage protagonist, "Veronica" adds emotional depth to its scares. The movie's clever use of sound design and visual effects creates genuinely unnerving moments that linger in the viewer's mind.

6. 10 Trivia Facts:

1. The film is loosely based on a real-life case from 1991 known as the "Vallecas Case."

2. Director Paco Plaza interviewed the actual police officers involved in the real case for research.

3. The movie uses a mix of practical effects and CGI to create its supernatural elements.

4. "Veronica" gained international attention when Netflix viewers claimed it was "too scary to finish."

5. The film features several references to 1990s pop culture, enhancing its period setting.

6. Sandra Escacena, who plays Veronica, had never acted in a film before.

7. The movie won the Goya Award for Best Sound in 2018.

8. The Ouija board used in the film was specially designed to avoid copyright issues.

9. Plaza intentionally shot the film to look like it was made in the 1990s, using period-appropriate lenses and lighting techniques.

10. The character of Sister Death is based on a real nun who taught at Plaza's school when he was young.

9. Pan's Labyrinth (El Laberinto del Fauno)

1. **Movie Title**: Pan's Labyrinth (El Laberinto del Fauno)

2. **Year of Release**: 2006

3. **Cast and Director**:

  - Director: Guillermo del Toro

  - Cast: Ivana Baquero, Sergi López, Maribel Verdú, Doug Jones

4. **Synopsis**:

  Set in post-Civil War Spain in 1944, "Pan's Labyrinth" intertwines the harsh realities of fascist Spain with a dark fantasy world. The story follows Ofelia, a young girl who moves with her pregnant mother to live with her new stepfather, a sadistic army officer tasked with rooting out rebel forces. Ofelia discovers an ancient labyrinth where she meets a mysterious faun who tells her she is a princess of an underground realm. To prove her royalty and return to her kingdom, Ofelia must complete three dangerous tasks. As the lines between reality and fantasy blur, Ofelia navigates both the horrors of war and the challenges of her magical quests, leading to a poignant and tragic conclusion that questions the nature of sacrifice and innocence.

5. **Why This Movie Is Recommended**:

  "Pan's Labyrinth" is a visually stunning and emotionally powerful film that seamlessly blends dark fantasy with historical drama. Del Toro's imaginative creature designs and rich, Gothic aesthetics create a unique and unforgettable world. The film's exploration of the cruelty of war and the power of imagination resonates on multiple levels. It challenges viewers with its unflinching portrayal of violence while offering moments of breathtaking beauty. The movie's ability to evoke both wonder and horror, often simultaneously, sets it apart as a modern masterpiece of fantastical cinema with strong horror elements.

6. **10 Trivia Facts**:

  1. Guillermo del Toro turned down the opportunity to direct "The Chronicles of Narnia" to make this film.

  2. The Pale Man character was inspired by del Toro's lucid dreams as a child.

  3. Doug Jones, who played both the Faun and the Pale Man, learned all his Spanish lines phonetically.

  4. The film won three Academy Awards: Best Cinematography, Best Art Direction, and Best Makeup.

  5. Del Toro left his notebooks full of designs for the film in a taxi, but they were returned to him intact.

  6. The movie is thematically linked to del Toro's earlier film "The Devil's Backbone."

  7. Ivana Baquero, who played Ofelia, was originally considered too old for the role at 11, but impressed del Toro so much that he rewrote the character as older.

  8. The film's original title translates to "The Faun's Labyrinth," not "Pan's Labyrinth."

  9. Del Toro chose to use minimal CGI, relying heavily on practical effects and makeup.

  10. The director sees the film as a spiritual successor to his earlier work "Cronos," completing an unofficial trilogy about the Spanish Civil War.

10. Sleep Tight (Mientras Duermes)

1. Movie Title: Sleep Tight (Mientras Duermes)

2. Year of Release: 2011

3. Cast and Director:

- Director: Jaume Balagueró

- Cast: Luis Tosar, Marta Etura, Alberto San Juan

4. Synopsis:

"Sleep Tight" follows César, a concierge at an upscale Barcelona apartment building who harbors a disturbing obsession with Clara, one of the tenants. Outwardly polite and helpful, César leads a secret life of psychological torture, sneaking into Clara's apartment while she sleeps to sabotage her life in subtle ways. His goal is to make her as miserable as he is, driven by his inability to feel happiness. As Clara's life slowly unravels due to César's machinations, he must also contend with other residents who grow suspicious of his behavior. The film builds tension as César's actions become increasingly bold and dangerous, leading to a chilling climax that questions the nature of evil and happiness.

5. Why This Movie Is Recommended:

"Sleep Tight" is a masterclass in slow-burn psychological horror that gets under the viewer's skin. Director Jaume Balagueró crafts a deeply unsettling narrative that plays on primal fears of violation and vulnerability in one's own home. Luis Tosar's nuanced performance as César is both captivating and deeply disturbing, creating one of the most memorable villains in recent Spanish cinema. The film's exploration of the banality of evil and the nature of happiness adds depth to its suspenseful plot. With its claustrophobic setting and meticulous pacing, "Sleep Tight" creates an atmosphere of creeping dread that lingers long after the credits roll.

6. 10 Trivia Facts:

1. The film was written by Alberto Marini, who was inspired by his own experience of finding a stranger in his apartment.

2. Director Jaume Balagueró is better known for his work on the "[REC]" series.

3. The movie was shot entirely on location in a real apartment building in Barcelona.

4. Luis Tosar spent time observing real concierges to prepare for his role.

5. The film won three Goya Awards, including Best Actor for Luis Tosar.

6. Balagueró intentionally shot the film to make the audience uncomfortable, often using unsettling camera angles.

7. The movie's Spanish title, "Mientras Duermes," translates to "While You Sleep."

8. The film was produced by Filmax, a company known for its contributions to Spanish horror cinema.

9. "Sleep Tight" marked a departure for Balagueró from his usual supernatural horror themes.

10. The film's success further cemented Spain's reputation as a major producer of quality horror cinema in the 21st century.

11. The Skin I Live In (La piel que habito)

1. Movie Title: The Skin I Live In (La piel que habito)

2. Year of Release: 2011

3. Cast and Director:

  - Director: Pedro Almodóvar

  - Cast: Antonio Banderas, Elena Anaya, Marisa Paredes

4. Synopsis:

"The Skin I Live In" follows Dr. Robert Ledgard, a brilliant plastic surgeon haunted by past tragedies. He develops a new type of skin that can withstand any kind of damage. His test subject is a mysterious woman named Vera, whom he keeps captive in his mansion. As the narrative unfolds through flashbacks, we learn the disturbing truth about Vera's identity and the lengths to which Ledgard has gone in his obsessive quest. The film explores themes of identity, revenge, and the consequences of playing god, blurring the lines between victim and perpetrator in a twisted tale of psychological and body horror.

5. Why This Movie Is Recommended:

Almodóvar's foray into psychological horror is a visually stunning and deeply unsettling experience. The film masterfully combines elements of mad scientist narratives, body horror, and revenge thrillers to create a unique and provocative story. Its exploration of identity, gender, and obsession is both thought-provoking and disturbing. The performances, particularly from Banderas and Anaya, are captivating, bringing depth to complex and morally ambiguous characters. With its polished aesthetics and shocking twists, "The Skin I Live In" challenges viewers' expectations and leaves a lasting impact.

6. 10 Trivia Facts:

  1. The film is loosely based on Thierry Jonquet's novel "Mygale" (Tarantula).

  2. This was the first collaboration between Almodóvar and Antonio Banderas in 21 years.

  3. Almodóvar wrote the screenplay in Spanish and had it translated to English before translating it back to Spanish for filming.

  4. The film won the BAFTA Award for Best Film Not in the English Language.

  5. Almodóvar cited Alfred Hitchcock's "Vertigo" as an inspiration for the film's themes of obsession and identity.

  6. The director described the movie as "a horror story without screams or frights."

  7. The film's visual style was influenced by the work of artist Louise Bourgeois.

  8. Almodóvar originally considered Penélope Cruz for the role of Vera.

  9. The movie features several references to other films, including "Eyes Without a Face" and "Frankenstein."

  10. Despite its disturbing themes, the film was a commercial success in Spain and internationally.

12. Julia's Eyes (Los ojos de Julia)

1. Movie Title: Julia's Eyes (Los ojos de Julia)

2. Year of Release: 2010

3. Cast and Director:

  - Director: Guillem Morales

  - Cast: Belén Rueda, Lluís Homar, Pablo Derqui

4. Synopsis:

"Julia's Eyes" follows Julia, a woman with a degenerative eye condition that's slowly robbing her of her sight. When her twin sister Sara, who suffered from the same condition, dies under mysterious circumstances, Julia is convinced it wasn't suicide as the police claim. As she investigates her sister's death, Julia's eyesight begins to deteriorate rapidly. She becomes aware of a shadowy presence that seems to be stalking her, visible only to those whose eyesight is failing. Racing against time and her own failing vision, Julia must uncover the truth about her sister's death and confront the mysterious figure before she loses her sight completely.

5. Why This Movie Is Recommended:

"Julia's Eyes" is a masterful thriller that uses its protagonist's impending blindness to create a unique and terrifying atmosphere. The film plays with light, shadow, and perspective to immerse viewers in Julia's increasingly dark world. Its clever use of sound design adds to the tension, creating scares that don't rely solely on visual elements. The movie's exploration of vulnerability and the fear of the unseen adds depth to its suspenseful plot. With strong performances, particularly from Belén Rueda, and a twisting narrative that keeps viewers guessing, "Julia's Eyes" offers a fresh and engaging take on the psychological thriller genre.

6. 10 Trivia Facts:

1. The film was produced by Guillermo del Toro, who was a fan of Morales' previous work.

2. Belén Rueda, who plays Julia, also starred in "The Orphanage," another Spanish horror film produced by del Toro.

3. The movie uses a variety of cinematographic techniques to simulate Julia's deteriorating vision.

4. "Julia's Eyes" won three Gaudí Awards, including Best Actress for Belén Rueda.

5. The film's original Spanish title, "Los ojos de Julia," translates directly to "Julia's Eyes."

6. Director Guillem Morales wrote the script with Oriol Paulo, who later directed "The Body" and "Mirage."

7. The movie features a cameo appearance by Spanish horror icon Ángela Molina.

8. The film's success further established Spain as a major producer of quality horror cinema in the 21st century.

9. Many scenes were shot using specialized lenses to distort the image and represent Julia's failing eyesight.

10. The movie draws inspiration from classic thrillers like "Wait Until Dark" and "Rear Window."

13. Shrew's Nest (Musarañas)

1. Movie Title: Shrew's Nest (Musarañas)

2. Year of Release: 2014

3. Cast and Director:

- Directors: Juanfer Andrés and Esteban Roel

- Cast: Macarena Gómez, Nadia de Santiago, Hugo Silva

4. Synopsis:

Set in 1950s Spain, "Shrew's Nest" tells the story of Montse, a agoraphobic seamstress who hasn't left her apartment in years, and her younger sister, who she has raised since childhood. Their claustrophobic existence is disrupted when a injured young man, Carlos, collapses on their doorstep. Montse takes him in and tends to his wounds, but her fragile mental state and growing obsession with Carlos lead to increasingly disturbing behavior. As Carlos tries to escape and Montse's sister begins to rebel against her control, the apartment becomes a nightmarish trap filled with dark secrets and escalating horror.

5. Why This Movie Is Recommended:

"Shrew's Nest" is a claustrophobic and intense psychological horror that masterfully builds tension within its confined setting. The film's 1950s period detail adds to its unsettling atmosphere, creating a sense of isolation that mirrors Montse's mental state. Macarena Gómez delivers a tour-de-force performance as Montse, making her both terrifying and sympathetic. The movie's exploration of family dynamics, mental illness, and the effects of a repressive society adds depth to its horror elements. With its clever plot twists and visceral scenes of bodily horror, "Shrew's Nest" offers a unique and memorable entry in the Spanish horror canon.

6. 10 Trivia Facts:

1. The film was produced by Álex de la Iglesia, director of "The Day of the Beast."

2. "Shrew's Nest" marks the feature directorial debut of both Juanfer Andrés and Esteban Roel.

3. The movie's Spanish title, "Musarañas," refers to both shrews (small mammals) and a colloquial term for obsessive thoughts.

4. Most of the film was shot in a single apartment set, adding to its claustrophobic feel.

5. Macarena Gómez spent time with a psychologist to prepare for her role as the mentally unstable Montse.

6. The film won three Goya Awards, including Best New Director for Andrés and Roel.

7. The directors cited Roman Polanski's "Repulsion" as an influence on the film's atmosphere.

8. The movie's 1950s setting allowed the filmmakers to explore themes of repression in Franco-era Spain.

9. Despite its horror elements, the film also incorporates dark humor, particularly in its later scenes.

10. "Shrew's Nest" premiered at the 2014 Toronto International Film Festival in the Contemporary World Cinema section.

14. The Nameless (Los sin nombre)

1. Movie Title: The Nameless (Los sin nombre)

2. Year of Release: 1999

3. Cast and Director:

 - Director: Jaume Balagueró

 - Cast: Emma Vilarasau, Karra Elejalde, Tristán Ulloa

4. Synopsis:

"The Nameless" follows Claudia, a mother whose daughter, Angela, was brutally murdered five years ago. When Claudia receives a phone call from someone claiming to be Angela and begging for help, she is plunged back into her nightmare. Aided by a retired policeman and a journalist, Claudia investigates a sinister cult called "The Nameless," which may be connected to her daughter's disappearance and apparent resurrection. As they delve deeper into the cult's activities, they uncover a world of ritualistic violence and occult practices. The film builds to a haunting climax that questions the nature of evil and the lengths a mother will go to for her child.

5. Why This Movie Is Recommended:

"The Nameless" is a chilling and atmospheric thriller that marked Jaume Balagueró's impressive debut in feature films. The movie stands out for its bleak tone and unflinching exploration of human depravity. Balagueró masterfully creates a pervasive sense of dread that lingers throughout the film. The movie's complex plot, which blends elements of detective noir with occult horror, keeps viewers engaged and guessing. With its strong performances, particularly from Emma Vilarasau, and its willingness to delve into truly dark territory, "The Nameless" offers a uniquely disturbing experience that showcases the strengths of Spanish horror cinema.

6. 10 Trivia Facts:

 1. The film is based on the 1981 novel "The Nameless" by English horror writer Ramsey Campbell.

 2. This was Jaume Balagueró's first feature-length film, launching his career in horror cinema.

 3. The movie won the Best Film award at the Sitges Film Festival in 1999.

 4. Balagueró significantly changed the ending of the book for the film adaptation.

 5. The film's success helped establish Filmax as a major producer of Spanish horror films.

 6. "The Nameless" was shot entirely on location in Barcelona and its surroundings.

 7. The movie's bleak tone and ending were controversial upon its release.

 8. Balagueró cited David Fincher's "Seven" as an influence on the film's visual style.

 9. The film features early career appearances by several actors who would become prominent in Spanish cinema.

 10. "The Nameless" was one of the films that kicked off the new wave of Spanish horror in the late 1990s and early 2000s.

15. Witching and Bitching (Las brujas de Zugarramurdi)

1. Movie Title: Witching and Bitching (Las brujas de Zugarramurdi)

2. Year of Release: 2013

3. Cast and Director:

  - Director: Álex de la Iglesia

  - Cast: Hugo Silva, Mario Casas, Pepón Nieto, Carolina Bang

4. Synopsis:

"Witching and Bitching" follows a group of bumbling thieves who, after a chaotic heist involving one of the robbers' young sons, find themselves fleeing to a remote village on the French border. Unknown to them, the village of Zugarramurdi is home to a coven of cannibalistic witches preparing for an ancient ritual. As the thieves become entangled with the witches, they face a series of increasingly bizarre and horrifying obstacles. The film escalates into a manic, supernatural showdown blending elements of horror, comedy, and action, all while exploring themes of gender conflict and family dynamics.

5. Why This Movie Is Recommended:

"Witching and Bitching" showcases Álex de la Iglesia's unique talent for blending horror with dark comedy and social commentary. The film's frenetic pacing and over-the-top setpieces create a rollercoaster ride of absurd humor and genuine scares. De la Iglesia's distinctive visual style brings the witches' world to life with grotesque imagination. While the comedy is often broad, the film doesn't shy away from moments of real horror and tension. Its exploration of gender dynamics adds a layer of satire to the supernatural proceedings. For viewers who enjoy their horror with a heavy dose of humor and social commentary, "Witching and Bitching" offers a wildly entertaining and uniquely Spanish take on the witch movie subgenre.

6. 10 Trivia Facts:

  1. The film is loosely inspired by the real-life witch trials that took place in Zugarramurdi in the 17th century.

  2. It won eight Goya Awards, including Best Special Effects and Best Makeup and Hairstyles.

  3. The elaborate witch gathering scenes required over 200 extras.

  4. De la Iglesia cited "The Witches of Eastwick" and "The Evil Dead" as influences.

  5. The movie features cameos from several Spanish cinema icons, including Santiago Segura and Carlos Areces.

  6. The film's makeup effects were created by DDT Studios, known for their work on "Pan's Labyrinth."

  7. "Witching and Bitching" was shot in various locations across Spain, including Navarre and Madrid.

  8. The movie's original Spanish title translates directly to "The Witches of Zugarramurdi."

  9. De la Iglesia wrote the script with his frequent collaborator Jorge Guerricaechevarría.

  10. The film premiered at the 2013 San Sebastian International Film Festival to critical acclaim.

16. The Bar (El bar)

1. Movie Title: The Bar (El bar)

2. Year of Release: 2017

3. Cast and Director:

- Director: Álex de la Iglesia

- Cast: Blanca Suárez, Mario Casas, Carmen Machi, Secun de la Rosa

4. Synopsis:

"The Bar" takes place almost entirely within a small café in the center of Madrid. A group of strangers find themselves trapped inside when people outside the bar start dying mysteriously. As panic sets in, the patrons realize that anyone who tries to leave is shot by an unseen sniper. Tensions rise as the group tries to figure out what's happening and why they're being targeted. Suspicions, accusations, and conflicts erupt among the diverse cast of characters as they face the possibility of a deadly contagion or a calculated attack. The film blends elements of thriller, horror, and dark comedy as the situation escalates and the trapped individuals are forced to confront both external threats and their own darker natures.

5. Why This Movie Is Recommended:

"The Bar" showcases Álex de la Iglesia's talent for creating tense, claustrophobic scenarios filled with dark humor and social commentary. The film's single-location setting is used to great effect, ratcheting up the tension and forcing character conflicts to the forefront. De la Iglesia masterfully balances suspense, horror, and comedy, keeping viewers on edge while also providing moments of absurd levity. The diverse ensemble cast brings depth to their roles, allowing the film to explore societal tensions and human nature under extreme circumstances. With its mix of genres and its commentary on modern fears and prejudices, "The Bar" offers a unique and engaging entry in the Spanish horror-thriller canon.

6. 10 Trivia Facts:

1. The film was shot in chronological order to help the actors build tension naturally.

2. Most of the movie was filmed on a single set, which was a fully functional bar built in a studio.

3. De la Iglesia cited "The Exterminating Angel" by Luis Buñuel as an influence on the film's concept.

4. The movie premiered at the 67th Berlin International Film Festival.

5. De la Iglesia used the confined setting to explore themes of xenophobia and class conflict in Spanish society.

6. The film's makeup and special effects were created by Pan's Labyrinth veteran DDT Studios.

7. "The Bar" was one of the most-watched Spanish films on Netflix in 2017.

8. The script was co-written by De la Iglesia and his frequent collaborator Jorge Guerricaechevarría.

9. The film's tight shooting schedule required extensive rehearsals before filming began.

10. De la Iglesia incorporated elements of real conspiracy theories into the plot to add to the atmosphere of paranoia.

17. Tombs of the Blind Dead (La noche del terror ciego)

1. Movie Title: Tombs of the Blind Dead (La noche del terror ciego)

2. Year of Release: 1972

3. Cast and Director:

 - Director: Amando de Ossorio

 - Cast: Lone Fleming, César Burner, María Elena Arpón, José Thelman

4. Synopsis:

"Tombs of the Blind Dead" introduces the Templar Knights, undead creatures who rise from their graves to hunt the living. The film follows a group of tourists who accidentally awaken these blind, skeletal horsemen. The Templars, executed centuries ago for their occult practices, lost their eyes to scavenging birds and now hunt by sound. As the protagonists struggle to survive, they uncover the dark history of the Templars and their unholy rituals. The movie blends elements of traditional zombie films with medieval folklore, creating a unique and atmospheric horror experience that spawned several sequels.

5. Why This Movie Is Recommended:

"Tombs of the Blind Dead" is a landmark film in Spanish horror cinema, creating a memorable and influential monster in the undead Templars. Director Amando de Ossorio crafts a genuinely eerie atmosphere, using the Spanish countryside and ancient architecture to great effect. The film's slow-moving but relentless antagonists, predating the modern zombie craze, offer a unique take on the undead that still feels fresh today. With its blend of historical elements and supernatural horror, "Tombs of the Blind Dead" offers both scares and a sense of dark folklore. Its influence can be seen in many subsequent Spanish and international horror films, making it a must-watch for fans of the genre.

6. 10 Trivia Facts:

 1. This film is the first in the "Blind Dead" series, which includes four movies in total.

 2. Director Amando de Ossorio created the Templar zombies as a reaction against the "childish" vampire films of the time.

 3. The movie was shot on location in Portugal, including in the medieval town of Berzocana.

 4. The film's success helped kickstart the Spanish horror boom of the 1970s.

 5. To create the eerie slow-motion effect of the Templars' movement, the scenes were shot with the actors moving in slow motion rather than using camera tricks.

 6. The movie was released in the United States under the title "Revenge from Planet Ape" to capitalize on the popularity of "Planet of the Apes."

 7. De Ossorio built the Templar costumes himself, using skulls made of plaster.

 8. The film's score, composed by Antón García Abril, has been praised for enhancing the movie's creepy atmosphere.

 9. "Tombs of the Blind Dead" was one of the first Spanish horror films to gain international recognition.

 10. The movie's plot was loosely inspired by the real-life history of the Knights Templar.

18. Paco Plaza's Verónica

1. Movie Title: Verónica

2. Year of Release: 2017

3. Cast and Director:

- Director: Paco Plaza

- Cast: Sandra Escacena, Bruna González, Claudia Placer, Iván Chavero

4. Synopsis:

Set in 1991 Madrid, "Verónica" follows the titular teenage girl who uses a Ouija board with her friends during a solar eclipse to try and contact her deceased father. However, the séance goes wrong, and Verónica finds herself besieged by dangerous supernatural presences that threaten her and her younger siblings. As the malevolent forces grow stronger, Verónica desperately seeks help from a blind nun known as Sister Death. Racing against time, she must uncover the nature of the evil she has unleashed and find a way to protect her family before it's too late. The film builds tension through a combination of supernatural occurrences and the very real pressures of Verónica's life as she struggles to care for her younger siblings in her mother's absence.

5. Why This Movie Is Recommended:

"Verónica" stands out for its intense atmosphere and creative scares that go beyond typical possession tropes. Director Paco Plaza, co-creator of "[REC]", brings his expertise in found-footage horror to create a more traditional but equally terrifying narrative. The film's strength lies in its character development, particularly in Sandra Escacena's powerful performance as Verónica. By grounding the supernatural elements in the real-world struggles of its teenage protagonist, "Verónica" adds emotional depth to its scares. The movie's clever use of sound design and visual effects creates genuinely unnerving moments that linger in the viewer's mind.

6. 10 Trivia Facts:

1. The film is loosely based on a real-life case from 1991 known as the "Vallecas Case."

2. Director Paco Plaza interviewed the actual police officers involved in the real case for research.

3. The movie uses a mix of practical effects and CGI to create its supernatural elements.

4. "Verónica" gained international attention when Netflix viewers claimed it was "too scary to finish."

5. The film features several references to 1990s pop culture, enhancing its period setting.

6. Sandra Escacena, who plays Verónica, had never acted in a film before.

7. The movie won the Goya Award for Best Sound in 2018.

8. The Ouija board used in the film was specially designed to avoid copyright issues.

9. Plaza intentionally shot the film to look like it was made in the 1990s, using period-appropriate lenses and lighting techniques.

10. The character of Sister Death is based on a real nun who taught at Plaza's school when he was young.

19. The House That Screamed (La residencia)

1. Movie Title: The House That Screamed (La residencia)

2. Year of Release: 1969

3. Cast and Director:

- Director: Narciso Ibáñez Serrador

- Cast: Lilli Palmer, Cristina Galbó, John Moulder-Brown

4. Synopsis:

Set in a remote French boarding school for girls in the late 19th century, "The House That Screamed" follows Teresa, a new student who arrives at the strict institution run by Madame Fourneau. As Teresa tries to adjust to the oppressive atmosphere, she becomes aware of a series of mysterious disappearances among the students. The school's isolation, the sadistic behavior of Madame Fourneau's disturbed son Luis, and the tension between the girls create an atmosphere of dread and suspicion. As more girls vanish and Teresa uncovers dark secrets about the school and its inhabitants, the film builds to a shocking and gruesome climax that reveals the true horror at the heart of the institution.

5. Why This Movie Is Recommended:

"The House That Screamed" is a pioneering work in Spanish horror cinema, blending elements of Gothic horror with giallo-style mystery and psychological thriller. Director Narciso Ibáñez Serrador creates a claustrophobic and oppressive atmosphere that keeps viewers on edge throughout. The film's exploration of repressed sexuality and power dynamics adds depth to its horror elements. With its stylish cinematography, strong performances (particularly from Lilli Palmer as Madame Fourneau), and shocking finale, the movie offers a unique and influential entry in the genre. Its impact can be seen in many subsequent films, including Dario Argento's "Suspiria," making it a must-watch for horror enthusiasts.

6. 10 Trivia Facts:

1. The film is considered one of the precursors to the slasher genre, predating many of the American slasher films of the 1970s and 1980s.

2. Director Narciso Ibáñez Serrador was primarily known for his work in television before making this film.

3. The movie was shot in Barcelona, Spain, despite being set in France.

4. "The House That Screamed" was one of the first Spanish horror films to gain significant international distribution.

5. The film's original Spanish title, "La residencia," simply means "The Residence."

6. Lilli Palmer, who played Madame Fourneau, was a well-known German actress making a rare appearance in a horror film.

7. The movie's themes and style influenced many subsequent European horror films, particularly in Italy.

8. Despite its reputation now, the film was initially controversial in Spain due to its content.

9. Ibáñez Serrador wrote the screenplay under the pseudonym Luis Peñafiel.

10. The film's success helped pave the way for the boom in Spanish horror cinema in the 1970s.

20. Who Can Kill a Child? (¿Quién puede matar a un niño?)

1. Movie Title: Who Can Kill a Child? (¿Quién puede matar a un niño?)

2. Year of Release: 1976

3. Cast and Director:

- Director: Narciso Ibáñez Serrador

- Cast: Lewis Fiander, Prunella Ransome, Antonio Iranzo

4. Synopsis:

"Who Can Kill a Child?" follows Tom and Evelyn, an English couple on holiday in Spain, as they visit a small island off the coast. Upon arrival, they find the island seemingly deserted except for eerily behaving children. As they explore further, they discover that the children have murdered all the adults on the island, driven by a mysterious force that compels them to violence. Tom and Evelyn must fight for survival against the homicidal children while grappling with the moral dilemma posed by the film's title. As the situation escalates, the couple is forced to confront the unthinkable to ensure their own survival.

5. Why This Movie Is Recommended:

"Who Can Kill a Child?" is a disturbing and thought-provoking horror film that pushes the boundaries of the genre. Director Narciso Ibáñez Serrador creates an atmosphere of creeping dread, using the idyllic island setting to great effect in contrast with the horrific events. The film's central question poses a moral dilemma that adds depth to the horror, forcing viewers to confront uncomfortable ethical questions. With its unflinching approach to its controversial subject matter and its skilled building of tension, the movie offers a unique and haunting experience. Its influence can be seen in many subsequent films dealing with evil children, making it a significant work in the horror genre.

6. 10 Trivia Facts:

1. The film is based on the novel "The Children's Game" by Juan José Plans.

2. The movie opens with a montage of real footage showing children suffering in various conflicts, setting a somber tone.

3. It was shot on location on the island of Menorca, Spain.

4. The film was initially banned in several countries due to its controversial subject matter.

5. Director Narciso Ibáñez Serrador used many non-professional child actors from the local area.

6. The movie's original Spanish title translates directly to "Who Can Kill a Child?"

7. It has been influential on many subsequent horror films, including "Children of the Corn."

8. The film was remade in 2012 as "Come Out and Play."

9. Ibáñez Serrador chose to film many scenes from the adult characters' point of view to increase the sense of threat from the children.

10. Despite its controversial nature, the film has been praised for its social commentary on the cyclical nature of violence.

United Kingdom

1. The Wicker Man

1. Movie Title: The Wicker Man

2. Year of Release: 1973

3. Cast and Director:

  - Director: Robin Hardy

  - Cast: Edward Woodward, Christopher Lee, Diane Cilento, Britt Ekland

4. Synopsis:

Sergeant Howie, a devout Christian police officer, travels to the remote Scottish island of Summerisle to investigate the disappearance of a young girl. Upon arrival, he finds the islanders unhelpful and evasive, practicing a form of Celtic paganism under the guidance of their leader, Lord Summerisle. As Howie delves deeper into the mystery, he uncovers disturbing rituals and practices that challenge his faith and morality. The investigation takes a sinister turn as he realizes the true nature of his presence on the island, leading to a shocking and unforgettable climax that has become one of the most iconic scenes in horror cinema.

5. Why This Movie Is Recommended:

"The Wicker Man" is a masterpiece of folk horror that blends mystery, psychological tension, and pagan folklore into a uniquely unsettling experience. Its exploration of the clash between Christian and pagan beliefs creates a rich, thought-provoking narrative. The film's atmospheric setting, memorable performances, and haunting soundtrack contribute to a growing sense of dread that culminates in one of the most shocking endings in horror history. Its influence on the folk horror subgenre and British cinema, in general, is immeasurable, making it a must-see for any horror enthusiast.

6. 10 Trivia Facts:

  1. Christopher Lee considered this his best film and worked on it for free.

  2. The famous wicker man was over 60 feet tall and cost £3,000 to construct.

  3. The film was partially inspired by David Pinner's 1967 novel "Ritual."

  4. Britt Ekland's voice was dubbed in parts of the film, and a body double was used for her nude scene.

  5. The movie was shot almost entirely on location in Scotland.

  6. Original prints of the film were allegedly used as landfill for the M3 motorway.

  7. Director Robin Hardy and screenwriter Anthony Shaffer researched actual pagan rituals for authenticity.

  8. The film's original cut was 102 minutes long but was shortened to 87 minutes for its theatrical release.

  9. "The Wicker Man" was initially released as the B-movie in a double bill with "Don't Look Now."

10. Despite its cult status today, the film was a commercial failure upon its initial release.

2. 28 Days Later

1. Movie Title: 28 Days Later

2. Year of Release: 2002

3. Cast and Director:

- Director: Danny Boyle

- Cast: Cillian Murphy, Naomie Harris, Christopher Eccleston, Brendan Gleeson

4. Synopsis:

Jim, a bicycle courier, wakes up from a coma 28 days after a highly contagious virus has devastated the UK. He finds London deserted and soon encounters the "Infected" - humans turned into rabid, violent beings by the virus. Jim joins a group of survivors, including Selena and Frank, as they navigate the dangerous streets of London in search of safety. Their journey takes them to a military blockade outside Manchester, where they discover that the remaining soldiers may pose as much of a threat as the Infected. As they fight for survival against both the Infected and desperate humans, the film explores themes of social collapse, human nature, and the lengths people will go to in order to survive.

5. Why This Movie Is Recommended:

"28 Days Later" reinvigorated the zombie genre with its gritty, realistic approach and fast-moving Infected. Danny Boyle's kinetic direction and the use of digital video create a raw, immediate feel that heightens the tension and horror. The film's exploration of societal breakdown and human nature in crisis adds depth to the visceral scares. Its influence on subsequent zombie films and TV shows is undeniable, making it a pivotal work in the genre. The strong performances, particularly from Cillian Murphy, and the haunting score contribute to an unforgettable post-apocalyptic nightmare.

6. 10 Trivia Facts:

1. The film was shot on standard definition digital video cameras to give it a gritty, realistic look.

2. To create the deserted London scenes, the crew had to film very early in the morning and only had about an hour before the city became too busy.

3. Cillian Murphy worked as a bike courier in London to prepare for his role.

4. The "Infected" weren't called zombies during production to differentiate them from traditional slow-moving zombies.

5. The film's budget was only £5 million, relatively low for a movie of its scale.

6. Danny Boyle drew inspiration from George A. Romero's zombie films and John Wyndham's novel "The Day of the Triffids."

7. The original script had a much darker ending, which was filmed but later changed.

8. The production team consulted with scientists about the plausibility of the "Rage" virus.

9. The scene where Jim walks across Westminster Bridge was filmed with just a skeleton crew of 10 people.

10. Christopher Eccleston, who plays Major Henry West, was considered for the role of Jim before it went to Cillian Murphy.

3. Don't Look Now

1. Movie Title: Don't Look Now

2. Year of Release: 1973

3. Cast and Director:

   - Director: Nicolas Roeg

   - Cast: Julie Christie, Donald Sutherland, Hilary Mason, Clelia Matania

4. Synopsis:

   After the tragic drowning of their young daughter, John and Laura Baxter travel to Venice, where John has been commissioned to restore an ancient church. In the labyrinthine city, they encounter two elderly sisters, one of whom claims to be psychic and in contact with their deceased daughter. As strange events unfold, including recurring sightings of a small figure in a red coat similar to the one their daughter wore when she died, John's rationality is tested. The couple grapples with grief, skepticism, and the possibility of supernatural forces at work. As John's visions intensify, the film builds to a climax that blends psychological horror with shocking revelations, challenging perceptions of reality and fate.

5. Why This Movie Is Recommended:

   "Don't Look Now" is a masterpiece of atmospheric horror that transcends genre conventions. Nicolas Roeg's innovative editing techniques and use of symbolism create a disorienting, dreamlike atmosphere that keeps viewers on edge. The film's exploration of grief, psychic phenomena, and the nature of perception adds psychological depth to its supernatural elements. Outstanding performances from Julie Christie and Donald Sutherland bring authenticity to the couple's emotional journey. The movie's influence on subsequent psychological thrillers and horror films is significant, and its enigmatic nature continues to spark discussion and analysis decades after its release.

6. 10 Trivia Facts:

   1. The film is based on a short story by Daphne du Maurier, who also wrote the stories that inspired Hitchcock's "Rebecca" and "The Birds."

   2. The famous love scene between Julie Christie and Donald Sutherland was so convincing that rumors persisted for years that it wasn't simulated.

   3. The movie was shot entirely on location in Venice, adding to its authentic and eerie atmosphere.

   4. The recurring motif of the color red was inspired by Nicolas Roeg seeing a red-coated child in photos of Venice during pre-production.

   5. The film's iconic poster was designed by the Italian photomontage artist Ferruccio Orioli.

   6. Donald Sutherland allegedly had a real-life psychic experience during filming, seeing an apparition of his daughter.

   7. The movie's non-linear narrative structure was revolutionary for its time and influenced many subsequent films.

   8. Julie Christie was initially reluctant to do the film due to the explicit nature of the love scene.

   9. The dwarf actress who plays the mysterious red-coated figure was actually a 39-year-old schoolteacher.

   10. Director Nicolas Roeg claimed that the film's enigmatic nature was partly due to substantial cuts made to reduce its running time.

4. The Descent

1. Movie Title: The Descent

2. Year of Release: 2005

3. Cast and Director:

  - Director: Neil Marshall

  - Cast: Shauna Macdonald, Natalie Mendoza, Alex Reid, Saskia Mulder, MyAnna Buring, Nora-Jane Noone

4. **Synopsis**:

A year after losing her husband and daughter in a car accident, Sarah joins five friends on a caving expedition in the Appalachian Mountains. What starts as an adventure turns into a nightmare when a cave-in blocks their exit, forcing them to venture deeper into the uncharted system. As they struggle to find another way out, they discover they are not alone in the darkness. The group encounters humanoid cave-dwelling creatures, blind but with acute hearing, that begin to hunt them. Trapped in the claustrophobic underground labyrinth, the women must fight for survival against the creatures and their own fears, while also confronting the tensions and secrets within their group.

5. **Why This Movie Is Recommended**:

"The Descent" is a masterclass in sustained tension and claustrophobic horror. Director Neil Marshall expertly builds an atmosphere of dread even before the creatures appear, using the cave setting to evoke primal fears of darkness and confinement. The all-female cast delivers powerful performances, bringing depth to their characters' relationships and individual struggles. The film's exploration of grief, betrayal, and survival instinct adds psychological complexity to its visceral scares. With its innovative use of lighting, intense action sequences, and shocking twists, "The Descent" stands as one of the most effective and influential horror films of the 21st century.

6. **10 Trivia Facts**:

  1. The film was shot almost entirely in sequence to maintain the actors' sense of disorientation and fear.

  2. The cave sets were built at Pinewood Studios, with different levels to create the illusion of descending deeper.

  3. The actors underwent a week of intensive caving training before filming began.

  4. Director Neil Marshall was inspired by his own claustrophobia and fear of the dark.

  5. The crawlers (cave creatures) were played by dancers and gymnasts to achieve their unique, fluid movements.

  6. The US version of the film has a different ending from the UK release.

  7. To create authentic reactions, the actors often didn't see the crawler makeup until filming their scenes.

  8. The movie was shot in just 7 weeks.

  9. Shauna Macdonald, who played Sarah, was actually pregnant during some of the film's reshoots.

  10. The film's working title was "Cave," but it was changed to avoid confusion with another movie released the same year.

5. Peeping Tom

1. **Movie Title**: Peeping Tom

2. **Year of Release**: 1960

3. **Cast and Director**:

   - Director: Michael Powell

   - Cast: Carl Boehm, Anna Massey, Moira Shearer, Maxine Audley

4. **Synopsis**:

   Mark Lewis, a shy and reclusive focus puller for a London film studio, harbors a dark secret: he's a serial killer who films his victims' deaths to capture their final expressions of terror. Traumatized by his father's psychological experiments on him as a child, Mark is both fascinated and repulsed by fear. He befriends Helen, a young woman who lives in his building, and begins to form a genuine connection with her. As the police investigate the murders and Helen gets closer to uncovering Mark's secret, the film explores themes of voyeurism, the nature of fear, and the psychological impact of childhood trauma. The story builds to a tense climax as Mark's past and present collide, leading to a shocking and poignant conclusion.

5. **Why This Movie Is Recommended**:

   "Peeping Tom" is a groundbreaking psychological thriller that was far ahead of its time. Michael Powell's bold exploration of voyeurism and the dark side of filmmaking caused controversy upon its release but is now recognized as a masterpiece of British cinema. The film's meta-commentary on the act of watching and its psychological depth set it apart from other horror films of its era. Carl Boehm's nuanced performance as Mark Lewis brings sympathy to a deeply disturbed character. With its vibrant Technicolor cinematography and innovative approach to the serial killer genre, "Peeping Tom" remains a thought-provoking and influential work that continues to resonate with modern audiences.

6. **10 Trivia Facts**:

   1. The film was so controversial upon its release that it effectively ended Michael Powell's career in the UK.

   2. Martin Scorsese has cited "Peeping Tom" as a major influence and was instrumental in its rediscovery and re-evaluation.

   3. The movie was released the same year as Alfred Hitchcock's "Psycho," but initially received much harsher criticism.

   4. Michael Powell himself plays Mark's father in the home movie sequences.

   5. The film's exploration of voyeurism predates many of the themes later examined in films like "Rear Window" and "Blow-Up."

   6. Carl Boehm, who played Mark, was actually Austrian and spoke little English at the time of filming.

   7. The character of Mark Lewis was partly inspired by the real-life serial killer John Christie.

   8. The film's screenwriter, Leo Marks, was a former cryptographer for the British Special Operations Executive during World War II.

   9. Moira Shearer, who plays Mark's red-headed victim Vivian, was a famous ballet dancer known for her role in "The Red Shoes," also directed by Michael Powell.

   10. The movie was one of the first to suggest that the filmmaker and the viewer could be complicit in the violence depicted on screen.

6. The Innocents

1. Movie Title: The Innocents

2. Year of Release: 1961

3. Cast and Director:

- Director: Jack Clayton

- Cast: Deborah Kerr, Michael Redgrave, Megs Jenkins, Martin Stephens, Pamela Franklin

4. Synopsis:

Based on Henry James's novella "The Turn of the Screw," "The Innocents" follows Miss Giddens, a naive governess who takes charge of two orphaned children, Miles and Flora, at a remote English country estate. As she settles into her new role, Miss Giddens becomes convinced that the grounds are haunted by the ghosts of two former employees: the previous governess, Miss Jessel, and the valet, Peter Quint. She believes these malevolent spirits are exerting a corrupting influence on the children. As Miss Giddens attempts to protect her charges, the line between reality and imagination blurs, leaving both the characters and the audience to question whether the haunting is real or a product of the governess's increasingly fragile psyche.

5. Why This Movie Is Recommended:

"The Innocents" is a masterpiece of psychological horror that relies on atmosphere and suggestion rather than overt scares. Director Jack Clayton's use of deep focus cinematography and unsettling sound design creates a pervasive sense of unease. Deborah Kerr's nuanced performance as Miss Giddens perfectly captures the character's descent into paranoia. The film's exploration of sexual repression, childhood corruption, and the nature of evil adds layers of complexity to its ghost story framework. With its ambiguous narrative and haunting imagery, "The Innocents" remains one of the most sophisticated and chilling ghost stories in cinema history.

6. 10 Trivia Facts:

1. The screenplay was co-written by Truman Capote, who added more overt sexual undertones to the story.

2. The film's title comes from William Archibald's stage adaptation of Henry James's novella.

3. Director Jack Clayton insisted on shooting in CinemaScope to capture the vastness and isolation of the estate.

4. Deborah Kerr wore padded clothing to make her appear more physically and sexually repressed.

5. The film's iconic theme song, "O Willow Waly," was specially composed for the movie.

6. Martin Stephens, who played Miles, also starred in another classic British horror film, "Village of the Damned."

7. The movie was shot entirely in sequence to help build tension and character development.

8. Cinematographer Freddie Francis used candles and natural light extensively to create the film's eerie atmosphere.

9. The film's ambiguous ending has been the subject of critical debate for decades.

10. "The Innocents" was selected by Martin Scorsese for his list of the 11 scariest horror films of all time.

7. Hellraiser

1. Movie Title: Hellraiser

2. Year of Release: 1987

3. Cast and Director:

- Director: Clive Barker

- Cast: Andrew Robinson, Clare Higgins, Ashley Laurence, Doug Bradley

4. Synopsis:

Based on Clive Barker's novella "The Hellbound Heart," "Hellraiser" tells the story of Frank Cotton, who solves an antique puzzle box and inadvertently opens a portal to a realm of sadistic extra-dimensional beings known as Cenobites. Frank is torn apart but is later partially resurrected by his brother's wife, Julia, with whom he had an affair. As Julia lures men to the house to harvest their blood for Frank's full resurrection, Frank's niece Kirsty discovers the truth and accidentally summons the Cenobites. Led by the iconic Pinhead, the Cenobites demand a soul in exchange for Frank's. The film builds to a gruesome climax as Kirsty tries to survive the machinations of both her human and inhuman adversaries.

5. Why This Movie Is Recommended:

"Hellraiser" stands out in the horror genre for its unique blend of body horror, supernatural elements, and exploration of pleasure and pain. Clive Barker's directorial debut brings a fresh, visceral approach to horror, with groundbreaking special effects and a deeply unsettling atmosphere. The film's complex mythology and the iconic design of the Cenobites, especially Pinhead, have left an indelible mark on horror cinema. "Hellraiser" delves into themes of desire, suffering, and the extremes of human experience, offering a more philosophical take on horror that continues to fascinate and disturb audiences.

6. 10 Trivia Facts:

1. The Cenobites were originally called "Hierophants" in the early stages of production.

2. Doug Bradley, who played Pinhead, was initially offered the role of a moving man with two lines, but chose Pinhead instead.

3. The film was shot in 10 weeks on a budget of only $1 million.

4. Clive Barker based the Cenobites' design on punk fashion and Catholic iconography.

5. The famous line "We'll tear your soul apart" was improvised by Doug Bradley during filming.

6. The MPAA demanded multiple cuts to reduce gore before giving the film an R rating.

7. The puzzle box, known as the Lament Configuration, was designed by Simon Sayce and took six weeks to create.

8. Pinhead only has about seven minutes of screen time in the entire film.

9. The film's working title was "Sadomasochists from Beyond the Grave."

10. Clive Barker hand-painted some of the maggots used in Frank's resurrection scene.

8. The Haunting

1. Movie Title: The Haunting

2. Year of Release: 1963

3. Cast and Director:

- Director: Robert Wise

- Cast: Julie Harris, Claire Bloom, Richard Johnson, Russ Tamblyn

4. Synopsis:

Based on Shirley Jackson's novel "The Haunting of Hill House," the film follows Dr. John Markway, an anthropologist investigating paranormal activity at the notorious Hill House. He invites two women with psychic abilities, Eleanor Lance and Theodora, along with the house's skeptical heir, Luke Sanderson, to stay in the mansion. As they explore the house's dark history, Eleanor becomes increasingly unstable, forming a strong connection with the house's supernatural presence. The group experiences escalating paranormal phenomena, from loud noises to writing on the walls. As the house's malevolent influence grows stronger, particularly over the fragile Eleanor, the line between reality and imagination blurs, leading to a chilling climax that questions the nature of the haunting itself.

5. Why This Movie Is Recommended:

"The Haunting" is a masterclass in psychological horror, relying on suggestion and atmosphere rather than explicit scares. Director Robert Wise's use of unusual camera angles, distorted sound, and shadowy cinematography creates a pervasive sense of unease. The film's exploration of mental instability and the power of suggestion adds depth to its ghost story framework. Julie Harris's performance as the vulnerable Eleanor is particularly noteworthy, capturing the character's descent into madness. "The Haunting" remains one of the most influential haunted house films, demonstrating how effective horror can be when it leaves much to the viewer's imagination.

6. 10 Trivia Facts:

1. The film's exterior shots were filmed at Ettington Park Hotel in Warwickshire, England, which is reportedly haunted in real life.

2. Director Robert Wise used infrared film for the exterior shots to give the house a more ominous appearance.

3. The curved walls of the set were designed to create a sense of disorientation for both the characters and the audience.

4. Many of the film's scares were achieved through sound design rather than visual effects.

5. The character of Theodora is subtly implied to be lesbian, which was quite progressive for a film in 1963.

6. The film's famous "breathing door" effect was achieved by using a flexible door made of laminated wood.

7. "The Haunting" was selected for preservation in the United States National Film Registry by the Library of Congress in 2018.

8. Martin Scorsese named it as one of the scariest films of all time.

9. The film's ambiguous ending leaves it open to interpretation whether the hauntings were real or psychological.

10. Despite its current status as a classic, the film received mixed reviews upon its initial release.

9. Dracula

1. Movie Title: Dracula

2. Year of Release: 1958

3. Cast and Director:

- Director: Terence Fisher

- Cast: Christopher Lee, Peter Cushing, Michael Gough, Melissa Stribling

4. Synopsis:

This Hammer Films adaptation of Bram Stoker's classic novel begins with Jonathan Harker arriving at Count Dracula's castle under the guise of being a librarian. His true mission is to destroy the vampire, but he falls victim to Dracula's power. When Harker's friend, Dr. Van Helsing, comes to investigate his disappearance, he discovers the truth about Dracula and vows to end his reign of terror. The vampire count, meanwhile, has set his sights on Harker's fiancée, Lucy, and her sister-in-law, Mina. As Dracula's influence spreads, Van Helsing races against time to save the women and destroy the vampire, culminating in a dramatic confrontation at Dracula's castle.

5. Why This Movie Is Recommended:

Hammer's "Dracula" reinvented the vampire genre for a new generation, bringing vivid color and a more explicitly sexual undertone to the classic story. Christopher Lee's portrayal of Dracula as a charismatic, imposing figure became the definitive version for decades. The film's Gothic atmosphere, combined with its then-shocking levels of violence and sensuality, set a new standard for horror cinema. Peter Cushing's Van Helsing provides a worthy adversary, creating a compelling battle between good and evil. This adaptation's influence on subsequent vampire films cannot be overstated, making it a must-see for any horror fan.

6. 10 Trivia Facts:

1. Christopher Lee played Dracula in seven Hammer films, but spoke dialogue in only three of them.

2. The film was released in the US under the title "Horror of Dracula" to avoid confusion with the 1931 Universal version.

3. The movie was shot in just 25 days.

4. Christopher Lee and Peter Cushing became lifelong friends after working on this film.

5. The original UK release was given an X certificate, restricting it to adults only.

6. The film's vibrant color palette was revolutionary for horror movies of the time.

7. The cape worn by Christopher Lee was discovered in 2007 in a London costume shop and sold at auction for £35,000.

8. Director Terence Fisher insisted on Dracula being more physically active than in previous incarnations.

9. The disintegration scene at the end was achieved by painting Lee's face red and green and using different color filters.

10. Despite its current classic status, some critics at the time found the film too gory and sensational.

10. The Witch

1. Movie Title: The Witch (stylized as The VVitch: A New-England Folktale)

2. Year of Release: 2015

3. Cast and Director:

  - Director: Robert Eggers

  - Cast: Anya Taylor-Joy, Ralph Ineson, Kate Dickie, Harvey Scrimshaw, Ellie Grainger, Lucas Dawson

4. Synopsis:

Set in 1630s New England, "The Witch" follows a Puritan family banished from their colony due to a religious dispute. They establish a farm on the edge of a foreboding forest, but strange and sinister events begin to unfold. Their newborn son vanishes, crops fail, and accusations of witchcraft tear the family apart. The eldest daughter, Thomasin, becomes the focus of suspicion as her younger siblings exhibit increasingly disturbing behavior. As the family's isolation and paranoia grow, they face an evil force that may be supernatural, psychological, or both. The film builds to a haunting climax that blurs the lines between faith, delusion, and dark forces beyond human understanding.

5. Why This Movie Is Recommended:

"The Witch" is a masterpiece of slow-burning psychological horror that immerses viewers in the mindset of 17th-century New England. Director Robert Eggers' meticulous attention to historical detail, from the period-accurate dialogue to the authentic costumes and set design, creates an unparalleled atmosphere of dread and authenticity. The film's exploration of religious extremism, family dynamics, and the fear of the unknown adds layers of complexity to its horror elements. With outstanding performances, particularly from Anya Taylor-Joy, and a haunting score, "The Witch" offers a unique and deeply unsettling experience that lingers long after viewing.

6. 10 Trivia Facts:

  1. The film used only natural light and candlelight for authenticity, challenging the cinematography team.

  2. The dialogue is largely drawn from actual 17th-century journals, diaries, and court records.

  3. The goat "Black Phillip" became an unexpected horror icon after the film's release.

  4. Director Robert Eggers spent four years researching and writing the script to ensure historical accuracy.

  5. Anya Taylor-Joy had never acted in a film before "The Witch."

  6. The film was shot in northern Ontario, Canada, to capture the harsh wilderness setting.

  7. The Satanic Temple endorsed the film, calling it a "transformative Satanic experience."

  8. Ralph Ineson lost 30 pounds for his role as William to appear more gaunt and desperate.

  9. The film's score, composed by Mark Korven, used unusual instruments like the nyckelharpa and waterphone.

  10. "The Witch" was praised by horror author Stephen King, who called it "a real movie, tense and thought-provoking as well as visceral."

11. The Others

1. Movie Title: The Others

2. Year of Release: 2001

3. Cast and Director:

  - Director: Alejandro Amenábar

  - Cast: Nicole Kidman, Fionnula Flanagan, Christopher Eccleston, Elaine Cassidy, Eric Sykes

4. Synopsis:

Set in the aftermath of World War II, "The Others" follows Grace Stewart, a devoutly religious mother who lives in a remote country house with her two photosensitive children. When three new servants arrive at their home, strange occurrences begin to plague the family. Grace becomes convinced that her house is haunted and struggles to protect her children from the apparent supernatural presence. As the tension builds, long-held secrets come to light, challenging Grace's perception of reality. The film culminates in a shocking twist that recontextualizes everything that came before, offering a poignant meditation on grief, denial, and the nature of existence.

5. Why This Movie Is Recommended:

"The Others" is a masterclass in atmospheric horror that relies on psychological tension rather than gore or jump scares. Director Alejandro Amenábar crafts a deeply unsettling mood through his use of shadow, sound, and suggestion. Nicole Kidman delivers a powerhouse performance as the increasingly frantic Grace, anchoring the film's emotional core. The movie's exploration of themes like faith, motherhood, and the afterlife adds depth to its ghost story framework. With its clever script, stunning cinematography, and unforgettable twist ending, "The Others" stands as one of the most intelligent and affecting supernatural thrillers of the 21st century.

6. 10 Trivia Facts:

  1. The film was shot entirely in chronological order to maintain the sense of mystery for the actors.

  2. Nicole Kidman accepted the role just four days before filming began.

  3. The movie was filmed in Spain, despite being set on the British island of Jersey.

  4. Director Alejandro Amenábar also composed the film's haunting score.

  5. The house used in the film is a 19th-century palace called Palacio de los Hornillos in Cantabria, Spain.

  6. "The Others" was released the same year as "The Sixth Sense," which has a similar twist ending.

  7. The film's twist ending was kept so secret that only a handful of crew members knew about it during production.

  8. Amenábar wrote the script in Spanish and had it translated to English for filming.

  9. The movie's tagline, "Sooner or later they will find you," takes on a completely different meaning after you've seen the film.

  10. "The Others" was the first English-language film to win Best Film at Spain's Goya Awards.

12. Shaun of the Dead

1. Movie Title: Shaun of the Dead

2. Year of Release: 2004

3. Cast and Director:

- Director: Edgar Wright

- Cast: Simon Pegg, Nick Frost, Kate Ashfield, Lucy Davis, Dylan Moran, Bill Nighy

4. Synopsis:

Shaun, an unmotivated electronics store employee, finds his mundane life in London upended when a zombie apocalypse breaks out. Initially oblivious to the chaos around him, Shaun eventually realizes the danger and hatches a plan to rescue his mother and ex-girlfriend, then hole up in his favorite pub, The Winchester. Along with his slacker best friend Ed, Shaun must navigate the zombie-infested streets of North London, facing both the undead and his own personal shortcomings. As the situation grows dire, Shaun is forced to step up and become the hero his friends and family need, all while trying to reconcile with his ex and mend his relationships.

5. Why This Movie Is Recommended:

"Shaun of the Dead" brilliantly blends horror and comedy, creating a unique "rom-zom-com" that pays homage to classic zombie films while carving out its own identity. Edgar Wright's kinetic directing style and clever visual gags perfectly complement the sharp, referential script co-written with Simon Pegg. The film's ability to balance genuine scares with laugh-out-loud humor and touching character moments is remarkable. It also offers a subtle critique of modern urban life, drawing parallels between the zombie hordes and the daily grind. With its quotable dialogue, memorable characters, and perfect balance of heart and humor, "Shaun of the Dead" is a standout in both the horror and comedy genres.

6. 10 Trivia Facts:

1. The film contains numerous references to George A. Romero's zombie films, and Romero was so impressed that he offered Simon Pegg and Edgar Wright cameo roles in "Land of the Dead."

2. The Zombies' movements were inspired by the way Simon Pegg's wife walks when she's in heels.

3. "Shaun of the Dead" is the first in Wright and Pegg's "Cornetto Trilogy," followed by "Hot Fuzz" and "The World's End."

4. The film features cameos from many British comedians, including Martin Freeman, Reece Shearsmith, and Matt Lucas.

5. The Z-Word is never mentioned in the film; instead, the zombies are referred to as "those dead people."

6. Edgar Wright and Simon Pegg wrote a 29-page script full of pop culture references just for the scene where Shaun flips through TV channels.

7. The Winchester Pub was actually a working pub in North London, which closed shortly after filming.

8. Nick Frost's character Ed is named after Eddie Hitler, his character in the sitcom "Bottom."

9. The film's working title was "Tea Time of the Dead."

10. In a nod to "Dawn of the Dead," the music playing in the Winchester as the zombies attack is the same as the music playing in the mall in Romero's film.

13. A Field in England

1. Movie Title: A Field in England

2. Year of Release: 2013

3. Cast and Director:

  - Director: Ben Wheatley

  - Cast: Reece Shearsmith, Michael Smiley, Julian Barratt, Peter Ferdinando, Richard Glover, Ryan Pope

4. Synopsis:

  Set during the English Civil War in the 17th century, "A Field in England" follows a small group of deserters who flee from a battle through an overgrown field. Among them is Whitehead, an alchemist's assistant searching for his master. The group is captured by O'Neil, a mysterious alchemist who forces them to help him search for a supposed treasure buried in the field. As they dig and consume hallucinogenic mushrooms, reality begins to warp around them. The characters experience increasingly bizarre and terrifying visions, blurring the lines between reality, madness, and the supernatural. The film culminates in a series of mind-bending sequences that challenge perceptions of time, space, and sanity.

5. Why This Movie Is Recommended:

  "A Field in England" is a bold, experimental take on historical horror that defies easy categorization. Director Ben Wheatley's unique vision combines elements of psychological horror, dark comedy, and psychedelia to create a truly singular viewing experience. The stark black-and-white cinematography and period-accurate dialogue lend an air of authenticity to the surreal proceedings. The film's exploration of themes like power, faith, and altered states of consciousness adds depth to its unsettling atmosphere. While not for everyone, those who appreciate challenging, avant-garde cinema will find "A Field in England" a mesmerizing and deeply unsettling journey into the dark heart of English folklore and history.

6. 10 Trivia Facts:

  1. The film was released simultaneously in cinemas, on DVD, on TV, and on Video on Demand - a first for a UK film.

  2. Director Ben Wheatley insisted on using authentic 17th-century language throughout the script.

  3. The entire movie was shot in just 12 days in a single field.

  4. The psychedelic sequences were created using practical effects rather than CGI.

  5. The film's score incorporates sounds recorded on location, including wind in the grass.

  6. Actor Michael Smiley learned to dowse for real as part of his preparation for the role of O'Neil.

  7. The movie was partly inspired by the experimental films of Kenneth Anger.

  8. Some scenes were shot at 50 frames per second to create a slightly off-kilter feel.

  9. The film's budget was so low that the cast and crew camped in the field during production.

  10. Director Ben Wheatley has said that the film is meant to be watched multiple times to uncover its layers of meaning.

14. Kill List

1. Movie Title: Kill List

2. Year of Release: 2011

3. Cast and Director:

  - Director: Ben Wheatley

  - Cast: Neil Maskell, Michael Smiley, MyAnna Buring, Emma Fryer

4. Synopsis:

"Kill List" follows Jay, a former soldier turned contract killer, who is persuaded by his old partner Gal to take on a new assignment after a traumatic job in Kiev left him shaken. Jay, along with Gal, accepts a three-person hit list from a mysterious client. As they carry out their grim task, things take an increasingly bizarre and unsettling turn. Each target thanks Jay before being killed, and strange symbols begin to appear. Jay's mental state deteriorates as the job progresses, and he becomes more brutal in his methods. The film builds to a shocking climax at a cult gathering, where the true nature of the assignment and Jay's role in it is revealed, leading to a horrifying conclusion that blends occult horror with psychological trauma.

5. Why This Movie Is Recommended:

"Kill List" is a masterful blend of crime thriller, psychological horror, and occult mystery that subverts audience expectations at every turn. Director Ben Wheatley crafts an atmosphere of creeping dread that builds to an unforgettable climax. The film's ambiguous narrative and shocking tonal shifts keep viewers off-balance, creating a deeply unsettling viewing experience. Strong performances, particularly from Neil Maskell as the increasingly unhinged Jay, ground the film's more outlandish elements in a gritty realism. "Kill List" offers a unique and disturbing take on the hitman genre, infusing it with elements of folk horror and domestic drama. Its final act is one of the most talked-about and controversial in modern British cinema.

6. 10 Trivia Facts:

  1. The film was partly inspired by director Ben Wheatley's recurring nightmares.

  2. Many scenes were improvised, with the actors only given a rough outline of the plot.

  3. The shocking tunnel sequence was filmed in a real derelict Victorian tunnel in Yorkshire.

  4. The cult members' masks were inspired by English folk traditions and pagan rituals.

  5. Wheatley deliberately withheld information from the actors to create genuine reactions of confusion and unease.

  6. The film's ambiguous ending has sparked numerous theories and interpretations among viewers.

  7. "Kill List" was made on a budget of only £500,000.

  8. The movie features several references to 1970s British folk horror films like "The Wicker Man."

  9. Wheatley has stated that the film is meant to be experienced rather than fully understood.

  10. The director included subliminal images and sounds throughout the film to create a sense of unease.

15. Dog Soldiers

1. Movie Title: Dog Soldiers

2. Year of Release: 2002

3. Cast and Director:

- Director: Neil Marshall

- Cast: Kevin McKidd, Sean Pertwee, Emma Cleasby, Liam Cunningham, Darren Morfitt

4. Synopsis:

A squad of British soldiers is dropped into the Scottish Highlands for a routine training exercise against a Special Forces unit. However, they soon discover the mutilated remains of the Special Forces team and find themselves hunted by a pack of vicious werewolves. Teaming up with a local zoologist, the soldiers take refuge in an isolated farmhouse and must fight for survival as night falls and the werewolves attack. As their numbers dwindle and tensions rise, they uncover a conspiracy involving their own military. The soldiers must use their wit, teamwork, and limited resources to outlast the night and fend off the relentless werewolf assault.

5. Why This Movie Is Recommended:

"Dog Soldiers" breathes new life into the werewolf subgenre by combining it with intense military action. Director Neil Marshall creates a perfect balance of horror and humor, with sharp dialogue and well-drawn characters that elevate it above typical monster fare. The film's practical effects and impressive werewolf designs add to its visceral impact, proving that low-budget filmmaking can still deliver high-quality scares. With its claustrophobic setting, relentless pacing, and clever nods to classic horror films, "Dog Soldiers" offers a thrilling and often darkly funny take on the werewolf myth. It stands as a modern cult classic that showcases the best of British horror-action cinema.

6. 10 Trivia Facts:

1. The film was shot in Luxembourg, despite being set in Scotland.

2. The werewolf costumes were designed by effects artist Bob Keen, known for his work on "Hellraiser."

3. Director Neil Marshall appears in a cameo as a dead soldier in the film.

4. The movie's working title was "Silver."

5. Many of the interior farmhouse scenes were shot on a sound stage in London.

6. The film contains numerous references to other werewolf movies, including "An American Werewolf in London."

7. Actor Kevin McKidd performed many of his own stunts in the film.

8. The werewolves were portrayed by dancers and movement specialists to achieve their agile, animalistic movements.

9. "Dog Soldiers" was Neil Marshall's directorial debut and was made on a budget of just £2 million.

10. The film's success led to plans for a sequel, though it has yet to materialize.

16. The Wickerman (1973)

1. Movie Title: The Wickerman

2. Year of Release: 1973

3. Cast and Director:

- Director: Robin Hardy

- Cast: Edward Woodward, Christopher Lee, Diane Cilento, Britt Ekland, Ingrid Pitt

4. Synopsis:

Sergeant Howie, a devout Christian police officer, travels to the remote Scottish island of Summerisle to investigate the disappearance of a young girl. Upon arrival, he finds the islanders unhelpful and evasive, practicing a form of Celtic paganism under the guidance of their leader, Lord Summerisle. As Howie delves deeper into the mystery, he uncovers disturbing rituals and practices that challenge his faith and morality. The investigation takes a sinister turn as he realizes the true nature of his presence on the island, leading to a shocking and unforgettable climax that has become one of the most iconic scenes in horror cinema.

5. Why This Movie Is Recommended:

"The Wickerman" is a masterpiece of folk horror that blends mystery, psychological tension, and pagan folklore into a uniquely unsettling experience. Its exploration of the clash between Christian and pagan beliefs creates a rich, thought-provoking narrative. The film's atmospheric setting, memorable performances, and haunting soundtrack contribute to a growing sense of dread that culminates in one of the most shocking endings in horror history. Its influence on the folk horror subgenre and British cinema, in general, is immeasurable, making it a must-see for any horror enthusiast.

6. 10 Trivia Facts:

1. Christopher Lee considered this his best film and worked on it for free.

2. The famous wicker man was over 60 feet tall and cost £3,000 to construct.

3. The film was partially inspired by David Pinner's 1967 novel "Ritual."

4. Britt Ekland's voice was dubbed in parts of the film, and a body double was used for her nude scene.

5. The movie was shot almost entirely on location in Scotland.

6. Original prints of the film were allegedly used as landfill for the M3 motorway.

7. Director Robin Hardy and screenwriter Anthony Shaffer researched actual pagan rituals for authenticity.

8. The film's original cut was 102 minutes long but was shortened to 87 minutes for its theatrical release.

9. "The Wickerman" was initially released as the B-movie in a double bill with "Don't Look Now."

10. Despite its cult status today, the film was a commercial failure upon its initial release.

17. Under the Skin

1. Movie Title: Under the Skin

2. Year of Release: 2013

3. Cast and Director:

- Director: Jonathan Glazer

- Cast: Scarlett Johansson, Adam Pearson, Michael Moreland, Jeremy McWilliams

4. Synopsis:

An otherworldly woman, portrayed by Scarlett Johansson, prowls the streets of Scotland in a white van, seducing lonely men and luring them to a mysterious black void where they are consumed. As she continues her predatory routine, she begins to experience curiosity and perhaps empathy for her human prey. Her growing awareness of her own body and the world around her leads to a series of encounters that challenge her mission and identity. The film follows her journey of self-discovery and the consequences of her actions, building to a haunting climax that questions the nature of humanity and alienation.

5. Why This Movie Is Recommended:

"Under the Skin" is a bold, visually striking film that defies easy categorization. Director Jonathan Glazer creates a unique blend of art house cinema and science fiction horror that's both beautiful and deeply unsettling. Scarlett Johansson delivers a mesmerizing, mostly silent performance that captures the alien nature of her character. The film's use of hidden cameras and non-professional actors in many scenes lends an eerie realism to the proceedings. With its haunting score, striking visuals, and thought-provoking themes about identity, gender, and what it means to be human, "Under the Skin" offers a truly singular and unforgettable viewing experience.

6. 10 Trivia Facts:

1. Many of the men in the film were not actors but real people filmed with hidden cameras, unaware they were in a movie.

2. Scarlett Johansson wore a dark wig and drove around Glasgow in a van to prepare for her role.

3. The film took over a decade to make, with multiple rewrites and changes in cast and crew.

4. The alien liquid scenes were created using a mixture of lubricant and food coloring.

5. Mica Levi's haunting score was her first for a feature film.

6. The film is loosely based on Michel Faber's novel of the same name.

7. Glazer used thermal cameras for some scenes to create an otherworldly effect.

8. The beach scene, one of the most disturbing in the film, was shot with real families enjoying a day out.

9. Johansson performed many of her own driving stunts in the film.

10. The film's ending was shot in the Scottish Highlands in challenging weather conditions.

18. The Innocents (1961)

1. Movie Title: The Innocents

2. Year of Release: 1961

3. Cast and Director:

- Director: Jack Clayton

- Cast: Deborah Kerr, Michael Redgrave, Peter Wyngarde, Megs Jenkins, Martin Stephens, Pamela Franklin

4. Synopsis:

Based on Henry James's novella "The Turn of the Screw," "The Innocents" follows Miss Giddens, a naive governess who takes charge of two orphaned children, Miles and Flora, at a remote English country estate. As she settles into her new role, Miss Giddens becomes convinced that the grounds are haunted by the ghosts of two former employees: the previous governess, Miss Jessel, and the valet, Peter Quint. She believes these malevolent spirits are exerting a corrupting influence on the children. As Miss Giddens attempts to protect her charges, the line between reality and imagination blurs, leaving both the characters and the audience to question whether the haunting is real or a product of the governess's increasingly fragile psyche.

5. Why This Movie Is Recommended:

"The Innocents" is a masterpiece of psychological horror that relies on atmosphere and suggestion rather than overt scares. Director Jack Clayton's use of deep focus cinematography and unsettling sound design creates a pervasive sense of unease. Deborah Kerr's nuanced performance as Miss Giddens perfectly captures the character's descent into paranoia. The film's exploration of sexual repression, childhood corruption, and the nature of evil adds layers of complexity to its ghost story framework. With its ambiguous narrative and haunting imagery, "The Innocents" remains one of the most sophisticated and chilling ghost stories in cinema history.

6. 10 Trivia Facts:

1. The screenplay was co-written by Truman Capote, who added more overt sexual undertones to the story.

2. The film's title comes from William Archibald's stage adaptation of Henry James's novella.

3. Director Jack Clayton insisted on shooting in CinemaScope to capture the vastness and isolation of the estate.

4. Deborah Kerr wore padded clothing to make her appear more physically and sexually repressed.

5. The film's iconic theme song, "O Willow Waly," was specially composed for the movie.

6. Martin Stephens, who played Miles, also starred in another classic British horror film, "Village of the Damned."

7. The movie was shot entirely in sequence to help build tension and character development.

8. Cinematographer Freddie Francis used candles and natural light extensively to create the film's eerie atmosphere.

9. The film's ambiguous ending has been the subject of critical debate for decades.

10. "The Innocents" was selected by Martin Scorsese for his list of the 11 scariest horror films of all time.

19. Hellbound: Hellraiser II

1. Movie Title: Hellbound: Hellraiser II

2. Year of Release: 1988

3. Cast and Director:

- Director: Tony Randel

- Cast: Clare Higgins, Ashley Laurence, Kenneth Cranham, Imogen Boorman, Doug Bradley

4. Synopsis:

Picking up shortly after the events of the first film, "Hellbound: Hellraiser II" follows Kirsty Cotton as she's admitted to a psychiatric hospital run by the sinister Dr. Channard. Unbeknownst to Kirsty, Channard is obsessed with the Lament Configuration puzzle box and the realm it opens to. He resurrects Julia, Kirsty's evil stepmother, using the bloody mattress she died on. Together, they plan to access the realm of the Cenobites, led by the iconic Pinhead. Kirsty, along with a mute patient named Tiffany, must navigate the nightmarish landscape of Hell to stop Channard and save her father's soul. The film delves deeper into the mythology of the Cenobites and the nature of their hellish dimension, expanding the scope of the original in grotesque and imaginative ways.

5. Why This Movie Is Recommended:

"Hellbound: Hellraiser II" is a rare sequel that expands and enriches the mythology of its predecessor. It takes the visceral body horror and sadomasochistic themes of the original and amplifies them, creating a surreal and nightmarish vision of Hell. The film's exploration of the Cenobite realm is visually stunning and deeply unsettling, with practical effects that still impress today. It delves deeper into the characters' psyches, particularly Kirsty's, while introducing compelling new elements to the story. For fans of extreme horror and those fascinated by intricate dark fantasies, "Hellbound" offers a unique and unforgettable journey into the heart of otherworldly terror.

6. 10 Trivia Facts:

1. Clive Barker, creator of the Hellraiser series, wrote the story for this sequel but didn't direct it.

2. The film was shot in just eight weeks.

3. Doug Bradley's Pinhead has significantly more dialogue in this film compared to the original.

4. The actress who played Julia had to be convinced to return, as she initially didn't want to do a horror sequel.

5. The Leviathan, the god of Hell, was inspired by the Monolith from "2001: A Space Odyssey."

6. Kenneth Cranham, who played Dr. Channard, was not told about the extent of the prosthetics he would have to wear.

7. The film's budget was triple that of the original Hellraiser.

8. Some of the film's goriest scenes had to be cut to avoid an X rating in the US.

9. The Channard Cenobite's weapons were operated by puppeteers hiding behind the actor.

10. Despite mixed reviews upon release, the film has since gained a strong cult following.

20. 28 Weeks Later

1. Movie Title: 28 Weeks Later

2. Year of Release: 2007

3. Cast and Director:

- Director: Juan Carlos Fresnadillo

- Cast: Robert Carlyle, Rose Byrne, Jeremy Renner, Harold Perrineau, Catherine McCormack, Imogen Poots, Mackintosh Muggleton

4. Synopsis:

Set six months after the events of "28 Days Later," the sequel begins as NATO forces declare Britain safe from the Rage virus. The US Army oversees the repatriation process in a small, secured area of London. Don, a survivor who abandoned his wife during the initial outbreak, is reunited with his children who were out of the country. However, when his wife is found alive and brought to the safe zone, it triggers a new outbreak of the Rage virus. As the infection spreads rapidly through the supposed safe zone, a small group of survivors, including Don's children and a few military personnel, must navigate the chaos of London to escape. The film explores themes of guilt, family, and the breakdown of social order in the face of overwhelming crisis.

5. Why This Movie Is Recommended:

"28 Weeks Later" successfully builds on the intense, gritty world established in the first film while carving out its own identity. Director Juan Carlos Fresnadillo maintains the frenetic energy and visceral horror of the original while expanding the scope to create a more action-packed, but equally terrifying experience. The film's exploration of family dynamics and moral choices under extreme circumstances adds depth to the zombie-like horror. With its pulse-pounding sequences, strong performances, and bleak outlook on human nature, "28 Weeks Later" stands as one of the strongest entries in the zombie subgenre. It's a worthy sequel that in some ways surpasses its predecessor in terms of scale and intensity.

6. 10 Trivia Facts:

1. Danny Boyle, director of "28 Days Later," served as an executive producer and directed a few second unit scenes.

2. The film's opening sequence was shot in a single take.

3. Real British Army soldiers were used as extras in many scenes.

4. The production team had to get permission from the London Port Authority to film helicopter scenes over the Thames.

5. The firebombing scenes were filmed at Canary Wharf, with special permission from the business district.

6. Robert Carlyle's character was originally supposed to die in the opening sequence.

7. The film features early performances from future stars Jeremy Renner and Imogen Poots.

8. The movie was shot on 35mm film, unlike its predecessor which used digital video.

9. The infected in this film were instructed to move more aggressively than in the first movie.

10. A third film in the series, tentatively titled "28 Months Later," has been discussed but never materialized.

Germany

1. Nosferatu

1. Movie Title: Nosferatu, eine Symphonie des Grauens (Nosferatu: A Symphony of Horror)

2. Year of Release: 1922

3. Cast and Director:

  - Director: F.W. Murnau

  - Cast: Max Schreck, Gustav von Wangenheim, Greta Schröder

4. Synopsis:

Nosferatu is a silent German Expressionist horror film that loosely adapts Bram Stoker's "Dracula." The story follows Thomas Hutter, a real estate agent who travels to Transylvania to meet Count Orlok, a mysterious nobleman interested in purchasing property in Hutter's hometown. Hutter soon discovers Orlok is a vampire and barely escapes with his life. Orlok, obsessed with Hutter's wife Ellen, follows him back to Germany, bringing plague and death. As the town succumbs to the vampire's influence, Ellen realizes she must sacrifice herself to destroy the monster and save her community.

5. Why This Movie Is Recommended:

Nosferatu is a cornerstone of horror cinema, renowned for its haunting visuals and the unforgettable performance of Max Schreck as Count Orlok. The film's use of shadows, innovative special effects, and eerie atmosphere set a standard for vampire movies that persists to this day. Its exploration of themes like plague and societal decay gives it a depth that transcends its genre. As one of the earliest and most influential horror films, Nosferatu is essential viewing for any fan of the genre or student of film history.

6. 10 Trivia Facts:

  1. The film was almost lost forever due to a copyright lawsuit from Bram Stoker's estate.

  2. Max Schreck's unsettling performance led to rumors that he was an actual vampire.

  3. The film used real locations in Slovakia and Poland for Orlok's castle scenes.

  4. Nosferatu was the only production of Prana Film, which declared bankruptcy after the lawsuit.

  5. The film's iconic poster was designed by Albin Grau, who was also the art director and co-producer.

  6. Many of the film's exterior shots were filmed in Lübeck, Germany.

  7. The movie was remade in 1979 by Werner Herzog, starring Klaus Kinski.

  8. The film's success helped establish the vampire as a major horror movie monster.

  9. Nosferatu was one of the first films to use stop-motion animation for special effects.

  10. The film's score, composed by Hans Erdmann, is considered one of the first feature film scores.

2. Das Cabinet des Dr. Caligari (The Cabinet of Dr. Caligari)

1. Movie Title: Das Cabinet des Dr. Caligari (The Cabinet of Dr. Caligari)

2. Year of Release: 1920

3. Cast and Director:

  - Director: Robert Wiene

  - Cast: Werner Krauss, Conrad Veidt, Friedrich Fehér, Lil Dagover

4. Synopsis:

The Cabinet of Dr. Caligari tells the story of Francis, who recounts a series of murders in his town. The tale revolves around Dr. Caligari, a mysterious showman who arrives at a local fair with a somnambulist named Cesare, whom he keeps in a cabinet. Caligari claims Cesare can predict the future, but soon, Cesare's predictions of death start coming true. As Francis investigates, he uncovers a dark conspiracy involving Caligari and the sleepwalking Cesare. The film's twist ending calls into question the entire narrative, blurring the line between reality and madness.

5. Why This Movie Is Recommended:

The Cabinet of Dr. Caligari is a masterpiece of German Expressionist cinema and a landmark in horror film history. Its distorted, dreamlike sets and unconventional visual style create a sense of unease that perfectly mirrors the story's themes of madness and control. The film's exploration of authority, insanity, and the nature of reality continues to resonate with modern audiences. Its influence on horror, film noir, and even modern psychological thrillers is immeasurable, making it an essential watch for any serious film enthusiast or horror fan.

6. 10 Trivia Facts:

  1. The film's twist ending was added by producers against the writers' wishes.

  2. The movie's sets were painted on canvas, creating its distinctive, unreal look.

  3. It's considered the first true horror film and a precursor to the psychological thriller genre.

  4. Conrad Veidt, who played Cesare, later portrayed Major Strasser in "Casablanca."

  5. The film's style heavily influenced Tim Burton, particularly in "Edward Scissorhands" and "The Nightmare Before Christmas."

  6. The movie was banned in some countries due to fears it might influence fragile minds.

  7. The character of Dr. Caligari inspired the look of Batman's nemesis, The Joker.

  8. The film was shot entirely indoors on a tight budget.

  9. It was one of the first films to use a frame narrative structure.

  10. The movie's premiere was held in the Marmorhaus cinema in Berlin, which still exists today.

3. Vampyr

1. Movie Title: Vampyr

2. Year of Release: 1932

3. Cast and Director:

  - Director: Carl Theodor Dreyer

  - Cast: Julian West (Nicolas de Gunzburg), Maurice Schutz, Rena Mandel, Sybille Schmitz

4. Synopsis:

Vampyr follows Allan Gray, a student of the occult who arrives at a small inn in the village of Courtempierre. He experiences strange visions and encounters with shadows, leading him to investigate the supernatural occurrences in the area. Gray discovers an old castle inhabited by a lord whose daughter is gravely ill, seemingly under the influence of a vampire. As he delves deeper into the mystery, Gray uncovers a web of vampirism and dark magic. The film blends reality and dreams, creating a surreal atmosphere as Gray fights to save the lord's daughter and defeat the forces of evil.

5. Why This Movie Is Recommended:

Vampyr is a unique and influential entry in early horror cinema, notable for its dreamlike quality and innovative cinematography. Director Carl Theodor Dreyer's use of soft focus, shadows, and unconventional camera angles creates a haunting, otherworldly atmosphere that blurs the line between reality and nightmare. The film's subtle approach to horror, relying more on mood and suggestion than explicit scares, set a new standard for psychological horror. Its influence can be seen in later works of surrealist cinema and atmospheric horror films, making it a must-watch for fans of the genre and film history enthusiasts.

6. 10 Trivia Facts:

1. The lead actor, Julian West, was actually Baron Nicolas de Gunzburg, who financed the film.

2. Vampyr was Dreyer's first sound film, though it uses minimal dialogue.

3. The movie was shot in three language versions: English, French, and German.

4. Many scenes were filmed through a piece of gauze to create the film's distinctive hazy look.

5. The movie is loosely based on elements from J. Sheridan Le Fanu's "In a Glass Darkly."

6. Dreyer used primarily nonprofessional actors for the film.

7. The famous sequence of a man seeing himself in a coffin was achieved using a transparent bottom.

8. The film was a commercial failure upon release but has since been recognized as a classic.

9. Vampyr was shot entirely on location in France, adding to its authentic, eerie atmosphere.

10. The movie's original screenplay was much longer, but Dreyer cut it significantly during filming.

4. Der Golem, wie er in die Welt kam (The Golem: How He Came into the World)

1. Movie Title: Der Golem, wie er in die Welt kam (The Golem: How He Came into the World)

2. Year of Release: 1920

3. Cast and Director:

- Directors: Paul Wegener, Carl Boese

- Cast: Paul Wegener, Albert Steinrück, Lyda Salmonova, Ernst Deutsch

4. Synopsis:

Set in 16th-century Prague, the film tells the story of Rabbi Loew, who creates a giant golem out of clay to protect the Jewish community from persecution. Using ancient mystical powers, he brings the golem to life. Initially, the creature serves its purpose, averting a decree that would have expelled the Jews from the city. However, as the golem grows stronger, it becomes harder to control. When the Rabbi's assistant animates the golem for selfish reasons, it turns violent and rampages through the ghetto. The film culminates in a tense struggle to stop the golem before it destroys everything in its path, exploring themes of creation, power, and the consequences of playing God.

5. Why This Movie Is Recommended:

"The Golem" is a landmark of German Expressionist cinema and early horror. Its blend of Jewish mysticism, gothic atmosphere, and groundbreaking special effects create a unique and captivating viewing experience. The film's exploration of the dangers of unchecked power and the moral responsibilities of scientific advancement remains relevant today. Paul Wegener's portrayal of the golem is both terrifying and sympathetic, setting a standard for "monster" characters in future films. As a precursor to many classic monster movies, including "Frankenstein," "The Golem" is essential viewing for any horror or film history enthusiast.

6. 10 Trivia Facts:

1. This is actually the third "Golem" film made by Paul Wegener, but the only one to survive mostly intact.

2. The film's set design was inspired by medieval Prague, created by architect Hans Poelzig.

3. The golem costume, designed by Wegener himself, weighed over 40 pounds.

4. "The Golem" is considered one of the earliest examples of the "created monster" genre in film.

5. The movie's special effects, including the creation of the golem, were groundbreaking for their time.

6. Wegener based the story loosely on Gustav Meyrink's 1915 novel "Der Golem."

7. The film influenced later monster movies, particularly James Whale's 1931 "Frankenstein."

8. Despite its dark themes, the movie was marketed as suitable for children in some areas.

9. The film uses color tinting in certain scenes to enhance the mood and atmosphere.

10. "The Golem" was one of the first films to be distributed internationally by Hollywood studios.

5. M

1. Movie Title: M

2. Year of Release: 1931

3. Cast and Director:

  - Director: Fritz Lang

  - Cast: Peter Lorre, Otto Wernicke, Gustaf Gründgens

4. Synopsis:

"M" tells the story of a city gripped by fear as a serial killer preys on children. As the police intensify their search, the criminal underworld, feeling the pressure of increased law enforcement activity, decides to track down the killer themselves. The film follows both the police investigation and the criminals' hunt, creating a tense, psychological thriller. Peter Lorre plays Hans Beckert, the disturbed killer who is eventually caught and put on trial by a kangaroo court of criminals. The movie explores themes of justice, mob mentality, and the nature of evil, culminating in a powerful climax that questions societal responsibility for creating "monsters."

5. Why This Movie Is Recommended:

"M" is a masterpiece of early sound cinema that seamlessly blends elements of horror, thriller, and film noir. Fritz Lang's innovative use of sound, including the killer's haunting whistle, creates an atmosphere of constant unease. The film's exploration of the psychology of a serial killer was groundbreaking for its time and continues to influence modern thrillers. Peter Lorre's nuanced performance as the troubled Beckert is unforgettable, eliciting both revulsion and sympathy. "M" not only serves as a gripping crime drama but also as a poignant social commentary, making it a must-watch for cinephiles and horror fans alike.

6. 10 Trivia Facts:

1. "M" was Fritz Lang's first sound film and is considered by many to be his masterpiece.

2. The movie was inspired by the real-life case of serial killer Peter Kürten, the "Vampire of Düsseldorf."

3. Peter Lorre's performance in "M" launched his international career.

4. The letter "M" is never explicitly explained in the film but is believed to stand for "Mörder" (murderer).

5. Lang used actual criminals as extras in some scenes to add authenticity.

6. The film's famous whistling theme is "In the Hall of the Mountain King" by Edvard Grieg.

7. "M" was one of the first films to use a leitmotif for a character.

8. The movie was banned by the Nazis shortly after its release.

9. Lang claimed that "M" was his favorite of all his films.

10. The film's critique of mob justice and capital punishment was highly controversial at the time of its release.

6. Nekromantik

1. Movie Title: Nekromantik

2. Year of Release: 1987

3. Cast and Director:

  - Director: Jörg Buttgereit

  - Cast: Bernd Daktari Lorenz, Beatrice Manowski, Harald Lundt

4. Synopsis:

Nekromantik follows Rob, a street cleaner working for a company that removes corpses from accident scenes. Rob's girlfriend Betty shares his fascination with death, and together they indulge in necrophilic acts. Their relationship takes a dark turn when Rob brings home a decomposing corpse, which becomes a third party in their love life. As Betty becomes more attached to the corpse, Rob's life spirals out of control. When Betty leaves him, taking the corpse, Rob descends into a series of increasingly disturbing and violent acts, culminating in a shocking and controversial finale that blurs the line between life, death, and sexual ecstasy.

5. Why This Movie Is Recommended:

Nekromantik is not for the faint of heart, but it's a significant film in the evolution of extreme cinema. Buttgereit's unflinching exploration of taboo subjects pushes the boundaries of what's acceptable in film. Despite its shocking content, the movie offers a thought-provoking commentary on society's relationship with death and sexuality. Its low-budget, guerrilla-style filmmaking and provocative themes have made it a cult classic, influencing later transgressive filmmakers. For those interested in the outer limits of horror cinema and societal taboos, Nekromantik is an essential, if challenging, watch.

6. 10 Trivia Facts:

  1. The film was banned in several countries upon release and remains prohibited in some.

  2. Director Jörg Buttgereit used animal organs from a local butcher for the gore effects.

  3. The movie was shot on 8mm film, contributing to its gritty, realistic look.

  4. Nekromantik's controversial nature led to it being distributed underground for many years.

  5. The film's shocking climax was achieved using clever editing and practical effects.

  6. Buttgereit faced legal troubles in Germany due to the film's content.

  7. The movie's synthesizer score, composed by Daktari Lorenz, has gained a cult following.

  8. Nekromantik spawned a sequel in 1991, also directed by Buttgereit.

  9. The film was partially funded by Buttgereit's job at a local cinema.

  10. Despite its reputation, Nekromantik contains more dark humor than many viewers expect.

7. Der Student von Prag (The Student of Prague)

1. Movie Title: Der Student von Prag (The Student of Prague)

2. Year of Release: 1913

3. Cast and Director:

- Director: Stellan Rye

- Cast: Paul Wegener, John Gottowt, Grete Berger

4. Synopsis:

Set in 19th century Prague, the film tells the story of Balduin, a poor student who makes a Faustian bargain with the sorcerer Scapinelli. In exchange for 100,000 gold pieces and the chance to woo a countess, Balduin sells his reflection to Scapinelli. However, the reflection becomes an independent entity, a doppelgänger that begins to torment Balduin and sabotage his life. As Balduin's sanity unravels, he finds himself in a deadly game of cat and mouse with his own image. The film explores themes of identity, ambition, and the consequences of tampering with the natural order, building to a climactic confrontation between Balduin and his mirror self.

5. Why This Movie Is Recommended:

"Der Student von Prag" is a landmark in early cinema and German Expressionism. As one of the first feature-length horror films, it laid the groundwork for many tropes and themes that would become staples of the genre. The film's exploration of the doppelgänger concept is both psychologically complex and visually striking, especially given the technical limitations of the time. Paul Wegener's dual performance as Balduin and his reflection is particularly noteworthy. For film historians and horror enthusiasts, this movie offers a fascinating glimpse into the origins of horror cinema and the enduring power of German Expressionism.

6. 10 Trivia Facts:

1. This was one of the first films to use the doppelgänger motif, which became a staple in horror.

2. The movie was remade in 1926 and 1935, with the 1926 version also starring Paul Wegener.

3. It's considered one of the earliest examples of art cinema in Germany.

4. The film's script was written by Hanns Heinz Ewers, a noted author of fantasy and horror literature.

5. "Der Student von Prag" was one of the first films to use double exposure for special effects.

6. The movie was partially shot on location in Prague, adding to its authentic atmosphere.

7. At the time of its release, it was one of the longest German films ever made.

8. The film's success helped establish Paul Wegener as a major figure in early German cinema.

9. Its themes and visual style heavily influenced later German Expressionist classics like "The Cabinet of Dr. Caligari."

10. The movie draws inspiration from works by Edgar Allan Poe and E.T.A. Hoffmann.

8. Wir sind die Nacht (We Are the Night)

1. Movie Title: Wir sind die Nacht (We Are the Night)

2. Year of Release: 2010

3. Cast and Director:

- Director: Dennis Gansel

- Cast: Karoline Herfurth, Nina Hoss, Jennifer Ulrich, Anna Fischer

4. Synopsis:

"We Are the Night" follows Lena, a young petty thief in Berlin who catches the eye of Louise, the leader of a trio of female vampires. Louise transforms Lena into a vampire, introducing her to a world of luxury, power, and immortality. As Lena struggles to adapt to her new existence, she finds herself torn between her growing attraction to Tom, a police detective investigating a string of mysterious deaths, and her loyalty to her new vampire family. The film explores themes of female empowerment, the price of immortality, and the conflict between human morality and vampire nature. As the body count rises and the police close in, Lena must decide where her true allegiance lies.

5. Why This Movie Is Recommended:

"We Are the Night" offers a fresh, stylish take on vampire lore, set against the vibrant backdrop of modern Berlin. The film stands out for its strong female ensemble cast and its exploration of vampirism as a form of liberation and empowerment. Gansel's direction brings a sleek, almost music video-like quality to the action sequences, while still maintaining the dark, seductive atmosphere essential to vampire films. The movie balances horror elements with character drama and social commentary, making it appealing to both genre fans and casual viewers. Its unique perspective on vampire mythology and contemporary setting make it a noteworthy entry in 21st-century German horror cinema.

6. 10 Trivia Facts:

1. The film was in development for nearly a decade before finally being produced.

2. Director Dennis Gansel was inspired by the vampire nightclub scene in "Blade."

3. The movie features an almost exclusively female vampire cast, a rarity in the genre.

4. Many of the film's action sequences were shot in the abandoned Spreepark amusement park.

5. The vampires' inability to see their reflection was achieved through a combination of practical effects and CGI.

6. "We Are the Night" was one of the most expensive German productions of 2010.

7. The film's soundtrack features a mix of German and international electronic music artists.

8. Karoline Herfurth, who plays Lena, also appeared in the vampire film "Perfume: The Story of a Murderer."

9. The movie references several classic vampire films, including "The Hunger" and "Interview with the Vampire."

10. Despite its modern setting, the film incorporates several traditional vampire myths and weaknesses.

9. Goodnight Mommy (Ich seh, Ich seh)

1. Movie Title: Goodnight Mommy (Ich seh, Ich seh)

2. Year of Release: 2014

3. Cast and Director:

  - Directors: Veronika Franz, Severin Fiala

  - Cast: Susanne Wuest, Elias Schwarz, Lukas Schwarz

4. Synopsis:

Set in an isolated modern home, "Goodnight Mommy" follows twin boys, Elias and Lukas, who become suspicious of their mother when she returns home after facial reconstructive surgery. Her face covered in bandages and her behavior markedly changed, the boys begin to doubt her identity. As the mother's strict new house rules and seemingly cruel behavior escalate, the twins become convinced that this woman is an impostor. They decide to take matters into their own hands, leading to a series of increasingly disturbing confrontations. The film builds tension through its ambiguous narrative, leaving the audience questioning the reality of the situation until its shocking climax.

5. Why This Movie Is Recommended:

"Goodnight Mommy" is a masterclass in psychological horror, using its minimalist setting and small cast to create an atmosphere of claustrophobic dread. The film's crisp, sterile visuals contrast sharply with the psychological messiness of its story, creating a uniquely unsettling viewing experience. Franz and Fiala's direction keeps the audience off-balance, cleverly playing with perspective and unreliable narrators. The performances, particularly from the young twins, are exceptional, adding to the film's realism and horror. For fans of slow-burn psychological thrillers and art-house horror, "Goodnight Mommy" offers a deeply disturbing and thought-provoking experience that lingers long after viewing.

6. 10 Trivia Facts:

1. The film was Austria's submission for the Best Foreign Language Film at the 88th Academy Awards.

2. Directors Franz and Fiala are aunt and nephew, adding an interesting dynamic to their exploration of family horror.

3. The movie was shot chronologically to help the young actors understand the story's progression.

4. Many scenes were improvised, with the directors giving the actors general directions rather than specific lines.

5. The film's original German title, "Ich seh, Ich seh," translates to "I see, I see," referencing a children's game.

6. The house used in the film was actually a set built specifically for the movie.

7. "Goodnight Mommy" was remade as an English-language film in 2022, starring Naomi Watts.

8. The directors were inspired by Michael Haneke's style of creating tension through long, static shots.

9. The film's ambiguous ending has sparked numerous fan theories and interpretations.

10. Despite its disturbing content, the movie uses very little on-screen violence, relying instead on psychological horror.

10. Der Name der Rose (The Name of the Rose)

1. Movie Title: Der Name der Rose (The Name of the Rose)

2. Year of Release: 1986

3. Cast and Director:

- Director: Jean-Jacques Annaud

- Cast: Sean Connery, Christian Slater, F. Murray Abraham, Ron Perlman

4. Synopsis:

Set in a 14th-century Italian monastery, "The Name of the Rose" follows William of Baskerville, a Franciscan friar, and his novice Adso as they arrive to participate in a theological debate. Their visit coincides with a series of mysterious deaths among the monks. As William investigates, he uncovers a complex web of secrets, forbidden knowledge, and political intrigue centered around the monastery's vast library. The investigation is complicated by the arrival of Bernardo Gui, a ruthless inquisitor determined to root out heresy. As the body count rises and tensions escalate, William races to solve the murders and protect the library's secrets, leading to a climactic confrontation that threatens the very foundations of medieval Christian society.

5. Why This Movie Is Recommended:

While primarily a historical mystery, "The Name of the Rose" incorporates strong elements of Gothic horror that make it a unique entry in the genre. The film's atmospheric depiction of medieval monastic life, complete with its superstitions and power struggles, creates a palpable sense of dread and claustrophobia. Annaud's direction brings Umberto Eco's complex novel to life with stunning visuals and a tangible sense of time and place. The movie's exploration of the conflict between reason and faith, and the horror that can arise from dogmatism and the suppression of knowledge, adds depth to its more conventional mystery elements. For viewers interested in historical settings, complex mysteries, and the darker aspects of religious history, "The Name of the Rose" offers a rich and rewarding experience.

6. 10 Trivia Facts:

1. The film is based on Umberto Eco's bestselling novel of the same name.

2. The massive library set was inspired by M.C. Escher's artwork.

3. Sean Connery learned to write with a quill pen for his role as William of Baskerville.

4. The movie's monastery was actually a full-scale exterior set built near Rome.

5. Christian Slater was only 15 years old when filming began.

6. The film's dialogue is a mix of Latin, Italian, and English to create an authentic medieval atmosphere.

7. Ron Perlman's character, Salvatore, speaks a made-up language combining Latin, Italian, German, and English.

8. The elaborate makeup for some characters took up to five hours to apply.

9. Despite being set in Italy, much of the film was shot in Germany.

10. Umberto Eco, the novel's author, was initially skeptical about the film adaptation but later praised it.

11. Angst (Fear)

1. Movie Title: Angst (Fear)

2. Year of Release: 1983

3. Cast and Director:

 - Director: Gerald Kargl

 - Cast: Erwin Leder, Robert Hunger-Bühler, Silvia Rabenreither

4. Synopsis:

"Angst" follows a psychopath who is released from prison after serving a 10-year sentence for murder. Immediately upon release, he begins to plan his next killing spree. The film takes a deeply unsettling dive into the mind of the killer as he breaks into a family home and terrorizes its inhabitants. Through a combination of voice-over narration and visceral, unflinching visuals, the audience is forced to experience the events from the killer's perspective. The movie explores the nature of violence, mental illness, and the failure of the justice system to rehabilitate offenders, all while maintaining a relentless atmosphere of dread and tension.

5. Why This Movie Is Recommended:

"Angst" is a harrowing and intense exploration of psychopathy that pushes the boundaries of the horror genre. Kargl's innovative cinematography, including the use of bodycam-style shots decades before they became common, creates a uniquely immersive and disturbing experience. The film's unflinching portrayal of violence and its psychological effects is not for the faint of heart, but it offers a powerful and thought-provoking examination of the nature of evil. For those interested in psychological horror and the darker aspects of human nature, "Angst" is a landmark film that continues to influence filmmakers today.

6. 10 Trivia Facts:

1. The film was banned in several countries due to its graphic content.

2. "Angst" was inspired by the real-life case of mass murderer Werner Kniesek.

3. Gaspar Noé cites "Angst" as a major influence on his filmmaking style.

4. The movie uses a custom-made camera rig to achieve its unique, floating point-of-view shots.

5. Lead actor Erwin Leder went on a strict diet to achieve the gaunt look of the killer.

6. The film's score was composed by Klaus Schulze, a pioneer of electronic music.

7. "Angst" was Gerald Kargl's only feature film as a director.

8. The movie was shot in just 24 days.

9. For years, "Angst" was only available through underground distribution channels.

10. The film features minimal dialogue, relying heavily on visual storytelling and voice-over narration.

12. Anatomy (Anatomie)

1. Movie Title: Anatomy (Anatomie)

2. Year of Release: 2000

3. Cast and Director:

- Director: Stefan Ruzowitzky

- Cast: Franka Potente, Benno Fürmann, Anna Loos

4. Synopsis:

"Anatomy" follows Paula Henning, a talented medical student who wins a prestigious scholarship to a renowned anatomy program in Heidelberg. However, she soon discovers that the school harbors a dark secret: an underground society of doctors and students who perform illegal experiments on living subjects. As Paula delves deeper into the conspiracy, she uncovers a history of unethical practices and finds herself in increasing danger. The film blends elements of medical horror with a taut thriller plot, exploring themes of scientific ethics, ambition, and the abuse of power. Paula must use her medical knowledge and wits to survive and expose the truth before she becomes the next victim.

5. Why This Movie Is Recommended:

"Anatomy" stands out as a unique entry in the German horror genre, combining elements of body horror, medical thriller, and traditional slasher films. The movie's sterile hospital setting provides a chilling backdrop for its gruesome events, subverting the notion of medical professionals as healers. Ruzowitzky's direction keeps the tension high throughout, while Franka Potente delivers a strong performance as the determined protagonist. The film's exploration of medical ethics and the potential dark side of scientific advancement adds depth to its horror elements. For fans of medical thrillers and those interested in a distinctly German take on the horror genre, "Anatomy" offers a suspenseful and thought-provoking experience.

6. 10 Trivia Facts:

1. The film was a major box office success in Germany, spawning a sequel in 2003.

2. Many of the anatomical specimens shown in the film are real, borrowed from medical schools.

3. Director Stefan Ruzowitzky went on to win an Oscar for his 2007 film "The Counterfeiters."

4. The movie features early career performances from several actors who became major stars in German cinema.

5. "Anatomy" was one of the first German horror films to gain significant international distribution in the 2000s.

6. The film's success helped revitalize the German horror genre in the early 21st century.

7. Some medical professionals criticized the film for its portrayal of anatomy studies.

8. The movie features a cameo from German punk rock musician Bela B.

9. "Anatomy" was partially inspired by real-life scandals involving unethical medical practices.

10. The film's special effects were groundbreaking for German cinema at the time.

13. Possession

1. Movie Title: Possession

2. Year of Release: 1981

3. Cast and Director:

 - Director: Andrzej Żuławski

 - Cast: Isabelle Adjani, Sam Neill, Heinz Bennent, Margit Carstensen

4. Synopsis:

   Set in Cold War-era Berlin, "Possession" follows the disintegration of the marriage between Anna and Mark. As Mark returns from a mysterious assignment, he finds Anna wanting a divorce. What begins as a domestic drama quickly spirals into a nightmarish descent into madness, violence, and the supernatural. Anna's behavior becomes increasingly erratic and horrifying, involving self-harm, infidelity, and possible murder. As Mark investigates, he uncovers a terrifying secret involving Anna and a monstrous, tentacled creature. The film blends psychological horror, body horror, and political allegory, creating a surreal and disturbing exploration of marital breakdown, identity, and societal collapse.

5. Why This Movie Is Recommended:

   "Possession" is a unique and unforgettable entry in the horror genre, defying easy categorization. Żuławski's direction creates a fever dream of a film, with frantic camerawork and intense performances that keep viewers off-balance. Isabelle Adjani's tour-de-force performance, particularly in the infamous subway scene, is both mesmerizing and deeply unsettling. The film's ability to blend personal, political, and cosmic horror creates a rich tapestry of meaning that rewards multiple viewings. While not for all tastes due to its extreme nature and ambiguous narrative, "Possession" is a must-see for fans of avant-garde cinema and those seeking horror that challenges both emotionally and intellectually.

6. 10 Trivia Facts:

   1. Isabelle Adjani won the Best Actress award at the Cannes Film Festival for her role.

   2. The film was banned in the UK as part of the "video nasty" panic and wasn't available uncut until 1999.

   3. The creature in the film was designed by Carlo Rambaldi, known for his work on "E.T." and "Alien."

   4. Director Żuławski wrote the script while going through a difficult divorce.

   5. The film was shot entirely on location in Berlin, often near the Berlin Wall.

   6. "Possession" was made as a French-German co-production to secure funding.

   7. Sam Neill learned to speak German for his role, though most of his lines are in English.

   8. The movie's themes were partially inspired by the political climate of Poland in the early 1980s.

   9. Żuławski claimed that several crew members quit during filming due to the intense nature of the scenes.

   10. Despite its initial controversial reception, "Possession" has become a cult classic and is now considered a masterpiece of horror cinema.

14. Der Himmel über Berlin (Wings of Desire)

1. Movie Title: Der Himmel über Berlin (Wings of Desire)

2. Year of Release: 1987

3. Cast and Director:

 - Director: Wim Wenders

 - Cast: Bruno Ganz, Solveig Dommartin, Otto Sander, Peter Falk

4. Synopsis:

 While not traditionally categorized as horror, "Wings of Desire" incorporates elements of supernatural fantasy that resonate with the genre. The film follows two angels, Damiel and Cassiel, who watch over the divided city of Berlin. These invisible, immortal beings can hear the thoughts of humans but cannot interact with the physical world. Damiel becomes fascinated with a lonely trapeze artist named Marion and begins to yearn for human experiences. As he contemplates giving up his immortality for love, the film explores themes of existence, mortality, and the beauty and pain of human life. The angels' perspective provides a unique view of post-war Berlin, blending historical reality with metaphysical fantasy.

5. Why This Movie Is Recommended:

 Though more poetic than horrific, "Wings of Desire" offers a unique perspective on themes often explored in horror: death, immortality, and the supernatural. Wenders' masterful direction creates a hauntingly beautiful portrait of Berlin, with the angels' black-and-white perspective contrasting sharply with the colorful human world. The film's meditation on mortality and the value of human experience provides a thoughtful counterpoint to more traditional horror narratives about immortality. For viewers interested in the intersection of fantasy, philosophy, and cinema, "Wings of Desire" offers a deeply moving and visually stunning experience that expands the boundaries of what supernatural storytelling can achieve.

6. 10 Trivia Facts:

 1. The film was inspired by Rainer Maria Rilke's poetry, particularly the Duino Elegies.

 2. Peter Falk, playing himself, was a last-minute addition to the cast.

 3. The movie was shot in both black-and-white and color, with color representing human perception.

 4. Many scenes were improvised, with Wenders often giving actors their lines just before shooting.

 5. The film's original German title translates to "The Sky Over Berlin."

 6. "Wings of Desire" was remade in 1998 as "City of Angels" starring Nicolas Cage and Meg Ryan.

 7. The movie features appearances by several notable musicians, including Nick Cave and Crime & the City Solution.

 8. Wenders and his crew had to negotiate with East German authorities to film certain scenes near the Berlin Wall.

 9. The distinctive camera movements were achieved using a custom-built rig called the "angel's wing."

 10. The film won numerous awards, including the Best Director award at the Cannes Film Festival.

15. Funny Games

1. Movie Title: Funny Games

2. Year of Release: 1997

3. Cast and Director:

  - Director: Michael Haneke

  - Cast: Susanne Lothar, Ulrich Mühe, Arno Frisch, Frank Giering

4. Synopsis:

"Funny Games" follows a wealthy Austrian family - Georg, Anna, and their young son Georgie - as they arrive at their lakeside vacation home. Their idyllic retreat is shattered when two young men, Peter and Paul, insinuate themselves into the family's life and take them hostage. What follows is a nightmarish ordeal as the two sadistic intruders subject the family to a series of cruel and violent "games." The film unflinchingly depicts the psychological and physical torture inflicted on the family, while also directly challenging the audience's role as spectators to this violence. Through fourth-wall-breaking moments and manipulations of film conventions, Haneke forces viewers to confront their own complicity in consuming violent media.

5. Why This Movie Is Recommended:

"Funny Games" is a provocative and deeply unsettling critique of violence in media and society. Haneke's clinical direction and the film's stark violence create a visceral sense of horror that lingers long after viewing. The movie's meta-textual elements, including characters addressing the audience directly, add a layer of psychological complexity rarely seen in horror films. While extremely challenging to watch, "Funny Games" offers a powerful examination of the nature of screen violence and audience expectations. For viewers interested in thought-provoking, auteur-driven horror that pushes the boundaries of the genre, "Funny Games" is an essential, if harrowing, experience.

6. 10 Trivia Facts:

1. Haneke remade the film shot-for-shot in English in 2007 with Naomi Watts and Tim Roth.

2. The director has stated that if viewers start to watch the film, they should watch it through to the end, but if they don't like it, they should leave the cinema immediately.

3. The film was controversial upon release for its depiction of violence and its critique of audience complicity.

4. Haneke deliberately cast actors known for more sympathetic roles to subvert audience expectations.

5. The movie was filmed in sequence to maintain the emotional intensity of the performances.

6. "Funny Games" was inspired by real-life violent events and media coverage of them.

7. The film's title is ironic, as the "games" depicted are anything but funny.

8. Haneke has said that the film is a reaction to what he perceived as the trivialisation of violence in American cinema.

9. The movie features very little background music, adding to its stark, realistic tone.

10. Despite its graphic subject matter, much of the violence in "Funny Games" occurs off-screen, leaving it to the viewer's imagination.

16. Rammbock: Berlin Undead

1. Movie Title: Rammbock: Berlin Undead

2. Year of Release: 2010

3. Cast and Director:

- Director: Marvin Kren

- Cast: Michael Fuith, Theo Trebs, Anka Graczyk

4. Synopsis:

"Rammbock: Berlin Undead" is a unique take on the zombie genre set in the heart of Berlin. The story follows Michael, who travels to Berlin to return his ex-girlfriend's keys, only to find himself in the midst of a zombie outbreak. Trapped in an apartment complex with a teenage plumber's apprentice, Gabi, Michael must navigate the chaos and find a way to survive. As the infected overrun the city, the pair must use their wits and limited resources to fortify their position and search for other survivors. The film explores themes of isolation, survival, and human connection in the face of overwhelming odds, all within the confined spaces of urban Berlin.

5. Why This Movie Is Recommended:

"Rammbock" stands out in the overcrowded zombie genre for its tight focus and claustrophobic setting. At just over an hour long, the film is a lean, intense experience that makes the most of its limited budget with creative practical effects and taut direction. The movie's Berlin setting adds a unique flavor to the zombie apocalypse trope, utilizing the city's distinctive architecture to enhance the sense of confinement. For horror fans looking for a fresh take on zombie films or those interested in seeing how German cinema approaches the genre, "Rammbock" offers a compelling, efficient thriller that proves you don't need a huge budget to create effective horror.

6. 10 Trivia Facts:

1. The film's title "Rammbock" refers to a medieval battering ram, symbolizing the relentless nature of the zombie horde.

2. Despite being a zombie film, it contains very little gore, focusing instead on tension and suspense.

3. The movie was shot in just 16 days on a modest budget.

4. "Rammbock" was director Marvin Kren's feature film debut.

5. The film's infected are not traditional zombies but rather living people driven mad by a rage-inducing virus.

6. Much of the movie was filmed in and around a single apartment complex in Berlin.

7. The film received positive reviews internationally, unusual for a low-budget zombie movie.

8. "Rammbock" was part of a wave of German genre films in the early 2010s that helped revitalize the country's horror scene.

9. The movie's short runtime was partially due to budget constraints but ended up being praised for its efficiency.

10. Despite its critical success, "Rammbock" has not received a sequel, remaining a standalone entry in the zombie genre.

17. Der Todesking (The Death King)

1. Movie Title: Der Todesking (The Death King)

2. Year of Release: 1990

3. Cast and Director:

  - Director: Jörg Buttgereit

  - Cast: Hermann Kopp, Heinrich Ebber, Michael Krause

4. Synopsis:

  "Der Todesking" is an experimental horror film structured around the seven days of the week, each featuring a different story related to suicide and death. The segments are linked by images of a decomposing corpse, symbolizing the passage of time. Each vignette explores different aspects of mortality, from a woman corresponding with a serial killer to a man obsessed with violent films. The movie doesn't follow a traditional narrative, instead creating a collage of death-related imagery and concepts. Through its unconventional structure, the film examines society's relationship with death, the allure of self-destruction, and the thin line between life and death.

5. Why This Movie Is Recommended:

  "Der Todesking" is a challenging but rewarding film for those interested in avant-garde cinema and philosophical horror. Buttgereit's unflinching approach to taboo subjects and his artistic visual style create a unique viewing experience that goes beyond traditional horror. The film's episodic structure allows it to explore various facets of death and suicide, offering a multifaceted examination of these complex topics. While not for the faint of heart, "Der Todesking" provides thought-provoking commentary on mortality and the human condition. For fans of experimental cinema or those seeking horror that pushes boundaries both thematically and stylistically, this film is a must-see.

6. 10 Trivia Facts:

  1. The decomposing body shown throughout the film was created using time-lapse photography of a pig carcass.

  2. Buttgereit made the film as a reaction to what he saw as the glorification of death in mainstream media.

  3. The movie was shot on 16mm film, contributing to its gritty, realistic aesthetic.

  4. "Der Todesking" was initially banned in several countries due to its graphic content.

  5. The film features very little dialogue, relying primarily on visual storytelling.

  6. Buttgereit himself appears in a small role in one of the film's segments.

  7. The movie's unconventional structure was partially inspired by art house cinema of the 1960s and 70s.

  8. Despite its controversial nature, the film has been praised for its artistic merit and philosophical depth.

  9. The soundtrack, composed by Hermann Kopp, plays a crucial role in setting the film's haunting atmosphere.

  10. "Der Todesking" is often seen as a thematic companion piece to Buttgereit's earlier film "Nekromantik."

18. Die Wand (The Wall)

1. Movie Title: Die Wand (The Wall)

2. Year of Release: 2012

3. Cast and Director:

- Director: Julian Pölsler

- Cast: Martina Gedeck

4. Synopsis:

While not a traditional horror film, "Die Wand" (The Wall) incorporates elements of psychological horror and existential dread. The story follows an unnamed woman who finds herself suddenly and inexplicably cut off from the outside world by an invisible wall while vacationing in the Austrian mountains. Trapped in this alpine setting with only a dog, a cat, and a cow for company, she must learn to survive off the land. As time passes, the woman grapples with isolation, the struggle for survival, and the psychological toll of her mysterious imprisonment. The film explores themes of solitude, humanity's relationship with nature, and the resilience of the human spirit in the face of inexplicable circumstances.

5. Why This Movie Is Recommended:

"Die Wand" offers a unique blend of psychological horror, sci-fi concepts, and existential drama. The film's stunning alpine setting provides a beautiful yet isolating backdrop that enhances the protagonist's sense of alienation. Martina Gedeck's powerful solo performance carries the film, conveying a range of emotions as her character adapts to her surreal situation. The movie's slow-burn approach and ambiguous nature create a creeping sense of unease that lingers long after viewing. For those interested in philosophical horror or films that explore the psychological effects of isolation, "Die Wand" provides a thought-provoking and visually striking experience.

6. 10 Trivia Facts:

1. The film is based on the 1963 novel of the same name by Austrian author Marlen Haushofer.

2. Almost the entire movie features only one actor on screen, Martina Gedeck.

3. The film was shot on location in the Austrian Alps, adding to its authentic feel.

4. "Die Wand" won the Prize of the Ecumenical Jury at the Berlin International Film Festival.

5. The invisible wall concept has drawn comparisons to Stephen King's "Under the Dome."

6. Director Julian Pölsler had wanted to adapt the novel for over 20 years before finally making the film.

7. The movie features minimal dialogue, with much of the story told through voiceover narration.

8. Despite its fantastic premise, the film focuses more on the day-to-day realities of survival.

9. The ambiguous nature of the wall has led to numerous interpretations, from ecological allegory to psychological metaphor.

10. "Die Wand" was Austria's submission for the Best Foreign Language Film at the 85th Academy Awards.

19. Das Experiment (The Experiment)

1. Movie Title: Das Experiment (The Experiment)

2. Year of Release: 2001

3. Cast and Director:

  - Director: Oliver Hirschbiegel

  - Cast: Moritz Bleibtreu, Christian Berkel, Oliver Stokowski, Wotan Wilke Möhring

4. Synopsis:

"Das Experiment" is a psychological thriller based loosely on the Stanford Prison Experiment. The film follows Tarek, a taxi driver who volunteers for a social experiment recreating prison conditions. Twenty volunteers are randomly split into prisoners and guards, with the prisoners having to follow strict rules enforced by the guards. What begins as a scientific study quickly devolves into a nightmarish scenario as the participants become increasingly absorbed in their roles. Power dynamics shift, alliances form and break, and the line between reality and simulation blurs dangerously. As tensions escalate and violence erupts, the experiment spirals out of control, forcing participants to confront the darker aspects of human nature.

5. Why This Movie Is Recommended:

While not a traditional horror film, "Das Experiment" delves into the psychological horror of human behavior under extreme conditions. Hirschbiegel's taut direction and the claustrophobic setting create a palpable sense of tension that builds to a harrowing climax. The film's exploration of power dynamics, authority, and the potential for cruelty in ordinary people offers a chilling commentary on human nature. Strong performances, particularly from Moritz Bleibtreu, bring depth to the characters as they grapple with their evolving roles. For those interested in psychological thrillers that examine the darker side of humanity, "Das Experiment" provides a gripping and thought-provoking experience that lingers in the mind long after viewing.

6. 10 Trivia Facts:

1. The film is loosely based on Mario Giordano's novel "Black Box," which itself was inspired by the Stanford Prison Experiment.

2. "Das Experiment" was remade in 2010 as an American film starring Adrien Brody and Forest Whitaker.

3. The movie won several German Film Awards, including Best Actor for Moritz Bleibtreu.

4. Director Oliver Hirschbiegel went on to direct the Oscar-nominated film "Downfall."

5. The film's intense subject matter reportedly led to heated arguments among the cast and crew during filming.

6. "Das Experiment" was shot in a chronological order to help the actors experience the psychological progression of their characters.

7. The movie's success helped revitalize interest in German cinema internationally.

8. Several scenes were improvised to add to the realism of the situation.

9. The film sparked debates about ethics in psychological experiments and the nature of reality TV.

10. Despite its fictional nature, some viewers have mistaken the events of the film for a documentary.

20. Wir (We)

1. Movie Title: Wir (We)

2. Year of Release: 2020

3. Cast and Director:

  - Director: René Eller

  - Cast: Pauline Casteleyn, Aimé Claeys, Gaia Sofia Cozijn, Maxime Jacobs

4. Synopsis:

  "Wir" (We) is a disturbing coming-of-age thriller set in a seemingly idyllic town on the Dutch-Belgian border. The film follows a group of eight teenagers who, bored with their mundane lives, decide to engage in increasingly dangerous and illegal activities. What starts as harmless fun quickly escalates into a dark exploration of sex, drugs, and violence. The narrative is told from multiple perspectives, revealing different facets of the events as they unfold. As the teenagers push boundaries and challenge socictal norms, their actions lead to dire consequences, forcing them to confront the reality of their choices and the loss of innocence.

5. Why This Movie Is Recommended:

  "Wir" offers a provocative and unsettling look at youth culture and the potential for darkness in seemingly ordinary places. Eller's unflinching direction and the film's non-linear structure create a sense of unease that builds throughout the movie. The film's exploration of teenage rebellion taken to extreme ends provides a chilling commentary on societal pressures, group dynamics, and the search for identity. While not a traditional horror film, "Wir" incorporates elements of psychological horror and shocking imagery that will stay with viewers long after the credits roll. For those interested in challenging, boundary-pushing cinema that blends drama with horror elements, "Wir" offers a unique and confronting experience.

6. 10 Trivia Facts:

  1. The film is based on the controversial novel "Wij" by Dutch author Elvis Peeters.

  2. "Wir" faced controversy upon release due to its graphic depiction of teenage sexuality and violence.

  3. The movie features a cast of mostly non-professional actors to add authenticity to the performances.

  4. Director René Eller opted for a raw, naturalistic visual style to enhance the film's realism.

  5. The film's multiple perspective approach was inspired by Akira Kurosawa's "Rashomon."

  6. "Wir" premiered at the Rotterdam International Film Festival, where it garnered significant attention.

  7. The movie's title "Wir" (We) emphasizes the collective nature of the teenagers' actions and their group identity.

  8. Several scenes were improvised to capture genuine reactions from the young cast.

  9. The film's disturbing content led to walkouts at some festival screenings.

  10. "Wir" has been compared to other controversial youth-focused films like Larry Clark's "Kids" and Harmony Korine's "Gummo."

Russia

1. Viy

1. Movie Title: Viy (Вий)

2. Year of Release: 1967

3. Cast and Director:

- Directors: Konstantin Ershov, Georgiy Kropachyov

- Cast: Leonid Kuravlyov, Natalya Varley, Alexei Glazyrin

4. Synopsis:

Based on Nikolai Gogol's novella, "Viy" follows Khoma, a seminary student who encounters a witch in an isolated village. Forced to spend three nights praying for the soul of a deceased young woman, Khoma faces increasingly terrifying supernatural occurrences. Each night, the witch's spirit attempts to penetrate the protective circle Khoma draws around himself, culminating in a final confrontation with the monstrous Viy, king of the gnomes. The film blends Slavic folklore with Gothic horror elements, creating a uniquely Russian horror experience.

5. Why This Movie Is Recommended:

"Viy" is a landmark in Russian horror cinema, notable for being one of the few Soviet-era films to tackle supernatural themes. Its blend of folk horror, practical effects, and psychological tension creates a uniquely atmospheric experience. The film's striking visuals and imaginative creatures, impressive for their time, continue to captivate audiences. As an adaptation of a classic Russian literary work, it offers insight into Slavic folklore and superstitions, making it culturally significant as well as entertaining.

6. 10 Trivia Facts:

1. It's considered the first Soviet-era horror film.

2. The film faced censorship issues and was initially banned in some regions.

3. Many of the supernatural creatures were created using practical effects and puppetry.

4. The actress playing the witch, Natalya Varley, was a circus performer before becoming an actress.

5. The film's success led to a resurgence of interest in Gogol's original story.

6. Director Aleksandr Ptushko, known for his fantasy films, contributed to the special effects.

7. The movie was shot in Ukraine, near Kyiv.

8. It took nearly two years to complete due to the complex special effects.

9. The film has been remade several times, including a 2014 version starring Jason Flemyng.

10. Some scenes were considered so frightening that they were cut from the initial release.

2. Night Watch (Nochnoy Dozor)

1. Movie Title: Night Watch (Ночной дозор, Nochnoy Dozor)

2. Year of Release: 2004

3. Cast and Director:

- Director: Timur Bekmambetov

- Cast: Konstantin Khabensky, Vladimir Menshov, Valeri Zolotukhin

4. Synopsis:

Set in modern Moscow, "Night Watch" depicts a world where the forces of Light and Darkness maintain an uneasy truce. The Night Watch, comprised of Light Others, patrols the night to keep Dark Others in check. The story follows Anton Gorodetsky, a Night Watch agent who becomes entangled in a prophecy about a powerful Other who could tip the balance between good and evil. As Anton navigates this supernatural underworld, he must confront both external threats and his own moral ambiguities. The film blends urban fantasy with horror elements, creating a unique vision of a hidden world existing alongside our own.

5. Why This Movie Is Recommended:

"Night Watch" revolutionized Russian cinema with its ambitious scope and Hollywood-style visual effects. It offers a fresh take on vampire and supernatural lore, infused with distinctly Russian sensibilities. The film's gritty, stylized aesthetic and complex mythology set it apart from typical horror fare. Its exploration of moral ambiguity within the context of an age-old battle between good and evil adds depth to the supernatural thrills. As the first part of a trilogy, it introduces a rich, fully-realized world that horror and fantasy fans alike can immerse themselves in.

6. 10 Trivia Facts:

1. The film is based on the novel of the same name by Sergei Lukyanenko.

2. It was the highest-grossing Russian film ever at the time of its release.

3. Director Timur Bekmambetov went on to direct Hollywood films like "Wanted" and "Abraham Lincoln: Vampire Hunter."

4. The film's unique subtitles for international release were designed to be part of the visual experience.

5. A video game based on the film was released in 2006.

6. The movie's success led to a sequel, "Day Watch," released in 2006.

7. Fox Searchlight Pictures acquired the North American distribution rights, a rare feat for a Russian film.

8. The film's visual style was influenced by The Matrix and the works of Quentin Tarantino.

9. Many of the actors were relatively unknown at the time but became stars in Russia after the film's success.

10. The film uses a mix of Russian and English in its dialogue, reflecting Moscow's cosmopolitan nature.

3. The Bride (Nevesta)

1. Movie Title: The Bride (Невеста, Nevesta)

2. Year of Release: 2017

3. Cast and Director:

- Director: Svyatoslav Podgayevskiy

- Cast: Victoria Agalakova, Vyacheslav Chepurchenko, Alexandra Rebenok

4. Synopsis:

"The Bride" follows Nastya, a young woman who travels with her fiancé to his family home for their wedding. Upon arrival, she discovers his strange relatives and their unsettling traditions. As Nastya delves deeper into the family's history, she uncovers a terrifying secret involving a cursed wedding dress and a vengeful spirit. Trapped in the old mansion, she must fight to survive and break the cycle of horror that has plagued the family for generations. The film blends elements of traditional ghost stories with modern psychological horror, creating a tense and atmospheric experience.

5. Why This Movie Is Recommended:

"The Bride" stands out as a polished entry in contemporary Russian horror cinema. It skillfully combines classic haunted house tropes with uniquely Russian folkloric elements, resulting in a fresh and engaging narrative. The film's strong visual style, from the eerie mansion to the haunting wedding dress, creates a palpable sense of dread. Its exploration of family secrets and cursed legacies adds psychological depth to the supernatural scares. For horror fans looking to explore international offerings, "The Bride" provides a glimpse into the evolving landscape of Russian genre filmmaking.

6. 10 Trivia Facts:

1. The film was shot in various locations across Russia, including some historic mansions.

2. Director Svyatoslav Podgayevskiy is known as one of the leading figures in the new wave of Russian horror cinema.

3. The movie's success helped establish Podgayevskiy's production company, which focuses on horror films.

4. The ghostly bride's makeup and effects were created using a combination of practical and digital techniques.

5. The film drew inspiration from various international horror films, including Japanese ghost stories.

6. "The Bride" was one of the highest-grossing Russian horror films of its release year.

7. The movie features a blend of modern and period settings, reflecting its themes of past and present colliding.

8. Many of the cast members were relatively new to horror films, bringing fresh performances to the genre.

9. The film's marketing campaign in Russia included viral videos and interactive experiences.

10. Some scenes were shot in the famous Lenfilm studios in Saint Petersburg.

4. Gogol. The Beginning

1. Movie Title: Gogol. The Beginning (Гоголь. Начало)

2. Year of Release: 2017

3. Cast and Director:

- Director: Egor Baranov

- Cast: Alexander Petrov, Oleg Menshikov, Evgeny Stychkin

4. Synopsis:

"Gogol. The Beginning" is a supernatural thriller that reimagines the early life of famous Russian writer Nikolai Gogol. Set in the 19th century, the film portrays Gogol as a young clerk with a talent for writing and the ability to communicate with the dead. He teams up with a renowned detective to investigate a series of mysterious murders in a remote village. As they delve deeper into the case, they encounter dark forces from Slavic mythology. Gogol must confront his own supernatural abilities and the horrors that inspire his future literary works. The film blends historical fiction, horror, and detective genres to create a unique narrative.

5. Why This Movie Is Recommended:

This film offers a fresh and imaginative take on the life of one of Russia's most celebrated authors. By blending historical elements with supernatural horror, it creates a unique viewing experience that appeals to both literature enthusiasts and genre fans. The movie's high production values, including impressive period costumes and sets, immerse viewers in a richly detailed 19th-century Russia. Its clever integration of elements from Gogol's actual works into the plot adds an extra layer of enjoyment for those familiar with his writing. As part of a planned series, it sets up an intriguing universe that combines Russian literary history with dark fantasy.

6. 10 Trivia Facts:

1. The film is the first part of a trilogy, followed by "Gogol. Viy" and "Gogol. Terrible Revenge."

2. It was originally conceived as a television series before being adapted into a film trilogy.

3. Lead actor Alexander Petrov underwent extensive makeup to resemble the historical Nikolai Gogol.

4. The movie incorporates elements from several of Gogol's short stories, particularly those from his collection "Evenings on a Farm Near Dikanka."

5. Some of the supernatural creatures in the film are based on Slavic folklore that Gogol used in his actual writings.

6. The film's success led to a resurgence of interest in Gogol's works among younger Russian audiences.

7. Director Egor Baranov also directed all three films in the trilogy, maintaining a consistent vision.

8. The movie blends several genres, including detective fiction, horror, and historical drama.

9. Some scenes were shot in authentic 19th-century locations to enhance the period atmosphere.

10. The film's marketing campaign in Russia included interactive exhibitions about Gogol's life and works.

5. Faust

1. Movie Title: Faust (Фауст)

2. Year of Release: 2011

3. Cast and Director:

  - Director: Alexander Sokurov

  - Cast: Johannes Zeiler, Anton Adasinsky, Isolda Dychauk

4. Synopsis:

  Alexander Sokurov's "Faust" is a dark and surreal adaptation of Goethe's classic play. Set in a grimy, nightmarish version of 19th-century Germany, the film follows Heinrich Faust, a disillusioned intellectual searching for the meaning of existence. He encounters Mephistopheles, portrayed as a grotesque moneylender, who offers him ultimate knowledge and power in exchange for his soul. As Faust grapples with temptation and desire, particularly for the innocent Margarete, he descends into a hallucinatory world where reality and nightmare blur. Sokurov's vision transforms the familiar tale into a haunting exploration of human nature, ambition, and the costs of unchecked desire.

5. Why This Movie Is Recommended:

  While not a traditional horror film, "Faust" creates an atmosphere of existential dread and visual horror that rivals many genre entries. Sokurov's distinctive visual style, with its distorted imagery and sickly color palette, immerses viewers in a truly unsettling world. The film's philosophical depth adds layers of psychological horror to its more overt grotesqueries. As the final entry in Sokurov's tetralogy on power, it offers a unique perspective on the classic story. For those interested in arthouse horror or films that blur the lines between reality and nightmare, "Faust" provides a challenging and unforgettable experience.

6. 10 Trivia Facts:

  1. The film won the Golden Lion at the 68th Venice International Film Festival.

  2. It's the final part of Sokurov's tetralogy on power, following "Moloch," "Taurus," and "The Sun."

  3. The movie was primarily shot in the Czech Republic, with some scenes filmed in Iceland.

  4. Sokurov used specially crafted lenses to create the film's distorted, dreamlike visuals.

  5. The dialogue is primarily in German, despite being a Russian production.

  6. The film took nearly 10 years to finance and produce.

  7. Sokurov incorporated elements from various versions of the Faust legend, not just Goethe's play.

  8. The director described the film as a "thriller" rather than a straightforward adaptation.

  9. Many of the grotesque effects were achieved through practical means rather than CGI.

  10. The film's score incorporates works by Charles Gounod, whose opera was based on Goethe's "Faust."

6. Kolya: A Ghost Story

1. Movie Title: Kolya: A Ghost Story (Коля, История призрака)

2. Year of Release: 2020

3. Cast and Director:

- Director: Anton Megerdichev

- Cast: Yuri Borisov, Maryana Spivak, Oleg Maslennikov-Voitov

4. Synopsis:

"Kolya: A Ghost Story" follows the tragic tale of a young boy named Kolya who dies in a car accident. Unable to accept his death, Kolya's spirit remains tethered to the world of the living. The film explores the aftermath of his death, focusing on how his ghostly presence affects his grieving parents and the community around them. As strange occurrences begin to multiply, the line between the natural and supernatural worlds blurs. The movie delves into themes of grief, acceptance, and the enduring power of love beyond death, all while maintaining an atmosphere of otherworldly dread.

5. Why This Movie Is Recommended:

This film stands out for its emotional depth, blending heartfelt drama with supernatural elements. It offers a uniquely Russian perspective on the ghost story genre, incorporating local folklore and cultural beliefs about the afterlife. The movie's strength lies in its ability to evoke both fear and empathy, making the audience feel for the characters while still delivering chilling moments. Its exploration of grief and the inability to let go resonates on a universal level, elevating it beyond typical genre fare. The film's atmospheric cinematography and subtle use of special effects create a haunting visual experience.

6. 10 Trivia Facts:

1. The film was inspired by real-life stories of paranormal experiences following the loss of a loved one.

2. Director Anton Megerdichev is known for his work in various genres, making this his first foray into horror.

3. The movie was shot on location in a small Russian town, adding to its authentic atmosphere.

4. Many of the ghostly effects were achieved through practical means rather than CGI.

5. The film incorporates elements of Russian Orthodox beliefs about the afterlife.

6. Young actor playing Kolya underwent extensive training to portray the ghostly movements.

7. The movie's score was composed using traditional Russian instruments to enhance the cultural atmosphere.

8. Several scenes were shot during the "white nights" phenomenon in northern Russia, creating a unique visual aesthetic.

9. The film sparked discussions in Russia about cultural attitudes towards death and grieving.

10. "Kolya: A Ghost Story" was selected for several international film festivals, raising the profile of Russian horror cinema abroad.

7. The Mermaid: Lake of the Dead

1. Movie Title: The Mermaid: Lake of the Dead (Русалка: Озеро мертвых)

2. Year of Release: 2018

3. Cast and Director:

  - Director: Svyatoslav Podgayevskiy

  - Cast: Viktoriya Agalakova, Efim Petrunin, Sofia Shidlovskaya

4. Synopsis:

"The Mermaid: Lake of the Dead" blends Slavic folklore with modern horror elements. The story centers around Roma, a young man who encounters a mysterious young woman near a lake shortly before his wedding. Unbeknownst to him, she is a murderous mermaid spirit who falls in love with him and aims to drag him to the bottom of the lake. As Roma begins to fall under her spell, his fiancée Marina must uncover the dark history of the lake and find a way to break the mermaid's curse before it's too late. The film explores themes of love, jealousy, and the dangerous allure of the unknown.

5. Why This Movie Is Recommended:

This film offers a fresh take on mermaid mythology, drawing from lesser-known Slavic folklore rather than more familiar Western interpretations. Its atmospheric setting and strong visual effects create a haunting aquatic world that's both beautiful and terrifying. The movie successfully blends supernatural horror with elements of romance and drama, appealing to a wide audience. It stands out in the landscape of Russian horror for its unique subject matter and high production values. For viewers interested in folklore-based horror or looking to explore international offerings in the genre, "The Mermaid: Lake of the Dead" provides an engaging and culturally distinctive experience.

6. 10 Trivia Facts:

1. The film draws inspiration from Slavic legends of rusalkas, dangerous water spirits.

2. Many of the underwater scenes were shot in specially constructed tanks to achieve the desired otherworldly effect.

3. The actress playing the mermaid underwent extensive makeup and prosthetics work for her transformations.

4. Director Svyatoslav Podgayevskiy is considered one of the leading figures in the new wave of Russian horror cinema.

5. The film's success led to increased interest in Slavic folklore-based horror movies in Russia.

6. Some of the lake scenes were shot at real locations believed to be haunted according to local legends.

7. The movie incorporates elements of body horror in its depiction of the mermaid's transformations.

8. The film's marketing campaign in Russia included interactive "mermaid-spotting" events at lakes.

9. "The Mermaid: Lake of the Dead" was one of the few Russian horror films to receive a wide international release.

10. The movie's soundtrack blends traditional Slavic folk music with modern horror scores.

8. Palata No. 6 (Ward No. 6)

1. Movie Title: Палата №6 (Ward No. 6)

2. Year of Release: 2009

3. Cast and Director:

- Directors: Karen Shakhnazarov, Aleksandr Gornovsky

- Cast: Vladimir Ilyin, Aleksei Vertkov, Aleksandr Pankratov-Chernyi

4. Synopsis:

Based on Anton Chekhov's short story, "Ward No. 6" is a psychological thriller set in a mental hospital. The film follows Dr. Andrey Ragin, the head of a provincial psychiatric hospital, who becomes increasingly disillusioned with his life and work. He forms an unlikely friendship with a paranoid patient, Ivan Gromov, whose philosophical discussions begin to affect Ragin's own mental state. As Ragin's behavior becomes more erratic, the line between doctor and patient blurs, leading to a disturbing role reversal. The film explores themes of sanity, institutional power, and the thin line between reason and madness.

5. Why This Movie Is Recommended:

While not a traditional horror film, "Ward No. 6" creates a sense of psychological dread that rivals many genre entries. Its exploration of mental illness and the abuse of power in institutions is deeply unsettling. The film's claustrophobic setting and bleak atmosphere contribute to a growing sense of unease throughout. As an adaptation of Chekhov's work, it offers literary depth alongside its thrills. The strong performances and nuanced character development elevate the film beyond simple scares, making it a thought-provoking and disturbing experience that lingers long after viewing.

6. 10 Trivia Facts:

1. The film is a modern adaptation of Chekhov's 1892 short story, updated to a contemporary setting.

2. Director Karen Shakhnazarov is known for his diverse filmography, including historical dramas and comedies.

3. Many scenes were shot in a real, abandoned psychiatric hospital to enhance the authentic atmosphere.

4. The film was Russia's submission for the Best Foreign Language Film at the 82nd Academy Awards.

5. Some of the extras in the hospital scenes were played by actual psychiatric patients (under supervision).

6. The movie uses a documentary-style approach in some scenes, blurring the line between fiction and reality.

7. "Ward No. 6" premiered at the Toronto International Film Festival to critical acclaim.

8. The film explores themes that were controversial in Chekhov's time and remain relevant today.

9. Some of the dialogue is taken directly from Chekhov's original text, maintaining its literary roots.

10. The movie's success led to renewed interest in Chekhov's lesser-known works in Russia.

9. The Dyatlov Pass Incident

1. Movie Title: The Dyatlov Pass Incident (Тайна перевала Дятлова)

2. Year of Release: 2013

3. Cast and Director:

- Director: Renny Harlin

- Cast: Holly Goss, Matt Stokoe, Luke Albright, Ryan Hawley, Gemma Atkinson

4. Synopsis:

"The Dyatlov Pass Incident" is a found-footage horror film based on the real-life mysterious deaths of nine Russian hikers in the Ural Mountains in 1959. The movie follows a group of American students who travel to the Urals to investigate what happened to the original expedition. As they retrace the steps of the ill-fated hikers, they encounter increasingly strange and terrifying phenomena. The film blends historical fact with supernatural horror, exploring theories ranging from government conspiracies to alien encounters. As the modern-day students uncover more about the past, they find themselves facing a similar, horrifying fate.

5. Why This Movie Is Recommended:

This film stands out for its basis in a real, unsolved mystery that has fascinated people for decades. It successfully creates tension by playing on the viewers' knowledge of the true story's tragic end. The movie's remote, snowy setting adds to the sense of isolation and dread. While it employs found-footage techniques, it does so in a way that feels fresh within the context of the historical mystery. The blend of fact and fiction, along with the various theories presented, keeps viewers guessing until the end. For those interested in horror based on real events or fans of found-footage films looking for a unique entry in the genre, "The Dyatlov Pass Incident" offers a chilling and thought-provoking experience.

6. 10 Trivia Facts:

1. The film is based on the real Dyatlov Pass incident, which remains unsolved to this day.

2. Despite being set in Russia, the movie was primarily shot in Northern Russia and Bulgaria.

3. Director Renny Harlin is known for Hollywood action films, making this his first venture into found-footage horror.

4. The film incorporates actual photographs and documents from the 1959 incident.

5. Some of the theories presented in the movie are based on real speculations about the incident.

6. The filmmakers consulted with experts on the Dyatlov Pass incident during the script development.

7. The movie's release renewed interest in the real-life mystery, leading to new investigations.

8. Some scenes were shot in temperatures as low as -30°C (-22°F) to capture the harsh environment.

9. The film blends Russian and American perspectives, with both Russian and English dialogue.

10. "The Dyatlov Pass Incident" was released under different titles in various countries, including "Devil's Pass" in some regions.

10. The House of Voices (Тихий дом)

1. Movie Title: The House of Voices (Тихий дом)

2. Year of Release: 2016

3. Cast and Director:

- Director: Oleg Asadulin

- Cast: Alexandra Bortich, Ivan Shakhnazarov, Anastasia Akatova

4. Synopsis:

"The House of Voices" follows a group of young people who decide to participate in a unique psychological experiment. They agree to spend a week in complete isolation in a supposedly haunted house, with no outside contact. As the days pass, strange occurrences begin to plague the participants. They start hearing inexplicable voices and experiencing vivid, terrifying hallucinations. The line between reality and imagination blurs as the house seems to prey on their deepest fears and darkest secrets. As tensions rise and trust erodes, the group must confront both supernatural horrors and their own psychological demons to survive.

5. Why This Movie Is Recommended:

"The House of Voices" offers a fresh take on the haunted house subgenre by incorporating elements of psychological experimentation. Its focus on the characters' mental states and interpersonal dynamics adds depth to the supernatural scares. The film's claustrophobic setting and mounting tension create a palpable sense of unease throughout. It explores themes of isolation, trust, and the power of suggestion, making it as much a psychological thriller as a ghost story. For viewers who enjoy horror that blends mind games with paranormal activity, this film provides an engaging and unsettling experience.

6. 10 Trivia Facts:

1. The film was inspired by real psychological experiments on sensory deprivation and group dynamics.

2. Most of the movie was shot in a single location to enhance the sense of claustrophobia.

3. The actors underwent a brief period of isolation before filming to better understand their characters' mindsets.

4. Director Oleg Asadulin has a background in psychological thrillers, which influenced the film's tone.

5. The movie uses minimal special effects, relying more on suggestion and sound design to create scares.

6. Some of the "voices" in the film were created using a technique called "backmasking" (reverse audio).

7. The house used for filming has its own reputation for being haunted, adding to the atmosphere on set.

8. The film's working title was "Experiment: Fear" before being changed to "The House of Voices."

9. Several scenes were improvised by the actors to capture genuine reactions.

10. The movie sparked discussions in Russia about the ethics of psychological experiments and reality TV.

11. Sleepless Beauty (Ya ne splyu)

1. Movie Title: Sleepless Beauty (Я не сплю)

2. Year of Release: 2020

3. Cast and Director:

  - Director: Pavel Khvaleev

  - Cast: Polina Davydova, Evgeniy Gagarin, Sergey Topkov

4. Synopsis:

"Sleepless Beauty" follows Mila, a young woman who is kidnapped and subjected to a brutal experiment in sleep deprivation. Her captors, part of a shadowy organization, broadcast her torment live on the dark web. As Mila is forced to stay awake, she experiences increasingly disturbing hallucinations and psychological breakdowns. The film explores the deterioration of her mental state as reality and nightmares blend together. Meanwhile, viewers of the broadcast speculate and argue about the purpose of the experiment, adding a layer of social commentary to the horror. As Mila's ordeal continues, the true nature and purpose of her captivity become increasingly sinister and surreal.

5. Why This Movie Is Recommended:

"Sleepless Beauty" stands out for its innovative approach to psychological horror. By focusing on sleep deprivation, it taps into a universal fear and creates a uniquely unsettling atmosphere. The film's use of vivid, hallucinatory sequences pushes the boundaries of traditional horror visuals. Its commentary on internet culture and the ethics of voyeurism adds depth to the visceral scares. For viewers looking for a challenging, thought-provoking horror experience that blends psychological torment with social critique, "Sleepless Beauty" offers a fresh and disturbing take on the genre.

6. 10 Trivia Facts:

1. The film was shot in a real abandoned factory, adding to its claustrophobic atmosphere.

2. Director Pavel Khvaleev has a background in electronic music, which influenced the movie's unique soundscape.

3. The hallucination sequences were created using a combination of practical effects and CGI.

4. The movie premiered at the Moscow International Film Festival.

5. Lead actress Polina Davydova underwent sleep deprivation herself to prepare for the role.

6. The film incorporates elements of real sleep deprivation studies in its plot.

7. Some of the "viewers" in the dark web scenes were played by actual fans of the director's previous work.

8. The movie's Russian title "Я не сплю" directly translates to "I'm not sleeping."

9. Khvaleev cited David Lynch as an influence on the film's surreal elements.

10. The film sparked discussions in Russia about online privacy and the dark web.

12. The Blackout (Аванпост)

1. Movie Title: The Blackout (Аванпост)

2. Year of Release: 2019

3. Cast and Director:

  - Director: Egor Baranov

  - Cast: Pyotr Fyodorov, Aleksey Chadov, Svetlana Ivanova

4. **Synopsis**:

  "The Blackout" presents a post-apocalyptic scenario where most of the Earth has lost power and all contact with vast territories has disappeared. The story focuses on a small area in Eastern Europe that still has electricity. A group of survivors, including military personnel, scientists, and civilians, try to uncover the truth behind the global catastrophe. As they venture into the dark territory beyond their safe zone, they encounter terrifying creatures and face the possibility of an alien invasion. The film blends elements of science fiction, horror, and military action as the characters fight for survival and seek answers in a world plunged into darkness.

5. **Why This Movie Is Recommended**:

  While primarily a sci-fi action film, "The Blackout" incorporates strong elements of horror that will appeal to genre fans. Its unique premise of a partial apocalypse creates a tense, claustrophobic atmosphere. The movie's high production values and impressive visual effects set a new standard for Russian genre cinema. It successfully blends military action with supernatural terror, offering a fresh take on both alien invasion and post-apocalyptic narratives. For viewers who enjoy their horror with a sci-fi twist and appreciate large-scale, ambitious storytelling, "The Blackout" provides an intense and visually striking experience.

6. **10 Trivia Facts**:

  1. The film's budget was one of the largest for a Russian sci-fi movie at the time.

  2. Many of the exterior scenes were shot in Croatia to achieve the desired post-apocalyptic look.

  3. The movie's creature designs were kept secret during production to maintain suspense.

  4. Director Egor Baranov is known for blending genres, as seen in his "Gogol" trilogy.

  5. The film uses a mix of practical effects and CGI for its creature scenes.

  6. "The Blackout" was released internationally on Netflix, expanding its audience beyond Russia.

  7. The movie's success led to discussions about a potential sequel or TV series adaptation.

  8. Some of the military equipment used in the film was provided by the Russian armed forces.

  9. The film's script went through numerous revisions to balance its sci-fi, horror, and action elements.

  10. "The Blackout" received praise for its portrayal of strong female characters in a typically male-dominated genre.

13. Invasion (Вторжение)

1. Movie Title: Invasion (Вторжение)

2. Year of Release: 2020

3. Cast and Director:

  - Director: Fyodor Bondarchuk

  - Cast: Irina Starshenbaum, Rinal Mukhametov, Alexander Petrov

4. Synopsis:

  "Invasion" is a sequel to the 2017 film "Attraction," continuing the story of an alien encounter in Russia. The film follows Yulia, a young woman who has developed extraordinary abilities after contact with alien technology. As she struggles to control her powers, a new alien threat emerges, putting Earth in danger. The Russian military, along with Yulia and her allies, must face this invasion while uncovering the true intentions of the extraterrestrial visitors. The movie blends large-scale sci-fi action with elements of body horror and psychological suspense as Yulia's transformation progresses and the alien presence becomes more menacing.

5. Why This Movie Is Recommended:

  While primarily a sci-fi blockbuster, "Invasion" incorporates horror elements that will appeal to genre fans. Its exploration of body transformation and the psychological impact of alien contact adds depth to the spectacular visual effects and action sequences. The film offers a uniquely Russian perspective on the alien invasion trope, incorporating local settings and cultural elements. For horror enthusiasts who enjoy their scares mixed with high-stakes action and impressive visuals, "Invasion" provides an entertaining and sometimes unsettling experience. It's also a rare example of a big-budget Russian genre film that achieved international recognition.

6. 10 Trivia Facts:

  1. The film is one of the most expensive Russian productions ever made, with a budget of around $15 million.

  2. Many of the film's underwater scenes were shot in actual depth, not in tanks.

  3. Director Fyodor Bondarchuk is the son of famous Soviet filmmaker Sergei Bondarchuk.

  4. The movie's visual effects were created by the same team that worked on "Gravity" and "Blade Runner 2049."

  5. "Invasion" was released in IMAX format, a first for a Russian sci-fi film.

  6. The film incorporates elements of real scientific theories about extraterrestrial life.

  7. Some scenes were shot in Moscow's actual government buildings, adding to the film's authenticity.

  8. The movie's release was accompanied by a large-scale VR experience in Russian theaters.

  9. "Invasion" broke box office records in Russia for its opening weekend.

  10. The film's alien designs were kept strictly under wraps during production to maintain suspense.

14. Dark Planet (Обитаемый остров)

1. **Movie Title**: Dark Planet (Обитаемый остров)

2. **Year of Release**: 2008

3. **Cast and Director**:

   - Director: Fyodor Bondarchuk

   - Cast: Vasiliy Stepanov, Yuliya Snigir, Pyotr Fyodorov

4. **Synopsis**:

   Based on the Strugatsky brothers' novel "Prisoners of Power," "Dark Planet" is set in the year 2157. It follows Maxim, a space explorer from Earth who crash-lands on a distant planet. He discovers a post-apocalyptic world ruled by an oppressive regime that maintains control through mind-altering towers. As Maxim navigates this harsh new world, he uncovers dark secrets about the planet's history and the true nature of its ruling class. The film blends science fiction with elements of psychological horror as it explores themes of totalitarianism, mind control, and the corruption of power.

5. **Why This Movie Is Recommended**:

   While primarily a sci-fi epic, "Dark Planet" incorporates strong elements of psychological horror and dystopian dread that will appeal to genre fans. Its exploration of a totalitarian society and the use of mind control creates an atmosphere of constant unease and paranoia. The film's impressive visual design brings to life a unique and unsettling alien world. For viewers who enjoy their horror with a heavy dose of social commentary and philosophical questions, "Dark Planet" offers a thought-provoking and visually striking experience. It's also a significant entry in Russian genre filmmaking, showcasing high production values and ambitious storytelling.

6. **10 Trivia Facts**:

   1. The film is based on a novel by the Strugatsky brothers, who are considered the greatest Russian sci-fi writers.

   2. "Dark Planet" was originally planned as a single film but was split into two parts due to its scope.

   3. The movie's budget was one of the largest in Russian film history at the time.

   4. Many of the futuristic sets were built practically rather than relying on CGI.

   5. The film's visual style was influenced by Soviet-era science fiction films.

   6. Director Fyodor Bondarchuk faced challenges adapting the complex novel into a visual medium.

   7. The movie features a cameo by one of the original novel's authors, Boris Strugatsky.

   8. "Dark Planet" was shot in Crimea, with some locations chosen for their alien-like landscapes.

   9. The film's release was accompanied by a video game adaptation.

   10. Despite mixed critical reception, the movie was a box office success in Russia.

15. The Moth Diaries (Дневники мотылька)

1. Movie Title: The Moth Diaries (Дневники мотылька)

2. Year of Release: 2011

3. Cast and Director:

  - Director: Mary Harron

  - Cast: Sarah Bolger, Lily Cole, Sarah Gadon

4. Synopsis:

While not a Russian production, "The Moth Diaries" is based on a novel by Russian-American author Rachel Klein and has gained popularity among Russian horror fans. The film is set in an elite all-girls boarding school and follows Rebecca, a teenager still grieving her father's suicide. When a mysterious new student, Ernessa, arrives and befriends Rebecca's best friend Lucy, strange and disturbing events begin to occur. Rebecca becomes convinced that Ernessa is a vampire, but her obsession is dismissed as jealousy or mental instability. As the line between reality and fantasy blurs, Rebecca must confront her own fears and uncover the truth about Ernessa before it's too late.

5. Why This Movie Is Recommended:

"The Moth Diaries" offers a unique take on vampire lore, blending elements of gothic horror with coming-of-age drama. Its boarding school setting creates a claustrophobic atmosphere that enhances the growing sense of dread. The film explores themes of adolescent sexuality, friendship, and mental health, adding psychological depth to its supernatural elements. For viewers who appreciate subtle, atmospheric horror and complex female characters, "The Moth Diaries" provides a thought-provoking and visually haunting experience. Its popularity in Russia also makes it an interesting bridge between Western and Eastern European horror traditions.

6. 10 Trivia Facts:

1. The film is based on a novel by Rachel Klein, who drew inspiration from her own experiences at a boarding school.

2. Director Mary Harron is known for her work on "American Psycho," bringing a similar psychological intensity to this film.

3. The movie was filmed in Montreal, Canada, though the story is set in New England.

4. The film's vampire elements are more subtle and ambiguous than in traditional vampire movies.

5. "The Moth Diaries" premiered at the Venice Film Festival.

6. The movie incorporates themes and imagery from gothic literature, particularly works by Edgar Allan Poe.

7. Lead actress Sarah Bolger studied "Dracula" and other vampire literature to prepare for her role.

8. The film's atmospheric score was composed by Lesley Barber, known for her work on "Manchester by the Sea."

9. Despite being in English, the movie gained a significant following among Russian horror fans.

10. The film's ambiguous ending has sparked debates among viewers about the true nature of the events depicted.

16. Sputnik

1. Movie Title: Sputnik (Спутник)

2. Year of Release: 2020

3. Cast and Director:

- Director: Egor Abramenko

- Cast: Oksana Akinshina, Pyotr Fyodorov, Fedor Bondarchuk

4. Synopsis:

Set in the Soviet era, "Sputnik" follows Tatyana Klimova, a young doctor recruited to assess the sole survivor of a mysterious space incident. The cosmonaut, Konstantin, has returned to Earth, but he's not alone - he's brought an alien parasite back with him. As Tatyana studies the symbiotic relationship between Konstantin and the creature, she uncovers a sinister military plot. The film blends elements of sci-fi horror with psychological thriller as Tatyana races to understand the alien entity and save Konstantin, all while questioning the motivations of those around her. "Sputnik" explores themes of isolation, humanity, and the moral complexities of scientific discovery against the backdrop of Soviet-era secrecy.

5. Why This Movie Is Recommended:

"Sputnik" offers a fresh take on the alien invasion genre, combining body horror with psychological suspense. Its Soviet setting provides a unique backdrop that adds layers of paranoia and tension to the narrative. The film's strong character development and exploration of ethical dilemmas elevate it beyond typical monster movies. With its high production values and restrained approach to horror, "Sputnik" demonstrates the growing sophistication of Russian genre cinema. For fans of thoughtful sci-fi horror in the vein of "Alien" or "The Thing," this film provides a tense, atmospheric, and intellectually engaging experience.

6. 10 Trivia Facts:

1. "Sputnik" is director Egor Abramenko's feature film debut, expanded from his short film "The Passenger."

2. The film's creature design was inspired by deep-sea marine life.

3. "Sputnik" was one of the first Russian films to be released on VOD platforms due to the COVID-19 pandemic.

4. The movie pays homage to classic sci-fi horror films while maintaining its unique Soviet-era setting.

5. Much of the film was shot in a real, abandoned Soviet-era facility to enhance authenticity.

6. The actors underwent extensive research into Soviet-era space programs to prepare for their roles.

7. "Sputnik" received international acclaim, with rights sold to over 30 countries.

8. The film's score, composed by Oleg Karpachev, incorporates elements of Soviet-era electronic music.

9. Despite its sci-fi premise, the filmmakers focused on practical effects over CGI where possible.

10. "Sputnik" was selected as the opening film for the Tribeca Film Festival's sci-fi section in 2020.

17. Deadly Still (Пиковая дама: Зазеркалье)

1. Movie Title: Deadly Still (Пиковая дама: Зазеркалье, also known as Queen of Spades: Through the Looking Glass)

2. Year of Release: 2019

3. Cast and Director:

 - Director: Aleksandr Domogarov Jr.

 - Cast: Angelina Strechina, Daniil Muravyov-Izotov, Claudia Boccaccini

4. **Synopsis**:

 "Deadly Still" is a supernatural horror film that revolves around an old boarding school with a dark history. A group of teenagers discovers an antique mirror that once belonged to the infamous Countess of Spades, a malevolent entity from Russian folklore. When they perform an ancient ritual to summon her spirit, they unleash a terrifying force that begins to hunt them down. As the students struggle to survive and break the curse, they uncover disturbing secrets about the school's past and the true nature of the Countess. The film blends elements of urban legends, ghost stories, and psychological horror as the line between reality and nightmare blurs for the trapped teenagers.

5. **Why This Movie Is Recommended**:

 "Deadly Still" stands out for its effective use of Russian folklore in a modern horror context. The film creates a genuinely creepy atmosphere, utilizing the boarding school setting to enhance feelings of isolation and dread. Its blend of jump scares and psychological terror caters to various horror preferences. The movie also explores themes of guilt, trauma, and the dangers of toying with the unknown, adding depth to its supernatural premise. For fans of ghost stories and mirror-based horror like "Candyman" or "Oculus," "Deadly Still" offers a culturally distinctive and chilling entry in the subgenre.

6. **10 Trivia Facts**:

 1. The film is part of a series of Russian movies based on the legend of the Queen of Spades.

 2. The Queen of Spades is a figure from Russian folklore, often associated with death and fortune-telling.

 3. Many of the mirror scenes were achieved using practical effects rather than CGI.

 4. The movie was shot in an actual abandoned boarding school, adding to its eerie atmosphere.

 5. Director Aleksandr Domogarov Jr. comes from a family of well-known Russian actors.

 6. The film incorporates elements of the "Bloody Mary" urban legend, popular in many cultures.

 7. "Deadly Still" was a box office success in Russia, outperforming many international horror releases.

 8. The movie's release sparked renewed interest in Russian urban legends and folklore among younger audiences.

 9. Some of the child actors reported feeling genuinely scared during filming of certain scenes.

 10. The film's success led to discussions about a potential crossover with other Russian horror franchises.

18. The Savage (Дикий)

1. Movie Title: The Savage (Дикий)

2. Year of Release: 2021

3. Cast and Director:

- Director: Vladimir Ulyanov

- Cast: Vladimir Epifantsev, Stepan Devonin, Evgeniya Serebrennikova

4. Synopsis:

"The Savage" is a psychological horror-thriller set in the remote Siberian wilderness. The story follows a group of geologists on an expedition deep into the taiga. As they venture further into the isolated forest, they encounter a strange, feral man living alone in the wild. Initially viewing him as a curiosity, the team soon realizes that the man possesses a terrifying secret and may not be alone. As tensions rise within the group, they must confront not only the external threats of the hostile environment and its mysterious inhabitants but also their own inner demons. The film explores themes of civilization versus nature, the thin veneer of human society, and the primal fears that lurk in the depths of the human psyche.

5. Why This Movie Is Recommended:

"The Savage" stands out for its unique setting, utilizing the vast and intimidating Siberian landscape to create a palpable sense of isolation and dread. The film blends elements of wilderness survival thrillers with psychological horror, offering a fresh take on the "man versus nature" trope. Its exploration of primal fears and the fragility of civilized behavior in extreme situations adds depth to the visceral scares. For viewers who appreciate slow-burn horror that relies more on atmosphere and psychological tension than jump scares, "The Savage" provides a haunting and thought-provoking experience.

6. 10 Trivia Facts:

1. The film was shot on location in some of the most remote parts of Siberia.

2. The actor playing the feral man underwent extensive physical training to portray the character convincingly.

3. Many of the survival techniques shown in the film are based on real practices used in the Siberian wilderness.

4. The movie incorporates elements of Siberian folklore and shamanic traditions.

5. Some of the crew reported strange experiences during the isolated shoot, adding to the film's mystique.

6. "The Savage" premiered at the Moscow International Film Festival.

7. The film's sound design heavily features natural Siberian sounds to enhance the immersive experience.

8. Director Vladimir Ulyanov drew inspiration from his own experiences on geological expeditions.

9. The movie sparked discussions in Russia about the preservation of remote wilderness areas.

10. Some scenes were filmed in temperatures as low as -40°C (-40°F), challenging the cast and crew.

19. The Cellar (Подвал)

1. Movie Title: The Cellar (Подвал)

2. Year of Release: 2018

3. Cast and Director:

- Director: Igor Voloshin

- Cast: Jean-Marc Barr, Olga Simonova, Margarita Bychkova

4. Synopsis:

"The Cellar" is a psychological horror film that blurs the line between reality and nightmare. The story centers on a dysfunctional family who move into a new home with a mysterious cellar. As strange occurrences begin to plague the family, they discover that the cellar seems to have a mind of its own, trapping them in a labyrinth of their worst fears and darkest secrets. Each family member is forced to confront their personal demons as the cellar manipulates their perceptions and plays on their deepest anxieties. As they struggle to escape, they must uncover the truth about the house's dark history and their own troubled past.

5. Why This Movie Is Recommended:

"The Cellar" offers a unique blend of psychological horror and surrealism that sets it apart from typical haunted house stories. The film's strength lies in its ability to create a disorienting, nightmarish atmosphere where reality constantly shifts. Its exploration of family dynamics and personal trauma adds psychological depth to the supernatural elements. The movie's visual style, with its use of unsettling imagery and clever practical effects, creates a sense of unease that lingers long after viewing. For fans of mind-bending horror that challenges perceptions of reality, "The Cellar" provides a disturbing and thought-provoking experience.

6. 10 Trivia Facts:

1. Director Igor Voloshin is known for his work in arthouse cinema, bringing a unique aesthetic to the horror genre.

2. The film's cellar set was built entirely on a soundstage to allow for greater control over the surreal elements.

3. "The Cellar" incorporates elements of Jungian psychology in its exploration of the characters' subconscious fears.

4. The movie features minimal dialogue, relying heavily on visual storytelling and atmosphere.

5. Some scenes were shot using practical effects and forced perspective to create disorienting visuals.

6. The film's score, composed by Dmitry Evgrafov, uses unconventional instruments to create an unsettling soundscape.

7. "The Cellar" premiered at the Sitges Film Festival, known for showcasing innovative genre films.

8. The movie's ambiguous ending has sparked numerous fan theories and interpretations.

9. Some of the more surreal sequences were inspired by the works of David Lynch and Luis Buñuel.

10. The film's exploration of family trauma was partly inspired by the director's own experiences.

20. III (Три)

1. Movie Title: III (Три)

2. Year of Release: 2015

3. Cast and Director:

- Director: Pavel Khvaleev

- Cast: Polina Davydova, Lyubov Ignatushko, Evgeniy Gagarin

4. Synopsis:

"III" is an experimental horror film that defies easy categorization. The story follows two sisters, Ayia and Mirra, living in a remote village. When a mysterious plague begins to spread through the community, Mirra falls ill. In a desperate attempt to save her sister, Ayia turns to a local shaman who guides her through a series of mystical rituals. These rituals transport Ayia into the darkest recesses of Mirra's subconscious, where she must confront nightmarish visions and overcome terrifying obstacles. As Ayia delves deeper into this surreal mindscape, the line between reality and hallucination blurs, and she risks losing herself in the process.

5. Why This Movie Is Recommended:

"III" stands out for its unique visual style and unconventional narrative approach. The film blends elements of body horror, psychological thriller, and avant-garde cinema to create a truly singular viewing experience. Its exploration of folklore, mysticism, and the power of the subconscious mind offers a fresh take on horror themes. The movie's striking imagery and unsettling sound design create an immersive atmosphere of dread and disorientation. For viewers who appreciate experimental cinema and are looking for a horror experience that challenges traditional storytelling norms, "III" provides a visually stunning and deeply unsettling journey into the unknown.

6. 10 Trivia Facts:

1. Director Pavel Khvaleev has a background in electronic music, which heavily influenced the film's soundscape.

2. Much of the movie was shot in a small village in Tatarstan, Russia, adding to its authentic folk horror atmosphere.

3. The film's unique visual style was achieved through a combination of practical effects and digital manipulation.

4. "III" premiered at the Sitges Film Festival, where it gained attention for its innovative approach to horror.

5. The movie incorporates elements of Tatar folklore and shamanic practices.

6. Many of the surreal sequences were inspired by the director's own dreams and nightmares.

7. The film was made on a very low budget, with the crew taking on multiple roles during production.

8. "III" features minimal dialogue, relying primarily on visual storytelling and sound design to convey its narrative.

9. The movie's title, "III," refers to the three stages of the shamanic ritual depicted in the film.

10. Despite its experimental nature, the film gained a cult following and critical acclaim in international horror circles.

Sweden

1. Let the Right One In (Låt den rätte komma in)

1. Movie Title: Let the Right One In (Låt den rätte komma in)

2. Year of Release: 2008

3. Cast and Director:

  - Director: Tomas Alfredson

  - Cast: Kåre Hedebrant, Lina Leandersson, Per Ragnar

4. Synopsis:

  Set in the Stockholm suburb of Blackeberg in the 1980s, the film follows Oskar, a bullied 12-year-old boy who befriends Eli, a mysterious girl who only comes out at night. As their friendship deepens, Oskar discovers that Eli is actually a vampire trapped in the body of a child. The film weaves a haunting tale of loneliness, love, and the blurred lines between innocence and monstrosity. As a series of brutal murders rocks the community, Oskar finds himself drawn deeper into Eli's dark world, forcing him to confront his own desires for revenge and companionship.

5. Why This Movie Is Recommended:

  "Let the Right One In" brilliantly reimagines vampire lore through a coming-of-age story, blending horror with poignant drama. Its nuanced exploration of childhood alienation and the nature of evil sets it apart from typical vampire narratives. The film's stark winter setting creates a haunting atmosphere that perfectly complements its themes of isolation and moral ambiguity. With its subtle approach to horror, compelling performances from its young leads, and thought-provoking narrative, it stands as a landmark in both Swedish cinema and the horror genre at large.

6. 10 Trivia Facts:

  1. The film is based on the novel of the same name by John Ajvide Lindqvist, who also wrote the screenplay.

  2. The title is taken from a song by Morrissey, "Let the Right One Slip In."

  3. Lina Leandersson, who played Eli, had her voice dubbed by Elif Ceylan to make her sound more androgynous.

  4. The film spawned an American remake titled "Let Me In" in 2010.

  5. Director Tomas Alfredson used minimal CGI, opting for practical effects whenever possible.

  6. The movie's iconic pool scene took five days to shoot.

  7. Alfredson deliberately avoided watching other vampire films to keep his vision unique.

  8. The film won numerous awards, including the Founders Award for Best Narrative Feature at the 2008 Tribeca Film Festival.

  9. Despite its vampire theme, the word "vampire" is never used in the film.

10. The character of Håkan was significantly altered from the book version to make the film less controversial.

2. The Seventh Seal (Det sjunde inseglet)

1. Movie Title: The Seventh Seal (Det sjunde inseglet)

2. Year of Release: 1957

3. Cast and Director:

  - Director: Ingmar Bergman

  - Cast: Max von Sydow, Gunnar Björnstrand, Bengt Ekerot, Nils Poppe

4. Synopsis:

Set during the Black Death in 14th century Sweden, "The Seventh Seal" follows Antonius Block, a disillusioned knight returning from the Crusades. He encounters Death personified and challenges him to a game of chess to delay his fate. As the game progresses, Block journeys through a plague-ravaged landscape, grappling with questions of faith, mortality, and the meaning of life. Along the way, he encounters various characters, including a traveling theater troupe, each offering different perspectives on life and death. The film interweaves elements of existential drama with supernatural horror, creating a haunting meditation on human existence in the face of inevitable mortality.

5. Why This Movie Is Recommended:

While not a traditional horror film, "The Seventh Seal" incorporates elements of supernatural dread and existential terror that have deeply influenced the horror genre. Bergman's masterful direction creates an atmosphere of pervasive unease, with Death's constant presence looming over the characters. The iconic imagery, particularly the chess game with Death, has become a cultural touchstone. Its exploration of human fear in the face of mortality and the unknown makes it a fundamental work for understanding the psychological roots of horror cinema.

6. 10 Trivia Facts:

  1. The film's title refers to a passage from the Book of Revelation in the Bible.

  2. Bergman was inspired to make the film after seeing a painting in a church depicting a man playing chess with Death.

  3. The movie was shot in just 35 days.

  4. Max von Sydow was only 28 when he played the world-weary knight Antonius Block.

  5. The chess game in the film uses an actual chess problem, which ends in checkmate.

  6. Bergman wrote the script while hospitalized for stomach problems.

  7. The film's famous "Dance of Death" sequence was improvised on set.

  8. "The Seventh Seal" has been parodied numerous times, including in "Bill & Ted's Bogus Journey" and "Last Action Hero."

  9. Bergman claimed he was no longer afraid of death after making this film.

  10. The movie was initially a box office failure in Sweden but gained international acclaim.

3. Border (Gräns)

1. Movie Title: Border (Gräns)

2. Year of Release: 2018

3. Cast and Director:

- Director: Ali Abbasi

- Cast: Eva Melander, Eero Milonoff, Jörgen Thorsson

4. Synopsis:

"Border" follows Tina, a customs officer with an extraordinary sense of smell that allows her to detect contraband and even emotions. Tina's isolated life is disrupted when she encounters Vore, a mysterious man who shares her unusual physical appearance and abilities. As Tina begins to uncover the truth about her identity, she is drawn into a dark underworld that challenges her understanding of humanity and morality. The film blends elements of Scandinavian folklore with body horror and psychological thriller, exploring themes of identity, belonging, and the nature of good and evil.

5. Why This Movie Is Recommended:

"Border" offers a unique and unsettling take on horror, seamlessly blending supernatural elements with real-world issues. Its exploration of identity and otherness through the lens of Nordic mythology creates a deeply affecting and thought-provoking experience. The film's stunning makeup and prosthetic work, combined with powerful performances, bring its fantastical elements to visceral life. Its ability to evoke both empathy and revulsion makes it a standout in contemporary horror cinema, challenging viewers' perceptions and leaving a lasting impact.

6. 10 Trivia Facts:

1. The film is based on a short story by John Ajvide Lindqvist, author of "Let the Right One In."

2. Lead actress Eva Melander spent four hours in makeup each day to transform into Tina.

3. "Border" won the Un Certain Regard award at the 2018 Cannes Film Festival.

4. The film was Sweden's entry for Best Foreign Language Film at the 91st Academy Awards.

5. Director Ali Abbasi is Iranian-born but has lived in Sweden since 2002.

6. The movie's makeup team was nominated for an Academy Award for Best Makeup and Hairstyling.

7. Abbasi described the film as "a love story and a crime story" rather than a straightforward horror film.

8. The film's creature design was inspired by Scandinavian folklore about trolls.

9. "Border" was shot on location in various parts of Sweden, including Kapellskär and Värmland.

10. The film's success led to increased interest in adapting more of Lindqvist's work for the screen.

4. Hour of the Wolf (Vargtimmen)

1. Movie Title: Hour of the Wolf (Vargtimmen)

2. Year of Release: 1968

3. Cast and Director:

- Director: Ingmar Bergman

- Cast: Max von Sydow, Liv Ullmann, Gertrud Fridh, Georg Rydeberg

4. Synopsis:

"Hour of the Wolf" follows Johan Borg, a painter living on a remote island with his pregnant wife Alma. Johan is plagued by insomnia, alcoholism, and disturbing visions. As his mental state deteriorates, he becomes convinced that the island is inhabited by demonic entities. Alma struggles to understand and help her husband as he spirals deeper into his nightmarish world. The line between reality and hallucination blurs as Johan confronts his inner demons and the mysterious aristocrats who seem to haunt the island. The film explores themes of artistic madness, marital strain, and the terrifying power of the subconscious mind.

5. Why This Movie Is Recommended:

"Hour of the Wolf" is a masterclass in psychological horror, blending surrealism with deeply personal fears. Bergman's direction creates a pervasive sense of unease, using stark black-and-white cinematography to heighten the nightmarish atmosphere. The film's exploration of an artist's mental breakdown is both intimate and universally terrifying. Its influence can be seen in numerous psychological horror films that followed. For those interested in the intersection of art, madness, and horror, "Hour of the Wolf" is an essential and haunting experience.

6. 10 Trivia Facts:

1. The title refers to the hour between night and dawn, traditionally associated with heightened fear and supernatural activity.

2. This is Bergman's only horror film, though many of his works contain elements of psychological terror.

3. The film was partly inspired by Bergman's own experiences with panic attacks and insomnia.

4. Liv Ullmann was pregnant during filming, mirroring her character's condition.

5. The movie features several references to Mozart's opera "The Magic Flute," which Bergman later adapted for film.

6. Bergman considered this film one of his personal favorites among his own works.

7. The character of Johan Borg is named after Johan August Strindberg, a Swedish playwright known for his psychological dramas.

8. The film's structure, with Alma narrating directly to the camera, influenced later horror films like "The Blair Witch Project."

9. Some of the film's more surreal sequences were inspired by paintings by Francisco Goya.

10. "Hour of the Wolf" was shot back-to-back with another Bergman film, "Shame," using the same main actors and island location.

5. Evil Ed

1. Movie Title: Evil Ed

2. Year of Release: 1995

3. Cast and Director:

- Director: Anders Jacobsson

- Cast: Johan Rudebeck, Per Löfberg, Olof Rhodin, Camela Leierth

4. Synopsis:

"Evil Ed" follows Edward Tor Swenson, a mild-mannered film editor who is assigned to cut the violent scenes from a series of low-budget horror films called the "Loose Limbs" franchise. As Ed works on the gruesome footage, he begins to lose his grip on reality. The constant exposure to graphic violence takes its toll, and Ed starts hallucinating, seeing monsters and experiencing vivid, bloody visions. His mental state deteriorates rapidly, leading to a psychotic breakdown where he becomes a violent killer himself. The film blends gory horror with dark comedy, satirizing both the horror genre and censorship debates.

5. Why This Movie Is Recommended:

"Evil Ed" stands out as a unique entry in Swedish horror cinema, offering a meta-commentary on the genre itself. Its blend of over-the-top gore, dark humor, and satire makes it a cult favorite among horror fans. The film cleverly critiques censorship and the effects of media violence while reveling in the excesses of splatter films. For those who appreciate horror-comedies and aren't squeamish about graphic violence, "Evil Ed" provides an entertaining and subversive viewing experience that both celebrates and lampoons the horror genre.

6. 10 Trivia Facts:

1. The film was made as a response to the strict censorship of horror films in Sweden during the 1980s and early 1990s.

2. "Evil Ed" was shot over a period of three years due to budget constraints.

3. The movie contains numerous references to other horror films, including "The Evil Dead" and "A Nightmare on Elm Street."

4. Despite its low budget, the film gained international recognition and was distributed in over 20 countries.

5. The character of Ed was partially inspired by David Cronenberg's "Videodrome."

6. Many of the film's special effects were created using household items and food products.

7. Director Anders Jacobsson also worked as the film's editor and special effects artist.

8. The "Loose Limbs" franchise mentioned in the film is a parody of real-life low-budget horror series.

9. "Evil Ed" was one of the first Swedish films to receive widespread distribution on home video in the United States.

10. A special edition Blu-ray released in 2017 included over 3 hours of new and archival bonus features.

6. Frostbiten (Frostbite)

1. Movie Title: Frostbiten (Frostbite)

2. Year of Release: 2006

3. Cast and Director:

- Director: Anders Banke

- Cast: Petra Nielsen, Carl-Åke Eriksson, Grete Havnesköld, Emma Åberg

4. Synopsis:

Set in the northernmost town of Sweden during its month-long polar night, "Frostbiten" follows teenager Saga and her mother Annika, who move to the town for Annika's new job at the local hospital. Unbeknownst to them, the hospital's lead physician is conducting secret experiments related to vampirism. When a group of teenagers accidentally ingest pills containing vampire blood, they begin to transform, leading to chaos in the town. As the vampire infection spreads, Saga must fight to survive the long night and save her mother. The film blends traditional vampire lore with dark humor and the unique setting of the Arctic winter.

5. Why This Movie Is Recommended:

"Frostbiten" stands out for its fresh take on vampire mythology, using the Arctic setting to create a unique atmosphere. The film cleverly uses the month-long darkness as a perfect backdrop for vampire activity, adding a new dimension to the genre. Its blend of horror and comedy, along with its distinctly Swedish setting and sensibilities, offers a different flavor compared to mainstream vampire films. For fans of vampire movies looking for something off the beaten path, "Frostbiten" provides an entertaining and innovative experience.

6. 10 Trivia Facts:

1. "Frostbiten" was the first vampire film ever produced in Sweden.

2. The movie was shot in Kalix, Sweden, and Kiruna, the northernmost town in Sweden.

3. Director Anders Banke studied filmmaking in Russia and brings some Russian cinematic influences to the film.

4. The film's visual effects were created by Filmgate, known for their work on "Let the Right One In."

5. "Frostbiten" premiered at the 2006 Gothenburg Film Festival.

6. The movie pays homage to classic vampire films while also subverting many tropes of the genre.

7. The film's portrayal of vampirism as a virus spread through pills is a unique twist on vampire lore.

8. "Frostbiten" was one of the most expensive horror films produced in Sweden at the time of its release.

9. The movie's soundtrack features several Swedish punk and metal bands.

10. Despite being set during the polar night, much of the film was actually shot during summer months with simulated darkness.

7. Marianne

1. Movie Title: Marianne

2. Year of Release: 2011

3. Cast and Director:

 - Director: Filip Tegstedt

 - Cast: Thomas Hedengran, Peter Stormare, Tintin Anderzon, Sandra Larsson

4. **Synopsis**:

 "Marianne" follows Krister, a man haunted by guilt and grief after the death of his wife in a car accident. He moves with his teenage daughter to a small town in northern Sweden, hoping for a fresh start. However, Krister begins experiencing terrifying sleep paralysis episodes featuring a malevolent entity. As his mental state deteriorates, he struggles to distinguish between reality and nightmare. The line between psychological trauma and supernatural horror blurs, leaving both Krister and the audience questioning what is real. The film explores themes of guilt, grief, and the psychological toll of trauma, all set against the backdrop of the isolated Swedish countryside.

5. **Why This Movie Is Recommended**:

 "Marianne" offers a deeply psychological approach to horror, focusing on the internal struggles of its protagonist as much as external threats. Its exploration of sleep paralysis taps into a primal fear that many can relate to, creating visceral scares. The film's slow-burn approach and ambiguous nature challenge viewers, inviting multiple interpretations. With strong performances and a haunting atmosphere, "Marianne" showcases a more subtle, character-driven side of Swedish horror that lingers in the mind long after viewing.

6. **10 Trivia Facts**:

 1. "Marianne" was director Filip Tegstedt's debut feature film.

 2. The film was partly inspired by Tegstedt's own experiences with sleep paralysis.

 3. Peter Stormare, known for his roles in Hollywood films, plays a supporting role as a therapist.

 4. The movie was shot entirely on location in Östersund, Tegstedt's hometown in northern Sweden.

 5. "Marianne" blends elements of Swedish folklore with modern psychological horror.

 6. The film's sound design plays a crucial role in creating its unsettling atmosphere.

 7. Tegstedt used crowdfunding to help finance the post-production of the film.

 8. "Marianne" premiered at the 2011 Fantasia International Film Festival in Montreal.

 9. The film's portrayal of sleep paralysis has been praised for its accuracy by those who have experienced the phenomenon.

 10. Despite its supernatural elements, much of the horror in "Marianne" comes from the exploration of grief and mental health issues.

8. Ond tro (Evil Faith)

1. Movie Title: Ond tro (Evil Faith)

2. Year of Release: 2010

3. Cast and Director:

  - Director: Kristian Petri

  - Cast: Sonja Richter, Jonas Karlsson, Magnus Krepper

4. Synopsis:

"Ond tro" tells the story of Mona, a young woman who becomes involved with a religious cult led by the charismatic Gabriel. As Mona is drawn deeper into the cult's activities, she begins to question the true nature of Gabriel's teachings and the group's intentions. The film explores themes of faith, manipulation, and the blurred lines between spirituality and madness. As strange and disturbing events unfold, Mona must confront her own beliefs and the potential dangers of blind faith. The narrative weaves elements of psychological thriller with supernatural horror, creating an unsettling exploration of religious extremism and its consequences.

5. Why This Movie Is Recommended:

"Ond tro" stands out for its nuanced approach to religious horror, delving into the psychological aspects of cult mentality. The film creates a palpable sense of unease through its exploration of faith taken to extremes. Its commentary on the dangers of charismatic leadership and groupthink adds depth to the horror elements. With strong performances and a slowly building tension, "Ond tro" offers a thought-provoking and chilling experience that goes beyond simple scares to examine the nature of belief itself.

6. 10 Trivia Facts:

  1. The film's title "Ond tro" translates to "Bad Faith" or "Evil Faith" in English.

  2. Director Kristian Petri is known for his work in both fiction and documentary filmmaking.

  3. "Ond tro" was partially inspired by real-life cult incidents in Sweden and around the world.

  4. The movie explores the concept of "love bombing," a manipulation tactic used by some cults.

  5. Much of the film was shot on location in the Swedish countryside, adding to its isolated atmosphere.

  6. "Ond tro" premiered at the 2010 Gothenburg Film Festival.

  7. The film's score, composed by Johan Söderqvist, plays a crucial role in building tension.

  8. Lead actress Sonja Richter prepared for her role by studying accounts of real cult survivors.

  9. The movie sparked discussions in Sweden about the nature of faith and the potential dangers of extreme religious groups.

  10. "Ond tro" blends elements of Scandinavian noir with religious horror, creating a unique genre hybrid.

9. Isolerad (Isolated)

1. Movie Title: Isolerad (Isolated)

2. Year of Release: 2010

3. Cast and Director:

- Director: Anders Banke

- Cast: Peter Stormare, Anastasios Soulis, Johannes Brost

4. Synopsis:

"Isolerad" follows a group of young criminals who hijack a cash-in-transit van and take refuge in an old, abandoned factory. As they wait to make their escape, tensions rise within the group, exacerbated by their isolation and the pressure of their situation. However, they soon discover that they are not alone in the factory. A malevolent presence begins to stalk them, turning their hideout into a nightmarish trap. The film blends elements of crime thriller with supernatural horror, as the characters must confront both their own violent natures and an unknown, possibly otherworldly threat.

5. Why This Movie Is Recommended:

"Isolerad" offers a unique blend of crime drama and horror, creating a tense, claustrophobic experience. The film's use of its isolated setting builds a palpable sense of dread, while the interpersonal conflicts among the criminals add depth to the narrative. Its exploration of how extreme situations can bring out the worst in people adds a psychological layer to the horror elements. For those who enjoy genre-blending films that keep you guessing, "Isolerad" provides a gripping, intense viewing experience that balances human drama with supernatural terror.

6. 10 Trivia Facts:

1. "Isolerad" marks Anders Banke's second feature film after "Frostbiten."

2. The movie was shot entirely on location in an actual abandoned factory in Sweden.

3. Peter Stormare, known for his roles in Hollywood films, plays a key supporting role.

4. The film's title "Isolerad" means "Isolated" in English, reflecting the characters' situation.

5. "Isolerad" premiered at the 2010 Fantastic Fest in Austin, Texas.

6. The movie's sound design plays a crucial role in creating its unsettling atmosphere.

7. Director Anders Banke drew inspiration from both Scandinavian crime dramas and classic horror films.

8. The film explores themes of greed, paranoia, and the breakdown of social norms in isolated situations.

9. "Isolerad" features practical effects for its horror elements, minimizing the use of CGI.

10. The movie's ambiguous ending has sparked discussions among viewers about its true nature and meaning.

10. Psalm 21

1. **Movie Title**: Psalm 21

2. **Year of Release**: 2009

3. **Cast and Director**:

   - Director: Fredrik Hiller

   - Cast: Jonas Malmsjö, Niklas Falk, Björn Bengtsson, Julia Dufvenius

4. **Synopsis**:

   "Psalm 21" centers on Henrik Horneus, a young priest struggling with his faith after the death of his father. When he receives news that his father, also a priest, has died under mysterious circumstances in a remote northern village, Henrik travels there to investigate. As he delves into the village's dark secrets and his father's final days, Henrik encounters increasingly strange and terrifying phenomena. The line between reality and nightmare blurs as Henrik confronts both supernatural horrors and the depths of his own doubts and fears. The film explores themes of faith, family secrets, and the nature of evil, all set against the backdrop of the isolated Swedish wilderness.

5. **Why This Movie Is Recommended**:

   "Psalm 21" offers a unique blend of religious horror and psychological thriller, delving deep into questions of faith and the nature of evil. Its atmospheric use of the Swedish wilderness creates a sense of isolation and dread that permeates the film. The movie's exploration of a crisis of faith adds depth to its horror elements, creating a thought-provoking experience. With strong performances and striking visuals, "Psalm 21" provides a cerebral and chilling take on religious horror that stands out in the Swedish horror landscape.

6. **10 Trivia Facts**:

   1. The film's title refers to Psalm 21 in the Bible, which deals with themes of divine judgment.

   2. Director Fredrik Hiller also plays a supporting role in the film.

   3. "Psalm 21" was partly inspired by Swedish folklore and religious traditions.

   4. The movie was shot on location in northern Sweden, utilizing the natural landscape to create atmosphere.

   5. The film blends elements of Christianity with pagan mythology, creating a unique religious horror hybrid.

   6. "Psalm 21" premiered at the 2009 Fantastic Fest in Austin, Texas.

   7. The movie's score, composed by Johan Söderqvist, plays a crucial role in building tension.

   8. The film explores the concept of generational sin and inherited guilt.

   9. "Psalm 21" received praise for its visual effects, which were impressive given its relatively modest budget.

   10. The movie sparked discussions in Sweden about the portrayal of religion in horror films.

Romania

1. Morome□ii 2

1. Movie Title: Morome□ii 2

2. Year of Release: 2018

3. Cast and Director:

- Director: Stere Gulea

- Cast: Hora□iu Mălăele, Iosif Pa□tina, Dana Dogaru

4. Synopsis:

While not strictly a horror film, "Morome□ii 2" contains elements of psychological horror and existential dread. Set in post-World War II Romania, the film follows the Moromete family as they struggle to adapt to the new communist regime. The patriarch, Ilie Moromete, faces the dissolution of his family and way of life as collectivization threatens to strip away his land and identity. The creeping sense of inevitability and loss creates a haunting atmosphere throughout the film, as the characters grapple with forces beyond their control.

5. Why This Movie Is Recommended:

"Morome□ii 2" is recommended for its masterful portrayal of psychological tension and societal horror. While not a traditional horror film, it captures the dread and anxiety of a changing world with nuance and depth. The film's exploration of the loss of individual autonomy and the erosion of traditional values resonates with universal fears. Its rich character development and atmospheric storytelling create a sense of impending doom that rivals many conventional horror movies.

6. 10 Trivia Facts:

1. The film is a sequel to the 1987 movie "Morome□ii," also directed by Stere Gulea.

2. Both films are based on Marin Preda's novel of the same name.

3. The original "Morome□ii" is considered a classic of Romanian cinema.

4. Hora□iu Mălăele, who plays Ilie Moromete, is one of Romania's most respected actors and comedians.

5. The film was shot on location in Teleorman County, Romania, to capture the authentic rural setting.

6. "Morome□ii 2" premiered at the 2018 Transilvania International Film Festival.

7. The movie's production took over seven years from concept to completion.

8. It features a mix of professional actors and local villagers to enhance authenticity.

9. The film received funding from the Romanian National Film Center.

10. "Morome□ii 2" was Romania's submission for the Best International Feature Film at the 92nd Academy Awards, although it was not nominated.

2. Bucure☐ti NonStop

1. Movie Title: Bucureşti NonStop

2. Year of Release: 2015

3. Cast and Director:

- Director: Dan Chi☐u

- Cast: Ion Besoiu, Olimpia Melinte, Gheorghe Ifrim

4. Synopsis:

"Bucureşti NonStop" is a dark comedy-drama with elements of horror that intertwines several stories set in Bucharest over the course of one night. The film follows various characters including a taxi driver, a pharmacist, and a group of youths as they navigate the city's nocturnal underbelly. As the night progresses, the characters encounter increasingly surreal and unsettling situations, blurring the line between reality and nightmare. The city itself becomes a character, its dark corners hiding secrets and dangers that the protagonists must confront.

5. Why This Movie Is Recommended:

While not a traditional horror film, "Bucureşti NonStop" is recommended for its unsettling atmosphere and exploration of urban fears. The movie's nonlinear narrative and interconnected stories create a sense of unease and unpredictability. Its portrayal of Bucharest at night taps into universal anxieties about urban environments after dark. The film's blend of dark humor and genuine tension offers a unique viewing experience that challenges genre conventions.

6. 10 Trivia Facts:

1. The film was shot entirely at night over a period of 18 days.

2. Director Dan Chi☐u also wrote the screenplay.

3. "Bucureşti NonStop" premiered at the 2015 Transilvania International Film Festival.

4. The movie features a mix of established actors and newcomers.

5. Many scenes were improvised to capture the spontaneity of nightlife.

6. The film's soundtrack features a mix of Romanian and international music.

7. Some of the locations used in the film are actual 24-hour businesses in Bucharest.

8. The movie received funding from the Romanian National Film Center.

9. It was praised for its authentic portrayal of Bucharest's diverse neighborhoods.

10. The film's title, "NonStop," refers both to the 24-hour nature of city life and the relentless pace of the narrative.

3. Undeva la Palilula

1. Movie Title: Undeva la Palilula (Somewhere in Palilula)

2. Year of Release: 2012

3. Cast and Director:

  - Director: Silviu Purcărete

  - Cast: Aron Dimény, George Mihăiţă, Răzvan Vasilescu

4. Synopsis:

"Undeva la Palilula" is a surrealist dark comedy with horror elements set in a fictional Romanian town during the communist era. The story follows a young doctor assigned to a remote hospital in Palilula, a bizarre place where time seems to stand still and reality bends in unexpected ways. As he encounters the town's eccentric inhabitants and their strange customs, the doctor finds himself caught in a nightmarish world that blurs the line between the absurd and the terrifying. The film's dreamlike quality and unsettling imagery create a sense of unease that permeates every scene.

5. Why This Movie Is Recommended:

"Undeva la Palilula" is recommended for its unique blend of dark humor, surrealism, and horror. Director Silviu Purcărete, known for his work in theater, brings a theatrical and visually striking approach to the film. The movie's exploration of isolation, cultural disorientation, and the absurdities of bureaucracy resonates with both Romanian history and universal human experiences. Its haunting imagery and atmospheric storytelling create a lingering sense of unease that stays with viewers long after the film ends.

6. 10 Trivia Facts:

  1. This was the directorial debut of Silviu Purcărete, a renowned Romanian theater director.

  2. The film took over seven years to complete from conception to release.

  3. Many of the actors in the film had previously worked with Purcărete in theater productions.

  4. The fictional town of Palilula was entirely constructed for the film.

  5. The movie's surreal style has been compared to the works of Federico Fellini and Emir Kusturica.

  6. "Undeva la Palilula" won the FIPRESCI Prize at the 2012 Transilvania International Film Festival.

  7. The film's score, composed by Vasile Şirli, plays a crucial role in creating its unsettling atmosphere.

  8. Many of the bizarre customs depicted in the film were invented by Purcărete.

  9. The movie was partially funded by the Romanian National Film Center.

  10. Despite its surreal elements, the film is seen as a metaphor for Romania's transition from communism.

4. Ți se va întâmpla doar Ție

1. Movie Title: Ți se va întâmpla doar Ție (It Can Only Happen to You)

2. Year of Release: 2022

3. Cast and Director:

- Director: Iura Luncașu

- Cast: Anca Dumitra, Ada Galeș, Gabriel Spahiu

4. Synopsis:

"Ți se va întâmpla doar Ție" is a psychological thriller with horror elements that follows Ana, a successful lawyer whose life begins to unravel after a series of inexplicable events. What starts as minor incidents escalates into a terrifying ordeal as Ana becomes convinced that she's being targeted by an unseen force. As her paranoia grows, she starts to question her own sanity and the loyalty of those around her. The film blurs the line between reality and delusion, creating a tense atmosphere where the true horror lies in the uncertainty of Ana's perceptions.

5. Why This Movie Is Recommended:

This film is recommended for its masterful buildup of psychological tension and its exploration of paranoia and gaslighting. The movie's ability to create fear from everyday situations makes it particularly unsettling. Its commentary on the fragility of mental health and the ease with which one's life can spiral out of control adds depth to the horror elements. The strong performances, particularly from lead actress Anca Dumitra, bring authenticity to the psychological turmoil portrayed on screen.

6. 10 Trivia Facts:

1. The film marks Iura Luncașu's return to feature film directing after focusing on television for several years.

2. Many of the film's scenes were shot in Bucharest, showcasing both its modern and historic areas.

3. The movie premiered at the 2022 Transilvania International Film Festival.

4. Anca Dumitra, who plays Ana, is best known for her role in the popular Romanian TV series "Las Fierbinți."

5. The film's title is a play on the common phrase used to reassure people that bad things won't happen to them.

6. Some of the film's more intense scenes required specialized psychological preparation for the actors.

7. The movie received funding from the Romanian National Film Center.

8. It features a minimalist score that enhances the growing sense of unease throughout the film.

9. The film sparked discussions in Romania about mental health awareness.

10. Despite its thriller/horror elements, the movie also incorporates dark humor typical of Romanian New Wave cinema.

5. Pădurea spânzuraților

1. Movie Title: Pădurea spânzuraților **(Forest of the Hanged)**

2. Year of Release: 1964

3. Cast and Director:

  - Director: Liviu Ciulei

  - Cast: Victor Rebengiuc, Liviu Ciulei, Ștefan Ciobotărașu

4. Synopsis:

   While primarily a war drama, "Pădurea spânzuraților" contains elements of psychological horror that make it a haunting viewing experience. Set during World War I, the film follows Apostol Bologa, an ethnic Romanian serving as an officer in the Austro-Hungarian army. As he grapples with his conscience and national identity, Bologa faces the moral horror of war and the existential dread of impending doom. The titular "forest of the hanged" refers to the execution of deserters, a constant reminder of the price of disobedience and the fragility of life in wartime. The film's atmosphere of oppression and inevitability creates a sense of horror that transcends traditional genre boundaries.

5. Why This Movie Is Recommended:

   "Pădurea spânzuraților" is recommended for its profound exploration of the horrors of war and the human psyche. While not a conventional horror film, its ability to evoke a sense of dread and existential terror is masterful. The movie's stark black-and-white cinematography and haunting imagery create an atmosphere of impending doom that rivals many traditional horror films. Its themes of moral conflict, identity crisis, and the loss of humanity in wartime resonate deeply and leave a lasting impact on viewers.

6. 10 Trivia Facts:

   1. The film is based on the 1922 novel of the same name by Liviu Rebreanu.

   2. Director Liviu Ciulei also plays a significant role in the film as Captain Klapka.

   3. "Pădurea spânzuraților" won the Best Director award at the 1965 Cannes Film Festival, a first for Romanian cinema.

   4. The movie was shot on location in Romania, with many scenes filmed in Transylvania.

   5. It's considered one of the most important films in Romanian cinema history.

   6. The film's anti-war message was controversial at the time of its release.

   7. Victor Rebengiuc, who plays Apostol Bologa, went on to become one of Romania's most respected actors.

   8. The movie's success helped launch the Romanian New Wave in cinema.

   9. Many of the extras in the film were local villagers with no acting experience.

   10. The film's restoration in 2019 introduced it to a new generation of viewers.

Iran

1. Under the Shadow (سایه زیر)

1. **Movie Title:** Under the Shadow (Persian: سایه زیر, romanized: Zir-e Sayeh)

2. **Year of Release:** 2016

3. **Cast and Director:**

   - Director: Babak Anvari

   - Cast: Narges Rashidi, Avin Manshadi, Bobby Naderi

4. **Synopsis:**

Set in 1980s Tehran during the Iran-Iraq War, "Under the Shadow" follows Shideh, a mother struggling to cope with the terrors of war and a mysterious evil presence in her apartment. As her husband is called away to serve in the military, Shideh is left alone with her young daughter Dorsa. Strange occurrences begin to plague their home, coinciding with missile attacks on the city. Dorsa becomes convinced that a djinn is haunting them, while Shideh grapples with the reality of the war and the possibility of a supernatural threat. The film blends the horrors of war with traditional Middle Eastern folklore, creating a unique and terrifying experience.

5. **Why This Movie Is Recommended:**

"Under the Shadow" stands out for its masterful blend of sociopolitical commentary and supernatural horror. It uses the backdrop of the Iran-Iraq War to explore themes of oppression, particularly the struggles of women in a restrictive society. The film's slow-burn approach to horror, building tension through atmosphere and psychological dread rather than jump scares, creates a deeply unsettling experience. Its unique cultural perspective brings fresh elements to the haunted house subgenre, making it a must-watch for horror fans seeking something beyond Western tropes.

6. **10 Trivia Facts:**

   1. The film was Britain's submission for the Best Foreign Language Film at the 89th Academy Awards.

   2. Director Babak Anvari drew from his own childhood experiences during the Iran-Iraq War.

   3. The movie was shot in Jordan due to filming restrictions in Iran.

   4. It won the Outstanding Debut award at the 2017 BAFTAs.

   5. The film's dialogue is entirely in Persian, despite being a UK production.

   6. "Under the Shadow" was acquired by Netflix for streaming distribution.

   7. The apartment used in the film was custom-built on a soundstage.

   8. It was the first Iranian horror film to gain significant international recognition.

   9. The director insisted on casting Persian-speaking actors for authenticity.

10. The film draws inspiration from classic horror movies like "Rosemary's Baby" and "The Babadook".

2. A Girl Walks Home Alone at Night (رودمی خانه به تنها شب در دختری)

1. Movie Title: A Girl Walks Home Alone at Night (Persian: رودمی خانه به تنها شب در دختری, **romanized: Dokhtari dar šab tanhâ be xâne miravad)**

2. Year of Release: 2014

3. Cast and Director:

- Director: Ana Lily Amirpour

- Cast: Sheila Vand, Arash Marandi, Marshall Manesh

4. Synopsis:

Set in the fictional Iranian ghost town of Bad City, this black-and-white film follows the story of a lonely vampire known only as "The Girl". She stalks the streets at night, preying on men who disrespect or abuse women. The Girl's path crosses with Arash, a young man struggling to care for his heroin-addicted father. As an unlikely romance blooms between them, the film explores themes of loneliness, addiction, and gender dynamics in a surreal, noir-esque setting. The vampire's presence in the town serves as both a threat and a form of justice, challenging the societal norms of this desolate, oil-rich hellscape.

5. Why This Movie Is Recommended:

"A Girl Walks Home Alone at Night" is a unique blend of horror, western, and film noir, creating a genre-defying experience. Its striking black-and-white cinematography and carefully curated soundtrack contribute to an otherworldly atmosphere. The film subverts traditional vampire lore by presenting its protagonist as a vigilante figure, offering a fresh perspective on the genre. Its feminist undertones and exploration of Iranian diaspora culture add depth to the narrative. This stylish, unconventional approach to horror makes it a standout film for those seeking something beyond traditional scares.

6. 10 Trivia Facts:

1. It's often referred to as "the first Iranian vampire Western".

2. The film was shot entirely in California, despite its Iranian setting.

3. Director Ana Lily Amirpour was born in England to Iranian parents and raised in the US.

4. The vampire's iconic chador was inspired by Amirpour's childhood memories of women in Iran.

5. The character of The Girl was partially inspired by the director's love of skateboarding.

6. The film's soundtrack features a mix of Iranian pop and Western alternative music.

7. Amirpour created a graphic novel prequel to the film.

8. The director describes the fictional Bad City as "the love child of David Lynch and Sergio Leone".

9. The cat in the film, which plays a significant role, was cast before any of the human actors.

10. Despite its Iranian setting and characters, the film is primarily in English.

3. Fish & Cat (گربه و ماهی)

1. Movie Title: Fish & Cat (Persian: گربه و ماهی, romanized: Mahi va Gorbeh)

2. Year of Release: 2013

3. Cast and Director:

- Director: Shahram Mokri

- Cast: Babak Karimi, Saeid Ebrahimifar, Abed Abest

4. Synopsis:

"Fish & Cat" is an experimental horror film that blends elements of slasher movies with art-house cinema. The story revolves around a group of university students who gather at a lakeside camp for a kite-flying event. Nearby, two suspicious men run a small restaurant that is rumored to serve human flesh. As the narrative unfolds, the film explores the interactions between these characters in a non-linear fashion. The most striking aspect of the film is its presentation as one continuous 134-minute shot, which loops and repeats scenes from different perspectives, creating a disorienting and surreal atmosphere that blurs the lines between past, present, and future.

5. Why This Movie Is Recommended:

"Fish & Cat" is a unique and challenging film that pushes the boundaries of conventional horror storytelling. Its innovative single-shot technique creates a sense of unease and disorientation that perfectly complements the unsettling narrative. The film's non-linear structure and time-bending approach to storytelling keep viewers constantly guessing, making for an intellectually engaging experience. While it may not offer traditional scares, its oppressive atmosphere and the looming threat of violence create a persistent sense of dread. For those interested in experimental cinema and unconventional horror, "Fish & Cat" offers a truly singular viewing experience.

6. 10 Trivia Facts:

1. The entire film was shot in one continuous take, lasting 134 minutes.

2. Despite appearing as one shot, the film was actually filmed over three days.

3. The script was 350 pages long, significantly longer than the average 90-120 page screenplay.

4. The film's structure was inspired by M.C. Escher's impossible constructions.

5. "Fish & Cat" won the Special Orizzonti Award for Innovative Content at the 70th Venice International Film Festival.

6. The film's title is a reference to a Persian expression about a suspicious situation.

7. Director Shahram Mokri spent six months rehearsing with the actors before filming.

8. The film blends elements of the slasher genre with Iranian New Wave cinema.

9. Despite its horror elements, the film contains very little on-screen violence.

10. The movie's circular narrative structure has drawn comparisons to time loop films, despite not being a traditional time loop story.

4. The Night (شب)

1. Movie Title: The Night (Persian: شب, romanized: Shab)

2. Year of Release: 2020

3. Cast and Director:

- Director: Kourosh Ahari

- Cast: Shahab Hosseini, Niousha Noor, George Maguire

4. Synopsis:

"The Night" follows an Iranian couple, Babak and Neda, and their infant daughter as they spend a harrowing night in a mysterious Los Angeles hotel. After attending a dinner party and getting lost on their way home, the exhausted family checks into the Hotel Normandie. As the night progresses, they find themselves trapped in a nightmarish scenario where they are forced to confront the secrets and lies in their relationship. Strange occurrences and ghostly encounters push the couple to their psychological limits, blurring the lines between reality and hallucination. The hotel becomes a labyrinthine manifestation of their guilt and unresolved issues, forcing them to confront their past to survive the night.

5. Why This Movie Is Recommended:

"The Night" stands out for its atmospheric tension and psychological depth. It skillfully blends elements of Iranian cinema with Western horror tropes, creating a unique cultural perspective on the haunted hotel subgenre. The film's exploration of guilt, immigration, and marital secrets adds layers of meaning to its supernatural scares. Strong performances, particularly from Shahab Hosseini (known for his work in Asghar Farhadi's films), elevate the emotional impact of the story. Its slow-burn approach to horror, focusing on building dread rather than relying on jump scares, makes it a compelling watch for fans of psychological horror.

6. 10 Trivia Facts:

1. "The Night" is the first U.S.-produced film to receive a license for theatrical release in Iran since the 1979 revolution.

2. The film was shot on location at the actual Hotel Normandie in Los Angeles.

3. Director Kourosh Ahari was inspired by Stanley Kubrick's "The Shining" in his approach to hotel-based horror.

4. The movie is primarily in Persian, with some English dialogue.

5. Lead actor Shahab Hosseini won the Best Actor award at the Molins Film Festival for his performance.

6. The film's score, composed by Nima Fakhrara, incorporates traditional Iranian instruments.

7. "The Night" had its world premiere at the Santa Barbara International Film Festival in 2020.

8. The director used practical effects and minimal CGI to create a more realistic, grounded feel to the supernatural elements.

9. The story was partially inspired by the director's own experiences as an Iranian immigrant in the United States.

10. Despite being set in Los Angeles, much of the film has a distinctly Iranian aesthetic and storytelling style.

5. Zalava (زالاوا)

1. Movie Title: Zalava (Persian: زالاوا)

2. Year of Release: 2021

3. Cast and Director:

 - Director: Arsalan Amiri

 - Cast: Navid Pourfaraj, Pouria Rahimi Sam, Hoda Zeinolabedin

4. Synopsis:

 Set in 1978, just before the Iranian Revolution, "Zalava" takes place in a remote Kurdish village where the inhabitants believe they are being plagued by demons. The film follows Masoud, a skeptical gendarmerie sergeant who arrives to debunk these superstitious beliefs. He clashes with the villagers and a mysterious exorcist named Amardan, who claims he can capture the demons in a glass jar. As strange events unfold and tension rises in the village, Masoud finds his rational worldview challenged. The line between reality and superstition blurs, forcing him to confront the possibility that there might be some truth to the villagers' fears. The film explores the conflict between modern skepticism and traditional beliefs against the backdrop of pre-revolution Iran.

5. Why This Movie Is Recommended:

 "Zalava" offers a unique blend of folk horror and sociopolitical commentary, set against the rarely-seen backdrop of Kurdish Iran. Its exploration of the tension between rationality and superstition provides a fresh perspective on horror themes. The film's atmospheric building of dread and its ambiguous approach to the supernatural create a consistently unsettling viewing experience. Strong performances and thoughtful direction elevate the material beyond simple scares, offering insight into a specific time and place in Iranian history. For viewers interested in culturally specific horror that challenges genre conventions, "Zalava" is a must-watch.

6. 10 Trivia Facts:

 1. "Zalava" won the Grand Prize and FIPRESCI Award at the 36th Venice International Film Critics' Week.

 2. The film is director Arsalan Amiri's feature debut, though he has an extensive background as a screenwriter.

 3. Much of the dialogue in the film is in the Kurdish language, rather than Persian.

 4. The story is based on folk tales and superstitions from the director's childhood in Kurdistan.

 5. The film's period setting required careful attention to historical details in costumes and set design.

 6. "Zalava" was Iran's submission for the Best International Feature Film at the 94th Academy Awards.

 7. The director chose to keep the existence of demons ambiguous throughout the film to maintain tension.

 8. The glass jar used by the exorcist in the film became an iconic image in the movie's marketing.

 9. Despite its horror elements, the film also incorporates moments of dark humor.

 10. The character of Masoud was inspired by the director's uncle, who was a gendarme in Kurdistan during that era.

The End... Or Is It?

Well, well, well. Look who made it to the other side.

You've done it, brave soul. You've traversed the treacherous terrain of Planet Terror and lived to tell the tale. But at what cost, I wonder?

446 nightmares later, and here you are. Changed. Different. Your eyes a little wider, your nerves a little more frayed. The shadows in your room seem deeper now, don't they? The creaks in your house a little more... deliberate?

Don't worry. That's normal. Side effects of your journey may include increased heart rate, paranoia, and the unshakeable feeling that something is watching you from just beyond the corner of your eye. But it's worth it, isn't it? For the thrill. For the knowledge. For the delicious, spine-tingling fear that now courses through your veins.

You've peered into the abyss of global horror, and make no mistake – it peered right back at you. From the haunted forests of Japan to the cursed tombs of Egypt, from the blood-soaked streets of Italy to the paranormal plains of America – you've seen it all. Or have you?

Remember, dear thrill-seeker, in the world of horror, nothing ever truly ends. There's always another scare around the corner, another nightmare waiting to be born. And now, armed with this tome of terror, you're ready for whatever comes next.

So go ahead. Close this book. Put it back on your shelf. But know this – it won't stay there. It can't. The stories within, the horrors you've witnessed, they're a part of you now. They'll whisper to you in the dead of night, tempting you to open these pages once more, to relive the fear, to dive back into the delicious darkness.

And when that happens – because it will happen – Planet Terror will be waiting for you. Always waiting. Always watching.

Sweet dreams, brave soul. May your nightmares be... entertaining.

Made in the USA
Las Vegas, NV
26 December 2024